THE NEW
OXFORD BOOK OF
CAROLS

THE NEW OXFORD BOOK OF
CAROLS

EDITED BY
HUGH KEYTE
AND
ANDREW PARROTT

ASSOCIATE EDITOR
CLIFFORD BARTLETT

Music Department
OXFORD UNIVERSITY PRESS
Oxford   New York

Oxford University Press, Walton Street, Oxford OX2 6DP
Oxford New York Toronto
Delhi Bombay Calcutta Madras Karachi
Petaling Jaya Singapore Hong Kong Tokyo
Nairobi Dar es Salaam Cape Town
Melbourne Auckland
and associated companies in
Berlin Ibadan

Oxford is a trade mark of Oxford University Press

Published in the United States
by Oxford University Press, New York

British Library Cataloguing in Publication Data
Data available

Library of Congress Cataloging-in-Publication Data
The New Oxford Book of Carols
edited by Hugh Keyte and Andrew Parrott;
associate editor, Clifford Bartlett.
1 close score.
Includes bibliographical references
1. Carols. 2. Christmas music. I. Keyte, Hugh. II. Parrott,
Andrew. III. Bartlett, Clifford.
M2065.N48 1992   92–756468
ISBN 0–19–353323–5

Music and text origination by
Barnes Music Engraving Ltd., East Sussex,
and Hope Services, Abingdon, Oxfordshire

Printed in the United States of America
on acid-free paper

Items from this anthology are included on the EMI Classics
recordings 'The Carol Album' and 'The Christmas Album', performed
by the Taverner Consort, Choir, and Players, directed by Andrew Parrott

CONTENTS

PART I COMPOSED CAROLS

THE MIDDLE AGES

ENGLISH CAROLS 1400–1700

v

Contents

Contents

PART II TRADITIONAL CAROLS

ENGLISH TRADITIONAL

LUCK-VISIT SONGS

IRISH TRADITIONAL

Contents

APPENDICES, BIBLIOGRAPHY, AND INDEXES

INTRODUCTION

Books, like people, can often trace their origins back to the most unlikely places. The present anthology was conceived by the editors a few days before Christmas 1985, at the foot of an escalator funnelling close-packed commuters from the underground system up to the concourse of London's Waterloo Station. As part of a group singing carols for charity, each of us would from time to time do a stint hunting out requested items from a stack of different carol-books, experiencing anew the familiar inconveniences of the standard anthologies, while the rest continued to perform. Why, we kept asking ourselves with increasing exasperation, was there no single collection that presented the essential 'core' repertory of popular Christmas carols and hymns? Why such an abundance of sophisticated settings but such a dearth of straightforward harmonizations? Could it really be so difficult to provide original foreign-language texts or to devise decent translations? What was it about the hymns and carols of Christmas that required them always to be constrained within a voices-and-organ format and harmonized in a late-Victorian or Edwardian idiom?

A vision of the caroller's ideal anthology presented itself. It would be comprehensive, literate, and practical. The unassuming musical settings would be protean in their adaptability to different resources and venues, and yet preserve the essential character of the melodies. An editor would need to get back behind the modern arrangements and bowdlerizations to the genuine articles beyond, but it could hardly be a matter of more than fifty carols or so: a couple of months' work, perhaps. We might as well do their job ourselves.

Two months' work was exactly what Ralph Vaughan Williams anticipated in 1904, when Percy Dearmer persuaded him to take on the musical editorship of what would in the event emerge in 1906 as *The English Hymnal*. For two years he laboured to produce the book that was to have a profound effect on hymn-singing throughout the English-speaking world, hunting out fine tunes from a wide historical period, pitching them for congregations rather than for choirs, and allowing them to speak once more in something approaching their authentic accents. A quarter of a century later he collaborated with Martin Shaw and Percy Dearmer to produce the equally seminal *Oxford Book of Carols* (1928), the quality and balance of which instantly established it as the most satisfactory carol collection available, its historical annotations the best handy guide to the background of the repertory. Like Vaughan Williams in 1904, it was only when we began work that we discovered the extent of what we had taken on and were disabused of our naïve supposition that good, simple settings and reliable texts and translations lay easily to hand. We came to realize, too, how restricted the current repertory has become: whole genres which deserve to be widely known have been steadfastly ignored or laid aside, and in many individual cases a single 'standard' musical setting has replaced former glorious diversity. Our initial conception of a very basic and deliberately limited collection expanded enormously as we came to grips with the realities of the project, and a much broader scheme emerged, both utilitarian and innovative, which has remained essentially unchanged.

More or less the entire repertory current in the English-speaking world is represented and we have gone far beyond this (and our initial scheme) in five areas that seem to us to have been most unjustly neglected by modern anthologists: medieval Latin song; the fifteenth-century English carol; the German Christmas chorale; the Christmas hymns of the English 'gallery' composers; and those of their American 'primitive' and shape-note counterparts. One drawback of the expansion of our initial plan is that multiple purchase of the present volume will be beyond the resources of most choirs. With this in mind, *The Shorter New Oxford Book of Carols*—an anthology of items drawn from the complete collection and omitting the appendices and notes—is planned for publication in the near future.

The presentation of the current volume has been designed to allow the maximum of choice, both among the variants and alternatives that are provided and in the various ways in which the editorial settings in particular may be used. Underlying the whole book (and governing many of the choices of setting, as well as the performance notes) is the expectation that an increasing number of musicians will wish to perform the entire range of carols—not merely the earlier ones—in an historically based ('authentic') manner, grounded in the performance practices of the appropriate places and periods. A non-historical approach is always a viable alternative, however, and this too has been taken into account. Whether we shall succeed in expanding the existing repertory remains to be seen. What can hardly be doubted is the need for a new collection on the general lines of the old *Oxford Book of Carols*. Musical knowledge has increased enormously in the sixty or so years that have elapsed since its publication, and attitudes (as well as the circumstances in which carols are performed) are no longer the same. No natural successor has yet appeared, and we believe that our approach has the potential to revitalize what has in many respects become an inward-looking and enfeebled tradition. Radical change is arguably as necessary for the Christmas carol today as it was for hymnody in 1904.

The word 'carol' admits of so many definitions that any anthologist needs to establish a set of criteria that will govern selection. Ours are broad but strict: the content must be narrative, contemplative, or celebratory, the spirit must be simple, the form normally strophic. ('Carol' is used in this sense throughout the book, though the distinction between carol and hymn is retained where necessary.) We have in the main restricted ourselves to carols for Christmas and most of its associated feasts and seasons, ranging from Advent (the penitential period of preparation for Christmas) to Candlemas (the feast of the Presentation of the Virgin in the Temple, 2 February, forty days after Christmas, which marked the end of the season in the medieval church calendar). Carols of the Annunciation have the status of honorary Christmas carols, having been sung at this season from medieval times. (The feast falls on 25 March, nine months before Christmas Day, and was established in the western church by the eighth century; but it is also commemorated on the Ember Wednesday of the final week in Advent at what was known in medieval France as the Golden Mass, with the Annunciation narrative forming the Gospel.) Most hymns for Advent and the Epiphany have been excluded, since they will rarely be sung outside churches and are readily available in hymnals. We have also ruled out certain classes of carol that have been part of the Christmas repertory since the Middle Ages but have no direct link with the season (notably carols of the Passion and narrative carols of the life of Christ), though we are not so doctrinaire as to exclude such favourites as 'The Joys of Mary' (131) or 'Tomorrow shall be my dancing day' (132). Also omitted are certain 'general' carols that have attached themselves to Christmas, among them 'King Jesus hath a garden fair' and Elizabeth Poston's fine 'Jesus Christ the Apple Tree'. Through-composed settings are automatically debarred, save for a handful that combine a quasi-strophic form and a carol-like modesty, among them Harold Darke's 'In the bleak mid-winter' (111:1) and John Joubert's 'There is no rose of such virtue' (120); and the anonymous 'Swete was the song the Virgine soong' (44), though entirely non-strophic, could hardly be denied.

There are a few carols of no obvious distinction which are held in such universal affection that it would have been churlish to omit them. These aside, we believe that every item in the book is among the best of its kind. We have had to be highly select-ive, both in what we include and in the number of alternative versions and settings that are provided: we could effortlessly have filled a slim volume with variant melodies to *The Cherry Tree Carol* (128) and a plump one with the various tunes and settings to which 'While shepherds watched' (46) has been sung in the two centuries since it was written. Faced with a choice of this kind, we have normally balanced a tune or setting from Britain with a contrasting example from America, or one that is familiar with one that is little known.

Any carol-book stands or falls as much on the quality of its settings as on the choice of its repertory. In this respect the relationship of the anthologist to his carols differs markedly from that of the occasional arranger. The latter, clearly, is at liberty to mould text and melody to his will, but the former should surely be the servant and not the master of his material. A fine carol melody is in any case no *tabula rasa* awaiting a colourful arrangement to give it life. Whether composed or traditional, it already lives within a penumbra of latent harmony, and it seems to us a sterile exer-cise to clothe it (as so many anthologists do) with either textbook or quasi-modernist harmonies, the one inhabiting a stylistic no man's land, the other imposing an ersatz contemporaneity.

Our editorial arrangements normally take a historical approach, working out-wards from the melodies, striving in each case to identify the implicit harmonies and to evoke the time and place of origin. The natural vehicle for a tune is by no means always four-part vocal harmony, and we include far more settings for 'eccentric' forces than is usual. Our arrangement of the ballad tune for 'All hayle to the dayes' (138) is one of many that are dual-purpose: strictly speaking, the four-part setting is anachronistic, but we also allow for the more historical option of voice and con-tinuo. Where appropriate, we have cheerfully adopted features of historical styles that most arrangers are at pains to avoid. There is, for example, a harmonization in a crude 'shape-note' manner (139:1), and there are editorial completions of melody-and-bass gallery settings from eighteenth-century England (142, for instance) that bristle with 'forbidden' consecutive fifths and octaves. But all these are diligently modelled on existing repertory, and we know from experience that it is not the innocent ear that will baulk at them but the academic eye. There are also some tunes—those of certain English folk carols, for example—which are most naturally sung by an unaccompanied voice and for which no historically-based style is appropriate; here we have cast off our self-imposed constraints and have drawn on aspects of rustic and improvisatory practice that at least do the melodies no violence.

The book is divided into two main sections, part I containing 'composed' carols and part II 'traditional'. Within the first, the order is roughly chronological, though with some geographical grouping leading to a slightly zigzag sequence; in the second, the carols are arranged purely by country of origin. A carol's chronological position is determined by the date at which music and words first appeared together: 'Ding! dong! merrily on high' (108) is thus dated *c*.1900, despite its sixteenth-century tune. Composed and traditional settings of the same text are placed separately in parts I and II: 'A Virgin unspotted', for example, appears in William Billings's setting in part I (80) and in its folk settings in part II (143).

We begin with plainchant hymns and medieval carols from all over Europe, including a group now known chiefly from the Swedish–Finnish *Piae Cantiones* of 1582, deriving from much earlier central-European material. We then turn back to fifteenth-century England and continue through the sixteenth century to the early years of the seventeenth. (There would seem to be surprisingly few English carols from the period 1500–1750, but many that originated in this period passed into popular use and so appear in part II.) A group of three mid-sixteenth-century Spanish pieces follows, after which we pick up the central-European carol where we left it. Many of the Latin items here have medieval origins, but are mostly given in settings published by Michael Praetorius shortly after 1600. (His encyclopaedic publications took on a quasi-official status, and seem to have been an indispensable part of the libraries of all Lutheran churches with any musical pretensions.) This group leads naturally to carols in the German language, both Lutheran and Catholic, many of which are familiar through their use in the cantatas and chorale-based organ works of J. S. Bach. The remainder of part I follows in a chronological sequence, with no distinction between the handful of foreign carols and those in English.

The division of the book into 'composed' and 'traditional' sections is more a matter of convenience than the reflection of any deep distinction. Virtually all the *noëls* in the French section (188–95) consist of texts set by mainly clerical poets to existing melodies; yet the texts of some of the English medieval carols in the 'composed' section (23–6, for example) were very probably written by Franciscan friars for existing tunes in much the same way. ('Popular by destination' is the usual term for such pieces.) An analogous case is Luther's 'Vom Himmel hoch, da komm' ich her' (60), which began as a new text to a traditional dance-song; it was later given a solemn church tune and so (theoretically) defected from the 'traditional' category into the 'composed'. All the music in part II could, indeed, be parcelled out among the formal categories of 'traditional', 'folk', and 'popular', but we have always preferred the first when no vital distinction is involved. Such distinctions are periodically handed down on tablets of stone, which are just as frequently smashed, and reflect the strongly left- and right-wing polarity of much US 'folk-music' scholarship. For appraisals of the conveniently loose definitions that have prevailed for most of the twentieth century, see chapter IV ('The Carol as Popular Song') in R. L. Greene, *The Early English Carols* (1935; rev. 1977), the introduction to Margaret Dean-Smith, *A*

Guide to English Folk Song Collections 1822–1952 (1954), and the first chapter of A. L. Lloyd, *Folk Song in England* (1967). Unlike most folk-song scholars, Lloyd was a folk-singer son of folk-singer parents, and a commensurate weight is to be placed on the exasperated aside that follows his lucid survey of the three categories and their ramifications: 'At this point I rest my typewriter and think how abstract the matter of folk song definition is, and how boring for all those dogged scholars who dart into argument with voices sharpened, glasses glinting, using their conference papers as batons in a Tweedledum-Tweedledee fight, with never a notion that their science more than most should be all of a piece with life . . . Deep at the root, there is no essential difference between folk music and art music: they are varied blossoms from the same stock, grown to serve a similar purpose, if destined for different tables' (*Folk Song in England*, p. 19). Perhaps our two sections may be taken to represent the two complementary flower-beds. If something more precise is demanded, we might distinguish the carols in the 'traditional' section as those with complex ancestry, for they have in the main *evolved* into their present form, while those in the 'composed' section have mostly sprung from known stock in a relatively straightforward manner. The distinction is ultimately one of 'feel' rather than definition.

The history of the carol is not easily available to the general reader. Greene's *The Early English Carols* is invaluable in its particular field, and the lengthy introduction and notes (unindexed, alas) also cover much of the traditional carol repertory and the general background very usefully. Elsewhere, for the most part, information has to be searched out in editions of individual repertories, in chapters of specialist books, in scholarly articles and monographs, and in the pages of the journals of national folk-song societies. Most popular writing on the subject is marred by the same non-scholarly approach which perpetuates existing errors in carol settings: the long-term survival of the non-existent Carl Leuner (see 'Schlaf wohl, du Himmelsknabe du', 178) and the persistence of the mistranscribed conclusion of 'Infant holy, Infant lowly' (184) are very minor symptoms of a pervasive inertia. As long ago as 1948, in an article in the first volume of *The Journal of the American Musicological Society*, Leonard Ellingwood deplored the 'steady succession of handbooks to hymnals of various denominations put together by men who blithely and carelessly copy from each other as extensively as do our popular encyclopaedists, who examine no sources, who feel that a glib phrase suffices for the lack of basic fact'. His plea for scholars to 'leave upon occasion the ivory towers where so many of our studies are centered, and to make contributions where they are eagerly awaited by a large cross-section of contemporary society' has not gone entirely unheeded, at least in the US: the forthcoming companion to the recent new edition of the Episcopalian *Hymnal*, for example, is in the hands of an impressive team of practical-minded scholars. But carols have everywhere lagged far behind hymns in this respect, and there is consequently much ground to make up.

The historical notes that accompany each carol are one way in which we have tried to compensate for this deficiency. They vary considerably in length and complexity. In some cases (John Joubert's setting of 'There is no rose', 120, for example), little needs to be given beyond the source and meaning of the text and the circumstances of composition. In others, the origin of the text may throw fresh light on a familiar carol (Phillips Brooks was inspired to write 'O little town of Bethlehem', 101, standing one Christmas Eve in the field of the annunciation to the shepherds just outside Bethlehem) or the origins of a tune may be contentious (which came first, the melody of 'Adeste, fideles', 70, or the closely related operatic *air anglois* that appeared at around the same time?). There is often a wealth of ancillary anecdotal material, and this we have made a point of including on a generous scale: Mistral's account of Provençal processions of the three kings (186) or Laurie Lee's evocation of his childhood singing of the doubts of Joseph to an old farmer of the same name (128) may have little immediate effect on performance, but they point up the fertile soil of folk observance and traditional life from which so many carols sprang. In yet other cases, the background of a genre will scarcely rate a mention in the standard accounts, as with the German *Wechselgesang* tradition (see notes, 55), or the origins of an individual carol will have been obscured by the dissemination of myths and legends (as with 'Christians, awake!', 71). Scholarly work on the Christmas hymn and carol repertory is thin on the ground, and rare indeed are such clarifying articles as those by Richard S. Hill on 'Away in a manger' (see notes, 100) and John Wilson on the origins of the tune 'Antioch' (see notes, 76). Some of our more extended notes are thus more dense than we should have preferred, since they summarize material that is not easily available or is the result of our own researches.

The Appendices are another way of tackling the same problem of the lack of reliable background information. Of the many topics that could usefully have been covered, we have preferred to concentrate on one or two areas that have particular relevance to our selection of carols rather than attempting anything more encyclopaedic. Appendix 1 is a brief singer's guide to the pronunciation of fifteenth-century English. Appendix 2 shows the various ways in which Christmas (and other) hymns were performed in Germany and England before the current manner became standardized in the nineteenth century, with particular prominence given to aspects of historical organ accompaniment that have fallen out of use. Appendix 3 surveys the English 'gallery' and American 'primitive' traditions, and Appendix 4 focuses on certain nineteenth-century publications that virtually saved the English traditional carol, and prepared the way for its eventual acceptance as part of the common birthright of all classes of society.

What follows is in no way intended as a formal history of the carol, if only because the word 'carol' in the normal modern usage which we follow (see above) is little more than a catch-all term for a variety of forms and types that have no real historical continuity. (Modern scholars tend to restrict the term to the specific medieval poetic and musical form, derived from the sung and danced *carole*, in which a refrain precedes and follows each verse.) Nor is it a blow-by-blow account of the various genres included here. The first ('composed') section of the book is ordered on historical lines, and this sketch of the changing social background of performance and of the types of popular Christmas music current in the different periods provides a framework in which to set the bewildering variety of carols that it contains. The 'traditional' carols of the second part have less need of such a historically-based scheme, and are in any case organized by country. Yet the 'art music' bias of conventional musical education means that there is probably an even greater need of background here: Appendix 4 goes some way towards providing this for an important part of the English repertory, while less amply represented repertories are considered in the historical notes to specific carols.

The Middle Ages

The earliest music in our collection is a group of plainchant hymns (1–5). For several centuries, hymns were the only verse forms within the official liturgy, and this, together with the concision of the texts and the graceful tunes to which they came to be sung, made them particularly memorable. The hymn was long believed to have been introduced to the Western Church in the fourth century by St Ambrose. Though only a few of the attributions to him have withstood the scepticism of modern scholarship, it is accepted that he played a key role in establishing the type of serious, theologically based text that has been the rule for liturgical hymnody ever since. Hymns were allocated to specific services and seasons, mostly in the daily cycle known as the office—hence 'office hymns'. Ours are from the Sarum (Salisbury) rite, which was standard throughout southern England by the time of the Reformation. The texts differ from those later used in the Roman rite, which were revised in the seventeenth century, and the music is rather more melismatic. Phrases from the texts are extensively quoted in English medieval carols.

Plainchant hymns have an established place in the services of many churches today, but the tendency of modern choirs to regard monophonic and two-part music as beneath their dignity has led to the neglect of a whole treasury of Christmas song from the Middle Ages. Helen Waddell's *The Wandering Scholars* and Carl Orff's *Carmina Burana* helped to draw attention to a small part of the repertory, and other medieval songs are known from J. M. Neale's translations from *Piae Cantiones* (Holy Songs', 1582), but many more still await the general popularity they deserve.

Throughout medieval Europe, the Christmas period was celebrated with an elaboration and richness exceeded only by Holy Week and Easter. Almost every day of the Octave was a feast, with magnificent processions after vespers and before mass. The ritual climax was 1 January, which was not only the Octave (eighth day) of Christmas but also the universally accepted beginning of the New Year (whenever the official year happened to begin), the feast of the Circumcision of Christ (his name-day), and the original feast-day (*natale*) of the Virgin Mary. (This last died out in the course of the thirteenth century, but left an indelible print in the liturgy.) Sung dramas and all kinds of religious and secular celebrations were common, and the official liturgy was adorned with additions and expansions ('tropes') that were specific to the various feasts. A favoured place for these was the conclusion of matins, lauds, and, especially, vespers, where rhythmic verses were sung as substitutes for the concluding 'Benedicamus Domino' versicle and 'Deo dicamus gracias' response. At first these were called *versus* (verses), later *cantiones* (songs), and many of them came to be translated or imitated in the vernacular, especially in Bohemia and Germany, where the more popular were eventually adapted as chorales by both Lutherans and Catholics. Despite its late date, *Piae Cantiones* (produced by a Catholic student but edited by a Lutheran pastor) contains some of the best of these medieval songs, though often in untypical forms, and was the source from which, nearly three centuries later, they entered the English carol repertory. We have also taken several monophonic songs (9–11) from the one- and two-part settings that comprise what may be the earliest complete cycle of *Benedicamus* substitutes (see notes, 9), from Aosta in northern Italy.

A substantial section of the present book is devoted to the distinctive repertory of fifteenth-century English carols (24–38). Despite their calculatedly popular character and an excellent modern edition by John Stevens, these are still rarely heard outside specialist circles. They were evidently written for professionals to sing, but their popular idiom must have had a broader appeal than most polyphony of the period. Some were certainly intended for the Christmas banquets in ecclesiastical establishments, others perhaps for use as substitutes for office antiphons, in devotions at the crib, or in the Christmas post-vespers processions. In addition to the polyphonic carols we have included two monophonic examples (25 and 26), which give a rare hint of what Christmas music may have been like outside the Church.

The sixteenth and seventeenth centuries

Despite strong local traditions, there was an underlying unity of practice in the pre-Reformation Church throughout Europe. From the sixteenth century onwards this gave way to a diversity that reflected the different beliefs and liturgies that now prevailed within the fragmented Church.

For our present purposes, the Reformation was most fruitful in Germany, where long before Martin Luther's break with Rome there had been a strongly rooted tradition of vernacular song. Luther believed firmly in the power of music and its value in worship. He and his colleagues retained and adapted the existing repertory (which included the popular Latin *cantiones*) and provided sacred texts for many folk melodies, while also encouraging the creation of new hymns. The incomparable tradition of Christmas music thus established is surprisingly poorly represented in English-language carol-books. Even the great Christmas chorales familiar from the works of J. S. Bach are rarely given in the forms in which they were sung by congregations. Also unknown outside Lutheran circles is the rich tradition of *Wechselgesang* (antiphonal song; see notes, 55, and Appendix 2), which lapsed in most regions in the eighteenth century, was revived in Germany in the 1920s, and has now spread to American Lutherans. Later Germanic Christmas hymnody has scarcely impinged on the English-speaking world, and the few later carols that have been adopted have tended to be those composed virtually within the folk tradition: Gruber's 'Stille Nacht!' (86), for example, is as close to the world of the *Volkslied* as some of Schubert's simpler strophic songs.

For a long time after the Reformation the English Church was considerably less enthusiastic about Christmas than the Lutheran because of the constant need to appease its powerful Calvinist faction, which regarded the feast as a popish abuse. From 1644 to 1660 Christmas Day was theoretically abolished by Parliament, and a comparable ban in puritan Massachusetts was not formally rescinded until 1681. The *Book of Common Prayer* made no specific provision for seasonal hymns, and it was only with the inclusion of 'While shepherds watched' (46) in the 1700 *Supplement to the New Version of the Psalms* (which was bound up with prayer-books) that a Christmas hymn acquired an honorary official status. From this beginning there gradually developed a whole new repertory. In secular society, however, Christmas continued to thrive, notwithstanding the various 'Laments of Old Christmas' that are found from the fifteenth century onwards. Christmas songs survive from plays (such as the 'Coventry' carols, 40 and 41) or were written for domestic use ('Swete was the song', 44).

The eighteenth century

The carol tradition in France sprang from much the same roots as those of England and Germany: early translations of Christmas office hymns, for example, have many parallels among English fifteenth-century carols, and 'Puer nobis nascitur' (21) was as well known in France as in Germany. But the luck-visit songs of the French folk tradition tend to be much less rich, and the dominant *noël* developed into a stereotyped procedure of writing new texts for existing tunes. We include only those *noëls* which are so well known as to have become part of the English-speaking repertory. Many date from the eighteenth century or are sung to eighteenth-century forms of their tunes, and there is only a marginal overlap with the distinct and slightly earlier corpus of organ settings.

Noëls apart, the 'composed' repertory for two hundred years or so from the later seventeenth century is mostly drawn from English-language sources, and our additional representation of the gallery and 'primitive' traditions has taken this tendency yet further.

This was a period of sad decline for the traditional carol in England, though in some remote areas (notably Cornwall) a few examples written down as late as the mid-eighteenth century are direct descendants of medieval carols, and others continued to treat the Christmas story in the old ways (e.g., 'When God at first created man', 142; see also Appendix 4). Everywhere the old texts continued to circulate in updated forms in broadsides and chap-books, but the new ones that accompanied and gradually displaced them were increasingly hymn-like. New carols of a popular type and aimed at the domestic market appeared regularly in the pages of such publications as *Poor Robin's Almanac*, but these were hardly to be distinguished from any other convivial song and degenerated into gluttonous inventories of food and drink, lightly disguised as celebrations of charity and the Christmastide tradition of open house. In the more conservative pages of *The Gentleman's Magazine*, carols expressing the old sentiments (though not in the old form) were published each Christmas, and the text of 'Arise and hail the sacred day' (87) originated in a carol submitted by two Devonshire subscribers in 1748. The 'Christmas Carol' welcoming the 'King of Seasons all' which Dickens puts into the mouth of Mr Wardle in chapter 28 of *The Pickwick Papers* (1837) was part of a continuing tradition, and fits many a fine seventeenth-century ballad tune such as 'All hayle to the dayes' (138).

It was into the new mould of the congregational hymn, then, that much of the vigour of the old carol tradition was poured. From the closing decade of the seventeenth century onwards, the dreary unison chanting of metrical psalms before and after the service, 'lined out' by a stentorian parish clerk, slowly gave way to harmonized settings led by the gallery choirs which were springing up in rural parishes. On Christmas Day these psalms were replaced by Christmas hymns or carols, at first sung to the familiar psalm tunes. Local 'country' settings of hymns, anthems, etc. were produced in great numbers, mostly by the peripatetic singing teachers (many of them parish clerks) who helped to set up the new choirs. Some of the new Christmas hymns are in crude but vigorous home-grown idioms; others, such as John Wainwright's superb setting of John Byrom's 'Christians, awake!' (71) and Thomas Clark's tune 'Cranbrook' ('While shepherds watched', 46:v), are in the essentially

Handelian tradition that was much favoured by provincial Dissent; and there was a whole spectrum of styles between the two extremes.

In Protestant America, as in England, the change to harmony coincided with the adoption of the *New Version* and involved a long-drawn-out struggle between the urban reformers and the conservative rural churches. American composers began by imitating English music, drawing on seventeenth-century tunes (including those of Orlando Gibbons, echoes of which can still be heard in shape-note hymns of the nineteenth century) and on 'country' composers of the following century, whose publications supplied the English churches. Imitations of English models soon gave way to a distinctive native tradition, every bit as vigorous and stylistically much more wide-ranging. Eighteenth-century primitivism reached its apogee in the startlingly original music of the Congregationalist William Billings of Boston (1746–1800), and rural Calvinism found a multitude of voices in the work of the shape-note composers who followed him. Shape-note music survives within a living tradition of performance, but the work of the earlier American composers, though a matter of lively concern to academics and available in facsimile editions, has been virtually ignored in hymn-books and carol anthologies and is scarcely known in the mainstream churches.

Appendix 3 contains a fuller discussion of these English and American traditions. We have made a point of including a fair representation of carols from both the English and American repertories, with Christmas hymns by Billings (78–80) and by English composers of the early nineteenth century (88–91), including some from the Thomas Hardy Collection which the author immortalized in *Under the Greenwood Tree* (1872).

The Victorians

A major influence in the increasing popularity of hymns in England during the eighteenth century had been the Methodists, in whose services hymn-singing was an essential element. As part of the dominant Evangelical party's determination to renew the moribund national church, hymns (and carols) began to be included within, rather than alongside, the prayer-book services. Reform was in the ascendant from the beginning of the nineteenth century, when hymn-books began to pour off the presses in great numbers to supply the new need. The culmination of this was *Hymns Ancient and Modern* (1861), the first book acceptable to the whole Anglican Church. During the same period, Independents (Congregationalists) and Baptists finally overcame their distrust of non-scriptural texts, and hymns (rather than psalms and other biblical paraphrases) assumed a central place in their services. The gallery tradition was a victim of the zeal for reform. The west-end choirs and bands were independent institutions, often casually behaved, and in many villages serving both the parish and the Methodist churches. Among the sweeping changes made by the increasingly conscientious and authoritarian Anglican incumbents was their replacement by barrel-organs, harmoniums, or robed cathedral-style chancel choirs under direct clerical control.

Outside such remote and conservative regions as Cornwall, Yorkshire, and Wales, Christmas itself was still little regarded among British Protestants, and it was only with the spread of romantic medievalism in society in general and the decline of the Evangelical movement and rise of the Tractarian (and later Anglo-Catholic) parties that the carol, generally thought to be on the point of extinction, was revivified. The first churches to introduce traditional ('folk') carols into services seem to have been those of the 'English' branch of Anglo-Catholicism, supposedly following medieval precedent, and it was an Anglo-Catholic cleric, J. M. Neale, who promoted the medieval repertory with his own poetic yet scholarly texts for medieval melodies from *Piae Cantiones* (1582). These he published in collaboration with the leading Anglican advocate of plainchant, Thomas Helmore, in their *Carols for Christmas-tide* (1853–4). The carefully chosen title of *Hymns Ancient and Modern* summed up the new attitude succinctly, and it was echoed a decade later by Henry Ramsden Bramley and John Stainer in their *Christmas Carols New and Old* (1871).

The carol revival

The Victorian 'reinvention' of Christmas was in reality more the compression of the traditional celebrations of the old Twelve Days into two or three, and the conversion of what had always been a period of communal festivity into a more inward-looking celebration of the family. Tradition, once a matter of unconscious observance, came to be something eagerly sought after and, if necessary, revived. Like the newly intro- duced Christmas tree (see notes, 181), carols were regarded as redolent of the ideal- ized Christmas of yore, and this opened the way for a revival of the traditional carol, which was gradually admitted by churches of every type alongside (but distinct from) the now well-established Christmas hymn. The groundwork had been laid in publications of 1822 and 1833 by the Cornish antiquaries Davies Gilbert and William Sandys (see Appendix 4), and their discoveries were taken up and adapted to popular taste by Edmund Sedding (1860 and 1863), W. H. Husk (1864), H. R. Bramley and John Stainer (1871), and R. R. Chope (1877). Bramley and Stainer were respectively chaplain and organist of Magdalen College, Oxford, where the ser- vices were in the Evangelical tradition and the choir occupied a place in the public mind analogous to that of King's College, Cambridge, today. They presented tradi- tional carols in a 'respectable' form, the melodies regularized, the harmonies ecclesi- astical, the texts adapted to all degrees of churchmanship. The carol was thus—at last—fit for inclusion in the services of cathedrals, which had stood out longest against their introduction.

Alongside the revival of the traditional carol went the writing of new ones—a ris- ing tide of mostly very sorry stuff. In his preface to *Carols for Christmas-tide* (1853–4), Neale observed that 'It is impossible at one stretch to produce a quantity of new carols, of which words and music shall alike be original. They must be the gradual accumulation of centuries; the offerings of different epochs, of different countries, of different minds, to the same treasury of the Church.' The new carols that have lived have, indeed, overwhelmingly been new textings of old tunes or new settings of old (and especially medieval) texts. Neale himself produced several popular successes of the first type, the best known being 'Good King Wenceslas' (97).

Around the turn of the century, another Anglo-Catholic priest, G. R. Woodward, initiated the plundering of the European carol repertories (see notes, 104) in an attempt to satisfy the seemingly insatiable appetite of choirs for fresh seasonal mater- ial. To him we owe the enrichment of the native English tradition by some of the finest French, Basque, Provençal, Czech, and Bohemian traditional carols. In line

xxi

with the Arts and Crafts ideals which had by now permeated ecclesiastical aesthetics (the Evangelical wing excepted), there was a gradual turning away from 'Olde English Yuletiderie' (of which Woodward's own texts for 'Ding-dong ding!', 104, and 'Past three o'clock', 105, are by no means the most florid examples) towards genuine and comparatively undoctored medieval and traditional texts, set to music that was frequently rooted in the past. Some composers even incorporated medieval techniques in their settings, while others aimed at the spare textures and fluid declamation of folk-song; a fine example of the latter is Holst's 'Lullay, my liking' (109:1).

The Oxford Book of Carols

The carol was finally accorded the serious treatment normally reserved for higher forms of art in *The Oxford Book of Carols* (1928). It is worth considering the special qualities that have made this the bench-mark against which any new collection has automatically been measured, together with the reasons why it nevertheless now needs to be replaced.

Percy Dearmer was again the guiding spirit, as he had been for *The English Hymnal* (with Vaughan Williams, 1904) and *Songs of Praise* (with Vaughan Williams and Martin Shaw, 1926). He was responsible for the remarkable literary qualities of the book, and contributed translations under several separate sets of initials. His preface is still one of the best surveys of the field, so long as due allowance is made for his frank aversion to clerical poets, gloom, and the confusion of hymns with carols. Dearmer's characterization of carols as 'songs with a religious impulse that are simple, hilarious [joyful], popular and modern' should perhaps be read less as a definition than as a manifesto, a declaration of war on all that was convoluted, sanctimonious, esoteric, and quaint in the Christmas repertory of his day.

The new book had grown out of a specifically Christmas collection by Dearmer and Shaw, the *English Carol Book* (first series, 1913; second series, 1919). The bland settings are in many ways analogous to the scrubbed, whitewashed church interiors of the period, such as that of Dearmer's church, the fashionable St Mary's, Primrose Hill, where Shaw directed the music from 1908 to 1920. The earlier books had met with little success, and Vaughan Williams was again persuaded to take time off from composing to breathe life into the new enterprise. A surprising number of Shaw's harmonizations that have become familiar from *The Oxford Book of Carols* were taken over unchanged from its predecessor, and they have always suffered from their proximity to the handful of masterly settings by Vaughan Williams. The latter was a leading member of the Folk-Song Society, then at the zenith of its influence, and the new book embodied many of its ideals and enthusiasms. Whoever conceived the idea of opening out the earlier scheme to embrace non-English items and seasons other than Christmas, it was Vaughan Williams who had the breadth of knowledge to put it into practice. His influence is discernible, too, in the historical notes that accompany each item, which helped to draw the user into a new kind of relationship with both the carols and the editors. In retrospect, this 'practical book of carols to be sung', as Dearmer modestly called it, can be seen to have timed its arrival perfectly, encapsulating the spirit of the age as surely as Bramley and Stainer had encapsulated theirs half a century earlier. Its great achievement was to bring to popular attention the rough-hewn glories of the genuine traditional carol, allowing a healthy gust of outdoor air into the stuffy atmosphere of the cloister.

A limitation that was scarcely apparent in 1928 is the restriction of the editors' choice of American carols to the admirable 'O little town of Bethlehem' and *Three Kings of Orient*, omitting the entire traditional and 'primitive' repertory. Of the last, like virtually everyone else at the time, they were unaware, but Vaughan Williams at least must have known of the 1916–18 visit of Cecil Sharp and Maud Karpeles to the mountainous regions of Southern Appalachia, and the huge cache of folk-songs with which they returned, including carols of English descent. Their work has been continued by a succession of notable American scholars. George Pullen Jackson, writing on the American shape-note repertory, and a phalanx of scholars on William Billings and the New England primitive composers have not only placed the English gallery tunes that Shaw arranged in a broader perspective but have shown that all such 'primitive' melodies are mere shadows of their true selves if divorced from their characteristic styles of setting.

For all its virtues, *The Oxford Book of Carols* has always been somewhat at odds with the practical needs of many singers, as anyone will appreciate who has searched the index in vain for 'Adeste, fideles!' (a hymn, so therefore ineligible), 'Stille Nacht!', or 'Away in a manger' (both rejected as vulgar; Neale's 'Good King Wenceslas' narrowly escaped the same fate). The very success of the book meant that it was widely taken up, and used as a comprehensive Christmas collection, something the editors had never envisaged. As a result, singers over the years have been frustrated at its supposed shortcomings, while large tracts of the book have been generally ignored. Sixty-four years on, use and association have nevertheless so rooted the Oxford Book in the affections of English-speaking choirs that it has itself taken on something of the immutable quality of a Christmas tradition. Yet we are now further removed from the rural idylls of Dearmer, Shaw, and Vaughan Williams than they were from the high-Victorian religiosity of Bramley and Stainer. Changing taste has left high and dry many of the new carols in the last section of the book. Advances in historical research have made the overall selection appear restricted, and patchings and corrections for the medieval items (such as those of the 1964 revision) have ceased to be a reasonable option. The last six decades have also seen a radical transformation of the social background against which carols are sung, and the popular perception of the traditional carol is no longer clouded by romantic associations with nationalism and an imaginary medieval past.

The later twentieth century

Of the collections that have appeared since the Oxford Book, by far the most widely used have been those of the series *Carols for Choirs*, begun by Reginald Jacques and David Willcocks in 1961 and continued by Willcocks and John Rutter. These concentrate on arrangements suitable for both the collegiate or cathedral choir's carol service and the choral society's Christmas concert. One of the least widely used collections was Erik Routley's admirable *University Carol Book* (also 1961); with its simple settings, wide scope, and concern for neglected repertories, this was in many ways the nearest to our own conception. For whatever reason, it sank without trace—mown down in the stampede for *Carols for Choirs*, perhaps. Elizabeth Poston's

First and *Second Penguin Book of Christmas Carols* (1965 and 1970) set new standards of scholarship and discrimination and were the first popular collections to give adequate representation to the American carol. That it still remains comparatively little used is perhaps a consequence of the editor's decision not to tailor her arrangements to the SATB choirs that continue to dominate the market.

The brief flowering of the carol in the early twentieth century was a purely insular phenomenon, and, so far as our anthology is concerned, the American carol died with the nineteenth century (though both British and American composers continued to produce impressive through-composed settings of the carol–anthem type, those of Herbert Howells and Leo Sowerby being deservedly popular). The English adoption of past and tradition-based idioms signalled the approach of a general crisis which had been gathering for over a century. The romantic movement had seen music move away from the formal, shared language of classicism towards idiosyncratic dialects that were ill-matched with the directness and simplicity of the typical carol text. The English retreat to the past was also, perhaps, part of a more general cultural malaise, but it produced a climate in which new carols could, at least, be created. With settings such as Maxwell Davies's 'The Fader of heven' (122), written in 1961, the carol as presently defined would seem to have reached an impasse. Yet other less self-consciously modernistic idioms had continued to be used (by Britten, Gardner, and Joubert, among others), and this more unassuming line may prove to be the one that continues forward. As we write, we are aware of a loosening of ideological restraints among younger composers, so that simple, direct forms of expression are no longer frowned upon. It could even be that those who have written off the traditional carol as a dead form may once again prove to have been too hasty with their requiems.

EDITORIAL POLICY: TEXTS

We have normally chosen to base a text on a single source. Where a source is garbled, we have been as economical as possible in our emendations, which are usually noted. In a few instances, we have adapted more boldly: an editorial couplet has been added to 'Christians, awake!' (71), for example, so that (for the first time, to our knowledge) Byrom's poem may be sung complete.

An editor who begins to replace archaic words is setting foot on a dangerously slippery slope, for the process can all too easily lead to blandness: we have preferred to explain obscurities in footnotes. In the case of congregational hymns, however, we have been more flexible, and we generally follow the standard modern form of a text, where there is one.

Calculatedly offensive references to Jews have been removed or modified ('wicked Jews' becomes 'wicked men', for example) and the changes are noted. Marginal cases, such as the verse in a medieval *cantio* that calls on the 'wretched Jews' to convert to Christianity, are retained but marked with an asterisk (*) to indicate possible omission. We also asterisk verses for the usual purpose of indicating reasonable or conventional abbreviations of longer items, though without catering for those who, like a recent Anglican bishop, feel that the ideal hymn comprises 'two verses, one of which may be omitted'.

Orthography

Original spelling has been retained where desirable and practicable, but we have freely amended the spelling, punctuation, and layout of texts known to have been transcribed directly from a singer or a recording, noting only substantial changes.

The orthography of English medieval carols has not been updated, since we believe that the gains of retaining the original outweigh the losses: allusive, deliberately ambiguous, and regional spellings remain unobscured, and singers are encouraged to attempt a medieval pronunciation. Obsolete letters have, however, been replaced by their modern equivalents, and modern usage has been followed for i/j and u/v. Medieval Latin orthography is similarly retained, with no classicizing substitution of 't' for 'c' or 'ae/oe' for 'e' (thus *leticie* does not become 'laetitiae').

In early German carols and hymns we have sometimes given the Low German text; but when the carol is well known, and also in the many cases where this would be an odd match for the musical setting, we have felt free to substitute either a later version (using Praetorius's texts with his settings, for example) or modern High German.

When a modern composer has set an old text, we have nearly always followed his orthography. A rare exception is *Wither's Rocking Hymn* (114), where we have given the complete text in its original form in preference to the modernized selection of verses set by Vaughan Williams in the *Oxford Book of Carols*.

Punctuation

Punctuation in early sources tends either to be sparse or mainly rhetorical rather than syntactical. The conscientious editor may choose either to preserve the original indications or (as we have done) to provide modern syntactical punctuation that will make the grammatical structure, and thus the meaning, clear to the singer. This is particularly important in lyric verse, with its frequently elliptical grammar, and in traditional texts, where the syntax can often be very loose. (In a few folk carols there are passages that resist logical analysis, and here we have punctuated as helpfully as possible without imposing a spurious solution.) We have rarely modified the punctuation of recognized poets.

By the standards of modern prose we have chosen to over-punctuate, but this has been dictated by the special needs of singers, who may be sight-reading or coping with multitudes of unfamiliar verses; with such an editorial approach, a comma need not imply a hiatus of any kind. Singers' needs are normally greater in non-English texts, and we have treated these similarly (though German has its own rules). We have punctuated Latin as though it were English (see 'Quem pastores laudavere', 57, where a failure to punctuate often obscures the vital fact that lines 3 and 4 of verse 1 are direct speech).

Pronunciation

Appendix 1 provides a brief guide to fifteenth-century English pronunciation (carols 24–38), but we have not felt it appropriate to offer guidance for the wide range of other foreign, old, or dialect texts in this anthology. For the various historical pronunciations of Latin, see Harold Copeman's two related books, *Singing in Latin* and *The Pocket Singing in Latin* (1990).

Singing translations

In a simple, strophic form such as the Christmas carol the text has absolute primacy: however indissoluble text and tune may have become, it is the words that *are* the carol. This places a heavy responsibility on the translator, and one that is rarely taken sufficiently seriously. Even when the literal meaning of the original is adequately conveyed (and it is astonishing how cavalier translators can be), the rhyme scheme will often be ignored or bent wilfully out of true, as if it were a mere ornament to the verse. In reality, the counterpoint of verbal and musical rhyme is vital.

We have made determined efforts to find adequate translations, but for the most part have been compelled to do the job ourselves. This has involved original translation, the touching up of existing versions, and centonizing (a cento is 'a composition formed by joining scraps from other authors'—*OED*). We are only too aware of the shortcomings of the results, but they have, at least, the virtue of being accurate, low-key, and reasonably grateful to sing. It is also with the needs of singers in mind that we have favoured the kind of regularly stressed verse characteristic of many hymns: though this can be doggerel when spoken, it has a very different effect when sung. Where an original rhyme scheme is too tight for a strict English imitation, we have substituted one with a similar 'feel' (see, for example, 'Entre le bœuf et l'âne gris', 190).

In a few instances we have chosen not to provide a singing translation. We feel, for example, that no English version could do justice to the fusion of words and music in certain of the medieval *cantiones* (9–15), and have merely supplied literal prose translations. (Where an imitation or free translation is given it is usually accompanied by a literal prose version.)

EDITORIAL POLICY: MUSIC

The broad historical and geographical span of this collection has necessitated some flexibility in the editorial conventions we have adopted, and we have tried to strike a balance between the natural expectations of uniformity within the anthology as a whole and the different editorial conventions that are standard for particular repertories.

Ligatures and coloration are shown only in medieval and certain renaissance carols. They are indicated in the usual manner: by square brackets over the notes concerned, complete in the first case, broken in the second. Plainchant ligatures are shown by slurs.

Plicated notes in medieval music are printed small.

Preliminary staves, showing clefs, time signatures, and initial notes (omitting lengthy rests) are given when this is the most convenient way of indicating how the original notation has been changed. Elsewhere, changes of note values and notated pitch are mentioned in the notes.

Note values have usually been reduced in older carols so that crotchet/quarter-note movement prevails throughout the book.

Part ranges are generally given only when they are not obvious, and particularly when they do not conform to the normal SATB categories. They are shown by small solid noteheads between the key and time signatures.

Transposition. We have frequently adjusted the notated pitch in pre-nineteenth-century repertory, to allow for small differences from the modern standard of a' = 440 Hz and to bring the music to what we believe the intended pitch to have been. This will normally bring it within the most comfortable areas of the singers' ranges. The fifteenth-century English polyphonic carols (24–38) have been brought into ranges suitable for tenors and basses, but they may be retransposed to suit other groups.

Transposing treble clefs (𝄞) are used in the normal way to indicate that the part should be sung/played an octave lower than notated.

𝄞 indicates *either* that a part may be sung in the treble or tenor octave at will *or* that it is to be sung/played at both octaves simultaneously. Where the intention is not obvious from the context, it is explained in the performance note.

☞ indicates the melody line when it is not in the highest part throughout. (For an extreme example, see 'Psallite Unigenito', 52.)

Accidentals are indicated in four ways: an accidental of normal size placed before a note is in the source; an accidental of normal size placed before a note but in round brackets is purely cautionary; an accidental of small size placed before a note would almost certainly have been supplied by performers as a matter of course; an accidental placed over a note and above the staff is an editorial suggestion.

Square brackets are used for various editorial additions.

Ornamentation by the performer was expected in many repertories, especially before the mid-nineteenth century. The subject is too varied and complex to be dealt with in detail here, though for some special cases see 160, 189, and Appendix 3. Cadential trills were routine in the eighteenth century, though sources are inconsistent in their indication and notation. In the interests of visual clarity, we have therefore omitted initial appoggiaturas and final terminations, but both are usually to be understood.

Beaming follows syllabification: notes sung to separate syllables are beamed separately and groups of notes sung to a single syllable are beamed together (or grouped by means of slurs if any are longer than quavers/eighth-notes). Exceptions to this have been made in the fifteenth-century English polyphonic carols, where beaming has been designed to clarify the rhythmic complexities, and slurs have not been used lest they give the impression that a legato style of performance is intended.

Performance notes are intended to suggest possibilities, but do not aim to be comprehensive. They are designed to guide and stimulate rather than to limit, and we have kept them concise by excluding general information on performance practice that is easily available elsewhere. Many carols would normally have been sung as a single melodic line, though we have not always specified this. 'Choir' is used in the conventional way to indicate groups with more than one voice per part or choir with or without congregation/audience. Thus a performance note reading '(*i*) choir; (*ii*) voices and organ' means '*either* choir singing in harmony, *or* any number of voices, in unison or harmony, with or without congregation/audience, and with organ'.

Superscript notation

Superscript rhythms are an economical and generally flexible device for dealing with the difficulty of fitting the words of later verses to the underlay of the first. This is a perennial problem, particularly in traditional carols, where the number of syllables in a line of text can vary considerably between verses and where the conventions for accommodating differences are not always those we might expect. The system is especially valuable for choirs; solo singers may prefer to go their own way, perhaps choosing to adapt the melodic line in some problem passages. (The written-out verses of the sixteenth-century carol 'Thys endere nyghth', 39, reflect this practice.)

The basic principle is that superscript note values indicate the *duration of a syllable* and not necessarily the rhythm to be sung. For example,

means 'joy-' is sung to three beats and '-ful' to one, even if the melodic line has several notes in a context such as

Superscript can also indicate where a single note (e.g., ○) in verse 1 subsequently needs to be split into more than one note on the same pitch (e.g., ♩. ♩). This system means that in simple homophonic pieces such as carols the superscript can nearly always serve not just the tune but equally all the vocal parts.

The notation is normally used to mark departures from the way the first (underlaid) verse is sung. Where there are several texts (e.g., a text and its translation), the superscript notation always refers back to the first verse of the particular text or language being sung.

In the music itself, small notes and dotted slurs indicate the common deviations in later verses, any discrepancies caused by the simultaneous underlaying of more than one verse (or a verse and its translation), and such occasional irregularities as upbeat notes not sung in the first verse or notes which must be substituted later for first-verse rests. Verses 3 and 8 of 'The Cherry Tree [Part I]' (128:1), given separately in our setting, are underlaid in example 1 (opposite) to show how they relate to the music.

Superscript slurs are used to indicate a natural elision of syllables (for instance, 'reverently') and occasionally also as a less rigid alternative to superscript rhythms. Stylized superscript repeat marks (𝄆 𝄇) indicate the repetition of one or more words within a line, though they may not apply to all voices.

We have applied the superscript system with considerable flexibility, especially in cases where adherence to the letter of the law would lead to undue complexity. In certain highly irregular carols, for instance, a greater amount of notation is given than is strictly necessary. In the fifteenth-century English carols, on the other hand, the fit of the texts varies from voice to voice and is in any case a matter of taste; here we have merely indicated the points at which the barlines might fall, leaving the placing of syllables within bars to the performers' discretion.

HUGH KEYTE
ANDREW PARROTT

June 1992

Example 1

1. Jo - seph was an old man, and an old___ man___ was___ he When

he wed - ded Ma - ry in the land of Ga - li - lee, *(etc.)*

3 'Joseph and Mary walked through an orchard good,
Where was cherries and berries, so red as any blood.

3. Jo - seph and___ Ma - ry walked through an orch - ard___ good, Where was

cher - ries and ber - ries, so___ red as a - ny blood.

8 'Go to the tree, Mary, and it shall bow to thee,
And the highest branch of all shall bow to Mary's knee.'

8. 'Go to the tree,___ Ma - ry, and___ it shall bow___ to___ thee, And the

high - est branch of all___ shall___ bow to Ma - ry's knee.'

ACKNOWLEDGEMENTS

Had we realized quite what would be involved in the researching, sifting, ordering, assembling, arranging, translating, writing up, and editing of such diverse material on so large a scale, perhaps we would never have undertaken the task. With the expansion of our original scheme, we found ourselves moving into areas which required ever more specialist assistance. We were most fortunate that Mark Everist and Gareth Curtis were able to help in the preparation of the initial sections of the book, the one acting as advisor for the early medieval repertory (1–22) and providing many of the initial transcriptions, the other taking on an even closer involvement with the music and texts of the English medieval carols (23–38).

At a later stage, a concentrated assault was made on problematic areas, and here we had the help of two scholars of unusually wide musical knowledge and general culture. Tim Crawford resolved countless intractable difficulties during this period, contributing invaluable insights and information of all kinds. His work was ideally complemented by that of Clifford Bartlett, who produced the Bibliography and subsequently joined us as associate editor, bringing to the project an unrivalled grasp of source material and bibliographical procedure, a broad and deep musical knowledge, a long-standing interest in the carol, and a strong sense of the practicalities of editing such diverse material. He also made available the valuable resource of his extensive personal library, and the hospitality that he and his wife Elaine extended so freely through some very exhausting and lengthy periods was most appreciated.

The book would never have achieved publication in anything like its present form without the services of a skilled sub-editor. John Denny joined the editorial team at a point when the organizational problems arising from the sheer bulk of a half-completed anthology were threatening to overwhelm all concerned, and he immediately induced calm and order. His belief in the book and his vision of what it should be were as vital to its completion as his multi-faceted professional skills, his steady judgement, and his unfailing good nature. When, during the final stages, ill health forced him to take a back seat, it was as much a personal as a practical blow for the rest of us. We are very grateful that Emma Tristram, an old friend, was able to complete the editing of the Appendices and Introduction. Our editor at Oxford University Press, Paul Keene, has faced the complex task of assembling this huge work. His attention to detail and clear grasp of the book as a whole in the face of a tight publication schedule have earned him our unqualified respect.

To our colleague and executive editor Malcolm Bruno we owe a debt of thanks every bit as large as that due to John Denny. He was present at the conception of the book and saved it (more than once) when it promised to be stillborn; we hope that he now regards his role of *accoucheur* with a mixture of relief and justified pride. His patience and personal loyalty have matched his business acumen, and his purely musical contribution has been not inconsiderable. He has been supported throughout by the experience and judgement of a first-class literary agent, Andrew Best, now retired from Curtis Brown, London. He has played a central part at every stage of the book's development, and his commitment has never wavered. Our thanks as well to Julian Elloway, senior editor and manager of the Music Department at Oxford University Press, for his support and enthusiasm.

Among the many who have given freely of their time and expertise are some who have earned our particular gratitude. At their head stand Anthony Burton, curator of the Museum of Childhood, Bethnal Green (part of the Victoria and Albert Museum) and Malcolm Taylor, librarian of the Vaughan Williams Memorial Library, Cecil Sharp House. Part II of the book owes much to their help and advice on many aspects of folk-song and custom. We have benefited enormously from Anthony Burton's personal collection of Christmas literature and ephemera, and from the unique resources of the Vaughan Williams library, as well as from the many individuals and institutions with which Malcolm Taylor put us in contact.

Ted Barnes has made available his encyclopaedic knowledge of English plainchant and ritual, and Blaise Compton has done likewise in the field of English gallery music, besides proffering practical help of all kinds and information on a vast range of subjects. Peter Horton and David Klocko generously made available to us their unpublished doctoral theses (on S. S. Wesley and Jeremiah Ingalls, respectively) together with associated musical material, as did Nicholas Heppel his unpublished master's dissertation on music and liturgy in seventeenth-century Durham.

Phyllis Kinney and Meredydd Evans are a husband-and-wife team of scholar–performers whose love of Welsh folk music is as strong as their hospitable urge to share it; all the Welsh carols that we have been able to include are either their suggestions or have benefited from their assistance.

Robin Leaver has solved countless hymnological problems for us, and has given wise advice on contentious subjects. Ian Russell, editor of the *Folk Music Journal* of the English Folk Dance and Song Society, has been equally kind and tireless in his own field. Jack Sage has been unfailingly generous on all matters Spanish, as has John Stevens on problems in medieval literature and linguistics. Nicholas Temperley has responded with painstaking attention to specific requests for information, as well as giving us access to the Hymn Tune Index.

Emily Van Evera has played a highly valued part at all stages, and especially during the lengthy process of setting the carol melodies, homing in on stylistic weaknesses and in many cases drawing on her knowledge of pre-classical and traditional folk music to suggest improvements. John Wilson, treasurer of the Hymn Society of Great Britain and Ireland and doyen of British hymnologists, has most generously acted as a kind of telephonic oracle and guide in the later stages of the book, throwing out suggestions, leaping on errors and misconceptions, and drawing on a lifetime's experience to cast light on some of the more obscure regions of the hymn and carol repertory into which we had innocently strayed.

Finally, we must offer the warmest of thanks to Rollo Woods, whose retirement from university librarianship has been devoted to an orderly investigation of the many manuscript sources of gallery music that moulder unregarded in vestries and attics. The music he has uncovered in his home county of Dorset includes the carol settings used by Thomas Hardy's father, previously known only from incomplete sources, and these have been placed at our disposal as freely as his unique knowledge of the repertory and sources.

Many more individuals have helped us, and we have been touched time and again by the enthusiastic responses to our requests for information. Regrettably, we can do no more than name each one. Our thanks are due to the following: Elisabeth Agate; Wulf Arlt; Alison and Michael Bagenal; Charles Barber; Jeremy Barlow; Elaine Bartlett; Mary Berry; Jaromír Černý; Harvey Brough; Priscilla C. Bruno; David Butchart; Patrick Carnegy; Nym Cooke; Harold Copeman; James Dalton; Geoffrey Dancer; Oliver Davies; Fr. Ian Dickie; Graham Dixon; the late Eric Dobson; Pina Dombey; Canon Alan Fairhurst; David Fallows; Gillian Fox; Mrs W. French; Thomas Gretton; Inglis Gundry; Celia Harper; the late Frank Harrison; Rosemary Haslam; Richard S. Hartman; Wallace Harvey; Stephen Haynes; Trevor Herbert; Tessa Henderson; Walter Hillsman; Christopher Hogwood; Joyce Horn; Lawrence Hughes; David Isaac; Hilary Jones; Dana Josephson; Roberta Keller; Don Kennedy; Catherine King; Tess Knighton; Carl Kroeger; Robin Langley; Horst Leuchtmann; Richard Luckett; Wesley Milgate; Margot Leigh Milner; Rufus Müller; Rui Neri; Victoria Newbert; Geoffrey West.

Incalculable help has also been given by the staff of many specialist libraries and other institutions in Britain and the US: the British Library, especially Arthur Searle and the Manuscript Room, and the staff of the Music Room and the Music Reading Area and admissions desk, all of whom have given every possible help over a very long period; the University of London Library, especially Anthea Baird and the Music Library; the library of King's College, University of London; Peter Salinger and the library of the School of Oriental and African Studies, University of London; the library of University College, London; the Warburg Institute, University of London; Christopher Bornet and the library of the Royal College of Music, London; the City of Westminster Libraries, London, especially the Central Music Library, Buckingham Palace Road, and the Central Reference Library, St Martin's St; Dr Williams's Library, Gordon Square, London; Jane Ramsden and Christie's (South Kensington) Ltd.; the Masters' Library, Dulwich College, London; the Franciscan Friars of the Atonement Central Catholic Library, Westminster, London; Alison Taylor and the Museum of Methodism, City Road, London; the Revd Dr Gordon Huelin and the Society for Promoting Christian Knowledge, Holy Trinity Church, Marylebone Road, London; the Science Museum Library, London; Taverner Concerts Ltd., London; the Victoria and Albert Museum, London, especially Ronald Parkinson and the Collection of Designs, Prints and Paintings, and the V & A Picture Library; Janet Halton and the Moravian Church Library and Archive, Muswell Hill, London (the library is to be transferred to the Special Collections Division of the John Rylands University Library of Manchester); Robin Clutterbuck (Education Officer) and Buckfast Abbey, Buckfastleigh, Devon; Alison Sproston and the library of Gonville and Caius College, Cambridge; Trevor Ling and the Cathedral Library, Canterbury; Roy Saer and the Welsh Folk Museum, St Fagans, Cardiff; Roger Peers and the Dorset County Museum, Dorchester; the Thomas Hardy Collection, Dorset County Library, Dorchester; the Dorset County Record Office, Dorchester; the Devon Record Office, Exeter; the Revd the Mother Superior, St Mary's Convent, Fernham, Faringdon, Oxon; Kathleen Pinder, manager of the Tourist Information Centre, Ilkeley, Yorks; the Kent Archives Office, Maidstone; Michael Powell and Chetham's Library, Manchester; the John Rylands University Library of Manchester, especially Gareth Lloyd, Peter Knockles, and the Methodist Church Archive, Special Collections Division; Manchester Central Library, especially the Henry Watson Music Library, Richard Bond, David Taylor, and the Local Studies Unit, and Christine Linyard and the Language and Literature Library; the Norfolk Record Office, Norwich; the library of St Edmund's College, Old Hall Green, nr. Ware, Herts.; the Bodleian Library, University of Oxford, especially Peter Ward Jones, Robert Bruce, Martin Holmes, and the Music Reading Room; the library of the Faculty of Music, University of Oxford; Martin Olive and the library of the Local Studies Dept., Sheffield City Library; the Local Studies Dept., the Central Library, Stockport, Cheshire; Leslie Douch and the Royal Institution of Cornwall (the Cornish Museum), Truro; the Cornwall Record Office, Truro; the National Library of Ireland, Dublin; the library of Trinity College, Dublin; Fr Charles Davy, SJ, and Conglowes Wood College, Naas, Co. Kildare, Eire; Fintan Murphy and the County Museum, Enniscorthy, Co. Wexford, Eire; Catherine Massip and the Music Dept., Bibliothèque Nationale, Paris; B. Schotts Soehne, Mainz; Bayerische Nazionalmuseum, Munich; Germanisches Nazionalmuseum, Nuremberg; the National Library, Prague; the Hymn Tune Index, Music Dept., University of Illinois at Urbana; the Houghton Library of Harvard University, Cambridge, Massachussetts; The Hymn Society in the United States and Canada (archives), Oberlin College, Oberlin, Ohio; Dorothy Ricto and Concordia Publishing House (Lutheran), St Louis, Missouri; the staff of Talbott Library, Westminster Choir College, Princeton, New Jersey.

We very much hope that no individual or institution has been inadvertently omitted. If so, we apologize and offer our thanks with equal sincerity.

160:I. Music and text reproduced from *The Wexford Carols,* © 1982, by permission of Diarmaid Ó Muirithe, editor.

161:I & II. Reproduced from *The Wexford Carols*, © 1982, by permission of Diarmaid Ó Muirithe, editor.

162: Text reproduced from *The Wexford Carols*, © 1982, by permission of Diarmaid Ó Muirithe, editor.

164:I & II. Melody, Welsh text, and English translation from *National Songs of Wales.* © Copyright 1959 Boosey & Co. Reproduced by permission of Boosey & Hawkes Music Publishers Ltd.

165. Translation of v. 1 from *National Songs of Wales.* © Copyright 1959 Boosey & Co. Reproduced by permission of Boosey & Hawkes Music Publishers Ltd. Translation of v. 2 reproduced from *The Oxford Book of Carols* by permission of OUP.

166. Arrangement © National Museum of Wales (Welsh Folk Museum). Reproduced by permission of National Museum of Wales.

168. Text of v. 1 and melody from *The Penn School Collection.* Permission granted by Penn Center, Inc., St Helena Island, South Carolina. Text of vv. 2–12 reproduced by permission of Penguin Books Ltd.

171. Melody and text from *Ten Christmas Carols from the Southern Appalachian Mountains.* Copyright © 1935 (Renewed) G. Schirmer, Inc. International Copyright Secured. All Rights Reserved. Used by permission of G. Schirmer, Inc.

172. Melody and text from *Songs of the Hill-Folk.* Copyright © 1934 (Renewed) G. Schirmer, Inc. International Copyright Secured. All Rights Reserved. Used by permission of G. Schirmer, Inc.

173. Melody and text from *The Anglo-American Carol Study Book.* Copyright © 1948, 1949 (Renewed) G. Schirmer, Inc. International Copyright Secured. All Rights Reserved. Used by permission of G. Schirmer, Inc.

179. Translation of vv. 1–4 reproduced by permission of Stainer & Bell Ltd.

181:I. English translation from *The International Book of Christmas Carols* by Walter Ehret and George Evans. Copyright holders Walter Ehret and George Evans. Used by permission.

182. Original English translation from *The International Book of Christmas Carols* by Walter Ehret and George Evans. Copyright holders Walter Ehret and George Evans. Used by permission.

183. English translation from *The International Book of Christmas Carols* by Walter Ehret and George Evans. Copyright holders Walter Ehret and George Evans. Used by permission.

192. Translation of vv. 1–3 reproduced by permission of Novello and Co. Ltd. Translation of v. 4 reproduced from *Carols for Choirs 2* by permission of OUP.

195:II. Arrangement © The Church Pension Fund. Reproduced from *The Hymnal*, 1982.

196:II. Arrangement © 1922 B. Feldman and Co. Ltd., trading as H. Freeman and Co., London WC2H 0EA.

197:II. Arrangement © 1954, B. Feldman and Co. Ltd., trading as H. Freeman and Co., London WC2H 0EA.

198. Original English translation of v. 3 from *The International Book of Christmas Carols* by Walter Ehret and George Evans. Copyright holders Walter Ehret and George Evans. Used by permission.

199. English translation from *The International Book of Christmas Carols* by Walter Ehret and George Evans. Copyright holders Walter Ehret and George Evans. Used by permission.

201. Original English translation from *The International Book of Christmas Carols* by Walter Ehret and George Evans. Copyright holders Walter Ehret and George Evans. Used by permission.

PART I

Composed Carols

1

Verbum supernum, prodiens
High Word of God, eternal Light

(Advent)   *Sarum chant*

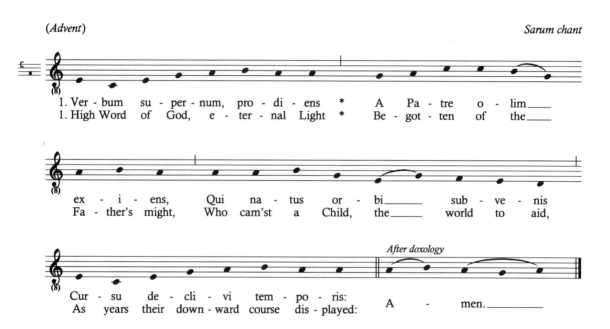

1. Ver - bum su - per - num, pro - di - ens * A Pa - tre o - lim___
1. High Word of God, e - ter - nal Light * Be - got - ten of the___

ex - i - ens, Qui na - tus or - bi___ sub - ve - nis
Fa - ther's might, Who cam'st a Child, the___ world to aid,

After doxology

Cur - su de - cli - vi tem - po - ris: A - men.___
As years their down - ward course dis - played:

2 Illumina nunc pectora
   Tuoque amore concrema;
   Audito et preconia
   Sint pulsa tandem lubrica.

2 Our hearts enlighten from above,
   And kindle with thine own true love;
   That, dead to earthly things, we may
   Be filled with heavenly things today.

3 Iudexque cum post aderis
   Rimari facta pectoris
   Reddens vicem pro abditis
   Iustisque regnum pro bonis,

3 So, when the Judge's sentence dire
   Condemns the lost to endless fire,
   And sweetest accents call the blest
   To enter on their heavenly rest,

4 Non demum arcemur malis
  Pro qualitate criminis;
  Sed cum beatis compotes
  Simus perennes celibes.

4 O may we not for wilful sin
  The due rewards of evil win;
  But grant us, Lord, thy face to see,
  And heaven enjoy eternally.

5 Laus, honor, virtus, gloria
  Dei Patri et Filio,
  Sancto simul Paraclito,
  In sempiterna secula. Amen.

5 To God the Father, God the Son,
  And Holy Spirit, three in one,
  Praise, honour, might and glory be,
  Both now and in eternity. Amen.

c. Tenth-century

vv. 1–4 tr. J. M. Neale (1818–66), adapted
v. 5 editors

The matins Advent hymn in the Sarum rite: it has no place in the Tridentine rite. St Thomas Aquinas (*c.*1227–74) used the same first line in his famous hymn for Corpus Christi to point up the connection between the doctrines of the incarnation and transubstantiation. The translation is adapted from Neale and Helmore's *Hymnal Noted* (1851).

In some sources the 'Amen' is given a tone lower.

PERFORMANCE Choir, antiphonally, the first line (to *) sung by one or two soloists on the side that sings verse 1, the doxology full.

2

Veni, Redemptor gencium
Come, thou Redeemer of the earth

(Christmas)

Sarum chant

1. Ve - ni,_____ Re - demp - tor_____ gen - ci - um,_____ * Os - ten - de par -
1. Come, thou_____ Re - deem - er_____ of_____ the earth, * And ma - ni - fest_____

-tum vir - gi - nis._____ Mi - re - tur om - ne_____ se - cu - lum:
thy vir - gin_____ birth._ Let ev - ery age_____ a - dor - ing fall:

Ta - lis de - cet_____ par - tus_____ De - um._____ A - men._____
Such birth be - fits_____ the_____ God_____ of_____ all._____

The bracketed notes for vv. 4, 5, and 6 apply to the Latin text only.

2 Non ex virili semine
   Sed mistico spiramine
   Verbum Dei factum caro,
   Fructusque ventris floruit.

2 Sprung from no seed of human race
   But by the Spirit's mystic grace,
   The promised fruit of Mary's womb,
   The Word of God, doth flesh assume.

3 Alvus tumescit virginis,
   Claustra pudoris permanent;
   Vexilla virtutum micant;
   Versatur in templo Deus.

3 The virgin womb that honour gained
   With virgin honour all unstained;
   The banners there of virtue glow;
   God in his temple dwells below.

4

4 Procedens de thalamo suo,
   Pudoris aula regia,
   Gemine gigas substancie
   Alacris ut currat viam.

5 Egressus eius a Patre,
   Regressus eius ad Patrem;
   Excursus usque ad inferos,
   Recursus ad sedem Dei.

6 Equalis eterno Patri
   Carnis tropheo accingere,
   Infirma nostri corporis
   Virtute firmans perpetim.

7 Presepe iam fulget tuum,
   Lumenque nox spirat novum
   Quod nulla nox interpollet,
   Fideque iugi luceat.

8 Deo Patri sit gloria,
   Eiusque soli Filio,
   Cum Spiritu Paraclito,
   Et nunc et in perpetuum. Amen.

St Ambrose (c.340–97)

4 Forth from his chamber goeth he,
   That royal home of purity,
   A giant, in twofold substance one,
   Rejoicing now his course to run.

5 From God the Father he proceeds,
   To God the Father back he speeds;
   His course he runs to death and hell,
   Returning on God's throne to dwell.

6 O equal to the Father, thou!
   Gird on thy fleshly mantle now;
   The weakness of our mortal state
   With deathless might invigorate.

7 Thy cradle here shall glitter bright,
   And darkness breathe a newer light
   Where endless faith shall shine serene
   And twilight never intervene.

8 All glory to the Father be;
   Glory, eternal Son, to thee;
   All glory, as is ever meet,
   To God the Holy Paraclete. Amen.

tr. J. M. Neale (1818–66), adapted

Ambrose was the great bishop of Milan who played an important part in St Augustine's conversion. Although he did not invent the hymn form, as was believed in medieval times, he certainly wrote many hymns and taught them to his flock. This Sarum version of one of the finest was sung only at first vespers of the Nativity, on Christmas Eve. It is not sung in the Tridentine rite. The translation is chiefly from Neale and Helmore's *Hymnal Noted* (1851). For Luther's translation see 'Nun komm, der Heiden Heiland' (58).

PERFORMANCE Choir, antiphonally, the first line (to *) sung by two soloists on the side that sings verse 1, the doxology full.

3

Christe, Redemptor omnium
O Christ, the Father's only Son

(*Christmas*)

Sarum chant

1. Chri - ste, Re - demp - tor___ om - ni - um, * Ex___ Pa - tre___
1. O Christ, the___ Fa - ther's_ on - ly_____ Son, * Whose death for___

Pa - tris___ u - ni - ce, So - lus an - te prin - ci - pi - um
all re - demp - tion_____ won, Be - fore the__ worlds, of___ God most_ high

After doxology

Na - tus in - ef - fa - bi - li - ter: A - men._____
Be - got - ten___ all___ in - ef - fa - bly:

2 Tu lumen, tu splendor Patris,
  Tu spes perhennis omnium;
  Intende quas fundunt preces
  Tui per orbem famuli.

2 The Father's light and splendour thou,
  Their endless hope to thee that bow;
  Accept the prayers and praise today
  That through the world thy servants pay.

3 Memento, salutis Auctor,
  Quod nostri quondam corporis
  Ex illibata virgine
  Nascendo, formam sumpseris.

3 Salvation's Author, call to mind
  How, taking form of humankind,
  Born of a virgin undefiled,
  Thou in man's flesh becam'st a child.

4 Hic presens testatur dies,
    Currens per anni circulum,
    Quod solus a sede Patris
    Mundi salus adveneris.

4 Thus testifies the present day,
    Through every year in long array,
    That thou, salvation's source alone,
    Proceededst from the Father's throne.

5 Hunc celem, terra, hunc mare,
    Hunc omne quod in eis est,
    Auctorem adventus tui
    Laudat exultans cantico.

5 Whence sky, and stars, and sea's abyss,
    And earth, and all that therein is,
    Shall still, with laud and carol meet,
    The Author of thine advent greet.

6 Nos quoque, qui sancto tuo
    Redempti sumus sanguine,
    Ob diem natalis tui
    Hympnum novum concinimus.

6 And we who, by thy precious blood
    From sin redeemed, are marked for God,
    On this, the day that saw thy birth,
    Sing a new song of ransomed earth.

7 Gloria tibi, Domine,
    Qui natus es de Virgine,
    Cum Patre et Sancto Spiritu,
    In sempiterna secula.
      Amen.

7 Eternal praise and glory be,
    O Jesu, virgin-born, to thee,
    With Father and with Holy Ghost,
    From men and from the heavenly host.
      Amen.

Sixth-century

tr. J. M. Neale (1818–66), adapted

The Christmas-season matins hymn in the Sarum rite. Both text ('Jesu, Redemptor omnium') and melody differ considerably in the Tridentine rite, where its use is not confined to matins. The translation is adapted from Neale and Helmore's *Hymnal Noted* (1851).

PERFORMANCE Choir, antiphonally, the first line (to *) sung by one or two soloists on the side that sings verse 1, the doxology full.

4

A solis ortus cardine
From lands that see the sun arise

Sarum chant

1. A so - lis or - tus car - di - ne * Et us - que ter - rae__
1. From lands that see__ the sun__ a - rise * To earth's re - mo - test__

li - mi - tem Chri - stum__ ca - na - mus_ Prin - ci - pem,__
bound - a - ries Let ev - ery heart a - wake,__ and_ sing__

After doxology

Na - tum Ma - ri - a__ Vir - gi - ne. A - men.__
The Son of Ma - ry,__ Christ__ the__ King.

2 Beatus Auctor seculi
  Servile corpus induit
  Ut, carne carnem liberans,
  Ne perderet quos condidit.

2 Behold, the world's Creator wears
  The form and fashion of a slave;
  Our very flesh our Maker shares,
  His fallen creature, man, to save.

3 Caste parentis viscera
  Celestis intrat gratia:
  Venter puelle baiulat
  Secreta, que non noverat.

3 For this, how wondrously he wrought!
  A maiden, in her lowly place,
  Became, in ways beyond all thought,
  The chosen vessel of his grace.

4 Domus pudici pectoris
   Templum repente fit Dei
   Intacta nesciens virum,
   Verbo concepit Filium.

4 She bowed her to the angel's word
   Declaring what the Father willed;
   And suddenly the promised Lord
   That pure and hallowed temple filled.

5 Enixa est puerpera
   Quem Gabriel predixerat,
   Quem matris alvo gestiens
   Clausus Iohannes senserat.

5 That Son, that royal Son she bore,
   Whom Gabriel announced before,
   Whom, in his mother's womb concealed,
   The unborn Baptist had revealed.

6 Feno iacere pertulit
   Presepe non abhorruit
   Parvoque lacte pastus est,
   Per quem nec ales esurit.

6 He shrank not from the oxen's stall,
   He lay within the manger-bed,
   And he whose bounty feedeth all
   At Mary's breast himself was fed.

7 Gaudet chorus celestium
   Et angeli canunt Deo,
   Palamque fit pastoribus
   Pastor, Creator omnium.

7 And, while the angels in the sky
   Sang praise above the silent field,
   To shepherds poor the Lord most high,
   The one great Shepherd, was revealed.

8 Gloria tibi, Domine,
   Qui natus es de Virgine,
   Cum Patre et Sancto Spiritu,
   In sempiterna secula.
        Amen.

8 Eternal praise and glory be,
   O Jesu, virgin-born, to thee,
   With Father and with Holy Ghost,
   From men and from the heavenly host.
        Amen.

Coelius Sedulius (fl. c.450)

vv. 1, 5, 8 tr. J. M. Neale (1818–66), adapted
vv. 2–4, 6, 7 tr. J. Ellerton (1826–93)

The Christmas-season hymn at lauds and vespers in the Sarum rite. The second half of the melody differs considerably in the Tridentine rite, where the hymn is sung only at lauds. The text consists of the first seven verses, beginning A–G, of Sedulius's alphabetical poem *Paean alphabeticus de Christo*, which celebrates the dual nature of Christ while tracing his life on earth. (Verse 8 is the appended Christmas doxology; the four verses H–L form the Epiphany office hymn 'Hostis Herodes impie'.) The translation is from Neale and Helmore's *Hymnal Noted* (1851), adapted, and *Church Hymns* (1871). For a harmonization of a German version of the 'A solis' melody with Luther's translation see 'Christum wir sollen loben schon' (61).

The 'temple' of verse 4 is Mary's womb. Tradition, following the *Protevangelium of James*, asserted that Gabriel visited her in the temple, of which she was a dedicated virgin. Verse 5 refers to the visit of Mary to Elizabeth (Matthew 1: 39–56), when John the Baptist leapt in his mother's womb in recognition of Christ in the womb of Mary.

PERFORMANCE Choir, antiphonally, the first line (to *) sung by two soloists on the side that sings verse 1, the doxology full.

5

Letabundus
Come rejoicing

(Christmas; Candlemas)

Sarum chant

1. Le - ta - bun - dus * Ex - ul - tet fi - de - lis cho - rus: 'Al - le -
1. Come re - joi - cing, * Faith-ful__ men, with rap - ture sing - ing: 'Al - le -

-lu - ia!' 2. Re - gem__ re - gum, In - tac - te pro - fu - dit tho - rus:
-lu - ia!' 2. Mon-archs' Mon - arch, From a__ ho - ly maid - en spring - ing:

Res mi - ran - da. 3. An - ge - lus con - si - li - i Na - tus est
Might-y__ won - der! 3. An - gel__ of the__ Coun - sel__ here, Sun from star

de__ vir - gi - ne, Sol de__ stel - la. 4. Sol oc - ca - sum ne - sci - ens,
he__ doth ap - pear, Born of__ maid - en: 4. He a__ sun who knows no__ night,

Stel - la sem - per__ ru - ti - lans, Sem - per__ cla - ra. 5. Si - cut__
She a star whose pa - ler__ light Fa - deth__ ne - ver. 5. As a__

si - dus__ ra - di - um__ Pro - fert__ Vir - go__ Fi - li - um,
star__ its__ kin - dred ray,__ Ma - ry__ doth her__ Child dis - play,

Pa - ri____ for - ma. 6. Ne - que____ si - dus ra - di - o,____
Like in____ na - ture. 6. Still un - dimmed the____ star shines on,____

Ne - que____ Ma - ter____ Fi - li - o Fit cor - rup - ta.
And the____ Maid - en____ bears a____ Son, Pure as____ e - ver.

7. Ced - rus al - ta Li - ba - ni Con - for - ma - tur____ y - so - po
7. Le - ba - non his Ce - dar____ tall To the hys - sop____ on____ the wall

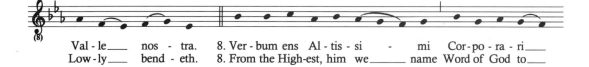

Val - le____ nos - tra. 8. Ver - bum ens Al - tis - si - mi Cor - po - ra - ri____
Low - ly____ bend - eth. 8. From the High - est, him we____ name Word of God to____

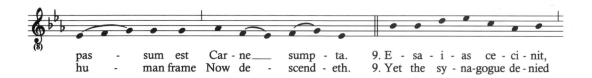

pas - sum est Car - ne____ sump - ta. 9. E - sa - i - as ce - ci - nit,
hu - man frame Now de - scend - eth. 9. Yet the sy - na - gogue de - nied

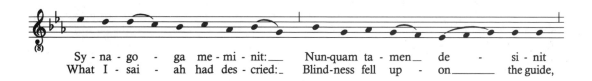

Sy - na - go - ga me - mi - nit:____ Nun - quam ta - men____ de - si - nit
What I - sai - ah had des - cried:____ Blind - ness fell up - on____ the guide,

Es - se____ ce - ca. 10. Si non su - is va - ti - bus, Cre - dat vel____ gen - ti - li - bus____
Proud, un - bend - ing. 10. If her pro - phets speak in vain, Let her heed the gen - tile strain,

Si - bi - li - nis___ ver - si - bus Hec pre - dic - ta.
And from mys - tic___ Si - byl gain Light and___ lead - ing.

11. In - fe - lix pro - pe - ra, Cre - de vel ve - te - ra: Cur dam - na - be - ris,
11. No lon - ger then de - lay: Hear what the Scrip-tures say. Why be cast a - way,

Gens mi - se - ra? 12. Quem do - cet lit - te - ra, Na - tum con - si - de - ra;
A race for - lorn? 12. Turn, and this Child be - hold: That ve - ry Son, of old

Ip - sum ge - nu - it Pu - er - pe - ra. A - men.___
In God's writ fore - told, A maid hath borne.

The Sarum version of one of the finest of all sequences. The chant varies only in detail from continental versions, but the Sarum books associate it with the Virgin rather than with Christmas: it is to be sung as the hymn at second vespers of Candlemas (2 February) when that feast falls before Septuagesima, and is one of the sequences allowable at the daily Lady Mass. In at least some monasteries and outside England it was sung at Christmas. The Council of Trent banned most sequences, but allowed the Benedictines to retain this one, so that it has never been entirely forgotten. The translation is adapted from *The Hymner* (1904).

In the Middle Ages a sequence was always sung between the *Alleluia* and gospel at festal masses. With its wide vocal range and tuneful chant it formed one of the musical climaxes of the service, emphasized in many places by the ringing of bells while it was sung.

The blindness of the synagogue (verses 9–12) was a common medieval theme, in the visual as well as the literary arts. The sibylline prophecies (verse 10) foretell the birth of a Saviour by a Great Virgin and were thought to emanate from female pagan visionaries of the ancient world. Verse 8: some sources have 'mens' (mind) for 'ens' (being).

Many new texts (*contrafacta*) were written to this melody during the Middle Ages, both in Latin and in the vernacular (see R. L. Greene, *Early English Carols*, 1977, pp. xcviii ff.).

PERFORMANCE Choir. As a sequence at mass, antiphon-ally, the first line (to *) sung by one or two soloists on the side that sings verse 1, the final verse perhaps full, and with no 'Amen'; otherwise, as a hymn, begun by one, two, or four soloists, and continued antiphonally.

6

Festa dies agitur

(*Christmas*)
Thirteenth-century
(Egerton MS)

VERSE

1. Fes - ta di - es a - gi - tur—
2. Gau-de - a - mus i - gi - tur— *Mun - do sa - lus red - di - tur—*
3. O quam fe - lix cre - di - tur—

In qua Sol___ ex - o - ri - tur, ___ Qui mun-dum re - plet lu - mi - ne.
In So - le, ___ qui di - ci - tur___ Ve - rus De - us___ in ho - mi - ne.
Ma - ter, ad___ quam mit - ti - tur___ Vox de ce - lo - rum cul - mi - ne!

REFRAIN

Mun - do sa - lus red - di - tur___ Chri - sto, na - to___ de Vir - gi - ne.

Philip the Chancellor? (d. 1236)

TRANSLATION 1 The festive day has come—salvation is restored to the world—on which the Sun has arisen, which fills the world with light. Salvation is restored to the world by Christ, the Virgin's Son.

2 Let us rejoice, therefore, . . . in the Sun, which is called true God made man.

3 How happy must she be, . . . that mother, to whom is sent a voice from the height of heaven.

A monophonic *conductus* from a manuscript collection of mostly thirteenth-century Latin and French songs (British Library, Egerton 274). (A *conductus* was the sung accompaniment to a minor liturgical action, such as the deacon's procession to the *pulpitum* to sing the gospel at mass.) The text may be by Philip the Chancellor (see notes, 8), who wrote some of the best-known Latin songs of the

thirteenth century. It celebrates the return of hope to a world cut off from paradise since Adam's fall. The 'Sol' of verses 1 and 2 is the 'Sun [or Daystar] of righteousness' who will 'arise with healing in his wings', heralded in Malachi's messianic prophecy (4:2) which closes the Old Testament.

There is no key signature in the source, and only at two points is a flat provided, to avoid the tritones in the *clos* endings ('lumine . . . Virgine' in verse 1). We marginally prefer flattening all the Bs, but flattening only these two is a viable alternative. The notation has no rhythmic implications, and the piece may be interpreted in various ways, of which one is in triple time, following the stress-patterns of the text (as indicated by the stems above the staff).

PERFORMANCE (*i*) Unison voices; (*ii*) solo voice(s) for the verses, unison voices for the refrain.

7

Dieus soit en cheste maison

(Christmas)

*Adam de la Halle (b. 1245–50,
d. 1285–8 or after 1306)*

TRANSLATION   May God be in this house, and wealth and joy in abundance.

1 Our Lord Noël sends us to his friends—that is, to lovers, and to the courtly and well-bred—to collect some coppers as a Christmas offering.

2 Our Lord is reluctant to ask for them himself, but to those who are noble and well mannered he has sent us in his place; we are some of his wards and children.

(tr. Stephen Haynes)

Adam de la Halle was one of the most prolific of the *trouvère* poets of late thirteenth-century France. Unlike most of his fellows, who provided only a melody line for their poems, he also wrote settings in parts. He is best known for his pastoral play with songs, *Le Jeu de Robin et de Marion*.

'Dieus soit en cheste maison' concludes the group of *rondeaux* in the beautifully decorated manuscript in the Bibliothèque Nationale, Paris (fonds français 25566), which is essentially a carefully arranged 'collected works' of Adam.

A *rondeau* was one of the poetic *formes fixes* (strict forms) which depended for much of their effect on a calculated tension between the fixed rhymes of the poetry and the different but equally fixed repetitions of the musical phrases.

'Dieus soit' is a very early example of a *chanson de quête* —a luck-visit song. The singers represent themselves as having been sent by their 'Lord Noël' (the equivalent of the English 'Sir Christmas'—see notes, 154), in a parody of what was a common trick of the medieval nobility, too hard up to pay their musicians: they would send them on a 'courtesy' visit to better-off neighbours, who would be obliged to feed and pay them as a sign of respect for their noble master.

PERFORMANCE   Three voices. (For the case against instruments see Christopher Page, *Voices and Instruments of the Middle Ages*, 1987.) The implications of *plicae* (indicated here by small notes) for performance remain obscure.

8

Angelus ad Virginem
Gabriel, fram Heven-King

I

(Latin)

(*Annunciation; Christmas*)

Thirteenth-century
(Arundel MS)

1. An - ge - lus ad Vir - gi - nem Sub - in - trans in con -

-cla - ve, Vir - gi - nis for - mi - di - nem De - mul - cens, in -

-quit:___ 'A - ve! A - ve Re - gi - na Vir - gi - num!

Ce - li Ter - re - que Do - mi - num Con - ci - pi - es, Et

pa - ri - es In - tac - ta Sa - lu - tem ho - mi -num; Tu___

Por - ta___ Ce - li___ fac - ta, Me - de - la Cri - mi - num.'

16

2 'Quomodo conciperem
   Que virum non cognovi?
Qualiter infringerem
   Quod firma mente vovi?'
'Spiritus Sancti gracia
Perficiet hec omnia.
Ne timeas,
Sed gaudeas
   Secura,
Quod castimonia
   Manebit in te pura
Dei potencia!'

3 Ad hec Virgo nobilis
   Respondens inquit ei:
'Ancilla sum humilis
   Omnipotentis Dei.
Tibi, celesti nuncio,
Tanti secreti conscio,
Consenciens
Et cupiens
   Videre
Factum quod audio,
   Parata sum parere
Dei consilio.'

4 Angelus disparuit
   Et statim puellaris
Uterus intumuit
   Vi partus salutaris.
Qui, circumdatus utero
Novem mensium numero,
Hinc exiit
Et iniit
   Conflictum,
Affigens humero
   Crucem, qua dedit ictum
Hosti mortifero.

5 Eya, Mater Domini,
   Que pacem reddidisti
Angelis et homini
   Cum Christum genuisti,
Tuum exora Filium
Ut se nobis propicium
Exhibeat
Et deleat
   Peccata,
Prestans auxilium
   Vita frui beata
Post hoc exilium.

Philip the Chancellor? (d. 1236)
(Arundel MS)

I

(English)

(Annunciation; Christmas)

Thirteenth-century
(*Arundel MS*)

1. Ga - bri - el, fram He - ven - King Sent to__ the Mai - de__

swee - te, Brou - te__ hir blis - ful ti - ding And fair__ he gan

hir__ gree - te: 'Heil_ be thu,__ ful__ of grace_ a - right!

For_ God - es__ Son, this He - ven - Light, For_ man - nes love Wil

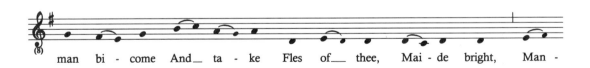

man bi - come And__ ta - ke Fles of__ thee, Mai - de bright, Man -

-ken free_ for to_____ ma - ke Of sen_ and dev - les_ might.'

2 Mildelich him gan andswere
   The milde Maide thanne:
'Wichewise sold ich bere
   A child withute manne?'
Th'angel hir seid: 'Ne dred tee nout;
Thurw th'Oligast sal been iwrout
This ilche thing
Warof tiding
   Ich bringe;
Al manken wurth ibout
   Thurw thine sweet childinge
And ut of pine ibrout.'

3 Wan the Maiden understood
   And th'angels wordes herde,
Mildelich, with milde mood,
   To th'angel hie andswerde:
'Ure Lords thewe maid iwis
Ich am, that heer aboven is;
Anentis me
Fulfurthed be
   Thi sawe
That ich, sith his wil is,
   A maid, withute lawe,
Of moder have the blis.'

4 Th'angel went awei mid than
   Al ut of hire sighte;
Hire womb arise gan
   Thurw th'Oligastes mighte.
In hir wes Crist bilok anon,
Sooth God, sooth man in fles and bon,
And of hir fles
Ibore wes
   At time,
Warthurw us kam good won;
   He bout us ut of pine,
And let him for us slon.

5 Maiden-Moder makeles,
   Of milce ful ibunde,
Bid for us him that tee ches,
   At wam thu grace funde,
That he forgive us sen and wrake,
And clene of evri gelt us make,
And heven-blis,
Wan ur time is
   To sterve,
Us give, for thine sake,
   Him so heer for to serve
That he us to him take.

Thirteenth-century
(Arundel MS)

II

Fourteenth-century
(Dublin Troper)

(Annunciation; Christmas)

1. An - ge - lus ad Vir - gi - nem Sub - in - trans in___ con - cla - ve,
1. Ga - bri - el, fram He - ven-King Sent to the Mai - de swee - te,

Vir - gi - nis for - mi - di - nem De - mul - cens, in - quit: 'A - ve!
Brou - te hir blis - ful___ ti - ding And fair he gan___ hir gree - te:

A - ve Re - gi - na Vir - gi - num! Ce - li Ter -
'Heil___ be thu, ful___ of grace___ a - right! For___ Go - des

III

(*Annunciation; Christmas*)

Fourteenth-century
(Cotton Fragments)

1. An - ge-lus ad Vir - gi - nem Sub - in - trans in__ con - cla - ve, Vir - gi-nis for-
1. Ga - bri-el, fram He - ven-King Sent to__ the Mai - de swee - te, Brou - te hir blis-

-mi - di - nem__ De - mul - cens, in - quit: 'A - ve! A - ve Re - gi - na__
-ful ti - ding And fair__ he gan__ hir gree - te: 'Heil__ be thu,__ ful of__

Vir - gi - num! Ce - li Ter - re - que Do - mi - num Con - ci - pi - es, Et
grace__ a - right! For__ God-es__ Son, this He - ven-Light, For man - nes__ love Wil

pa - ri - es__ In - tac - ta Sa - lu - tem ho - mi-num; Tu__
man bi - come__ And ta - ke Fles of__ thee, Mai - de bright, Man -

Por - ta Ce - li fac - ta, Me - de - la Cri - mi - num.'
-ken__ free for__ to ma - ke Of sen and dev - les might.'

TRANSLATION   1 The angel, coming secretly to the Virgin, calming the Virgin's fear, said: 'Hail! hail, Queen of Virgins! You shall conceive the Lord of Heaven and Earth and give birth, remaining a virgin, to the Salvation of mankind; you, made the Gateway of Heaven, the cure for sin.'

2 'How shall I conceive, since I know not a man? How shall I break what I have resolutely vowed?' 'The grace of the Holy Spirit shall perform all this. Fear not, but rejoice, confident that chastity will remain pure in you by the power of God.'

3 At this, the noble Virgin, replying, said to him: 'I am the humble servant of almighty God. To you, heavenly messenger, who know so great a secret, I give my assent and desire to see done what I hear, and am ready to obey God's will.'

4 The angel disappeared, and at once the girl's womb swelled up by the power of the birth of Salvation. He, having been contained in the womb for nine months, came out from it and entered the conflict, taking on his shoulder the Cross, by which he gave the blow to the mortal enemy.

5 O Mother of the Lord, who restored peace to angels and men when you gave birth to Christ, beg of your Son that he may show himself favourable to us and wipe away our sins, offering help to enjoy the blessed life after this exile.
(tr. editors)

TRANSLATION   1 Gabriel, sent from the King of Heaven to the sweet Maiden, brought her happy news and greeted her courteously: 'Hail be thou, [who art] indeed full of grace! For God's Son, this Light of Heaven, for love of man will become man and take human form from thee, fair Maiden, to free mankind of sin and the devil's power.'

2 The gentle Maiden then gently answered him: 'In what manner should I bear a child without a husband?' The angel said to her: 'Fear nothing: through the Holy Ghost shall this very thing be done of which I bring news; all mankind will be redeemed by means of thy sweet child-bearing and brought out of torment.'

3 When the Maiden understood and heard the angel's words, she answered the angel gently, with gentle spirit: 'I am indeed the bond-maid of our Lord, who is above. Concerning me may thy saying be fulfilled, that I, since it is his will, may as a maiden, contrary to natural law, have the joy of motherhood.'

4 With that, the angel went away, out of her sight; her womb began to swell through the power of the Holy Ghost. In her Christ was straightway enclosed, true God and true man in flesh and bone, and of her flesh was born in due time, whereby good hope came to us: he redeemed us from pain [of hell] and allowed himself to be slain for us.

5 Matchless Maiden-Mother, [who art] full of compassion, pray for us to him that chose thee, in whose sight you found grace, that he forgive us [our] sin and hostility and absolve us from all guilt, and, when our time comes to die, give us the bliss of heaven, for thy sake, so serving him here [below] that he take us to himself.
(tr. E. J. Dobson, adapted)

A *cantio* (song) of the angel's annunciation to Mary. Although possibly French, it was particularly popular in Britain, where it survives in several manuscripts. In the sixteenth century the members of St Mary's College, Aberdeen, were required to sing this and two antiphons in the intervals between twelve strokes of the great bell (presumably sounding the angelus) at six o'clock every evening, between vespers and supper, 'solemniter cum organis et cantu' ('solemnly, with organ and voices', probably implying alternate vocal and organ verses). In Chaucer's 'Milleres Tale', from *The Canterbury Tales*, the young clerk (cleric) of Oxenford is described as having a 'gay sautrye / On which he made a nightes melodye / So swetely that al the chambre long, / And *Angelus ad Virginem* he song'. This has been generally taken to mean that he accompanied himself on the psaltery as he sang, but the playing and the singing were possibly separate activities.

The compiler of *Speculum Laicorum* ('The Mirror of the Laity'), an English collection of edifying stories of the late thirteenth century, writes that 'Odo [of Cheriton] tells of a certain great cleric, Chancellor of Paris, who, among many other blessed things which he uttered, composed that sweetest song about the Virgin that begins: Angelus ad virginem'. Christopher Page (in '*Angelus ad virginem*: a new work by Phillippe the Chancellor?', *Early Music*, vol. XI, no. 1, January 1983, pp. 69–70) has suggested that the 'great cleric' could be Philip the Chancellor (d. 1236), who is credited with other well-known thirteenth-century *cantiones*, though whether he also composed the music is unknown.

Tune I and both texts are from the late thirteenth-century Arundel manuscript (British Library, Arundel MS 248), the only source that exists with both Latin and English texts. (The latter is an imitation rather than a strict translation.) There are minor discrepancies between the Latin texts in the English sources (they are listed in E. J. Dobson and F. Ll. Harrison, *Medieval English Songs*, 1979, whose edition we follow for the English, and John Stevens, '*Angelus ad virginem*: the history of a medieval song', 1981, which also gives a full list of the sources). This and another English paraphrase, 'The angel to the Vergyn said' (Bodleian Library, Oxford, Douce MS 302), were, Christopher Page suggests, probably the products of roaming Franciscan friars, who with their devotion to the Virgin and concern for the non-Latin-speaking laity could have brought the song to England in the first place.

The scribe of Arundel 248 wrote the tune out only once, with five verses of each text underlaid. The strict metrical pattern of the poem makes underlay unproblematic, but the rhythmic interpretation is difficult. As with other medieval songs (e.g., 'Dieus soit en cheste maison', 7), the significance of the *plicae* (transcribed as small notes) is unclear, and it is complicated here by the fact that when a des-cending note is plicated the main note is written twice (as in the incipit), while ascending plicated notes are not doubled. We favour an 'isosyllabic' reading (each syllable occupying one beat) with a plainsong-like lengthening of the last note of each phrase. This brings out the ornamentation written into the music (the four-note group on '-li' of 'Celi' at the end of verse 1 is an elaboration of the two notes on the first syllable of 'intacta' in the previous phrase), it permits additional ornamentation, and it allows subsequent stanzas to be stressed naturally.

Some editors have abstracted the middle voice of II for solo performance: there is no particular objection to this as long as it is presented as a modern derivation, but solo performances of songs of this kind would tend towards rhythmic freedom and an ornate line, and the Arundel version is arguably closer to what the composer conceived.

Setting II is one of three contained in Cambridge University Library MS Add. 710, the mid-fourteenth-century Dublin Troper. On fo. 127 is a monophonic version with a complete Latin text, and on the final leaf, fo. 130, are two three-part arrangements, one with partial text and the other, on the verso, untexted: this last is the one we give. The rhythm here is unambiguous. Bar 8 is a jumble of notes in the source; this embellishment (which it might be inappropriate to repeat in the later verses) is applied to the crucial word 'Ave', and is the most enterprising of the many ornamental figures in this ornate setting. Throughout, and also in setting III, the underlying melodic line would perhaps have been variously ornamented in subsequent verses.

Setting III is from another British Library source, the Cotton Fragments (XXIX, fo. 36ᵛ). These few smoke-blackened sheets are from a manuscript of 1349, relics of a fire that destroyed the Cotton Library in 1731. The notation is ambiguous, but a regular compound-time interpretation seems to us the only sensible one. (It preserves the prevailing consecutive sixths in bar 9, for example, which an isosyllabic reading will not.) The editorial barlines are intended only as a guide to phrasing.

Verse 2, Latin: Mary lived as a temple virgin before the Annunciation, according to the *Protevangelium of James*.

PERFORMANCE   I, solo voice, with instrumental drone *ad lib*.

II (*i*) three voices; (*ii*) voice (on melody) and two instruments. The melisma in bar 8 should possibly be sung only in verse 1 (on 'Ave')—see notes, above.

III (*i*) voice and instrument; (*ii*) two voices.

All three settings may be performed at any comfortable pitch. In the English text, *e/ed/es* final syllables are sounded except where elision is indicated.

9

Procedenti Puero–Eya! novus annus est
Verbum caro factum est–Eya! novus annus est

I

(*New Year*)

Thirteenth-century
(Florence MS)

VERSE

1. Pro - ce - den - ti__ Pu - e - ro— E - ya!__ no - vus__
2. In__ val - le mi - se - ri - e— Ve - nit__ nos re - di - me - re—

an - nus_____ est— Vir - gi - nis ex u - te - ro—

REFRAIN

Glo - ri - a lau - dis! *De - us__ ho - mo__ fac - tus__ est Et im - mor - ta - lis.*

3 Christus nobis natus est—
   Eya! novus annus est—
   Crucifigi passus est—
    Gloria laudis!

4 Cuius crucifixio—
   Eya! novus annus est—
   Nostra sit salvatio—
    Gloria laudis!

5 Redemptorem seculi—
   Eya! novus annus est—
   Laudant omnes populi—
    Gloria laudis!

6 Collaudemus Dominum—
   Eya! novus annus est—
   Salvatorem hominum—
    Gloria laudis!

Philip the Chancellor? (d. 1236)
(S. Gall MS)

TRANSLATION 1 To the Boy coming forth—rejoice! the New Year is come—from the womb of a virgin—glory and praise! God is made man and [remains] immortal.
  2 To this vale of misery . . . he comes to redeem us . . .
  3 Christ was born for us . . . he endured crucifixion . . .

4 And may his crucifixion . . . be our salvation . . .
5 The Redeemer of the Ages . . . all peoples praise . . .
6 Let us unite to praise the Lord . . . the Saviour of mankind . . .

II

(*New Year*)

Fourteenth-century
(*Aosta MS 9–E–19*)

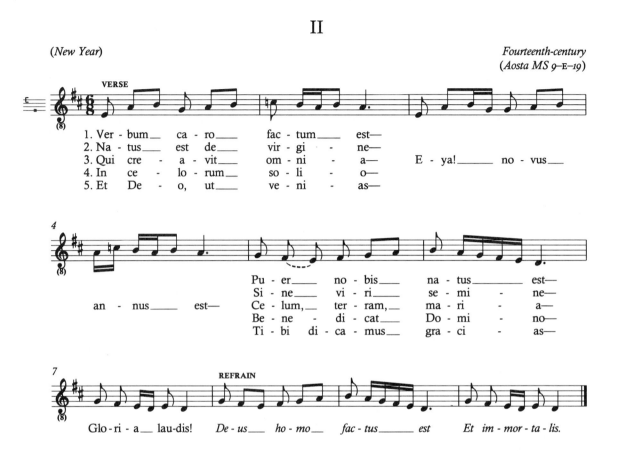

VERSE

1. Ver - bum __ ca - ro __ fac - tum __ est—
2. Na - tus __ est de __ vir - gi - ne—
3. Qui cre - a - vit __ om - ni - a—
4. In ce - lo - rum __ so - li - o—
5. Et De - o, ut __ ve - ni - as—

E - ya! __ no - vus __ an - nus __ est—

Pu - er __ no - bis __ na - tus __ est—
Si - ne __ vi - ri __ se - mi - ne—
Ce - lum, __ ter - ram, __ ma - ri - a—
Be - ne - di - cat __ Do - mi - no—
Ti - bi di - ca - mus __ gra - ci - as—

REFRAIN

Glo - ri - a __ lau-dis!   *De - us __ ho - mo __ fac - tus __ est   Et im - mor - ta - lis.*

TRANSLATION 1 The Word is made flesh—rejoice! the New Year is come—a Boy is born for us—glory and praise! God is made man but [remains] immortal.

2 He is born of a virgin . . . without human seed . . .

3 He who created all things . . . the heavens, the earth, the seas . . .

4 . . . on the heavenly throne . . . may he bless the Lord . . .

5 And unto [thee, O] God, for coming to us . . . Let us say: Thanks be to thee.

Versions of this popular New Year *cantio* (song) are found in a number of medieval sources (see *Analecta Hymnica*, vol. 20, p. 90). In a thirteenth-century manuscript at S. Gall, Switzerland (MS 383), it is ascribed to Philip the Chancellor (of the University of Paris), who probably wrote the words (and in some cases perhaps also the music) of some of the best-known Latin songs of that century.

The music of version I is taken from one of the major sources of thirteenth-century music, Biblioteca Medicea-Laurenziana, Florence, Plut. 29.1, copied in a commercial scriptorium in Paris within a few years of 1250 (see Mark Everist, *Polyphonic Music in Thirteenth-Century France*, 1989). The words of the first verse are the same as in the S. Gall manuscript, but its remaining three verses are conventional phrases that any singer might have extemporized ('Sine viri semine / natus est de Virgine. Sine viri copula / natus ante secula. Sit laus Regi Glorie / et pax Regno Gallie'— 'Without human seed he is born of a virgin. Without human procreation he was born before time. Praise be to the King of Glory and peace to the kingdom of France'.) The S. Gall melody lacks the first note, thus obscuring the quotation of the opening of the well-known melody of the hymn 'Ave maris stella'. We have accordingly set the superior S. Gall text to the Florence music; we have also amended the last two notes of bar 8 (E–F♯ in Florence).

This may seem an odd song to associate with 1 January, but the dual celebration of the Circumcision of Christ and of the original *natale* (feast-day) of the Virgin Mary had not entirely died out in Philip's time.

Version II is from the cycle of *Benedicamus* tropes appended to a fourteenth-century Aosta manuscript (9–E–19).

The troping of the liturgy, a medieval passion, was essentially an expansion of an existing text. The new text could take many forms: a few interpolated words, a learned gloss entwined with the original, a set of verses for some feast or season—in effect a newly created hymn hung upon an existing liturgical peg. It might be sung to a melismatic passage in the existing chant, to fresh chant, or to a new tune provided for it.

Each ecclesiastical office ended with a ritual exchange, to plainchant, between a single voice or a few voices (depending on the particular office and the status of the feast or season) and the whole choral body to the text 'Benedicamus Domino—Deo gracias' ('Let us bless the Lord—Thanks be to God'). The *Benedicamus* versicle became one of the most popular spots for extended verse tropes, with the *Deo gracias* response either incorporated in the final stanza (which may sometimes have been sung by all, possibly even in simple polyphony; see for example 21: 1) or sung by all to the existing chant. In the case of *Benedicamus* verses, such as the present ones, the precentor (or his equivalent) and/or his assistants (the 'cantors' or 'rulers of choir'), or some other designated persons, would sing to the end of the verse containing the versicle. The full choral body would respond, either with the final (*Deo gracias*) stanza or with the untroped *Deo gracias* response to its accustomed chant. Such songs continued to be sung as

straightforward hymns after the sixteenth-century abolition of large-scale troping. The *Piae Cantiones* repertory would certainly have been sung in this way, and many popular carols (for example, 'Unto us is born a Son', 21) are in fact *Benedicamus* verses, their origins betrayed only by a puzzling tendency to end with blessing of the Lord.

The present song is headed 'In circumcisione domini benedicamus ad vesperas' ('On the feast of the Circumcision of the Lord, the *Benedicamus* at vespers') and is one of several sets of *Benedicamus* verses in this manuscript that exist elsewhere as straightforward songs and seem to have been adapted (sometimes rather clumsily) as tropes. The adaptation in this case is a happy one, producing a tight, attractive song. The opening 'Verbum caro', not found in other versions, reflects the many allusions to the opening of St John's gospel in the liturgy of the Circumcision.

PERFORMANCE I and II, voices: verse, solo/soli, perhaps full in bars 3–4 and 7; refrain, full. The Gallic stress on the final syllable of Latin words is very noticeable in II, but should not be exaggerated in performance. We have been less cautious than usual in the vexed question of applying rhythm to the non-mensural notation, because comparison of the various versions seems to rule out other interpretations. (For a transcription of I in modal rhythm see Gordon A. Anderson, *Notre Dame and Related Conductus*, vol. 8, M32, 1979; for an equal-note transcription of II see Frank Ll. Harrison, 'Benedicamus, conductus, carol: a newly discovered source', *Acta Musicologica*, XXXVII, 1965, p. 44. For the S. Gall version see David Wulstan, *An Anthology of Carols*, 1968.)

10

Ad cantus leticie

I

(*Christmas*)

Fourteenth-century
(Aosta MS 9–E–17)

1. Ad can - tus le - ti - ci - e Nos in - vi - tat ho - di - e

Spes, et a - mor pa - tri - e Ce - les - - - tis.

2 Natus est Emanuel,
   Quem predixit Gabriel,
   Unde sanctus Daniel
      Est testis.

*3 Judea gens misera,
   Crede Lege propera,
   Potens esse libera
      Si credis.

4 Ergo nostra concio
   In cordis et organo
   Benedicat Domino
      Jubilo.

5 Et Deo, qui venias
   Donat et leticias,
   Nos eidem gracias
      Agamus.

(Aosta MS 9–E–17)

† Variant ending for verse 2.

TRANSLATION 1 Hope, together with love of our heavenly homeland, today invites us to songs of joy.
  2 Emmanuel is born, whom Gabriel foretold and of whom the blessed Daniel is witness.

3 Wretched Jewish race, hasten to believe the Law: you can be free if you will believe.
  4 So may our assembly with strings and organ joyfully bless the Lord.
  5 And unto God, who gives us blessings and joys, let us give thanks.

II

(*Christmas*)   (*Piae Cantiones, 1582*)

1. Ad can-tus lae-ti-ci - ae   Nos in-vi-tat ho-di -

1. Ad can-tus lae-ti-ci-ae   Nos in-vi-tat ho-di-

-e   Spes, et a-mor pa-tri-ae Coe-les - tis.

-e   Spes, et a-mor pa-tri - -ae Coe-les - tis.

2 Natus est Emanuel,
   Quod praedixit Gabriel,
   Unde sanctus Daniel
      Est testis.

3 Ergo nos cum gaudio
   Nostra simul concio
   Benedicat Domino
      Jubilo.

(*Piae Cantiones, 1582*)

TRANSLATION   (verses 1, 2, as text I, but '*which* Gabriel foretold and of *which*. . .') 3 With gladness, therefore, may we and all our company joyfully bless the Lord.

A *cantio* (song) in *binatim* style. *Cantus planus binatim*, literally 'doubled' (or 'twinned') plainchant, was a very common type of simple polyphony. In origin it was a technique of improvising a second voice to an existing melody (see C. Corsi and P. Petrobelli, *Le Polifonie Primitive in Friuli e in Europa*, 1989), often with a characteristic 'mirroring' of the line (see the opening of 'Veni, veni, Emanuel', 16: 1). Oral transmission always predominated.

Version I is in the form of a *Benedicamus* trope (see notes, 9), from a fourteenth-century manuscript in Aosta, where it is headed 'Benedicamus for Vespers of the Vigil of the Birth of our Lord'. The first four verses substitute for the versicle 'Benedicamus Domino', sung by the cantors; verse 5 para-phrases the response 'Deo gracias', and may well have been sung full. The music is written out for all five verses, with a variant ending for verse 2. The original notation gives no indication of rhythm: for this we have followed Frank Ll. Harrison's edition of a virtually identical copy (Aosta, MS 9–E–19) in *Acta Musicologica*, XXXVII, 1965, pp. 35–48. Version II is from *Piae Cantiones* (1582). Parallel sixths, unlike thirds, are unknown in medieval *binatim*, and the way they have replaced the fifths of version I suggests later adaptation.

Version I uses the medieval technique of voice-exchange known as *rondellus*; in the second phrase of II the exchange has disappeared, perhaps in the process of oral transmission (see notes, 11).

PERFORMANCE   I, two solo voices, the last verse full *ad lib.*; II, voices.

11

Laudemus cum armonia

Fourteenth-century
(Aosta MS 9–E–19)

(*Christmas*)

Lau - de - mus cum ar - mo - ni - a Sum - mi___ Pa - tris_ Splen - do - rem,
Quem sa - cra vir - go Ma - ri - a Pe - pe - rit Sal - va - to - rem

Su - um - que Ge - ni - to - rem, Cu - ius na - ti___ so - lemp - ni - a Re - co - len -

-tes men - te pi - a Ad ip - si - us ho - no - rem; Be - ne - di - ca - mus

Do - mi - no, Psal - len - tes 'Al - le - lu - ia!' Er - go____ ad -
Ut in - de_

-sis ex - o - ra - trix, De - i_____ pro_ no - bis ge - ni - trix,
cres - cat cas - ti - tas; De - o_____ di - ca - mus gra - ci - as.

TRANSLATION Let us praise with harmony the Splendour [Christ] of the most high Father, whom the blessed Virgin Mary bore as the Saviour and as her own Father, observing in his honour the festival of his birth with a holy mind; let us bless the Lord, singing 'Alleluya!' Be present therefore, our advocate, who bore God for our sake, that purity may henceforth increase; let us say: Thanks be to God.

This *cantio* (song) is one of several pieces we have taken from the complete cycle of *Benedicamus* tropes in a fourteenth-century manuscript in the Seminary Library in Aosta, Italy (9–E–19). It is also in another Aosta source (MS 9–E–17) and, since it has been found nowhere else, may have originated locally. It is assigned to vespers of Christmas Day. (Both manuscripts give 'ermonia', presumably a scribal error.) At bar 31 the lower voice reads:

The song is in *binatim* style (see notes, 10), and the final section (bars 32–40 and their repeat) uses *rondellus* or voice-exchange technique, the two simple phrases passing back and forth between the two parts. (The manuscript gives only the first four words of text for this section, and the music stops abruptly after 'Dei'—bar 37, first time—but this is enough to indicate the *rondellus* technique, and the rest of the text can be supplied from elsewhere in the manuscript, where it forms the conclusion of two tropes for other feasts.) This is one of many cases where the concluding 'Deo gracias' would appear to have been designed for polyphonic performance by the whole choral body.

PERFORMANCE Bars 1–32, four (or two) voices, bars 32–40, choir.

12

Verbum caro factum est: Dies est leticie

(Christmas; New Year?)

*Fourteenth-century
(Aosta MS 9–E–19)*

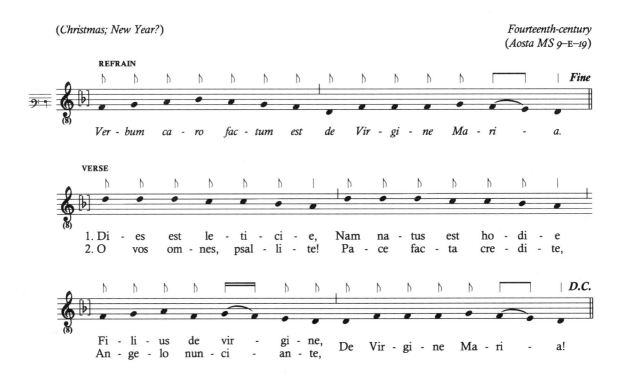

REFRAIN

Ver - bum ca - ro fac - tum est de Vir - gi - ne Ma - ri - a.

VERSE

1. Di - es est le - ti - ci - e, Nam na - tus est ho - di - e
2. O vos om - nes, psal - li - te! Pa - ce fac - ta cre - di - te,

Fi - li - us de vir - gi - ne, De Vir - gi - ne Ma - ri - a!
An - ge - lo nun - ci - an - te,

3 Lux venit de Lumine
   In intacta Virgine;
   Noël! noël! dicite
    De Virgine Maria!

4 Portam clausam graditur,
   Qui alcio geritur:
   Deus homo nascitur
    De Virgine Maria.

5 Fatur a pastoribus,
   Dum natus est parvulus,
   Rex potens fortissimus,
    De Virgine Maria.

6 O Jesu, quem credimus,
   Da salutem omnibus
   Super in celestibus
    De Virgine Maria!

(Aosta MS 9–E–19)

TRANSLATION   The Word is made flesh by the Virgin Mary.

1 This is a joyful day, for today a Son is born of a virgin, of the Virgin Mary.

2 Sing praises, everyone; believe that peace has come, through the message of an angel, by the Virgin Mary.

3 The Light [Christ] within a pure virgin comes from the Light [the Father]; sing Nowell! nowell! for the Virgin Mary.

4 He proceeds through the closed gate, he who is born from on high; God is born a man by the Virgin Mary.

5 It is told by the shepherds that a little Child is born; a great and mighty King is born of the Virgin Mary.

6 O Jesu, in whom we believe, grant us all salvation among those who dwell above in heaven, through the Virgin Mary.

This is one of four carols (two for the Christmas season) that follow the cycle of *Benedicamus* song-tropes for the whole year in a fourteenth-century manuscript in the Seminary Library in Aosta, Italy (9–E–19; see notes, 9). Frank Ll. Harrison argued that these rare examples of early carols were intended to have a function analogous to that of the tropes, and were perhaps sung with them, an appropriate carol preceding the appointed song-trope at the *Benedicamus* of matins, lauds, or vespers.

Unlike the *Benedicamus* pieces, the four carols in this Aosta manuscript are not designated for particular occasions. The Marian emphasis could imply use on New Year's Day, since, although Mary is prominent in the liturgy of the whole of the Christmas octave (25 December to 1 January), she received particular honour on the octave day, 1 January, which had been her original *natale*, or feast-day.

There are nine verses in the source. The 'closed gate' of verse 4 is the eastern portal of the city in Ezechiel's vision (Ezechiel 43:4; 44:2) which is traditionally associated with Mary's virginity: the King passes through it (i.e., Christ is born), after which it is sealed up for ever (Mary's perpetual virginity).

There is no connection with the song 'Dies est laeticiae' (18) beyond the opening words of the verse.

PERFORMANCE   Refrain, choir; verse, solo voice(s). The opening refrain should probably be sung first by solo voice(s) and repeated full.

13

Verbum caro factum est: In hoc anni circulo

(New Year; Christmas)

Verbum caro factum est de Virgine Maria.

1 In hoc anni circulo
Vita datur seculo,
Nato nobis Parvulo
De Virgine Maria.

2 O beata femina,
Cuius ventris Gloria
Mundi lavat crimina
De Virgine Maria.

3 Stella Solem protulit,
Sol salutem contulit,
Carnem veram abstulit
De Virgine Maria.

4 Fons de suo rivulo
Nascitur pro populo
Quem tulit de vinculo
De Virgine Maria.

5 Laus, honor, virtus Domino
Deo Patri et Filio,
Sancto simul Paracleto
De Virgine Maria.

Twelfth-century?
(Piae Cantiones, 1582)

TRANSLATION The Word was made flesh by the Virgin Mary.

1 In this rounding of the year life is given to the world; a little Boy is born to us by the Virgin Mary.

2 O blessed woman, the Glory of whose womb cleanses the sins of the world by the Virgin Mary.

3 A star brings forth the Sun, the Sun brings salvation, and takes unto itself very flesh by the Virgin Mary.

4 A Source from its own river is born for the people, whom it has brought from prison by the Virgin Mary.

5 Glory, honour, power be to the Lord God, Father and Son, and to the Holy Ghost, by the Virgin Mary.

This was one of the most popular of all medieval carols, known as early as the twelfth century. (A text, partly in Latin, partly in Provençal, occurs in a manuscript in the Bibliothèque Nationale, Paris, fonds latin 1139, fo. 48). Versions from all over Europe survive. Version II and the text are from *Piae Cantiones* (1582). Version I, in *binatim* style (see notes, 10), is from the Czech Jistebnice Cantional (1420), which shares much of its repertory with the 1582 publication. Version III is one of two florid early fifteenth-century settings of the tune, this one from the Trent MS 92 (fo. 13), a large anthology mostly of sacred music. Only two parts are given, with the indication that the third is to be improvised in *fauxbourdon*, as in some English fifteenth-century carols (see notes, 28). Just the first verse appears. A setting in Bologna University Library (MS 2216, p. 37) has the tune in the lowest of the three parts. There is a charmingly ornamented monophonic version in Turin, Biblioteca Nationale (MS F14, fo. 334^r).

PERFORMANCE I, refrain, choir; verse, two voices. II, refrain, choir; verse, solo voice(s). III, three solo voices, perhaps with choral refrain.

I

(Jistebnice Cantional, 1420)

II

(*Piae Cantiones, 1582*)

Ver - bum ca - ro fac - tum est de Vir - gi - ne; Ver - bum

ca - ro fac - tum est de Vir - gi - ne Ma - ri - a. (v.5)

1. In hoc an - ni cir - cu - lo_____ Vi - ta da - tur se - cu -

- lo,_____ Na - to no - bis Par - vu - lo De Vir - gi - ne;

Na - to no - bis Par - vu - lo De Vir - gi - ne Ma - ri - a.

2 O beata femina,
   Cuius ventris Gloria
   Mundi lavat crimina
   De Virgine Maria.

3 Stella Solem protulit,
   Sol salutem contulit,
   Carnem veram abstulit
   De Virgine Maria.

4 Fons de suo rivulo
   Nascitur pro populo
   Quem tulit de vinculo
   De Virgine Maria.

5 Laus, honor, virtus Domino
   Deo Patri et Filio,
   Sancto simul Paracleto
   De Virgine Maria.

Twelfth-century?
(*Piae Cantiones, 1582*)

Repeat signs apply to setting II only.

III

Fifteenth-century
(Trent MS)

(New Year; Christmas)

14

Verbum Patris hodie

I

(*Christmas*)

Thirteenth-century
(Sarum Antiphonal)

1. Ver - bum Pa - tris ho - di - e Pro - ces - sit de Vir - gi - ne;
2. Re - ful - gens pas - to - ri - bus Nun - ci - a - vit an - ge - lus

Ve - nit___ nos re - di - me - re, Et ce - les - ti pa - tri - e
Pa - cem___ pa - cis nun - ci - us: Tu Pas - tor ec - cle - si - e

Vo - lu - it nos red - de - re: Vir - tu - tes an - ge - li - ce
Pa - cem no - bis tri - bu - e: Fi - li - os et in - stru - e

Cum ca - no - re ju - bi - lo Be - ne - di - cant Do - mi - no.
Re - demp - to - ri de - bi - tas Ju - bi - lan - do gra - ci - as.

TRANSLATION 1 The Word of the Father today comes forth from a Virgin; he comes to redeem us and wishes to lead us back to the heavenly kingdom; let the angelic powers with jubilant song bless the Lord.

2 A shining angel, messenger of peace, announced peace to the shepherds. Thou Shepherd of the Church, grant us peace, and teach thy children to rejoice with thanks and gratitude to the Redeemer.

This is a *Benedicamus* trope (see notes, 9), widely known from at least the thirteenth century. Version I was sung at the end of lauds of Christmas Day in the Sarum use, which was celebrated immediately before the mass at dawn (*Missa in galli cantu*). It is the only 'official' (very freely) troped

Benedicamus, occurring in the manuscript antiphoners and in the printed breviary of 1531. Our edition is based on Salisbury Cathedral MS 152 (*Antiphonale Sarisburiense*, W. H. Frere, ed., 1901–24, pp. 53–4). The first verse, to be chanted by two priests of the highest form (i.e., senior clergy, occupying the rear stalls) wearing surplices, replaced the chanted 'Benedicamus Domino'. The priests would descend to sing, standing between the choir-stalls, facing the high altar. Verse 2 is the troped 'Deo gracias', and was to be sung by two corresponding clergy, similarly dressed, 'from either side of the choir'. (The Latin is as ambiguous as the English, but one from each side in both cases is probably intended.)

II

(*Christmas*)

Fifteenth-century?
(*Asti MS*)

1. Ver - bum Pa - tris ho - di - e Pro - ces - sit de Vir - gi - ne;
2. Pa - cem bo - nis om - ni - bus Nun - ti - a - vit an - ge - lus;

Vir - tu - tes an - ge - li - ce Cum ca - no - re ju - bi - lo
Re - ful - sit pa - sto - ri - bus Ve - lud so - lis cla - ri - tas.

Be - ne - di - ca - mus Do - mi - no.
De - o di - ca - mus gra - ti - as. Al - le - lu - ia.

TRANSLATION 1 The Word of the Father comes forth from a Virgin; the angelic powers with jubilant song [let us] bless the Lord.

2 The angel announced peace to all good men; light as of the sun shone on the shepherds. Let us give thanks to God. Alleluia.

Version II survives in a number of manuscripts in slightly different versions, with an upper part derived by the technique of *binatim* (see notes, 10). Our version is from Asti, Italy (Biblioteca del Seminario Vescovile, MS 17),

where the original melody is notated in black and the added one in red on the same staff (facsimile in Corsi and Petrobelli, *Le polifonie primitive in Friuli e in Europa*, 1989, p. 310). In verse 1 the author's desire to retain the words 'Benedicamus Domino' of the versicle creates a grammatical difficulty, a not unusual medieval confusion.

PERFORMANCE I (*i*) (liturgically) two pairs of singers, each singing one verse; (*ii*) choir. II, verse 1, two or more voices; verse 2, choir.

15

Verbum Patris umanatur

I

(New Year; Christmas) (Moosburg Gradual, 1355–60)

VERSE

1. Ver-bum Pa-tris u-ma-na-tur, O! O! Dum pu-el-la sa-lu-ta-tur, O! O! Sa-lu-

REFRAIN

-ta-ta fe-cun-da-tur vi-ri ne-sci-a.___ Ey! ey! ey-a! no-va gau-di-a!

II

Thirteenth-century
(Cambridge University MS)

VERSE

1. Ver-bum Pa-tris u-ma-na-tur, O! O! Dum pu-el-la sa-lu-ta-tur,

1. Ver-bum Pa-tris u-ma-na-tur, O! O! Dum pu-el-la sa-lu-ta-tur,

1. Ver-bum Pa-tris u-ma-na-tur, O! O! Dum pu-el-la sa-lu-ta-tur,

6

O! O! Sa-lu-ta-ta fe-cun-da-tur vi-ri ne-sci-a.___

O! O! Sa-lu-ta-ta fe-cun-da-tur vi-ri ne-sci-a.___

O! O! Sa-lu-ta-ta fe-cun-da-tur vi-ri ne-sci-a.___

40

2 Novus modus geniture, O! O!

Sed excedens vim nature, O! O!

Dum unitur creature Creans omnia.

3 Audi partum praeter morem, O! O!

Virgo parit Salvatorem, O! O!

Creatura Creatorem, Patrem filia.

4 In parente Savatoris, O! O!

Non est parens nostri moris, O! O!

Virgo parit, nec pudoris marcent lilia.

5 Homo Deus nobis datur, O! O!

Datus nobis demonstratur, O! O!

Dum pax terris nuntiatur celis gloria.

Thirteenth-century
(Cambridge University MS)

TRANSLATION 1 The Word of the Father is made man, when a maiden is greeted; she, being greeted, conceives without knowledge of a man. Ey! ey! eya! new joys!

2 This is a new manner of birth, but exceeding the power of nature, when the Creator of all things is united with his creation [man].

3 Hear of an unexampled birth: a virgin has borne the Saviour, a creature the Creator, a daughter the Father.

4 In the Saviour's birth there is no parent of our kind; a virgin gives birth, but the lilies of her chastity do not wither.

5 God-made-man is given to us; this gift is shown to us, while peace on earth is announced with glory in the heavens.

A rumbustious song, well suited to the New Year's festival of the subdeacons for which we suspect it was composed. Tags like 'Verbum Patris' were common in carols for New Year's Day.

Version I is from the Moosburg Gradual of 1355–60 (see notes, 21). Version II is an earlier setting of a different form of the melody, taken from a manuscript in the Cambridge University Library (MS Ff. I 17. fo. 4), a small collection of miscellaneous songs probably composed in England in the thirteenth century. (Verse 4 is omitted in this source.) The pattern of discordant passages resolving on to open fifths is a characteristic of the period, and is a calculated effect relying on the current Pythagorean tuning, in which major thirds are very wide and perfect fifths absolutely pure. The notation is non-mensural and bars 11–12 present a problem if an 'isosyllabic' interpretation is adopted, in which each syllable of text is given equal length, since the voices will have an odd flurry of notes here. We think it much more likely that the melody notes sung to 'He! he! hei!' here and 'Ey! ey!' in version I should be of double length, as we give them.

There is another, slightly earlier, two-part setting of 'Verbum Patris umanatur' from S. Martial, Limoges (Paris, Bibliothèque Nationale, fonds latin 3719).

PERFORMANCE I, verse, solo voice(s); refrain, choir. II, three voices.

16

Veni, veni, Emanuel
O come, O come, Emmanuel!

(*Advent*)

1 Veni, veni, Emanuel:
  Captivum solve Israel,
  Qui gemit in exilio,
  Privatus Dei Filio.

    Gaude! gaude! Emanuel
    Nascetur pro te, Israel.

2 Veni, O Jesse Virgula;
  Ex hostis tuos ungula,
  De specu tuos tartari,
  Educ, et antro barathri.

3 Veni, veni, O Oriens;
  Solare nos adveniens;
  Noctis depelle nebulas,
  Dirasque noctis tenebras.

4 Veni, Clavis Davidica;
  Regna reclude celica;
  Fac iter tutum superum,
  Et claude vias inferum.

5 Veni, veni, Adonaï,
  Qui populo in Sinaï
  Legem dedisti vertice
  In maiestate glorie.

    Thirteenth-century?

1 O come, O come, Emmanuel!
  Redeem thy captive Israel
  That into exile drear is gone,
  Far from the face of God's dear Son.

    Rejoice! rejoice! Emmanuel
    Shall come to thee, O Israel.

2 O come, thou Branch of Jesse! Draw
  The quarry from the lion's claw;
  From the dread caverns of the grave,
  From nether hell, thy people save.

3 O come, O come, thou Dayspring bright!
  Pour on our souls thy healing light;
  Dispel the long night's lingering gloom,
  And pierce the shadows of the tomb.

4 O come, thou Key of David, come,
  And open wide our heavenly home;
  Safeguard for us the heavenward road,
  And bar the way to death's abode.

5 O come, O come, Adonaï,
  Who in thy glorious majesty
  From Sinai's mountain, clothed in awe,
  Gavest thy folk the elder Law.

tr. J. M. Neale (1818–66)
rev. T. A. Lacey (1853–1931), adapted

Alternative translation of verse 1:

1   O come, O come, Emmanuel!

And ransom captive Israel

That mourns in lonely exile here

Until the Son of God appear.

tr. J. M. Neale (1818–66)

I

Thirteenth-century?
(Bibliothèque Nationale MS)

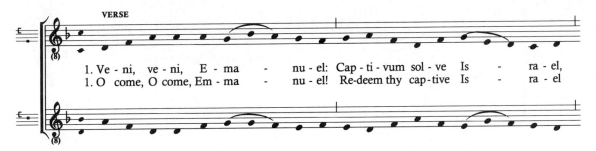

VERSE

1. Ve - ni, ve - ni, E - ma - nu - el: Cap - ti - vum sol - ve Is - ra - el,
1. O come, O come, Em - ma - nu - el! Re-deem thy cap-tive Is - ra - el

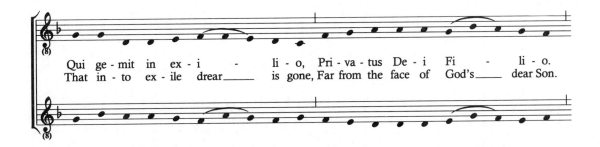

Qui ge - mit in ex - i - li - o, Pri - va - tus De - i Fi - li - o.
That in - to ex - ile drear___ is gone, Far from the face of God's___ dear Son.

REFRAIN

Gau - de! gau - de! E - ma - nu - el Na - sce - tur pro te, Is - ra - el.
Re - joice! re - joice! Em - ma - nu - el Shall come to thee, O Is - ra - el.

II

Thirteenth-century?
(Bibliothèque Nationale MS, arr. editors)

VERSE

1. Ve - ni, ve - ni, E - ma - nu - el: Cap - ti - vum sol - ve
1. O come, O come, Em - ma - nu - el! Re - deem thy cap - tive

Is - ra - el, Qui ge - mit in ex - i - li - o, Pri -
Is - ra - el That in - to ex - ile drear___ is gone, Far

REFRAIN

-va - tus De - i Fi - li - o. Gau - de! gau - de! E -
from the face of God's___ dear Son. Re - joice! re - joice! Em -

-ma - nu - el Na - sce - tur pro te, Is - ra - el.
-ma - nu - el Shall come to thee, O Is - ra - el.

44

The text is based on the series of 'O' antiphons sung at vespers on the days leading up to Christmas—in the Tridentine rite from 17 to 23 December (see *Liber Usualis*). The antiphons date back at least to the reign of Charlemagne (771–814), and there is an English poem based on them by Cynewulf (*c*.800). More verses were added to the original seven, including one for Christmas Day, but there can be no doubt that the seven were designed as a group, since their initial letters, ignoring the 'O', spell out the reverse acrostic 'SARCORE'—'ero cras', 'I shall be [with you] tomorrow', a hidden counterpart of the joyful iteration of 'cras' which rings like a bell through the liturgy of the last week of Advent.

This metrical version of five of the seven antiphons (for 23, 19, 21, 20, and 18 December) was in use in the thirteenth century. It is more an imitation than a direct versification: the sometimes despairing conclusions to the antiphons ('come and lighten us who sit in darkness and in the shadow of death') are converted into a confident refrain ('Gaude . . .'). J. M. Neale translated it in 1851, revising it in 1853, and it quickly became popular. An improved version by T. A. Lacey appeared in *The English Hymnal* (1906). Neale's original verse 1, which we give as an alternative, is retained by most American hymnals.

'Emanuel' means 'God with us' (see Isaiah 7:14, quoted in Matthew 1:23). 'Israel' is used in the conventional sense of 'Christians', and the Babylonian exile is a metaphor for fallen man, banned from paradise.

The 'Branch of Jesse' (verse 2) refers to the messianic prophecy in Isaiah 11:1: 'Behold there shall come forth a rod out of the stem of Jesse, and a branch shall grow out of his roots.' Carved or painted 'Jesse trees' would typically show a plant rooted in the loins of the sleeping Jesse, father of David, with the ancestors of St Joseph on the various branches, culminating in the infant Christ. The verse looks forward to the harrowing of hell by Christ before his resurrection, and the destruction of Satan's power over man.

'Oriens' (verse 3) is a light that rises over the horizon, whether the morning sun or the daystar, invoking Malachi 4:2: 'But unto you that fear my name shall the Sun of righteousness arise with healing in his wings . . .'. (See also Luke 1:78 and Isaiah 9:2).

The 'Key of David' (verse 4) refers to the messianic prophecy of Isaiah 22:22: 'And the key of the house of David will I lay upon his shoulder; so he shall shut, and none shall open.' Christ, 'of the house and lineage of David', was able to unlock the gates of heaven, barred since the Fall, and close those of hell, to which all humanity had been destined.

'Adonai' (verse 5) means 'Lord', and was one of the titles substituted by devout Jews for the unutterable Name of God. The rest of the verse concerns the giving of the Ten Commandments to Moses, the 'elder law' which is now to be interpreted in the light of further revelation: 'A new commandment give I unto you . . .' (John 13:34).

The tune was first published, with Neale's revised text, in part II of his and Helmore's influential *Hymnal Noted* (1854), and stated to be from a source in the National Library, Lisbon. In an article of 1881, Helmore revealed that the source was in fact a French missal, and that Neale himself, now dead, had copied the tune. Helmore's memory may have been at fault, since a letter to the press in 1909 by H. Jenner claimed that it had been his father, Bishop Jenner, who had supplied Helmore with both text and music, which he had copied at Lisbon in 1853. Searches failed to locate the hymn in the Lisbon library, and doubts about the authenticity of the tune were only laid to rest in 1966, when Mary Berry (then Mother Thomas More) discovered the tune in another French source, a fifteenth-century Franciscan processional (Bibliothèque Nationale, fonds latin 10581), which was probably copied for a nunnery. Fos. 87ᵛ onwards contain a series of troped verses (interpolations) to the responsory 'Libera me, Domine', sung during the procession to the burial place after a funeral mass, and these are set to what we know as the 'Veni, veni, Emanuel' melody. Each verse is set out in *binatim* style on two pages (see notes, 10), with the familiar melody on the left and a simple countermelody on the right.

The processional confirms the French origin of the tune, but leaves open the question of which text was originally sung to it. Jenner's letter corroborates Helmore's initial assertion that the source was in the Lisbon library, which remains virtually uncatalogued. The neat fit of the tune with, particularly, the repeated 'gaude' of the refrain makes us suspect that 'Veni, veni, Emanuel' was the original text, and it can only be a matter of time before the Lisbon source is uncovered. (We are grateful to Dr Rui Neri, who searched on our behalf.)

Setting I is the Bibliothèque Nationale version, with the words of the hymn substituted. Setting II is our harmonization.

PERFORMANCE   I (*i*) verse, two voices; refrain, choir; (*ii*) choir. II (*i*) voices and organ; (*ii*) choir.

17

Qui creavit celum
He who made the earth so fair
(Song of the Nuns of Chester)

Thirteenth-/fourteenth-century?
(Huntington Library MS)

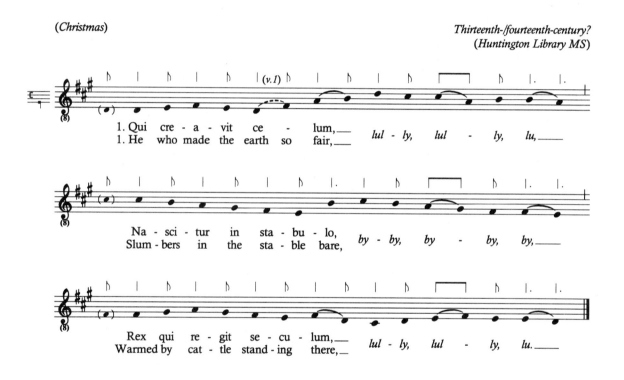

1. Qui cre - a - vit ce - lum,—— *lul - ly, lul - ly, lu,——*
1. He who made the earth so fair,—— *lul - ly, lul - ly, lu,——*

Na - sci - tur in sta - bu - lo, *by - by, by - by, by,——*
Slum - bers in the sta - ble bare, *by - by, by - by, by,——*

Rex qui re - git se - cu - lum,—— *lul - ly, lul - ly, lu.——*
Warmed by cat - tle stand - ing there,—— *lul - ly, lul - ly, lu.——*

2 Joseph emit panniculum, *by-by, by-by, by;*
Mater involvit Puerum, *lully, lully, lu,*
Et ponit in presepio, *by-by, by-by, by.*

2 Oxen, lowing, stand around, *lully, lully, lu,*
In the stall no other sound, *by-by, by-by, by,*
Mars the peace by Mary found, *lully, lully, lu.*

3 Inter animalia, *lully* . . .
Iacent mundi gaudia, *by-by* . . .
Dulcis super omnia, *lully* . . .

4 Lactat mater Domini, *by-by* . . .
Osculatur parvulum, *lully* . . .
Et adorat Dominum, *by-by* . . .

5 Roga, mater, Filium, *lully* . . .
Ut det nobis gaudium, *by-by* . . .
In perenni gloria, *lully* . . .

6 In sempiterna secula, *by-by* . . .
In eternum et ultra, *lully, lully, lu,*
Det nobis sua gaudia, *by-by* . . .

3 Joseph piles the soft, sweet hay, *lully* . . .
Starlight drives the dark away, *by-by* . . .
Angels sing a heavenly lay, *lully* . . .

4 Jesus sleeps in Mary's arm, *lully* . . .
Sheltered there from rude alarm, *by-by* . . .
None can do him ill or harm, *lully* . . .

5 See his mother o'er him bend, *lully* . . .
Hers the joy to soothe and tend, *by-by* . . .
Hers the bliss that knows no end, *lully* . . .

English version by Irene Gass, adapted

Thirteenth-/fourteenth-century?
(*Huntington Library MS*)

TRANSLATION 1 He who created the sky is born in a stable, the King who rules the age.
2 Joseph buys a tiny swaddling-cloth; the mother wraps the Child and places him in the manger.
3 Among the animals lie the world's joys, sweet above all things.
4 The Mother of the Lord gives milk, she kisses her Infant and worships the Lord.
5 Mother, ask your Child to grant us joy in eternal glory.
6 Throughout the ages, to eternity and beyond, may he give us his joys.

The editors of *The Oxford Book of Carols* (1928) memorably described this enchanting song as a 'lullaby, in which the nuns of St Mary's gave vent to their womanly instincts'. (Another medieval expression of maternal love of the infant Christ was cradle-rocking, which began in Rhineland nunneries and eventually became a craze in churches all over the Germanic countries—see notes, 55.)

Formally, 'Qui creavit' is a puzzle. If we ignore the refrains, the verse has a rhyme scheme typical of the freer type of early sequence: ABA AAB CCC DAA AAC CCC. The refrains are perhaps a Christmas adaptation of the common practice of repeating each line of a sequence tutti to a single vowel (rather as 'Noël' was sung as substitute for certain 'Alleluia' refrains in the Christmas liturgy). On the other hand, the refrains have their own music, where such repetitions on a vowel always repeat that of the line they follow. Perhaps the song began as a simple free sequence, developed the refrain lines, and was eventually given a new or revised musical setting.

'Qui creavit' is found in a single source, a manuscript processional copied for the Benedictine nunnery of St Mary, Chester, in the early fifteenth century (now in the Henry E. Huntington Library, San Marino, California, MS EL.34.87; modern edition, with a facsimile of this carol: *The Processional of the Nuns of Chester*, J. Wickham Legg, ed., 1899). The song is probably older than that: perhaps of the thirteenth or fourteenth century.

In the manuscript the music is written out in full for each verse. In line 2 the seventh note—B in our transcription—is doubled in verses 2–6. The notation gives no other clue as to rhythm, and our feeling is that, whether or not the song was conceived in duple rhythm, by the fifteenth century it would probably have been sung in triple. Modern editors have treated the song fairly roughly: one book gives duple rhythm for the main text, triple for the 'lully' and 'by-by' refrains; the original *Oxford Book of Carols* suppressed the regular alternation of 'lully' and 'by-by' (perpetuated in Irene Gass's free translation), while the 1964 revision sets the refrains in *falso-bordone*, a solo technique which might just conceivably have been applied to the verses, but hardly to what must be full refrains.

What the song is doing in a processional is not known. Such pieces were frequently used as *Benedicamus/Deo gracias* substitutes (see notes, 9), at least on the Continent, but inclusion in a procession is unusual. According to Legg, the Chester book shows little sign of having been used, the fairly frequent verbal and musical mistakes (typical of books of smaller houses, and of nunneries in general) being uncorrected. It seems to have been copied from the processional of an English Benedictine monastery, as it follows the Sarum use in most respects, and the rubrics all assume male participants. Many of the processions are so sketchily indicated that the book may best be seen as a record of differences from Sarum, to be used in conjunction with a full processional.

'Qui creavit' seems to have been inserted into the manuscript at random, not with the other Christmas processions but between those of St Benedict (21 March) and Shere (Maundy) Thursday. It is followed by the versicle 'Puer natus est nobis' and the collect 'Concede, qucsumus', both without music. The versicle is not found in Sarum, though the Chester book also gives it at the conclusion of the return into quire of the processions for 'christenmas day . . . if it falle on Sunday' and 'Sunday affter yole day'. The collect is the Sarum one for the conclusion of the procession before mass on Christmas Day and throughout the octave (until 1 January).

The unnamed procession connected with 'Qui creavit' may have been for the blessing of the crib, the ceremony between Christmas matins and midnight mass which was instituted, or formalized, by St Francis in 1223. This was a permitted but theoretically extra-liturgical ceremony which rarely found its way into the liturgical books. The crib was normally placed outside the quire, for the benefit of the laity, and 'Qui creavit' could have formed part or all of a short procession from quire to a spot just outside the screen.

Churches that retain the practice of blessing the crib may like to incorporate the Chester song on occasion. The procession would begin in quire in the usual way, 'Qui creavit' being sung on the way to the crib with the figure of Christ, and the form of blessing there would follow local custom. For the return to quire we give (below) the antiphon 'Hodie Christus natus est' from the Chester processional, plus versicle, response, and collect to be sung at the conclusion. (In medieval usage the three solo cantors, male or female, of 'Hodie' would walk together in procession, and would sing the versicle from mid-quire, facing the altar.) In large churches the outward and returning processions could be augmented with hymns or other chant.

Antiphon at the return into quire

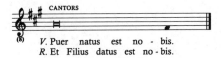

V. Puer natus est no - bis.
R. Et Filius datus est no - bis.

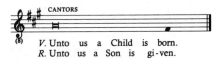

V. Unto us a Child is born.
R. Unto us a Son is gi - ven.

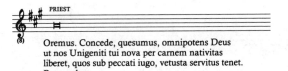

Oremus. Concede, quesumus, omnipotens Deus
ut nos Unigeniti tui nova per carnem nativitas
liberet, quos sub peccati iugo, vetusta servitus tenet.
Per eundem

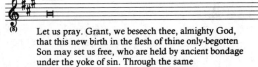

Let us pray. Grant, we beseech thee, almighty God,
that this new birth in the flesh of thine only-begotten
Son may set us free, who are held by ancient bondage
under the yoke of sin. Through the same

Christum Dominum nos - trum. R. A - men.

Jesus Christ our Lord. R. A - men.

PERFORMANCE 'Qui creavit': (i) three soloists alternating
with choir (lully, etc.); (ii) choir throughout. Antiphon, etc.:
voices, with three cantors and priest.

18

Dies est laeticiae
Earth with joy this day doth ring

(Piae Cantiones, 1582, arr. editors)

1. Di - es est lae - ti - ci - ae   In or - tu re - ga - li;   Nam pro - ces - sit
1. Earth with joy this   day doth ring,   Songs of praise de - vi - sing;   From a maid comes

ho - di - e De ven - tre vir - gi - na - li   Pu - er ad - mi - ra - bi - lis,
forth our King   Like a bright star   ris - ing.   What se - duc - tive   in - fan - cy!

To - tus de - lec - ta - bi - lis   In hu - ma - ni - ta - te,   Qui in - aes - ti -
All de - lec - ta - bi - li - ty,   Grace in ev - ery ges - ture;   But no hu - man

-ma - bi - lis   Est, et in - ef - fa - bi - lis   In di - vi - ni - ta - te.
eye may see   His con-cealed di - vi - ni - ty,   God in hu - man ves - ture.

2   Orto Dei Filio
        Virgine de pura
    Ut rosa de lilio,
        Stupescit natura,
    Quem parit iuvencula
    Natum ante secula,
        Creatorem rerum,
    Quod uber munditiae
    Dat lac pudicitiae,
        Antiquo dierum.

2   God is born from virgin's womb:
        Reason is confounded;
    Rose on lily-stem doth bloom:
        Nature stands astounded.
    Born before all time was he;
    Though a child, eternity
        Is his habitation:
    He who suckles tenderly,
    Equal in the Trinity
        Saw the world's creation.

3   Mater haec est filia:
        Pater hic est natus,
    Quis audivit talia,
        Deus homo natus,
    Servus est et Dominus,
    Qui ubique cominus
        Nescit comprehendi,
    Praesens est et eminus,
    Stupor eius geminus
        Nequit apprehendi.

3   Can such wonders truly be?
        Mary's Child hath taught her:
    Child and Father both is he,
        Mother she, and daughter.
    His high place the Lord forsakes
    And a servant's office takes,
        Gladly condescending:
    Of twin natures he partakes,
    God incarnate for our sakes,
        Past all comprehending.

4   In obscuro nascitur
   Illustrator solis,
Stabulo reponitur,
   Princeps terrae molis.
Fasciatur dextera
Quae affixit sydera
   Et coelos ascendit;
Concrepat vagitibus
Qui tonat in nubibus
   Ac fulgur accendit.

5   Christe, qui nos proprius
   Manibus fecisti,
Et pro nobis omnibus
   Nasci voluisti,
Te devote petimus,
Laxa quod peccavimus,
   Ne nos interire
Post mortem nos miseros,
Ne simul ad inferos
   Patiaris ire.

Fourteenth-century?
(Piae Cantiones, 1582)

4   Lord of sky and earth and sea,
   On the straw reclining;
Cold and dark his birth, yet he
   Set the bright sun shining.
Wrapped in swaddling bands he lies
Who the heavens did devise,
   Gave the stars their stations;
Lo! he shakes with childish cries
Who with thunder from the skies
   Shook the earth's foundations.

5   Christ, whose hands with craftsman's skill
   Lovingly did frame us,
And wast born, of thy free will,
   That thou mightst reclaim us:
Weak and sinful though we be,
In our last extremity
   Do thou never leave us;
Grant that we may numbered be
With thy saints eternally;
   In thy courts receive us!

(Free tr., editors)

'Dies est laeticiae' has always been one of the most popular of all Christmastide *cantiones* (songs) in German-speaking countries, and in the sixteenth century was sung on Christmas and New Year's Days and on the Epiphany. Luther often praised it in his sermons, calling it 'a work of the Holy Spirit'.

The tune is found in many forms, the *Piae Cantiones* version (1582), with eight stanzas (of which we give five), being one of the strongest. It was sung to several Christmas texts, among them 'Eia! mea anima', written for the tune by Johann Mauburn (*Rosetum Exercitiorum Spiritualium*, 1494), and our harmonization is in debt to Praetorius's setting of this in his *Musae Sioniae* (VI, 1609).

We do not give any of the chorale versions, but attractive settings are readily available, including those by Praetorius (*Musae Sioniae*, V and VI), a good plain one in Schein's *Cantional* (1645, 'Der Tag der ist so freudenreich'), one for keyboard in Scheidt's *Tabulatur-Buch* (1650, no. 8, 'Ein Kindelein so löbelich'), a five-part *cantus firmus* setting in Eccard's *Geistlicher Lieder* (1597), and a four-part setting by Bach (BWV 294). There are chorale preludes on the tune by Buxtehude, Pachelbel, and Bach.

PERFORMANCE   Choir or unison voices with organ *ad lib.* (The editorial natural in bar 10 does not apply in monophonic performances.)

19

Corde natus ex Parentis
Of the Father's heart begotten

I

(Christmas)

(Piae Cantiones, 1582, arr. editors)

†1. Of the Fa-ther's heart be-got-ten Ere the world from cha - os rose, He is Al-pha and O-me-ga, He the Source and he the Close Of what-ev-er is, or has been, Or the fu-ture years dis-close, Sae-cu-lo-rum sae-cu-lis.

Saec-cu-lo-rum sae - cu - lis.

After doxology

-close, Sae-cu-lo-rum, sae-cu-lo-rum sae-cu-lis. A - men.

† For an alternative translation of verse 1 see p. 56. 'Saeculorum saeculis' = 'Unto the ages of ages' [eternity].

II

(*Christmas*)

(*Piae Cantiones, 1582, adapted and arr. editors*)

†1. Of the Father's heart be-got-ten Ere the world from cha-os rose,

He is Al-pha and O-me-ga, He the Source and he___ the Close

Of what-ev-er is, or has___ been, Or the fu-ture

Sae-cu-lo-rum sae-cu-lis.___

After doxology

years dis-close, Sae-cu-lo-rum, sae-cu-lo-rum sae-cu-lis. A-men.

† For an alternative translation of verse 1 see p. 56. 'Saeculorum saeculis' = 'Unto the ages of ages' [eternity].

54

2 At his word was all created;
   He commanded, it was done:
Earth, and heaven, and depths of ocean,
   In their threefold order one;
All that grows beneath the shining
   Of the orbs of moon and sun

3 He assumed this mortal body,
   Frail and feeble, doomed to die,
That the race from dust created
   Might not perish utterly,
Which the dreadful Law had sentenced
   In the depths of hell to lie

4 O that birth, for ever blessèd!
   When the Virgin, full of grace,
By the Holy Ghost conceiving,
   Bore the Saviour of our race,
And the Child, the world's Redeemer,
   First revealed his sacred face

5 O ye heights of heaven, adore him!
   Angel-hosts, his praises sing!
Powers, dominions, bow before him,
   And extol your God and King!
Let no tongue today be silent,
   Every voice in concert ring

6 This is he whom once the sibyls
   With united voice foretold,
His the birth that faithful prophets
   In their pages did unfold;
Let the world unite to praise him,
   Long-desired, foreseen of old

7 Hail, thou Judge of souls departed!
   Hail, thou King of them that thrive!
On the Father's throne exalted
   None in might with thee may strive,
Who at last, to judge returning,
   Sinners from thy face shall drive

8 O ye elders, lead the anthems:
   Laud your God in ancient lays!
Youths and maidens, hymn his glory!
   Infants, bring your songs of praise!
Guileless voices, in sweet concord
   Unto all the length of days,

9 Let the storm and summer sunshine,
   Gliding stream and sounding shore,
Sea and forest, frost and zephyr,
   Night and day their Lord adore;
All Creation joined to praise thee
   Through the ages evermore,

10 Christ, to thee, with God the Father,
      And, O Holy Ghost, to thee,
   High thanksgiving, endless praises,
      And eternal glory be;
   Honour, power, and all dominion,
      And eternal victory

tr. editors, partly a cento after J. M. Neale (1818–66)
and Roby Furley Davis (1866–1937)

† *Alternative translation of v. 1:*

1 Of the Father's love begotten
   Ere the worlds began to be,
He is Alpha and Omega,
   He the Source, the Ending he
Of the things that are, that have been,
   And that future years shall see,
      Evermore and evermore.

tr. J. M. Neale (1818–66)

III

(*Christmas*)   *York chant*

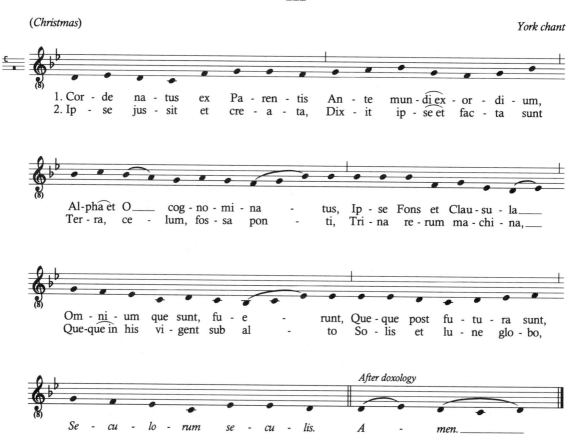

1. Cor - de   na - tus   ex   Pa - ren - tis   An - te   mun - di ex - or - di - um,
2. Ip - se   jus - sit   et   cre - a - ta,   Dix - it   ip - se et   fac - ta   sunt

Al-pha et O___   cog - no - mi - na - tus,   Ip - se Fons et Clau - su - la___
Ter - ra,   ce - lum, fos - sa   pon - ti,   Tri - na   re - rum ma - chi - na,___

Om - ni - um   que sunt,   fu - e - runt,   Que - que post   fu - tu - ra   sunt,
Que - que in his   vi - gent sub   al - to   So - lis   et   lu - ne   glo - bo,

After doxology

Se - cu - lo - rum   se - cu - lis.   A - men.___

3 Corporis formam caduci,
Membra morti obnoxia
Induit, ne gens periret
Primoplasti ex germine,
Merserat quem Lex profundo
Noxialis Tartaro
  Seculorum seculis.

4 O beatus ortus ille!
Virgo cum puerpera
Edidit nostram salutem
Feta Sancto Spiritu,
Et Puer, Redemptor Orbis,
Os sacratum protulit
  Seculorum seculis.

5 Psallat altitudo celi,
Psallite omnes angeli,
Quidquid est virtutis usquam
Psallat in laudem Dei!
Nulla linguarum silescat,
Vox et omnis consonet
  Seculorum seculis.

6 Ecce, quem vates vetustis
Concinebant seculis,
Quem prophetarum fideles
Pagine spoponderant,
Emicat promissus olim:
Cuncta conlaudent eum
  Seculorum seculis.

7 Macte Judex mortuorum,
Macte Rex viventium,
Dexter in Parentis arce
Qui cluis virtutibus,
Omnium venturus inde
Justus ultor criminum
  Seculorum seculis.

8 Te senes et te juventus,
Parvulorum te chorus,
Turba matrum virginumque,
Simplices puellule,
Voce concordes pudicis
Perstrepant concentibus,
  Seculorum seculis.

9 Fluminum lapsus et unde,
Litorum crepidines,
Imber, estus, nix, pruina,
Silva et aura, nox, dies
Omnibus te concelebrent
Seculorum seculis,
  Seculorum seculis.

10 Tibi, Christe, sit cum Patre
Hagioque Pneumate,
Hymnus, decus, laus perhennis,
Gratiarum actio,
Honor, virtus, victoria,
Regnum eternaliter,
  Seculorum seculis. Amen.

vv. 1–9 Aurelius Clemens Prudentius (348–c.410)
v. 10 medieval

Prudentius was a Romano-Spanish lawyer who, in his retirement, wrote outstanding religious poetry, extracts from which were incorporated into the church's offices in early medieval times.

The liturgical offices are, basically, prayers and praises offered at significant points of the day. The ideal of the sanctification of daily life which led to their institution in the fifth century was also the inspiration of Prudentius's *Cathemerinon* (Greek for 'diurnal' or daily prayer book), a collection of hymns to be sung at various times of the day (sunrise, the lighting of the lamps, etc.) as well as on certain occasions in the year. Among them is a thirty-seven stanza 'Hymnus omnis horae' ('Hymn for every hour [of the day]'), beginning 'Da, puer, plectrum', from which 'Corde natus' is taken. The final stanza (III, verse 9) concludes with the words 'seculorum seculis'. This was added to the final melisma of those stanzas that were taken into the liturgy, and the doxology (verse 10) was added at the same time. In verse 5 the first word is changed to 'Psallant' in liturgical sources.

In the Mozarabic (Spanish) rite and in some other European rites, verses from 'Corde natus' were sung on Marian feasts and on 1 January (the Circumcision of Christ and also a Marian feast until the thirteenth century). In England it occurs in Leofric's Collectar (eleventh century). In the Hereford use verses were sung at the lesser hours during Christmastide: our verses 1, 2, and 10 at prime, 4, 5, and 10 at terce, 6, 7, and 10 at sext, and 8, 9, and 10 at none. In the York use our verses 1, 2, 4, 5, 8, and 10 were sung at compline throughout Christmastide.

Our translation draws on verses by J. M. Neale (in *Carols for Christmastide*, 1853–4, and *The Hymnal Noted*, part II, 1854, both edited by Neale and Helmore), as extended and adapted by Sir Henry Williams Baker (1821–77) for *Hymns Ancient and Modern* (1861), and on Davis's freer but more poetic translation in *The English Hymnal* (1906). We give Neale's original verse 1 as an alternative since it is widely sung, especially in the US. (If it is sung, the refrain 'Ever-more and evermore' should be substituted throughout.)

The tune began as a *Sanctus* trope (see notes, 9) to the words 'Divinum mysterium', in praise of the Blessed Sacrament, and perhaps evolved from the chant of the Christmas sequence 'Votis Pater'. The final melisma is shorter in the earliest manuscripts, but the florid version in a fifteenth-century source in the Prague Národní Muzeum (XIII. E8) is similar to the one in *Piae Cantiones* (1582) (see ex. 1).

A two-part setting in the Las Huelgas manuscript (Burgos, *c*.1325) has an added upper voice and ends with a much longer melisma.

It was Neale and Helmore who first brought together Prudentius's text (in translation) and the *Piae Cantiones* tune. The original 'Divinum mysterium' text matches the tune well, the two main stresses of each line of text falling on the first beat of the notional bars of 6/8 (which is stretched to 9/8 at three cadences: see ex. 2). Prudentius's text is in quite a different metre, however, and is at odds with the natural stress of the music. We have papered over the cracks in setting I by barring according to the verbal stress, which disturbs the music but is preferable to the normal solution in which both text and tune are mis-stressed. Most American hymnals iron out the triple time of the *Piae Cantiones* tune to produce a 'chant' version (II). There is no historical justification for the result, but it neatly side-steps the problem of stress, since the chant is able to adapt itself to the text without distortion. We prefer this to setting I, but the ideal solution is perhaps to sing Prudentius's great hymn to the fine chant that was written for it (III), of which we give the York form. The hymn was sung liturgically by Lutherans, and settings of a rhythmicized version of the tune by Praetorius may be found in his *Hymnodia Sionia* (1611).

PERFORMANCE   I, II: (*i*) unison voices; (*ii*) voices with organ; (*iii*) choir.

III, voices.

EX. 1: *Národní Muzeum MS*

Fi - de ro - bo - ra - - - - - tur,___

EX. 2: *Piae Cantiones*

Di - vi-num mys - te - ri - um___ Mo - do de - cla - ra - tur, Et mens in - fi -

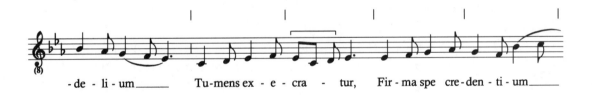

- de - li - um___ Tu - mens ex - e - cra - tur, Fir - ma spe cre - den - ti - um___

_____ Fi - des ro - bo - ra - - - - tur.___

20

Personent hodie
On this day earth shall ring

(Christmas; Holy Innocents?)

1 Personent hodie
  Voces puerulae
  Laudantes iucunde
    Qui nobis est natus,
    Summo Deo datus,
  Et de virgineo
    Ventre procreatus.

2 In mundo nascitur;
  Pannis involvitur;
  Praesepi ponitur
    Stabulo brutorum
    Rector supernorum;
  Perdidit spolia
    Princeps Infernorum.

3 Magi tres venerunt;
  Munera offerunt;
  Parvulum inquirunt,
    Stellulam sequendo,
    Ipsum adorando,
  Aurum, thus et myrrham
    Ei offerendo.

4 Omnes clericuli,
  Pariter pueri,
  Cantent ut angeli:
    'Advenisti mundo:
    Laudes tibi fundo
  Ideo: Gloria
    In excelsis Deo.'

  (Piae Cantiones, 1582)

1 On this day earth shall ring
  With the song children sing
  To the Son, Christ the King,
  Born on earth to save us;
  Him the Father gave us.
    Ideo gloria in excelsis Deo!

2 His the doom, ours the mirth,
  When he came down to earth;
  Bethlehem saw his birth;
  Ox and ass, beside him,
  From the cold would hide him.
    Ideo gloria in excelsis Deo!

3 God's bright star, o'er his head,
  Wise men three to him led;
  Kneel they low by his bed,
  Lay their gifts before him,
  Praise him and adore him.
    Ideo gloria in excelsis Deo!

4 On this day angels sing;
  With their song earth shall ring,
  Praising Christ, heaven's King,
  Born on earth to save us;
  Peace and love he gave us.
    Ideo gloria in excelsis Deo!

English version by
Jane M. Joseph (1894–1929)

I

(*Piae Cantiones, 1582, arr. editors*)

1. Per - so - nent ho - di - e Vo - ces pu - e - ru - lae Lau -

Lau - dan - tes iu - cun - de

- dan - tes iu - cun - de Qui no - bis est na - tus,

Lau - dan - tes iu - cun - de Qui no - bis est_____ na - tus,

Qui no - bis est_____ na - tus,

Sum - mo De - o da - tus, Et de vir -, vir -, vir -, et de vir -,

Et de vir -, et

Sum - mo De - o_____ da - tus, Et de vir -,_____ vir -, vir -, et de vir -,

Sum - mo De - o da - tus, Et de vir -,

vir -, vir -, et de vir - gi - ne - o

de vir -, et de vir - gi - ne - o Ven - tre pro - cre - a - tus.

_ vir -, vir -, et_____ de vir - gi - ne - o

et de vir -, et de vir - gi - ne - o

II

(Christmas; Holy Innocents?)

*(Piae Cantiones, 1582,
arr. Gustav Holst, 1874–1934)*

Moderato maestoso

1. On this day   earth shall ring
1. Per - so - nent   ho - di - e

With the song   child - ren sing   To the Son,   Christ the King,
Vo - ces pu —   e - ru - lae   Lau - dan - tes   iu - cun - de

Born on earth to   save   us;   Him the Fa - ther gave   us.
Qui no - bis est   na - tus,   Sum - mo De - o   da - tus,

PIANO
or ORGAN

TRANSLATION 1 Let children's voices resound today, merrily praising him who has been born, sent by almighty God and brought forth from a virgin's womb.

2 He was born into the world, wrapped in swaddling clothes, and placed in the manger in a cattle shed, the Lord of the heavens, the Prince [who] destroyed the spoils of hell.

3 Three wise men appeared; they offered gifts and asked for a boy-child, following a star; they worshipped him, offering him gold, frankincense, and myrrh.

4 Let all the clerics, and likewise the boys, sing like the angels: 'You have come to the world; therefore I pour out praises to you: Glory to God in the highest!'

Text and melody are from *Piae Cantiones* (1582). The song is found in only one other source, Rhezelius's (Swedish) *Någre Psalmer* (1619), where it is translated into the vernacular. The second note of bar 14 (setting I) is missing in *Piae Cantiones*, as are the words 'munera offerunt' in verse 3, though these have been entered by hand in the copy used for the 1967 facsimile edition.

The song is well known in England in the oddly grandiose but still popular setting by Holst (II). This was written in 1916–17 for one of the Whitsun music festivals he ran (see notes, 109) and was originally a setting for voices and orchestra of Jane Joseph's English text, which is only loosely based on the Latin. It was published in 1924, and appeared in *The Oxford Book of Carols* (1928) with piano reduction and the Latin text.

Setting I is harmonized in a late sixteenth-century Germanic style, so far as the medieval tune will allow. In monodic performance the editorial accidental added to the melody in bar 9 should be omitted (and perhaps also the one in bar 17, though we do not know how far the singers of 1582 would have updated their monophonic medieval repertory).

'Personent hodie' is a parody (imitation with new text) of a medieval song to St Nicholas which begins 'Intonent hodie voces ecclesie'. No version of the model is known with exactly this melody, but the one in the Moosburg Gradual (completed 1360; see notes, 21) is close. (It is transcribed and discussed in *Analecta Hymnica*, XXI, p. 86, no. 128, and is also reproduced in the notes to G. R. Woodward's edition of *Piae Cantiones*, 1910.) The repeated syllables in the model have a *raison d'être*, whereas in 'Personent hodie' they are merely decorative. The saint's life abounded in trinities: the third verse of 'Intonent hodie' speaks of (one of) three boys, drowned in a barrel, whom the saint restored to life, the words 'submersum puerum'

('the drowned boy') being sung as 'submersum, -sum, -sum puerum', a jokey representation of the dead trio. Verse 4 concerns three girls whom he saved from prostitution by giving each a bag of gold as dowry, and has 'Reddens vir-, vir-, virginibus' where verse 1 of 'Personent' has 'Et de vir-, vir-, vir-'.

St Nicholas, later subsumed into the modern Santa Claus, was the patron of children, and in some places it was on his day, 6 December, rather than on Holy Innocents' Day, 28 December, that the choristers with their boy bishop took over the services: the repetitions in 'Intonent' are part of the general lightheartedness of such occasions. Could 'Personent' have been intended for Innocents' Day? Verse 1 specifically calls on boys' voices to sing, and the alternative—that this might be a purely school song (like others in the collection)—is ruled out by verse 4, in which 'all the clerics' are called on to sing 'together with the boys.'

PERFORMANCE I (*i*) unison voices (omitting the editorial accidentals in bar 9 and perhaps also bar 17); (*ii*) choir.

II, unison voices and piano or organ (or orchestra; see above).

21

Puer nobis nascitur
Unto us is born a Son

I

(*Christmas*)

(*Moosburg Gradual, 1355–60,
arr. editors*)

VERSES 1–3 (v.1)

1. Pu - er no - bis na - sci - tur, Rec - tor an - ge - lo - rum;
2. In pre - se - pe po - ni - tur Sub fe - no a - si - no - rum;
3. Qui na - tus ex Ma - ri - a Di - e ho - di - er - na:

(v.3)

In hoc mun - do pa - sci - tur Do - mi - nus Do - mi - no - rum.
Cog - no - ve - runt Do - mi - num Chri - stum, Re - gem Ce - lo - rum.
Per - duc nos cum gra - ci - a Ad gau - di - a su - per - na.

VERSE 4

4. O et O et O et O; O et O et O!

O et O et O et O; Be - ne - di - ca - mus Do - mi - no.
[De - o di - ca - mus gra - ci - as.]

(*see notes*)

TRANSLATION 1 Unto us a Boy is born, the Ruler of the Angels; the Lord of Lords is nurtured in this world.

2 He is placed in a manger where asses feed; they recognized the Lord Christ, King of Heaven.

3 You who were born of Mary on this day: lead us joyfully to the highest joys [of paradise].

4 O and O, etc.; Let us bless the Lord [Let us say 'Thanks be to God'].

65

II

(*Christmas; Holy Innocents*)

(*Piae Cantiones, 1582, arr. editors*)

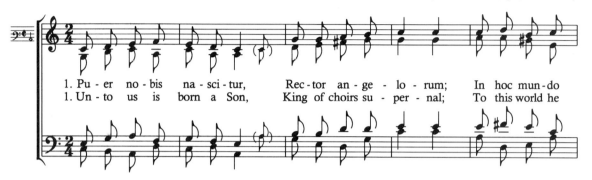

1. Pu - er no - bis na - sci - tur, Rec - tor an - ge - lo - rum; In hoc mun - do
1. Un - to us is born a Son, King of choirs su - per - nal; To this world he

pa - sci - tur Do - mi - nus Do - mi - no - rum, Do - mi - nus Do - mi - no - rum.
deigns to come Of lords the Lord e - ter - nal, of lords the Lord e - ter - nal.

2 In praesepe positum
  Sub foeno asinorum
 Cognoverunt Dominum
  Christum, Regem Coelorum.

*3 Hunc Herodes timuit
  Magno cum tremore;
 In infantes irruit
  Hos caedens in furore.

4 Qui natus ex Maria
  Die hodierna:
 Duc nos, tua gratia,
  Ad gaudia superna.

2 Lo! he lies within a stall
  Where cattle fed before him;
 King of heaven and Lord of all,
  They know him and adore him.

*3 Rage did Herod then impel,
  Whom fearful trembling fillèd;
 On the little boys he fell
  And every one he killèd.

4 Born of Mary on this day,
  By thy grace translate us
 To the realm above, we pray,
  Where endless joys await us.

5 'Te salvator A et O,'
   Cantemus in choro;
   Cantemus in organo:
     'Benedicamus Domino.'

(*Piae Cantiones, 1582*)

5 Every voice in quire now blend
   To hymn our Saviour, Source and End;
   In sweet concord sing we so:
     Benedicamus Domino.

v. 1 tr. G. R. Woodward, adapted
vv. 2–5 tr. editors

One of the most charming of all medieval *cantiones* (songs), known in English-speaking countries only in the unusual duple-time form of *Piae Cantiones* (1582). Elsewhere it is usually in triple time. (In France it was sung as a Latin *noël* from the sixteenth century; the organ settings by Lebègue and Dandrieu are both of a pastoral character. The very similar Catholic chorale version is usually sung in modern Germany to the text 'Uns ist geborn ein Kindelein'.) Our two versions are from the Moosburg Gradual (1355–60), which is the earliest known source, and the familiar one from *Piae Cantiones*, with optional harmonies.

The song is a *Benedicamus* substitute (see notes, 9), with an unusual feature. The last verse in *Piae Cantiones* implies that 'Benedicamus Domino' was sometimes sung in harmony ('in organo'): the response would then be sung, normally either in chant by all or in a polyphonic setting by soloists. But the Moosburg Gradual has what must be an indication of a third possibility. The last verse is marked 'R' (response), which elsewhere in the manuscript indicates a refrain: but no later source has a refrain, and the repetition of 'Benedicamus Domino' after each verse would be unique in the song repertory and very odd liturgical practice. What the scribe seems to be indicating, in shorthand, is that the final verse is to be repeated with the response 'Deo dicamus gracias' substituted for 'Benedicamus Domino'. Immediately after the last verse he gives the words 'Deo dicamus gracias' with new music (the top part in our bars 13–15) which, by what can hardly be coincidence, fits neatly in two-part harmony with the music of the last line of the verses: the implication is that both the 'Benedicamus' and 'Deo gracias' are to be sung with this simple harmony. Several interpretations of the 'shorthand' are possible, and we favour the most obvious: that the entire song was performed by a group of soloists (presumably the cantors), who would break into polyphony in the final phase. (A third part, which we have added, would perhaps have been improvised.) The whole last verse was then repeated full (since all would normally sing the response), with 'Deo dicamus gracias' substituted in the last line.

The Moosburg Gradual is a large manuscript volume copied for the Augustinian College of St Castulus in Moosburg in Germany (now Cod. MS 2° 156 in the Munich University Library). It actually comprises several liturgical books, of which the Cantional contains thirty-three songs and the Troper a few more. Many of the songs derive from the twelfth- and thirteenth-century *organum* repertory of St Martial and Notre-Dame (de Paris) and occur in other sources before and after the Moosburg codex; others are signed by the scribe, Johann Decanus von Perchausen. ('Puer nobis nascitur' is not so signed.) The 'O et O' has its counterpart in other Moosburg songs: 'Eya et eya', 'A et E, O et I', etc., and these seem to be nothing more arcane than ululations of joy. Later sources of 'Puer nobis nascitur' have 'Alpha, I et E et O', 'A et I et E et O', and 'O et A et A et O', suggesting that the 'alpha and omega' theme (as in text II) evolved as a rationalization of earlier practice.

The slight variations in the music of verses 1 (bar 3) and 3 (bar 5) are intentional. The former is perhaps best regarded as an ornament on an important word, while the stepwise motion in verse 3 may illustrate 'graceful leading'. Songs from manuscripts in which only the first verse is set were probably varied in a comparable way.

The third verse in *Piae Cantiones* (II) is a later addition, typical of the 'narrative' intrusions into non-narrative songs which were often designed to tie the song to a particular feast, in this case Holy Innocents' Day (28 December). On other occasions it is perhaps better omitted.

PERFORMANCE I (*i*) (reflecting probable historical practice) a small group of voices, in unison until the two-/three-part final phrase of verse 4, a large group then repeating verse 4 in a similar manner, substituting 'A et A' etc. and 'Deo dicamus gracias' (see above); (*ii*) unison voices: the 'Deo dicamus gracias' may be (*a*) omitted, (*b*) substituted in a repeat of verse 4 (with 'A et A' etc.), or (*c*) sung after verse 4 in unison (to the top part in the last phrase) or in two or three parts.

II (*i*) unison voices; (*ii*) choir; (*iii*) unison voices and organ.

22

Omnis mundus iucundetur

(Christmas)   *(Praetorius, 1607, adapted)*

*2 Mater plorat cum adorat Deum factum hóminem:
     Natus ridet quando videt charam matrem vírginem.

*3 Rident sata, virent prata, nato Regi párvulo;
     Gaudent montes, saltant fontes, magno Mundi Dómino.

v. 1 fourteenth-century (Piae Cantiones, 1582)
vv. 2, 3 seventeenth-century (Dankó, 1893)

TRANSLATION   1 Let all the world rejoice at the birth of the Saviour; the chaste Mother, who conceived him by the word of Gabriel, rejoices.

With sonorous voices and sincere hearts let us rejoice and be glad today: today Christ is born of Mary the Virgin. Rejoice! let us rejoice and be glad therefore.

2 The Mother weeps as she adores God made man; her Son laughs when he sees his dear virgin mother.

3 The crops laugh, the fields become green at the birth of the King as a little child; the hills rejoice, the fountains leap for the great Lord of the World.

This Christmas *cantio* (song) probably dates from the fourteenth century, and it remained popular well into the seventeenth. The earliest surviving source, to a German translation of the text beginning 'Alle werlet freuet sich', is in a late fifteenth-century manuscript in Wrocław, Poland (MS I, 8, fo. 113).

As with other songs that remained in vogue for centuries, this one developed and branched into many different forms. In the seventeenth century we find it in both duple and triple time, and two new German translations are found in Catholic song-books. We have adapted Praetorius's version (from his *Musae Sioniae*, V, 1607, no. 93; see notes, 53) by imposing the rhythm of the version in *Piae Cantiones* (1582),

which fits the Latin text more fluently. (The *Piae Cantiones* tune differs in having A–B–A–G for G–B–C–D in bars 10–11, 15–16, 20–1, 25–6, and 30–1.) An error in the *Piae Cantiones* text—'synceris' for 'sonoris'—is corrected from Praetorius.

'Omnis mundus iucundetur' was never a verse-and-refrain song. It consists of two sections, bars 1–4 (repeated), and bars 5–32. But the first section is so like a verse to modern ears that we have lengthened the song by adding two optional verses from the seventeenth-century Hungarian Christmas song 'Coelo rores pluunt flores', taken from Joseph Danko's *Vetus Hymnarium Ecclesiasticum Hungaricae* (1893). (The Lutheran chorale adaptation 'Seid fröhlich und jubilieret' also turns 'Omnis mundus' into a refrain song.)

PERFORMANCE   (*i*) (with verses 2 and 3 *ad lib.*) bars 1–4 (repeated), four voices, or choir, with organ and/or other instruments; bars 5–32, the same, with additional forces (congregation, audience, etc.).

(*ii*) (omitting verses 2 and 3) voices and organ.

(*iii*) (preferably with verses 2 and 3) two antiphonal groups dividing the setting between them, the groups alternating at bars 1 (second time), 5, 12, 17, and 22, and all combining at bar 27.

23

Lullay, lullay: Als I lay on Yoolis Night

(Christmas)

Fourteenth-century
(Cambridge University MS)

REFRAIN

Lul - lay, lul - lay, lay, lay, lul - lay:__ Mi dee - re mo - der, sing lul - lay.

VERSE

1. Als I lay on Yoo - lis Night, A - lone__ in_____ my long-ing, Me
2. The mai - den wold with - out - en song Hir child__ o_____ sleep to bring: The

thought I saw a well fair sight, A may__ hir_____ child__ rok-king:
child him thought sche ded him wrong And bad__ his_____ mo - der sing.

3 'Sing nou, moder,' said the child,
   'Wat schal to me befall
  Heerafter, wan I cum til eld,
   For so doon modres all.

4 'Ich a moder, trewely,
   That kan hir credel keep,
  Is wun to lullen luvely,
   And sing hir child o sleep.

5 'Sweete moder, fair and free,
   Be cause that it is so,
  I pray thee that thou lulle me,
   And sing sumwat therto.'

6 'Sweete sune', saide sche,
   'Weroffe schuld I sing?
  Ne wist I nere yet more of thee
   But Gabriels greeting.

REFRAIN
Lul - lay, lul - lay, lay, lay, lul - lay:___ Mi dee - re mo - der, sing lul - lay.

Fine

VERSE
(4)
7. 'He grett me good - li on his knee, And said - e,_____ "Hail, Ma - rie! Hail,
8. 'I wun - dred mich - il in my thought, For man_ wold___ I right none; "Ma -

9
D.C.
full of grace! God is with thee; Thou be - ren_____ schalt Mes - sie."
- rie," he said - e, "dred thee nought; Let God_ of_____ heven a - lone!

9 ' "The Holi Gost schal doon al this,"
   He said, withouten wun,
   That I schuld beren mannis blis,
   And Godis owne Sun.

10 'He saide, "Thou schalt bere a King
    In King Davitis see;"
    In all Jacobes wuniing
    Ther Loverd schuld he be.

11 'He saide that Elizabeth,
    That barain was bifore,
    "A knave child conceyved hath:
    To me leeve thou the more!"

12 'I answered blethely,
    For that his word me paid,
    "Lo, Godis servant heer am I:
    Be et as thou me said."

13 'Ther, als he saide, I thee bare
    On midewenter night,
    In maidenhede withouten kare,
    Be grace of God almight.

14 'Ther schepperds waked in the wold,
    Thei herd a wunder mirth
    Of angles ther, as theim thei told
    The tiding of thi birth.

15 'Sweete sune, sikirly,
    No more kan I say;
    And, if I koude, fawn wold I
    To doon al at thi pay.'

16 Serteynly this sight I say,
    This song I herde sing,
    Als I me lay this Yoolis Day
    Alone in my longing.

Fourteenth-century
(Dobson, 1979)

TRANSLATION   1 As I lay on Christmas Night, alone in my desire, it seemed to me I saw a very lovely sight, a maid rocking her child.

2 The maiden wanted to put her child to sleep without singing; to the child it seemed she wronged him, and he told his mother to sing.

3 'Sing now, mother,' said the child, 'what is to befall me in the future when I am grown up, for all mothers do that.

4 'Every mother, truly, who knows how to watch over her cradle, is accustomed to lull lovingly and sing her child to sleep.

5 'Sweet mother, fair and gracious, since that is so, I pray you lull me and sing something as well.'

6 'Sweet son,' said she, 'of what should I sing? I never knew anything more about you than Gabriel's greeting.

7 'He greeted me courteously, kneeling, and said "Hail, Mary! Hail, full of grace! God is with thee; thou shalt bear the Messiah."

8 'I wondered greatly in my mind, for I by no means desired a husband. "Mary," he said, "do not fear; leave the God of Heaven to his ways.

9 ' "The Holy Ghost is to do all this," he said, without delay, that I should bear man's bliss and God's own Son.

10 'He said, "Thou shalt bear a King in King David's seat [Bethlehem]"; in all the house of Jacob he was to be Lord.

11 'He said that Elizabeth, who until then had been barren, "has conceived a male child—so give me more credence."

12 'I answered gladly, for his words pleased me: "Lo, I am here, God's servant; be it as thou hast said to me."

13 'There [in King David's seat], as he said, I bore you on Midwinter Night, in virginity without pain, by the grace of almighty God.

14 'Where shepherds were watching in the uplands they heard a wondrous song of angels there, as they told them the tidings of your birth.

15 'Sweet son, assuredly I can say no more, and if I could, I would gladly, to do everything as you wish.'

16 Certainly I saw this sight, I heard this song sung, as I lay this Christmas Day alone in my desire.

(tr. *E. J. Dobson, adapted*)

A lullaby carol in the form of a vision. We give a mere sixteen verses (1–15, 37) of the thirty-seven in R. L. Greene's *Early English Carols* (1977). The primary source is a manuscript in Edinburgh (National Library of Scotland MS Advocates 18.7.21, one of three that preserve the words without the music) written by a Franciscan friar, John Grimestone, 'cum magna sollicitudine' ('with great care') in the north-east Midlands in 1372. E. J. Dobson believes that verses 16–36, in which Christ responds to Mary by himself foretelling his future life, are a later addition (*Medieval English Songs*, 1979); his freely emended text is 'modified in spelling and regularized in metre'.

The melody is from a manuscript owned by Thomas Turke, one of the inaugural fellows of Winchester College in 1395. It contains two- and three-part songs in Latin, French, and English, Latin sermons and religious tracts, and tables of eclipses for the years 1415–62. In 1418, when Turke became a monk, he presented the manuscript to John Morton, an ecclesiastical administrator at Salisbury. The manuscript (Cambridge University Library Add. 5943) has only the refrain and one verse.

For another carol of conversation between Virgin and Child see 'Thys endere nyghth' (39).

PERFORMANCE   Voices. Refrain: first time, solo repeated full; subsequently, full. Verse: solo. The little decorative figures in bars 7 and 11 need not be used throughout, and similar ornaments could be introduced elsewhere. All final *e*s are sounded except where indicated.

24

Lullay, lullow: I saw a swete semly syght

(Christmas)

Fifteenth-century
(Ritson's MS)

¹ child (bairn)   ² maiden

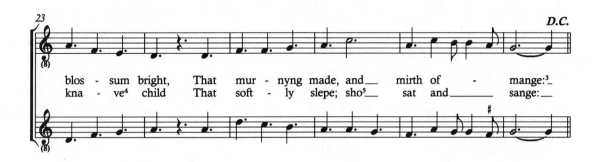

blos - sum bright,   That mur - nyng made, and__ mirth of - mange:[3]_
kna - ve[4] child   That soft - ly slepe; sho[5]__ sat and_____ sange:__

[3] who lamented and rejoiced together   [4] boy   [5] she

This carol is probably only the beginning of a longer one (the rest having been lost), which appears to have been similar in theme to 'Als I lay on Yoolis Night' (23) and 'Thys endere nyghth' (39). Text and music are from Ritson's manuscript (British Library, Add. MS 5665), which was copied in the first quarter of the sixteenth century and contains Latin masses and motets and English sacred and secular songs as well as a large number of carols. The volume may have a connection with Exeter Cathedral, as eight of the carols are by Richard Smert, who was vicar-choral there from 1428 to about 1466 (see notes, 36), and five are attributed to John Trouluffe, a canon of St Probus, Exeter, in the late 1460s and 70s.

PERFORMANCE Two voices, with refrains full *ad lib*. (A tone higher than notated may suit tenors better.) For a guide to pronunciation see Appendix 1.

25

Nova! nova!

(*Annunciation; Christmas*)

Fifteenth-century
(*Hunterian Museum MS*)

REFRAIN

No - va! no - va! 'A - ve' fit ex 'E - va'.[1]

Fine **VERSES 1–2**

1. Ga - bri - ell off hye de - gre, He___ cam down from Tri - ni - te To Na - za - reth in Ga - li - le.
2. He met a may - dn in a place, He kne - lyd down a - fore hir face, He seyd: 'Heile, Ma - ry, ful of grace!'

No - va! no - va!

D.C.

VERSES 3–4

3. When the maiden herd tell off this Sche was full sore a-baschyd I - wys, And wened that sche had don a-mysse.
4. Then seid the an - gell: 'Dred not thue, Ye shall con-ceyve in___ all ver - tu A Chyld whose name shall be Jhe-su.'

No - va! no - va!

D.C.

[1] News! news! 'Ave' is made from 'Eva'.

VERSES 5–6

5. 'It is not yit syx moneth a - goon___ Sen E - li - za - beth con-cey - ved
6. Then seid the may - den ve - re - ly: 'I am youre ser - vaunt right tru - e -

D.C.

John, As it was pro - phy - sed be forne.' *No - va! no - va!*
- ly. *Ec - ce an - cil - la Do - mi - ni.'[2]*

---

[2] Behold the handmaid of the Lord.

An Annunciation carol from a fifteenth-century manuscript of unknown origin (Glasgow University, Hunterian Museum MS 83) which, among its miscellaneous contents, includes two carols and a Christmas song. Similar texts, without music, are found in two Oxford sources (Balliol College MS 354 and Bodleian Library MS Eng. poet. e. 1) and we have drawn freely on these to amend the more obvious corruptions in the Glasgow source (e.g., 'Ffrom Nazareth to Galile' in verse 1; 'vi wekes' in verse 5). Only verse 1 is set, to what may have been an existing popular tune; the note lengths are very confused. (A parallel case is 'Nowell: Tydynges trew', 26.) David Wulstan has suggested (in *An Anthology of Carols*, 1968) that all the Fs should be natural (i.e., that the Bs as notated in the MS should be

B flats); on the other hand, the Lydian flavour may reflect a folk origin. (Regarding this rare mode in English folk music, see A. L. Lloyd, *Folk Song in England*, 1967.) The two text-only manuscripts interpolate the word 'With' at the beginning of the fourth line of each verse; this may easily be incorporated by adding a ♩ E at the end of bar 11, etc. The refrain embodies the popular medieval conceit that the Virgin Mary was the new Eve, the 'Ave Maria' of the Annunciation signalling the end of man's domination by Eve's sin.

PERFORMANCE Refrain, full; verse, solo (perhaps freely adapting the tune from verse 2 onwards—see notes, 39). Some fifteenth-century carols begin with a solo refrain, repeated full, and this may be effective here. For a guide to pronunciation see Appendix 1.

26

Nowell: Tydynges trew ther be cum new

(Annunciation; Christmas)

Fifteenth-century
(Bodleian Library MS)

REFRAIN

'No - well, no - well, no - - well!' This is the

sa - lu - ta - ci - on off the aun - gell Ga - bri - ell. *Fine*

VERSES 1–3

1. Tyd - ynges trew ther be cum new, sent frome__ the Tri - ni -
2. Whan he fyrst pre - sent - id was be - fore__ hyre fayere vi -
3. 'Hayle, vir - gyne ce - les - ti - all, the mek - est that e - ver

- te Be[1]__ Ga - bri - ell to Na - za - ret, ci - te off Ga - li - le. A
- sag, In the most de - muere and good - ly wys he ded to hyre o - mag, And
was; Hayle, tem - ple off__ de - i - tie and myr-rour off all grace; Hayle,

clene may - den and pure vir - gyn tho-row hyre hu - mi - li -
seid, 'La - dy, frome heven so hy, that__ Lord - es he - ry -
vir - gyne puer,[3] I the en - sure,[4] with - in full ly - tyl

- te, Hath con - cey - veyd the per - son se - cond in de - y - te. *D.C.*
- tag[2] The wich off the__ borne wold be, I am sent on mes - sag.
space[5] Thou shalt re - ceyve and hym con-ceyve that shal bryng gret so - lace.'

[1] by [2] offspring [3] pure [4] assure [5] while

35 VERSES 4-6

4. So - den - ly⁶ she, a - bashid tru - ly, but not al thyng⁷ dys -
5. Than___ a - geyne to hire cer - teyn⁹ an - swer - ed the aun -
6. Thane___ a - geyne to the aun - gell she an - swer - ed wo - man -

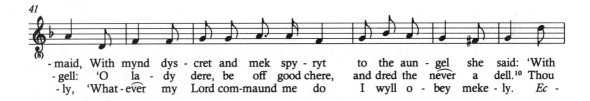

41

- maid, With mynd dys - cret and mek spy - ryt to the aun - gel she said: 'With
- gell: 'O la - dy dere, be off good chere, and dred the never a dell.¹⁰ Thou
- ly, 'What - ever my Lord com-maund me do I wyll o - bey meke - ly. Ec -

47

what ma - ner shuld I chyld bere, the wich e - ver a
shalt con - ceyve in thi bo - dy, may - den, very God hym -
- ce,___ sum hu - mi - li - ma an - cil - la Do - mi -

53   D.C.

maid Have ly - vid chast all my lyf past and ne - ver mane a - said?'⁸
- self, In whos byrth heven and erth shal joy, call - id· E - ma - nu - ell.'
- ni; Se - cun - dum ver - bum tu - um,' she seid, 'fi - at mi - hi.'¹¹

⁶ immediately ⁷ in any way ⁸ assayed (approached) a man ⁹ certainly ¹⁰ not a whit ¹¹ 'Behold, I am the most humble handmaid of the Lord; be it unto me according to thy word' (after Luke 1:38)

An Annunciation carol from a manuscript in the Bodleian Library, Oxford (MS Eng. poet. e. 1), a large and varied collection which probably belonged to Beverley Minster in Yorkshire. The seven verses (we omit verse 6) are set to what was probably an existing popular tune, though the scribe notes: '. . . yf so be that ye wyll have a nother tewyn it may be at yowr plesur . . .'. The music is written very roughly—only verse 1 is underlaid—and the rhythms are clearly corrupt, so that a variety of interpretations are possible. (A parallel case is 'Nova! nova!', 25. For an alternative transcription see John Stevens's *Mediaeval Carols, Musica Britannica*, IV, rev. 1958.) Where the text does not fit the tune satisfactorily we have made small emendations from other manuscript sources.

PERFORMANCE Refrain, full; verse, solo (perhaps freely adapting the tune from verse 3 onwards—see notes, 39). Some fifteenth-century carols begin with a solo refrain, repeated full, and this may be effective here. For a guide to pronunciation see Appendix 1.

27

Hayl, Mary, ful of grace

(*Annunciation; Christmas*)

Fifteenth-century
(*Trinity roll*)

-der___ om - ni - po - tent; Now is God with - yn the
blode___ to - ge - dre___ ranne; Ma - ry bare bothe___ God and

went[1] Whan the an - gel___ seide 'A - ve'.
manne Thorw ver - tu and___ thorw dyng - ny - te.

*3 So seith the Gospel of Syn Johan:
God and man is made but one
In flesch and blode, body and bone,
O[2] God in personys thre.

*4 'And the prophete Jeremye
Told in his prophecie
That the sone of Marie
Schuld deye for us on rode tre.[3]

5 'Moche joye to us was graunt[4]
And in erthe pees yplaunte[5]
Whan that born was this faunte[6]
In the londe of Galile.

6 'Mary, graunte us the blys
Ther thy Sonys wonynge ys;[7]
Of that we han ydone amys[8]
Pray for us pur[9] charite.

Fifteenth-century
(*Trinity roll*)

[1] now has God entered thee   [2] one   [3] the tree of the rood
[4] much joy was granted us   [5] and peace planted on earth
[6] infant   [7] where thy Son's dwelling is   [8] for what we
have done amiss   [9] through

An Annunciation carol from an early fifteenth-century manuscript roll in the library of Trinity College, Cambridge (MS 0.3.58). It is the first item in the roll, and decay has partly or completely obscured some notes. The text (with small differences) is also in Richard Kele's *Christmas Carolles newely Inprynted* (*c*.1550). Text and music (again with small differences) are in the Selden manuscript (see notes, 29). Here a later hand (probably that of John Alcock, bishop of Worcester from 1476–86 and later joint Lord Chancellor,

Master of the Rolls, etc.) has drawn his device of a cock opposite verse 5, and added another verse at the end: 'Hayl, blyssyd lady, qwych hays born / God Son in Trinite; / In the, laydy, he tuk hys plays / Qwen the angel sayd "Ave" .' The addition may reflect Alcock's personal devotion to the Virgin, and was presumably intended to be sung between verses 5 and 6.

Verses 1 and 2: it was believed that Mary conceived through the ear as she heard Gabriel's words. Verse 4, 'the prophete . . . told': he didn't.

PERFORMANCE   Refrain, three voices or choir; verse, two voices. For a guide to pronunciation see Appendix 1.

28

Ther is no rose of swych vertu

(*Christmas*)

Fifteenth-century
(*Trinity roll*)

REFRAIN

Ther is no rose of_____ swych[1]____ ver - tu

Fine

As is the rose_____ that_ bare_____ Jhe - su.

VERSE

1. Ther is_____ no_ rose of swych____ ver -
2. For in_____ this_ rose con - tey - nyd_____

- tu As_ is_____ the_ rose_____ that bare Jhe - su.
was He - ven_____ and_ erthe_____ in ly - tyl space,

[1] such

82

3 'Be³ that rose we may weel see
  That he is God in personys thre,
      *Pari forma.*⁴

4 The aungelys sungyn the sheperdes to:
  'Gloria in excelsis Deo.'⁵
      *Gaudeamus.*⁶

5 'Leive⁷ we al this worldly merthe,
  And folwe we this joyful berthe:
      *Transeamus.*⁸

Fifteenth-century
(Trinity roll)

² a wonderful thing   ³ by   ⁴ of the same form   ⁵ glory to God on high   ⁶ let us rejoice   ⁷ leave   ⁸ let us go

From the same early fifteenth-century manuscript as 'Hayl, Mary, ful of grace' (27). It is the last item, and discoloration and decay make some of the music difficult to decipher: in bar 13, a hole has swallowed the second note of the lower voice. Our added middle part in the refrain is of a kind that might have been improvised. (The resulting succession of ⁶₃ chords is characteristic of the English technique known as faburden, which is in fact the addition of parts *above* and *below* a melody: three-part realizations with treble tune such as the present one have more in common with the related technique of *fauxbourdon.*)

The use of the first verse as a refrain is unusual in a carol, and recalls what was sometimes done in processional performances of sequences. The identification of Mary with the rose was a common medieval conceit which forms the

basis of several surviving English carols and a multitude of Latin hymns. The Latin in the first three verses is from the sequence 'Letabundus' (5). 'Gaudeamus' (verse 4) is perhaps from the Christmastide office (*Introit*) antiphon 'Gaudeamus, omnes fideles: Salvator noster natus est in mundum . . .' ('Rejoice, all we faithful: our Saviour is born into the world . . .'). 'Transeamus' is the first word of the shepherds' response to the angels' 'Gloria in excelsis': 'Let us go now even unto Bethlehem, and see this thing which is come to pass' (Luke 2:15).

See 'There is no rose' (120) for a modern setting of this text by John Joubert. There is also a setting by Britten in *A Ceremony of Carols*, for high voices and harp.

PERFORMANCE Refrain, two or three voices, or choir; verse, two voices. For a guide to pronunciation see Appendix 1.

29

Alleluya pro Virgine Maria

(Christmas)

Fifteenth-century
(Selden MS)

REFRAIN

Al - le - le - lu - ya pro Vir - gi - ne_____ Ma - ri - a.

Fine

VERSE

1. Di - va na - ta - li - ci - a Nos - tra pur - gat_____
2. Na - to sa - cri - fi - ci - a Re - ges dant tri -
3. Mor - tis vin - cla_____ tru - ci - a Sol - vit di - e -

TRANSLATION Alleluya for the Virgin Mary.

1 The divine birth cleanses our faults, lest we be given over to punishment.

2 To the Son the kings give triple offerings after the revilings of Herod.

3 He loosed the fierce chains of death on the third day by the power of his resurrection.

From the Selden manuscript (Bodleian Library, Oxford, Selden b. 26), the first part of which (originally separate) is an important mid-fifteenth-century source of songs and carols. Many are addressed to the Virgin, and it has been suggested that the manuscript was connected with the choir of the Lady Chapel in the nave of Worcester Cathedral. This carol is one of six that seem to have been copied from the Selden manuscript into another which probably belonged to the Chapel Royal (British Library MS Egerton 3307). Bar 25, upper voice: first note twice the length in Selden.

A setting of the text by Peter Maxwell Davies forms part of his *O Magnum Mysterium* (1961), as does 'The Fader of heven', 122).

PERFORMANCE Refrain, two voices or choir; verse, two voices. For a guide to pronunciation see Appendix 1.

30

Alleluya: A nywe werk is come on honde

(*Christmas*)

Fifteenth-century
(*Selden MS*)

¹ hand

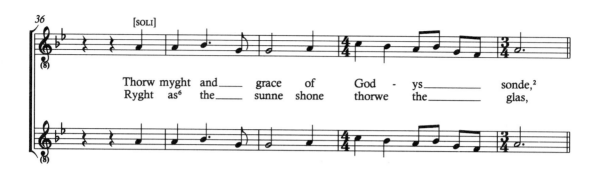

Thorw myght and___ grace of God - ys___ sonde,[2]
Ryght as[6] the___ sunne shone thorwe the___ glas,

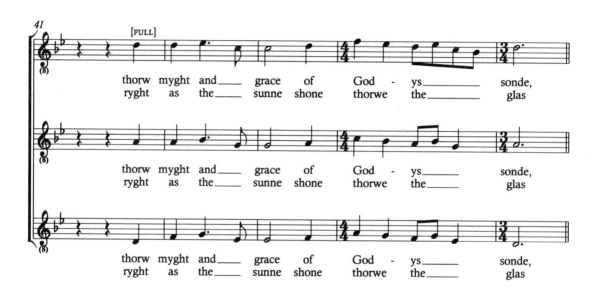

thorw myght and___ grace of God - ys___ sonde,
ryght as the___ sunne shone thorwe the___ glas

thorw myght and___ grace of God - ys___ sonde,
ryght as the___ sunne shone thorwe the___ glas

thorw myght and___ grace of God - ys___ sonde,
ryght as the___ sunne shone thorwe the___ glas

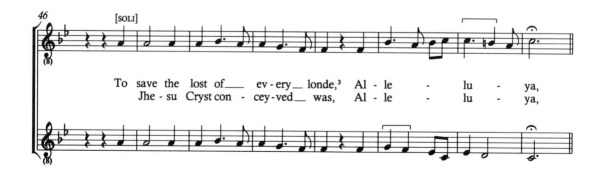

To save the lost of___ ev - ery__ londe,[3] Al - le - lu - ya,
Jhe - su Cryst con - cey-ved__ was, Al - le - lu - ya,

[2] messenger (Gabriel) [3] land [6] just as

al - le - lu - ya, For now is
Of Ma - ry

al - le - lu - ya,

al - le - lu - ya, For now is
Of Ma - ry

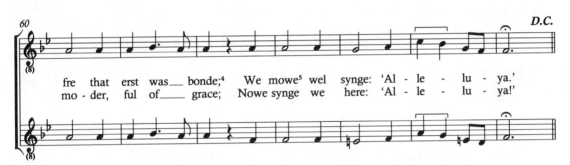

fre that erst was___ bonde;[4] We mowe[5] wel synge: 'Al - le - lu - ya.'
mo - der, ful of___ grace; Nowe synge we here: 'Al - le - lu - ya!'

3 Nowe is fulfylled the prophecie
Of David and of Jeremie,[7]
And also of Ysaie,[8]

Alleluya,
Synge we therfore bothe loude
and hye:
'Alleluya, alleluya!'

4 'Alleluya!' this swete songe,
Oute of a grene branche hit spronge.
God sende us the lyf that lasteth longe!

Alleluya.
Nowe joye and blysse be hem amonge
That thus cunne[9] synge: 'Alleluya'.

Fifteenth-century
(Selden MS)

[4] for now is free what formerly was bound [5] may
[7] Jeremiah [8] Isaiah [9] can

From the Selden manuscript (see notes, 29), which gives six verses. This is one of the finest and most complex carols from the first half of the fifteenth century. The three-part, faburden-like repetitions are unusual in placing the tune in the middle rather than the highest voice. The 'grene branche' in verse 4 is Mary. The omitted verses (between our verses 3 and 4) concern the recognition by Simeon. The image of the sun shining through glass (verse 2) was frequently related to Christ's conception: as the light passes through the glass without harming it, so the Holy Spirit impregnated Mary while leaving her *virgo intacta*. The prophecies of verse 3 are presumably those of the psalm verses used in the Christmas liturgy: of Jeremiah 23:5 and 33:15, and of Isaiah 7:14, 9:2 and 6, and 40:1–5.

PERFORMANCE Two-part sections, solo voices; three-part sections, choir, or three voices. Both refrains are sung each time. For a guide to pronunciation see Appendix 1.

31

Make we joye nowe in this fest

(*Christmas*)

Fifteenth-century
(Selden MS)

REFRAIN

Make we joye___ nowe in___ this fest___ In quo

Chri - stus na - tus est. E - - - ya. *Fine*

VERSE [SOLI]

1. A Pa - tre u - ni - ge - ni - tus Thorw a___ mai -
2. A - gnos - cat om - ne___ se - cu - lum. A bryght sterre

- den___ is com to us. Synge we___ to here___ and sey: 'Wel -
thre___ kynges have made come For___ to seke___ with here pre -

3 *A solis ortus cardine,*
  So myghty a lord was none as he,
  For to oure kynde he hath yeve gryth,
  Adam parens quod polluit.

4 *Maria ventre concepit;*
  The Holy Gost was ay here with.
  In Bedleem yborne he ys,
  Consors paterni luminis.

5 *O lux beata Trinitas!*
  He lay bytwene an oxe and asse,
  Thou moder and maiden fre;
  Gloria tibi, Domine!

Fifteenth-century
(Selden MS)

TRANSLATION Let us rejoice now on this feast on which Christ was born.
  1 The Only-begotten of the Father is come to us by a maiden; let us sing to her and say [to him]: 'Welcome! Come, Saviour of the [gentile] peoples!'
  2 Let every age acknowledge that a bright star made three kings come to seek, with their presents, the high Word coming forth.
  3 From where the sun rises [to where it sets] there was no lord as mighty as he, for he has given peace to our race, which was defiled by our father Adam.
  4 Mary has conceived in her womb; the Holy Spirit was truly with her. He is born in Bethlehem, sharer in the fatherly light.
  5 O Light of the Holy Trinity! He lay between an ox and an ass, thou Mother and noble Maiden; Glory to thee, O Lord!

From the Selden manuscript (see notes, 29). The text also occurs, without music, in another Bodleian manuscript (MS Eng. poet. e. 1; see notes, 26) and, set to different music, in Ritson's manuscript (see notes, 24). The Latin lines in the verses are nearly all the openings of office hymns of Advent, Christmas, and the Epiphany; verse 5 quotes a Trinity hymn and the opening of the Christmastide doxology. The way these Latin tags are incorporated as first and fourth lines of couplet-rhymed stanzas is unique among fifteenth-century carols. A clue to the origin of the text may lie in the fact that three of the hymns quoted are in the York use but not in Sarum.
  (For a modern setting of this text see carol 119.)

PERFORMANCE Refrain, two voices or choir; verse, two voices. For a guide to pronunciation see Appendix 1.

32

What tydynges bryngest thou, messangere?

(*New Year; Christmas*†)

Fifteenth-century
(Selden MS)

REFRAIN [FULL]

'What tyd - ynges bryngest_ thou, mes - san - gere, Of

mes - san - gere, Of

Fine VERSE [SOLI]

Chri - stis byth[1]_ this_ Yer - es_ Day?'[2]

1. 'A
2. 'A

Chri - stis_

Babe_ ys born of_ hye_ na - tore,[3] Is Prinse of
seme - ly syght hit_ is_ to_ se: The berde[8] that

Pes,[4] and e - ver shal_ be; Off he - ven and_ erthe he_
hath this Babe_ y - borne Con - ceyv - ed a_ Lord of_

† See notes.

[1] birth [2] New Year's Day [3] nature [4] peace [8] maiden

hath___ the___ cure; Hys Lord-shyp___ is e - ter - ni -
hygh___ de - gre And mai - den___ as heo⁹___ was___ by -

- te.
- forne. Such won - der tyd - yngys___ ye___ mow_ here.'⁵

tyd - yngys

[FULL]
'What tyd - ynges bryngest___ thou, mes - san - gere?'

mes - san - gere?'

[SOLI]
'That man is___ made now God - ys___ fere,⁶ Wham
'That maide and___ moder ys wone___ y - fere¹⁰ And

D.C.
syn had made but fen - des___ praye.'⁷
al - wey lady of hye___ a - ray.'

⁵ may hear ⁶ companion ⁷ whom sin had made the prey of fiends
⁹ she ¹⁰ one together

*3 'This maide began to gretyn[11] here
        Chylde,
     And saide: "Haile, Sone, haile, Fader
        dere!"
     He saide: "Haile, moder, haile, maide
        mylde!"
     This gretynge was in queynte[12] manere.
     Such wonder tydyngys ye mow here.'
     'What tydynges bryngest thou,
        messangere?'
     'Here gretyng was in suche manere
     Hit turned mannys peyne[13] to play.'

4 'A wonder thynge is now befalle:
     That Lorde that formed sterre[14] and
        sunne,
     Heven and erth and angelys alle,
     Nowe in mankynde is by gunne.[15]
     Such wonder tydyngys ye mow here.'
     'What tydynges bryngest thou,
        messangere?'
     'A faunt that is not of on yere[16]
     Ever hath ybe[17] and shal be ay.'

Fifteenth-century
(Selden MS)

[11] greet [12] quaint [13] man's pain [14] star [15] now
begins as a man [16] an infant not one year old [17] been

From the Selden manuscript, which probably originated at
Worcester Cathedral (see notes, 29). The Trinity roll (see
notes, 27) preserves what may be an earlier version of the
setting. It lacks the interpolation 'What tydynges . . . ' in the
verses and gives the last note of each phrase as (in our
reduction) ♩ followed by ⁊⁊ ; as with 'Nowell syng we'
(34) this may or may not reflect a real difference in
performance, and it could be that the 'joins' at bars 30–1
and 35–6 in our Selden version are not to be read literally.
The interpolation in the Selden manuscript is only an
incipit, marked 'ut supra' ('as above'), leaving it unclear
whether the repeat is of bars 1–5 or of the whole refrain;
comparison with other carols suggests the shorter version,
which we give. Our added middle parts in the refrain and
interpolation are of a kind that might have been improvised
in faburden style (see notes, 28). The text also occurs, with
variants and a fifth verse, in another Bodleian manuscript

(Douce 302) which may also pre-date the Selden source.
    Carols were sung in the hall at Worcester during the
Christmas season, including New Year's Day, which may
explain the New Year refrain in what is otherwise a
Christmastide carol. (The Trinity manuscript has 'Yolys
[Christmas] Day'.) We know that carols were also sung
there at the annual feast for civic officials on the Epiphany
(6 January) at which some kind of ceremony involving
'messengers' was observed, so perhaps this carol was
presented dramatically at a similar observance on 1 January,
the two soloists representing the messenger. (See 'Nowell:
Dieus wous garde, byewsser', 36 and 'Nowell: The borys
hede', 37, for other carols that were possibly acted.)

PERFORMANCE Refrain and interpolation (bars 31–5), two-
or three-part choir (or solo voices); verse, two voices. For a
guide to pronunciation see Appendix 1.
    In a dramatic presentation, the two soloists would re-
present the messenger. When sung on Christmas Day,
change 'Yeres' to 'Yolys' in the refrain.

33

Nowel: Owt of your slepe aryse

(Christmas)

Fifteenth-century
(Selden MS)

¹ for God has now taken on manhood   ² husband

2 And thorwe a maide faire and wys[3]
  Now man is made of ful grete pris;[4]
  Now angelys knelen to mannys servys,
  And at this tyme[5] al this byfel.

3 Now man is bryghter than the sonne;
  Now man in heven an hye shal wone;[6]
  Blessyd be God this game is begonne,
  And his moder emperesse of helle.

4 That ever was thralle, now ys he fre;[7]
  That ever was smalle, now grete is she;[8]
  Now shal God deme[9] bothe the and me
  Unto his blysse yf we do wel.[10]

*5 Now man may to heven wende;
  Now heven and erthe to hym they bende;
  He that was foo[11] now is oure frende;
  This is no nay that Y yowe telle.[12]

6 Now, blessyd brother,[13] graunte us grace
  A[14] domesday to se thy face
  And in thy courte to have a place,
  That we mow[15] there synge 'Nowel'.

Fifteenth-century
(Selden MS)

[3] wise [4] worth [5] Christmas [6] now man shall live in heaven on high [7] he [man] who was in thrall for ever is now free [8] Mary [9] judge [10] act righteously [11] foe [12] there is no denying what I tell you [13] Christ [14] at [15] may

From the Selden manuscript (see notes, 29). A two-part setting of the same text survives incomplete in a manuscript in Cambridge University Library (Ll.1.11). Another manuscript in the same library (Ee.1.12) has the text only of a different carol, written around 1492 by the Canterbury friar and prolific carol poet James Ryman, which has a very similar first verse: perhaps the present text is also by Ryman. It seems to have been inspired by a verse in Romans 12, which was read as an epistle in Advent: 'The night is far spent, the day is at hand: let us therefore cast off the works of darkness, and let us put on the armour of light.' 'Bereth the belle' (verse 1) implies leadership. Bells were hung on the lead horse of a team and on the leading sheep of a flock (the 'bell-wether'), and were awarded as the prize at country races.

The refrain is written monophonically in the source, but the refrain indications at the verse-end suggest that it is to be sung canonically; precisely how is a matter of some dispute, and ours is one of several possible interpretations.

PERFORMANCE Refrain, choir or three voices; verse, three voices. For a guide to pronunciation see Appendix 1.

34

Nowel syng we bothe al and som

(Christmas)

Fifteenth-century
(Selden MS)

98

bought   to   blysse,   Bothe   all_____ and sum.
dyde   us   dyght,   Bothe   alle_____ and summe.

and   sume.
and   summe.

3 *Puer natus* to us was sent,
   To blysse us bought, fro bale us blent,
   And ellys to wo we hadde ywent,
      Bothe alle and summe.

4 *Lux fulgebit* with love and lyght,
   In Mary mylde his pynon pyght,
   In here toke kynde with manly myght,
      Bothe alle and summe.

5 *Gloria tibi* ay and blysse:
   God unto his grace he us wysse,
   The rent of heven that we not mysse,
      Bothe alle and summe.

Fifteenth-century
(Selden MS)

TRANSLATION Let us sing 'Nowell', each and every one, now that the King of Peace is come.

1 This has come to pass, in love and joy: Christ has now prepared his grace for us, and with his body has redeemed us unto bliss, each and every one.

2 From the fruit of the womb of radiant Mary both God and man come to rest in her; he rescued us from disease, each and every one.

3 A Boy-child was sent to us; he redeemed us unto bliss and took us away from sorrow, and we would otherwise have come to grief, each and every one.

4 The Light will shine with love and light; in gentle Mary he set up his pennon [flag]; in her he boldly assumed manhood, each and every one.

5 Glory to thee [O Lord] always, and joy! May God guide us to his grace, so that we shall not lose the reward of heaven, each and every one.

From the Selden manuscript (see notes, 29). The music, with different words, is found also in the Trinity roll (see

notes, 27), where the chief difference is that each phrase ends with (in our reduction) ♩ followed by ♪♪ ; this may or may not reflect a real difference in performance. Our added middle part in the refrain is of a kind that might have been improvised in faburden style (see notes, 28).

The palindromic arrangement of rhymes is unusual: verses 1 and 5 correspond, as do 2 and 4, while 3 stands alone. Each Latin tag is the opening of an item in the liturgy of Christmas Day. 'Rex Pacificus' is the first antiphon of first vespers, and the rest, in order, are: the second antiphon of second vespers, the last antiphon of second vespers, the office (*Introit*) of the mass of the day, the office of the mass at dawn, and the seasonal doxology to the office hymns ('Gloria tibi, Domine. . .'), which that day is sung for the first time.

PERFORMANCE Refrain, two- or three-part choir (or solo voices); verse, two voices. For a guide to pronunciation see Appendix 1.

35

Synge we to this mery cumpane

(Christmas)

Fifteenth-century
(Selden MS)

REFRAIN

Synge we to this_____ me - ry_____ cum - pa -

Synge we to this me - ry cum - pa -

Fine

- ne: 'Re - gi - na_____ Ce - li, le - ta - re.'[1]

- ne: 'Re - gi - na Ce - li, le - ta - re.'[1]

VERSE

1. Ho - ly Mai - de, bless - yd_____ thou____ be; God - ys Sone is
2. Thow art Em - per - esse of_____ He - ven fre; Now art thou Mo - der

born_____ of_____ the, The Fa - der of He - ven, thus ly -
in_____ ma - ges - te Y - knytte in the bless - ed____ Tri -

born_____ of the,
in ma - ges - te,

[1] rejoice, Queen of Heaven

D.C.

-ve² ____ we;   'Re - gi - na ____ Ce - li,   le - ta - re.'
-ni - tie;   'Re - gi - na   Ce - li,   le - ta - re.'

3 Hayl, wyf, hayl maide, bryght of ble!³
   Hayl, doughter, hayl, suster, ful of pite!
   Hayl, cosyn⁴ to the Persones Thre!
   Regina Celi, letare.

4 Lo, this curteys Kynge of degre
   Wole⁵ be thy Sone with solempnite;
   Mylde Mary, this ys thy fee;⁶
   Regina Celi, letare.

5 Therfore knele we on oure kne;
   Thy blysful berthe now worshype we
   With this songe of melode:
   Regina Celi, letare.

Fifteenth-century
(Selden MS)

² believe   ³ fair of face   ⁴ next of kin   ⁵ will   ⁶ due

From the Selden manuscript (see notes, 29). A similar text, without music, is found in a British Library manuscript (Sloane 2593), and a quite different setting of another carol with the same refrain is in Ritson's manuscript (see notes, 24).

'Regina celi, letare' is the opening of the Eastertide antiphon of the Virgin, here used presumably because it continues: 'Quia quem meruisti portare... resurrexit...' ('For he whom thou wast worthy to bear... hath arisen...').

'Thy blysful berthe' (verse 5) is, obviously, the birth of Christ to Mary (blissful because painless and/or because bringing bliss to mankind).

Our added middle part in the refrain is of a kind that might have been improvised in faburden style (see notes, 28).

PERFORMANCE   Refrain, two- or three-part choir (or three voices); verse, two voices. For a guide to pronunciation see Appendix 1.

36

Nowell: Dieus wous garde, byewsser

(*Christmas*)

Richard Smert (*fl. 1428–77*)

here, Syre Crist - es - masse.'

'Well-come, my lord Ser___ Crist - es - masse, Well - come to us

'Well-come, my lord Ser Crist - es - masse, Well - come to us

'Well-come, my lord Ser Crist - es - masse, Well - come to us

all, bothe___ more___ and___ lasse, Com nere,___ no - well.'

all, bothe___ more___ and___ lasse, Com___ nere,___ no - well.'

all, bothe___ more and___ lasse, Com nere,___ no - well.'

VERSE [SOLI]

1. 'Dieus wous garde, byews - ser,[1] tyd - ynges Y_____ yow___ bryng: A mayde
2. 'Crist - e is now born of a pu - re___ mayde; In an
3. 'Beu - vex bien par tut - te la com - pa - ny,[4] Make gode

†1. 'Dieus wous garde, byews - ser,[1]___ tyd-ynges Y_____ yow bryng: A mayde

[1] God keep you, fine sir (*Dieu vous garde, beau sire*)   [4] a health to everyone
† Bass underlay for vv. 2 and 3 follows that of v. 1.

hathe born a chylde____ full____ yong, The weche² caus -
oxe stall - e he____ ys____ layde; Where - for____ syng____
chere and be ryght____ me - ry, And syng____ with____

hathe born a____ chylde full____ yong, The_ weche² caus -

-eth____ yew for_____ to____ syng: No - - well.'
we____ all atte_____ a - brayde;³ No - - well.'
us____ now joy - ful - ly:

-eth yew for_____ to syng: No - - - well.'

[FULL]   REFRAIN [SOLI]
'No - - well.' 'No - well,____ no -

'No - - well.'

'No - - well.' 'No - well, no -

- well, no - well,____ no - - - - well.'

- well,____ no - well,____ no - - - - well.'

² which ³ together

Richard Smert was rector of Plymtree in Devon from 1435 to 1477 and a vicar-choral of Exeter Cathedral from 1428 to about 1466. This carol is from Ritson's manuscript (see notes, 24), which contains a number of Smert's carols. Headed 'in die nativitatis' ('on Christmas Day'), it may reflect a ceremony of welcoming a personified 'Sir Christmas' into the company. Such characters occur in other carols, and are common in mummers' plays, one of which begins: 'Here comes I, Father Christmas, welcome or welcome not, / I hope Old Father Christmas will never be forgot' (E. K. Chambers, *The Medieval Stage*, 1903). (See also 'Christemas hath made an end', 154: 1)

Whether the present carol was meant to be acted is uncertain. Frank Ll. Harrison (in *Now Make We Merthe*, vol. 2, 1968) believed that it was, pointing out that carols of this kind would be appropriate at the Christmas celebrations of the cathedral singing-men in their common hall. 'Syre Cristesmasse's' two-part music could be sung by

himself and an attendant (perhaps one of several, bearing candles, etc.), beginning outside the closed doors, with the three-part music of the welcoming company taken by chorus. (Other 'dramatic' carols are 'Nowell: The borys hede', 37, also by Smert, and 'What tydynges bryngest thou, messangere?', 32.)

The form of the refrain is unclear in the manuscript, which gives bars 47–8 as an incipit, referring back to the opening, followed by bars 54–61. This could mean that the whole of bars 1–29 followed by 54–61 should be sung after each verse, but common sense suggests the form we give, with bars 1–29 forming an introduction. Bar 40: the manuscript has E–D for D–C in the lower part.

PERFORMANCE Two-part sections, solo voices ('Syre Cristesmasse' and companion); three-part sections and refrain, choir (company in hall). The carol could perhaps be a tone higher. For a guide to pronunciation see Appendix 1.

37

Nowell: The borys hede
(The Exeter Boar's Head Carol)

(*Christmas*)

Richard Smert (fl. 1428–77)

gode Y thyngke_____ to_____ telle.

gode_ Y thyngke_____ to_____ telle.

gode_____ Y thyngke_____ to telle.

VERSE [SOLI]

1. The bor - ys hede_____ that we_____ bryng_____
2. A bore ys a_____ so - ve - rayn_____
3. This bor - ys hede_____ we_____ bryng_____ with_____

1. The bor - ys hede_____ that_____ we bryng_____
2. A bore ys a_____ so - ve - rayn_____
3. This bor - ys hede_____ we bryng_____ with

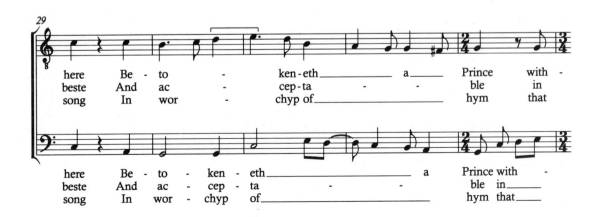

here Be - to - ken-eth_____ a_____ Prince with -
beste And ac - cep-ta - - ble in
song In wor - chyp of_____ hym that

here Be - to - ken - eth_____ a Prince with -
beste And ac - cep - ta - - ble in_____
song In wor - chyp of_____ hym that_____

¹ must ² most and least [of social degree]

From Ritson's manuscript (see notes, 24), which contains a number of Smert's carols (see notes, 36). It is headed 'in die nativitatis' ('on Christmas Day'). Frank Ll. Harrison has suggested (in *Now Make We Merthe*, 1968) that Smert's carol could have been written for his fellow singing-men of Exeter Cathedral feasting in their common hall, the two soloists accompanying the entrance of the boar's head. (See 'Nowell: Dieus wous garde, byewsser', 36, and 'What tydynges bryngest thou, messangere?', 32, for other carols that were possibly acted.) It is the grandest of the handful of surviving boar's head carols (see notes, 124), and unique in making the dish a symbol of Christ; the others are mostly content to be convivial—one (without music, alas) has a burden beginning 'Po, po, po, po!', a fifteenth-century pig-call.

Bars 45–7: top part a third higher in the manuscript.

PERFORMANCE Two-part sections, solo voices (bearers of boar's head); three-part sections and bars 45–7, choir (company in hall). The carol could perhaps be sung a tone higher. For a guide to pronunciation see Appendix 1.

38

Mervele noght, Josep

(*Immaculate Conception; Christmas*)

Fifteenth-century
(*Ritson's MS*)

¹ though

² grows big [with child]   ³ condescension

⁴ otherwise I should have secretly stolen away   ⁵ die

From Ritson's manuscript (see notes, 24), and marked 'in die nativitatis' ('on Christmas Day'). Such rhythmic and metrical complexity is typical of carols of the later fifteenth century.

Verses 1 and 3 are spoken by Joseph, verses 2 and 4 and the refrain by the announcing angel (see Matt. 1:18–25). The unbinding of Joseph's forefathers (verse 4) looks forward to their release from purgatory before Christ's Resurrection, the subject of medieval 'Harrowing of Hell' dramas.

PERFORMANCE   Two-part sections, solo voices; three-part sections, choir, or three voices. Both refrains are sung each time. For a guide to pronunciation see Appendix 1.

39

Thys endere nyghth I saw a syghth

(*Christmas; Epiphany*)

Sixteenth-century
(*British Library MS*)

Thys en-dere nyghth[1] I saw___ a syghth, A sterre as bryghth as___ day,

Thys en-dere nyghth[1] I saw a syghth, A sterre as bryghth___ as day, And e-

Thys en-dere nyghth[1] I saw a syghth, A___ sterre as bryghth as day,___ And

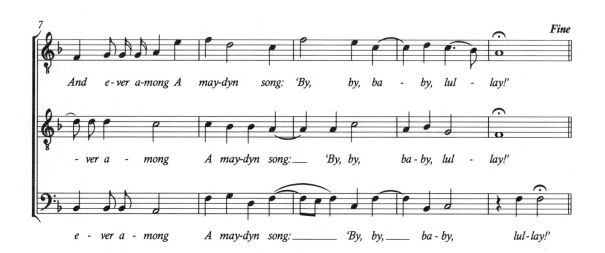

And e-ver a-mong A may-dyn song: 'By, by, ba-by, lul-lay!'

-ver a - mong A may-dyn song:___ 'By, by, ba-by, lul - lay!'

e - ver a - mong A may-dyn song:___ 'By, by,___ ba-by, lul-lay!'

[1] the other night [a few nights ago]

VERSES (TENOR)
VERSE 1

1. Thys Vyr - gyn clere² Wyth - ow - tyn pere Un - to hur Son gan say: 'My Son, my Lorde, My Fa - ther dere, Why ly - est thow in hay? Me thenke by ryght Thow kyng and knyght Shulde lye in ruche³ a - ray; Yet, ne - ver-the-lesse, I wyll nott cesse To syng: "By, by, lul - lay!" '

D.C.

VERSE 2

2. Thys Babe full bayne⁴ Aun - swer - yd a - gayne, And thus me thought he sayd: 'I am a Kyng A - bove__ all thyng, Yn hay yff⁵ I be layd; For ye shall see That kyng - es thre Shall cum on Twel - fe Day; For thys be - hest Geffe me [thy] brest, And sing: "By, Ba - by, lul - lay!" '

D.C.

² pure ³ rich ⁴ disobedient ⁵ though

VERSE 3

3. 'My Son, I say, Wyth - owt - tyn nay, Thow art my der - lyng der; I shall the kepe Whyle thow dost slepe And make the goode chere; And all thy whylle[6] I wyll__ ful - fill, Thow wotyst hyt well, yn fay,[7] Yet more then thys, I wyll the kys And syng: "By, Ba - by, lul - lay!" '

D.C.

VERSE 4

4. 'My mo - der swete, When I have slepe, Then take me up at last, Up - -pon your kne That ye sett me And hand - ell me full soft; And yn your arme Lap[8] me__ ryght warme, And kepe[9] me nyght and day, And, yff I wepe And can - nott slepe, Syng: "By, Ba - by, lul - lay!" '

D.C.

⁶ will   ⁷ thou knowest it well, in faith   ⁸ wrap   ⁹ preserve

VERSE 5

5. 'My Son, my Lorde, My Fa - ther dere, Syth all ys at thy wyll,[10] I
pray the, Son, Graunte me a bone,[11] Yff hyt be ryght and skylle:[12] That chylde or
man [That] may or can Be me - ry on thys day,[13] To blys them
bryng, And I shall syng: "By, by, Ba - by, lul - lay!"'

D.C.

VERSE 6

6. 'My mo - ther shene,[14] Of he - vyn quene, Your ask - yng[15] shall I
spede, So[16] that the myrth Dys-please me nott Yn [word - es] nor in
dede; Syng what ye wyll, So[16] that ye full - fyll My ten
com - maund - e - ment - es ay;[17] Yow for to
please Let them nott sesse To syng: "Ba - by, lul - lay!"'

D.C.

[10] since all is at thy command   [11] boon   [12] reasonable   [13] Epiphany   [14] bright   [15] request   [16] provided   [17] always

A touching dialogue between the infant Jesus and his mother, on whose lap he sits. It was a popular carol, and the text survives in four manuscripts, two from the fifteenth century and two from the sixteenth. There is a related dialogue-carol with a different burden ('Lullay, my child, and wepe no more', no. 151 in Greene, *The Early English Carols*, 1977) but a similar first verse: a doleful carol in which the child, bitterly cold, foretells his Passion and death and considers Adam's fall. Both are perhaps products of the friars, who did much to popularize carols in England, as elsewhere, sometimes adapting existing secular songs. The last two verses, in which the child is endowed with the full consciousness of his divine nature, are certainly the product of a clerical hand.

A British Library manuscript (Royal App. 58) from the first quarter of the sixteenth century is the only musical source for 'Thys endere nyghth', and we have therefore made it our primary textual source. (See John Stevens, *Music and Poetry in the Early Tudor Court*, 1961, pp. 129–32, for discussion of the manuscript, which is a single part-book from a set of four, and contains a mixture of French chansons published around 1530 together with some of the earlier lute and keyboard music in an English source. There are four fifteenth-century carols and a number of songs, all with music.) The three-voice refrain, marked 'corus', has a regular duple pulse and contrasts with the solo verses which, most unusually, are written out in full

and adapt the refrain melody to a basically triple rhythm. The verses are in fact a careful notation of what was probably the normal soloists' practice: the tune is subtly varied each time, not only for purely musical reasons (notably at the 'By, by' conclusion to each verse) but also to match the changing stress of the words. There are obvious implications for the performance of carols such as 'Nova! nova!' (25) and 'Nowell: Tydynges trew' (26).

The references to the 'bright star' and the three kings mean that the carol was almost certainly written for the Epiphany (6 January). It is partly an apologia for merrymaking: the last six lines of verse 5 can be paraphrased as 'Whoever is merry on this (Epiphany) day, bring them to heavenly bliss, and I (in heaven) will sing (to you): "By, by . . ." '. 'Them' in the final verse, line 9, refers to the merrymakers, including, of course, those who sing this carol. Mary refers to Christ as her Father (verses 1 and 5) because, as a co-equal member of the Trinity, he was creator of the universe (see also 'Dies est laeticiae', 18, verses 2 and 3).

For other carols with similar themes see 'Lullay, lullay: Als I lay on Yoolis Night' (23) and 'Lullay, lullow: I saw a swete semly syght' (24).

PERFORMANCE Three voices. In the manuscript the 'middle' singer of the refrain takes the verses.

40

Lully, lulla, thow littel tyne child
(The Coventry Carol)

(*Holy Innocents*)

Sixteenth-century
(*Sharp, 1825*)

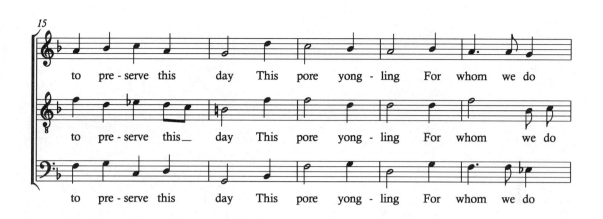

to pre - serve this day This pore yong - ling For whom we do

to pre - serve this_ day This pore yong - ling For whom we do

to pre - serve this day This pore yong - ling For whom we do

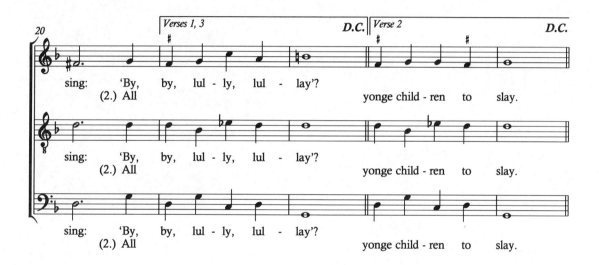

Verses 1, 3 D.C. ‖ *Verse 2* D.C.

sing: 'By, by, lul - ly, lul - lay'? yonge child - ren to slay.
(2.) All

sing: 'By, by, lul - ly, lul - lay'? yonge child - ren to slay.
(2.) All

sing: 'By, by, lul - ly, lul - lay'? yonge child - ren to slay.
(2.) All

2 Herod the King
   In his raging
      Chargid he hath this day
   His men of might
   In his owne sight
      All yonge children to slay.

3 That wo is me,
   Pore child, for thee,
      And ever morne and say[2]
   For thi parting
   Nether say nor singe:
      'By, by, lully, lullay.'

Sixteenth-century
(Sharp, 1825)

[2] grieve and sigh

The Pageant of the Shearman and Tailors is part of the cycle of mystery plays which was performed in Coventry each year on the feast of Corpus Christi. Only two plays survive from what was the most admired of all the English cycles (not to be confused with the *Ludus Coventriae* cycle, which is from an unknown location), to which royal visits were several times made in the fifteenth century.

The Coventry cycle is one in which the plays were undoubtedly performed in the streets on pageant carts: there is a splendid stage direction—'Here Erode ragis [Herod rages] in the pagond [pageant] and in the strete also'.

The first mention of the plays is in 1392, but the earliest known manuscript, copied over a period of about twenty years, was signed 'nevly corrected be [by] Robart Croo' on 14 March 1534. The songs (see also 'As I out rode', 41) were added to the end of Croo's manuscript by Thomas Mawdycke in 1591: this and the shepherds' carol are the only vernacular songs from English mystery plays to have survived with text and music intact—or, rather, semi-intact, as the manuscript was unfortunately destroyed when the Birmingham Free Reference Library was burnt out in 1879. The music can be recovered only from a horrendously inaccurate piece of engraving in Thomas Sharp's *Dissertations on the Pageants or Dramatic Mysteries, anciently performed in Coventry* . . . (1825). Sharp had published a previous edition of the play in 1817, and all modern editions derive from these two books. (See Hardin Craig, *Two Coventry Corpus Christi Plays*, second edn., 1957, for a comprehensive edition, and Peter Happé, *English Mystery Plays: A selection*, 1975, for a good popular edition.)

The Pageant of the Shearmen and Tailors falls into two halves, introduced by Isaiah and separated by a dialogue between two prophets. The first part covers the annunciation to Mary, the Nativity, and the annunciation to the shepherds, the second the adoration of the three kings, the flight into Egypt, and the massacre of the innocents. Sharp's 1825 publication prints the heading to Mawdycke's songs: 'Theise Songes belong to the Taylors and Shearmens Pagant. The first and the laste the shepheards sing and the second or middlemost the women singe.' The order is odd, because the 'first' and 'laste' songs belong to the shepherds' scene at the end of the first half, where they are separated by dialogue, whilst the 'second or middlemost'—the present song (which has had the title 'The Coventry Carol' wished on it by modern editors)—comes very near the end of the play: 'Here the Wemen cum in wythe there chyldur, syngyng [to] them; and Mare and Josoff goth away clene. [The song follows.] First Woman: I lolle [lull] my chylde wondursly swete, And in my narmis [arms] I do hyt kepe, Be-cawse thatt yt schuld not crye.' Their singing is to put the children to sleep lest Herod's soldiers locate them by their crying. When the soldiers do burst in, the third woman in particular puts up a stout resistance, menacing the soldiers with the 'womanly geyre [gear]' of her 'pott-ladull'. But to no avail: (First soldier) 'Who hard [heard] eyver soche a cry of women thatt there chyldur have lost?'

The song thus comes at a highly dramatic moment in the play, and its plaintive music is the more effective for the careful mingling of humour and brutality in which it is set. It is also the emotional climax of the long play, which ends with a brief scene in which the soldiers report back to Herod.

The singers would probably have been a boy and two men: audiences were used to male performers representing women. Unlike the companion shepherds' song, this one was probably newly written for the play, though it is thought that the words and music of the refrain were taken from elsewhere. Its reconstruction is not easy, and involves juggling with the contradictory versions of the three verses and refrains given by Sharp. We are in agreement with most good modern editions except that we take seriously what Sharp prints in the soprano at the end of verse 2. For a quite different solution to the notational problems see J. Caldwell, *The Oxford History of English Music*, I, p. 265.

For another setting of the text see 'Lullay, thou tiny little child' (171).

PERFORMANCE Three voices.

41

As I out rode this enderes night
(The Coventry Shepherds' Carol)

(*Christmas*)

Sixteenth-century
(Sharp, 1825)

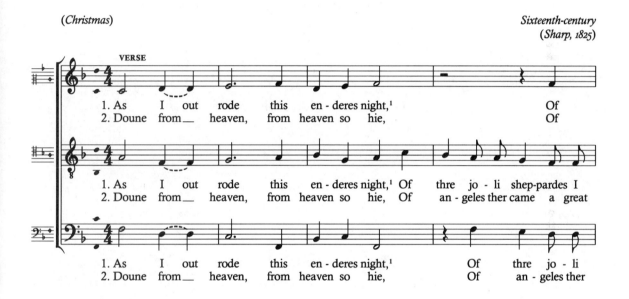

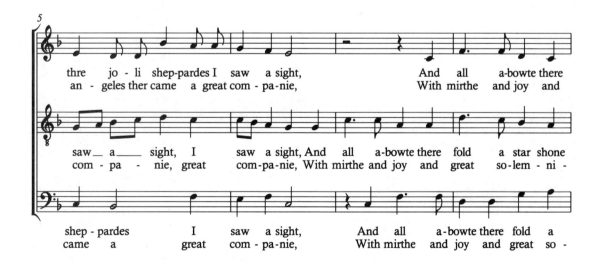

¹ the other night [a few nights ago]

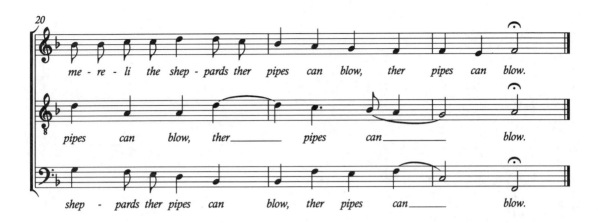

One of two songs (see also 'Lully, lulla, thow littel tyne child', 40) that were added to the text of the Coventry Pageant of the Shearmen and Tailors in 1591. There is a reference in the 1534 text to a song 'Ase I outen rodde', which may have been an earlier setting of the present text, and this suggests that the new setting (despite its mid-century idiom) was specially composed for the play. R. L. Greene (in *The Early English Carols*, 1977) points to a whole genre of shepherd carols of this and other types, many of them with the onomatopoeic 'terli, terlow': pipes or 'horns' (perhaps rustic shawms) were particularly associated with shepherds. The shepherds' scene ends the first half of the play, as the massacre of the innocents ends the second, so that the inclusion of the only composed music in these scenes seems to have been a conscious dramatic decision.

The two verses are headed 'Song I' and 'Song II' in Thomas Sharp's *Dissertations on the Pageants or Dramatic Mysteries, anciently performed in Coventry . . .* (1825 edn.), and, as in Croo's 1591 manuscript of the play (now destroyed), they are for some reason separated by the women's lullaby (see notes, 40).

The two Coventry plays that have survived (the Shearmen and Tailors', and the Weavers') are remarkable for the complexity of some of the scenes, which could have involved more than one pageant cart and, at least in the present case, certainly involved the street, in which Herod famously raged. The birth of Christ occurs during the shepherds' scene, and the two themes interact with some dramatic ingenuity. Immediately previously, Mary has told Joseph that the birth is imminent, and sends him to the town to fetch midwives. The shepherds are then seen (Mary presumably being hidden by a curtain or other device), three brothers who meet up and shelter from the cold weather. As they eat and drink a star appears in the sky, and the third shepherd (all three are gifted in biblical exegesis) immediately realizes its import:

A ha! Now ys cum the tyme that old fathurs
    [prophets] hath told,
Thatt in the wynturs nyght soo cold
A chyld of meydyn borne be he wold
In whom all profeciys schalbe fullfyld.

The angels are heard singing 'Glorea in exselsis Deo' 'above in the clowdis'. This confirms the fulfilment of prophecy, and the first shepherd suggests:

> . . . now goo we hence
> To worschippe thatt chyld of hy manyffecence,
> And that we ma syng in his prescence
> 'Et in tarra pax omynibus.'

There the Scheppardis syngis 'Ase I owt rodde', and Josoff seyth

> 'Now, Lorde, this noise that I do here [the shepherds'
>   song],
> With this grett solemnete,
> Gretly amendid hath my chere . . .'

The angels are again heard singing their 'Glorea' and Mary shows Joseph her new-born child. The angels are now seen as they sing to the shepherds, who approach and worship Christ. As they leave, Mary thanks them:

> Now, herdmen kynd,
> For your comyng
> To my chyld schall I prae,
> Asse he ys heyvin Kyng,
> To grant you his blessyng,
> And to hys blys that ye may wynd [wend, go]
> At your last day.

There the Scheppardis syngith ageyne [verse 2] and goth forthe of the place . . .

This is the end of the first half, and the two prophets enter for their linking dialogue.

The shepherds' singing is thus cleverly integrated into the play and has a genuine dramatic function; and, despite the third-person text, it reflects the action that has just occurred—the appearance of the star in verse 1 and of the angels in verse 2.

PERFORMANCE   Three voices. The youngest of the shepherds was presumably played by a boy. The carol could perhaps be sung a tone higher.

42

We happy hirdes men

(*Christmas*)

Sixteenth-century
(Shanne MS)

2 Gladd tidinges they us toulde:
The Kynge of all mankynde
Newe borne and in clothes fould,[2]
They saie we shall him fynde

¹ also   ² swaddled

3 At Bethlem in a staull,
   And eke his mother free.[3]
Great comforth to us all;
   O blissèd maie he be!

4 Nowe let us with much joie
   In haist to Bethlem trudge,
To se that blissèd Boie
   That once[4] must be our Judge.

5 When we to Bethlem came,
   We sawe as it was saide:
That Child of glorious fame
   In maunger he was laide.

6 We sheperdes downe did fall,
   And songe with voice on hie;
The angells said, 'We shall
   Singe *Glorie in excelsie*.'

7 All haile, O Christ, O Kynge!
   All haile, O Virgin's Sonne!
We praie the us to bringe
   In heaven, with the to woon,[5]

8 Wheere we the Father may
   See, with the Holye Goest,
Him magnifie all waie,
   With all the heavenlie hoste.

Sixteenth-century
(Shanne MS)

[3] noble [4] one day [5] dwell

A charming if rather crudely composed song of the mid-sixteenth century, which was perhaps written for a shepherd scene in a play. It exists complete in a commonplace-book of the Roman Catholic Shanne family of Methley, near Leeds (British Library Add. MS 38599). The triplex and bassus parts are also in altus and bassus part-books, dated 1637, in Carlisle Cathedral. A folk-song version, apparently deriving from the three-part song, survives in the Clague collection of Manx folk-songs (printed in the *Journal of the Folk-Song Society*, vol. 8, p. 281, transcribed by Annie Gilchrist).

The Shanne manuscript, although earlier than the Carlisle books, seems to have been taken from an inferior source. The only oddity in Carlisle is the prolongation of the bass for three beats in bars 3 and 7; it has a more satisfactory version of the point on 'For angells bright and cleare', which can be sung by all three parts, whereas the Shanne manuscript has E–C for the Carlisle E–E in the bass, bar 6, and the same figure in the tenor, but has E–E in the triplex bar 7; and it has C–A, in octaves with the bass, for the Carlisle E–C in the triplex bar 11. In view of these superior readings we have also preferred the Carlisle ♩ Es in the triplex, bar 2. The text in the Carlisle books is very close to that of the Shanne manuscript, but omits verse 5 and has a different close: 'And glorify alway / Him that of might is most.'

The Shanne book includes direful prophecies, accounts of various marvellous events, and the cast list of 'A verie fyne Historie or Stage Plaie called "Cannimore and Lionley"', which was given four performances in a barn in Whit week, 1614, with five members of the Shanne family taking part. 'We happy hirdes men' is in a group of fourteen songs at the end of the book, headed 'Certaine pretie songes hereafter followinge, Drawn together by Richard Shanne, 1611', though their first editor, Hyder E. Rollins, believed they were copied in about 1624. The identity of Richard Shanne is not known.

The Carlisle books formed part of a collection of Elizabethan music copied *c*.1635 by Thomas Smith (1615–1702), later Bishop of Carlisle; the insides of the front covers are signed and dated 'Thomas Smith, Jan. 8: Ann: 1637', and must have been copied during his time at Queen's College, Oxford, which he entered as an undergraduate in 1631 and where he was by 1637 a fellow and tutor. He was appointed a canon of Carlisle Cathedral in 1660, dean in 1671, and was consecrated bishop in 1684, remaining there until his death. He presented an organ to the cathedral and left his books to its library (see John P. Cutts, *Bishop Smith's Part-Song Books*, 1972).

PERFORMANCE Three voices. The mezzo-soprano clef of the highest voice suggests that it was taken by a boy.

Final *es* and *ess* were no longer sounded when the song was written.

Editorial repeat marks above the last line of verses 2–7 indicate suggested text repeats for the bass.

43

Come, love we God!

(Epiphany; Christmas)

Sixteenth-century
(Shanne MS, arr. editors)

1. Come, love we God! of might is most[1] The Fa-ther, the Sonne, the Ho - lie Goost,
2. The Fa-ther sent downe his one-lie Soune, Which of a maide was man be cum

Reg - nan-te jam__ in e - the-ra;[2] The which mayd man, both more and lesse,[3]
Cum__ pu - ra con - ti - nen-ti - a.[6] In Beth - lem, Jui-de,[7] two beast be-tweene,

And cre - at him to his lick-nesse;[4] *O quan - ta, O quan-ta sunt_ hec o - pe-ra!*[5]
This Child was borne, [that] I of meane;[8] *O no - va, O no-va stel - la lu - mi-na!*[9]

[1] the most mighty (Father, etc.)   [2] now reigning in heaven   [3] of higher and lower degree   [4] likeness   [5] O how many
are these works!   [6] with pure countenance   [7] Judah   [8] of whom I speak   [9] O light of a new star!

3   The hirdemen came with theyr offring,
    Ffor to present that pretie thinge[10]
        Cum summa reverentia.[11]
    They offred theyr giftes that Child untill;[12]
    They weere received with full good will;
        Quam grata sunt hec munera![13]

4   These kynges came from the east cuntrie,
    Which knewe then, by Astronomie
        Et Balam vaticenia,[14]
    That then was born the Kynge of Blisse;
    His mother a maid both was and is:
        O Dei mirabilia.[15]

5   To seeke that Babe they tooke the waie;
    They had good speede in theyr jurney,
        Stella micanta per via.[16]
    When they came wheere as Herod leay,
    The starr was hid that ledd the way
        Ob tetra regis crimina.[17]

6   Hee questioned them of theyr cunninge;[18]
    'What novells,'[19] he said, 'or what tydinge
        Vos fertis [ex Arabia]?'[20]
    They said was borne both God and man:
    'We will him worshipp as Soveraigne,
        Cum digna Deo latria.'[21]

7   'Come heare again!' Herod did saie;
    'Howe that ye speede[22] in youre jurney
        Mihi fiat notitia:[23]
    I will him worshipp'—he though[t] not so;
    He ment with fraud them for to sloo:[24]
        O ficta amicitia![25]

8   They past the towne; they saw the starre,
    Which ledd them till they found the barne,[26]
        Sugentem matris ubera;[27]
    They offred him gould, mirr, and sence;
    He tooke them with great diligence,[28]
        Quam digna est infancia.[29]

9   They tooke theyr leeve of that sweet thinge,[30]
    And thought to come by[31] Herod Kynge,
        Apparente voce angelica:[32]
    'Turne home,' he saith, 'leave Herodes will:
    He thinkes with fraud youe for to kyll,
        Per cauta homicidia.'[33]

10 They turnd againe full merilie,
    Ich[34] one into his owne cuntrie,
        Alacri terra tenera[35]
    They had heavens blisse at theyr endinge,[36]
    The which God graunt us, ould and younge,
        In clara poliregia.[37]

(*Shanne MS, 1611*)

[10] [to the Child]   [11] with great reverence   [12] unto
[13] how pleasing are these gifts!   [14] and the prophecy of
Balaam [Numbers 24: 17–18]   [15] O wonders of God!
[16] the star lighting their way   [17] because of the loathsome
crimes of the king   [18] knowledge   [19] news   [20] do you
bring [from Arabia]   [21] with worship worthy of God
[22] how did you fare   [23] tell me   [24] slay   [25] O feigned
friendship!   [26] bairn [child]   [27] suckling at his mother's
breast   [28] delight   [29] as befits a child   [30] [the Child]
[31] come to   [32] the angelic voice appearing   [33] by secret
murder   [34] each   [35] eager for his dear land   [36] death
[37] in the noble city of the King

From the same source as 'We happy hirdes men' (42), and
headed 'A Christmas carroll by Sir Richard Shanne priest'.
This is not the Richard Shanne who compiled the
manuscript, but (judging from the style of the music) a
member of the family living in the first part of the sixteenth
century. Only the tenor is given, perhaps under the mis-
apprehension that it is the melody. The Latin tags are not
drawn from the liturgy. For a link with a fifteenth-century
carol see R. L. Greene, *Early English Carols*, 1977, no. 23C
and notes.

PERFORMANCE   (*i*) Solo, at any convenient pitch; (*ii*) three
voices; (*iii*) choir.

44

Swete was the song the Virgine soong

I

(*Christmas*)

Sixteenth-century
(arr. Thomas Hamond, d. 1662)

¹ also   ² deftly

II

Sixteenth-century
(*Egerton MS*)

(*Christmas*)

Sweet was the song the Vir-gin sung When she to Beth-lem Ju - da came And

was de - li - ver'd of her Sonne, That bless - ed Jhe - sus hath to Name.

'Lul-la, lul - la, lul - la-by, Lul - la, lul - la, lul - la - by, Swet

Babe!' quoth she; 'My Sonne and eke[1] a Sa-viour borne, Which hath vouch - sa - fed from an

[1] also

high To vi-sitt us that wer for-lorne. La lul-la, la lul-la, la___ lul - la -

- by, Sweet Babe!' sung she, And rockt him feat - lie²___ one hir knee.

² deftly

This song has become well known through Geoffrey Shaw's arrangement in *The Oxford Book of Carols* (1928), which is good enough to have convinced many people that it was a genuine sixteenth-century setting.

It is not certain which, if any, of the four surviving sources represents the original form of the song, but the consort-song version for soprano and four viols (British Library Add. MS 17786–91, edited in *Musica Britannica*, vol. XXII, rev., no. 64), copied in Oxford *c.*1610–20, probably derives from an Elizabethan source and may represent the composer's original conception or, at least, incorporate his tune and bass. Setting I, not hitherto published, is Hamond's arrangement for four voices of the consort song. It retains the melody and bass, with minor modifications, the inner parts being newly and skilfully composed. Bars 29–30 are a creative misunderstanding: in the consort song the second-lowest viol plays the true bass here, but Hamond, copying from parts, was unaware of this and found himself forced into an unusual and bitter-sweet cadence.

Thomas Hamond was a gentleman and amateur musician living at Hawkedon, near Bury St. Edmunds, Suffolk. In that area there were two other country houses in which music was an important part of daily life: Rushbrooke Hall, where George Kirbye was resident composer, and Hengrave Hall, John Wilbye's country base: Hamond certainly was in touch with Kirbye, and probably with Wilbye as well. Hamond's manuscripts are described in Craig Monson's *Voices and Viols in England, 1600–1650*,

1982. He opened and closed one of them (Bodleian Library, Oxford, MS F 7–10; mostly four-part songs copied from the publications of Dowland, Weelkes, and Pilkington) with pieces he described as his own, though that was an exaggeration in the case of 'Swete was the song', the closing item.

Setting II is from the British Library manuscript Egerton 2971, a small book containing songs, mostly richly ornamented, for voice and bass viol, and music for lyra viol. Thurston Dart dated the book between 1610 and 1620 (*Galpin Society Journal*, XIV, 1961, pp. 30–3). Another version, for voice, with the bass line in (lyra) viol tablature, possible implying a chordal accompaniment, is in William Ballet's Lute Book (library of Trinity College, Dublin, MS D.1.21/II), which was probably copied in the 1590s. (This version of the tune is the one used by Geoffrey Shaw.) A setting for four voices and lute of practically the same text is the last piece in John Attey's *First Booke of Ayres* (1622, the last publication of its kind) which Peter Warlock called 'a flawless work of serene beauty which forms a fitting conclusion to this golden period of English song' (*The English Ayre*, 1926).

PERFORMANCE I, four voices, perhaps with lute and/or viols.

II, voice and viol. A bass viol could either play the bass line alone (a common way of performing ayres) or supply chords 'lira-way'; a lute or harpsichord might supply chords (with or without the viol). The bass figuring is editorial. The embellishments are possibly just for the repeat.

45

Thus angels sung
(The Angels' Song)

(*Christmas*)

Orlando Gibbons (*1583–1625*)
(*arr. editors*)

1. Thus an-gels sung, and thus sing we: 'To God on high all__ glo-rie__

bee! Let him on__ earth his peace be - stow And un-to men his fa-vours show.'

2 If angels sung at Jesus' birth
   Then we have greater cause for mirth,[1]
   For it was all for our poor sake
   He did our human nature take.

3 Dear Christ, thou didst thyself abase
   Thus to descend to human race
   And leave thy Father's throne above:
   Lord, what could move thee to such love?

[1] joy

4   Man, that was made out of the dust,
    He found a paradise at first:
    But see! the God of heaven and earth,
    Laid in a manger at his birth.

5   Surely the manger where he lies
    Doth figure forth his sacrifice;
    And, by his birth, may all men see
    A pattern of humility.

6   Stupendous Babe, my God and King!
    Thy praises will I ever sing,
    In joyful accents raise my voice,
    And in the praise of God rejoice.

7   My soul, learn by thy Saviour's birth
    For to abase thyself on earth,
    That I may bee exalted high
    To live with him eternally.

v. 1 George Wither (1588–1667)
vv. 2–7 anon. (Sandys, 1833, adapted)

One verse only is set to song 34 in *The Hymnes and Songes of the Church* (1623), the volume on which Wither (see notes, 114) and Gibbons collaborated. The book was a successor to Wither's 1621 *Songs of the Old Testament . . .*, and it was followed by *The Psalmes of David Translated into Lyrick-Verse* (1632), the three together forming an unsuccessful attempt to provide an alternative to the banality of Sternhold and Hopkins, whose widely used metrical 'Old Version' of the psalms and canticles had done much to alienate the lettered classes from the Church (see Appendix 3). Wither's verse in the 1623 volume is, as always, uneven, but the best is on a high level and continues to be unjustly neglected, while Gibbons's contribution is one of the treasures of English hymnody: after neglect (only two songs were included in the first edition of *Hymns Ancient and Modern*, 1861), it has regained something like its proper place (eleven in *The English Hymnal*, 1908).

'The Song of Angels' (now generally called 'The Angel's Song') is a paraphrase of Luke 2:14. It is headed:

This is the third Evangelicall *Song* mentioned in the *New Testament*; and it was sung by a Quire of *Angells* (at the birth of our blessed Saviour *Jesus Christ*) whose rejoycing shall bee made compleat by the redemption of mankinde. In this *Song* they first glorifie God, and then proclaime that happie Peace and reconciliation, which his Sonnes Nativitie should bring unto the World, rejoycing therin; and in that unspeakable *good will*, and deare *Communion* which was thereby established between the *God head*, the *Manhood*, and *Them*. We therefore ought to joyne with them in this *Song*, and sing it often to praise God, and quicken faith and charitie in our selves.

Gibbons's tune has links with two others in the 1623 publication, nos. 9 and 44, but internal evidence suggests that the present tune was the original from which they were

derived. The song is one of the few from the collection that has continued to be sung from the time of its publication to the present day, though changes were made to both text and tune in the eighteenth century. Wither's single verse was extended, usually by two others of a non-Christmas character, thus respecting his recommendation that we should 'sing it often'. We have turned it into a Christmas hymn by adding six stanzas from the twelve-verse text of 'Hark! hark what news the angels bring' (see notes, 75) given by William Sandys in his *Christmas Carols, Ancient and Modern* (1833), which is clearly a corrupt version of an untraced original.

The opening of the tune was too subtle for Georgian taste, and the first phrase was replaced by a new one in straightforward triple time:

The rest of the tune was notated in triple time, with much consequent mis-stressing. The earliest occurrences are in three related books: Michael Broome's *Collection of Church Musick I, c.*1725 (see R. A. Crawford, *The Core Repertory . . .*, 1984, p. xxiii), Francis Timbrell's *Divine Musick Scholar's Guide* (*c.*1720–35), and Matthew Wilkins's *Book of Psalmody* (*c.*1730); it persists in some present-day Dissenting hymnals. John Arnold, in his influential *The Compleat Psalmodist* (1750 edn.) gives a different triple-time first line and has a seven-bar fugue on the fourth.

Like all the Gibbons tunes, this one consists only of melody and bass (to which we have added inner parts), leaving performing options open.

PERFORMANCE   (*i*) Unison voices and organ, with optional four-part choir; (*ii*) solo voice and continuo.

46

While shepherds watched their flocks by night

(*Christmas*)

1 While shepherds watched their flocks
   by night,
   All seated on the ground,
   The angel of the Lord came down,
   And glory shone around.

2 'Fear not,' said he (for mighty dread
   Had seized their troubled mind),
   'Glad tidings of great joy I bring
   To you and all mankind.

3 'To you in David's town this day
   Is born of David's line
   The Saviour, who is Christ the Lord;
   And this shall be the sign:

4 'The heavenly Babe you there shall find
   To human view displayed,
   All meanly wrapped in swathing bands,
   And in a manger laid.'

5 Thus spake the seraph; and forthwith
   Appeared a shining throng
   Of angels, praising God, who thus
   Addressed their joyful song:

6 'All glory be to God on high,
   And to the earth be peace;
   Good will henceforth from heaven to men
   Begin and never cease.'

Nahum Tate? (1652–1715)

I

after Christopher Tye (c.1500–73)
(arr. Richard Alison, fl. 1592–1606)

134

II

after George Frideric Handel (1685–1759)

1. While shep-herds watched their flocks by night, All seat-ed on the ground, The an-gel of the Lord came down, And glo-ry shone a-round, and glo-ry shone a-round.

III

(*Christmas*)

Traditional (*arr. editors*)

1. While shep-herds watched their flocks by night, All___ seat - ed on___ the ground,
   The an - gel of the Lord came down, And___ glo - ry shone a - round.

2. 'Fear not,' said he___ (for might - y dread Had seized their troub - led mind),

'Glad ti - dings of great___ joy___ I bring To___ you and___ all___ man - kind.
'Glad ti - dings___ of great_____

IV

(Christmas)

(Joseph Watts, 1749)

1. While shep - herds watched their flocks__ by night, All seat - ed__

The an - gel of the

on__ the ground, The an - gel of the Lord came down, the

The an-gel of the Lord came down, the an - gel

Lord____ came down,

an - gel of the Lord came down, And glo - ry shone a - round. - round.

of the Lord came down,

V

(Christmas)

Thomas Clark (1775–1859)

1. While shep-herds watched their flocks by night, All seat-ed___ on___ the___ ground, The an-gel of the Lord came down,___ The an-gel of the Lord came down,___ the an-gel of the Lord came down, of the Lord came down, And glo-ry shone a- -round, and glo-ry shone a-round, and glo-ry shone a-round.

The an-gel of the Lord came down,___ of the Lord came down, and glo-ry shone a-round, and glo-ry shone a-round, and glo-ry shone a-round.

VI

(*Christmas*)

c.1830
(*Dunstan, 1928*)

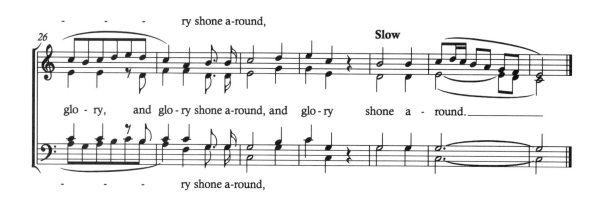

Slow

ry shone a-round,

glo - ry, and glo - ry shone a-round, and glo - ry shone a - round.____

- - - ry shone a-round,

VII

(Christmas)

John Foster (1762–1822)

1. While shep-herds watched their_ flocks by__ night, All seat - ed__ on the

And_ glo - ry shone a -

ground, The an - gel of__ the__ Lord came down, And

And_ glo - ry shone a -

This 'Song of the angels at the Nativity of our Blessed Saviour' is a very accomplished paraphrase of Luke 2: 8–14, and has been one of the central Christmas hymns for English-speaking Protestants since its first appearance in 1700. The text was first published as one of the sixteen hymns (all liturgical or scriptural paraphrases) that open the 1700 Supplement by the Irishmen Nahum Tate and Nicholas Brady to their 1696 *New Version of the Psalms of David*; in the course of the following century these metrical translations gradually supplanted the much lampooned 'Old Version' of Sternhold and Hopkins. Though Tate's authorship of 'While shepherds watched' seems to have been universally assumed from the time of the hymn's earliest appearances outside the *New Version* (where the hymn is unattributed), we can find no solid evidence to support this.

We have modernized the original 'humane' in verse 4 and have also substituted the now near-universal 'who' for 'and' in verse 5 line 3, but have ignored the rest of the multitude of other small changes that have passed in and out of fashion. 'Swathing bands' (verse 4) is sometimes replaced by the more common 'swaddling bands' or 'swaddling clothes'. 'Meanly' (in the same line) reflects the non-Biblical tradition that Joseph could afford only a tiny cloth (see carol 17, verse 2).

Congregational hymns were virtually unknown before the eighteenth century. The Supplement provided one for Christmas, two for Easter, three for the communion, and (added shortly after 1708) Thomas Ken's hymns for morning and evening. These 'authorized' hymns provided seasonal and occasional substitutes for the metrical psalms which were commonly sung alongside (rarely within) the prayer-book services. They might be sung before and after matins and evensong (the usual country custom); or after the Litany which came between matins and the ante- or full communion service; or (particularly in urban churches) before and after the sermon. The psalm tunes which a particular congregation knew—often pitifully few in number—would normally also be used for the hymns, and this practice continued as the tune repertory expanded later in the century.

'While shepherds watched' is in common measure (or metre), with lines of 8.6.8.6 syllables, and this meant that by far the widest number of tunes could be drawn upon. Indeed, no other hymn has been sung to so many tunes and settings. Out of what are probably hundreds we select seven: some because they are in common use, others for their intrinsic merit and rich associations. It would be good if the near-hegemony now enjoyed by the excellent tune I ('Winchester' or 'Winchester New') could give way to a little of the earlier diversity.

The hymn's common measure was only one reason for its vast number of tunes. Another was its status in the Church of England as the only legally authorized Christmas hymn (see Nicholas Temperley, *The Music of the English Parish Church*, 1979, vol. 1, pp. 121, 123, 208). The 1700 Supplement, like the *New Version* itself, gained a kind of honorary liturgical status from being 'allowed by the monarch in council' and 'permitted to be used in churches', and it was in consequence routinely bound up with copies of *The Book of Common Prayer*. 'While shepherds watched' was thus disseminated across the country, and it was not

until the 1782 'University Press' edition of the *New Version* that it was joined by Wesley's (altered) 'Hark! the herald angels sing' (92) and Philip Doddridge's 'High let us swell our tuneful notes', by which time other Christmas texts were already in circulation among both Dissenters and Anglicans.

The Winchester psalm tune (I) predates the hymn by more than a century, and could have been associated with it from as early as 1708, when the melody (with no dotted rhythm in bar 3) and a bass were printed in the sixth edition of the Supplement as one of the 75 tunes for use with the 12 hymns and the 26 alternative psalm translations 'in particular measures'. 'While shepherds watched' is there set to 'St James' (see *The English Hymnal*, rev. ed., 1933, no. 341), but with the rubric 'or any other tune of 8 and 6 syllables [i.e., in common measure]'. ('Winchester' is given with Psalm 84, 'O God of hosts, the mighty Lord'.)

The tune had first appeared in a four-voice, tenor-tune setting by George Kirbye (d. 1634), which Thomas East printed with Psalm 81 in his *Whole Booke of Psalms, with their wonted Tunes, as they are sung in churches, composed into foure parts . . . Compiled* [arranged] *by sondry authors* (London, 1592). This particular 'wonted tune' lies at the centre of a spider's web of interlinked psalm tunes which has been mapped out by Nicholas Temperley (see his article 'Kindred and affinity in hymn tunes', *Musical Times*, September 1972, pp. 905–7). This is the most extensive of known tune families in the English 'composed' tradition (though overshadowed by the numerous great clans of folk tunes), and by tracing links between the thirteen members, Temperley demonstrates various quasi-Darwinian processes by which new psalm tunes evolved. Where congregations sang without accompaniment and (theoretically) in unison, mutations were the routine result of communal 'descants' to the tunes, and Temperley strongly suspects that the four-line 'Winchester' tune evolved in this manner from a descant to an eight-line tune by Christopher Tye (to the eighth of his fourteen verse paraphrases of the opening chapters of *The Actes of The Apostles*, 1553, modern edition in *Early English Church Music*, vol. 19, 1977). He also shows that many musical phrases are common currency within the 'extremely restricted form' of the early psalm tune, and characterizes 'Winchester' thus: '[It] has conventional cadence tags for its second and fourth lines. Its third line is little more than a scale . . . preceded by a rising fourth which turns it into a tag that was commonly used in contrapuntal imitation [and was so treated by Tye]. Only the first line has some individuality.' This first line is the one part of the tune that seems to have been freshly composed (or is perhaps a new mutation), and gives the whole much of its character.

Kirbye's 1592 setting has the melody in the tenor and cannot be adapted without destroying its character, so we have chosen instead an arrangement by Richard Alison (another of the 1592 'sondry authors') in his *Psalmes of David in Meter, the plaine song* [melody] *beeing the common tunne to be sung and plaide upon the lute, orpharyon, citterne or bass violl, severally or altogether, the singing part to be either for tenor or treble to the instruments, according to the voyce, or for foure voyces* (1599). Little is known about Alison, but he describes himself in this volume as 'Gent. Practitioner in the Art of

Musicke' and as 'living in the Duke's place neere Aldegate'. The dedication is to Anne, Countess of Warwick, and refers to 'your H[ighness's] husband, sometimes my good Lord and Master', which suggests that Alison may have been a page or gentleman retainer in the Warwick household.

Although it is not spelled out, Alison's Elizabethan customers would realize that the 'altogether' option could effectively be expanded to a standard mixed consort with either solo voice or four voices. The consort consisted of violin or treble viol playing the treble line; flute (or perhaps recorder) playing either the alto or tenor line; bandora, which would here play from the bass; lute; cittern; and bass viol. (The scoring for four voices and such a consort is specified in William Leighton's *Teares or Lamentacions of a Sorrowfull Soule*, 1614, for Leighton's own simple settings which begin the book.)

The vigorous tune II is widely sung in the US. It is adapted from the soprano aria 'Non vi piaque ingiusti dei' in Handel's *Siroe, Rè di Persia* (1728). We have been unable to discover who made the arrangement, but suspect Lowell Mason (1792–1872).

Tune III is a major-mode version of the 'Chestnut' tune of 'God rest you merry, gentlemen' (151:1), and is said to have been the most common of all the tunes sung to 'While shepherds watched' before the present century.

Tune IV is the wonder-working melody that features in a number of narratives by Thomas Hardy. It soothes a savage beast (in the story of William Dewy's encounter with the enraged but pious bull in *Tess of the D'Urbervilles*), annihilates the devil and his minions (in the poem 'The Paphian Ball'), and, most miraculously of all, causes young Dorsetmen to give up their Christmas Eve drinking (in 'The Dead Quire'). What is so special about the tune? Nicholas Temperley (in his article 'The origins of the fuging tune', *RMA Research Chronicle*, 1981, pp. 1–32) is fairly cool: '. . . one of the most successful tunes of this germinal period . . . largely free from gross harmonic blunders, which may account for its great popularity . . . either by skill or luck or a combination of the two, the section of imitative counterpoint does not produce any great departure from the general harmonic idiom . . . no great violence is done to the verbal rhythm . . .'; all true, but Hardy clearly saw something more:

> *While shepherds watched their flocks by night,*—
> Thus swells the old familiar sound
> In many a quaint symphonic flight . . .
> Something supernal has the sound
> As verse by verse the strain proceeds . . .
> ('The Dead Quire')

It is an odd fact, if we remember William Dewy's bull-quelling violin performance in *Tess*, that one of the carol-books in the Dorset County Museum (TH2, 1841; see notes, 87), written by Hardy's father, one of the models for William Dewy, contains the top two parts seemingly arranged for a single violin, though this may tell us more about violin-and-bass performance than about cattle management.

The setting was first published by Joseph Watts in *A Choice Collection of Church Musick* (1749). We have incor-

porated one correction from the version printed in William East's *Second Book of the Voice of Melody* (1750) and another from James Evison's *Compleat Book of Psalmody* (second edn., 1751), both avoiding consecutive fifths.

Tune V, now universally known as 'Cranbrook', is one of the earliest and certainly the best known of the enormous number composed by the remarkable cordwainer (shoemaker) and musician Thomas Clark, who became the leading Dissenting composer of the late Georgian period. The setting we give is the earliest we have found—perhaps Clark's original—from an undated manuscript reproduced in Wallace Harvey's *Thomas Clark of Canterbury* (1981). We prefer this to the blander revisions that the composer made for successive publications. Clark included the tune in a form close to the manuscript in his first publication, *A Set of Psalm and Hymn Tunes* (London, 1805).

Clark's preferred text was Philip Doddridge's 'Grace! 'tis a charming sound', but 'While shepherds watched' has a long association with the tune despite the awkward lie of the words. (We have adapted the setting to improve the fit.) Salvationists sing the tune to Isaac Watts's 'Come, ye that love the Lord', but it is better known throughout the English-speaking world to the Yorkshire words 'On Ilkla Moor baht 'at'. (For another piece by Clark see 'Joy to the world!', 76: II.)

Setting VI was published by Ralph Dunstan in his *Cornish Song Book* (1929), where he gives the source only as 'from a manuscript in my possession of *c.*1830'. He suggests that the complexity of this church-gallery setting (see Appendix 3) precludes the singing of more than the one verse, but this seems unduly timorous to us, and we have adjusted the parts to accommodate later verses. We have transposed the setting down a tone.

The tune of VII is known in its native Yorkshire as 'Foster' or 'Old Foster'. As an essential item in public house carol-singing (see below) it is now almost invariably associated with the words of 'While shepherds watched', and features in most local carol-books in a variety of forms, some debased, some richly transformed through the process of oral transmission. Quite unknown, however, is the original setting, which we give here, where the text was the Sternhold and Hopkins metrical 'Old Version' of Psalm 47, 'Ye people all with one accord'. It is the weightiest piece in the second of the twin volumes of John Foster's only known publication, *A 2d Collection of Sacred Music Consisting of Anthems, Psalms & Hymns* (*c.*1820; only one copy known, in Sheffield Local History Library). The composer lies buried in the centre of the nave of St Mary's Parish Church, Ecclesfield, which in 1820 was still a village but is now a northern dormitory suburb of Sheffield. The nearby mining village of High Green, where Foster lived, was dominated by two local industrial families, the Newtons and the Ridleys. Both families were Methodist, and generous in their support of choirs, instrumental bands, and at least one full-scale orchestra for the recreation of their employees. It may be that Foster had some musical connection with the families or with a local Methodist chapel. A long-lived vicar of Ecclesfield recalled that he 'belonged to an old-established family in these parts', was 'a musician of local celebrity' and a 'humorist', and that an achievement of his forty years as a 'very influential' local coroner was the repression of bull-baiting and cock-fighting (Alfred Gatty, *A Life at One Living*, 1884, p. 25).

His setting of Psalm 47, Old Version, is one of the most expansively scored pieces in his very diverse publication, calling for choir, organ ('or pianoforte'), and an orchestra of strings, flute, two oboes, two horns, trumpet, and drum. For a little-known provincial musician it is a surprisingly accomplished piece of work. His keyboard part, which we give here, is a reduction of the orchestral accompaniment.

There is a continuing tradition of carol-singing in certain pubs in the Sheffield area which is said to have begun when the gallery choirs and bands were ejected from the parish churches in favour of harmoniums and barrel-organs. 'Old Foster' is a particular favourite at the Fountain Inn at Ingbirchworth, near Barnsley, and here, as everywhere in the singing pubs, the original has floridly mutated over the years. (A version was recorded in 1973 by Ian Russell, of the Survey of Language and Folklore, now the Centre for English Cultural Tradition and Language, at Sheffield University, and issued on a record, *The People's Carol: I*. A transcription of a similar mutation is published in *The Joy of Christmas: Words and music of traditional and local carols compiled and presented by Worral Male Voice Choir*, 1982.)

The Hutchens MS of Cornish Christmas carols, prepared for Davies Gilbert *c.*1825, has a fine triple-time tune for this text (see Appendix 4). For the justly if sometimes extravagantly praised setting by Daniel Read (1757–1836) to his fuging tune 'Sherburne' (*The American Singing Book*, 1785) see R. A. Crawford, *The Core Repertory* . . . , 1984, no. 84.

PERFORMANCE I (*i*) solo voice and lute, orpharion and/or cittern, with or without bass viol; (*ii*) solo voice or four voices with mixed consort (see above). Alison's setting is also suitable for congregation and organ, when it may be treated as a normal modern hymn-tune. (Elizabethan congregations sang hymns in unison and unaccompanied.)

II, voices and organ.

III, choir.

IV, V, voices, with instruments *ad lib.* (see Appendix 3). The change of metre in IV at bar 7 is probably ○ = ○

VI (*i*) as IV/V; (*ii*) choir and organ.

VII (*i*) choir and organ or piano; (*ii*) choir and orchestra.

47

O remember Adam's fall
Remember, O thou man

I

(*Christmas*)

Seventeenth-century?
(Bedford, 1733)

Loud / **FULL** / **SOLI** / **Soft**

1. O re-mem-ber A-dam's fall, O thou man, O___ thou man! O re - mem-ber
2. O re-mem-ber, O thou man, O thou man, O___ thou man, O re - mem-ber,

A-dam's fall From___ heaven to hell! O re-mem-ber A-dam's fall, How we_ were con -
O thou man, Thy___ time mis-spent! O re-mem-ber, O thou man, How thou from thy

- dem-ned all In - to hell per - pe - tu - al, There for to dwell.
God didst run, And his pre-scence thou didst shun, There - fore re - pent!

3 O remember God's goodness,
O thou man, O thou man!
O remember God's goodness
    And promise made!
O remember God's goodness,
All our evil to redress
(When we were remediless)
    And be our aid.

4 Oh, the angels all did sing,
O thou man, O thou man!
Oh, the angels all did sing,
    On heaven's high hill!
Oh, the angels all did sing:
'Praise be to our glorious King,
And on earth, in ev'rything,
    To men good will!'

5 Oh, the shepherds startled were,
O thou man, O thou man!
Oh, the shepherds startled were
    At this strange thing!
Oh, the shepherds startled were
When near Bethlehem they did hear
That Christ Jesus was born there
    To be our King!

6 To the stable they did go,
O thou man, O thou man!
To the stable they did go,
    This thing to see;
To the stable they did go,
Devoutly asking if 'twas so,
If Christ had been born or no,
    To set us free.

7 In a stable he was born,
O thou man, O thou man!
In a stable he was born
    For lost man's sake;
In a stable he was born:
For us wretches, and forlorn,
Our Redeemer thought no scorn
    Our flesh to take.

8 O give thanks to God alway,
O thou man, O thou man!
O give thanks to God alway,
    Joyfully!
O give thanks to God alway
For this, our happy day;
Let all men sing and say:
    'Holy, holy!'

Sixteenth-century?
(vv. 1–7 Bedford, 1733
v. 8 Ravenscroft, 1611, adapted)

II

(Christmas)

Thomas Ravenscroft?
(c.1582–c.1635)

1. Re - mem - ber, O thou man, *O thou man, O thou man,* Re - mem - ber
O thou man, *Thy time is spent:* Re-mem-ber, O thou man, How thou art__
dead and gone, And I did what I can: *There - fore re - pent!*

[sic]

† See notes on performance.

2 Remember Adam's fall,
   O thou man, O thou man,
   Remember Adam's fall
     From heaven to hell!
   Remember Adam's fall,
   How we were condemnèd all
   In hell perpetual,
     There for to dwell.

3 Remember God's goodnesse,
   O thou man, O thou man,
   Remember God's goodnesse,
     And his promise made!
   Remember God's goodnesse;
   How he sent his Sonne, doubtlesse,
   Our sinnes for to redresse:
     Be not affraid!

4 The angels all did sing,
 O thou man, O thou man,
 The angels all did sing
 Upon the shepheards' hill;
 The angels all did singe
 Praises to our heavenly King,
 And peace to man living
 With a good will.

5 The shepheards amazèd was,
 O thou man, O thou man,
 The shepheards amazèd was
 To heare the angels sing,
 The shepheards amazèd was
 How it should come to passe
 That Christ our Messias
 Should be our King.

6 To Bethlem did they goe,
 O thou man, O thou man,
 To Bethlem did they go
 The shepheards three;
 To Bethlem did they goe
 To see whether it were so or no,
 Whether Christ were borne or no
 To set man free.

7 As the angels before did say,
 O thou man, O thou man,
 As the angels before did say,
 So it came to passe;
 As the angels before did say,
 They found a Babe, whereas[1] it lay
 In a manger, wrapt in hay,
 So poore he was.

8 In Bethlem he was borne,
 O thou man, O thou man,
 In Bethlem he was borne,
 For mankind's sake;
 In Bethlem he was borne,
 For us that were forlorne,
 And therefore tooke no scorne
 Our flesh to take.

9 Give thanks to God alway,
 O thou man, O thou man,
 Give thanks to God alway,
 With heart most joyfully.
 Give thanks to God alway
 For this our happy day;
 Let all men sing and say:
 'Holy! holy!'

Sixteenth-century?
(Ravenscroft, 1611)

---

[1] where

'O remember Adam's fall' (1) is one of ten pieces that form the 'Appendix. A Specimen of Hymns for Divine [i.e., service] Musick', in *The Excellency of Divine Music: A sermon* [preached on 5 November 1733] *before several members of such societies who are lovers of psalmody. To which is added, a specimen of easy, grave tunes, instead of those which are used in our profane and wanton ballads. By Arthur Bedford, M. A. Chaplain to the most noble John, Duke of Bedford, and to the Haberdasher's Hospital at Hoxton.*

Bedford was a leading figure in the religious-society movement, begun in the later seventeenth century, which played a part in the development of parish church choirs (see Appendix 3). He advocated the dispersal of skilled singers among congregations to lead the psalms, and suggested that the singers could also group together as a choir to sing a short anthem before the Sunday services and 'whatever Psalms, Hymns and Anthems they pleased' afterwards. To provide for this, he proposed the regular publication of cheap, broadside-style collections of acceptable tunes, and this seems eventually to have borne fruit in an anonymous quarterly publication, *Divine Recreations, being a collection of psalms, hymns, and canons*, which has been ascribed to him and which ran to three numbers in 1736–7. To Bedford's text we have added verse 8, adapted from Ravenscroft's verse 9.

Ravenscroft's version (II) is 'A Christmas Carroll' in the 'Country Pastimes' section of his *Melismata: musical phansies fitting to court, citie and countrey humours to 3, 4 and 5 voyces* (1611). This was the third of a series of collections of rounds, canons, and songs with Greek or pseudo-Greek titles. The soprano part (only) appears in the revised third edition of *Cantus, Songs and Fancies to thre, foure, or five parts, both apt for voices and viols* (Aberdeen, 1682) by John Forbes (father and son). It is not known whether Ravenscroft's tune is traditional or newly composed: many of the pieces in this section of *Melismata* appear to be imitations rather than transcriptions of country pieces. Traditional or not, both this and setting I belong to an English folk genre, prominent *c.*1600, in which the melody, alternating between solo and 'chorus', characteristically centres on the tonic, then the supertonic, and climaxes on a descending phrase from the dominant (compare Ravenscroft's 'Martin said to his man', the ballad 'Franklin is fled away', the trade song 'Soop [sweep], chimney, soop' in Gibbons's *The Cries of London*, and—without refrain—the ballad 'Go from my window'.)

The complete text is given to a single voice, the other three joining in with quasi-refrains. The form looks more like an invention of the composer than a reflection of any traditional practice. Although Ravenscroft does not mention it, there is the obvious possibility of performance by four voices throughout.

The carol appears with two quite different tunes in two Cornish manuscripts of the early nineteenth century, the Hutchens manuscript (Cornwall Record Office, Truro, DG 92, no. 20) and the Davey manuscript of 1825 (see Appendix 4).

'Remember, O thou man' is the 'ancient and time-worn hymn' that the Mellstock choir sang to Fancy Day in Thomas Hardy's *Under the Greenwood Tree* (1872), 'embodying a quaint Christianity in words orally transmitted from father to son through several generations . . .' The

choir presumably sang it to a descendant of Ravenscroft's setting, though, curiously, it does not survive in the books that were used at Stinsford and Puddletown by Hardy's father and grandfather; the relevant page is a blank. (See notes, 87.) According to Hardy's sister, Katherine, he obtained the (engagingly corrupt) words, quoted in full in the novel, from their mother (see W. R. Rutland, *Thomas Hardy*, 1938). The Mellstock choir (and, no doubt, Hardy's forefathers) had to rehearse the carol particularly thoroughly:

'Number seventy-eight was always a teaser—always,' said William [Dewy] . . . 'I can mind him since I was growing up a hard boy-chap.'

'But he's a good tune, and worth a mint o' practice,' said Michael.

'He is; though I've been mad enough wi' that tune at times to seize him and tear en all to linnet [lint]. Ay, he's a splendid carrel—there's no denying that.'

'The first line is well enough,' said the Sprinks; 'but when you come to "O, thou man," you make a mess o't.'

'We'll have another go into en, and see what we can make of the martel [mortal]. Half-an-hour's hammering at en will conquer the toughness of en; I'll warrant it.'

The difficulty was presumably caused by an unfamiliar idiom, and the problem of accommodating the irregular text.

PERFORMANCE I, voices, with optional doubling instruments in the full sections (see Appendix 3). Following contemporary convention, Bedford marks 'soft' and 'loud' merely to indicate 'soli' and 'full', which we have substituted. (This need not imply a choir.)

II (*i*) solo soprano, with three viols and perhaps continuo—lute, organ, etc.—with three lower voices joining in the 'refrains', printed in italic; (*ii*) four voices, singing throughout, with optional doubling/continuo instruments (see Appendix 3). When sung, the bass line should be performed in rhythmic unison with the other parts.

48

Riu, riu, chiu

(Immaculate Conception; Christmas)

Mateo Flecha the elder? (1481–1553)
(Villancicos de diversos autores, 1556)

22   *Fine*

Dios guar - do   el   lo - bo   De___ nues - tra   cor - de - ra.

Dios guar - do   el   lo - bo, el   lo - bo   De___ nues - tra   cor - de - ra.

Dios guar - do   el   lo - bo,   el   lo - bo   De___ nues - tra   cor - de - ra.

guar - do   el   lo - bo,   el   lo - bo   De___ nues - tra   cor - de - ra. 1. El

27   VERSE [SOLO]

lo - bo   ra - bio - so   La___ qui - so   mor - der,   Mas   Dios po - de - ro -
2. Es - te ques na - çi - do   Es___ el gran Mo - nar - cha,   Chris - to   pa - tri -
3. Mu-chas pro - fe - çi - as   Lo han___ pro - fe - ti - za - do;   Ya un en nues - tros

32

-so   La   su - po de - fen - der;   Qui - so - le ha - zer que No   pu - die - sse pe -
-ar - cã   De___ car - ne ves - ti - do;   Ha - nos re - di - mi - do Con   se   ha - zer chi -
di - as   Lo   he - mos al - can - ça - do.   A Dios hu - ma - na - do Ve - mos en el

38   *D.S.*

-car,   Ni aun o - ri - gi - nal   Es - ta   Vir - gen no   tu - vie - ra.
-qui - to: Aun - que e - ra in - fi - ni - to   Fi - ni - to se hi - zie - ra.
sue - lo   Y al hom-bre en el   cie - lo   Por - que el le qui - sie - ra.

4   Yo vi mil garçones
    Que andavan cantando,
    Por aqui bolando*
    Haziendo mil sones,
    Diziendo a gasconés:
    'Gloria sea en el çielo
    Y paz en el suelo,
    Pues Jesus nasçiera.'

5   Este viene a dar
    A los muertos vida
    Y viene a reparar
    De todos la caida.
    Es la Luz del Dia*
    Aqueste moçuelo;
    Este es el Cordero*
    Que San Juan dixera.

*An asterisk in the text indicates that the small-note variants should be sung.

6   Mira bien que͡ os quadre,

Que͡ ansina lo͡ oyera:

Que Dios no pudiera

Hazerla mas que madre;

El que͡ era su Padre*
           ⌣

Oy della nasçio
              ⌣

Y͡ el que la crio

Su* hijo se dixera.

7   Pues que ya tenemos

Lo que desseamos,

Todos juntos vamos,*

Presentes llevemos;

Todos le daremos*
              ⌣

Nuestra voluntad,

Pues a se͡ igualar

Con* el hombre viniera.

Juan del Encina? (*1468–1529/30*)
(*Villancicos de diversos autores, 1556*)

TRANSLATION *Riu, riu, chiu,* the guard [shepherd] by the river: God protected our Ewe from the wolf.

1 The furious wolf tried to bite her, but almighty God protected her well: he made her in such a way that she could know no sin, a virgin unstained by our first father's [Adam's] fault.

2 This new-born Child is a mighty monarch, the patriarchal Christ clothed in flesh; he redeemed us by making himself tiny: he who was infinite became finite.

3 Many prophecies foretold his coming, and now in our time we have seen them fulfilled. God became man, we see him on earth, and we see man in heaven because he [God] loved him.

4 I saw a thousand young men [angels] singing as they flew, making a thousand sounds, chanting to Basques [all good Spaniards]: 'Glory be in the heavens, and peace on earth, now that Jesus is born!'

5 He comes to give life to the dead and to atone for man's fall: this very Babe is the Light of Day, the Lamb of whom St John spoke.

6 Look to it! it concerns you all: God made her [Mary] a mere mother; he who was her father was born of her today; and he who created her calls himself her son.

7 Now we have gained what we desired let us go together to present to him our gifts; let each resign his will to the God who was willing to come down to earth to become man's equal.

(*tr. editors, after Robert Pring-Mill*)

Words and music are from *Villancicos de diversos autores*, a collection of Spanish songs for two to five voices published in Venice in 1556. The *villancico* is a refrain song, in many ways the Spanish equivalent of the carol, which has flourished from the fifteenth century to the present day. Musically, the classic *villancico* was very like the fifteenth-century English carol, though refrains were not invariably repeated between verses. The tuneful, frequently dance-like character of the music survived two major sixteenth-century changes: a musical shift from homophony to madrigalian polyphony, and a gradual poetic move away from predominantly secular, often rustic themes and simple language towards religious subjects and baroque opacity. The 1556 print stands at the mid-century watershed, most of the texts matching the refreshing simplicity of the music, but others reflecting something of the self-consciously intellectual preoccupations of the Valencian court of 1530–50, from which it derives.

None of the 'various composers' is named in the print. This song (and carol 50) have been attributed to Mateo Flecha the elder (see notes, 50). Twelve of the fifty-four songs are sacred—all for Christmas—and grouped together; at least two are based on the texts and chant of movements from the Christmas liturgy (see carol 49 for one; the other quotes the introit of the main mass of Christmas). This, with the striking stylistic unity of the whole Christmas group, raises the possibility that a single musician—and Flecha, as court composer from 1534 to 1544, would have been an obvious candidate—may have been commissioned to create them as a set, for use within the liturgy; *villancicos* were certainly used in this way in the following century.

'Riu, riu, chiu' was a traditional call of Spanish shepherds when guarding their flocks in a riverside fold. Elsewhere in the print, the catchy tune is found in a variant form with a secular shepherd-song, and it may derive from a genuine example. Lines 3–4 of the refrain, together with verse 1, are built around a strong image which is the key to what follows. The shepherd is God the Father; the precious ewe-lamb that he protects is the Virgin Mary; the furious wolf is Satan, whose bite will infect with the taint of Original Sin; and Mary's defence, like the impregnable wall of a sheepfold, is her own Immaculate (that is, sinless) Conception, which allowed Christ to be born fully human but untainted by Adam's fall. (The odd image of Mary as a lamb is an oblique reference to this doctrine.)

PERFORMANCE Refrain, four voices (there is no evidence of instrumental doubling in this repertory); verse, solo voice.

49

Verbum caro factum est: Y la Virgen le dezia

(Christmas)

Sixteenth-century
(*Villancicos de diversos autores*, 1556)

REFRAIN ... Fine

Ver - bum ca - ro fac - tum est Por___ que to - dos__ hos sal - veis.

Por que to - dos

Por___ que to - dos hos sal - veis.

VERSE

1. Y___ la Vir-gen___ le de - zi - a: 'Vi - da de la vi - da mi - a,
2. O___ ri - que-zas___ te-rre - na - les, ¿No da - reis u - nos pa - ña - les

D.C.

Hi - jo mi - o, ¿que os ha - ri - a, Que__ no__ ten - go en que os e - cheis?'
A Je - su__ que en-tre a - ni - ma - les Es na - sçi - do__ se - gun veis?

TRANSLATION The Word is made flesh for the salvation of you all.

1 And the Virgin said unto him: 'Life of my life, what would I [not] do for you, my Son? Yet I have nothing on which to lay you down.'

2 Oh, worldly riches! will you not give some swaddling clothes to Jesus, who is born among the animals, as you can see?

From the same source as 'Riu, riu, chiu' (48). The refrain (both text and music) is closely based on the short responsory *Verbum caro* sung at terce on Christmas Day (see *Liber Usualis*, p. 407).

PERFORMANCE Refrain, four voices or choir; verse, four voices.

50

E la don, don Verges Maria

(Christmas)

Mateo Flecha the elder? (1481–1553)
(*Villancicos de diversos autores*, 1556)

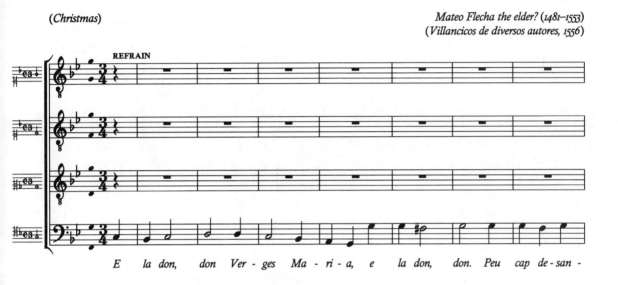

E la don, don Ver - ges Ma - ri - a, e la don, don. Peu cap de - san -

- que que nos dan - sa - ron. E la don, don Ver - ges Ma - ri - a, e la don

2 Digas nos qui to la dit
   Que verges na ya parit,
   Que nos may avem ausit
   Lo que tu diu giran tom.

3 A eo dian los argeus
   Que cantavan altas veus
   La *Grolla necelsis Deus,*
   Quen Belem lo trobaron.

4 Per señau nos an birat
   Que verets enbolicat
   De drapets, molt mal faxat:
   Lo ver Diu petit garçon.

5 Vin, Perot, y a Diu veray
   Y a la Verge sa may.
   Un sorron li portaray,
   Que sera ple de coucom.

6 Ara canta tu, Beltran,
   Per amor deu sant Infan,
   Y apres cantara Joan
   Y donar nos an coucom.

7 Ube cantare sus dich
   Per Jesus, mon bon amich,
   Que nos saunara la nit
   De tot mal quan hom fedorm.

Sixteenth-century
(*Villancicos de diversos autores, 1556*)

TRANSLATION She is our Lady, our Lady, the Virgin Mary. On pale feet they [angels?] danced for us.
  1 'O fellow shepherds, tonight a virgin has given birth to a beautiful boy, without rival in this world.'
  2 'Tell us who told you that a virgin has given birth, for we've never heard of anything like it!'
  3 'The angels, singing "Gloria in excelsis Deo" at the tops of their voices, said they found him in Bethlehem.'
  4 'He has been given to us as a sign, and you will see him, crudely wrapped in swaddling bands—God himself, as a little boy.
  5 'Come, Perot, and you will see God and the Virgin, his mother. Bring him a bag full of dates.
  6 'Now, Beltran, sing for the love of the holy Infant, and then John will sing, and we will give them dates.
  7 'Then we will sing for our good friend, the Lord Jesus, who this night will save us from all evil known to man.'
(*tr. Tess Knighton, adapted*)

This is one of the most delightful of the group of twelve Christmas *villancicos* in the 1556 *Villancicos de diversos autores*: see notes to 'Riu, riu, chiu' (48), which it immediately precedes in the print and with which it has much in common. Mateo Flecha the elder, to whom the music of these two songs is usually attributed (three others in the book are known to be by him) was particularly prized at the Valencian court for his jokey, quodlibet-like Christmas *ensaladas*.

Both settings are possibly based on the tunes of popular dance-songs. The texts are stylistically very different, but both are the work of professional poets exploiting a 'peasant' style and using popular tunes, a tradition that was common to Spain and Provence. 'E la don, don' is one of four Catalan *villancicos* in the print, and by far the richest in Provençal words and phrases. (We have tacitly corrected obvious misprints, and some of the translation is speculative. For a thoroughly 'corrected' text, see Leopoldo Querol Rosso's version in his *Cancionero de Uppsala*, 1980, p. 56.)

The 'don, don' of the refrain is a Catalan form of 'dona' (lady), but the repetition is perhaps also onomatopoeic, suggesting the pounding of the feet of the angelic dancers. The verses are in the form of a dialogue between a shepherd who has heard the angelic annunciation of Christ's birth and his companions who have not, though a single singer would probably have sung them all. The peasant idiom, the rustic gifts, and the use of Christian names are characteristic of both Spanish and Provençal Christmas songs.

The setting is for *voces aequales* (equal voices), the combination of clefs indicating a limited overall compass and perhaps allowing for different vocal scorings. The nature of the text suggests performance by adult males; we have accordingly transposed the piece down by a fifth, but performance at a higher written pitch by SSAT is also an option.

PERFORMANCE Refrain, four voices; verse, solo voice.

51

Gaudete!

(*Piae Cantiones*, 1582;
Jistebnice Cantional, 1420)

(*Christmas*)

REFRAIN

Gau - de - te! gau - de - te! Chri - stus est na - tus

Fine

Ex Ma - ri - a Vir - gi - ne: gau - de - te!

VERSE

1. Tem - pus ad - est gra - ti - ae, Hoc quod op - ta - ba - mus;
2. De - us ho - mo fac - tus est, Na - tu - ra mi - ran - te;
3. E - ze - chi - e - lis por - ta Clau - sa per - tran - si - tur;
4. Er - go nos - tra con - ci - o Psal - lat jam in lus - tro;

D.C.

Car - mi - na lae - ti - ci - ae De - vo - te red - da - mus.
Mun - dus re - no - va - tus est A Chri - sto reg - nan - te.
Un - de Lux est or - ta, Sa - lus in - ve - ni - tur.
Be - ne - di - cat Do - mi - no: Sa - lus Re - gi nos - tro.

Fourteenth century
(*Piae Cantiones*, 1582)

TRANSLATION Rejoice! rejoice! Christ is born of the Virgin Mary; rejoice!

1 The time of grace has come for which we have prayed; let us devoutly sing songs of joy.

2 God is made man, while nature wonders; the world is renewed by Christ the King.

3 The closed gate of Ezekiel has been passed through; from where the Light has risen [the East] salvation is found.

4 Therefore let our assembly sing praises now at this time of purification; let it bless the Lord: greetings to our King.

This superb song is one of the most popular of the Christmas pieces in *Piae Cantiones* (1582), and has even crossed the great divide to the world of 'folk rock' in an admirable recording by Steeleye Span in 1973.

The basis of 'Gaudete!' is a medieval *cantio* (song) which is found in several forms, with and without a refrain, with a variety of verses, and sometimes (as here) in the form of a *Benedicamus* substitute (see notes, 9). We have not found the *Piae Cantiones* verses elsewhere, and the song may have been one of those revised for publication by the editor, Finno: it is notably less Marian than his likely sources. (Since Finno did not print the music of the verses it is impossible to know whether he intended a carol—refrain, verse, refrain —or a refrain song—verse, refrain, verse.)

Verse 3 refers to the eastern gate of the city in Ezekiel's vision: 'Then the Lord said unto me: This gate shall be shut, it shall not be opened, and no man shall enter in by it; because the Lord, the God of Israel, hath entered by it, therefore shall it be shut' (Ezekiel 44:2). The gate is a traditional symbol of Mary as perpetual virgin: the entry of the God of Israel is interpreted as Christ's birth into the world, which supposedly did not impair her physical virginity, and after this she did not conceive again.

The *Piae Cantiones* verses derive from the Bohemian song 'Ezechielis porta'. Seven verses are found in two manuscripts in the Národní Muzeum, Prague, which reflect much of the very conservative *Piae Cantiones* repertory: the Jistebnice Gradual (c.1450, XII F 14) and Cantional (1420, II C 7).

The Gradual has the verse tune only, very roughly notated. There is no music with the Cantional text, but a note indicates that it is to be sung to that of the vernacular Christmas song 'Za ciesaře Augusta panna porodila', given on page 74 of the manuscript. (The song survives as the Czech folk carol 'Za ciesaře Augusta Panna velestkvouci'.) The Cantional version is more developed (or more accurately notated) than the one in the Gradual, and has its own refrain melody. The verse tune is very close to that which is sung today, and includes the rather surprising opening upbeat. (See *Old French and Czecho-Slovakian Carols*, arr. Richard Donovan, 1931.) It is also found as a chorale tune in some German books, including Praetorius's *Musae Sioniae* (V, 1607), set to the Christmas text 'Eia, mea anima'.

The *Piae Cantiones* refrain text does not occur elsewhere, and may be Finno's adaptation of the medieval refrain. Its stresses barbarously mis-match those of the setting, the melody of which was widely sung in Germany to Luther's grace before meat, 'Danket dem Herren, denn er ist so freundlich', which matches it perfectly. This tune had developed out of one of the simple four-part tenor-tune settings written for the performance of classical Latin verse and of the modern imitations that featured in many school dramas. (Classical versification depends on length of syllable and not on stress, but the long and short notes of the settings could as easily correspond to stressed and unstressed syllables as to the long and short syllables for which they were intended.) Several composers produced sample settings in the important metres, to which any other verses in that metre could equally well be sung. One by Ludwig Senfl, printed with Martial's 'Vitam quae faciunt beatiorum' and Catullus's 'Vivamus mea Lesbia atque amemus' (Senfl, *Varia Carmina Genera*, 1534), was included in many subsequent didactic collections. In Johann Spangenberg's *Grammaticae Latinae Partes* (1546) Senfl's melody appears in the tenor, set to Luther's grace, with a new melody in the soprano. It was this soprano tune to which the grace became generally sung and which would appear in 1582 in *Piae Cantiones* as the refrain melody of 'Gaudete!'.

Earlier settings lack accidentals; this need not imply uninflected performance, but the careful keyboard intabulations of 'Danket dem Herren' by Ammerbach (1571 and 1583) sharpen only the final leading note.

PERFORMANCE Refrain, choir or four voices, with instruments *ad lib.* (see notes, 54); verse, solo voice(s).

52

Psallite Unigenito

(Christmas)

Sixteenth-century
(Praetorius, 1609)

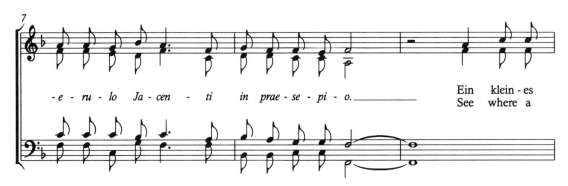

Kin - de - lein ligt in dem Krip - pe - lein, al - le lie - be En - ge-
Child so dear Lies in the man-ger here; An - gels, e - ver ho - vering

al - le lie - be En - ge - lein die - nen dem
An - gels, e - ver ho - vering near, Ser - ving, the

-lein die - nen dem Kin - de - lein und sin - gen ihm fein: Psal - li -
near, Ser - ving the Child so dear, Sing with voi - ces clear: †Singt und___

Psal -
Singt

Psal - li - te U - ni - ge - ni - to, Chri - sto, De - i
Singt und klingt Je - su, Gott - es Kind und Ma - ri - en

Kin - de - lein, Psal - li - te U - ni - ge - ni - to, Chri - sto, De - i
Child so dear, Singt und klingt Je - su, Gott - es Kind und Ma - ri - en

- te
klingt

- li - te_____ U - ni - ge - ni - to,
und_____ klingt_____ Je - su, Gott - es Kind

† See notes.

Traditional (tr. editors)

TRANSLATION (*Psallite Unigenito . . .*) Sing praises to the Only-begotten, to Christ the Son of God, to the Lord Redeemer, to the little Child laid in the manger.

(*Singt und klingt . . .*) Sing and play to Jesus, God's Child and Mary's dear Son, to our beloved Jesus, laid in the stall with oxen and asses.

Praetorius published this in his *Musae Sioniae* (VI, 1609, no. 85; see notes, 53), but it is in fact a contrafactum (retexting) of an anonymous French chanson, 'Ho la hé, par la vertu goy', first published in *Trente et Six Chansons musicales . . .* (Paris, 1530), which appears in a mid-sixteenth-century German source, Regensburg, Proske Bibliothek, A. R. 940/1.

The music circulated in Germany both as an instrumental piece and with the macaronic Latin/German text. At some stage the music was rewritten, in triple time and in a more straightforward manner, though preserving the melody of the chanson. The rewritten version reached the song-books before the original, appearing first in the *Alte catholische geistliche Kirchengesänge* (1599). Praetorius alone gives the original (he also gives the rewritten version, no. 94 in the same volume). (See W. Brennecke, 'Psallite: Singt und Klingt', in *Die Musikforschung*, V, 1952, p. 160.)

For the repeat of the 'Psallite' section all the Catholic books provide a German text. The *Catholische geistliche Gesänge* (1608) heads the two 'Psallite' sections 'Chorus latinus' and 'Teutscher Chorus'. Although the 'German chorus' text properly belongs to the rewritten version, it may be substituted for the Latin in bars 16–24; alternatively, it could be substituted for both Latin sections in a repeat of the entire piece.

PERFORMANCE Four voices or choir, with instruments *ad lib.* In a choral performance bars 9–17 could be taken by soloists.

En! natus est Emanuel
Lo! born is our Emmanuel

(Christmas)

Michael Praetorius (1571–1621)

VERSE 1

1. En! na - tus est E - ma - nu - el,_____ Do - mi - nus,
1. Lo! born is our Em - ma - nu - el,_____ Christ the Lord,

Quem prae - dix - it Ga - bri - el, Do - mi - nus._____
As fore - told by Ga - bri - el, Christ_____ the Lord._____

REFRAIN

Sal -
the

Sal - va - tor
the Sa - viour

Do - mi - nus_____ Sal - va - tor nos - ter_____ est,_____ Sal -
Christ the Lord,_____ the Sa - viour of man - kind,_____ the

Sal -
the

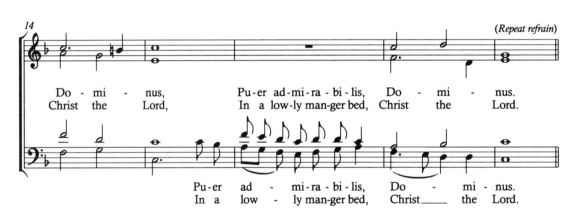

23

(Repeat refrain)

Ex Ma - ri - a Vir - gi - ne, Do - mi - nus.____
Of the Vir - gin Ma - ry born, Christ____ the Lord.____

Do - mi - nus.
Christ____ the Lord.

All Praetorius's harmonizations in this book are from parts V and VI of the largest of his publications, the *Musae Sioniae* ('The Muses of Sion', 1605–10, the nine volumes corresponding to the number of the choirs of angels, or heavenly muses). Parts IV–VI are a comprehensive treatment of liturgical hymnody, of which the melodies and performing traditions (and frequently the texts) varied from province to province in the Lutheran Church, often preserving local pre-Reformation usage. (See Appendix 2.) Lutheran hymnody was continuing its rapid sixteenth-century growth, the body of chorales sanctioned by Luther himself being supplemented by psalmody (in imitation of the Genevan churches), newly written texts, and hymns adapted (as were many of Luther's) from the Catholic tradition. Praetorius draws freely on the latter source in particular (the influential Mainz *Catholisch Cantual* of 1605 is one book which he seems to have used), though whether he was following or leading existing Lutheran practice is not always clear. The chorales of part V (1607), set for two to seven voices in a variety of styles, allow for a great variety of performance practice involving choir and congregation in alternation and combination, while much of the writing in parts VI–VIII is in the simple homophonic manner for which Praetorius had a particular genius.

Praetorius was a rigorous autodidact, and by the end of a fairly short life, which included posts at the courts of Wolfenbüttel, Kassel, Dresden, and Halle, he had assimilated all the current styles and techniques. The rich synthesis of German and Italian musical practice in his later works had no counterpart among his contemporaries. More relevant to his chorale settings was his exceptional interest in composers of the half-century before his birth, whose music he often published alongside his own. He had a particular devotion to the chorale settings of Johann Walther (1496–1570), who had worked with Luther on the first song-books of the Reformed church. Praetorius shared the deep and strictly orthodox faith of his theologian father (once a colleague of Walther), writing religious tracts (now lost) and regretting not having taken holy orders. Chorales form the basis of most of his huge published output, and the overwhelming preponderance of choral—often polychoral—music reflects his belief that this, rather than the increasingly fashionable solo and *concertato* genres, was the true music of heaven.

The sacred works appeared in carefully structured publications, mostly in linked sets, and with prefaces which will yield invaluable and otherwise lost information about German and Italian performance practice when they are eventually collated with the introductions to the larger individual works and with the *Syntagma Musicum* ('Musical Treatise') of 1614–18. On the secular side, *Terpsichore* (1612), the celebrated collection of French dance tunes, is the sole survivor of eight volumes of instrumental and vocal music which were at least prepared for publication.

'En! natus est Emanuel', with its refrain-like repeats of 'Dominus' and its infectious rhythm, has obvious parallels with 'Psallite Unigenito' (52) from the same volume of *Musae Sioniae* (VI, 1609). Like 'Psallite' it is rather archaic in style and may also derive from a chanson of the sixteenth century. Another parallel is that Praetorius provides two updated arrangements in the same volume (compared with one of 'Psallite'), the first (no. 96) in duple time with Latin and German text, the second (no. 97) in triple time with a different German text. The Latin text was sometimes sung to the tune of 'Resonet in laudibus' (55).

The opening musical phrase may have inspired Nicolaus Herman when he wrote the tune of his popular Christmas hymn 'Lobt Gott, ihr Christen alle gleich' (*c.*1554, published 1560).

PERFORMANCE Four voices or choir, with instruments *ad lib.*

54

Puer natus in Bethlehem
A Boy is born in Bethlehem
Ein Kind geborn zu Bethlehem

I

(*Christmas*)

1 Puer natus in Bethlehem;
   Unde gaudet Ierusalem.
   Alleluia!

2 Assumpsit carnem Filii
   Dei Patris altissimi.

3 Per Gabrielis nuncium
   Virgo concepit Filium.

*4 De matre natus virgine,
   Sine virili semine.

*5 Sine serpentis vulnere
   De nostro venit sanguine.

*6 In carne nobis similis,
   Peccato sed dissimilis.

7 Tanquam sponsus de thalamo,
   Processit matris utero.

8 Hic iacet in praesepio
   Qui regnat sine termino.

9 Cognovit bos et asinus
   Quod puer erat Dominus.

1 A Boy is born in Bethlehem;
   Rejoice, therefore, Jerusalem!
   Alleluya!

2 Our human flesh doth he take on,
   High Word of God, the eternal Son.

3 When Mary Gabriel's words received,
   Within her was her Son conceived.

*4 From virgin's womb doth he proceed
   No human father doth he need.

*5 From serpent's wound immune was he,
   Yet shared he our humanity.

*6 'Tis flesh like ours he's clothèd in,
   Though free from man's primeval sin.

7 As from his chamber strides the groom,
   So comes he from his mother's womb.

8 Within the manger doth he lie,
   Who reigns eternally on high.

9 The ox and ass that Child adored
   And knew him for their heavenly Lord.

Thirteenth-century?
(arr. Michael Praetorius,
1571–1621, adapted)

1. Pu - er na - tus in Beth - le - hem, Beth - le - hem; Un - de gau - det Ie - ru - sa - lem. Al - le - lu - ia! al - le - lu - ia! al - le - lu - ia!

1. A Boy is born in Beth - le - hem, Beth - le - hem; Re - joice, there - fore, Je - ru - sa - lem! al - le - lu - ia! al - le - lu - ia!

Beth - le - hem;

*10 Et angelus pastoribus
    Revelat quis sit Dominus.

*10 To shepherds did an angel come
    To tell them there was born a Son.

11 Magi de longe veniunt;
   Aurum, thus, myrrham offerunt.

11 The wise men came from lands afar
   To offer incense, gold and myrrh.

167

12 Intrantes domum invicem,
    Natum salutant hominem.

13 In hoc natali gaudio,
    Benedicamus Domino.

14 Laudetur sancta Trinitas,
    Deo dicamus gratias.

Thirteenth-century?
(vv. 1, 3–14 Piae Cantiones, 1582
v. 2 Hereford Breviary, 1505)

12 They stooped to enter, one by one,
    To greet in turn the new-born Son.

13 At this glad birth, with one accord
    Let us rejoice and bless the Lord!

14 To Holy Trinity be praise, [be praise,
        be praise,]
    And thanks be given to God always.

tr. editors

II

(Christmas)

1 Ein Kind geborn zu Bethlehem;
   des freuet sich Jerusalem.
     Halleluja!

2 Hier liegt es in dem Krippelein;
   ohn' Ende ist die Herrschaft sein.

3 Die König' aus Saba kamen her;
   Gold, Weihrauch, Myrrhe brachten sie dar.

4 Sie gingen in das Haus herein, [ins
       Haus herein]
   und grüssten das Kind und die Mutter sein.

5 Sie fielen nieder auf ihre Knie
   und sprachen: 'Gott und Mensch ist hie.'

6 Für solche gnadenreiche Zeit,
   sei Gott gelobt in Ewigkeit.

Fifteenth-century
(Praetorius, 1609, modernized)

1 A Boy is born in Bethlehem;
   Rejoice, therefore, Jerusalem!
     Alleluya!

2 Within a manger doth he lie,
   Who reigns eternally on high.

3 From distant Saba came three Kings,
   Gold, incense, myrrh their offerings.

4 They stooped to enter, one by one,
   To greet the Mother and the Son.

5 Then to the Child they bowed the knee,
   Declaring: 'God and Man is he!'

6 For this most joyful time give praise,
       [give praise, give praise,]
   And glory give to God always.

tr. editors

II

(Christmas)

Thirteenth-century?
(arr. J. S. Bach, 1685–1750)

1. Ein Kind ge - born zu Beth - le - hem, Beth -
1. A Boy is born in Beth - le - hem, Beth -

- le - hem; des freu - et sich Je - ru - sa - lem. Hal -
- le - hem; Re - joice, there - fore, Je - ru - sa - lem! Al -

- le - lu - ja! hal - le - lu - ja!
- le - lu - ya! al - le - lu - ya!

III

Thirteenth-century?
(Piae Cantiones, 1582, arr. editors)

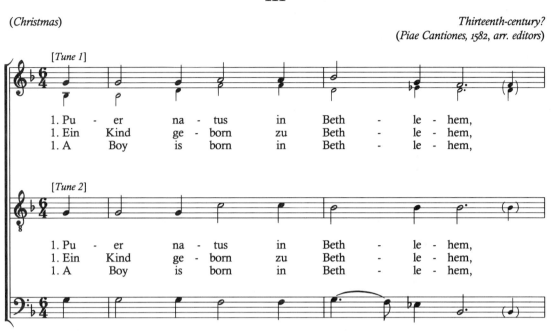

[Tune 1]

1. Pu - er na - tus in Beth - le - hem,
1. Ein Kind ge - born zu Beth - le - hem,
1. A Boy is born in Beth - le - hem,

[Tune 2]

1. Pu - er na - tus in Beth - le - hem,
1. Ein Kind ge - born zu Beth - le - hem,
1. A Boy is born in Beth - le - hem,

(H)al -

Beth - le - hem;___ Un - de gau - det Ie - ru - sa - lem.
des freu - et sich Je - ru - sa - lem. (H)al -
Re - joice, there - fore, Je - ru - sa - lem!

Beth - le - hem;___ Un - de___ gaud - et Ie - ru - sa - lem.
des freu - et sich Je - ru - sa - lem. (H)al -
Re - joice,___ there - fore, Je - ru - sa - lem!

1   Ein Kind geborn zu Bethlehem;
    des freuet sich Jerusalem.
        Halleluja!

2   Hier liegt es in dem Krippelein;
    ohn' Ende ist die Herrschaft sein.

3   Die König' aus Saba kamen her;
    Gold, Weihrauch, Myrrhe brachten sie dar.

4   Sie gingen in das Haus herein, [ins
        Haus herein]
    und grüssten das Kind und die Mutter sein.

5   Sie fielen nieder auf ihre Knie
    und sprachen: 'Gott und Mensch ist hie.'

6   Für solche gnadenreiche Zeit,
    sei Gott gelobt in Ewigkeit.

1   A Boy is born in Bethlehem;
    Rejoice, therefore, Jerusalem!
        Alleluya!

2   Within a manger doth he lie,
    Who reigns eternally on high.

3   From distant Saba came three Kings,
    Gold, incense, myrrh their offerings.

4   They stooped to enter, one by one,
    To greet the Mother and the Son.

5   Then to the Child they bowed the knee,
    Declaring: 'God and Man is he!'

6   For this most joyful time give praise,
        [give praise, give praise,]
    And glory give to God always.

Fifteenth-century
(Praetorius, 1609, modernized)

tr. editors

One of the most venerable of all Christmas *cantiones* (songs), 'Puer natus in Bethlehem' has retained its popularity down the centuries. It is probably of Bohemian origin, and we take the Latin text from *Piae Cantiones* (1582). This version is much longer than earlier ones, and verses 4, 5, 6, and 10, according to Lossius (see below), are the result of 'improvements' by Hermann Bonn (*c.*1504–48), a pupil of Luther and an industrious translator of hymns. The added verses are notably more 'theological' in tone, and may be omitted. The German text is the standard modern one (taken from Friedrich Blume, *Geschichte der evangelischen Kirchenmusik*, 1964).

The earliest source is a late thirteenth-century antiphoner from Bobbio, in Italy (Codex Taurinen, F 1 4; see *Analecta Hymnica*, vol. XX, no. 111, p. 99; and see vol. I, no. 178, p. 163 for five later Prague manuscripts). This gives only three verses, corresponding to verses 1, 2, and 9, set to an ancestor of the usual tune. A quite different tune is in the second earliest source, a processional from a Bohemian Benedictine nunnery, dated 1320 and now in Prague. This is thought to be the original melody, and it recurs in the Jistebnice Cantional (1420) and in two sixteenth-century song-books.

Verses 13 and 14 confirm that for most of its life 'Puer natus' was a substitute for the versicle 'Benedicamus Domino' and the response 'Deo dicamus gratias' at the conclusion of the office (see notes, 9). It is also found, in a ten-stanza form, as a sequence in the Hereford Breviary of 1505.

We give two settings of the usual tune: setting I is from Praetorius's *Musae Sioniae* (vol. VI, 1609, no. 34, with the bass of bars 10–11 adapted from vol. V, 1607, no. 84; see notes, 53). Setting II is from Bach's Epiphany Cantata 'Sie werden aus Saba alle kommen' (BWV 65), where it is sung to a translation of verse 11. (Another commonly sung German translation is 'Geborn ist uns ein Kindelein'.)

The 'usual tune' had an unusual origin, and in the sixteenth century was often found as a pair of linked tunes, one of which ('tune 2' in setting III) was the original and generated the other ('tune 1') as an upper part. The latter eventually broke free of its parent and became the standard tune. Setting III is our combination of these melodies. *Piae Cantiones* prints a two-part version with tune 2 in the tenor and tune 1 beneath it in the bass. This is in fact a reversal of their natural order, since 2 was the original tenor melody and 1 the part that evolved above it. They are found in the correct order in the song-books of Triller (the 1599 edn. of his 1555 *Ein schlesich Singbüchlein . . .*) and Lossius (*Psalm-*

odia, 1553). Triller and Lossius (1561 edn.) give the two tunes with a bass beneath, and Lossius places the Latin text beneath tune 2 (the original) and the German beneath tune 1, instructing that each verse be sung twice, first by the boys to tune 2 with the Latin text, then by 'the whole chorus' to tune 1 with the German. His instructions place the hymn squarely in the *Wechselgesang* ('antiphonal song') tradition (see Appendix 2). (We have made small amendments to both the text and the two tunes as they appear in *Piae Cantiones*. Verse 2 as given there has a defective rhyme, and we replace it with the corresponding verse from the Hereford Breviary.)

There are endless harmonizations of 'Puer natus' in sixteenth-century and later song-books. (See list in G. R. Woodward's edition of *Piae Cantiones*, 1910, pp. 227–8.) Praetorius published settings in *Musae Sioniae*, V (1607) and VI (1609); and there is a large-scale setting in his *Polyhymnia Caduceatrix et Panegyrica* (1619). There are chorale preludes on the tune by Buxtehude, Walther, and Bach.

PERFORMANCE I, voices, with organ and/or other instruments *ad lib.*

II, choir and organ, perhaps with the instrumentation of Bach's Cantata (see above).

III. Each verse may be sung twice, first in Latin and then in English/German:

Latin: sopranos sing tune 2, (*i*) unaccompanied, (*ii*) with organ continuo, or (*iii*) with other voices or instruments; in this last case the small-note alto part should be sung or played and tune 1 sung as the tenor.

English/German: voices and organ (other instruments *ad lib.*). The audience/congregation sings tune 1.

In some sources only one tune (2) is to be sung, with alternating Latin (lines 1, 3) and vernacular (lines 2, 4) texts.

To form a high choir of instruments and voices for the Latin verses, the parts (in descending order) are as follows:

alto (small notes), instruments, up an octave with voice(s) *ad lib.*;
tune 2, voice(s), at treble pitch;
tune 1, instruments, at notated (treble) pitch with voice(s) *ad lib.*;
bass, instruments, up an octave with voice(s) *ad lib.*

Superscript repeat signs in the text indicate which portions should be repeated at the end of the first phrase. Initial small-note crotchets within these repeat signs indicate that an extra upbeat should be sung for this repeat (bar 4 in settings I and II; bar 2 in setting III).

55

Resonet in laudibus
Let the voice of praise resound
Joseph, lieber Joseph mein
Joseph, dearest Joseph mine

I

(Christmas)

Fourteenth-century?
(Aosta MS 9–E–19)

1. Re - so - ne - mus lau - di - bus_ Cum jo-cun - di - ta - ti - bus_ Ec - cle - si - am fi -

-de - li - bus. Ap - pa - ru - it___ quem ge - nu - it___ Ma - ri - a.

2 Deus fecit hominem
  Ad suam imaginem
  Et similitudinem.

3 Deus fecit omnia,
  Celum, terram, maria,
  Cunctaque nascentia.

4 Ergo nostro concio
  In chordis et organo
  Benedicat Domino,

5 Et Deo qui venias
  Donat et leticias
  Nos eidem gracias.

Fourteenth-century
(Aosta MS 9–E–19)

TRANSLATION 1 Let us make the church resound with the merry praises of the faithful. He whom Mary bore hath appeared.
  2 God made man in his own image and likeness.
  3 God made all things, the heavens, the earth, the seas, and whatever has been born.
  4 Therefore let our company bless the Lord with strings and instrument,
  5 and let it give thanks to the same God, who gives us pardon and joys.

II

(*Christmas*)

Fifteenth-century
(S. Gall MS)

VERSE

1. Re - so - net in lau - di - bus Cum ju - cun - dis plau - si - bus Si - on cum fi -
1. Let the voice of praise re-sound, Signs of joy be all a-round, Heaven and earth with

REFRAIN

-de - li - bus: Ap - pa - ru - it quem ge - nu - it Ma - ri - a!
songs a-bound: A Child is born, the Christ, the Son of Ma - ry!

2 Christus natus hodie
   Ex Maria Virgine
† Sine virili semine:

3 Pueri, concinite,
   Nato Regi psallite,
   Voce pia dicite:

4 Sion, lauda Dominum,
   Salvatorem hominum,
   Purgatorem criminum:

2 Our salvation is begun;
   Mary now doth bear a Son;
   Earthly father hath he none:

3 Come, ye choirs, and reverently
   Praise your King on bended knee;
   Sing in sweetest harmony:

4 Sion, praise your God alway,
   Earth's Redeemer, born today!
   All our sins he'll purge away,
   The Child that's born, . . .

† ♩♩♩ for III.

174

5 Deo laus et gloria,
Virtus et victoria,
Perpete memoria:

(Mainz Cantual, 1605)

5 Triumph-songs to God we raise;
His the glory, his the praise
Unto all the length of days:

tr. editors

III

(Christmas)

(Mainz Cantual, 1605,
arr. editors)

1. Re - so - net in lau - di - bus Cum ju - cun - dis
1. Let the voice of praise re - sound, Signs of joy be

plau - si - bus Si - on cum fi - de - li - bus: Ap -
all a - round, Heaven and earth with songs a - bound: A

[**Fine** *ad lib.*
or v.s. for optional refrain]

-pa - ru - it quem ge - nu - it Ma - ri - a!
Child is born, the Christ, the Son of Ma - ry!

Is - ra - el: Ex Ma - ri - a Vir - gi - ne est
Is - ra - el: Vir - gin-born this bless - ed morn, our

na - tus Rex. Mag - num No - men Do - mi - ni E -
King is he. O pro - claim the might - y name: Em -

- ma - nu - el, Quod an - nun - ci - a - tum est per Ga - bri - el.
- ma - nu - el! Ga - bri - el from hea - ven came that name to tell.

IV

JOSEPH:

2 Gerne, liebe Muhme mein,
   helf' ich dir wiegen dein Kindelein!
   Gott, der wird mein Lohner sein
   im Himmelreich, der Jungfrau Kind Maria.

(FIRST) ATTENDANT:

3 Freu' dich nun, du christlich' Schar!
   Gott, der Himmelskönig klar,
   macht uns Menschen offenbar
   der uns gebar die reine Magd Maria.

(SECOND) ATTENDANT:

4 Alle Menschen sollen gar
   ganz in Freuden kommen dar,
   dass ein jeder recht erfahr',
   den uns gebar die reine Magd Maria.

(THIRD) ATTENDANT:

5 Uns erschien Emanuel,
   wie uns verkündet Gabriel,
   und bezeugt Ezechiel:
   Du Mensch ohn' Fehl', dich hat gebor'n
      Maria!

(FOURTH) ATTENDANT:

6 Ew'gen Vaters ew'ges Wort,
   wahrer Gott, der Tugend Hort,
   irdisch hier, im Himmel dort
   der Seelen Pfort', die uns gebar Maria.

FULL (*or* THE FOUR ATTENDANTS):

7 Süsser Jesu, auserkorn,
   weisst wohl, dass wir war'n verlorn:
   Stille deines Vaters Zorn.
   Dich hat geborn die reine Magd Maria.

JOSEPH:

2 Gladly, dear one, lady mine,
   I will rock this child of thine;
   Heavenly light on us both shall shine
   In paradise, as prays the mother Mary.

(FIRST) ATTENDANT:

3 Peace to all that have good will!
   God, who heaven and earth doth fill,
   Comes to turn us away from ill,
   And lies so still within the crib of Mary.

(SECOND) ATTENDANT:

4 All shall come and bow the knee;
   Wise and happy they shall be,
   Loving such a Divinity,
   As all may see in Jesus, Son of Mary.

(THIRD) ATTENDANT:

5 Now is born Emmanuel
   As foretold by Ezekiel,
   Promised Mary by Gabriel;
   Ah! who can tell thy praises, Son of Mary!

(FOURTH) ATTENDANT:

6 Thou my heart with love hast stirred,
   Thou, the Father's eternal Word,
   Virtue's shining treasure-hoard,
   Who ne'er demurred to be the Son of Mary.

FULL (*or* THE FOUR ATTENDANTS):

7 Sweet and lovely little one,
   Princely, beauteous, God's own Son,
   Without thee were we all undone:
   Our love is won by thine, O Son of Mary.

8 Himmlisch' Kind, o grosser Gott,
  leidest in der Krippen Not.
  Machst die Sünder frei vom Tod,
  du englisch' Brot, das uns gebar Maria.

(*Leipzig University MS, c.1400, modernized*)

8 Heavenly Child, thou Lord of all,
  Meanly housed in ox's stall,
  Free our souls, in Satan's thrall:
  On thee we call, thou blessèd Son of Mary.

tr. Percy Dearmer (1867–1936), adapted editors

(*Christmas*)

(*Mainz Cantual, 1605,
arr. editors*)

This has long been one of the most popular of all Christmas songs in Germany, where it is sung to two quite distinct texts: 'Resonet in laudibus', which dates probably from the fourteenth century, and 'Joseph, lieber Joseph mein', which may be even older.

'Resonet in laudibus' may have begun as a *Benedicamus* substitute (see notes, 9). It survives in that form in the earliest source, the Moosburg Gradual (University Library, Munich, MS 2° 156), which was copied between 1355 and 1360. Each verse in this monophonic version has a refrain drawn from the ancient hymn 'Magnum Nomen Domini' (56). Possibly even earlier is our version I, from another fourteenth-century manuscript, in Aosta in Italy (Seminary Library, MS 9–E–19), which contains *Benedicamus* substitutes for the entire year. Setting II, in which the melody is nearer the classic form, is a *binatim* setting (see notes, 10) from a mid-fifteenth-century manuscript copied at the Swiss monastery of S. Gall (MS 392).

Versions I and II represent the 'simple' form of the song, while settings III and IV, both from the early seventeenth century, represent the antiphonal *Wechselgesang* tradition. 'Joseph, lieber' (IV) is sung in English-speaking countries, though mostly in unsatisfactory versions; 'Resonet in laudibus' (III) is known by only distantly connected English texts, of which J. M. Neale's 'Christ was born on Christmas Day' is the best known, and it is nearly always shorn of its refrain. In either form this song is one of the glories of German hymnody and deserves better treatment.

The text 'Joseph, lieber Joseph mein' is first found in a Leipzig University manuscript (MS 1305) of *c*.1400. This quasi-dramatic song has a refrain similar to the one in the Moosburg gradual, drawing on 'Magnum Nomen Domini'. 'Joseph, lieber' was incorporated into various church dramas and may have been devised specifically for such use. The melodies of settings III and IV are from a Catholic book, the Mainz *Catholisch Cantual* (1605). The text of III is from the same source, while for IV we have preferred a modern High-German transliteration of the early Leipzig version.

The roots of the *Wechselgesang* tradition are in pre-Reformation Bohemia, from where it was adopted and brought to its fullest flowering by German Lutherans in their Christmas Night ante-communion services which replaced the former masses at midnight and dawn. Its essence is the alternation or 'exchange' (*Wechsel*) of whole sections of extended songs between different groups of voices and instruments placed strategically around the church (see Appendix 2): clergy, the unison *chorus choralis* and congregation, polyphonic *chorus musicus*, organ, and often other groups such as boys in high galleries (as in 'Quem pastores laudavere', 57) or singing actors (as in the present carol; see below). The songs were often complex constructions, 'assemblies' of different carols in Latin and German which gave extensive opportunity for antiphony, mostly between fairly substantial sections and therefore quite different from the line-by-line antiphony of the macaronic tradition (see notes, 59, and Appendix 2).

'Resonet' (III) and 'Joseph, lieber' (IV) were frequently sung in combination or separately as *Wechselgesänge* of a fairly straightforward type, their intertwined Latin and German texts concluding with a refrain; the different short sections were taken by different groups. Performance customs were so diverse that almost any division of the sections between different groups is possible.

Lutherans in America, who have revived the *Wechselgesang* in a modified and vernacular form, tend to give verses to children's choir and divide refrains between choir and congregation so that the last section is congregational. The Leipzig University MS contains a short drama around the church crib, in the course of which a *Wechselgesang* is to be sung, interweaving the Latin and German texts with a strophic form of 'Magnum Nomen'. Brief rubrics for a similar performance at about this time are quoted by Heinrich Hoffman von Fallersleben (*Geschichte der deutschen Kirchenlieder*, 1861, p. 418). (For other ways of singing 'Joseph, lieber Joseph mein' see C. A. P. Wackernagel, *Das deutsche Kirchenlied* . . . , Leipzig, 1864–77, vol. II, nos. 605–10.)

'Resonet in laudibus' was particularly associated with the medieval custom of cradle-rocking which flourished in Rhineland nunneries. By the late Middle Ages cradles were being enthusiastically rocked at Christmas vespers and matins throughout Germany and the Low Countries. Typically, the cradle would stand before the altar, with a brightly coloured Christ-child visible within, and the priest would rock it in time to the triple-time music of the appropriate *Wiegenlied* (cradle-song) carols, with the lullaby refrain 'Eia! eia!' and sometimes also 'Susani! susani!' (see 'Schlaf wohl, du Himmelsknabe du', 178, and 'Vom Himmel hoch, o Englein, kommt!', 64, for example.) In one church in the Netherlands in the sixteenth century there were two cradles, one on the altar and a small one in the congregation, hung about with bells, which the children in the congregation would rock whenever the priest rocked the larger one. Cradles were also carried about the streets by groups of carol-singing children, who would rock them in a similar manner while singing cradle-songs.

'Joseph, lieber' was sung not only at Christmastime but also at weddings, the loving family relationship it depicts being seen as the archetype of the perfect Christian marriage. Perhaps it was in connection with a marriage—or as a private joke?—that Mozart wrote the original second movement of his early Symphony in E flat, K132, which quotes the later, decorated version of the tune with which he was familiar.

Vigorous dancing was associated with 'Resonet in laudibus' in late medieval times. Witzel, in his *Psaltes Ecclesiasticus* (1550), describes the old custom of erecting a crib in church depicting the town of Bethlehem, around which on Christmas Eve and during Christmas Night boys would leap to express their joy, singing 'Resonet in laudibus' and clapping their hands, presumably in time to the music: the 'plausibus' ('with the clapping of hands') of verse 1 was thus not always a figure of speech. (See also Suso's account of dancing with angels to 'In dulci jubilo', 59, in what sounds like a true *carole*.)

Simple dramatic presentations of 'Resonet in laudibus' (in many cases nearer to *tableaux vivants* than true dramas) were kept up in both Catholic and Lutheran churches until the early eighteenth century, and could be adapted for modern carol services or Christmas masses. The characters could be in costume, with singers and musicians grouped around Mary and Joseph on either side of a large cradle containing an image of the infant. There could be four attendants (SATB voices) to sing the designated verses. The singing of 'A solis ortus cardine' (4) and/or 'Christum wir sollen loben schon' (61) begins the drama, perhaps with a processional entrance, each verse sung first in Latin and then in German. Mary rocks the cradle (with bells?) in time to the singing of verse 1 of 'Resonet', sung by full choir with instruments and organ; she ceases her rocking, rises, and sings verse 1 of 'Joseph, lieber Joseph mein' to her husband, with continuo accompaniment. (A short ritornello could be inserted here, and at equivalent spots.) Joseph helps her to rock during verse 2 of 'Resonet', and then stands to sing verse 2 of 'Joseph, lieber', and for all the remaining verses he and Mary continue to rock the cradle, together or in turn. The attendants' verses follow, and, when the two intertwined settings are completed, the refrain should be sung, from either III or IV; the congregation could join unison choir and organ for 'Magnum Nomen Domini'.

Among a number of hymns and songs inspired by 'Resonet' are 'En! natus est Emanuel' (53), and Nicolai's tune for his own 'Wie schön leuchtet der Morgenstern' (69). Among the many vocal settings are two by Johann Walther

(à 4, 1544; à 5, 1551), Lucas Osiander (à 4, 1586), Michael Praetorius (*Musae Sioniae*, V, 1607, nos. 87, 90, 101; VI, 1609, nos. 46, 47, 48, 54), Seth Calvisius (à 6, in E. Bodenschatz, *Florilegium Portense*, 1618), and there is an eight-part setting by Hieronymus Praetorius (1560–1629), to be sung in alternation with the verses of his 1622 *Magnificat* (modern edition 1980), in accordance with German Christmas custom. (The first version of Bach's *Magnificat* is a late example of this tradition.)

PERFORMANCE   I, verses 1–4, soli; verse 5, full; refrains, full.

II, verse, soli; refrain, full.

III, IV (without refrains): (*i*) choir, with instruments and/or organ *ad lib.*; (*ii*) unison voices and organ.

III, IV (with refrains): (*i*) as simple hymns, verse, choir with instruments and/or organ *ad lib.*; refrain, full, unison voices and organ, or with different groups taking all sections but the last, which may be full; (*ii*) as a *Wechselgesang* (the two combined): see notes above; (*iii*) dramatic presentation: see notes above.

When a congregation participates, transposition down a tone is advisable.

56

Magnum Nomen Domini Emanuel
O proclaim the mighty Name Emmanuel!

(*Christmas*)

Fourteenth-century?
(Praetorius, 1609, arr. editors)

Mag - num No - men Do - mi - ni___ E - ma - nu - el,
O pro - claim the might - y Name___ Em - ma - nu - el!

Quod an - nun - ci - a - tum est___ per Ga - bri - el!
Ga - bri - el from hea - ven came___ that Name to tell.

Ho - di - e ap - pa - ru - it, ap - pa - ru - it in
And___ to - day he comes___ to dwell, he comes___ to dwell in___

Is - ra - el;
Is - ra - el;   Per Ma - ri - am Vir - gi - nem in
____ Is - ra - el;   Vir - gin - born in Beth - le - hem, that
Is - ra - el;

Beth - le - hem. E - ja! e - ja! Vir - go De - um
fair ci - ty. E - ia! e - ia! Maid - en's womb a

ge - nu - it, Si - cut di - vi - na vo - lu - it cle -
God___ doth bear; The heaven - ly Fa - ther's ten - der care doth

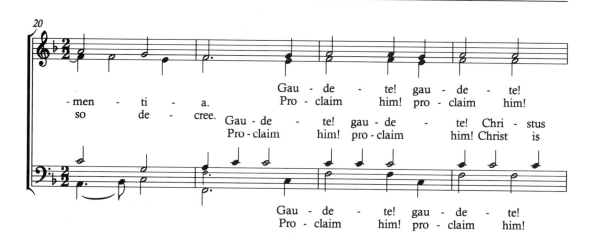

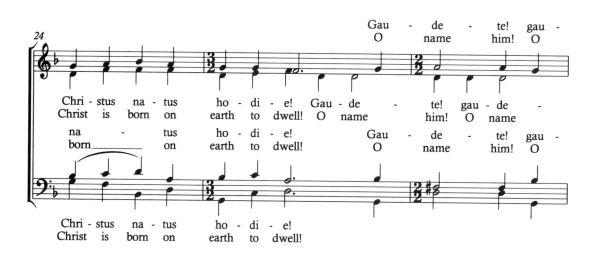

Scarcely known in Britain, this noble Christmas hymn has a special place in German hymnody, both Catholic and Lutheran. Besides being sung in its own right, it forms the conclusion to each verse of some of the classic *Wechselgesänge* ('antiphonal songs'—see notes, 55). Its non-strophic structure suggests an ancient origin, and it did, indeed, develop out of a rhyming plainchant antiphon. (See Wulf Arlt, *Ein Festoffizium* . . . , 1970, where it is given and discussed as the antiphon to the first psalm at compline on New Year's Day at Beauvais Cathedral.) Bars 1–13 derive from the chant melody, and the text is almost identical. In German pre-Reformation churches, certain plainchant items entered the burgeoning congregational repertory as a result of being sung jointly, usually in translation, by the *chorus choralis* (plainchant choir) and congregation (see Appendix 2).

We take the melody and text from Praetorius's *Musae Sioniae* (VI, 1609, no. 54). The earliest source in which 'Magnum Nomen' occurs in its modern form is the Leipzig University MS no. 1305 (*c*.1400). It there forms part of a *Wechselgesang* based on 'Resonet in laudibus' and 'Joseph, lieber Joseph mein' (see notes, 55).

A curious feature of the hymn is that it takes on a different form when it is part of a *Wechselgesang*: of the four sections, the last (bars 21–9) is never found, and the other three (sometimes slightly extended) are frequently re-ordered, with the third (14–21) often forming the conclusion. The opening of the melody of 'Magnum Nomen' is also different in *Wechselgesänge*, always echoing the opening of 'Resonet in laudibus': perhaps the 'Resonet' sequence was the earliest of such constructs when the tradition grew up in Bohemia, and 'Magnum Nomen' retained the 'Resonet' opening when it was later incorporated in other songs.

PERFORMANCE (*i*) Choir, with instruments or organ *ad lib.*; (*ii*) voices and organ; (*iii*) in antiphony between groups of voices and instruments, etc., with congregation joining in in bars 21–9; or a Latin antiphonal verse could be followed by a full repeat, with congregation, in the vernacular.

57

Quem pastores laudavere
Shepherds sang their praises o'er him

Fourteenth-century
(arr. Michael Praetorius, 1571–1621,
adapted editors)

(Christmas)

1. Quem pas - to - res lau - da - ve - re, Qui - bus an - ge - li dix - e - re:
1. Shep-herds sang their prai - ses o'er him, Called by an - gels to a - dore him:

'Ab - sit vo - bis jam ti - me - re: Na - tus est_ Rex Glo - ri - ae!'
'Have no fear, but come be - fore him: Born_ is now_ your glo - rious King!'

2 Ad quem magi ambulabant,
   Aurum, thus, myrrham portabant;
   Immolabant haec sincere
   Leoni victoriae;

2 Eastern sages came to view him,
   Judah's conquering Lion knew him,
   Gold, and myrrh, and incense to him
   As their tribute offering.

*3 Exsultemus cum Maria
    In coelesti hierarchia:
    Natum promant voce pia
    Dulci cum melodia;

4   Christo Regi, Deo nato,
    Per Mariam nobis dato,
    Merito resonet vere:
    'Laus, honor, et gloria!'

Fourteenth-century
(*Praetorius, 1607, adapted*)

*3 On this Child, rejoicing, gaze we;
    Led by Mary, anthems raise we;
    Reverently, with angels, praise we
    With the sweetest melody.

4   Christ our King, from Mary springing,
    God made man, salvation bringing,
    Thee we worship, ever singing:
    'Honour, praise, and glory be!'

Free tr., editors

TRANSLATION Even in its original three-verse form (verses 1, 2, and 4) the literal sense of this text is difficult to tease out, mainly because the principal verb ('resonet') is in the penultimate line: '[v. 1] Unto him whom the shepherds praised, told by the angels "Be not afraid: the King of Glory is born!"; [v. 2] unto him to whom the magi journeyed, to whom they brought gold, frankincense and myrrh, to whom, the victorious Lion [of Judah; see Revelation 5:5], they offered these things with sincerity; [v. 4] unto [him,] Christ the King, the Son of God, given to us through Mary, let "Praise, honour and glory!" right worthily resound!'

Verse 3 was a later addition to this elegant grammatical construction, and takes no account of its single-sentence context. Best seen as a free-standing interpolation, it reads: 'Let us rejoice with Mary in the heavenly hierarchy [of angels]: they praise the Infant in reverent tones [and] with sweet melody.'

The original verses emphasize the kingship of the new-born Christ. This theme is underlined by the reference in verse 4 to the Palm Sunday processional hymn 'Laus, honor et gloria', which was sung at town gates, the west doors of cathedrals, etc., in symbolic re-enactment of Christ's quasi-royal entry into Jerusalem shortly before his death; compare also the acclamations in Revelation 5:12–13.

'Quem pastores' has two distinct manners of performance in both the Catholic and Lutheran liturgies: as a conventional hymn, and (until the eighteenth century in most places) as part of one of the distinctive *Wechselgesänge* ('antiphonal songs'—see notes, 55) of Germanic Christmas hymnody. When performed *in Wechsel* it is sung by four boys (or groups of boys in unison, or even small consorts or choirs) who stand holding candles, ideally in high galleries on four sides of the church. Each sings one line of each

four-line stanza, so that the tune seems to revolve in the air, as if sung by circling angels, and each 'angelic' verse evokes the 'pastoral' response of the equivalent verse of the hymn 'Nunc angelorum gloria' from the main choir below.

The Lutherans associated such performances with vespers of Christmas Eve and the torchlit *Christnacht* (Christmas Night) ante-communion service, when the annunciation to the shepherds was a central theme. In other contexts 'Quem pastores' could be sung alone in the normal manner, as we give it here. The setting is from volume V (1607) of Praetorius's *Musae Sioniae* (see notes, 53); as in all his settings, the melody of the fourth strain rises to the dominant, something we have found in no other source. We have adapted it so that it ends on the tonic in the usual way. Verse 3, as we have already noted, was a later addition, and may be omitted. (Praetorius begins it ♩ ♩ ♩ 'Et exsultemus . . . '.)

An effective and apparently unique manner of performance is given by Johann Hermann Schein (1586–1630) in his *Cantional* (1627/45), and could be applied to the present setting. (Schein may have been reflecting practice at the Leipzig Thomaskirche, of which he was cantor, or he may have been adapting the usual lengthy *Wechselgesang* for use in smaller churches with limited forces and shorter liturgies.) 'Nunc angelorum' is not given, and 'Quem pastores' is divided among three choirs (presumably in high galleries), each of which sings one of the first three lines of each verse, all three combining for the final line.

PERFORMANCE (*i*) Choir, with instruments *ad lib.* (see Appendix 2); (*ii*) voices and organ; (*iii*) three choirs (see above).

58

Nun komm, der Heiden Heiland
Saviour of the Gentiles, come!

I

(Advent)

Sixteenth-century
(arr. Seth Calvisius, 1556–1615)

1. Nun komm, der Hei - den__ Hei - land, der Jung - frau - en Kind er - kannt,
1. Sa - viour of the Gen - tiles, come! Born for us the Vir - gin's Son;

des sich wun-der' al - le__ Welt, Gott solch Ge-burt ihm__ be-stellt.
God doth grant this won - drous birth: Awe and won-der fill__ the earth. A - men.

After doxology

II

Sixteenth-century
(arr. J. S. Bach, 1685–1750)

1. Nun__ komm, der__ Hei - den__ Hei - land, der__ Jung - frau - en
1. Sa - viour of__ the__ Gen - tiles, come! Born__ for us__ the

Kind er - kannt, des sich wun - der' al - le Welt,
Vir - gin's Son; God doth grant this won - drous birth:

Gott solch' Ge - burt ihm be - stellt. A - men.
Awe and won - der fill the earth.

After doxology

2 Er ging aus der Kammer sein,
   dem kön'glichen Saal so rein,
   Gott von Art und Mensch ein Held;
   sein' Weg er zu laufen eilt.

3 Sein Lauf kam vom Vater her
   und kehrt' wieder zum Vater,
   fuhr hinunter zu der Höll'
   und wieder zu Gottes Stuhl.

4 Dein Krippen glänzt hell und klar,
   die Nacht gibt ein neu' Licht dar.
   Dunkel muss nicht kommen drein,
   der Glaub' bleibt immer im Schein.

5 Lob sei Gott, dem Vater, g'tan;
   Lob sei Gott sei'm ein'gen Sohn,
   Lob sei Gott, dem Heil'gen Geist,
   immer und in Ewigkeit.

2 His high chamber leaveth he,
   Royal seat of purity,
   God and man, in substance one,
   Who a Hero's course will run.

3 Down from heaven he doth descend:
   Back to heaven he will ascend;
   When he's conquered death and hell
   On his Father's throne he'll dwell.

4 Shines thy crib so bright and clear,
   Night doth set a new star here;
   Darkness hence must keep away:
   Faith dwells in the light of day.

5 Praise be to the Father sung,
   Praise to God his only Son,
   Praise to God the Paraclete,
   Now and ever, as is meet.

St Ambrose (339–97)
tr. Martin Luther (1483–1546), modernized

tr. editors, partly after J. M. Neale (1818–66),
George MacDonald (1824–1905), et al.

The text is Luther's own translation of the Advent office hymn 'Veni, Redemptor gencium' (2), which is sung nowadays during both the Advent and Christmas seasons. It appeared in the first Lutheran hymn-book, *Etlich cristlich Lider Lobgesang und Psalm* (Wittenberg, 1523–4), which also included his translation of 'A solis ortus cardine', 'Christum wir sollen loben schon' (61). The melody is an adaptation (possibly also by Luther himself) of the plainchant, and was printed in the Erfurt *Enchiridion* of 1524.

Setting I is by Seth Calvisius (or Kalwitz) in his *Hymni Sacri Latini et Germanici* (1594). Setting II is the conclusion of Bach's Cantata 36, *Schwingt freudig euch empor*, where the text is the last verse of 'Nun komm, der Heiden Heiland'.

There is no acceptable existing English translation that fits this rather awkward metre, so we have retranslated the text, adapting and conflating a number of existing attempts, to allow the noble melody to be sung by English-speaking congregations.

PERFORMANCE I, voices and instruments and/or organ; II, choir and organ, perhaps with Bach's instrumentation.

---

2 *O Jesu parvule,*

   nach dir ist mir so weh.

      Tröst mir mein Gemüte,

   o Puer optime;

      durch alle deine Güte,

   o Princeps Gloriae,

   trahe me post te!

3 *O Patris caritas!*

   O Nati lenitas!

      Wir wärn all' verloren

   per nostra crimina;

      so hat er uns erworben

   coelorum gaudia;

   eia, wärn wir da!

4 *Ubi sunt gaudia?*

   Nirgends mehr denn da,

      da die Engel singen

   nova cantica,

      und die Schellen klingen

   in Regis curia;

   Eia, wärn wir da!

   vv. 1, 2, 4 fourteenth-century
   v. 3 Valentin Triller (d.1573)
   (Praetorius, 1607)

---

2 *O Jesu parvule,*[5]

   I yearn for thee alway!

      Comfort me and stay me,

   O Puer optime;[6]

      By thy great love I pray thee,

   O Princeps Gloriae,

   Trahe me post te![7]

3 *O Patris caritas!*

   O Nati lenitas![8]

      Condemned we had remainèd

   Per nostra crimina;[9]

      But he for us hath gainèd

   Coelorum gaudia:[10]

   In paradise afar,

   Where joys unending are.

4 *Ubi sunt gaudia*[11]

   More deep than heaven's are?

      In heaven are angels singing

   Nova cantica,[12]

      In heaven the bells are ringing

   In Regis curia.[13]

   O that we were there!

   tr. editors

---

[5] O infant Jesus [6] O best of boys [7] O Prince of Glory, draw me after you [to heaven] [8] O love of the Father! O mercy of the Son! [9] through our sins [10] the joys of heaven [11] Where are joys(?) [12] new songs [13] in the courts of the King

59

In dulci jubilo
Good Christian men, rejoice!

(Christmas)

I

Thirteenth-century?
(arr. Michael Praetorius, 1571–1621)

1. *In dul - ci ju - bi - lo,*[1]_____ nun sing - et und seid
   Let songs___ and glad - ness

   froh!_____ Un - sers Her - zen Won - ne leit *in prae - se - pi -*
   flow!_____ All our joy re - cli - neth___

   - o,[2]_____ und leuch - tet als die Son - ne *ma - tris in gre - mi -*
   And like the sun he shi - neth

   - o,[3]_____ *Al - pha es et O!*[4]_____ *Al - pha es___ et O!*_____

[1] with sweet jubilation   [2] in a manger   [3] in [your] mother's lap   [4] You are Alpha and Omega.

193

II

(*Christmas*)

Thirteenth-century?
(*arr. J. S. Bach, 1685–1750*)

1. *In dul - ci ju - bi - lo,*[1] _____ nun sing - et und_ seid froh!_____
Let songs and glad - ness flow!_____

in prae - se - pi - o,[2] _____

Un - sers Her - zen Won ____ ne leit   *in prae - se - pi - o,*[2] _____ und
All our joy_ re - cli ____ neth_   *in_ prae - se - pi - o,*[2] And

in_ prae - se - pi - o,[2]

ma - tris in gre - mi - o.[3] _____

leuch - tet als_ die Son ____ ne   *ma - tris_ in gre ____ mi - o.*[3]
like_ the sun_ he shi ____ neth   *ma - tris_ in gre - mi - o.*[3]

ma - tris_ in gre ____ mi - o.[3]

[1] with sweet jubilation   [2] in a manger   [3] in [your] mother's lap

194

Alpha es et O!

Alpha es et O!

Alpha es et O!

Alpha es et O!⁴

Alpha es et O!

2 *O Jesu parvule,*
    nach dir ist mir so weh.
        Tröst mir mein Gemüte,
    o Puer optime;
        durch alle deine Güte,
    o Princeps Gloriae,
    trahe me post te!

3 *O Patris caritas!*
    O Nati lenitas!
        Wir wärn all' verloren
    per nostra crimina;
        so hat er uns erworben
    coelorum gaudia;
        eia, wärn wir da!

4 *Ubi sunt gaudia?*
    Nirgends mehr denn da,
        da die Engel singen
    nova cantica,
        und die Schellen klingen
    in Regis curia;
    Eia, wärn wir da!

2 *O Jesu parvule,*[5]
    I yearn for thee alway!
        Comfort me and stay me,
    O Puer optime;[6]
        By thy great love I pray thee,
    O Princeps Gloriae,
    Trahe me post te![7]

3 *O Patris caritas!*
    O Nati lenitas![8]
        Condemned we had remainèd
    Per nostra crimina;[9]
        But he for us hath gainèd
    Coelorum gaudia:[10]
    In paradise afar,
    Where joys unending are.

4 *Ubi sunt gaudia*[11]
    More deep than heaven's are?
        In heaven are angels singing
    Nova cantica,[12]
        In heaven the bells are ringing
    In Regis curia.[13]
    O that we were there!

vv. 1, 2, 4 fourteenth-century
v. 3 Valentin Triller (d.1573)
(Praetorius, 1607)

tr. editors

[4] You are Alpha and Omega.   [5] O infant Jesus   [6] O best of boys   [7] O Prince of Glory, draw me after you [to heaven]
[8] O love of the Father! O mercy of the Son!   [9] through our sins   [10] the joys of heaven   [11] Where are joys(?)
[12] new songs   [13] in the courts of the King

III

Thirteenth-century?
(*Piae Cantiones, 1582,
arr. John Stainer, 1840–1901*)

(*Christmas*)

1. Good Christ-ian men, re - joice___ With heart and soul___ and voice!___

Give ye heed to what we say: News! news! Je - sus Christ is born to-day!

Ox and ass be - fore him bow, And he is in___ the man - ger now:

Christ is born to - day!___ Christ is born to - day!

2   Good Christian men, rejoice
With heart and soul, and voice!
Now ye hear of endless bliss:
Joy! joy!
Jesus Christ was born for this!
He hath oped the heavenly door,
And man is blessèd evermore:
Christ was born for this!

3   Good Christian men, rejoice
With heart and soul, and voice!
Now ye need not fear the grave:
Peace! peace!
Jesus Christ was born to save!
Calls you one and calls you all,
To gain his everlasting hall:
Christ was born to save!

English version by J. M. Neale (1818–66)

'In dulci jubilo' is usually said to have been taught to the mystic Heinrich Seuse (Suso) by angels. Suso (*c.*1295–1366) was a German Dominican monk, who at the age of eighteen assumed the role of 'Servant of the Eternal Wisdom'. He was a friend of the poet and fellow Dominican Johannes Tauler (see notes, 179) and studied with the great mystic Meister Eckhart. Suso achieved fame as a spiritual director of women's convents and for his *Das Büchlein der ewigen Weisheit* ('The Little Book of the Eternal Wisdom'), written in 1328. This autobiography is written in the third person, Suso always referring to himself as 'the Servant'. It contains accounts of repeated visionary experiences, many involving heavenly music, the most famous concerning 'In dulci jubilo':

After he had spent many hours in contemplating the joys of the angels and daybreak was at hand, there came to him a youth, who bore himself as though he were a heavenly musician sent to him by God; and with the youth there came many other noble youths, in manner and bearing like the first, save only that he seemed to have some pre-eminence above the rest, as if he were a prince-angel. Now this same angel came up to the Servant right blithely, and said that God had sent him down to him, to bring him heavenly joys amid his sufferings; adding that he must cast off all his sorrows from his mind and bear them company, and that he must also dance with them in heavenly fashion. Then they drew the Servant by the hand into the dance, and the youth began a joyous song about the infant Jesus, which runs thus: 'In dulci jubilo', etc. When the Servant heard the beloved name of Jesus sounding thus so sweetly, he became so joyful in his heart and feeling that the very memory of his sufferings vanished. It was a joy to him to see how exceedingly loftily and freely they bounded in the dance. The leader of the song knew right well how to guide them, and he sang first, and they sang after him in the jubilee of their hearts. Thrice the leader repeated the burden of the song, 'Ergo meritis', etc. This dance was not of the kind that are danced on earth, but it was a heavenly movement, swelling up and falling back again into the wild abyss of God's hiddenness . . . (*The Life of Blessed H. Suso, by Himself*, ch. 7, tr. T. F. Knox, 1865, adapted).

Suso does not suggest that the song was unknown to him, and this account follows others in which heavenly musicians perform known plainchant antiphons, responsories, etc. What his autobiography does tell us is that some version of the song existed before 1328, though the refrain 'Ergo meritis' is not known. The combination of a leader, a repeated refrain, and what sounds like a round-dance brings the angelic performance very close to the *carole* (see Introduction). There is an account of rougher human dancing to 'Resonet in laudibus' (see notes, 55), and it may be that religious dance-songs were a more widespread phenomenon than has been supposed.

'In dulci jubilo' is believed to be the oldest of all German macaronic (mixed-language) hymns, and it is almost unique in that the sense of the verse flows on regardless of changes of language: in 'Puer natus in Bethlehem' (54) the two languages are merely in opposition, the song having originally been sung *either* in Latin *or* in German.

The earliest source, with both text and music, is a Leipzig University MS of *c.*1400 (MS 1305, which also contains the earliest version of 'Joseph, lieber Joseph mein', 55:IV), where 'In dulci jubilo' is a single-stanza dance-song. This had expanded to four stanzas by the fifteenth century, with the vernacular lines in a variety of Low German and Dutch dialects. The final verse began 'Mater et filia' and was too Marian for Protestant use; Joseph Klug therefore omitted it when he gave the song its first Lutheran printing in the 1533 edition of his *Geistliche Lieder*. However, Valentin Triller reinstated it in a new Protestant adaptation (which has frequently been attributed to Luther) in his Leipzig song-book of 1545. He also moved this adapted fourth stanza to become the new stanza three, a reordering which improved the flow of sense and has been followed ever since. The first harmonized setting was in Georg Rhau's *Newe deudsche geistliche Gesenge* (Wittenberg, 1544), with the melody in the tenor; countless others followed.

Setting I is one of many by Praetorius, from *Musae Sioniae* (V, 1607, no. 83; see notes, 53). Bach's setting (II, BWV 368, originally in F) is probably from a lost cantata. It was published as no. 150 in *Johann Sebastian Bach's vierstimmige Choralgesänge*, collected by C. P. E. Bach (1769).

Setting III is Stainer's harmonization of the tune as it occurs (with Swedish/Latin text) in *Piae Cantiones* (1582), transcribed by Thomas Helmore. It was an error by Helmore which produced the 'News! news!' (bar 7), a rather pleasing addition which we retain. Neale had already written his free English imitation of the hymn when Helmore gave him his transcription, so he added the extra words and published it in their *Carols for Christmas-tide* (1853–4). Stainer's harmonization first appeared in *Christmas Carols New and Old* (1871).

Other settings by Praetorius include a fine five-part one in *Musae Sioniae*, VI (1609, no. 161). His *Polyhymnia Caduceatrix et Panegyrica* (1618–19) contains another for vast forces which include a choir of trumpets. Choral settings of this favourite hymn are too numerous to list, but among those for organ are two by Bach (BWV 608 and 729; 751 is by Johann Michael Bach) and others by Buxtehude, F. W. Zachau (his Fugue in G), and Walther.

PERFORMANCE   I (*i*) voices, with instruments *ad lib*; (*ii*) voices and organ. II, choir and organ. III, choir.

60

Vom Himmel hoch, da komm' ich her
From highest heaven I come to tell

I

(Christmas)

Martin Luther (1483–1546)
(arr. Michael Praetorius, 1571–1621)

1. 'Vom Him - mel hoch, da komm' ich her, ich bring' euch gu - te neu - e Mär,
1. 'From high - est heaven I come to tell The glad - dest news that e'er be - fell;

der gu - ten Mär bring' ich so viel, da - von ich sing'n und sa - gen will.
These ti - dings true to you I bring, And glad - ly of them say and sing.

II

Martin Luther (1483–1546)
(arr. J. S. Bach, 1685–1750)

1. 'Vom Him-mel hoch, da komm' ich her, ich bring' euch gu - te neu - e Mär, der
1. 'From high - est heaven I come to tell The glad - dest news that e'er be - fell; These

guten_ Mär bring' ich_ so___ viel, da - von ich___ sing'n und sa - gen will.
ti - dings true_ to__ you_ I__ bring, And_ glad - ly_ of__ them say_ and sing.

III

Traditional
(arr. editors)

1. 'Vom Him-mel hoch, da_ komm' ich her, ich bring' euch gu - te__ neu - e Mär, der
1. 'From high-est heaven I__ come to_ tell The glad - dest news that e'er_ be - fell; These

gu - ten Mär bring' ich so viel, da - von ich sing'n und_ sa - gen will.
ti - dings true to you I bring, And glad - ly of them say__ and sing.

2 'Euch ist ein Kindlein heut' gebor'n
von einer Jungfrau, auserkor'n;
ein Kindelein so zart und fein,
das soll eu'r Freud' und Wonne sein.

2 'To you today is given a Child,
Born of a chosen virgin mild;
That blessèd Child, so sweet and kind,
Shall give you joy and peace of mind.

3 'Es ist der Herr Christ unser Gott,
der will euch führ'n aus aller Not,
er will eu'r Heiland selber sein,
von allen Sünden machen rein.

3 ''Tis Christ, our Lord and God indeed,
Your help and stay in every need;
Your Saviour he is come to be,
From every sin to set you free.

4 'Er bringt euch alle Seligkeit,
die Gott, der Vater, hat bereit',
dass ihr mit uns im Himmelreich
sollt leben nun und ewiglich.

4 'All blessèdness to you he bears
Which God the Father's love prepares;
The heavenly kingdom ye shall gain,
And now and ever with us reign.

5 'So merket nun das Zeichen recht,
die Krippen, Windelein so schlecht:
Da findet ihr das Kind gelegt,
das alle Welt erhält und trägt.'

5 'Now hear the sign, and mark with care
The swaddling clothes and crib so bare;
There shall ye find this Infant laid
Who all the world upholds and made.'

6 Des lasst uns alle fröhlich sein
und mit den Hirten geh'n hinein,
zu seh'n, was Gott uns hat beschert,
mit seinem lieben Sohn verehrt.

6 Then let us all our gladness show,
And with the joyful shepherds go
To see what God for us hath done,
In sending us his glorious Son.

7 Merk auf, mein Herz, und sieh dort hin:
Was liegt doch in dem Krippelein?
Was ist das schöne Kindelein?
Es ist das liebe Jesulein.

7 Awake, my soul! my heart, behold
Who lieth in that manger cold!
Who is this lovely baby boy?
'Tis Jesus Christ, our only joy.

8 Sei uns willkomm'n, du edler Gast!
Den Sünder nicht verschmähet hast
und kommst ins Elend her zu mir,
wie soll ich immer danken dir?

8 Now welcome, ever-blessèd guest,
To sinful souls with guilt oppressed;
In mercy come to our distress!
How can we thank thy gentleness?

9 Ach Herr, du Schöpfer aller Ding',
wie bist du 'worden so gering,
dass du da liegst auf dürrem Gras,
davon ein Rind und Esel ass.

9 Ah, Lord, who all things didst create,
How cam'st thou to this poor estate,
To make the hay and straw thy bed,
Whereon the ox and ass are fed?

10 Und wär' die Welt vielmal so weit,
von Edelstein und Gold bereit',
so wär' sie doch dir viel zu klein,
zu sein ein enges Wiegelein.

11 Der Sammet und die Seiden dein,
das ist grob' Heu und Windelein,
darauf du Kön'g, so gross und reich,
her prangst als wär's dein Himmelreich.

12 Das hat also gefallen dir,
die Wahrheit anzuzeigen mir:
Wie aller Welt Macht, Ehr' und Gut
vor dir nichts gilt, nichts hilft noch tut.

13 Ach, mein herzliebes Jesulein,
mach dir ein rein sanft' Bettelein,
zu ruh'n in meines Herzens Schrein,
dass ich nimmer vergesse dein'!

14 Davon ich all'zeit fröhlich sei,
zu springen, singen immer frei
das rechte Susaninne schon,
mit Herzen Lust den süssen Ton.

15 Lob, Ehr' sei Gott im höchsten Thron,
der uns schenkt' seinen ein'gen Sohn;
des freuen sich der Engel Schar'
und singen uns solch's neues Jahr.

Martin Luther (1483–1546),
modernized

10 Nay, were the world ten times so wide,
With gold and gems on every side,
Yet were it all too small to be
A narrow cradle, Lord, for thee.

11 Thy samite and thy silk array
Are swathing-bands and coarsest hay
Which thou, O King, dost bathe with light
As though enthroned in heaven bright.

12 And all this woe hath come to thee
That thou might'st show the truth to me;
For all the power and wealth of earth
To thee are vile and nothing worth.

13 Ah, Jesu, my heart's treasure blest,
Make thee a clean, soft cradle-nest
And rest enshrined within my heart,
That I from thee may never part.

14 So shall I ever more rejoice,
And dance and sing with heart and voice
The truest lullaby e'er known,
A song of love, of sweetest tone.

15 To God on high all praise be done
Who gave for us his only Son
Whose birth the angels carol clear
And sing us all a glad New Year.

vv. 1–2, 4–13 tr. H. R. Bramley (1833–1917), adapted
vv. 3, 14–15 tr. editors

Luther wrote this hymn for his own family celebration of Christmas Eve. It was sung to the tune of a folk-song (III), 'Ich komm aus fremden Landen her', of which Luther's first verse is a parody. The text was published, with this tune, in Klug's *Geistliche Lieder* (1535).

The folk model is actually a *Kranzellied* ('crowning-song'), to which boys would dance together for the reward of a crown presented by the girls. Perhaps dancing was also involved in the first performance of the carol: certainly it formed part of a dramatic presentation, the first five verses being sung by a man dressed as an angel and standing by the domestic crib. The children responded with verses 6–14, and the angel joined in the concluding doxology. Luther was probably inspired by the crib and shepherd dramas of the medieval Church (see notes, 55), which continued to be popular. (Crib ceremonies were later introduced into Lutheran services and flourished in the seventeenth century.)

The grander tune (of settings I and II) was possibly composed by Luther himself, and was given with the hymn in Valentin Schumann's Leipzig song-book of 1539. For a time the two tunes happily coexisted, and they even appeared in harness as the double *cantus firmus* of a five-voice setting of the present hymn by Georg Forster (*c.*1510–68), published in Rhau's *Newe deudsche geistliche Gesenge CXXII* (1544). But the later tune gradually displaced its more homely companion.

(Both tunes were also associated with other texts).

The poet John Wedderburn, brother of James and Robert, worked with Luther in Wittenberg around 1540, and an English (or, rather, Scots) translation appeared in the Wedderburns' *Ane Compendious Buik of Godly and Spirituall Sangis* (generally known as *The Gude and Godlie Ballatis*) of 1567. (Verses 13 and 14 from this were later set by Peter Warlock and Britten as the carol 'Balulalow'.)

Setting I is from Praetorius's *Musae Sioniae* (VI, 1609; see notes, 53). Bach's setting (II) is the closing chorale from Part I of his *Christmas Oratorio*. We have omitted the instrumental interludes and adjusted the end of bar 6, where the vocal and instrumental parts diverge. Setting III is our arrangement of the original folk melody.

PERFORMANCE I, voices and organ with instruments *ad lib.*

II, choir and organ; or as in the *Christmas Oratorio* (see above).

III (*i*) voices; (*ii*) voices and instruments. The original forces are not known. One of the many performance possibilities might be: verses 1–5, tenor (angel) accompanying himself on harp; verses 6–14, children's voices with lute(s); verse 15, full, the children singing the tune (and perhaps also the alto) and the angel singing tenor.

61

Christum wir sollen loben schon
From lands that see the sun arise

(*Christmas*)

Chant
(arr. Lucas Osiander, 1534–1604)

1. Chris-tum wir sol - len lo - ben schon, der rei - nen Magd Ma - ri - en Sohn, so weit die lie - be Son - ne leucht' und an al - ler
1. From lands that see the sun a - rise To earth's re - mo - test boun - da - ries Let e - very heart a - wake, and sing The Son of Ma -

2 Der selig Schöpfer aller Ding'
   zog an ein's Knechtes Leib gering,
   dass er das Fleisch durch Fleisch erwerb',
   und sein' Geschöpf' nicht all's verderb'.

3 Die göttlich' Gnad' von Himmel gross
   sich in die keusche Mutter goss,
   ein Mägdlein trug ein heimlich Pfand,
   das der Natur war unbekannt.

4 Das züchtig' Haus des Herzen zart
   gar bald ein Tempel Gottes ward,
   die kein Mann rühret noch erkannt
   von Gott's Wort sie man schwanger fand.

5 Die edle Mutter hat gebor'n,
   den Gabriel verhiess zuvorn,
   den Sankt Johanns mit Springen zeigt,
   da er noch lag in Mutter Leib.

6 Er lag im Heu mit Armut gross,
   die Krippen hart ihn nicht verdross,
   es ward ein' kleine Milch sein Speis,
   der nie kein Vöglein hungern liess.

2 Behold, the world's Creator wears
   The form and fashion of a slave;
   Our very flesh our Maker shares,
   His fallen creature, man, to save.

3 For this, how wondrously he wrought!
   A maiden, in her lowly place,
   Became, in ways beyond all thought,
   The chosen vessel of his grace.

4 She bowed her to the angel's word,
   Declaring what the Father willed;
   And suddenly the promised Lord
   That pure and hallowed temple filled.

5 That Son, that royal Son she bore
   Whom Gabriel announced before,
   Whom, in his mother's womb concealed,
   The unborn Baptist had revealed.

6 He shrank not from the oxen's stall,
   He lay within the manger-bed;
   And he whose bounty feedeth all
   At Mary's breast himself was fed.

7 Des Himmels Chor sich freuen drob
und die Engel singen Gott lob,
den armen Hirten wird vermeld't
der Hirt und Schöpfer aller Welt.

8 Lob, Ehr und Dank sei dir gesagt
Christ, gebor'n von der reinen Magd
mit Vater und dem heil'gen Geist,
von nun an bis in Ewigkeit.
[Amen.]

Coelius Sedulius (fl. c.450),
tr. Martin Luther (1483–1546)

7 And, while the angels in the sky
Sang praise above the silent field,
To shepherds poor the Lord most high,
The one great Shepherd, was revealed.

8 Eternal praise and glory be,
O Jesu, virgin-born, to thee,
With Father and with Holy Ghost,
From men and from the heavenly host.
[Amen.]

vv. 1, 5, 8 tr. J. M. Neale (1818–66), adapted
vv. 2–4, 6, 7 tr. J. Ellerton (1826–93)

'Christum wir sollen' is Luther's translation of 'A solis ortus cardine' (4), sung at lauds on Christmas Day. It consists of the first seven verses of Sedulius's alphabetical poem, with an added doxology. The translation appeared in the first Lutheran hymn-book, *Etlich cristlich Lider Lobgesang und Psalm* (Wittenberg, 1523–4), one of four hymns by Luther of the eight in the book. It exemplifies the description of Luther in John Julian's *Dictionary of Hymnology* (1892) as 'the [St] Ambrose of German hymnody . . . He had an extraordinary faculty of expressing profound thought in the clearest language.'

Note-against-note settings of plainchant, such as Osiander's, are thought to have been an influence behind the simpler type of harmonization which began to replace the older motet-like settings towards the end of the sixteenth century. They were, nevertheless, intended for the *chorus musicus* to sing, and not for congregation and organ, though there is no reason why today's organists should not use such settings for congregational accompaniment. Osiander's setting was published in his *Fünfftzig Geistliche Lieder und Psalmen mit vier Stimmen auf contrapunctsweise* . . . (Nuremberg, 1586). Other settings are in Praetorius's *Musae Sioniae*, V (1607) and Schein's *Cantional* (1627/45). There is an elaborate stanzaic setting in *Musae Sioniae*, VI (1609).

The Catholic custom of singing 'Amen' after the doxology of a hymn was not widely observed by early Lutherans, and soon passed completely from general use. Klug does, however, print 'Amen' (without music) at the end of 'Christum wir sollen', and other hymns with doxologies, in his 1533 edition.

PERFORMANCE (*i*) Choir, with instruments and/or organ *ad lib.*; (*ii*) unison voices and organ.

62

Als ich bei meinen Schafen wacht'
While by my sheep I watched at night

I

(*Christmas*)

(*Auserlesene catholische geistliche Kirchengesänge, 1623, arr. editors*)

1. Als ich bei mei - nen Scha - fen wacht', ein En - gel mir die
1. While by my sheep I watched at night, Glad ti - dings brought an

Bot - schaft bracht'. *Des bin ich froh, bin ich froh, froh, froh,*
an - gel bright. *Then all be - low, all be - low, Sing i -*

froh! o, o, o! Be - ne - di - ca - mus Do - mi - no, be - ne - di - ca - mus Do - mi - no.
- o!

II

(*Christmas*)

Seventeenth-century
(*Trier Gesangbuch, 1871, arr. editors*)

The origin of the text is not known. It would appear to be a *Benedicamus* substitute (see notes, 9), and perhaps dates from *c*.1500. In the sixteenth century it was sung to an undistinguished chorale melody, but a fresh setting in the early seventeenth century gave it a new lease of life, and it has continued to be popular ever since: today it is one of the indispensable Christmas carols in the US.

The echo setting (I) appeared first in the Cologne *Auserlesene catholische geistliche Kirchengesänge* (1623). The echo form suggests that the new setting may have been a *Wechselgesang* ('antiphonal song'—see notes, 55) for two spatially separated groups. Equally possibly it may have been made for a shepherd drama (see notes, 177), with off-stage echo. The conservative Cologne book gives no

2 Er sagt', es soll geboren sein
zu Bethlehem ein Kindelein.
Des bin ich froh, (etc.)

3 Er sagt', das Kind liegt dort im Stall
und soll die Welt erlösen all'.

4 Als ich das Kind im Stall geseh'n,
nicht wohl konnt' ich von dannen geh'n.

5 Das Kind zu mir sein' Äuglein wandt',
mein Herz gab ich in seine Hand.

6 Demütig küsst' ich seine Füss',
davon mein Mund ward zuckersüss.

7 Als ich heimging, das Kind wollt' mit
und wollt' von mir abweichen nit.

8 Das Kind legt' sich an meine Brust
und macht' mir da all' Herzenslust.

9 Den Schatz muss ich bewahren wohl,
so bleibt mein Herz der Freuden voll.

c.1500?
(Auserlesene catholische geistliche
Kirchengesänge, 1623, modernized)

2 'For you,' he said, 'this blessèd morn
In Bethlehem a Child is born.'
Then all below / How great my joy! (etc.)

3 'Go where he lies within a stall,
The infant Redeemer of us all.'

4 There in the stall he sleeping lay;
There by his side I longed to stay.

5 Sweetly he gazed into my face:
I in his hands my heart did place.

6 Gently I kissed his tiny feet,
Which to my lips were honey-sweet.

7 Then to my home I made my way:
Yet still that Child with me did stay.

8 Within my arms that Child did rest:
Oh! how my heart with love was blest.

9 Close shall I guard this darling Boy,
Thus shall my heart be filled with joy.

v. 1 tr. Theodore Baker (1848–1934)
vv. 2–9 tr. editors

accidentals in bars 1 and 3, but they are found in subsequent seventeenth-century books, and were almost certainly always sung.

Setting II presents a later, cruder version of the tune, from the Trier *Gesangbuch* (1871), which is the basis of the carol as sung in the US.

There is a setting by Martin Shaw, to Herrick's 'What sweeter music can we bring', in *The Oxford Book of Carols* (1928).

The text has been cruelly mangled in English versions, the rich fantasy of the language (which evokes the medieval *Minnelieder*—secular love-songs) being reduced to a few conventional angel-and-shepherd verses. The poem makes little sense unless sung complete. We provide a full translation, with two different refrains (one underlaid in each setting), both free imitations of the German.

PERFORMANCE I (*i*) two solo voices, with or without organ or other instruments; (*ii*) choir(s). Ideally there should be two separated groups.

II, voices and organ.

63

Es steht ein' Lind' im Himmelreich
There stood in heaven a linden tree

(Annunciation; Christmas)

Fifteenth-century
(arr. editors)

1. Es steht ein' Lind' im Him - mel - reich, der blü - hen
1. There stood in heaven a lin - den tree, But, though 'twas

al - le Ä - ste, und En - gel sin - gen all - zu -
ho - ney - la - den, The an - gels cried: 'No bloom shall

- gleich, Ma - ri - a sei die Be - ste.
be Like that of one fair maid - en.'

2 Es kam ein Bote klar und rein
    her auf diese Erde,
  ging zur verschloss'nen Tür herein
    mit englischer Gebärde:

2 Sped Gabriel on wingèd feet,
    And passed through bolted portals
  In Nazareth, a maid to greet,
    Blessed o'er all other mortals.

3 'Gegrüsset seist du, Maria,
   du Krone aller Frauen.
   Du sollst ein Kind gebären ja
   und jungfräulich drauf trauen.'

4 'Wie kann ich gebär'n ein Kindelein
   und eine Jungfrau heissen?
   Niemand begehrt das Herze mein;
   das sollst du mir beweisen!'

5 'Das will ich dir beweisen wohl,
   du edle Königinne.
   Der Heil'ge Geist erscheinen soll
   in gottgewollter Minne.'

6 'Gabriel kehrt' wieder hin
   zu der Himmel Pforten.
   'Ich bin ein' Dirn' des Herren mein,
   mir g'scheh nach deinen Worten.'

7 'Gabriel kam wieder ein;
   er seid gar gute Märe,
   dass Maria Mägdlein fein
   Gottes Mutter wäre.

Traditional
(*Wackernagel, 1863–77, modernized*)

3 'Hail Mary!' cried the angel mild,
   'Of womankind the fairest:
   A maiden ay shalt thou be styled,
   Although a babe thou bearest.'

4 'But how should I a mother be
   While yet a maid remaining?
   No man with love hath looked on me:
   'Tis strange past all explaining!'

5 'Most noble queen, no man on earth
   Shall share in thy conceiving:
   Thou shalt by God be brought to birth,
   The Holy Ghost receiving.'

6 'So be it!' God's handmaid gan cry,
   'According to thy telling.'
   To heaven the angel then did fly,
   To his celestial dwelling.

7 This news filled all the heavens with glee:
   'Twas passed from one to other
   That 'twas Mary, and none but she,
   That God would call his mother.

vv. 1–3, 6, 7 tr. G. R. Woodward (1848–1934),
adapted
vv. 4, 5 tr. editors

The words derive from the ancient folk ballad 'Es steht ein' Lind' in jenem Tal', known as 'Die Liebesprobe' ('The test of love') and dating at least from the fourteenth century. The tune first appeared together with the sacred text in Heinrich Laufenberg's manuscript collection *Geistliche Lieder* of *c*.1430 (once in the Bibliothèque Municipale, Strasbourg, but destroyed in 1870 during the Franco–Prussian War; the text is printed in Wackernagel's *Der*

deutsche Kirchenlied, 1864–77). We give a modernized version of the text, omitting one of Laufenberg's verses. Verse 1, line 4, reads 'dass Jesus sei der Beste' in Lutheran sources. We have also trimmed Woodward's translation, still widely sung in England, of some of its more extreme archaisms.

PERFORMANCE   (*i*) Solo voice; (*ii*) choir, with organ *ad lib.*

64

Vom Himmel hoch, o Engel, kommt!
Come, angels, come! from heaven, appear!

(Christmas)

(Auserlesene catholische geistliche Kirchengesänge, 1623, arr. editors)

1. Vom Him - mel hoch,_ o En - gel, kommt! E - ia! e - ia! Su - sa - ni, su - sa - ni, su - sa - ni! Kommt singt und klingt, kommt pfeift_ und trombt! Hal - le - lu - ja,_ hal - le - lu - ja! Von Je - sus singt_ und Ma - ri - a.

1. Come, an - gels, come!_ from heaven, ap - pear! Come sing, come pipe, come trum - pet here! Al - le - lu - ia,_ al - le - lu - ia! Et in_ ex - cel - sis glo - ri - a!

2   Kommt ohne Instrumenten nit,
    Eia, (etc.)
    bringt Lauten, Harfen, Geigen mit!
    Halleluja, (etc.)

3   Lasst hören euer Stimmen viel
    mit Orgel und mit Saitenspiel!

4   Hier muss die Musik himmlisch sein,
    weil dies ein himmlisch' Kindelein.

5   Die Stimmen müssen lieblich gehn
    und Tag und Nacht nicht stille stehn.

6   Sehr süss muss sein der Orgel Klang,
    süss über allen Vögelsang.

7   Das Lautenspiel muss lauten süss,
    davon das Kindlein schlafen müss'.

8   Sing Fried' den Menschen weit und breit,
    Gott Preis und Ehr' in Ewigkeit.

*(Auserlesene catholische geistliche
Kirchengesänge, 1623, modernized)*

2   Your instruments of music bring:
    Eia, (etc.)
    The lute and harp, and bowèd string!
    Alleluia, (etc.)

3   Let strings and organ all agree
    To weave a solemn harmony.

4   Celestial music sound on high,
    For here a heavenly Child doth lie!

5   Your angel voices gently blend
    In psalms and songs that have no end.

6   Let sweetest organ-tones be heard,
    More sweet than any singing-bird!

7   With softest touch let lutes reply,
    To soothe the Child with lullaby.

8   Sing peace to men, where'er they be:
    Sing praise to God eternally!

tr. editors

One of the most appealing of all the cradle-rocking carols (see notes, 55). We have taken the words and melody from *Auserlesene catholische geistliche Kirchengesänge* (1623), as reprinted in L. Erk and F. M. Böhme, *Deutscher Liederhort* (3 vols., 1893–4, no. 1938).

The editors of *The Oxford Book of Carols* (1928) married the tune with the (music-less) fifteenth-century carol 'A little child there is yborn' so successfully that we hesitated before divorcing them: the German text is irresistible, however, and it is odd that it is scarcely known outside Germany. It is the poetic equivalent of Raphael's golden-haloed, curly-haired choir of angels, with its multitude of renaissance instruments.

Carols of this kind would be sung in Christmas services when the cradle-rocking occurred. 'Eia' (in this context meaning 'hush') and 'susani' (from the Low German 'Suse, Ninne!'—'Sleep, child!') would be devoutly addressed to the Christ-child in his cradle.

PERFORMANCE (*i*) Choir, with instruments and/or organ *ad lib.*; (*ii*) solo voice with instruments and/or organ; (*iii*) voices and organ.

65

Ein Kindlein in der Wiegen
He smiles within his cradle

(Christmas)

Traditional?
(Corner, 1649, arr. editors)

1. Ein Kind - lein in der Wie - gen, ein klei - nes Kin - de -
1. He smiles with - in his cra - dle, A babe with face__ so

- lein;____ das glei - sset wie ein Spie - gel nach a - de -
bright;____ It beams most like a mir - ror A - gainst a

- li - chem Schein,____ das klei - ne Kin - de - lein.
blaze__ of light:____ This babe__ so burn - ing bright.

2 Das Kindlein, das wir meinen,
   das heisst: Herr Jesu Christ,
   das verleih' uns Fried' und Einigkeit
   wohl hie zu dieser Frist,
   das geb' uns Jesu Christ!

3 Und wer das Kindlein will wiegen,
   das kleine Kindelein,
   der muss das nicht betrüben,
   er muss demüthig sein
   mit Maria der Jungfrau rein!

4 O Jesu, liebstes Kindelein,
   du kleines Kindelein,
   wie gross ist es, die Liebe dein!
   Schleuss' in das Herze mein
   die grosse Liebe dein!

Fourteenth-century?
(Corner, 1649)

2 This babe we now declare to you
   Is Jesus Christ our Lord;
   He brings both peace and heartiness:
   Haste, haste with one accord
   To feast with Christ our Lord.

3 And who would rock the cradle
   Wherein this Infant lies,
   Must rock with easy motion
   And watch with humble eyes,
   Like Mary pure and wise.

4 O Jesus, dearest Babe of all
   And dearest Babe of mine,
   Thy love is great, thy limbs are small.
   O, flood this heart of mine
   With overflow from thine!

tr. Robert Graves (1895–1985)

Both words and tune come from the *Geistliche Nachtigall der Catholischen Teutschen* ('Spiritual Nightingale of the Catholic Germans') of David Gregor Corner (1585–1648), published in Vienna in 1649. This is a collection of 546 hymns with 267 tunes, some marked with Corner's initials showing that he wrote the words (and perhaps also the tunes). Corner was a theologian and priest from Silesia who became rector of the University of Vienna. The title suggests that at least some of the hymns and melodies are traditional. 'Ein Kindlein in der Wiegen', which is headed 'Ein neues auch ächtiges Kindlwiegen' ('A new devotional cradle-song'), does not bear his initials, and the melody may well be a folk tune. The text is thought to date from the fourteenth century, and is found with a quite different tune in the

Schöne christenlichen catholisch weihnächt- oder kindtlesswiegen Gesäng of Haym von Themar (1590), who calls it 'Ein gar Alt frölich, auch Andächtig Weyhenächt Liedlein' ('A very old, joyful, but also devotional, little Christmas song'). The references to rocking the cradle may mean that the carol was specifically connected with the children's cradle-rocking custom that played a prominent part in German Christmas services (see notes, 55).

The translation was made by the English poet and novelist Robert Graves for *The Oxford Book of Carols* (1928).

PERFORMANCE (*i*) Solo voice and continuo; (*ii*) choir, with organ *ad lib.*

66

Es ist ein Roess entsprungen
Of Jesse's line descended
Es ist ein Reis entsprungen
A great and mighty wonder

I

(Christmas)

Fifteenth-century?
(Praetorius, 1609)

aus ei - ner___ Wur - zel
By an - cient___ si - byls

1. Es ist ein Roess ent - sprun - gen
1. Of Jes - se's line de - scend - ed,

aus ei - ner Wur-zel
By an - cient si - byls

aus ei - ner Wur - zel
By an - cient si - byls

aus Jes - se___ kam die
From no - ble___ root new -

zart, als uns die Al - ten sun - gen,
sung, With thorn-less branch ex - tend - ed,

aus Jes - se kam die
From no - ble root new -

aus Jes - se kam___ die
From no - ble root___ new -

2 Das Roesslein, das ich meine,
   darvon Esaias sagt,
hat uns gebracht alleine
   Mary die reine Magd
aus Gottes ewgem Raht
hat sie ein Kind gebohren
bleibend ein reine Magd.

2 That Flower of ancient splendour,
   Of which Isaiah spake,
Mary, the Rose-branch tender,
   Puts forth for mankind's sake;
Obedient to God's will,
A little Child she bears us,
Yet is a maiden still.

3 Das Blümelein so kleine,
   das duftet uns so süss;
mit seinem hellen Scheine
   vertreibts die Finsternis:
wahr Mensch und wahrer Gott,
hilft uns aus allem Leide,
rettet von Sünd und Tod.

3 The frozen air perfuming,
   That tiny Bloom doth swell;
Its rays, the night illuming,
   The darkness quite dispel.
O Rose beyond compare,
Bloom in our hearts' midwinter:
Restore the springtime there!

vv. 1, 2 fifteenth-century? (Praetorius, 1609)
v. 3 Friedrich Layritz (1808–59)

Free tr., editors

Alternative translation

1 Lo! how a Rose, e'er blooming,
    From tender stem hath sprung,
Of Jesse's lineage coming
    As seers of old have sung;
It came, a blossom bright,
Amid the cold of winter
When half-spent was the night.

2 Isaiah 'twas foretold it,
    The Rose I have in mind;
With Mary we behold it,
    The Virgin Mother kind:
To show God's love aright
She bore to us a Saviour
When half-spent was the night.

3 O Flower, whose fragrance tender
    With sweetness fills the air,
Dispel in glorious splendour
    The darkness everywhere;
True man, yet very God,
From sin and death now save us
And share our every load.

vv. 1, 2 tr. Theodore Baker (1851–1934)
v. 3 tr. Harriet R. K. Spaeth (1845–1925)

II

(*Annunciation; Christmas*)

1 Es ist ein Reis entsprungen
    aus einer Wurzel zart,
wie uns die Alten sungen;
    von Jesse kam die Art
und hat ein Blümlein bracht
mitten im kalten Winter
wohl zu der halben Nacht.

2 Das Reislein, das ich meine,
    so uns das Blümlein bringt,
Maria ists, die Reine,
    von der Jesaias singt;
nach Gottes ewgem Rath
hat sie ein Kind geboren
und bleibt doch reine Magd.

3 Das schrieb uns ohne Mängel
      Lucas mit treuer Hand,
   wie Gabriel der Engel
      vom Himmel ward gesandt
   zu einer Jungfrau rein,
   die Gott sich auserwählte,
   sie sollt ihm Mutter sein.

4 Der Engel unverdrossen
      fuhr in der Juden Land
   gen Nazareth; verschlossen
      Marien er da fand
   in ihrem Kämmerlein.
   Er sprach sie an so freundlich:
   'Gegrüsst sei, Jungfrau rein,

5 'du bist voll aller Gnaden,
      der Herr will mit dir sein,
   hoch über aller Frauen
      will er dich benedein.'
   Die edle Jungfrau zart,
   von dieses Engels Grüssen
   wie sie erschrocken ward!

6 'Du sollst dich nicht entsetzen,'
      sprach er, 'o Jungfrau schon!
   Mein Wort lass dich ergetzen,
      ich komm aus Himmels Thron,
   bring frohe Botschaft dir.
   Du hast bei Gott Genade
   gefunden, glaube mir.'

7 'Ein Kindlein wirst du tragen
      in deinem keuschen Leib,
   davon die Schriften sagen,
      du überselig Weib!
   sein Nam ist Jesus Christ:
   der Herr will ihm verleihen
   seines Vaters David Sitz.'

8 Da sprach die Jungfrau reine
      gar züchtig mit Verstand:
   'Wie soll mir das geschehen,
      die keinen Mann erkannt?'
   Der Engel sprach zu ihr:
   'Diess Wunder wird verschaffen
   der heilge Geist an dir.

9 'Es wird dich überschatten
      des Allerhöchsten Kraft
   und unverletzt bewahren
      deine reine Jungfrauschaft,
   denn dieses Kindlein schon,
   das von dir wird geboren,
   ist Gottes ewger Sohn.'

10 Da sprach mit Freud und Wonne
      die edle Jungfrau rein,
   als sie vernahm, sie solle
      des Herren Mutter sein,
   gar willig, unverzagt:
   'Ich bin des Herren Dienerin,
   mir gescheh wie du gesagt.'

11 Aus heilgen Geistes Kräften
   Maria bald empfieng
den ewgen Himmelsfürsten:
   schau an das Wunderding!
Neun Mond er bei ihr war;
sie wurde Gottes Mutter,
blieb Jungfrau immerdar.

12 Wohl zu denselben Zeiten
   der starke Fürst und Held
Augustus, Römscher Kaiser,
   beschrieb die ganze Welt,
den Zins von Allem nahm,
da Joseph mit Maria
auch hin gen Bethlem kam.

13 Herbergen waren theuer,
   sich fand kein Aufenhalt
als eine alte Scheuer;
   da war die Luft gar kalt.
Wohl in derselben Nacht
Marie gebar den Fürsten,
der Frieden hat gebracht.

14 Lob, Ehr sei Gott dem Vater,
   dem Sohn und heilgen Geist;
Maria, Gottes Mutter,
   auch deine Hülfe leist
und bitt dein Kindelein,
dass Gott durch seine Güte
uns gnädig will verzeihn.

15 Wir bitten dich von Herzen,
   du edle Königin,
bei deines Sohnes Schmerzen,
   wenn wir einst fahren hin
aus diesem Jammerthal;
du wollest uns geleiten
bis in der Engel Saal.

16 So singen wir all' 'Amen!'
   das heisst: 'Nun werd' es wahr,
dass wir begehrn allsammen:'
   O Jesu, hilf uns dar
in deines Vaters Reich!
Darin wolln wir dich loben:
O Gott, uns das verleih!

Fifteenth-century?
(vv. 1–15 Simrock, 1865,
v. 16 Alte catholische
geistliche Kirchengesänge, 1599)

TRANSLATION 1 A branch has sprung up from a tender root, as the ancients sang to us [foretold]. The plant rises from Jesse and has produced a flower in the cold midwinter and in the dead of night.

2 The dear branch of which I tell, which brings forth the beloved flower, is the Virgin Mary, of whom Isaiah sings; complying with God's eternal will, she has given birth to a child and yet remains a pure maiden.

3 It was truly described for us by the trusty hand of Luke how the angel Gabriel was sent from heaven to a pure virgin whom God chose for himself to be his mother.

4 The willing angel came into the land of Jewry, to Nazareth; there, unconcealed, he found Mary in her chamber. He cheerfully addressed her thus: 'Hail, pure virgin!

5 'Thou art full of all grace; the Lord wishes to be with you. High above all women he wishes to glorify you.' The noble, tender virgin, by this angelic greeting how startled she was!

6 'Be not afraid,' he said, 'fair virgin! Rejoice at my words! I come from the throne of heaven to bring you good tidings. You have found favour with God, believe me.

7 'You shall bear a child within your chaste body, as the scriptures foretold, you highly favoured maiden! His name is Jesus Christ: the Lord will grant him the seat of his father, David.'

8 Then spoke the pure virgin, most modestly and with understanding: 'How may this happen to me who have known no man?' The angel replied: 'This wonder will the Holy Spirit accomplish upon you.

9 'The power of the Most High will overshadow you, and preserve intact your pure virginity, for this wondrous Child which shall be born of you is God's eternal Son.'

10 Then, with joy and rapture, the noble virgin spoke, perceiving that she was truly to be the mother of the Lord, utterly meek and undismayed: 'I am the handmaid of the Lord: as you have spoken, so may it happen to me.'

11 By the power of the Holy Spirit Mary directly received the eternal Prince of Heaven: behold a wonder! Nine months did he remain within her; she was made the Mother of God, yet remained eternally a virgin.

12 At this same time the powerful prince and hero Augustus, Emperor of Rome, made a census of the whole world, that everyone might be taxed; and so Joseph, with Mary, made his way towards Bethlehem.

13 Inns were costly; no lodging was to be found except an old stable, where the air was very cold. In that selfsame night Mary bore the Prince who has brought peace.

14 Praise and glory be to the Father, the Son, and the Holy Spirit. Mary, God's mother, lend your aid, too, and beg of your dear Child that God through his goodness may mercifully pardon us.

15 From the heart we beg you, O noble Queen, through the sufferings of your Son, that when we at last depart from this vale of tears you will conduct us into the angelic mansions.

16 So sing we all 'Amen!' That is: 'Would that it were so, what we beg of you altogether.' O Jesu, assist us unto your Father's kingdom! There will we praise you: O God, grant us this!

III

(*Christmas*)

1 A great and mighty wonder,
A full and holy cure!
The Virgin bears the Infant
With virgin-honour pure.
Repeat the hymn again:
'To God on high be glory,
And peace on earth to men!'

2 The Word becomes incarnate
And yet remains on high!
And cherubim sing anthems
To shepherds, from the sky.

3 While thus they sing your Monarch,
Those bright angelic bands,
Rejoice, ye vales and mountains,
Ye oceans, clap your hands!

4 Since all he comes to ransom,
By all is he adored,
The Infant born in Bethlehem,
The Saviour and the Lord.

5 And idol forms shall perish,
And error shall decay,
And Christ shall wield his sceptre,
Our Lord and God, for ay.

St Germanus (634–c.733)
tr. J. M. Neale (1818–66)

221

Both words and melody are believed to have originated in the diocese of Trier in the fifteenth or early sixteenth century as a Christmas or Twelfth Night folk carol. The text is found in many different forms: a nineteen-stanza version appears in the *Gebetbüchlein des Frater Conradus* ('Father Conrad's Little Prayer-Book') of 1582/8, and versions with music were printed in many Catholic song-books between 1599 (*Alte catholische geistliche Kirchengesänge*) and 1678 (*Sirenes Symphoniacae*). The 1599 book has twenty-three stanzas; the *Catholische geistliche Gesänge* (Cologne, 1608) has only six, with a Latin translation beginning 'De stirpe David nata' given pride of place.

The setting is from Praetorius's *Musae Sioniae* (VI, 1609; see notes, 53). He gives only two stanzas but baulked at the final line of verse 2; his solution was simply to substitute the last line of verse 1.

At its most extended, the carol is a catch-all narrative of the Annunciation, Conception, Visitation, Birth, shepherds, and magi, enclosed by verses 1–2 and 14–16 in our text II, which is selected from the twenty-two-stanza version entitled 'Winterblümlein' ('The little flower of winter') in Karl Simrock's *Deutsche Weihnachtslieder* (1865), with the final verse taken from the 1599 song-book. The structure suggests that, like so many folk-songs and carols, this one may have grown through a succession of accretions, perhaps beginning life as verses 1–2 and 14–16, then growing into an Annunciation carol by the addition of a further ten stanzas, and later accumulating the much shorter groups of stanzas that deal with the Visitation, Birth, shepherds, and magi.

In medieval iconography, the tree of Jesse is often depicted as a rose plant. The messianic prophecy of Isaiah 12 declares that 'There shall come forth a rod out of the stem of Jesse, and a branch shall grow out of his roots.' Allowing for the characteristic mirror-imaging of Hebrew verse, this means that a rod/branch (the Virgin Mary) will grow from the stem/root of Jesse (father of King David and

patriarch of Christ's genealogy in popular medieval forms) and will bear a 'little flower' (the Christ-child). It is not clear whether *Ros'* (rose) or *Reis* (branch) was the original reading of line 1. *Roess* is given by Praetorius, *Ros'* by other sixteenth- and seventeenth-century sources except Corner (*Geistliche Nachtigall*, Vienna, 1649), and is not incompatible with Isaiah and the Jesse tree if we read it as meaning a rose plant or tree. The quite different image of Christ as a tiny child within an enveloping rose flower (Mary) is sometimes found in German medieval art, and this, together with the *Roeslein* or *Reislein* of verse 2 (which is an affectionate diminutive of *Ros'* / *Reis*: Mary, and not the *Blümlein*, her offspring) has tripped up many a translator (see the alternative translation by Theodore Baker, which is widely sung in the US). Our own translation is an attempt to bring the intended image into sharp focus. (Our last three lines are a departure from the German, which may be rendered: 'True Man, true God, we crave / That thou from ills defend us / From sin and death us save!')

Text III has no connection with the German. It is J. M. Neale's fine English version of a poem by St Germanus, which is sung as a hymn in the Greek liturgy for Christmas Day. Neale's translation was published in his *Hymns of the Eastern Church* (1861), and the editors of *The English Hymnal* (1908) adapted it to fit Praetorius's setting by using the original third verse as a refrain, omitting its first line ('And we with them triumphant . . .'). It works well, and is at least as often sung in England as the original text.

Herbert Howells's well-known carol-anthem 'A spotless rose' sets a translation of 'Es ist ein Roess'.

PERFORMANCE (*i*) Choir; (*ii*) voices, with organ and/or instruments *ad lib*. Various shortened versions of text II are possible: verses 1, 2, 14–16; 1–11, 14–16; 1–5, 7, 8, 10, 11, 14; 1–3, 11–14 or 11–16.

67

O Jesulein süss! o Jesulein mild!
O Little One sweet! O Little One mild!

I

(Christmas)

Seventeenth-century
(arr. Samuel Scheidt, 1587–1654)

1. O Je - su-lein süss! o Je - su-lein mild! Deines Va - ters Willen hast
1. O Lit - tle One sweet! O Lit - tle One mild! Thy Fa - ther's will thou

du____ er - füllt; bist kom - men aus dem Him - mel - reich, uns
hast____ ful - filled; Thou hast come down from heaven's bright sphere To

ar - men Men-schen wor - den gleich, o Je - su-lein süss! o Je - su-lein mild!
be like us poor mor - tals here. O Lit - tle One sweet! O Lit - tle One mild!

II

(Christmas)

Seventeenth-century
(arr. J. S. Bach, 1685–1750)

1. O Je - su - lein süss! o Je - su - lein mild! Deines Va - ters
1. O Lit - tle One sweet! O Lit - tle One mild! Thy Fa - ther's

Willen hast du er - füllt; bist kom - men aus dem
will thou hast ful - filled; Thou hast come down from

Him - mel - reich, uns ar - men Men - schen wor - den
heaven's bright sphere To be like us poor mor - tals

gleich, o Je - su - lein süss! o Je - su - lein mild!
here. O Lit - tle One sweet! O Lit - tle One mild!

o Je - su - lein mild!
O Lit - tle One mild!

2 O Jesulein süss! o Jesulein mild!
   Deins Vaters Zorn hast du gestillt,
   du zahlst für uns all unser Schuld,
   und bringst uns hin deins Vaters Huld,
   o Jesulein süss! o Jesulein mild!

3 O Jesulein süss! o Jesulein mild!
   Mit Freuden hast du die Welt erfüllt,
   du kommst herab vom Himmelssaal,
   und trostst uns in dem Jammerthal,
   o Jesulein süss! o Jesulein mild!

4 O Jesulein süss! o Jesulein mild!
   Sei unser Schirm und unser Schild,
   wir bitten durch dein Geburt im Stall,
   beschütz uns all vor Sündenfall,
   o Jesulein süss! o Jesulein mild!

5 O Jesulein süss! o Jesulein mild!
   Du bist der Lieb ein Ebenbild,
   zünd an in uns der Liebe Flamm,
   dass wir dich lieben allzusamm,
   o Jesulein süss! o Jesulein mild!

6 O Jesulein süss, o Jesulein mild!
   Hilf, dass wir thun alls, was du willt,
   was unser ist, ist Alles dein,
   ach lass uns dir befohlen seyn,
   o Jesulein süss! o Jesulein mild!

(Schemelli, 1736)

2 O Little One sweet! O Little One mild!
   Thy Father's anger hast thou stilled;
   Our guilt thou bearest in our place,
   To win for us thy Father's grace.
   O Little One sweet! O Little One mild!

3 O Little One sweet! O Little One mild!
   With joy thy birth the world has filled;
   From heaven thou comest to men below
   To comfort us in all our woe.
   O Little One sweet! O Little One mild!

4 O Little One sweet! O Little One mild!
   Be thou our guard, be thou our shield;
   By this thy birth we humbly pray:
   O keep us free from sin this day.
   O Little One sweet! O Little One mild!

5 O Little One sweet! O Little One mild!
   In thee love's beauties are all distilled;
   O light in us love's ardent flame,
   That we may give thee back the same.
   O Little One sweet! O Little One mild!

6 O Little One sweet! O Little One mild!
   Help us to do as thou has willed.
   Lo! all we have belongs to thee;
   Ah, keep us in our fealty!
   O Little One sweet! O Little One mild!

vv. 1–4 tr. editors
vv. 5, 6 tr. Percy Dearmer (1867–1936), adapted

The origins of both text and tune are lost in a great forest of interlocking carols connected with worship at the crib and with the tradition of cradle-rocking (see notes, 55). It first emerged as an identifiable carol in Scheidt's *Tabulatur-Buch* (1650), a collection of chorale settings specifically for organists. This version (I) may be sung chorally, but is more effective as a unison hymn accompanied by organ. At bars 4 and 8 Scheidt writes ♩. ♩ ♩ .

The carol later appeared in Leipzig Vopelius's *Gesangbuch* (1682) and in the Dresden *Gesangbuch* of 1723. It was from Vopelius that Bach knew the work and made an arrangement (II, BWV 493) for Schemelli's *Musikalisches Gesangbuch* (Leipzig, 1736). Georg Christian Schemelli (*c.*1676–1762), whose son had attended the Thomasschule where Bach taught, persuaded Bach to supervise the music, which consisted of sixty-nine tunes for use with the 954 hymns. The publication was for the domestic rather than the ecclesiastical market, and Bach merely furnished the melodies with a figured bass. Solo performance will therefore come closest to Bach's expectations. For four-part performance we have realized Bach's figuring, the characteristic fullness of which has produced inner parts virtually identical with those of *The Oxford Book of Carols* (1928).

PERFORMANCE   I (*i*) unison voices and organ; (*ii*) choir and organ.

II (*i*) solo voice and continuo; (*ii*) choir, with organ *ad lib.*

68

Wachet auf!
Wake, O wake!

I

(Advent)

Philipp Nicolai (1556–1608)
(arr. J. S. Bach, 1685–1750)

1. 'Wa - chet auf!' ruft uns die Stim - me der
1. 'Wake, O wake!' With ti - dings thrill - ing The

Wäch - ter, sehr hoch auf der Sin - ne; 'Wach
watch - men's cry the air is fill - ing: 'A -

auf, du Stadt Je - ru - sa - lem!' Mit - ter - nacht heisst
-rise, Je - ru - sa - lem, a - rise! Mid - night strikes! no

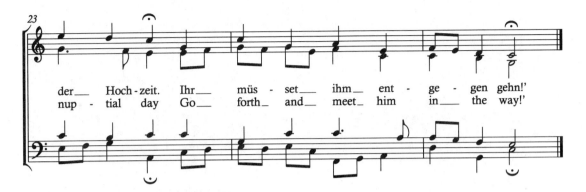

der__ Hoch-zeit. Ihr__ müs-set__ ihm__ ent-ge__gen gehn!'
nup-tial day Go__ forth__ and__ meet__ him in__ the way!'

2 Zion hört die Wächter singen,
  das Herz tut ihr vor Freuden springen,
    sie wachet und steht eilend auf.
'Ihr Freund kommt vom Himmel prächtig,
  von Gnaden stark, von Wahrheit mächtig:
    ihr Licht wird hell, ihr Stern geht auf!'
Nun komm, du werte Kron,
Herr Jesu, Gottes Sohn!
Hosianna!
Wir folgen all'
zum Freudensaal
und halten mit das Abendmal.

3 'Gloria!' sei dir gesungen
  mit Menschen- und englischen Zungen,
    mit Harfen und mit Zimbeln schon.
Von zwölf Perlen sind die Pforten,
  an deiner Stadt sind wir Konsorten
    der Engel hoch um deinen Thron.
Kein Aug' hat je gespürt,
kein Ohr hat je gehört
solche Freude.
Des sind wir froh,
io! io!
ewig *in dulci jubilo.*

Philipp Nicolai (1556–1608)

2 Sion hears the watchmen singing,
  Her heart for joy within her springing;
    She wakes, and eagerly attends;
See her Friend, from heaven descending,
Adorned with truth and grace unending!
    Her light shines clear, her star ascends.
Appear, thou precious Crown!
God's Son, to earth come down!
Sing 'Hosanna!'
Now rise we all
To that glad hall
Where to thy feast thou dost us call.

3 Men and angels there adore thee
  With harp and cymbal, bowed before thee,
    With 'Gloria!' in highest tone.
Twelve bright pearls, thy city's portals,
Stand open, that thy ransomed mortals
    May join the angels round thy throne.
What joy above doth flow,
Unheard, unseen below!
We heavenward go,
Such joy to know:
Io! io!
Ever *in dulci jubilo!*

vv. 1, 2 tr. Francis Crawford Birkitt (1864–1933),
adapted
v. 3 tr. editors

II

Philipp Nicolai (1556–1608)

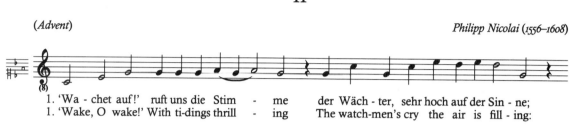

1. 'Wa - chet auf!' ruft uns die Stim - me der Wäch - ter, sehr hoch auf der Sin - ne;
1. 'Wake, O wake!' With ti-dings thrill - ing The watch-men's cry the air is fill - ing:

'Wach auf, du Stadt Je - ru - sa-lem!' Mit - ter - nacht heisst die - se Stun - de;
'A - rise, Je - ru - sa-lem, a - rise! Mid - night strikes! no more de - lay - ing:

sie ruf - en uns mit hel - lem Mun - de: 'Wo seid ihr, klu - gen Jung-frau - en?
The hour has come!' we hear them say - ing; 'Where are ye all, ye vir - gins wise?

Wohl auf, der Bräut-gam kommt; steht auf, die Lam - pen nehmt! Hal - le - lu - ja!
The Bride - groom now is nigh: Stand forth! your lamps raise high! Hal - le - lu - jah!

Macht euch be - reit zu der Hoch - zeit. Ihr müs - set ihm ent - ge - gen gehn!'
In bright ar - ray This nup - tial day Go forth and meet him in the way!'

2 Zion hört die Wächter singen,
   das Herz tut ihr vor Freuden springen,
      sie wachet und steht eilend auf.
   'Ihr Freund kommt vom Himmel prächtig,
   von Gnaden stark, von Wahrheit mächtig:
      ihr Licht wird hell, ihr Stern geht auf!'
   Nun komm, du werte Kron,
   Herr Jesu, Gottes Sohn!
   Hosianna!
   Wir folgen all'
   zum Freudensaal
   und halten mit das Abendmal.

3 'Gloria!' sei dir gesungen
   mit Menschen- und englischen Zungen,
      mit Harfen und mit Zimbeln schon.
   Von zwölf Perlen sind die Pforten,
   an deiner Stadt sind wir Konsorten
      der Engel hoch um deinen Thron.
   Kein Aug' hat je gespürt,
   kein Ohr hat je gehört
   solche Freude.
   Des sind wir froh,
   io! io!
   ewig *in dulci jubilo*.

Philipp Nicolai (1556–1608)

2 Sion hears the watchmen singing,
   Her heart for joy within her springing;
      She wakes, and eagerly attends;
   See her Friend, from heaven descending,
   Adorned with truth and grace unending!
      Her light shines clear, her star ascends.
   Appear, thou precious Crown!
   God's Son, to earth come down!
   Sing 'Hosanna!'
   Now rise we all
   To that glad hall
   Where to thy feast thou dost us call.

3 Men and angels there adore thee
   With harp and cymbal, bowed before thee,
      With 'Gloria!' in highest tone.
   Twelve bright pearls, thy city's portals,
   Stand open, that thy ransomed mortals
      May join the angels round thy throne.
   What joy above doth flow,
   Unheard, unseen below!
   We heavenward go,
   Such joy to know:
   Io! io!
   Ever *in dulci jubilo*!

*vv. 1, 2 tr. Francis Crawford Birkitt (1864–1933),
adapted
v. 3 tr. editors*

Nicolai was not primarily a hymn-writer. His contemporaries admired him as an eloquent preacher and a powerful, often bitter polemicist of orthodox Lutheranism, besieged as it was by Catholicism on one side, Calvinism on the other. He published only four chorales, but two of these are universally known and hold a special place in Lutheran hymnody—'Wachet auf!' and 'Wie schön leuchtet der Morgenstern' (69). The one stands alongside hymns like Luther's 'Ein' feste Burg ist unser Gott' at the summit of the classic Lutheran tradition; the other was the instigator of a quite new tradition of deeply personal but publicly sung love-hymns to Christ which flowered in the Pietist movement. The magnificent tunes are known as the 'king' and 'queen' of chorale melodies. They are almost certainly by Nicolai himself, and look back to the Meistersinger tradition of many of the early chorale melodies in the way they are constructed from a common stock of musical phrases and motifs.

These joyful hymns were written in harrowing circumstances, in the wake of the bubonic plague which ravaged the Westphalian town of Unna, of which Nicolai was pastor, between July 1597 and January 1598. They were published together in an appendix to his devotional work *Frewden Spiegel dess ewigen Lebens* ('Mirror of the Joy of Eternal Life'). The preface is dated 10 August 1598, and the book was published in Frankfurt the following year. At the height of the plague he witnessed, from his parsonage adjoining the cemetery, thirty or more burials a day; yet, from mournful contemplation of death, he found himself mysteriously led on to ecstatic meditation on the afterlife:

> There seemed to me to be nothing more sweet, delightful, and agreeable than the contemplation of the noble, sublime doctrine of Eternal Life obtained through the Blood of Christ. This I allowed to dwell in my heart day and night, and searched the Scriptures . . . and read also the sweet treatise [*De Civitate Dei*] of the ancient doctor St Augustine . . . Daily I wrote out my meditations, and found myself . . . comforted in heart, joyful in spirit, and truly content . . . [I thought to leave behind me the *Frewden Spiegel*] as the token of my peaceful, joyful, Christian departure, or (if God should spare me in health) to comfort other sufferers.

Although the plague had largely abated in Unna by January 1598, on 10 September, at Tübingen, it claimed another victim—the fifteen-year-old Wilhelm Ernst, Count of Waldech, beloved ex-pupil of Nicolai, who had tutored him from the age of five during his nine years as preacher to the Waldech court.

Once again, personal sorrow was sublimated in fervent contemplation of the afterlife, and the pair of hymns that Nicolai wrote in memory of the boy contain no hint of grief. The initial letters of their verses are acrostics, spelling out the initials of the boy's name, those of 'Wachet auf!' standing in reverse for *Graf zu Waldech*.

Both are bridal songs celebrating the count's union with Christ in death in the traditional metaphor of a mystical marriage. Printed as they were with the *Frewden Spiegel*, we may take them also as a memorial to the 1,300 of Nicolai's flock who had perished, and who perhaps form the bridal throng that ascends in 'Wachet auf!' and praises Christ the beloved in 'Wie schön leuchtet.'

Weddings were ceremonial occasions in Nicolai's time. According to both Jewish and German custom, the bridegroom would be led with music by his company of bachelors to the house of the bride, where her bridesmaids would greet him in song. The two groups would then unite, and, after the ceremony, would process, again with music, to the marriage supper. This is the dominating image of 'Wachet auf!' The subtitle reads: 'Of the voice at Midnight and the Wise Virgins who meet their Heavenly Bridegroom. Mat. 25.' During Advent the Church contemplates the Second Coming of Christ and the Last Things of the Book of Revelation which will follow that event. This is the context in which Nicolai develops Christ's parable of the Wise Virgins. They, the bride's attendants, are individual Christians. The bride (the 'Stadt Jerusalem' in verse 1, 'Zion' in verse 2) is the Church. The groom is Christ. On the symbolic level, the call to be prepared, the joyful greeting of Christ, and his union with the bride represent the ideal response of Christians to the Nativity, to the Day of Judgement, and to the approach of Christ in the hour of death.

There are, in addition, two strokes of genius. First, Nicolai underlines the theme of erotic/spiritual love by adapting the secular image of the Watcher, who in the medieval *Wächterlieder* sings as he stands in a high turret to warn a pair of illicit lovers beneath the walls of the approach of dawn. The image was suggested by Matthew 25:13—'Watch, therefore, for ye know neither the day nor the hour whereon the Son of Man cometh.' This verse, Christ's prophecy of his Second Coming, had a prominent place in the medieval German liturgy. In the chorale the watchmen warn not lovers but the bride and her attendants of the approach of the groom at midnight, the traditional hour of Christ's birth: but the coming of light (dawn/the torches of the groom's procession) is the common theme.

The second stroke is to make the entire chorale the song of the handmaids of the bride (Sion, the Church), so that we, the singers, are at the centre of a very baroque religious drama, played out between heaven and earth, with the towering walls of Jerusalem between, and torchlit processions descending and ascending. In verse 1 we describe the watchmen's call; in verse 2 we relate Sion's joyful reaction, greet the descending Groom, and anticipate the joys of the perpetual marriage supper of the Lamb in heaven; and in verse 3 we praise the Groom as the united companies of bride and Groom soar to the heavenly Jerusalem, where praise and bliss are unending.

Although the text of 'Wachet auf!' is nowhere specifically connected with Christmas, the melody suggests that Nicolai was thinking of it in that context. His tunes for both chorales begin with figures which recall the plainchant psalm tone 5 (the Lutherans retained the tones), but particularly the triadic opening of several Christmas chorale melodies, including 'Quem pastores' (57), 'In dulci jubilo' (59) (with the opening words of which 'Wachet auf!' concludes), and 'Resonet in laudibus' (55).

Some German churches keep up an old tradition of playing a chorale from the tower at set times each day, and 'Wachet auf!' is one of those that are often played.

Bach's setting (I) forms the final movement of his Cantata no. 140 (notated there in E♭).

PERFORMANCE   I (*i*) unison voices and organ; (*ii*) choir and organ, perhaps a tone higher.

II, solo voice or unison voices.

69

Wie schön leuchtet der Morgenstern
How fair the Morning Star doth shine

I

(Christmas; General)

Philipp Nicolai (1556–1608)
(arr. J. S. Bach, 1685–1750)

1. Wie schön leuch-tet_ der Mor-gen-stern, voll Gnad' und_ Wahr-heit
1. How fair the_ Morn-ing Star doth shine: 'Tis Da- vid's_ Son,_ of

von_ dem Herrn, die sü - sse Wur-zel_ Jes - se. Du Sohn Da-vid_ aus
Ja-cob's line, With truth and vir-tue_ bless - ed; Sweet branch that_ doth from

Ja-kobs Stamm, mein Kö - nig_ und mein Bräu - ti-gam, hast mir mein Herz be-
Jes - se spring, My Bride-groom and_ my heaven-ly_ King, My heart hast thou pos-

- ses - sen. Lieb - lich, freund - lich, schön und herr - lich, gross und ehr - lich,
- sess - ed! De - scend, sweet Friend, Prince - ly, glo - rious, Brave, vic - to - rious,

reich an__ Ga - ben, hoch und sehr präch - tig__ er - ha - ben.
Gifts be - stow - ing, Lord - ly, no - ble__ past__ all know - ing.

II

(*Christmas; General*) *Philipp Nicolai (1556–1608)*

1. Wie schön leuch - tet der Mor - gen - stern, voll Gnad' und Wahr - heit von dem Herrn,
1. How fair the Morn - ing Star doth shine: 'Tis Da - vid's Son, of Ja - cob's line,

die sü - sse Wur - zel Jes - se. Du Sohn Da - vid aus Ja - kobs Stamm,
With truth and vir - tue bless - ed; Sweet branch that doth from Jes - se spring,

mein Kö - nig und mein Bräu - ti - gam, hast mir mein Herz be - ses - sen.
My Bride-groom and my heaven - ly King, My heart hast thou pos - sess - ed!

Lieb - lich, freund - lich, schön und herr - lich, gross und ehr - lich,
De - scend, sweet Friend, Prince - ly, glo - rious, Brave, vic - to - rious,

reich an Ga - ben, hoch und sehr präch - tig er - ha - ben.
Gifts be - stow - ing, Lord - ly, no - ble past all know - ing.

2 Ei, mein' Perle, du werte Kron',
  wahr' Gottes und Marien Sohn,
    ein hochgebor'ner König!
  Mein Herz heisst dich ein *lilium;*
  dein süsses *Evangelium*
    ist lauter Milch und Honig.
    Ei, mein Blümlein,
      Hosianna!
      Himmlisch' Manna,
    das wir essen,
  deiner kann ich nicht vergessen.

3 Geuss sehr tief in mein Herz hinein,
  du heller Jaspis und Rubin,
    die Flamme deiner Liebe,
  und erfreu mich, dass ich doch bleib'
  an deinem auserwählten Leib
    ein lebendige Rippe.
    Nach dir ist mir,
      gratiosa
      coeli rosa,
    krank und glimmend,
  mein Herz mit Liebe verwundet.

2 Hail! Mary's Son, my Pearl, my Crown:
  Hail! Son of God, to earth come down,
    Of kingly race descended:
  Bloom in my heart, thou *Fleur-de-lys;*
  Thy Gospel, sweetest Word to me,
    Is milk and honey blended;
    In thee we see
      Heavenly Manna
      (Sing 'Hosanna!'),
    Food supernal,
  Leading up to life eternal.

3 Thou Ruby fair, thou Jasper bright,
  My inmost heart set thou alight
    With love beyond all telling;
  Prepare a place in thy blest side
  Where I, a living rib, may bide,
    In thy dear body dwelling.
    Ay me! For thee,
      Gratiosa
      Coeli Rosa,
    With what anguish,
  Fev'rish, sick with love, I languish.

4 Von Gott kommt mir ein Freudenschein,
wenn du mich mit den Äugelein
  gar freundlich tust anblicken.
O Herr Jesu, mein trautes Gut,
dein Wort, dein Geist, dein Leib und Blut
  mich innerlich erquicken.
    Nimm mich freundlich
      in dein' Arme',
      dass ich warme
    werd' von Gnaden;
auf dein Wort komm ich geladen.

4 A heavenly light upon me plays
When Christ on me doth turn his gaze,
  With loving eyes to view me;
Thy precious Word and Spirit, Lord,
Thy body broken, blood outpoured,
  Sustain me and renew me.
    Hold me! fold me
      Gently to thee;
      Warm me throughly;
    O espouse me:
With what gifts thy Word endows me!

5 Herr Gott, Vater, mein starker Held,
du hast mich ewig vor der Welt
  in deinem Sohn geliebet.
Dein Sohn hat mich ihm selbst vertraut,
er ist mein Schatz, ich bin sein Braut,
  sehr hoch in ihm erfreuet.
    Eia, eia,
      himmlisch' Leben
      wird er geben
    mir dort oben;
ewig soll mein Herz ihn loben.

5 Lord God, who from eternity
In thy dear Son hast lovèd me
  With love that fadeth never:
Now hath he raised me up on high
He is my love, his bride am I;
  Nothing our love can sever.
    Eia! eia!
      Heaven inviteth,
      He delighteth
    There to raise me
Where for ever I shall praise thee.

6 Zwingt die Saiten in Cythara
und lasst die süsse Musica
  ganz freudenreich erschallen,
dass ich möge mit Jesulein,
dem wunderschönen Bräut'gam mein
  in steter Liebe wallen.
    Singet, springet,
      jubilieret,
      triumphieret,
    dankt dem Herren;
gross ist der König der Ehren.

6 O strike the lute! let all around
To music's sweetest strains resound,
  The joyful echoes waking!
From Jesus will I never stray,
But with my wondrous Bridegroom stay,
  All earthly ties forsaking.
    Loudly, proudly,
      Voices raising,
      Heaven praising,
    Thanks outpour ye
Unto Christ, the King of Glory!

<table>
<tr>
<td>

7 Wie bin ich doch so herzlich froh,

dass mein Schatz ist das A und O,

der Anfang und das Ende.

Er wird mich doch zu deinem Preis

aufnehmen in das Paradeis,

des klopf' ich in die Hände.

Amen, Amen,

komm du schöne

Freudenkrone,

bleib du nicht lange;

deiner war' ich mit Verlangen.

</td>
<td>

7 What joy my loving heart doth know,

Because my love is A and O,

The first, the last, unending.

To me he gives the highest prize,

And leads me into Paradise,

To joys all else transcending.

Amen! amen!

Joy surrounds thee,

Beauty crowns thee,

Make no staying:

Come! o come! make no delaying!

</td>
</tr>
</table>

after Philipp Nicolai (1556–1608)

free tr. editors
vv. 1–3, 6 after G. R. Woodward (1849–1934)

This is the companion to Nicolai's 'Wachet auf!' (68). Both hymns commemorate the young Count of Waldech with an acrostic: the initial letters of the seven verses of 'Wie schön leuchtet' spell out '*W*ilhelm *E*rnst, *G*raf *u*nd *H*err [Count and Lord] *z*u *W*aldech'.

The subtitle of the hymn is 'A Spiritual Bridal Song of the Beloved Soul concerning Jesus Christ, her Heavenly Bridegroom, founded on the 45th Psalm of the Prophet David'. This psalm, beginning 'My heart is inditing of a good matter', was written for the wedding of a king, possibly Solomon, and contains the real or imagined songs of the procession of the groom and (from the words 'Hearken, O daughter') of the bride's party which awaits him. There is an obvious parallel with the wedding processions of 'Wachet auf!', in which the heavenly bridegroom (Christ) descends with his companions to lead the bride and her party of wise virgins (Sion, the Church) to the heavenly marriage feast; the more so because, as commentators on the psalm agree, in verse 6 the Hebrew poet moves beyond praise of the earthly king to praise the King of Heaven: 'Thy throne, O God, is for ever and ever; the sceptre of thy Kingdom is a right sceptre.' Nicolai concentrates mainly on the second part of the psalm. Whereas 'Wachet auf!' was the public song of the entire bridal party, 'Wie schön leuchtet' is the love-song of the bride herself (the individual Christian soul).

The only Christmas references are in the first two verses. The 'Morning Star' of the opening has nothing to do with

the star of the magi: this is Christ, the 'dayspring from on high' (Luke 1:78) and the 'Sun of righteousness' (Micah 4:2). The image is of the sun or a bright star rising in the morning sky, and represents Christ's birth into a world of darkness, or, in this chorale, the bridegroom's torchlit procession coming to the bride, (The 'Jesulein' of verse 6 is an affectionate diminutive, and does not imply the infant Christ.)

For a long time the chorale was sung not at Christmas but at weddings and deathbeds. But, with the spread of the Pietist movement in the eighteenth century, and its concern for the personal relationship between believer and Saviour, the old inhibitions about using so personal a text in public worship vanished.

There is a precedent for singing only part of the hymn in Samuel Scheidt's setting of verses 1–3 for three voices, with optional double choir (*Werke*, VIII, 1957). Bach's Cantata no. 1 is based on Nicolai's chorale, and sets verses 1 and 7. Our version I comes from a lost cantata and was first published as no. 91 in *Johann Sebastian Bach's vierstimmige Choralgesänge* (1765), collected by C. P. E. Bach and notated there in E major.

PERFORMANCE I, voices and organ; II, solo voice or unison voices. Like 'Wachet auf!', this was (and still is in some German churches) a favourite tune for playing from church towers. It remains a frequent choice for carillons in Germany and the Low Countries.

70

Adeste, fideles
O come, all ye faithful

I

(Christmas)

Anon. (An Essay on the Church Plain Chant, 1782, arr. Thomas Greatorex, 1757–1831, adapted)

1. A - de - ste, fi - de - les, Lae - ti, tri - um - phan - tes, Ve - ni - te, ve -
1. O come, all ye faith - ful, Joy - ful and tri - um - phant, O come ye, O

(D.C. ad lib.)

- ni - te in Beth - le - hem! Na - tum vi - de - te Re - gem An - ge -
come ye to Beth - le - hem! Come and be - hold him, Born the King of

- lo - rum! Ve - ni - te, a - do - re - mus! Ve - ni - te, a - do - re - mus! Ve -
An - gels! O come, let us a - dore him! O come, let us a - dore him! O

II

Anon. (*Douai MS, c.1740;*
bass adapted from
An Essay on the Church Plain Chant, 1782)

(*Christmas*)

1. A - de - ste, fi - de - les, Lae-ti, tri - um - phan - tes, Ve - ni - te, ve -

-ni - te in Beth - le - hem! Na - tum vi - de - te

(*v.6*) Re-gem An - ge - lo - rum! Ve - ni - te, a - do - re - mus! Ve - ni - te, a - do -

-re - mus! Ve - ni - te, a - do - re - mus__ Do - mi - num!

† ♩ in vv. 2, 6, and 7.

2 Deum de Deo,
   Lumen de Lumine,
   Gestant puellae viscera
   Deum verum, genitum non factum.
      Venite, adoremus! (etc.)

2 God of God,
   Light of Light,
   Lo! he abhors not the Virgin's womb;
   Very God,
   Begotten, not created.
      O come, let us adore him! (etc.)

*3 En grege relicto,
   Humiles ad cunas
   Vocati pastores appropriant;
   Et nos ovanti gradu festinemus.

*3 See how the shepherds
   Summoned to his cradle,
   Leaving their flocks, draw nigh to gaze!
   We, too, will thither
   Bend our hearts' oblations.

*4 Stella duce, Magi,
   Christum adorantes,
   Aurum, thus, et myrrham dant munera;
   Jesu infanti corda praebeamus.

*4 Lo, star-led chieftains,
   Magi, Christ adoring,
   Offer him incense, gold and myrrh;
   We to the Christ-child
   Bring our hearts' oblations.

*5 Pro nobis egenum
   Et foeno cubantem,
   Piis foveamus amplexibus;
   Sic nos amantem quis non redamaret?

*5 Child, for us sinners,
   Poor and in the manger,
   Fain we embrace thee with love and awe;
   Who would not love thee,
   Loving us so dearly?

6 Cantet nunc 'Io!'
   Chorus angelorum;
   Cantet nunc aula caelestium:
   † 'Gloria in excelsis Deo!'

6 Sing, choirs of angels!
   Sing in exultation!
   Sing, all ye citizens of heaven above:
   'Glory to God
   In the highest.'

7 Ergo qui natus
   Die hodierna,
   Jesu, tibi sit gloria,
   Patris aeterni Verbum caro factum.

7 Yea, Lord, we greet thee,
   Born this happy morning;
   Jesu, to thee be glory given,
   Word of the Father
   Now in flesh appearing.

vv. 1, 2, 6, 7 anon. (eighteenth-century)
vv. 3, 5 Abbé E. J. F. (de) Borderies (1764–1832)
v. 4 anon. (nineteenth-century)

vv. 1, 2, 6, 7 tr. F. Oakeley (1802–80), adapted
vv. 3, 4, 5 tr. W. T. Brooke (1848–1917), adapted

Superscript notation applies to setting I only.
† See performance note.

The genesis of this universally loved Christmas hymn is shrouded in obscurity. The tune and four Latin verses (1, 2, 6, 7) are found in the manuscripts of John Francis Wade, a plainchant scribe well known in English Catholic circles. He is thought to have been primarily resident at the English College at Douai, France, but is known to have worked in Lancashire in 1751 and to have been connected with various prominent Catholic musicians of the foreign embassy chapels in London, among them Samuel Webbe (1740–1816) and Thomas Arne (1720–78).

The English College was founded in 1568 in order to educate English Roman Catholics for the secular priesthood. After the French Revolution it dispersed to two locations, St Edmund's College near Ware, Hertfordshire, and Ushaw College, Durham. Since most of the eighteenth-century documents and books of the English College were either confiscated or destroyed during the Revolution, little information about Wade is available from what would have been its most likely source. An obituary in *The Laity's Directory* (J. P. Coghlan, London, 1787) merely states that he was employed (presumably at the English College) to teach 'the Latin and Church song' (i.e., plainchant), and that his 'beautiful manuscripts abound in our churches'.

Our tune II is found in a Douai manuscript which was almost certainly copied by Wade and which probably dates from *c*.1740. Wade alternated between duple- and triple-time treatments of the tune, and he was perhaps responsible for the modern form in 4/4, first printed, in chant notation and with a bass part, in *An Essay on the Church Plain Chant* (Coghlan, 1782, 1789). (The *Essay* is thought to have been the work of Wade and Samuel Webbe.) Our setting II adapts the bass part printed there to the *c*.1740 version of the melody. It was presumably the *Essay* version that Webbe used when performing the hymn in the Portuguese Embassy chapel where he was organist and where, in 1795, it made such an impression on the Duke of Leeds that he commissioned an arrangement from Thomas Greatorex, director of the popular 'Concerts of Antient Music' of which the Duke was a patron. The arrangement (which we adapt in our setting I) was in B♭, for SATB soloists, choir, and orchestra, and was first performed at one of these concerts on 10 May 1797; it was repeated on many subsequent occasions, making the hymn famous far beyond the Catholic circles to which it had been initially confined. The 'Ancient Concerts' also gave the hymn its somewhat mysterious title, as Vincent Novello, Webbe's successor as organist of the Portuguese Embassy chapel, relates in the *Congregational and Chorister's Psalm and Hymn Book*, 1843:

> This piece obtained the name of 'The Portuguese Hymn' from the accidental circumstance of the Duke of Leeds ... having heard the hymn first performed at the Portuguese Chapel, and who, supposing it to be peculiar to the service in Portugal, introduced the melody at the Ancient Concerts, giving it the title of the 'Portuguese Hymn', by which appellation this very favourite and popular tune has ever since been distinguished; but it is by no means confined to the choir of the Portuguese Chapel, being the regular Christmas hymn 'Adeste Fideles', that is sung in every Catholic chapel throughout England.

The earliest manuscript source of the hymn is reproduced in facsimile in Dom Jean Stéphan's article 'The Adeste Fideles: a study on its origin and development' (*Publications*, Buckfast Abbey, Devon, 1947). He dates it 1743/4 (but *c*.1740 is rather more likely), and calls it 'the Jacobite manuscript' because the words 'Regem nostrum Jacobum' (James III, the Old Pretender) appear in a 'duet-plainchant' setting of 'Domine salvum fac Regem'. Furthermore, Stéphan suggests that the triple-time original of the tune is an offspring or parody of a duple-time 'air anglois', 'Rage inutile'. This 'English air' comes from a comic opera produced in 1744 by Charles Simon Favart (1710–92) for Duclos' play *Le Comte d'Acajou* (see ex. 1). The likeness is too close to be coincidental, and since at least one of Wade's manuscripts probably predates the play, or is at least coeval, it is possible that both tunes in fact derived independently from another source, as yet unidentified. G. E. P. Arkwright, writing in the *Musical Antiquary* (April 1910), suggested that 'Adeste' was adapted from an aria by Handel, 'Pensa ad amare', from *Ottone* (1723), but this was a red herring. More recent research suggests that Thomas Arne might have had a hand in it: manuscript evidence of an Arne–Wade connection is not wanting, and the floating tradition that the hymn was sung 'for the first time' in the Channel Row Dominican Priory, Dublin, shortly after the Jacobite uprising of 1745 links in conveniently with Arne's Dublin sojourn of 1742–4. (There was a close relationship between this convent and Douai.)

Samuel Webbe gives no attribution with his arrangement in his *Collection of Motetts or Antiphons* (1792), and Vincent Novello attributes the melody in his *Congregational and Chorister's Psalm and Hymn Book* to John Reading, with the date 1680 and a note that Reading was a pupil of Dr Blow. The John Reading taught by Blow was born in 1685/6, so Novello must have confused him with an earlier John Reading (d. 1692), organist of Winchester Cathedral. However, nothing extant by either Reading in any way resembles 'Adeste Fideles'.

EX. 1: *Le Comte d'Acajou, 1744*

Rage in-u-ti-le! J'aime Zir-phi-le,

Et mon a-mour m'af-fran-chit en ce jour. Mon

coeur est tri-om-phant, Mon coeur en-fin res-sent un

feu. J'é-tois un en-fant; je suis en Dieu.

Among the many subsequent choir-books that contain the hymn are the following: 1750, Henry Watson Library, Manchester; 1751, for the English College, Lisbon, and entitled *Cantus diversi . . .*, now in Stonyhurst College, Lancashire; 1754, *Vesperale Novum*, Smith College, Massachusetts; 1760, *Antiphonae*, at St Edmund's College, Old Hall Green, near Ware; 1761, St Mary's Priory, Fernham, Oxfordshire; 1767, a vesperal bound in with a copy of *The Evening-Office of the Church, in Latin and English* (Coghlan, 1760). (*The Evening-Office*, one of a number of books Wade is believed to have published anonymously, contains the first printing of the four-verse text. The second edition, published in 1773, bears at the foot of the title-page the printed inscription 'Printed for J. F. W.'.) In each of these books there is a single melodic line which would probably have been accompanied by organ. The first version is in clear triple time. Subsequent versions exhibit metrical/ notational differences. Moreover, changes in notation in Wade's later manuscripts often appear arbitrary. These versions frequently depart from the notation of identical plainchant given in contemporary English Catholic plainchant treatises such as *The Art of Singing* (Thomas Meighan, 1748) and *The True Method to Learn the Church-Plain-Song* (James Marmaduke, London, 1748). The 1760 version, for example, has a refrain that entirely resists duple or triple classification (see ex. 2).

EX. 2: *1760 MS*

In the so-called 'Jacobite' manuscript the hymn is headed 'Prosa in Nativitate Domini', and the word 'rep[etitur]' ('repeat') appears at the half-way point of the music (an asterisk in later books), implying that the whole of each verse is to be sung by soloist(s) and the second half repeated full. Indeed, in Webbe's setting in his *Collection of Motetts* each verse is to be sung by solo voice and organ continuo, the second half repeated by the choir, while Greatorex's 'Portuguese Hymn' arrangement repeats both halves (see performance notes, below).

According to Stéphan, the text was possibly inspired by the Christmas matins invitatory, with its refrain 'Christus natus est nobis / Venite adoremus'. Verses 3 and 5 are two of three additional stanzas by the Abbé Étienne Jean François Borderies. He came across the hymn during his exile in England in 1793 and published all seven verses in

the *Office de S. Omer* (1822). Verse 4 seems also to be of Gallic origin, the earliest known source being a *Thesaurus Animae Christianae* (Mechelin, Belgium, *c.*1850), in which it is printed with the four original verses and the three by Borderies as a 'Second Sequence for Christmas "Ex Graduale Cisterciense" ' ('from a Cistercian gradual'). The usual modern French sequence of verses is 1, 3, 5, and 4.

Oakeley's translation of the four original verses was made for use at his church, Margaret Chapel (now All Saints'), Margaret Street, London. It was considerably revised in F. H. Murray's *Hymnal for Use in the English Church* (1852). W. T. Brooke translated the four additional verses and combined them with Oakeley's translation in the *Altar Hymnal* (1884). Both Murray's and Brooke's versions were further revised before reaching the form given in *The English Hymnal* (1906), which we follow.

The first known publication of the Latin text in America was in a broadside of 1795 (a copy is in the Newberry Library, Chicago). Words and music were printed in Benjamin Carr's *Musical Journal*, II, no. 29, 29 December 1800. The first appearance in a tune-book (to a Watts text) was as a tenor setting in Nehemiah Shumway's *The American Harmony* (2nd ed., 1801) (see R. Crawford, *The Core Repertory*, 1984).

In England the hymn's popularity grew steadily. The text was printed in countless broadsides (sometimes with surprising new 'translations from the Portuguese'). The tune was the fourth most common one on church barrel-organs built between *c.*1790 and 1860, surpassed only by the 'Old Hundreth', 'Hanover', and 'Tallis's Canon'. (See Nicholas Temperley, *The Music of the English Parish Church*, 1979.) In the course of the nineteenth century it became associated exclusively with Wade's words, a process completed in America only in the 1950s. It is now sung in similar form in churches of all denominations.

PERFORMANCE I (*i*) SATB soloists, choir, and organ (orchestra in the original). Bars 1–8 are sung first by one soloist (the other soloists taking subsequent verses in turn) and then repeated by all four; the four soloists sing bars 9–20, the written-out repeat (bars 21–32) being sung by full choir and organ (a congregation or concert audience could join in the full section); (*ii*) choir or four soloists, with congregation taking the repeats; (*iii*) voices and organ, without repeats. The ritornello can be used with any of these schemes. Ornaments should be sung by soloists or small groups only.

In verse 4 Greatorex has a fermata at bar 19, perhaps implying a short cadenza by (some of) the soloists; and in the same verse, in the repeat (bar 31) he writes *Adagio*—doubled note lengths might be best (*a tempo* at the editorial ritornello). In verse 6 Greatorex sets the last line as 'Gloria in excelsis, in excelsis Deo', with ♪ ♪♪ on 'Gloria'. (See the Bibliography entry under 'Greatorex' for details of an edition of his setting.)

II, unison voices and organ.

71

Christians, awake!

(Christmas)

John Wainwright (c.1723–68)
(arr. editors)

1. Christ - ians, a - wake! Sa - lute the hap - py morn

Where - on the Sa - viour of the World was born!

Rise to a - dore the my - ste - ry of___ love

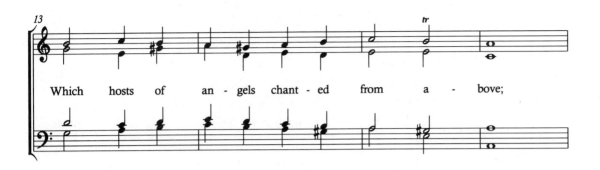

Which hosts of an - gels chant - ed from a - bove;

With them the joy - ful ti - dings first be - gun Of

God in - car - nate and the Vir - gin's Son.

2 Unto the watchful shepherds it was told,
   Who heard the angelic herald's voice: 'Behold!
   I bring good tidings of a Saviour's birth
   To you and all the nations of the earth:
   This day hath God fulfilled his promised word,
   This day is born a Saviour, Christ the Lord!

*3 'In David's city, shepherds, ye shall find
    The long-foretold Redeemer of mankind;
    Joseph and Mary, in a stable there,
    Guard the sole object of the Almighty's care;
    Wrapped up in swaddling-clothes, the Babe divine
    Lies in a manger: this shall be your sign.'

*4 He spake, and straightway the celestial choir
    In hymns of joy, unknown before, conspire.
    The praises of redeeming love they sung,
    And heaven's whole orb with Hallelujahs rung;
    God's highest glory was their anthem still,
    Peace on the earth, and mutual good will.

5 To Bethlehem straight the enlightened shepherds ran
    To see the wonder God had wrought for man,
    And found, with Joseph and the blessèd Maid,
    Her Son, the Saviour, in a manger laid:
    To human eyes none present but they two,
    Where heaven was pointing its concentred view.

6 Amazed, the wondrous story they proclaim,
    The first apostles of his infant fame;
    While Mary keeps and ponders in her heart
    The heavenly vision which the swains impart,
    They to their flocks, still praising God, return,
    And their glad hearts within their bosoms burn.

7 Let us, like these good shepherds, then, employ
    Our grateful voices to proclaim the joy;
    Like Mary, let us ponder in our mind
    God's wondrous love in saving lost mankind:
    Artless and watchful as these favoured swains,
    While virgin meekness in our heart remains.

*8 Trace we the Babe, who has retrieved our loss,
   From his poor manger to his bitter Cross,
   Treading his steps, assisted by his grace,
   Till man's first heavenly state again takes place,
   And, in fulfilment of the Father's will,
   The place of Satan's fallen host we fill.

9 Then may we hope, the angelic thrones among,
   To sing, redeemed, a glad triumphal song.
   He that was born upon this joyful day
   Around us all his glory shall display;
   Saved by his love, incessant we shall sing
   Of angels and of angel-men the King.

John Byrom (1692–1763), adapted

ORGAN INTERLUDES   *(Hugh Keyte)*

INTERLUDE 1

INTERLUDE 2

INTERLUDE 3

INTERLUDE 4

INTERLUDE 5

INTERLUDE 6

INTERLUDE 7

INTERLUDE 8

This is one of the finest of English eighteenth-century hymns, well able to stand beside Wesley's 'Lo! he comes' (72) and 'Adeste, fideles' (70).

John Byrom, a true polymath and a respected citizen of his native Manchester, came under the influence of the saintly personalities of the young John and, especially, Charles Wesley when teaching them the successful short-hand system he had invented. When his wife inherited her brother's property in 1738, he was able to devote himself to the literary life, and one of the fruits of this was his posthumously published *Miscellaneous Poems* (1773). This volume contains a number of hymns, including a version of 'Christians, awake!', and was highly praised by John Wesley.

The hymn was written as a Christmas present for Byrom's daughter, Dorothy, probably in 1749. A small sheet of paper in Byrom's hand is preserved in Chetham's Library, Manchester (A.7.63), and may be the one she received (unless it is an earlier draft). It contains the fifty-two-line poem, with several revisions, substantially as it appeared in the *Miscellaneous Poems*. It is headed 'Christmas Day', and Byrom has later added 'For Dolly'.

A great strength of the poem is its directness and simplicity, which contrasts with Byrom's usual manner. He was, in fact, affecting to write a waits' carol of the traditional kind, and the opening calls to 'awake' and 'rise' are to be taken literally, as sung beneath the windows of a house by a party of carollers on their Christmas Night tour of the parish. The conceit soon became a reality, as Byrom recorded in his notebook: 'Christmas Day 1750. The singing men and boys with Mr Wainwright came here and sang "Christians Awake".' The Byroms lived in central Man-

chester, in a half-timbered house (demolished *c*.1821) in Hanging Ditch, between Hunter's Lane and Old Mill Gate, very close to the collegiate church (now the cathedral) where John Wainwright was assistant organist. There is a tradition that the first performance of the hymn in a parish church was at St Mary's, in nearby Stockport, on Christmas Morning. This seems to stem from the testimony, in the 1880s, of a Stockport solicitor, Aaron Eccles, as reported in Henry Heginbotham's *Stockport, Ancient and Modern* (London, 1892, vol. 2, p. 365). The Wainwright family had close connections with the music at St Mary's, and John was probably still active there (if not necessarily directing the music) in 1750, when he composed the hymn.

Wainwright published his setting in 1767 in his *Collection of Psalm-Tunes, Anthems, Hymns, and Chants, for 1, 2, 3, and 4 voices*, heading it 'A Hymn for Christmas Day, the words by Dr Byrom of Manchester'. By this time his melody had already been pirated by the Baptist divine and psalmodist Caleb Ashworth (of Daventry, Northampton), who named his remarkably crude three-part arrangement of it after Mottram, a village near Manchester, in his *Collection of Tunes* (1760). The name 'Stockport' was given to the tune after Wainwright's death by the Manchester Unitarian minister Ralph Harrison, who included Wainwright's setting in his hymn-book *Sacred Harmony* (1784–6), which was used at Stockport for many years. (The name 'Yorkshire', which infuriates Mancunians, was given by the editors of *Hymns Ancient and Modern*, 1861, who knew neither author nor composer, but noted that the hymn was especially popular in that county. It had clearly circulated widely in the north before this date: Gilbert printed an accurate version of the music in his *Ancient Christmas Carols* (2nd ed., 1823), 'sent to the author out of Yorkshire', and Sandys printed it again, from a similar source, in his *Christmastide*, *c.*1853, when it had still not caught on in the south, attributing the words to Anthony Greatorex, father of the composer Thomas Greatorex, and the music to Samuel Webbe.)

The choir at Stockport was an exceptional institution, singled out for praise by the composer John Alcock, organist of Lichfield Cathedral:

'I have frequently had the pleasure of hearing several psalm-tunes, hymns, anthems, &c. sung by companies of singers in the most exact manner possible [a high compliment in eighteenth-century terms], particularly at Stockport, in Cheshire, at the opening of the organ [in 1755] where I heard Mr Purcell's *Te Deum* and *Jubilate*, and two grand anthems, with all the instrumental parts, performed by tradesmen, most of them from Manchester, amongst which, were only two professors [professionals] of music . . .' (preface to *The Pious Soul's Heavenly Exercise*, 1756).

Wainwright's setting is scored for melody and bass until the final strain (bar 20, last note), which breaks into four-part harmony. The bass is both figured and texted, and allows for organ accompaniment and unaccompanied or instrumentally doubled performance in the 'gallery' style (see Appendix 3) since organs were still rarities in parish churches. We have provided inner parts in bars 1–20 (omitting the figuring), and have reversed the treble and tenor in the final strain, as was standard practice from the late eighteenth century when earlier tenor-melody settings were republished. If the parts are sung as Wainwright wrote them, some sopranos should double the melody (see performance note).

There has never been a satisfactory singing version of the text. What the collegiate church choir sang in 1750 we do not know. Byrom, despite the 'waits' conceit, never divided it into the six-line stanzas for which the tune is written and in which so many of his poems are cast. The original poem has only one division, separating the 'narrative' and 'response' sections (between our verses 6 and 7), but the sense falls into a succession of four- and six-line groups. Many of the latter (e.g., our verse 7) have been ruthlessly truncated or broken up by editors. The only revision by Byrom himself

was a forty-six-line version published, together with 'God, who at sundry times', in an undated broadsheet, perhaps from 1751, a copy of which is in Manchester Public Library, and in Harrop's *Manchester Mercury and General Advertiser* (no. 41, 19 December 1752). The two-part division was retained: Byrom obviously regarded his work more as a poem to be read than as a hymn to be sung. Two notably un-wait-like couplets were removed: 'Joseph and Mary, a distressed Pair, / Guard the sole Object of th'Almighty's Care, / To human Eyes none present but they two / Where Heav'n was pointing its concentred View'; and the first couplet of our verse 6 was omitted in error, and reappeared in *Miscellaneous Poems*.

The texts of most modern hymn-books derive from an unsatisfactory six-stanza adaptation of the newspaper revision. This was probably the work of James Montgomery (see notes, 96), Thomas Cotterill's assistant for the eighth edition (1819) of his *Selection of Psalms and Hymns*, where it is no. 212. The same version is in Montgomery's own influential *Christian Psalmist* (1825) and was adopted by *Hymns Ancient and Modern*. It seems to us that Byrom's poem deserves to be sung complete, at least on occasion, and we have added a couplet of our own (which concludes verse 8) to make the original fifty-two lines up to fifty-four, giving nine stanzas. We have transposed the couplet beginning 'Joseph and Mary . . .' to verse 3, altering 'a distressed pair' to 'in a stable there'; 'Of the' (verse 2, line 4) replaces 'Upon', to match the musical stress (Byrom vacillated between the two); the last couplet of verse 3 in Byrom's manuscript reads 'Wrapt up in swadling Cloaths, be this the Sign, / A cratch contains the holy Babe divine' (we follow the prints); and we have substituted 'our' for 'the' in verse 7, line 6, to make the meaning clear.

We have added a complete set of organ interludes for the hymn, in a slightly later style, leaving the organist to provide a giving-out if required. (See Appendix 2.)

PERFORMANCE (*i*) Four-part choir and organ, with unison congregation *ad lib.*; (*ii*) unison voices and organ, the choir in four-part harmony in the final strain. If the treble and tenor parts are reversed to restore Wainwright's original setting (see note) some sopranos should continue to sing the melody here.

72

Lo! he comes, with clouds descending
Lo! he comes, an infant stranger

I

(*Advent*)

Martin Madan (*1726–90*)
(*arr. editors*)

1. Lo! he____ comes,____ with____ clouds____ de - scend - ing,
Thou - sand,____ thou - sand____ saints,____ at - tend - ing,

Once_____ for fa - voured____ sin - ners____ slain;____
Swell_____ the tri - umph____ of____ his____ train.____

[SOLI] [FULL] [SOLI]

Hal - le - lu - jah! hal - le - lu - jah! hal - le -

252

-lu - jah! God_____ ap - pears, on earth to_____ reign.
earth to reign.

2 Every eye shall now behold him
    Robed in dreadful majesty;
Those who set at nought and sold him,
    Pierced, and nailed him to the tree,
        Deeply wailing
    Shall the true Messiah see.

*3 Every island, sea, and mountain,
    Heaven, and earth, shall flee away;
All who hate him must, confounded,
    Hear the trump proclaim the Day:
        Come to judgement!
    Come to judgement! Come away!

*4 Now Redemption, long expected,
    See in solemn pomp appear!
All his saints, by man rejected,
    Now shall meet him in the air!
        Hallelujah!
    See the Day of God appear!

*5 Answer thine own Bride and Spirit,
    Hasten, Lord, the general doom!
The new heaven and earth to inherit,
    Take thy pining exiles home!
        All creation
    Travails, groans, and bids thee come!

6 The dear tokens of his Passion
    Still his dazzling body bears,
Cause of endless exultation
    To his ransomed worshippers:
        With what rapture
    Gaze we on those glorious scars!

7 Yea, amen! let all adore thee,
    High on thy eternal throne!
Saviour, take the power and glory:
    Claim the kingdom for thine own!
        O come quickly!
    Hallelujah! come, Lord, come!

vv. 1, 2, 5–7 Charles Wesley (1707–88)
vv. 3, 4 John Cennick (1718–55)

II

(Christmas)

Martin Madan (1726–90)
after Thomas Olivers (1725–99)

1. Lo! he___ comes, an in - fant___ stran - ger, Of a low - ly
2. Lo! he___ comes, the great___ Cre - a - tor, Call - ing all the

[CONTINUO]

mo - ther___ born, *p* Swathed and___ cra - dled in_____ a man - ger,
world___ to___ own Him, the___ Judge and Lord_____ of na - ture,

Of his pris - tine glo - ry___ shorn! *f* Hal - le - lu - jah!
Seat - ed on his Fa - ther's throne.

hal - le - lu - jah! hal - le - lu - jah! Praise ye___ God's in - car - nate Word!
Praise ye___ him, the li - ving Lord!

3 Lo! he comes, by man unfriended,
      Fain[1] with stabled beast to rest;
   Shepherds, who their night-fold tended,
      Hailed alone the new-born guest!
         Hallelujah! hallelujah! hallelujah!
      Praise ye Jesse's tender rod!

4 Lo! he comes, around him pouring
      All the armies of the sky;
   Cherub-, seraph-host, adoring,
      Swell his state and loudly cry:
         'Hallelujah! hallelujah! hallelujah!
      Praise ye Christ, the Son of God!'

5 Lo! he comes, constrained to borrow
      Shelter from yon stabled shed,
   He who shall, through years of sorrow,
      Have not where to lay his head.
         Hallelujah! hallelujah! hallelujah!
      Praise him, slighted by his own!

6 Lo! he comes, all grief expelling
      From the hearts that him receive;
   He to each with him a dwelling
      In his Father's house will give.
         Hallelujah! hallelujah! hallelujah!
      Praise him on his glory's throne!

7 Lo! he comes, to slaughter fated
      By a tyrant's stern decree:
   From the sword, with blood unsated,
      Forced in midnight haste to flee.
         Hallelujah! hallelujah! hallelujah!
      Praise him in affliction's hour!

8 Lo! he comes: at his appearing
      All his foes before him fall;
   Proudest kings, his summons hearing,
      On the rocks for shelter call.
         Hallelujah! hallelujah! hallelujah!
      Praise him, girded round with power!

9 Lo! he comes; but who the weakness
      Of his coming may declare,
   When, with more than human meekness,
      More than human woes he bare?
         Hallelujah! hallelujah! hallelujah!
      Praise him, emptied of his might!

10 Lo! he comes; what eye may bear him,
      In his unveiled glory shown?
   Mightiest angels, marshalled near him,
      Serve, and him their mightier own.
         Hallelujah! hallelujah! hallelujah!
      Praise him, with his crown of light!

11 Man, of human flesh partaking,
      Offspring of the Virgin's womb,
   Who, the hopeless wanderer seeking,
      Deigned in lowly guise to come:
         Hallelujah! hallelujah! hallelujah!
      Praise ye the incarnate Word!

12 Son of the eternal Father,
      Who again in power shall come,
   Round him all mankind to gather,
      And pronounce unerring doom:
         Hallelujah! hallelujah! hallelujah!
      Praise ye him, the living Lord!

Richard Mant (1776–1848)

[1] obliged

Wesley's incomparable Advent hymn (text I, verses 1, 2, 6, and 7) was written in the early days of Methodism. Charles, 'the poet of Methodism' and brother of John, was inspired by a hymn by the Moravian John Cennick (1718–55) to compose three imitations on different subjects. The one that has lived shares Cennick's theme, the Last Things, a traditional subject of meditation during the penitential season of Advent. Cennick's hymn begins memorably: 'Lo! he cometh; countless trumpets / Blow before his bloody sign / Midst ten thousand Saints and Angels / See the crucified shine! / Allelujah / Welcome, welcome, bleeding Lamb!'

Wesley found the hymn in the fifth edition of Cennick's *Collection of Sacred Hymns* (1752). What attracted him was the unusual form of the stanzas and the vivid, high-flown verse which, despite the disconcerting dips into bathos, radiates bardic fervour when compared with most hymns of the time. Verses from both 'Lo! he comes' and its model were combined in Wesley's *Hymns of Intercession for all Mankind* (1758).

The familiar modern version of the tune first appeared in a publication by the Revd Martin Madan, a minor example of that familiar religious type, the passionate-natured, dissipated man of the world who undergoes a sudden conversion and devotes his life to Christ. As a law student in London he had gone to hear Wesley preach, with the sole purpose of studying his mannerisms for a later impersonation in a drinking club to which he belonged. Immediately converted, he was soon labouring energetically in the social and spiritual morass that was eighteenth-century London. He became well known as a writer of polemics on social and political matters, as an occasional composer, and, above all, as an eloquent though low-key preacher in the Calvinist–Methodist tradition. In 1746 he was appointed the first chaplain and director of music at the Lock Hospital, a charitable institution near Hyde Park Corner that cared for women suffering from (usually fatal) venereal infections. It was Madan's experience of the problems of these women, mostly driven on to the streets by a combination of poverty and a shortage of marriageable men, that eventually led to the publication for which he is chiefly remembered, *Thelyphthora, or a treatise on female ruin* (1780), which advocates polygamy as the lesser evil. Forced to resign from the hospital in the resulting furore, Madan spent the rest of his life quietly in Kew, translating literary and theological works from the Latin.

Madan's other important publication, which contains his setting of 'Lo! he comes' (II), is his influential *Collection of Psalm and Hymn Tunes never published before . . . To be used at the Lock Hospital* (1769; there were later, expanded editions from c.1775 onwards). The 'Lock Collection', as it was known, is unusually coherent for the period, since Madan, wearing one hat, had selected the psalms and hymns to be used in the hospital chapel and, wearing another, had chosen, arranged, and sometimes composed the music to which they were sung. Much of the music is in the current *galant* idiom, with duets, trios, figured bass, and 'symphonies' (instrumental ritornellos), all in a light and deliberately non-learned style. We have reversed the two vocal parts for convenience of layout.

The origins of the tune that Madan gives for 'Lo! he comes', called 'Helmsley', are not easy to unravel. In his *Popular Music of the Olden Time* (1853–9), William Chappell deplores it as a light secular tune introduced into church. It was the Methodists who (like Luther before them) deliberately harnessed 'the Devil's tunes' in the service of the Lord, and this one was constructed by Thomas Olivers, a close associate of the Wesleys, from a tune he is said to have heard whistled in the street. His melody, set to 'Lo! he comes', first appeared in the second edition of Charles Wesley's *Select Hymns with Tunes Annex'd* (1765), with the title 'Olivers':

Chappell claimed that the source of the tune was 'a hornpipe danced by Miss Catley in *The Golden Pippin*'. This cannot be so, because Kane O'Hara's burletta was first produced (at Covent Garden) in 1773, post-dating Wesley's *Select Hymns*. But there is a little group of related melodies, including a song in the published score of *The Golden Pippin*, which must have provided Olivers' source. The earliest version we have found is a country dance, one of five dances appended to Walsh's 1761 score of Thomas Arne's highly successful *Thomas and Sally*, first produced at Covent Garden on 28 November 1760. This has obvious links with the first half of Olivers' tune (none of the versions has anything related to the second half, and this is presumably original):

The Golden Pippin was unsuccessful at Covent Garden in 1773, but successfully revived there in 1776. Neither production is known to have contained a hornpipe, but both contained the song 'Where's the mortal can resist me?' sung by the celebrated soprano Anne Catley and clearly derived from Arne's dance (a piano score of the 1776 revival was published in *The Pianoforte Magazine*, X, 1800):

Where's the __ mor - tal __ can __ re - sist __ me?

Queens must __ ev - 'ry __ hon - our __ gain

Where did this version of the tune come from? Many London sheet-music versions (and a set of keyboard variations) appeared from 1773 onwards, some with the *Golden Pippin* text, others, including one published in 1773, in which the song is described as a 'Favourite Song sung by Mr Mahon in Dublin, and by Miss Catley, in The Golden-Pippin', with a quite different text beginning 'Guardian Angels, now protect me: Send, ah send the youth I love!' Mahon was presumably from the family of Dublin musicians of that name, several members of which migrated to become prominent in the London musical scene. Between 1763 and 1770 Anne Catley was herself in Dublin, where she could hardly have avoided professional contact with the Mahons. Perhaps Mahon arranged the song from Arne's country dance, and Anne Catley brought it back with her to London in 1770, possibly introducing it into *The Golden Pippin* as a condition of her participation.

The tune that Olivers heard whistled in the street, and which he adapted to Wesley's hymn in 1765, was therefore probably Arne's country dance. Even if there had already been an edition of the concert song in Dublin (and we have failed to trace one), it is unlikely to have become known to London street-whistlers. Differences between Arne's tune and Olivers' could have resulted from the whistler's defective memory, or Olivers' inaccurate transcription, or his arrangement of what he transcribed.

Until *c.*1830, most hymn-books followed the centonized text in the Lock Collection. Thereafter, many compilers made their own selection of verses from Cennick and Wesley, and different versions proliferated. In the present century we have lost this variety, as successive hymn-book committees have chiselled out the Cennick verses. As a tiny blow for diversity and choice, we give the six verses that Madan prints, together with Wesley's original third verse (which he omits), and with our own choral setting (I) of the melody in its usual modern form. Our verses 1, 2, 6, and 7 constitute Wesley's original hymn (with the last line of verse 1 restored: Madan rewrote it); our verse 5 is from another hymn that Wesley based on Cennick; and verses 3 and 4 are from Cennick's 'Rise, ye dearly purchased sinners' (with Madan's rewritten final lines retained).

Setting II is Madan's original, with which we give a different and admirable text written in imitation of Wesley's hymn by Bishop Richard Mant. Mant's hymn was published, with the title 'The Infant Stranger' and set to an arrangement of Madan's tune, in the SPCK *Christmas Carols* of 1833, edited (anonymously) by himself. His the text was included in *A Good Christmas Box*, the famous chap-book collection of Christmas carols published in 1847. In both cases the verses were assigned alternately to 'First Company' and 'Second Company': this probably reflects the practice in certain London churches in which groups of boy and girl charity children sang from separate galleries, though Mant may just possibly have been thinking of the customary division of seating in churches between men and women on either side of the central aisle.

PERFORMANCE   I, voices and organ; II, sopranos (soli or full) and organ continuo. (Text II may be sung to setting I, with or without Mant's division into 'companies'.)

73

Lift up your heads in joyful hope

I

(*Christmas*)

Eighteenth-century
(arr. Martin Madan, 1726–90)

1. Lift up your heads in joy - ful hope: Sa - lute the hap - py mom! Sa - lute the hap - py mom! Each heaven - ly power Pro - claims the glad hour: Lo! Je - sus the Sa - viour is born, lo! Je - sus the Sa - viour is born.

2 All glory be to God on high,
    To him all praise is due,
  The promise is sealed,
  The Saviour's revealed,
    And proves that the record is true.

3 Let joy around like rivers flow,
    Flow on, and still increase;
  Spread o'er the glad earth
  At Jesus his birth,
    For heaven and earth are at peace.

4 Now the good will of heaven is shown
    Towards Adam's helpless race;
  Messiah is come
  To ransom his own,
    To save them by infinite grace.

5 Then let us join the heavens above,
    Where hymning seraphs sing;
  Join all the glad powers,
  For their Lord is ours,
    Our prophet, our priest, and our king.

Eighteenth-century
(Madan, 1769)

A carol that was once very popular, and fell into disuse during the Victorian period. Its earliest known appearance is in Martin Madan's 'Lock Collection' (1769; see notes, 72), where the fine melody is given a three-part setting (I, here transposed down a tone) headed 'set by M. M.', which implies that the melody (at least) was taken from an earlier source.

The carol subsequently appeared in no fewer than fifty-two publications, at least two-thirds of them in the US. 'Lift up your heads' was the text most commonly connected with the tune in these publications, but eight others are found, most of them connected with Christmas.

Andrew Law's arrangement (II, again transposed down a tone) is from his *Collection of Hymn Tunes* (1783), the earliest of the American sources. It was considered progressive for its time, being a four-part arrangement with the melody in the treble throughout.

Interlude 1 is from William Gresham's *Psalmody Improved*

(1797 or earlier), where it appears with an arrangement of Madan's hymn for unison voices and organ continuo; interlude 3 is from William Gawler's *Harmonia Sacra* of 1781, where it appears with the 'York' psalm tune and is notated in G. (For the performance of interludes see Appendix 2.)

PERFORMANCE   I, high voices and organ. The octave writing in bars 5–7 in the second voice is presumably to be sung as written, singers without a high G taking the lower notes.

II, choir. The second voice is less an alto than a kind of second treble (partly derived from Madan).

Appoggiaturas in both settings are probably long (♩ ♩).

The two settings could effectively be combined, with verses 1, 3, and 5 being sung by the choir and/or congregation to setting II, verses 2 and 4 by high voices to setting I.

II

Eighteenth-century
(arr. Andrew Law, 1749–1821,
after Martin Madan, 1726–90)

(*Christmas*)

1. Lift up your heads in joy-ful hope: Sa-lute the

hap - py___ morn! Sa-lute the hap-py___ morn! Each

hea-ven-ly power Pro-claims the glad hour: Lo! Je-sus the

Sa - viour is born, lo! Je-sus the Sa-viour is born.

ORGAN INTERLUDES

INTERLUDE 1

William Gresham (fl. 1797)

INTERLUDE 2

Editors

INTERLUDE 3

William Gawler (1750–1809)

74

Hark! hear you not a chearful noise

(Christmas)

Matthew Wilkins? (d. 1773)

A___ thou - sand___ Heav'n - ly___ ec - choes cry!

SYMPHONY (*editorial*)

ORGAN

2 So loud they sung it down to earth,
Innocent children heard their mirth
And sung with them what none can say
For joy: their Prince was born that day.

3 Their Prince, their God, like one of those
Is made a child, and wrapt in cloaths;
All this in time was fully done:
We have a Saviour, God the Son.

Wilkins, c.1760

From *A Book of Psalmody, containing a choice collection of Psalm Tunes, Hymns and Anthems, in Two, Three, and Four parts by the best masters ancient and modern, with a short Introduction to the scale of musick. Collected, printed, taught and sold by Matthew Wilkins of Great Milton near Thame Oxfordshire* (*c*.1760). A second edition of this volume, *A Collection of Church Music*, was published *c*.1775 by Elizabeth Wilkins, Matthew's widow. (Confusingly, there was a quite different earlier publication by Matthew, *c*.1730 and *c*.1750, which was also called *A Book of Psalmody*.) Little is known of Wilkins beyond what his title-pages reveal.

The *c*.1760 book is exactly what the title claims: an impressive and wide-ranging collection of music of a consistently high standard, including the early fuging tune that so haunted the imagination of Thomas Hardy (see 'While shepherds watched', 46: IV).

The text of this 'Hymn for Christmas Day' is unattributed. We have altered 'light' to 'like' in verse 1, line 3. An identical text (with 'light') was set twice by William Billings (see notes, 78): as a hymn, 'Hadley' (only verse 1 given), and later as a set piece based on 'Hadley' in *The Continental Harmony* (1794). One of these ascribes the text to 'Dr Watts', but it is not to be found among Isaac Watts's published verse.

Billings may have obtained the text from Wilkins, but we suspect that both took it from an earlier source which we have not discovered—certain features of Wilkins's setting seem archaic, notably the descant-like soprano, which is more like those of Gibbons's psalm tunes than the independent soprano parts of the time. It may even be an arrangement, using an existing tenor and bass: the usual country way of setting a (tenor) tune was to add first the bass, then the alto, and finally the soprano, with increasing dissonance as each is added; in the present case the bass is markedly more expert than the upper voices at certain points—which in no way diminishes the appeal. (See Appendix 3.) Perhaps Wilkins's model was a two-part setting (these were very common in country publications) or, just possibly, a devotional song for voice and continuo. We have transposed the setting down a tone.

PERFORMANCE (*i*) Choir, with the tenor doubled at the higher octave, and instruments *ad lib.* (see Appendix 3). Wilkins's printed key, G, may be preferred. The repeat marks in verses 2 and 3 are for SAB voices only; (*ii*) solo voice (tenor line) and continuo, at any appropriate pitch, and ignoring the repeat marks in verses 2 and 3. The organ symphony is appropriate to this option.

75

Hark! hark what news the angels bring

I

(Christmas)

Seventeenth-century?
(Smith, 1732, arr. editors)

VERSE

1. Hark! hark what news the an - gels bring: Glad ti - dings

an - gels

of a

of a new - born King Who is the Sa - viour

of a new - born King

of man - kind, In whom we shall sal - va - tion find.

REFRAIN

Hal-le - lu-jah! hal-le - lu-jah! Hal-le - lu-jah! hal-le - lu-jah! Hal-le - lu - jah! hal-le - lu-jah!

264

2   This is the day; this blessèd morn
    The Saviour of mankind was born;
    Born of a maid, a virgin pure,
    Born without sin, from guilt secure.

3   If angels sing at Christ his birth,
    Sure we have greater cause for mirth;
    For why? It was for our sake
    Christ did our human nature take.

4 My soul, learn by thy Saviour's birth
  For to debase thyself on earth,
  That thou mayst be exalted high
  To live with him eternally.

5 I do resolve, while here I live,
  As I'm in duty bound, to give
  All glory to the Deity,
  One God alone in persons three.

(A Compleat Book of Psalmody, 1769)

II

(Christmas)

1 Hark! hark what news the angels bring:
  Glad tidings of a new-born King,
  Born of a maid, a virgin pure,
  Born without sin, from guilt secure.

2 Hail mighty Prince, eternal King!
  Let heaven and earth rejoice and sing!
  Angels and men with one accord
  Break forth in songs: 'O praise the Lord!'

*3 Behold! he comes, and leaves the skies:
   Awake, ye slumbering mortals, rise!
   Awake to joy, and hail the morn
   The Saviour of this world was born!

*4 Echo shall waft the strains around
   Till listening angels hear the sound,
   And all the heavenly host above
   Shall join to sing redeeming love.

vv. 1, 2 Stephenson, c.1775
vv. 3, 4 anon. (A Good Christmas Box, 1847)

Joseph Stephenson? (fl. 1760–75)

† Verses 2–4 begin here.

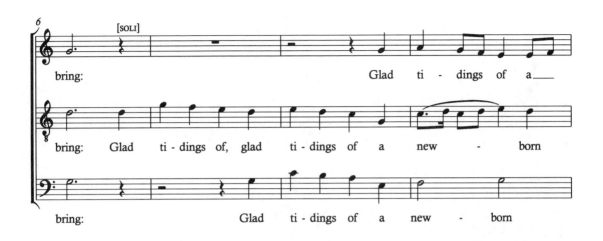

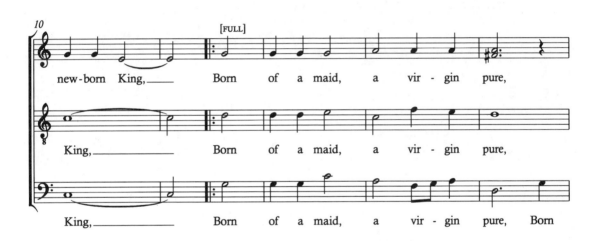

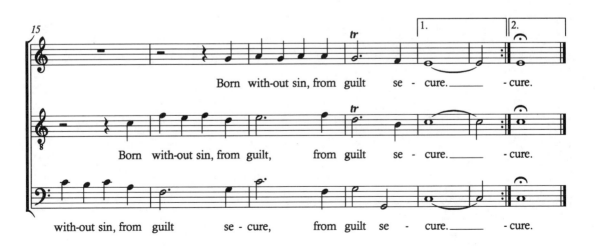

III

Walton waits' version (1919)
after Joseph Stephenson (fl. 1760–75)

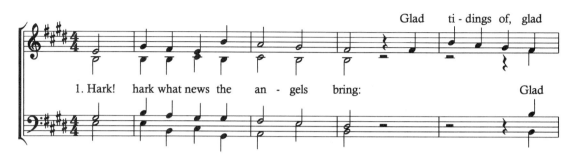

Glad ti-dings of, glad

1. Hark! hark what news the an-gels bring: Glad

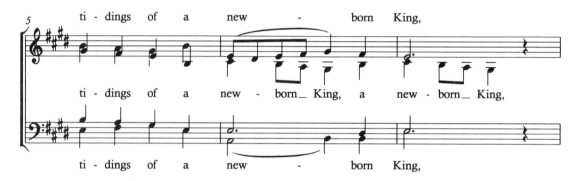

ti-dings of a new - born King,

ti-dings of a new-born King, a new-born King,

ti-dings of a new - born King,

Born

Born of a maid, a vir-gin pure,

Born with-out sin, born

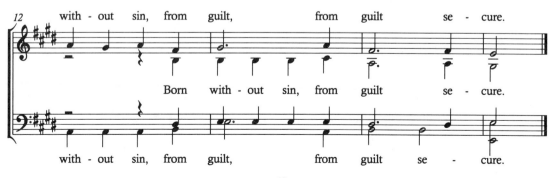

with-out sin, from guilt, from guilt se - cure.

Born with-out sin, from guilt se - cure.

with-out sin, from guilt, from guilt se - cure.

2 Hail mighty Prince, eternal King!
Let heaven and earth rejoice and sing!
Angels and men with one accord
Break forth in songs: 'O praise the Lord!'

*3 Behold! he comes, and leaves the skies:
Awake, ye slumbering mortals, rise!
Awake to joy, and hail the morn
The Saviour of this world was born!

*4 Echo shall waft the strains around
Till listening angels hear the sound,
And all the heavenly host above
Shall join to sing redeeming love.

vv. 1, 2 Stephenson, c.1775
vv. 3, 4 anon. (A Good Christmas Box, 1847)

Setting I was published in the form of a verse for melody and bass followed by a four-part 'Hallelujah!' in Benjamin Smith's *Harmonious Companion* (1732). The composer was certainly not Smith, who writes at the head of his table of contents: 'I did propose to publish the Names of the Authors of the Tunes, but finding that Article very difficult, and of little use, I hope I shall be excus'd from omitting them.' (We sympathize.)

This setting appears to be from the time of Purcell, and verse and 'Hallelujah!' were very possibly composed as a unit, perhaps for domestic use as a divine hymn. The verses were probably conceived for solo voice and continuo, but at least some of the buyers of Smith's volume would have performed it chorally, either in two parts, with the melody doubled at the upper octave, or (following a common custom) adding one or two upper parts themselves. The hymn appeared in identical form in the 1769 edition of James Evison's *Compleat Book of Psalmody*, in which all the other tunes are in four parts. This may strengthen the case for solo or choral two-part performance; for four-part performance we provide optional soprano and alto parts. The symphony is also editorial.

Twenty-three years after Smith's volume, the 'Hallelujah!' refrain was printed as the conclusion to the anonymous anthem 'They that put their trust in the Lord' in William Crisp's *Divine Harmony* (1755). Crisp ascribes the entire anthem to the northern composer James Green (*fl.* 1713–51): it had indeed appeared in the sixth edition of Green's *Collection of Choice Psalm Tunes* (1729), but it was also printed in various collections without the 'Hallelujah!', and it is thus that we find it in the earliest known source, the first edition of John Chetham's *Book of Psalmody* (1718). The likelihood is that the 'Hallelujah!' was originally composed in connection with the present hymn, and that anthem and 'Hallelujah!' were only brought together by Green (who provided a quite different 'Hallelujah!' conclusion in his tenth edition of 1744).

Setting II is taken from the fourth edition (*c.*1775) of *Church Harmony Sacred to Devotion* by Joseph Stephenson, parish clerk of Poole, in Dorset. Headed 'A Christmas Hymn', it is an orthodox fuging tune, but with a surprising opening which would seem to owe a debt to the English madrigalists, whose works were by no means unknown in the eighteenth century.

Versions of setting II as sung in the West Country were printed by both Gilbert and Sandys, each with interesting crudities resulting from absorption into the oral tradition (and, in Sandys's case, from the omission of a bar by the printer). There is also an arrangement, with a clumsily added soprano, by the American composer Daniel Bayley, published in his *New Harmony of Zion, or Complete Melody* (Newburyport, 1788).

Version III is a transcription of Stephenson's setting after 150 years of living rough. It was taken down by H. E. D. Hammond in 1919 from the singing of the Walton (Buckinghamshire) waits, and is bound into a copy of Sandys in the Vaughan Williams Memorial Library in London. Hammond calls it 'The Old Hark Hark', which is what it is known as in the singing pubs of South Yorkshire, where it is a particular favourite. Apart from 'On Ilkla Moor' (originally a psalm tune—see notes, 46:v), there can hardly be another 'composed' setting that has so thoroughly penetrated the oral tradition.

A different setting of the words as sung in Leicestershire is given in *The University Carol Book* (1961).

PERFORMANCE I, *verse*: (*i*) tenor or soprano and continuo; (*ii*) in two parts, soprano and tenor voices on the melody, with basses, and doubling instruments *ad lib.*; (*iii*) voices in four parts, the melody sung at both octaves, and with instruments *ad lib.*; (*iv*) choir, with the treble and tenor parts exchanged so that the tune is uppermost, the treble tune possibly doubled at the lower octave in the verse only; instruments *ad lib. Refrain*: voices (no octave doubling) with organ and/or instruments. (See Appendix 3.)

II, choir, soli and full as indicated.

III, choir, full throughout. The key is presumably the one in which the Walton waits sang it, perhaps with boys on the top line and men (tenor, baritone, bass) below. It could be sung SATB if transposed up to G. The transcription does not mention octave doublings, but these probably occurred; and instrumental doubling would also be effective (see Appendix 3).

76

Joy to the world!

(Christmas)

1 Joy to the world! the Lord is come:
   Let earth receive her King!
   Let ev'ry heart prepare him room,
   And heav'n and nature sing!

2 Joy to the earth! the Saviour reigns:
   Let men their songs employ,
   While fields and floods, rocks, hills and
     plains
   Repeat the sounding joy.

*3 No more let sins and sorrows grow,
   Nor thorns infest the ground:
   He comes to make his blessings flow
   Far as the curse is found.

4 He rules the world with truth and grace,
   And makes the nations prove
   The glories of his righteousness
   And wonders of his love.

Isaac Watts (1674–1748)

I

Pre-1833
(rev. William Holford, c.1834,
arr. editors)

II

(Christmas)

Pre-1833
(arr. Thomas Clark, 1775–1859,
after Holford, c.1834)

1. Joy to the world!_ the Lord is come: Let earth re-ceive her King! Let ev-'ry_ heart_ pre-pare_ him_ room,_ And heav'n and na-ture_ sing,_ and heav'n and na-ture sing,_ and heav'n, and heav'n_ and na-ture_ sing!

As their title suggests, Watts's *Psalms of David imitated in the language of the New Testament* (1719) are not conventional translations. Some psalms are omitted as unsuitable for Christian worship, others are given in several different paraphrases, and latent Christian interpretations of these Old Testament songs are generally made explicit: the well-known hymn 'Jesus shall reign where'er the sun', for example, is from Psalm 72. In some cases Watts even substitutes 'Britain' for 'Israel', rather as a medieval illustrator would set a biblical scene in his own country.

'Joy to the world!' is drawn from 'To our Almighty Maker, God', Watts's paraphrase of Psalm 98, beginning with verse 2. There is no explicit reference to Christmas, but the heading reads: 'The Messiah's Coming and Kingdom'. There is a setting by William Billings (see notes, 78) in his *Music in Miniature* (1779) and another is attributed to him in Jonathan Huntington's *The Apollo Harmony* (1807). Thomas Cotterill published a much altered text in his *Selection of Psalms and Hymns* (1819), which perhaps encouraged others to make their own adaptations, for the hymn appeared as 'The Lord is come: let heaven rejoice' in *The Mitre Hymn Book* (1836) and as 'Joy to the world, the Lord is nigh' in the Catholic-Apostolic (Irvingite) *Hymns for the Use of the Churches* (1864). As a result, several different versions are still in use. We, like most modern editors, have preferred Watts's original.

The tune, usually known as 'Antioch', has been ascribed to a number of composers and is often wrongly described as 'arranged from Handel' and is attributed to Lowell Mason (1792–1872). Its origins and development have been traced by John Wilson in his article 'The Origins of the Tune "Antioch"' (Bulletin of the Hymn Society of Great Britain and Ireland, no. 166, June 1986), which we summarize here—partly because it has been conspicuously ignored by several subsequent US hymnals. (See below for a possible caveat, which would reverse Wilson's 'earliest known form' and 'first stage of revision', while confirming his case for an English provenance.) Its first known printings were in the 1830s and it has much in common with Dissenting 'repeating' tunes of that date, which retained the idiom of the previous century. In the *Collection of Tunes* (1833) by the Methodist Thomas Hawkes, of Wilton, Somerset, it is given in what is presumably its original form (see ex. 1, below), with the title 'Comfort' and

headed 'author unknown'; it is recommended to be sung with two Charles Wesley hymns, 'O joyful sound of gospel grace!' and 'How large the promise, how divine'. The same tune, with rather fuller harmony and again associated with 'O joyful sound', is also found a little later in another compilation by a Methodist, the third volume (*c.*1835) of the non-denominational *Congregational Harmonist* by Thomas Clark, of Canterbury (see notes, 46:v), who does not mark it as one of his own compositions.

The tune is transformed in one of the most successful of early nineteenth-century tune-books, *Voce di melodia* (*c.*1834) by William Holford, conductor of the choir of St Clement's proprietary chapel, Lever Street, Manchester. This was the companion tune-book to the huge *Selection of Psalms and Hymns extracted from various collections* (1827) by the Revd William Nunn, proprietor of the chapel, which was influential in introducing the work of many of the best Dissenting hymn-writers to Anglicanism. Holford's book almost certainly appeared just before the 1835 (third) edition of the *Selection*. This revision of 'Comfort' produced what we may loosely call the 'Antioch' version of the tune (I).

A new source has recently been discovered, with the tune and setting of 'Comfort' as in *Voce di melodia*. It is no. 87 (p. 949) of vol. III of the undated four-volume collection of psalm and hymn-tunes *Psalmodia Britannica . . . arranged, or the existing arrangements revised, by Charles Rider*. The front boards of vols. 3 and 4 of the British Library copy (a.263) have 'Mr Charles Rider, Fairfield' inscribed in gold letters, and a shorter and seemingly linked collection with many Lancashire tune-names (in the same library) is by 'Charles Rider, Manchester': publication in Manchester around 1826–32 has been suggested for the big collection, though it may prove to be later. For the present, it is equally possible that Rider revised the tune and Holford merely took it from him, or vice versa; or both may have taken the revised version from some earlier and as yet undiscovered book.

It may even be that their supposed revision is closer to the original than Hawkes's version. The second half of Hawkes's first strain (see ex. 1 bars 2–4) looks suspiciously like a fragment of the treble of an earlier tenor-tune setting which—by a familiar but unconscious process (see Appendix 3)—has been incorporated in the tune by gallery singers and/or congregation; the 'missing' notes of the

EX. 1: *'Comfort'* (*Hawkes, 1833*)

O joy - ful sound of gos - pel_____ grace! Christ shall in me ap - pear.

I, e - ven____ I,____ shall see____ his____ face;____ I shall be ho - ly____

here,____ I shall be ho - ly____ here,____ I shall____ be ho - ly here.

♩ ♩♩ ♩ ♩♩

modern form, B♭ A G F, form Hawkes's bass at this point. If this were so, it would follow that: (*i*) the tune as harmonized by Hawkes was an adaptation (his own? West Country? Methodist?), and was already at one or more removes from its original form, the setting having been modified through oral transmission; (*ii*) the descent of a complete octave in the first strain of the modern form, first found in the books of Rider and Holford, was not a revision at all, but derived from the as yet undiscovered original print or a direct descendant; (*iii*) we cannot in that case be sure that the later strains in Rider and Holford do not also reflect the original; (*iv*) the tune may even have been composed and first published in the Manchester area; and (*v*) John Wilson's conviction that it is of English origin is, if anything, strengthened.

Holford attributes the tune unequivocally to Handel, presumably because of the resemblance of the opening phrase to the choruses 'Glory to God' and 'Lift up your heads' in *Messiah*; and, in the hallowed antiquarian tradition, he strengthens the attribution by rewriting the fifth and sixth strains with staggered upper and lower voices (which we retain in our arrangement—see bars 12–16) to bring out what was at best a faint echo of the string ritornello introducing the recitative 'Comfort ye, my people' in *Messiah*. Holford may have been influenced in this by the name of the tune, though 'Comfort' is in fact a typical Dissenting tune-name of the time. The opening figure is by no means unique in melodies of its type, and any resemblance to Handel was probably coincidental or, at least, unconscious, since Handel's idiom in general, and the music of *Messiah* in particular, was Holy Writ to Dissenting musicians.

In 1836 the Rider/Holford version appeared in tune-books on both sides of the Atlantic. John Houldsworth, of Halifax, included it in the third edition of his *New and Enlarged Edition of Cheetham's Harmony* (Halifax, 1832), with rather fuller harmony and an adventurous ascent for solo tenor in the fourth strain which we have incorporated in our own setting (I, bars 10–12). A version deriving from

Houldsworth is in Edward Booth's *Wesleyan Psalmist* (1843), with no mention of Handel.

The crucial marriage with Watts's text also occurred in 1836. Lowell Mason (1792–1872), the leading Presbyterian hymn-composer in America, made several arrangements, the first of which appeared in the third of his series of booklets entitled *Occasional Psalm and Hymn Tunes, selected and original* (Boston, 1836). Mason retained the attribution to Handel, changed the tune-name to 'Antioch', and united it with Watts's hymn for the first time. Mason's setting owes much to Holford, but all feeling of the eighteenth century has finally been lost from the harmony. It quickly became a national favourite, and Mason produced successive versions of it in his *Modern Psalmist* (1839), *Carmina Sacra* (1841), and *The National Psalmist* (1848).

From America the 'Antioch' version, allied to Watts's text, made its way back home, though it never established itself in the seasonal repertory outside Evangelical circles. But the original 'Comfort' version is still kept alive in those sections of the British Churches that take pride in their eighteenth-century heritage, in a revision by Thomas Clark (setting II). Here it is cleverly modified to take in the essence of Holford's and Houldsworth's changes (the expressive pause in bar 15 comes from the latter) while preserving the character of the original and playing down the 'Comfort ye' mutation. The revision was produced for the 1854 edition of *The Union Tune Book* (1837), for which Clark was commissioned to reharmonize the tunes, and it appears there with Watts's text though with the tune-name 'Jerusalem' (from a less than happy association with the hymn 'Jerusalem, my happy home'). With small differences, Clark's revision appeared also in *The Primitive Methodist Hymnal* (1889) and in *Companion Tunes to Gadsby's Hymn Book* (1927) with the 'Jerusalem' text and entitled 'Jerusalem/Comfort'.

PERFORMANCE I, choir and/or congregation with organ, and instruments *ad lib.*

II, choir, with instruments or organ *ad lib.*

77

Come, let us all with heart and voice

(*Christmas*)

c.1780?
(*Herman French Collection*)

SYMPHONY

VERSE

1. Come, let us all___ with heart and voice Join with the an-gels, and re - -joice! Join__ with the an-gels, and re-joice! Join__ with the an-gels, join__ with the an-gels in their songs; Join with our hearts as well as

2 Then let us all in praise unite
   To him who left yon world of light;
   He left his Father's glorious throne
   For us a Saviour to be born.

3 'All glory,' then again begin,
   'To him who thus was sent from heaven!
   For ever be his Name adored,
   Of Christ, our Saviour and our Lord!'

c.1780?
(Herman French Collection)

This fine setting, undated and unsigned, is found in three related scores from the Devon village of Widecombe, where the local Methodists and Baptists used to combine their singers and instruments to form the Christmas Night carol party. All three are in the collection of West Country gallery manuscripts built up by the late Herman French and kindly made available to us by Mrs W. French. We have not found the text or setting in any other source, and the tune does not appear in the register of *Fuging Tunes in the Eighteenth Century* by Nicholas Temperley and Charles G. Manns (1983). One of the three manuscripts (HF6 in the catalogue-in-progress by Rollo Woods) seems to be a copy score for the other two: it is rough, with many corrections,

and with unsolved problems in bars 10 and 27–8. We have tacitly corrected the obvious errors, and have simply guessed at bar 10. Possible errors that we have left uncorrected are in bars 3 (instrument I, last note, C?), 7 (sixth bass note, D?), and 15 (second tenor note, C?). The scores have no instrumental indications, but see Appendix 3 for the Widecombe band.

PERFORMANCE Choir and instruments. In the vocal sections the instruments double the voices, ornamenting the lines as appropriate (see Appendix 3, and carols 89 and 96:III for examples).

78

As shepherds in Jewry

(Christmas)

William Billings (1746–1800)

1. As shep - herds in Jew - ry were guard - ing their sheep, Pro -
2. 'Though A - dam the first in re - bel - lion was found, For -

- mis - cuous-ly seat - ed,[1] e - stran - ged from sleep, An an - gel from hea - ven pre -
- bid - den to tar - ry on hal - low - ed ground; Yet A - dam the se - cond[2] ap -

CHORUS

- sent - ed to view, And thus___ he ac - cost - ed the trem - bl - ing few: 'Dis -
- pears to re-trieve The loss___ you sus -tained___ by the de - vil and Eve. Then,

[1] i.e., mingled with their flock   [2] Christ

3   'A token I leave you, whereby you may find

This heavenly stranger, this friend to mankind;

A manger's his cradle, a stall his abode,

The oxen are near him and blow on your God.

Then, shepherds, be humble, be meek and lie low,

For Jesus your Saviour's abundantly so.'

4 This wonderous story scarce cooled on the ear
When thousands of angels in glory appear;
They join in the concert, and this was the theme:
'All glory to God and good will towards men!'
Then, shepherds, strike in, join your voice to the choir,
And catch a few sparks of celestial fire!

5 'Hosanna!' the angels in ecstasy cry;
'Hosanna!' the wondering shepherds reply;
'Salvation, Redemption are centured[3] in one:
All glory to God for the birth of his Son!
Then, shepherds, adieu! we commend you to God;
Go visit the Son in his humble abode!'

6 To Bethlehem city the shepherds repaired
For full confirmation of what they had heard;
They entered the stable with aspect so mild,
And there they beheld both the Mother and Child.
Then make proclamation, divulge it abroad,
That gentle and simple[4] may hear of the Lord!

William Billings (1746–1800)

[3] cinctured (encompassed) [4] those of high and low degree

William Billings, the outstanding American composer of the eighteenth century, was 'a singular man, of moderate size, short of one leg, with one eye, without an address, and with an uncommon negligence of person.' Time has rendered the language of this contemporary description ambiguous: in reality he had one leg shorter than the other, did indeed have only one eye, and lacked not a home but a winning manner. His powerful personality and coherent musical aesthetic come over strongly in the trenchantly expressed introductions to his six published volumes of music, and the sheer quality, bulk, and variety of what he achieved, as an essentially spare-time composer and in the teeth of personal and financial difficulties, is astonishing.

Disdain for personal appearance proved no bar to acceptance by polite society. Billings dominated musical Boston, teaching singing, directing the choirs of fashionable churches, and composing. He was at least predominantly self-taught in music. He began working at the age of fourteen as a tanner, and in later life accepted civic posts such as scavenger, hog-reeve, and sealer of leather.

His six publications divide his output between them by genre. The first, the massive *New England Psalm Singer* (1770), was the first American hymn collection to consist of the works of a single composer; the last, *The Suffolk Harmony* (1786), is a short collection of varied small-scale settings. All six are for unaccompanied choir, reflecting the conservatism of the Congregational churches for which he worked, though he himself favoured the use of organ and gallery band, and wrote an anthem (since lost) with organ accompaniment to celebrate the installation of an instrument in First Boston Congregational Church; circumstances, however, forbade that line of development. Within the *a cappella* limitations he produced a surprising variety of idiom and form. He had an Ivesian contempt for pedantry: 'I don't think myself confin'd to any Rules for composition . . . it is best for every composer to be his own carver' (from the Introduction to *The New England Psalm Singer*).

The 'crudity' of Billings's writing has regularly been linked with the fact that he was self-taught as a composer, like most of his New World contemporaries and the shape-note composers who succeeded them (see Appendix 3). But, as his writings reveal, he was the conscious inheritor of a vigorous English tradition of country psalmody, some of it much rougher than anything he wrote.

'As shepherds in Jewry', headed 'Emanuel. For Christ-mas' in *The Psalm-Singer's Amusement* (1781), is one of Billings's most exhilarating works, resembling nothing so much as an English glee. David McKay and Richard Crawford point out (in *William Billings of Boston*, 1975) that all the texts in the volume except this and 'Modern Music' are by named authors, '. . . and it is certain that [Billings] wrote the two unattributed texts'. There is nothing here to rival the stanza beginning 'Exult, ye oxen' in Billings's 'Methinks I hear' (in *The Singing Master's Assistant*, 1778), but the verse has the same raw colonial vigour that we find in the music—witness the oxen that, splendidly, 'blow on your God' (verse 3).

Puritan prejudice against Christmas stood in the way of what would surely otherwise have been widespread dissemination of 'As shepherds in Jewry', though it had been printed in three minor hymn collections when it was found by Jeremiah Ingalls (1764–1838), who arranged it in three parts for his *Christian Harmony* (1805). It is this arrangement that has been popularized by the Yale Glee Club, and continues to appear, ascribed to Ingalls, in American and British publications. *The Christian Harmony, or Songster's Companion* was the northern collection that set the pattern for the many southern hymn collections that were soon to follow.

Ingalls somewhat emasculated Billings's text, and subjected the setting to a process now generally called 'southernization', which many other northern hymn settings would subsequently undergo. What George Pullen Jackson (in *White Spirituals of the Southern Uplands*, 1933) memorably calls 'the servile and eventless northern alto' is either wrestled into shape (for the democratic southern shape-note singers held that all parts were born equal) or else, as with 'Emanuel', is eliminated in favour of a three-part texture. Redundant as many northern alto parts might appear, the loss in the present case was great, as Billings uses the alto skilfully to bind together his varied scorings, almost as the horns are used in classical orchestration, and the scoring in the first four bars of the chorus is a small example of the sensitivity to the choral palette that sets Billings apart from his less adventurous contemporaries.

Like 'A virgin unspotted' (80), this setting moves to a rapid compound time for the chorus (technically an 'extension' in this case, as it is sung to different words each time). This is widely described as 'a Billings fingerprint', though it is sometimes found in English country psalmody from around the same time. Billings rarely seems to expect an arithmetical proportion between the verse and chorus notations, merely (as here) a feeling that the chorus is faster.

PERFORMANCE   Choir, with octave doubling of the tenor (see Appendix 3).

79

Shepherds, rejoice!

(*Christmas*)

William Billings (1746–1800)

1. 'Shep - herds, re - joice! lift up_ your_ eyes, And send your_ fears_ a -
2. 'No gold, nor pur - ple swad - dling bands, Nor roy - al_ shi - ning_

-way; News from the re - gion of_ the_ skies: Sal -
things; A man - ger for_ his cra - dle_ stands, And

-va - tion's born_ to - day! Je - sus, the God_ whom
holds the_ King_ of kings. Go, shep-herds, where the_

an - gels fear,_ Comes down to_ dwell with you; To -
In - fant lies,_ And_ see his_ hum - ble throne; With

-day he__ makes his en - trance here, But__ not as__ mon - archs do.
tears of__ joy__ in all__ your eyes, Go,__ shep - herds, kiss__ the__ Son.'

3 Thus Gabriel sang, and straight around
The heavenly armies throng;
They tune their harps to lofty sound
And thus conclude the song:
'Glory to God that reigns above,
Let peace surround the earth;
Mortals shall know their Maker's love
At their Redeemer's birth.'

4 Lord! and shall angels have their songs
And men no tunes to raise?
O may we lose these useless tongues
When they forget to praise!
'Glory to God that reigns above,
That pitied us forlorn!'—
We join to sing our Maker's love,
For there's a Saviour born.

Isaac Watts (1674–1748)

'Shepherds, rejoice!', an energetic setting of what is probably an original tune, comes from the first of Billings's six publications (see notes, 78). Only the first word of each line is printed. The setting is headed 'Boston. For Christmas'. (A peculiarity of the hymn is that the first two stanzas are spoken by Gabriel.)

The text, from Book I of Isaac Watts's *Horae Lyricae* (1687), was as great a favourite in America as it was in England, where it appeared in countless broadsheets and was frequently set by less sophisticated composers.

There is a later (and quite different) setting of the same tune, to words by Billings himself, beginning 'Methinks I hear a Heav'nly Host', in *The Singing Master's Assistant* (1778). The new text, much influenced by Watts, was probably an attempt to produce words that scanned better to the tune.

The *Diary of William Bentley, D.D., Pastor of the East Church, Salem, Massachusetts* (4 vols., republished 1905–14),

has interesting details of how hymns, including some by Billings, were incorporated in services:

Dec. 25 1785. Christmas. The service as follows: to introduce the morning service. Two short anthems, Hail, Hail, etc., and Methinks I see,—Boston. [This must be Billings's later setting.] Before the sermon, Shepherds rejoice, etc. [perhaps the present setting]. After sermon, Anthem, Behold, etc . . .

25 Dec. 1792. For the first time in this place the Clarionet, and Violin introduced into Church-Music—there is now no ground of complaint against the Catholics.

PERFORMANCE Choir, with octave doubling of the tenor (see Appendix 3). The hiatus at bars 8–9 is found in both settings of 'Boston', and may be intended either literally or as a way of notating a mid-tune breather of shorter duration.

80

A virgin unspotted

(*Christmas*)

William Billings (1746–1800)

1. A virgin un-spot-ted, the pro-phet[1] fore-told, Should
2. Through Beth-le-hem ci-ty, in Ju-ry,[2] it was That

bring forth a Sa-viour, which now we be-hold, To be our Re-deem-er from
Jo-seph and Ma-ry to-ge-ther did pass, And for to be tax-ed when

death, hell and sin, Which A-dam's trans-gres-sion in-vol-ved us in.
thi-ther they came, Since Cae-sar Au-gus-tus com-mand-ed the same.

REFRAIN

Then__ let us be__ mer-ry, put sor-row a-way: Our__

[1] Isaiah [2] Jewry

Sa - viour,   Christ   Je - sus,   was   born   on   this   day.

3 But Mary's full time being come, as we
    find,[3]
  She brought forth her first-born to save all
    mankind;
  The inn being full, for this heavenly guest
  No place there was found where to lay him
    to rest.

4 But Mary, blest Mary, so meek and so
    mild,
  Soon wrapped up in swaddlings this
    heavenly Child:
  Contented, she laid him where oxen do
    feed;
  The great God of nature approved of the
    deed.

5 To teach us humility all this was done;
  Then learn we from hence haughty pride
    for to shun;
  A manger's his cradle who came from
    above,
  The great God of mercy, of peace and of
    love.

6 Then presently[4] after, the shepherds did
    spy
  Vast numbers of angels to stand in the
    sky;
  So merrily talking, so sweet they did
    sing:
  'All glory and praise to our heavenly
    King!'

Traditional
(Billings, 1778)

[3] in the gospels   [4] immediately

From *The Singing Master's Assistant* (1778), the second of
Billings's six publications (see notes, 78). 'A virgin unspotted' is one of the most widespread of all English folk
carols, the melody existing in countless variants (see notes,
143). Both text and tune had crossed the Atlantic at least by
the eighteenth century. Billings prints only verse 1; the
others are from John Arnold, *The Compleat Psalmist*
(fourthedn., London, 1756).

Billings's melody seems to be original, despite echoes of
the folk melody in the refrain. No exact proportion between
the notation of verse and refrain seems intended: the
quavers of the refrain should perhaps be a little faster than
the crotchets of the verse (cf. 'As shepherds in Jewry', 78.)

PERFORMANCE   Choir, with octave doubling of the tenor
(see Appendix 3).

81

The Lord descended from above

(*Christmas*)

Supply Belcher (1752–1836)

rode,   And   on   the   wings   of   might-y   winds   Came
fly - ing,   fly - - ing,
fly - - ing all a-broad.   -broad.

Thomas Sternhold (d.1549)

Supply Belcher was a member of the eighteenth-century school of New England composers of which William Billings was the leading light (see notes, 78). He was born in Stoughton (now Sharon), Massachusetts, where he ran a tavern, and later moved to Farmington, Maine, where he taught in the local schools. He loved fugal counterpoint, and this, together with a certain expansiveness of melodic line, earned him the nickname 'The Handel of Maine'.

The Sternhold and Hopkins version of Psalm 18:9–10 was popular for Christmas settings in Puritan America (it was used occasionally in England, too) because it was one of the few pieces of versified Scripture that could be applied to Christmas. Billings set it several times, and a setting by James Lyon (1735–94) in his *Urania* (1761) was one of a number of pieces sung by a chorus of 350 voices with 50 instrumentalists in Philadelphia in 1786. Belcher's setting is from *The Harmony of Maine*, which he published in 1794.

Two unusual features are the comparative equality of treble and tenor voices in the full sections, and the suspension in bar 8 (a great rarity). The sustained notes held regardless of dissonance (bars 4, 11, 27) are typical of his free treatment of harmony. (We have made the minimum of amendments, since it is not always possible to distinguish printer's errors from the composer's intentions: bar 2, alto, note 2, G for A; bar 8, tenor, note 3, B for A; bar 22, bass, note 2, E for C; bar 30, bass, note 2, F for E; in bar 29 the treble and tenor rhythm is printed ♩ ♪♪♫ ; in bars 11½–12 perhaps the treble should be one degree lower, the alto similarly at '-ness of' in bars 12–13.)

PERFORMANCE   Choir (with no octave doubling). The hiatus in bars 14–15 may have been contracted in performance to |♩. ♩| as was certainly the custom in shape-note music (see notes, 82).

82

Ye nations all, on you I call

(Christmas)

William Walker (1809–75)

1. Ye nations all,__ on you I call: come, hear this de - cla - ra - tion, And
don't re - fuse__ this glo-rious news of Je - sus and sal - va - tion! To
roy - al Jews came first the news of Christ the great__ Mes - si - ah, As

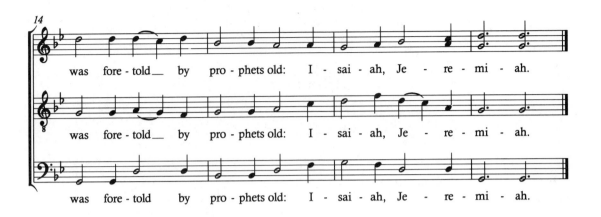

was fore-told__ by pro-phets old: I - sai - ah, Je - re - mi - ah.

was fore-told__ by pro-phets old: I - sai - ah, Je - re - mi - ah.

was fore-told by pro-phets old: I - sai - ah, Je - re - mi - ah.

2 To Abraham the promise came, and to his seed for ever,
   A light to shine in Isaac's line, by Scripture we discover.
   Hail, promised morn! the Saviour's born, the glorious Mediator—
   God's blessèd Word, made flesh and blood, assumed the human nature.

3 His parents, poor in earthly store to entertain the stranger,
   They found no bed to lay his head but in the ox's manger;
   No royal things, as used by kings, were seen by those that found him,
   But in the hay the stranger lay, with swaddling bands around him.

4 On the same night a glorious light to shepherds there appearèd;
   Bright angels came in shining flame: they saw and greatly fearèd.
   The angels said: 'Be not afraid! although we much alarm you,
   We do appear good news to bear, as now we will inform you.

5 'The city's name is Bethlehem, the which God hath appointed;
   This glorious morn a Saviour's born, for him God hath anointed.
   By this you'll know, if you will go to see this little stranger:
   His lovely charms in Mary's arms, both lying in a manger.'

6 When this was said, straightway was made a glorious sound from heaven;
   Each flaming tongue an anthem sung: 'To men a Saviour's given!
   In Jesus' name, the glorious theme, we elevate our voices;
   At Jesus' birth be peace on earth; meanwhile all heav'n rejoices.'

7   Then with delight they took their flight, and wing'd their way to glory;
    The shepherds gazed, and were amazed to hear the pleasing story.
    To Bethlehem they quickly came, the glorious news to carry,
    And in the stall they found them all, Joseph, the Babe, and Mary.

8   The shepherds then return'd again to their own habitation;
    With joy of heart they did depart, now they have found salvation.
    'Glory,' they cry, 'to God on high, who sent his Son to save us!
    This glorious morn the Saviour's born: his name it is Christ Jesus.'

William Walker? (1809–75)

'Singin' Billy' Walker was a highly successful singing teacher, composer, and compiler of several shape-note books (see Appendix 3) whose memory is still revered in parts of the American south. His musical activities sprang to a large extent fom his religious convictions, and the singing-schools he established were mostly among the Southern Baptist communities. He was born on Tyger River, near Cross Keys, Union County, South Carolina, and spent most of his life in the little town of Spartanburg in the same state. Walker was of Welsh descent, and was called 'Singin' Billy' to distinguish him from two other Spartanburg William Walkers, a father and son known as 'Hog Billy' and 'Pig Billy'. Walker preferred to distinguish himself by adding the initials A. S. H. after his name, standing for 'Author, *Southern Harmony*'.

The Southern Harmony, from which 'Ye nations all' is taken, was one of the early shape-note collections, first published in New Haven in 1835. It is a four-shape book, and was in some ways superseded by Walker's later seven-shape *Christian Harmony*, which appeared just after the Civil War in 1867. But *The Southern Harmony* remained popular, even though no new edition appeared after 1854: George Pullen Jackson, author of *White Spirituals of the Southern Uplands* (1933), was amazed to stumble across a *Southern Harmony* singing in 1931. Partly as a result of Jackson's book, there was a reprint of *The Southern Harmony* in 1939 and another in 1966, and it is in regular use at the annual singing at Benton, Kentucky. Many of the individual pieces have also been kept alive in the books of the Primitive Baptists. There were originally twenty-five pieces by Walker himself, but the number had grown to forty by the third edition of 1854. The authors of the words are rarely named.

'Ye nations all' is the most popular of Walker's pieces, and has the tune-name 'The Babe of Bethlehem'. It is here transposed down a tone. The swinging pentatonic melody in the middle part is one of a large family of related Dorian and Aeolian tunes given by Jackson in the notes on this song, in his *Spiritual Folk-Songs of Early America* (1937, no. 51), the seventeen variants being sung to eleven spiritual and six secular texts. Jackson believed that Walker recorded the carol from oral tradition and added the treble and bass himself. 'Gap-scaled' tunes of this sort were popular in the early days among the Calvinist sects, before the introduction of tune-books, and drew on the folk traditions of the various European settlers. (Gapped scales are characteristic of primitive music: this one is essentially the 'bagpipe' pentatonic—five-note—scale corresponding to the black notes on the piano.)

We give the text as Walker prints it, merely substituting 'the which' for 'in which' in verse 5, line 1. Lines 3 and 4 of that verse resist punctuation. They seem to mean: 'You will recognize him by this, if you go to see the little stranger: he is lying in all his beauty in the arms of Mary, and they both [rather than both of Mary's arms] are lying in a manger.'

PERFORMANCE   Choir, with the usual shape-note octave doublings (see Appendix 3). The rests in bar 9 should perhaps be ignored. Jackson says that shape-note singers have a common custom of 'not tolerating any dead spaces or long rests . . . which are felt as needed to make the rhythmic form mathematically correct or quadratic . . . the leaders and singers deliberately disregard the rest-beat and proceed as though it did not exist.'

83

Glory to God on high

(Christmas)

Jeremiah Ingalls (1764–1838)

good will to men, to___ an-gels joy,_____ good will to

good will to men, to___ an-gels joy,_____ good will to

men, to an-gels joy,_____ good will to

men, to an-gels joy,_____ good will to

men, to an - gels joy, At our Re - deem - er's birth!

men,_ to___ an - gels joy, At our Re - deem - er's birth!

men, to an - gels joy, At our Re - deem - er's birth!

men, to an - gels joy, At our Re - deem - er's birth!

Isaac Watts (1674–1748)

Jeremiah Ingalls was born in Andover, Massachusetts, in 1764. By 1791 he had moved to Newbury, Vermont, where he married and set about fathering his eleven children. Described as 'short and corpulent', he worked as a cooper and farmer until, in 1800, he built his own tavern which he ran for the next decade. (Supply Belcher also ran a tavern—see notes, 81: then, as now, singing and drinking often went together.)

In 1805 Ingalls brought out his only publication, *The Christian Harmony, or, Songster's Companion*. It may have been the expense of this and the only moderate sales (at $1 a copy it was not cheap) that led to the financial difficulties that afflicted him a few years later and which are thought to have been the reason for his removal from the diaconate and expulsion from Newbury Congregational Church. He moved with his family to a farm between Rochester and Hancock in the Green Mountains and remained there until his death.

A singing-school master all his life, Ingalls wrote incidental music for various local events in Newbury and played both sacred and secular music on his 'bass viol' (cello or double bass, as in English gallery bands—see Appendix 3), the use of which he introduced to both the Newbury and Rochester churches.

The Christian Harmony is in many ways untypical of tune-books of the time in its use of unusual metres, in its mainly three-voice texture (rather than the four voices normal in previous northern books), in its liberal use of dance-like triple-time tunes and folk melodies, and in its great length. No comparable collections appeared in the north, but it seems to have been the inspiration of the distinctive southern type of song-book. Of the 137 pieces it contains, twenty-three are lifted complete from other sources, and for the rest 'Ingalls evidently considered as fair game any music, sacred or secular, printed or oral, with which he was familiar' (David Klocko, in his introduction to the modern facsimile edition, 1981).

The tune, called 'Redemption', may have been inspired by the opening of Abraham Maxim's minor-mode hymn-tune 'Machias', which Ingalls found in the 1803 edition of *The Village Harmony* (1795). The rest of Ingalls's melody is his own. The text is a verse of Watts's hymn 'Behold, the grace appears', from his *Hymns and Spiritual Songs* (Book I, 1707).

PERFORMANCE   Voices, with octave doubling of the tenor (see Appendix 3); cello or double bass *ad lib*.

The generally high tessitura in Ingalls's book suggests a low pitch standard. Performance in G is more exciting, but F may be closer to what was intended.

84

Hail the blest morn!

I

(Christmas)

(arr.?) William Caldwell (fl. 1834–7)

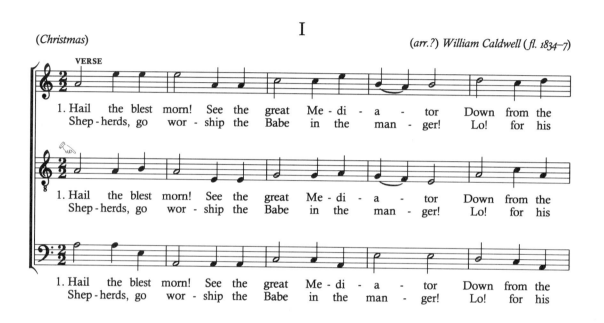

morn - ing, Dawn on our dark - ness and lend us thine aid; Star in the

East, the ho - ri - zon a - dorn - ing, Guide where our in - fant Re - deem - er was laid!

2 Cold on his cradle the dewdrops are shining,
   Low lies his bed with the beasts of the stall;
Angels adore him, in slumber reclining,
   Wise men and shepherds before him do fall.

3 Say, shall we yield him, in costly devotion,
   Odours of Edom and off'rings divine,
Gems from the mountain and pearls from the ocean,
   Myrrh from the forest and gold from the mine?

4 Vainly we offer each ample oblation,
   Vainly with gold would his favour secure;
Richer by far is the heart's adoration,
   Dearer to God are the prayers of the poor.

v. 1 anon.
Refrain and vv. 2–4 after Reginald Heber (1783–1826)

II

(*Christmas*)   (*Songs for All Time*)

VERSE

1. Hail the blest morn!__ See the great Me - di - a - tor
Shep - herds, go wor - ship the Babe in the man - ger!

Down from the re - gions of glo - ry de - scend!
Lo! for his guard__ the bright an - gels at - tend.

REFRAIN

Bright - est and best of the sons of the morn - ing, Dawn on our dark - ness and

lend us thine aid; Star in the East,__ the ho - ri - zon a - dorn - ing,

Guide where our in - fant Re - deem - er was laid!

2 Cold on his cradle the dewdrops are shining,
    Low lies his bed with the beasts of the stall;
   Angels adore him, in slumber reclining,
    Wise men and shepherds before him do fall.

3 Say, shall we yield him, in costly devotion,
  Odours of Edom and off'rings divine,
  Gems from the mountain and pearls from the ocean,
  Myrrh from the forest and gold from the mine?

4 Vainly we offer each ample oblation,
  Vainly with gold would his favour secure;
  Richer by far is the heart's adoration,
  Dearer to God are the prayers of the poor.

v. 1 anon.
Refrain and vv. 2–4 after Reginald Heber (1783–1826)

The tune first appeared, with this text, in Caldwell's *Union Harmony or Family Musician* (Maryville, Tennessee, 1837), with the name 'Star in the East'. All that is known of Caldwell is what he tells us in his preface, that he had been a singing-teacher for fifteen years before the publication. He also tells us that the purpose of the book was not a narrow denominational one: it was to provide a selection suitable for 'the different branches of the church of Christ in the Southern and Western country'—hence 'Union'.

'Hail the blest morn!' is one of forty-two tunes to which Caldwell attaches his own name, but he warns in his preface that 'many of the tunes over which the name of the Subscriber [Caldwell] is set are not entirely original, but he has harmonised, and therefore claims them . . . Many of the airs which the author has reduced to the [shape-note notational] system and harmonised, have been selected from the unwritten music in general use in the Methodist church, others from the Baptist and many more from the Presbyterian taste.' George Pullen Jackson comments: 'We may therefore look upon him as a recorder of religious folk-tunes from the oral tradition, long before folk-tunes as such were identified in America as a specific musical form. And the folkish character of many of these recorded tunes is perfectly evident in their primitive five-tone modes and their melodic trend.'

We have taken the setting (I) from William Walker's shape-note book *The Southern Harmony* (1835; see notes, 82). The sometimes quite extended octave writing (e.g., bars 15–16) may reflect an improvised practice in the churches and outdoor meetings of the early nineteenth century that is otherwise all but lost to us (see Appendix 3).

A touching major-mode version of the melody (II) was collected from Mrs Rachel Ritchie in Kentucky (*Songs For All Time*), and is ideal for solo or unison performance.

The text is a puzzle. The source of verse 1 is unknown, but the refrain and verses 2–4 are the first four verses of the Epiphany hymn 'Brightest and best of the sons of the morning' by Bishop Heber. The same text appears in the Presbyterian *Psalms and Hymns for the Worship of God* (Richmond, 1867), where it is misattributed to Tate and Brady. Verse 1 is markedly inferior to Heber's verses, and may simply have been added to free his verse 1 to function as a refrain, an idea that could have been suggested by his repetition of verse 1 as verse 5. There is an additional awkwardness in that the new verse 1 is uncompromisingly for Christmas Day whilst the remainder is for the Epiphany. We have allowed most of the variations from Heber's text to stand, only restoring 'Edom' for 'Eden' in verse 3 and 'would' for 'we' in verse 4, line 2.

The episcopate was anathema to members of the Calvinist sects, so they were presumably ignorant of the fact that this, the most popular carol in the southern books, was by a bishop of the Church of England (though in fact, like all Heber's hymns, it was written while he was vicar of Hodnet, Shropshire, before his three years as Bishop of Calcutta; ironically, the hymn was much criticized when it was first published in the *Christian Observer* in 1811, mainly on the grounds of its metre, which—intentionally—suggests a dance: it was rejected by the editors of the first edition of *Hymns Ancient and Modern*, 1861, while in the current *English Hymnal* it is set to a staid chorale). Christmas itself was unacceptable to the more extreme Puritans, who saw it as the old pagan Saturnalia in a thin Christian disguise (but see Chester Raymond Young, 'The observance of old Christmas in Southern Appalachia', in *An Appalachian Symposium*, ed. J. W. Williamson, 1977, for evidence of a more open attitude in the south).

PERFORMANCE I, voices, with the usual shape-note octave doublings (see Appendix 3).

II, solo, or unison voices; perhaps solo verses, unison refrains. For an example of the way in which solo singers embellished tunes of this kind see George Pullen Jackson, *Spiritual Folk-Songs of Early America* (1937), p. 153, no. 135 ('Amazing grace!').

85

Hark! hark! glad tidings charm our ears

(Christmas)

Anon.
(arr. William Walker, 1809–75)

*2 Our frailties long he deigned to share,
   The heir of heaven, of pain the heir;
   By miracles his power he tried,
   Preached, fasted, sighèd, groaned and died.
   He lived that men might live in peace;
   He died that death and sin might cease;
   He rose to prove to hell's fierce pow'rs:
   Blest immortality is ours.

Anon.
(*v. 1 Walker, 1835; v. 2 Wyeth, 1813*)

From William Walker's *The Southern Harmony* (1835; see notes, 82). It is an arrangement of the first section of the anonymous 'Redemption Anthem' that appeared for the first time in John Wyeth's influential shape-note book, *Repository of Sacred Music* (1813). A truncated hymn version, attributed to 'Stephenson', was included in Ananias Davisson's *Kentucky Harmony* (1816), one of many pieces from Wyeth that were taken over by the first of the important southern books (see Appendix 3).

Walker's source was presumably the *Kentucky Harmony*, though he attributes the setting to 'A. Benham sr'; he pro-

duced a three-part setting by the simple expedient of omitting the alto; he also omits the treble at the opening. He gives only one verse, while indicating that two are to be sung, and we have taken the second from Wyeth. We have also transposed the music down a tone, divided three bars of 2/4 so as to produce two bars (16–17) of 3/4, and substituted Gs for B♭s in bar 7 of the bass part.

PERFORMANCE Voices, with the usual shape-note octave doublings (see Appendix 3).

86

Stille Nacht! heilige Nacht!
Silent night! holy night!

I

(Christmas Night)

1 Stille Nacht! heilige Nacht!
Alles schläft; einsam wacht
nur das traute heilige Paar.
Holder Knab im lockigten Haar,
schlafe in himmlischer Ruh!
schlafe in himmlischer Ruh!

2 Stille Nacht! heilige Nacht!
Gottes Sohn, o wie lacht
Lieb' aus deinem göttlichen Mund
da uns schlägt die rettende Stund,
Jesus, in deiner Geburt!
Jesus, in deiner Geburt!

3 Stille Nacht! heilige Nacht!
die der Welt Heil gebracht
aus des Himmels goldenen Höhn.
Uns der Gnaden Fülle läßt sehn
Jesum in Menschengestalt,
Jesum in Menschengestalt.

4 Stille Nacht! heilige Nacht!
wo sich heut alle Macht
väterlicher Liebe ergoß,
und als Bruder huldvoll umschloß
Jesus die Völker der Welt,
Jesus die Völker der Welt.

1 Silent night! holy night!
Sleeps the earth, calm and quiet;
Lovely Child, now take thy rest:
On thy mother's gentle breast
Sleep in heavenly peace!
Sleep in heavenly peace!

2 Silent night! holy night!
When thou smil'st, love-beams bright
Pierce the darkness all around;
Son of God, thy birth doth sound
Our salvation's hour!
Our salvation's hour!

3 Silent night! holy night!
From the heaven's golden height
Christ descends, the earth to free;
Grace divine! by thee we see
God in human form!
God in human form!

4 Silent night! holy night!
God above at that sight
Doth with fatherly love rejoice,
While earth's peoples, with one voice,
Jesus their brother proclaim!
Jesus their brother proclaim!

300

5 Stille Nacht! heilige Nacht!
   lange schon uns bedacht,
   als der Herr vom Grimme befreit
   in der Väter urgrauer Zeit
   aller Welt Schonung verhieß,
   aller Welt Schonung verhieß.

6 Stille Nacht! heilige Nacht!
   Hirten erst kundgemacht
   durch der Engel Alleluja;
   tönt es laut bei Ferne und Nah:
   'Jesus der Retter ist da!
   Jesus der Retter ist da!'

Joseph Mohr (1792–1849)

5 Silent night! holy night!
   Adam's sin damned us quite,
   But the Son, to set us free
   From the Father's stern decree,
   Now in his mercy is born!
   Now in his mercy is born!

6 Silent night! holy night!
   Shepherds first with delight
   Heard the angelic 'Alleluia!'
   Echoing loud, both near and far:
   'Jesus, the Saviour, is here!
   Jesus, the Saviour, is here!'

Free tr., editors

(See performance notes)

Franz Xaver Gruber (1787–1863)
(reconstructed by the editors)

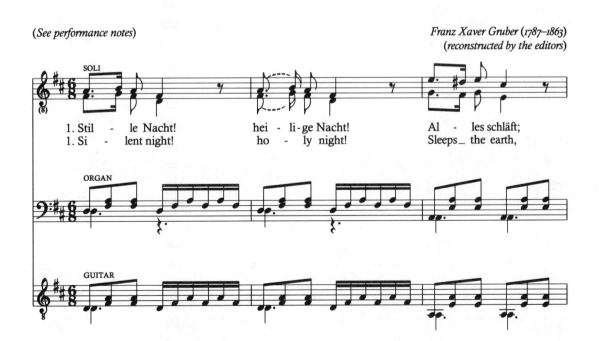

II

Modern version
after Franz Xaver Gruber (1787–1863)
(arr. editors)

(Christmas Night)

1. Si - lent night! ho - ly night! All is calm, all is bright
2. Si - lent night! ho - ly night! Shep - herds quake at the sight;
3. Si - lent night! ho - ly night! Son of God, love's pure light,

Round yon Vir - gin Mo - ther and Child; Ho - ly In - fant so ten - der and mild,
Glo - ries stream from hea - ven a - far, Heaven - ly hosts sing: 'Al - le - lu - ia!
Ra - diant, beams from thy ho - ly face With the dawn of re - deem - ing grace,

Sleep in hea - ven - ly peace! Sleep in hea - ven - ly peace!
Christ the Sa - viour is born! Christ the Sa - viour is born!'
Je - sus, Lord, at thy birth! Je - sus, Lord, at thy birth!

(tr. John F. Young, 1820–85)

The well-known story of how 'Stille Nacht!' came to be written is more fable than fact. The received version is that on Christmas Eve 1818 the organ in the parish church of the little Lower Austrian (now Bavarian) town of Oberndorf had breathed its last, and the curate (Mohr) and assistant organist (Gruber) between them saved the day by quickly writing a carol to be sung at midnight mass with guitar accompaniment. However, none of the many contemporary accounts suggests that there was any kind of emergency, and the organ remained in use for some years. 'Stille Nacht!' is in fact typical of the folk-like songs that organists in Austria and Bavaria would compose each year for the midnight service, and what Mohr and Gruber did was in no way out of the ordinary—except that they produced a carol of Schubertian charm which has captivated listeners from that first performance on.

There was always a strong folk element at the midnight mass in Austria and Catholic Germany, inspired by the cradle- and shepherd-songs that had grown up in the medieval tradition of cradle-rocking (see notes, 55). 'Stille Nacht!' is unmistakably in this tradition.

Gruber, an open, generous man, seems to have distributed copies of his carol to interested enquirers in the early days without even troubling to add his name. One such copy came into the hands of a glove-maker and folk-music enthusiast, Josef Strasser, who with his family singing group exploited the piece as a newly discovered Tyrolean 'folk carol'. In the audience for their Leipzig concert of 15 December 1832 was one A. R. Friese, who published the carol as the last of his *Vier ächte Tyroler Lieder* ... ('Four Authentic Tyrolean Songs for a soprano soloist or for four voices with optional piano accompaniment. Sung by the Strasser Family from the Ziller Valley. Faithfully transcribed from these excellent natural singers', Dresden, n.d.). Friese published a further arrangement *c.*1833. Only after much controversy and recourse to the law was the authorship of Mohr and Gruber established, a process that was hampered by the fact that the opening of the melody is almost identical to a *Volkslied* from the Innviertel, Gruber's homeland, which begins 'Geh i hinaus, zu an schen Haus'.

It was in the Dresden publications that the melodic variant appeared which continues to be sung everywhere except in Germany and Austria (compare bar 9 in settings I and II), seemingly as a result of a mistranscription by the Strassers from Gruber's soprano clef to treble. It was in this form that the carol spread to America, where it quickly became popular. Like 'Joy to the world!' (76), it was for a long time considered vulgar in England and was omitted from most hymn- and carol-books. (Its later popularity is said to owe something to the singing of Bing Crosby in the film *The Bells of St Mary's*, 1945.)

Gruber continued to perform it each Christmas, and a number of his arrangements survive, all of them giving the solo parts to high voices. Two of the arrangements are for orchestra: in the first (dated 12 December 1836, the year after he took up a new post in Hallein) the band consists of strings, flute, two clarinets, bassoon, two horns, and organ; the second (*c.*1845) is for a smaller orchestra of strings, two

horns, and organ. (Both manuscripts are now in the archives of the City of Hallein, and are printed in vol. 4 of *Denkmäler der Musik in Salzburg, Einzelausgaben* 4, 1987. This series also contains other music by Gruber, which shows him to be a capable composer.)

Painstaking research by Dr Joseph Gassner (*Silent Night, Holy Night: History and circulation of a carol*, ed. A. Schmaus and L. Kriss-Rettenbeck, 1968) has disposed of many myths and dated all the known autograph manuscripts. (Charles Cudworth's 'The true "Stille Nacht"', *Musical Times*, 105, 1964, p. 892, is an excellent background essay, despite minor errors of fact.) The original 1818 score has been lost, though five later autographs survive; we have drawn on two of these. One is in the Salzburg Museum Carolino Augusteum (HS 679) and is entitled 'Kirchenlied auf die heilige Christnacht ...' ('Church song for Christmas Night for soprano and alto [soli and choir] with quiet organ accompaniment ... 1818'). The date is misleading, since the arrangement was probably made by Gruber as part of his response to a request in 1854 from the Berlin Royal Chapel for the original version: whatever Gruber sent has disappeared, but this, in which the guitar writing seems to have been transferred directly to the keyboard, is as close to the original as we are now likely to get. The other is the 1836 Hallein arrangement, in which the upper parts are almost identical.

Mohr's contribution should not be underestimated. His poem, simple and euphonious as custom demanded, has unusual qualities which must have inspired Gruber. We give all six verses with our reconstruction (I), even though three (verses 1, 2, 6) became the norm at an early date in Austria, as elsewhere. The three-verse translation (II) is from C. L. Hutchin's *Sunday School Hymnal and Service Book* (Medford, Mass., 1876).

PERFORMANCE I (*i*) The original version (SATB and guitar): TB soli to bar 12 and SATB chorus thereafter, using the unornamented versions of bars 11 and 15 shown small above the staff. (*ii*) A 'standard' Gruber parish-choir setting (SATB and organ): SA chorus to bar 12 and SATB chorus thereafter. Organ plays the SA staff as right hand and the bass-clef staff as left hand. (*iii*) The '1818' autograph (SA and organ): SA soli to bar 12 and SA chorus thereafter. The 'quiet [8'] organ' as (*ii*).

II, choir, with organ *ad lib.*

87

Arise, and hail the sacred day!

(*Christmas*)

Eighteenth-century
(*Thomas Hardy Collection,
reconstructed by the editors*)

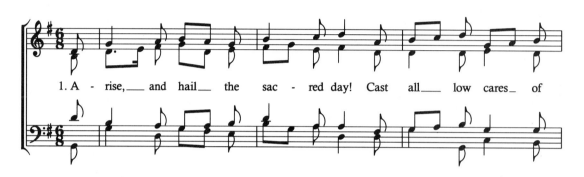

1. A - rise,___ and hail___ the sac - red day! Cast all___ low cares___ of

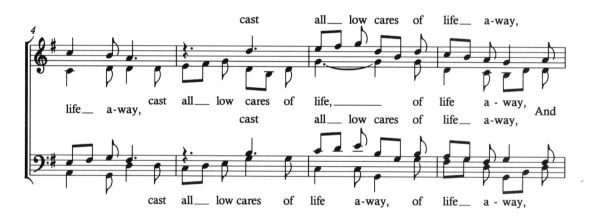

cast all___ low cares of life___ a-way,

life___ a-way, cast all___ low cares of life,_____ of life a - way, And

cast all___ low cares of life___ a-way,

cast all___ low cares of life a-way, of life___ a-way,

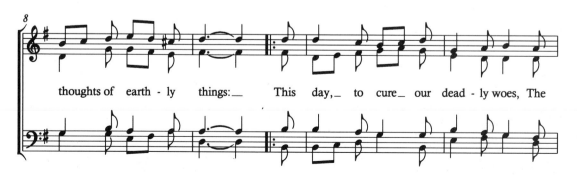

thoughts of earth - ly things:___ This day,___ to cure___ our dead - ly woes, The

2 If angels on that sacred morn
   Our Saviour, Jesus Christ, was born
      Poured forth their seraph's songs,
   How should a people, then, on earth,
   Triumph in honour of his birth
      To whom all praise belongs?

3 Then let us with the angels join
   And praise the glorious power divine
      With hallelujah high,
   With endless thanks to God above
   In showing forth his boundless love
      To all eternity!

After 'Mr Oats' (fl. 1748)
(Thomas Hardy Collection)

'You two counter-boys [altos], keep your ears open to Michael's fingering, and don't ye go straying into the treble part along o' Dick and his set [singers], as ye did last year; and mind this especially when we be in "Arise and hail"'—old William Dewy, the cellist leader of the Mellstock gallery band, giving last-minute instructions to the choir as they file out of the tranter's house just before midnight to begin their Christmas Night carolling of the parish, in Thomas Hardy's *Under the Greenwood Tree* (1872, chapter 4). The music referred to is probably 'Arise, and hail the joyful day', a straightforward four-part setting found in two of the four surviving carol-books that now form part of the Thomas Hardy Memorial Collection in the Dorset County Museum, Dorchester. (It has been published as no. 1 in *The Mellstock Carols*, ed. A. D. Townsend, 1989; bar 10 there could well have tempted the poor 'counter-boys' on to the tune—a constant hazard, which arose because singers generally learned their parts by rote.)

'Arise, and hail the sacred day!' is found in three of the four books in the museum collection, incomplete in each case and consisting of a score with soprano and tenor voices only. (Why the copying was never completed is a mystery.) The most useful of the three sources was compiled *c.*1820 by the local musician James Hook, and passed to Thomas Hardy (father of the novelist) *c.*1850. It consists mostly of songs and dance music, but 'Arise, and hail' appears at the end (with an incomplete violin part).

There can be little doubt that the two surviving vocal parts were being copied in from a complete four-part version, and the violin part and one of the other Hardy books can help to amplify the two parts a little. The violin begins by doubling the soprano line, but from bar 6 it doubles the missing alto an octave higher. (The first note of the second half returns to the treble line.) The single soprano of Hook's 'Duett' section (bars 15–18) can similarly be complemented from one of the other books, which has the same soprano part as Hook for the first seven notes and the alto for the remaining seven.

The version being copied into the Hardy books has little in common stylistically with the gallery tradition, and the long melisma in bars 14–15 is highly unusual (the only other example we know of is the melody of 'While shepherds watched' in the Hutchens manuscript in the Cornwall Record Office, Truro; see notes, 128). It is evidently a fairly sophisticated four-part arrangement of the three-part version of this carol printed in *The Musical Companion* (London, *c.*1775) by Joseph Stephenson of Poole, Dorset, perhaps taken from a publication we have not discovered. Stephenson's book contains some remarkably crude service music and two anthems, plus four Christmas carols in a rather more assured style which may not be by him (he

indicates his authorship of the rest of the music, but these have no attribution).

The Hardy family musicians were much in demand for weddings, Christmas parties, etc., not least because they performed gratis: see the tale 'Absent-mindedness in a Parish Choir', in Thomas Hardy's *Life's Little Ironies* (1894), in which a sleeping band at Christmas Day evensong is abruptly awoken for the final hymn, plays a hornpipe by mistake, and is replaced by a harmonium. The gallery choir and band at Stinsford, where the Hardys played, was disbanded in 1841, and the Puddletown band, in which the family then played, in 1845. 'Arise, and hail' seems to have been copied at a late stage, perhaps after 1845, when the Christmas Night carolling also ceased; so the curious title 'Christmas Piece' and the entry in what is mostly a book of songs and dances may mean that it was sung domestically in the Hardy household during various parties and celebrations in the course of the twelve days.

The text derives from a 'Hymn for Christmas-Day', published in the *Gentleman's Magazine* in November 1748 (pp. 516–17), 'The words by Mr Oats. Set to [quite different] Musick by Mr T. Wright, both of Devonshire.' This later appeared in William East's *Second Book of the Voice of Melody* (1750), and other settings of the text are found in Uriah Davenport's *Psalm-Singer's Pocket Companion* (1755), John Broderip's *Second Book of New Anthems and Psalm Tunes* (1750, reissued 1764), and William Tansur's *Royal Melody Compleat* (at least by the third edition, 1764–6). The text continued to be popular, and a good version in five verses was printed in *A Good Christmas Box* (1847).

PERFORMANCE Choir, with instruments *ad lib.* (see Appendix 3). Four strings would have been most likely in the Hardy household, the style suggesting a straightforward doubling—the upper instruments at pitch, without ornamentation, the cello taking the lower octave where possible. (A double bass is an alternative.)

88

Rejoice, ye tenants of the earth

(*Christmas*)

William Gifford (fl. c.1805)

1. Re - joice,_____ ye te - nants of the earth, And ce - le -

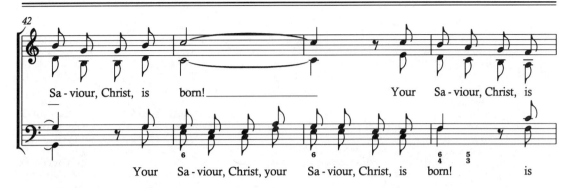

2 Behold! a meteor, shining bright,
   Conducts the eastern sages right
      To Judah's distant land,
   And guides to Bethlehem their road,
   Then fixes o'er his low abode,
      Directed by his hand;

3 And there they find the new-born King,
   To whom they did their offerings bring
      And worship at his feet,
   While angels, flying from their home,
   Proclaim that he alone is come,
      Salvation to complete.

4 For us these acclamations fly,
   For us he's born, below to die,
      That he may reign above:
   Then let us all our voices raise
   And sound abroad our Saviour's praise
      For his unbounded love.

William Gifford? (*fl. c.1805*)

'Four breaths, and then the last,' said the leader authoritatively, '"Rejoice, ye Tenants of the Earth," number sixty-four.'

At the close, waiting yet another minute, he said in a clear loud voice, as he had said in the village at that hour and season for the previous forty years—

'A merry Christmas to ye!'

When the expectant stillness consequent upon the exclamation had nearly died out of them all, an increasing light made itself visible in one of the windows of the upper floor . . . the blind went upward from before it, revealing to thirty concentrated eyes a young girl framed as a picture by the window architrave . . .

Opening the window, she said lightly and warmly—

'Thank you, singers, thank you!' . . .

'How pretty!' exclaimed Dick Dewy . . .

'As near a thing to a spiritual vision as ever *I* wish to see!' said tranter Dewy . . .

All the rest, after clearing their throats and adjusting their hats, agreed that such a sight was worth singing for.

Thus, in Thomas Hardy's *Under the Greenwood Tree* (1872), does the Mellstock choir first set eyes on Fancy Day, the new village schoolmistress, not knowing that her fine touch on the vicar's harmonium will be their undoing. (See also 'Remember, O thou man', 47:II, which features in the same novel.) The carol also appears in Hardy's narrative poem 'The Paphian Ball', in which the men of the Mellstock band are duped to play for the devil's ball instead of for the carollers; happily, a band of (presumably celestial) musicians steps in and meets with general approval:

'We've heard you many times,' friends said,
'But like *that* never you have played!
Rejoice, ye tenants of the earth,
And celebrate your Saviour's birth
Never so thrilled the darkness through,
Or more inspired us so to do!' . . .

The setting (in D) is by William Gifford, of South Petherton in Somerset, and was printed in his *Twelve New Psalm Tunes in 3, 4, 5 & 6 parts with symphonies and a thoroughbass for the organ, pianoforte with two Christmas hymns . . .* (London, 1805). It is headed '2nd Christmas Hymn. Written by the Author', and gives flutes and violins as alternatives on the upper instrumental parts.

'Rejoice, ye tenants' was an extremely popular carol in the West Country. Various parts (not the bass) are in the Hardy family manuscripts (see notes, 87), and two complete scores from the Devon village of Widecombe (transposed down a tone to C) are in the Herman French collection of carol manuscripts. It is also found in a manuscript book belonging to the Antell family and presented by W. A. Pickard-Cambridge to the Dorset County Record Office. The Antells were related by marriage to the Hardys, and an Antell was a model for Jude (the Obscure).

PERFORMANCE Choir and instruments—two flutes or violins, cello, and organ. The organ could be omitted if the cello plays throughout. Bassoon could effectively substitute for cello if flutes are used. (D is a better key for instruments).

The instruments play at pitch in the symphonies, and double the voices as follows: flute/violin 1 doubles the soprano and might ornament the line as appropriate (see carols 89 and 96:III for examples); flute/violin 2 doubles the alto at the higher octave in the full sections; the cello/bassoon should double the bass at the lower octave whenever possible in the full sections, with ornamentation as flute/violin 1.

(See also Appendix 3.)

89

Rouse, rouse from your slumbers!

(Christmas)

Nineteenth-century
*(Dunstan, 1929,
arr. editors)*

1. Rouse, rouse from_ your slum - bers!_ Pre - pare a glad_ voice And join_ with the num - bers_ That do_ now re - joice! Be no lon - ger_ si - lent,_ But_ now_ join_ with them: Arch - an - gels_ are_ bring-ing, arch - an - gels_ are_ bring-ing Glad ti - dings to_ men!
2. What bliss - ful_ glad ti - dings Is_ this that we_ hear? Har - mo - nious re - joi - cings Re - sound on_ the ear: 'Tis mu - sic_ trans - port - ing,_ Che - ru - bic,_ pro - found; Cre - a - tion's_ vast re - gions, cre - a - tion's vast_ re - gions It_ thun - ders_ a - round.

Join to   sing re - deem   -   -   ing   love!'

An - gel trumps the   mes - sage bring: 'Wel - come down the   new - born King!'

† Dunstan: 'Violin octave lower' (and at bar 36).

An - gel trumps the mes - sage bring: 'Wel - come down the new - born King!

Wel - come down_____ the new - - - born_ King!"

3   Hark! hark to the chorus,
      Salvation the theme,
   Which certain poor shepherds
      Did hear on the plain:
   ''Tis Jesus the Saviour,
      Come, see where he's born,
   In Bethlehem city
      On this happy morn!'

4   Then straightway the shepherds
      To Bethlehem steered,
   Stupendously led by
      A star that appeared;
   There Joseph and Mary
      They saw with surprise,
   And, laid in a manger,
      The King of the Skies.

Traditional
(*JRIC, 1923, adapted*)

A version of this carol was transcribed with some ceremony on Christmas Eve, 1921, from an old lady of eighty-seven, Mrs Ellen Lobb, of Penrose, 'just across Newquay Bay' in Cornwall. The carol had been taught to her by her grandfather, a Mr Tippet, when she was a child. An account of the occasion was given the following October in a paper to the Royal Institution of Cornwall by Ingeborg Lady Molesworth St Aubyn. 'Mrs Lobb's Carol' was then harmonized and printed in the *Journal of the Royal Institution of Cornwall* as a 'traditional Cornish carol' (vol. XXI, pt. 2, 1923).

Mrs Lobb's memory must have been at fault in verse 2, where we have replaced her fourth line ('It sounds from this sphere') and substituted 'thunders' for 'ushers' in the last line; and we have substituted 'with surprise' for 'a surprise' in verse 4.

When Ralph Dunstan later included it in his *Cornish Song Book* (1929), he retained the quite uncharacteristic setting of the verse while replacing the refrain with 'a reliable version from [among the] old MSS in my possession. My own MS copy, which must have been transcribed over 60 years ago [before 1869] has (in addition to the vocal parts) the instrumental parts for bassoon and flute . . .'. Dunstan doubted that the refrain originally belonged to this carol, and he may have been right. We have reharmonized the verse melody (a distant member of the 'Virgin unspotted' family, 143), making no attempt at a 'gallery' style, since Dunstan's refrain setting is almost certainly a 'cleaned-up' version of the original (see notes, 91).

Dunstan gives violin and cello as alternatives to flute and bassoon in the refrain, though whether this was in the manuscript is unclear. (For a comparable setting see 'Angels, from the realms of glory', 96:III.) In bars 36–9 he has the sopranos doubling the tenors and then the altos the basses, at the higher octave, producing a texture that we have never met elsewhere in this repertory. We have removed the upper voices, but have refrained from altering the instrumental parts.

PERFORMANCE   Choir and instruments (see Appendix 3). The nature of the flute/violin part (it moves from doubling the soprano to the tenor in the first phrase of the refrain) suggests that only the two instruments specified are called for.

90

Awake, and join the cheerful choir

(Christmas)

c.1825?
(Dorset County Museum MS)

1. A - wake, and join the_ cheer - ful choir Up - on this joy - ful
2. The_ shi - ning host in_ bright ar - ray De - scends from heaven to

morn!_ up - on_ this_ joy - ful morn! And glad Ho - san - nas
earth,_ de - scends from_ heaven to earth, And joy - ful news to

loud - ly sing For joy a Sa - viour's born! and glad Ho - san - nas_
us they bring Of our dear Sa - viour's birth, and joy - ful news to_

loud - ly sing For joy a Sa - viour's born! for joy_____ a
us they bring Of our dear Sa - viour's birth, of our_____ dear

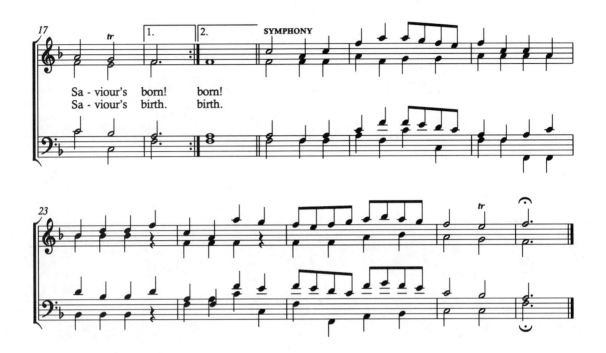

Sa - viour's born! born!
Sa - viour's birth. birth.

3 Let all the choirs on earth below
   Their voices loudly raise,
   And gladly join the cheerful band
   Of angels in the skies.

4 But let us join the cheerful song
   With joy and pious mirth,
   And all, with grateful heart and voice,
   Proclaim the Saviour's birth.

Anon.
(*W. A. Pickard-Cambridge, 1926*)

An infectious hornpipe setting which was popular in the Puddletown area. We take the setting from an accurate manuscript carol-book, headed 'George Hanford Book 1830', in the Dorset County Museum (Box File 2, Folk-Music, Church Music L.1957/53). An identical version (apart from the cadential variations), but without the symphony, is in two manuscript books from Puddletown, where the Hardys played when the Stinsford choir was disbanded in 1841: 'W. C. Crocker [altered to 'James Saunders', presumably inherited on Crocker's death] Puddletown October 15 1827', and 'James Saunders His Book [copied from] 1823', which is mostly copied from the Crocker book. The melody and three verses (the normal quota) are also in a Hardy family carol-book (Thomas Hardy Memorial Collection 1458.57) used 'on the roads' at Stinsford and compiled 1820–30, and a complete setting in

the best of the Hardy sources, the Antell manuscript in the Dorset County Record Office. We take the text from W. A. Pickard-Cambridge's *Collection of Dorset Carols* (1926), which gives four stanzas and a different tune, as sung at Bloxworth. A very similar version of the tune, sung to the same text, is one of the *Wiltshire Folk Songs and Carols* (Bournemouth [1904]) 'taken down from the mouths of old men' by Revd Geoffrey Hill.

PERFORMANCE Choir and strings. The upper instruments double the voices in both the solo and full sections (see Appendix 3). No opening symphony is indicated, but it is presumably intended that the one at the end should be played. For examples of ornamentation see carols 89 and 96:III.

91

Sound, sound your instruments of joy!
(Seraphic Minstrels)

(Christmas)

W. B. Ninnis
(fl. c.1810–30?)

1. Sound, sound your in-stru-ments of joy! [_____]

sound, sound your in-stru-ments of joy! _____

(See notes)

To tri-umph shake____ each string!____ to tri-umph shake each string!

Let shouts of u-ni-ver-sal joy,____

Let shouts, let shouts____ of
Let shouts of

Let shouts of u-ni-ver-sal joy,____

320

u - ni - ver - sal joy Wel - come, wel - come, wel - come a new - born King!

2 See! see the glad'ning dawn appears,
  Bright angels deck the morn;
  Behold! the great I AM is given;
  The King of Glory born.

3 Surprising scene! stupendous love!
  The Lord of Life, descend!
  He left his glorious realms above
  To be the sinner's friend.

4 Let heav'n and earth and sea proclaim
  Thy wondrous love abroad,
  And all the universal frame
  Sing praises to our God.

c.1810–30?
(vv. 1, 2, 4 Barnicoat, 1927;
v. 3 Dunstan, 1925)

We know nothing at all about the composers of the great majority of gallery carols (see Appendix 3), and in this case nothing more than Ninnis's name survives. 'Seraphic Minstrels' is preserved in two modern publications: in C major in Ralph Dunstan's *Second Book of Christmas Carols* (1925) and in D in a less well-known collection of *Old Cornish Carols* (1927), edited by Ben Barnicoat. Comparison of the two versions confirms what cannot be demonstrated elsewhere, that Dunstan 'improved' his material wholesale. A Cambridge Mus. Doc., he worked on the assumption that conventional rules of four-part harmony are always appropriate, and corrected any 'mistakes' made by the untutored country composers. Barnicoat, whom we follow, knew better: 'In transcribing for present-day use, every care has been taken to preserve the original harmonies, and only in isolated instances (where, perhaps, the manuscript is not quite clear) has any possible departure been made'. Of the 53 notes in Barnicoat's alto part, 30 differ in Dunstan, as do 28 of the 55 notes in the tenor; Dunstan's tune remains virtually intact.

Barnicoat's carols are all taken from a large collection of manuscripts written and collected by his grandfather, Francis Woolcock (1810–88), of Tregony, Cornwall. There is a setting of the text, headed 'A Hymn for Christmas Day' in Samuel Pearce, *Sacred Music* . . . (*c.*1776). 'I AM' (verse 2) is a Hebraic circumlocution for the name of God.

PERFORMANCE Choir, with instruments and/or organ *ad lib.* (see Appendix 3). The bass runs in bars 3–4 and 7 are probably instrumental, but can be taken vocally in purely choral performances. The text repeats in verses 2–4 are indicated above the lines. 'Sing praise, sing praise' should be sung in verse 4.

92

Hark! the herald angels sing

I

(*Christmas*)

Felix Mendelssohn (1809–47)
(arr. editors)

1. Hark! the he - rald an-gels sing: 'Glo-ry to the new-born King! Peace on earth and

mer-cy mild, God and sin - ners re - con-ciled!' Joy - ful, all ye na - tions rise!

Join the tri-umph of the skies! U - ni-ver-sal Na-ture say: 'Christ the Lord is

born to-day!' Hark! the he - rald an - gels sing: 'Glo - ry___ to the new-born King!'

2 Christ, by highest heaven adored,
Christ the everlasting Lord:
Late in time behold him come,
Offspring of a Virgin's womb.
Veiled in flesh the Godhead see!
Hail the incarnate Deity,
Pleased as man with man to dwell:
Jesus, our Emmanuel!

3 Come, Desire of Nations, come:
Fix in us thy humble home!
Rise, the Woman's conquering Seed,
Bruise in us the Serpent's head!
Adam's likeness, Lord efface:
Stamp thy image in its place!
Second Adam, from above,
Reinstate us in thy love!

4 Mild, he lays his glory by,
Born that man no more may die,
Born to raise the sons of earth,
Born to give them second birth.
Hail the heaven-born Prince of Peace!
Hail the Sun of Righteousness!
Light and life to all he brings,
Risen with healing in his wings.

Charles Wesley (1707–88) and others

ORGAN INTERLUDES

Samuel Sebastian Wesley (1810–76)

INTERLUDE 1

INTERLUDE 2

324

II

'C. B.' (Madan, 1769)

(Christmas)

1. Hark! hark the he - rald_ an - gels_ sing: 'Glo - ry
2. Hail! hail the heav'n-born Prince of__ Peace! Hail_____ the

to_____ the new - born_ King!_ Peace on earth and mer - cy
Sun____ of Right - eous - ness!_ Light and life_ to all____ he

mild,_ God and_ sin - ners re - con - ciled!'
brings, Ris'n with heal - ing in__ his wings.

Joy - ful,_ all ye__ na - tions, rise! Join the_
Mild, he_ lays his__ glo - ry_ by, Born that_

Charles Wesley (1707–88) and others

This 'Hymn for Christmas-Day' has always been the most popular of Charles Wesley's hymns, appearing in more hymn-books, old and new, than any other.

The original text, first published in Wesley's *Hymns and Sacred Poems* (1739), is cast in ten four-line stanzas, without refrain, beginning 'Hark, how all the welkin rings / Glory to the King of Kings . . .'. Of these we give eight with setting I (1, 2, 3, 4, 7, 9, 6, and 5 in the original) and four with setting II (1, 2, 5, and 6).

Verse 4 (II, 2) makes reference to Malachi 4:2, a prophecy of the Messiah: 'But unto you that fear my name shall the Sun of righteousness arise with healing in his wings.' The previous line refers to another messianic prophecy: 'For unto us a child is born . . . and his name shall be called Wonderful, Counsellor, the mighty God, the everlasting Father, the Prince of Peace' (Isaiah 9:6).

The version of the hymn that is almost universally sung today has evolved through a series of changes by subsequent editors. The leader of the Calvinist faction in early Methodism, George Whitefield, began the process in his *Hymns for Social Worship* (1753), in which he omitted the original verses 8 and 10 (which reflect the orthodox doctrine of the Fall, to which he was antagonistic), replaced Wesley's original opening couplet with the stronger, now familiar lines, and substituted 'heaven-born' for 'heav'nly' in Wesley's verse 5.

II is a fine setting for high voices and organ from Martin Madan's 'Lock Collection' (*A Collection of Psalm and Hymn Tunes . . .*, 1769; see notes, 72), which treats the hymn in eight-line stanzas (though retaining the original four-line numbering). The composer is given as 'C. B.', and may well be the great historian Charles Burney, who held organist's posts in London and King's Lynn between 1749 and 1760. (Three psalm tunes by him were included in the *Psalms of David*, published in 1790 by H. Drummond and Burney's pupil Edward Miller.) We have added some appoggiaturas from the 1807 edition of the Lock Collection, and replaced the conventional *piano* and *forte* indications with the 'soli' and 'full' that they imply.

'C. B.', or perhaps Madan, altered the last couplet of Wesley's verse 2 to 'With th'angelic host proclaim / Christ is born in Bethlehem', which we retain in this setting, along with other minor alterations; but for several reasons those lines seem to us inferior, and we restore Wesley's original in Mendelssohn's setting (I). The use of the opening couplet as refrain, a common device in the eighteenth century ('Christians, awake!', 71, is apparently still sung in this manner in parts of Yorkshire), first occurred when the hymn was finally included in an Anglican publication, among the 'hymns' added to the Supplement to the 1782 edition of Tate and Brady's *New Version of the Psalms*. The Supplement consisted of sixteen 'hymns' of various sorts, 'While shepherds watched' (46) being the only other Christmas hymn, plus extra metrical versions of the psalms. The *New Version* and its Supplement were bound up with all copies of *The Book of Common Prayer*, which meant that the hymns acquired a semi-liturgical status and were universally known. Small changes were made for this edition,

and a final change appeared in *Hymns Ancient and Modern* (1861), where Wesley's 'Pleased as Man with Men t'appear / Jesus, our Immanuel here' in his verse 4 was replaced with the present lines. The now standard versions of the three eight-line verses and refrain were thus established, and even accepted by the Methodists.

John Wesley, ironically, resented any modification of his or his brother's hymns, and fulminated against the practice in his preface to the 1779 edition of *A Collection of Hymns for the use of the people called Methodists*: 'Many Gentlemen have done my Brother and me (though without naming us) the honour to reprint many of our hymns. Now they are perfectly welcome to do so, provided they print them just as they are. But I desire they would not attempt to mend them—for they really are not able.' He goes on to suggest that the original texts be printed in the margin, 'that we may no longer be held responsible either for the nonsense or for the doggerel of other men'. This uncompromising attitude did not, however, inhibit him from radically 'mending' the work of others, notably Herbert and Watts.

Inclusion in the Supplement meant that large numbers of settings of 'Hark! the herald' were made of the four-line stanzas plus refrain, mostly for country choirs. We have found no outstanding country setting, and 'C. B.'s' is the best of those written for urban churches—in this case the female inmates of the institution of which Madan was chaplain. But this could hardly do for the majority of churches, which had mixed choirs, and until the mid-nineteenth century Wesley's hymn was in the position that Richard S. Hill described 'Away in a manger' (100) as being in at one stage—'a poem in search of a melody'. Mendelssohn's music, on the other hand, was a melody in search of a poem. It comes from his four-movement *Festgesang* for male chorus and brass, an occasional piece commissioned by the Gutenberg Festival that was held in Leipzig in 1840 to mark what was believed to be the 400th anniversary of the invention of printing. Mendelssohn toyed with the idea of adaptation to a more generally useful text in a letter to his London publishers, but was certain that 'it will never do to sacred words'. Wesley's sacred words were nevertheless soon wedded to the second movement ('Lied'—song—which is repeated as the fourth) in a curious, almost monorhythmic adaptation which appeared in *The Congregational Psalmist* (1858–79), the book that Dr Henry Allon and H. J. Gauntlett produced for the vast Union Chapel in Islington, London, with its celebrated psalmody class. This did not catch on, but the one that did, by W. H. Cummings, also treated Mendelssohn's rhythm in a fairly cavalier fashion, for some reason: certainly not to produce a better fit with the words. Cummings was a singer, organist, musical antiquarian, and committee man, a founding father of many of Britain's national musical institutions. His adaptation, made during his youthful period as organist of the parish church of Waltham Abbey, Essex, was first published in 1856. It gained national attention through inclusion in R. R. Chope's *Congregational Hymn and Tune Book* (1857) and in *Hymns Ancient and Modern* (1861), in which the editors sensibly moved the bar-

lines so that the tune begins on the first and not the third
beat: we do the same. Cummings's arrangement, with its
arbitrary clipping of Mendelssohn's melodic wings, is now
sung everywhere, which is a pity.

In bars 9–12 the original is:

(see the *Collected Works*, ed. J. Reitz, Leipzig, 1844–77, vol.
15). If desired, some voices could sing these Ds in each verse
of our arrangement, to the words of line 5 (omitting line 6).

We provide three interludes by a grandson of Charles
Wesley and contemporary of Mendelssohn, Samuel Sebastian Wesley. They are taken from his *Selection of Psalm
Tunes, adapted expressly to the English organ with pedals* (second edn., 1842). All three have been transposed down a tone
and will inevitably need to be simplified in the hands of all
but the most virtuosic performers. Interlude 1 was written
for the tune 'St Mary's', 2 and 3 for the 'Old Hundredth'.

PERFORMANCE   I, voices and organ. It may be performed
with Mendelssohn's brass parts (2 trumpets, 4 horns, 3
trombones, ophicleide). There was no organ in the original,
but it could effectively double the brass. One performance
scheme might be to sing verses 1 and 4 with full forces,
verse 2 with organ only, and verse 3 with men's voices and
brass. (When organ alone provides the accompaniment it is
probably best to substitute Gs for the bass Ds on the first
beat in bars 1 and 5.)

See Appendix 2 for the performance of givings-out and
interludes.

II, high voices and organ.

93

Once, in royal David's city

(Christmas)   *Henry John Gauntlett (1805–76)*

1. Once, in roy - al Da - vid's ci - ty, Stood a low - ly cat - tle shed
2. He came down to earth from hea - ven Who is God and Lord of all,

Where a mo - ther laid her ba - by In a man - ger for his bed;
And his shel - ter was a sta - ble, And his cra - dle was a stall;

Ma - ry was that mo - ther mild, Je - sus Christ her on - ly child.
With the poor and mean and low - ly Lived on earth our Sa - viour ho - ly.

ALTERNATIVE VERSE 4
SOPRANOS

4. For— he is our child - hood's pat-tern: Day by day like_ us_ he_ grew;
He— was lit - tle, weak and_ help-less, Tears and smiles like_ us_ he_ knew;

ALTOS

(Organ tacet)

And he_ feel - eth for our sad-ness, And he_ sha - reth_ in_ our_ glad-ness.

3 And through all his wondrous childhood
   He would honour and obey,
Love and watch the lowly maiden
   In whose gentle arms he lay;
Christian children all must be
   Mild, obedient, good as he.

4 For he is our childhood's pattern:
   Day by day like us he grew;
He was little, weak and helpless,
   Tears and smiles like us he knew;
And he feeleth for our sadness,
   And he shareth in our gladness.

5 And our eyes at last shall see him
   Through his own redeeming love,
For that Child, so dear and gentle,
   Is our Lord in heaven above;
And he leads his children on
   To the place where he is gone.

6 Not in that poor, lowly stable
   With the oxen standing by
We shall see him, but in heaven,
   Set at God's right hand on high,
When, like stars, his children, crowned,
   All in white shall wait around.

Mrs Cecil Frances Alexander (1823–95)

The poem was conceived as one of a sequence of *Hymns for Little Children* (1848), which Mrs Alexander wrote after overhearing a group of her godchildren complaining of the dreariness of the catechism. Some of the other famous hymns are 'Do no sinful action' (illustrating the baptismal promises), 'Yea, all things bright and beautiful', and 'There is a green hill far away' (both illustrating lines from the Creed). 'Once, in royal David's city' glosses the words '. . . who was conceived by the Holy Ghost, born of the Virgin Mary'. Mrs Alexander dedicated her hymns thus: 'To my little godsons I inscribe these simple lines, hoping that the language of verse, which children love, may help to impress on their minds what they are, what I have promised for them [at their baptism], and what they must seek to be.'

Like her other well-known hymns, 'Once, in royal David's city' is now established in the normal congregational repertory. It also traditionally opens the Christmas Eve Festival of Nine Lessons and Carols in the chapel of King's College, Cambridge, being sung during the entrance procession (formerly, with great effect, from the west end of the chapel).

The tune, called 'Irby', first appeared in a pamphlet issued by Gauntlett in 1849, *Christmas Carols: Four Numbers*, and it was reprinted among his settings of all the hymns in the 1858 edition of Mrs Alexander's work, 'set to music with piano accompaniment'—something of a lost labour, since this is the only tune that has lived on. Gauntlett himself made an admirably simple four-part arrangement for the first edition of *Hymns Ancient and Modern* (1861). This later passed into general use in the slightly more elaborate version that we give here, the ascending bass in bars 9 and 11 deriving from the Newcastle composer Henri Friedrich Hémy's setting in *The Crown of Jesus Music* (1864). We have moved the barlines so that each line of text begins on a first beat rather than a third; the third-beat beginning seems too prescriptive, and the word-stress will prevail in either case.

PERFORMANCE Voices and organ. The alternative version of verse 4 might also be sung by male voices for verse 2.

94

The Shepherds' Farewell to the Holy Family

(Octave of the Epiphany; Christmas)

Hector Berlioz (1803–69)

Allegretto (♩. = 50)

Oboes

CHOIR (& Strings)
p

PIANO/ORGAN *or* ORCHESTRA
f

Clarinets

1. Il___ s'en va loin de___ la
1. Born___ a - mong us___ in the

p

ter - re Où dans l'é - ta - ble il vit___ le jour. De son
man - ger, His dwell - ing - place the Child___ must flee; Though he

B. { De
   { Though

poco f

père et de___ sa mè - re Qu'il res - te le con - stant___ a -
fa - ceth fear_ and dan-ger, With lo - ving pa - rents safe___ is

son père et de___ sa mè - re Qu'il res - te le con-stant a -
he fa - ceth dan-ger, With lo - ving pa - rents safe___ is

poco f

vous bé - nisse, heur - eux__ é - poux! Que ja - mais de l'in - jus-
home and peace, a - las!__ ex - iled, His good an - gel watch be-

B. Que ja - mais de l'in - jus-
His good an - gel watch be-

- ti - ce Vous ne puis - siez__ sen - tir__ les coups! Qu'un bon an - ge
- side you, On moun - tain steep, in de - sert wild! No - thing harm you,

- ti - ce Vous ne puis - siez__ sen - tir les coups!
- side you, On moun-tain steep, in de-sert wild!

vous a - ver - tis - se   Des dan - gers pla - nant sur vous!   Qu'un bon an - ge
nought a - larm you,   Faith - ful pair and bless - ed Child!   No - thing harm you,

vous a - ver - tis - se   Des __ dan - gers __ pla - nant sur vous! __   Des dan -
nought a - larm you,   Faith - ful pair __ and bless - ed Child! __   Faith - ful

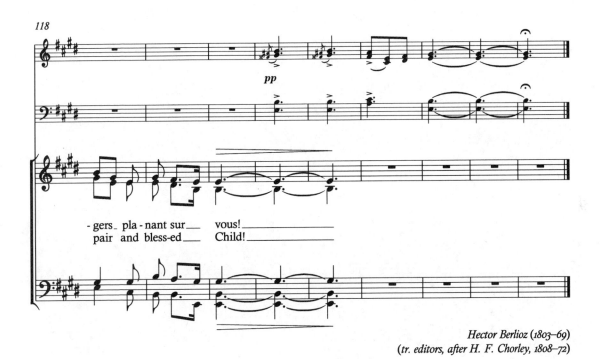

- gers pla - nant sur___ vous!_____
pair and bless-ed___ Child!_____

Hector Berlioz (1803–69)
(tr. editors, after H. F. Chorley, 1808–72)

A song of the shepherds, expressing their love and concern for the Holy Family who are fleeing to Egypt from the wrath of Herod. The Flight into Egypt has traditionally been celebrated at the end of the octave of the Epiphany (13 January) or just afterwards, though this piece is often sung at Christmas.

The well-known chorus began life as a party joke and was the germ from which grew one of Berlioz's finest works. In October 1850 he entered a short *Andantino* for organ into the autograph album of his host, the architect Louis Duc, but refused to sign his own name, ascribing the piece instead to an imaginary 'Pierre Ducré'. He reworked the organ piece as the chorus *L'Adieu des bergers à la Sainte Famille* ('The Shepherds' Farewell to the Holy Family'), writing his own text, and conducted the work a month later, on 12 November, at a concert of the Grande Société Philharmonique de Paris in the Salle Ste-Cécile. The lithographed chorus parts survive, with the title *L'Adieu des bergers à la Sainte Famille, fragment de la Fuite en Égypte mystère en 6 actes. Par Pierre Ducré maître de la musique de la Ste Chapelle de Paris (1679).* The chorus was deliberately written in what Berlioz conceived as a 'pure and simple' antique style, and the autograph score even calls for antique instruments: 'flûtes douces', 'oboë di caccia', and 'chalumeaux', later altered to flutes, oboes, and clarinets. The six-act drama ('mystère') was at this stage entirely

imaginary, and Berlioz was intent on exposing the ignorance of reviewers who constantly attacked his works as modernist and compared them unfavourably with the composers of the old schools. Amazingly, they accepted the work at face value, and Berlioz, having later added an introductory *Ouverture* and closing scene for tenor solo, *Le Repos de la Sainte Famille*, triumphantly announced himself as the true composer and had the work published as *La Fuite en Égypte, fragments d'un mystère en style ancien … attribué à Pierre Ducré, Maître de Chapelle imaginaire, et composé par Hector Berlioz* (Paris, 1852). He dedicated it to John Ella (1802–88), music critic of the London *Morning Post* and founder of the Musical Union. In 1853–4 Berlioz expanded the short cantata to form the oratorio *L'Enfance du Christ* (op. 25), which appeared in 1855 with the French text and a German translation by Peter Cornelius. An English translation by the critic H. F. Chorley appeared in the first London vocal score (1856), but was superseded by another by Paul England when Novello issued their vocal score in 1903. Both versions are so far from Berlioz's charming original that we have attempted to improve on them.

PERFORMANCE   Choir and orchestra or organ/piano. The strings double the voices, two oboes and two clarinets playing the little ritornelli and joining the strings in the third verse.

95

See, amid the winter's snow

(Christmas)

John Goss (1800–80)

VERSE
Unison

1. See, a-mid the win - ter's snow, Born for us on earth be - low,
2. Lo! with-in a man - ger lies He who built the star - ry skies,

See, the ten - der Lamb ap-pears, Pro-mised from e - ter - nal years!
He who, throned in height sub-lime, Sits a - mid the Che - ru - bim.

REFRAIN
Harmony

Hail, thou e - ver - bless - ed morn! Hail, Re-demp - tion's hap - py___ dawn!

Sing through all Je - ru - sa - lem:___ 'Christ is born in Beth - le - hem!'

3 Say, ye holy shepherds, say:
   What your joyful news today?
   Wherefore have ye left your sheep
   On the lonely mountain steep?

4 'As we watched at dead of night,
   Lo! we saw a wondrous light;
   Angels, singing "Peace on earth",
   Told us of the Saviour's birth.'

5 Sacred Infant, all-divine,
   What a tender love was thine
   Thus to come from highest bliss
   Down to such a world as this!

6 Teach, oh teach us, holy Child,
   By thy face so meek and mild,
   Teach us to resemble thee
   In thy sweet humility!

Edward Caswall (1814–78)

Edward Caswall was one of the many Anglican priests who joined the Roman Church under the influence of John Henry Newman. After the death of his wife he joined Newman at the Birmingham Oratory, where he was noted for his work among the poor and for his often outstanding translations of Latin hymns from the Roman breviary, which long remained standard vernacular versions. 'See, amid the winter's snow' was first published in a volume of *Easy Hymn Tunes* in 1851, not long after Caswall's conversion. The text was reprinted in his *Masque of Mary, and other poems* (1858) and again in *Hymns and Poems* (1873), a compendium of the earlier books.

The setting by the composer and organist Sir John Goss appeared in Bramley and Stainer's *Christmas Carols New and Old* (1871). Percy Dearmer, in his preface to *The Oxford Book of Carols* (1928), was properly dismissive of most of the twenty-four newly composed settings in *Christmas Carols*, but he pays grudging tribute to Goss's gem: 'little perhaps, except the tune by Sir John Goss, deserves to survive'—as, indeed, it has.

PERFORMANCE   Voices and organ.

96

Angels, from the realms of glory

I

(Christmas)

French traditional
(arr. Martin Shaw 1875–1958)

Christ the new-born King!_____ wor-ship Christ the new-born King!

1 Angels, from the realms of glory,
   Wing your flight o'er all the earth;
   Ye who sang Creation's story
   Now proclaim Messiah's birth!

   Come and worship Christ the new-born King!

2 Shepherds, in the field abiding,
   Watching o'er your flocks by night:
   God with man is now residing,
   Yonder shines the Infant Light.

3 Sages, leave your contemplations:
   Brighter visions beam afar.
   Seek the Great Desire of Nations:
   Ye have seen his natal star.

4 Saints, before the altar bending,
   Watching long in hope and fear:
   Suddenly the Lord, descending,
   In his temple shall appear.

5 Though an infant now we view him,
   He shall fill his Father's throne,
   Gather all the nations to him;
   Every knee shall then bow down.

James Montgomery (1771–1854)

II

Henry Smart (1813–79)

1. Angels, from the realms of glory, Wing your flight o'er all the earth;

Ye who sang Cre - a - tion's sto - ry Now pro-claim Mes - si - ah's birth!

Come and wor - ship, come and wor - ship, wor - ship Christ the___ new - born King!

2 Shepherds, in the field abiding,
    Watching o'er your flocks by night:
  God with man is now residing,
    Yonder shines the Infant Light.

3 Sages, leave your contemplations:
    Brighter visions beam afar.
  Seek the Great Desire of Nations:
    Ye have seen his natal star.

4 Saints, before the altar bending,
    Watching long in hope and fear:
  Suddenly the Lord, descending,
    In his temple shall appear.

5 Though an infant now we view him,
    He shall fill his Father's throne,
  Gather all the nations to him;
    Every knee shall then bow down.

James Montgomery (1771–1854)

III

Nineteenth-century
(Dunstan, 1929)

(*Christmas*)

1. An - gels,— from— the realms of— glo - ry, Wing— your

flight— o'er all the earth; Ye— who sang— Cre -

- a - tion's— sto - ry Now— pro - claim, now— pro -

- claim,— now— pro - claim— Mes - si - ah's birth!

Come   and wor-ship,   come   and wor-ship,

come and_ wor-ship,   wor - ship Christ_ the   new - born____ King!

wor - ship Christ____ the new - born King!

IV

(*Christmas*)

Nineteenth-century
(Heath, 1889, arr. editors)

1. An - gels, from the realms of glo - ry, Wing your flight o'er all the earth;_ Ye who sang Cre-

new - born King! wor - ship Christ the new - born King!

James Montgomery was the son of an Ayrshire clergyman of the Moravian Brethren. He had an odd career, but by the end of his life his popularity as a hymn-writer rivalled that of Isaac Watts and Charles Wesley. After failing at school he was apprenticed to a baker, but ran away and was taken on in 1792 by Mr Gales, publisher of the *Sheffield Register*. When Gales fled to France in 1794, fearful of the consequences of his repeated eulogies of the French Revolution, Montgomery took over the newspaper, changed its name to the *Sheffield Iris*, and was its editor for thirty-one years. Although he toned down the radical politics of the paper, he had the dissenter's love of freedom and was twice imprisoned for libel, once for printing a song in honour of the storming of the Bastille (which had in fact been published by his predecessor) and a second time for intemperate coverage of a riot in Sheffield. The paper was taken over by a rival in 1825, after which Montgomery devoted himself exclusively to religious verse. He produced some 400 hymns and skilfully adapted many more; in many cases his are the versions that are generally sung today.

'Angels, from the realms of glory' first appeared in the *Iris* on Christmas Eve 1816, at a time when most new Christmas carols consisted of tedious catalogues of eating and swilling. It appeared in various hymn-books from 1819 on, and quickly became popular throughout England, as the many local settings and its inclusion in countless broadsheets show. It is now sung almost exclusively to the tune of the old French carol 'Les anges dans nos campagnes' (I; see notes, 195). The editors of *The Oxford Book of Carols* (1928), who had little sympathy with the gallery tradition, chose the French tune simply because of the coincidental similarity of the opening stanzas. Their substitution of the refrain 'Gloria in excelsis Deo' from 'Les anges' for Montgomery's 'Come and worship Christ the new-born King' is incongruous with the poem's eighteenth-century idiom.

Tune II is Henry Smart's splendid 'Regent Square', to which the carol is commonly sung in the US. (The hymn usually sung to this tune in England is 'Light's abode, celestial Salem'). Smart was one of the old school of hymn accompanists, a wayward and largely self-taught musician with a genius for organ extemporization. He was organist of various leading London churches, among them St Luke's, Old Street (where the appointment was by com-petition: the other aspirants, hearing of his candidature, faded quietly away), and St Pancras Parish Church, where he stayed for five years and, though completely blind, created a standard of congregational singing without rival in London. 'Regent Square' was composed for the Presbyterian *Psalms and Hymns for Divine Worship*, which Smart edited in 1867, and was named after the most prominent Presbyterian church in London, in Regent Square.

Settings III and IV are both anonymous church-gallery settings (see Appendix 3). III survives only in Dunstan's *Cornish Song Book* (1929). The refrain is a rare written-out example of the kind of instrumental ornamentation that was improvised by the more skilled gallery musicians. (For another example, see 'Rouse, rouse from your slumbers', 89.) Notwithstanding the classical idiom, this has its roots in Renaissance 'division' technique, whereby the notes of the melody are divided up into notes of shorter length. Schoolteachers, doctors, tradesmen, and the younger sons of the gentry often had a place in gallery bands, and the players for whom this setting was made must surely have been able to tackle at least the foothills of the string quartet repertory.

IV, virtually a little cantata, was published without attribution in William Eade's *Cornish Carols* (pt. I, ed. R. H. Heath, Redruth, 1889). The full section (bars 19 to end) was also published, from a different source, by Ralph Dunstan in his *Cornish Song Book* (1929). Most unusually, this is not the refrain, which has already been sung by the soloists, but a free reworking of the entire solo verse and refrain. The organ harmonies (small notes, bars 5–18) and ornaments are editorial.

PERFORMANCE I, choir; II, voices and organ; III, choir (with no octave doublings) and instruments—see Appendix 3. Presumably Dunstan's source specified violin and bassoon, though his alternatives are perfectly acceptable. A second violin and viola could be added, doubling the alto and tenor lines at the upper octave. In the verse the instruments should double the voices, violin 1 playing the soprano line at pitch and up an octave *ad lib.*, the bassoon playing the bass at the lower octave whenever possible, and the inner parts playing up an octave as before, all with minimal ornamentation; IV, soprano and tenor soli, choir, congregation *ad lib.* (bars 19 to end), organ, and instruments *ad lib.*

97

Good King Wenceslas looked out

(St Stephen's Day)

Fourteenth-century
Piae Cantiones (1582)
(arr. John Stainer, 1840–1901)

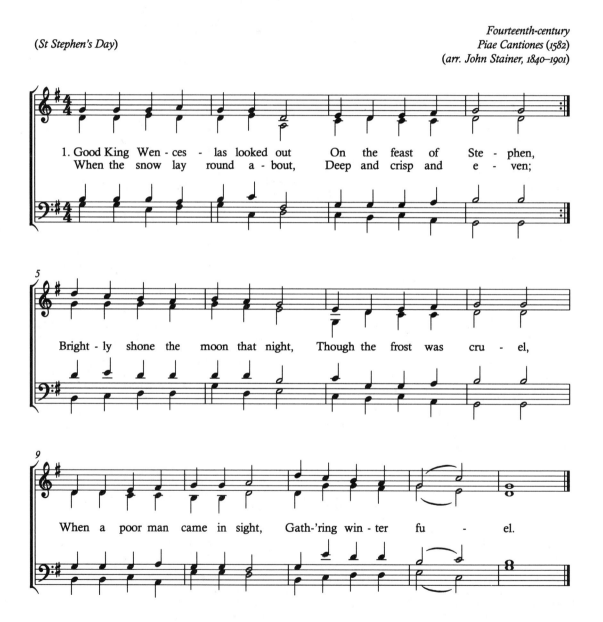

1. Good King Wen - ces - las looked out   On the feast of Ste - phen,
When the snow lay round a - bout,   Deep and crisp and e - ven;
Bright - ly shone the moon that night,   Though the frost was cru - el,
When a poor man came in sight,   Gath-'ring win - ter fu - el.

2   'Hither, page, and stand by me;
      If thou know'st it, telling—
   Yonder peasant, who is he?
      Where and what his dwelling?'
   'Sire, he lives a good league hence,
      Underneath the mountain,
   Right against the forest fence,
      By Saint Agnes' fountain.'

3   'Bring me flesh, and bring me wine!
      Bring me pine logs hither!
   Thou and I will see him dine
      When we bear them thither.'
   Page and monarch forth they went,
      Forth they went together,
   Through the rude wind's wild lament
      And the bitter weather.

4   'Sire, the night is darker now,
      And the wind blows stronger;
   Fails my heart, I know not how,
      I can go no longer.'
   'Mark my footsteps, good my page,
      Tread thou in them boldly:
   Thou shalt find the winter's rage
      Freeze thy blood less coldly.'

5   In his master's steps he trod,
      Where the snow lay dinted;
   Heat was in the very sod
      Which the saint had printed.
   Therefore, Christian men, be sure,
      Wealth or rank possessing,
   Ye who now will bless the poor
      Shall yourselves find blessing.

J. M. Neale (1818–66)

J. M. Neale, a distinguished liturgist and the greatest of English hymn translators, wrote the words to fit this splendid tune, which dates from the fourteenth century. He found it in *Piae Cantiones* (1582), where it is a spring song, 'Tempus adest floridum'. His text has been criticized on various grounds: one of its most puzzling aspects is the trouble to which page and master go to carry pine logs to the peasant who lives 'right against the forest fence'—perhaps the peasant did not have the right to gather firewood. It was first published in Neale and Helmore's *Carols for Christmas-tide* (1853–4), and it appeared with Stainer's arrangement in *Christmas Carols New and Old* (1871).

Wenceslas is the Germanized form of Vaclav. Vaclav the Good, who is celebrated here, reigned in Bohemia from 922 to 929. He was not noted for any Christian virtues, but was an ardent Catholic proselytizer and was canonized for political reasons after his murder by followers of his brother. The latter transferred his remains to St Vitus's Cathedral in Prague, where he became a cult figure, a resort of pilgrims, and finally Bohemia's (and modern Czecho-slovakia's) patron saint.

Neale's carol is not based on any known incident in the saint's life: it is probably no more than a pious illustration of the virtue of charity—St Stephen's Day (Boxing Day, 26 December) is a traditional day for giving to the poor.

PERFORMANCE   Choir.

98

What child is this

(*Christmas*)

Traditional
(arr. John Stainer, 1840–1901)

1. What child is this_ who, laid to rest,_ On Ma - ry's lap_ is sleep - ing, Whom

an - gels greet_ with an - thems sweet While shep - herds watch_ are keep - ing?

This, this_ is Christ the King, Whom shep - herds guard_ and an - gels sing:

Haste, haste_ to bring him laud,_ The Babe,_ the Son_ of Ma - ry!

2 Why lies he in such mean estate
    Where ox and ass are feeding?
Good Christians fear: for sinners here
    The silent Word is pleading.
Nail, spear shall pierce him through,
The Cross be borne for me, for you;
Hail! hail the Word Made Flesh,
The Babe, the Son of Mary!

3 So bring him incense, gold and myrrh;
    Come, peasant, king, to own him!
The King of Kings salvation brings:
    Let loving hearts enthrone him!
Raise, raise the song on high!
The Virgin sings her lullaby.
Joy! joy! for Christ is born,
The Babe, the Son of Mary!

William Chatterton Dix (1837–98)

William Chatterton Dix led a busy professional life as general manager of a marine insurance company in Bristol, his home town, but found time to write many original hymns and to versify existing prose translations of hymns from the Greek and Ethiopian Churches. He wrote 'What child is this' to the tune of 'Greensleeves' in about 1865, and it appeared with Stainer's setting in Bramley and Stainer's *Christmas Carols New and Old* (1871; see 'The old yeare now away is fled', 135, for a seventeenth-century variant of the tune). The carol is hardly sung now in England, though it remains popular in the United States.

PERFORMANCE (*i*) Choir; (*ii*) voices and organ.

99

Three Kings of Orient

(*Epiphany*)

John Henry Hopkins (1820–91)

GASPARD:

2 Born a king on Bethlehem plain,
Gold I bring to crown him again,
King for ever, ceasing never
Over us all to reign.

[CHORUS] *O Star of Wonder,* (etc.)

MELCHIOR:

3 Frankincense to offer have I,
Incense owns a Deity nigh;
Prayer and praising all men raising,
Worship him, God on high.

[CHORUS] *O Star of Wonder,* (etc.)

BALTHAZAR:

4 Myrrh is mine; its bitter perfume
Breathes a life of gathering gloom;
Sorrowing, sighing, bleeding, dying,
Sealed in the stone-cold tomb.

[CHORUS] *O Star of Wonder,* (etc.)

GASPARD, MELCHIOR, BALTHAZAR:

5 Glorious now behold him arise,
King, and God, and sacrifice.
Heaven sing: 'Alleluia';
'Alleluia' the earth replies.

[CHORUS] *O Star of Wonder,* (etc.)

John Henry Hopkins (1820–91)

Hopkins was rector of Christ's Church, Williamsport, Pennsylvania, when he published his little collection of *Carols, Hymns, and Songs* in 1865. The collection was successful enough to pass through two more editions, but only this carol has become widely known. It was included in Bramley and Stainer's *Christmas Carols New and Old* (1871) and has remained popular in England ever since.

Hopkins's collection is a model of clarity and simplicity, and his preface is agreeably splenetic: 'Compilers of other Collections are at liberty to transfer any of the pieces in this little volume provided they leave what they take unaltered. If any change be made in either words or music without my permission, I shall prosecute the offender to the extent of the law.' He clearly feared the worst, and with reason: as we write we have before us seven modern carol-books that include his carol—not one reproduces his original; not one preserves the very qualities for which the carol has been so admired.

The dramatized performances that are occasionally to be seen in churches seem to us misconceived, especially those in which the gifts are presented to the Christ-child. The kings are travelling, looking forward to the King, his Passion, death and, finally, to his Resurrection; the gifts are symbols of this, and nothing in the text suggests that the kings actually present them.

PERFORMANCE Hopkins's performance instructions are as lucid as his verse: 'Each of verses 2, 3, and 4 is sung as a solo, to the music of Gaspard's part in the 1st and 5th verses, the accompaniment and chorus being the same throughout. Only verses 1 and 5 are sung as a trio. Men's voices are best for the parts of the three kings, but the music is set in the G clef for accommodation of children.' We suggest full choir in the refrains. The accompaniment can be either organ or piano (Hopkins does not specify the instrument).

100

Away in a manger

I

(Christmas)   William J. Kirkpatrick (1838–1921)

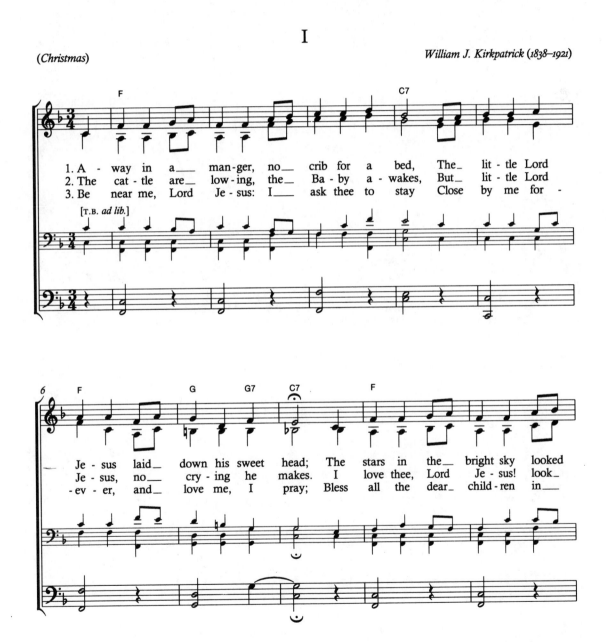

1. A - way in a__ man-ger, no__ crib for a bed, The_ lit - tle Lord
2. The cat - tle are_ low-ing, the_ Ba - by a - wakes, But_ lit - tle Lord
3. Be near me, Lord Je - sus: I_ ask thee to stay Close by me for -

Je - sus laid_ down his sweet head; The stars in the_ bright sky looked
Je - sus, no_ cry - ing he makes. I love thee, Lord Je - sus! look_
-ev - er, and_ love me, I pray; Bless all the dear_ child - ren in__

down where he lay— The_ lit - tle Lord Je - sus, a - sleep on the hay.
down from the sky, And stay by my cra - dle till__ morn - ing is nigh.
thy ten - der care, And take us to hea - ven to__ live with thee there.

Anon. (vv. 1, 2 Kirkpatrick, 1895;
v. 3 Gabriel, 1892)

II

(Christmas)

James R. Murray (1841/2–1905)

1. A - way in a man - ger, no crib for a bed, The lit - tle Lord
2. The cat - tle are low - ing, the poor Ba - by wakes, But lit - tle Lord

[T.B. ad lib.]

Je - sus laid down his sweet head; The stars in the sky___ looked
Je - sus, no cry - ing he makes. I love thee, Lord Je - sus! look

down where he lay— The lit - tle Lord Je - sus, a - sleep on the hay.
down from the sky, And stay by my cra - dle to watch lul - la - by.

Anon. (Murray, 1887)

Both words and tune II continue to be erroneously ascribed in the US to Martin Luther, the latter also sometimes to an apparently non-existent 'R. Mueller'. The great authority on the carol was Richard S. Hill, distinguished head of the reference section of the Library of Congress, Washington, DC, who set out his findings in an article in *Notes* (the journal of the American Music Library Association), 'Not so far away in a manger: Forty-one settings of an American carol' (vol. III, no. 1, Dec. 1945). He believed that the untraced (and probably untraceable, because unpublished) original hymn derived from one of the many children's dramatic presentations mounted by American Lutherans in 1883 to mark the 400th anniversary of the birth of their founder, and that it was originally a recited poem, not a song. The misattributions he put down to a combination of American lack of artistic self-esteem and innocent misunderstanding of a lost programme or printed account of the play, in which the poem was presumably presented as written by Luther for his children to recite, just as in real life he wrote 'Vom Himmel hoch, da komm' ich her' (60) for them to sing.

Verses 1 and 2 first appeared in a *Little Children's Book for Schools and Families*, issued in Philadelphia in 1885 with the authority of the General Council of the Evangelical Lutheran Church in North America, with a tune (one of at least forty-one to which the text has been sung down the years) which is no longer current. The third verse first appeared (unattributed) in 1892 in a Lutheran collection edited by Charles H. Gabriel, *Gabriel's Vineyard Songs* (Louisville, Kentucky). Bishop William F. Anderson later averred that it was written, in response to his request, by John T. McFarland, secretary of the Lutheran Board of Sunday Schools, sometime between 1904 and 1908. Perhaps the bishop misunderstood McFarland, who merely undertook to *supply* him with a third verse.

What is now the standard American tune (II) was associated with the words on their second appearance, in *Dainty Songs for Little Lads and Lasses* (Cincinnati, 1887) by James R. Murray, who had become nationally famous while a private in the Federal army for his ballad 'Daisy Deane'. Murray undoubtedly imagined that he had set a genuine Luther poem, as he headed it 'Luther's Cradle Hymn (Composed by Martin Luther for his children, and still sung by German mothers to their little ones)'. This last was a pious invention: German mothers remain resolutely unacquainted with the hymn. Murray signed the setting with his initials, thus giving the impression that he had merely arranged a melody by Luther; the setting quickly became popular, and in order to establish copyright he published it the following year in his *Royal Praise for the Sunday School*, heading it 'Music by J. R. M.'.

The tune sung in England (I) is by another American, William J. Kirkpatrick, a prolific writer of hymn-tunes who also fought on the Northern side in the Civil War. His setting was first published in *Around the World with Christmas. A Christmas exercise. Words arranged by H. E. Hewitt. Music by John Sweeney and Wm. J. Kirkpatrick* (Cincinnati, etc., 1895), one of the countless 'entertainments, playlets, services, or cantatas' that Hill uncovered in his researches.

The simple settings for voice(s) and keyboard that both Murray and Kirkpatrick provided are refreshing alternatives to the sophisticated SATB settings sometimes heard in carol services today. For choral performance we have added equally simple tenor and bass parts.

PERFORMANCE I and II (*i*) solo, unison, or two-part voices, with piano, harmonium, guitar, etc. (omitting the middle stave); (*ii*) choir.

101

O little town of Bethlehem

I

(Christmas)

Traditional
(arr. Ralph Vaughan Williams, 1872–1958)

1. O lit - tle town of_ Beth - le - hem, How still we_ see thee_ lie! A -
-bove thy deep and_ dream-less_ sleep The si - lent_ stars go_ by. Yet_
in thy dark streets shi - neth The_ e - ver-last - ing_ Light: The_
hopes and fears of_ all_ the_ years Are met in_ thee to - night.

II

Lewis H. Redner (1831–1908)

(Christmas)

1. O lit-tle town of Beth-le-hem, How still we see thee lie! A-bove thy deep and dream-less sleep The si-lent stars go by. Yet in thy dark streets shi-neth The e-ver-last-ing Light: The hopes and fears of all the years Are met in thee to-night.

III

(*Christmas*)

Henry Walford Davies (1869–1941)

1. O lit - tle town of Beth - le-hem, How still we see thee_ lie! A -

-bove thy_ deep and_ dream-less_ sleep The_ si - lent_ stars go by. Yet_

in thy_ dark streets shi - neth The_ e - ver - last - ing Light: The_

hopes and fears of__ all__ the_ years Are met_____ in thee to - night.

2 O morning stars, together
      Proclaim the holy Birth!
   And praises sing to God the King,
      And peace to men on earth;
   For Christ is born of Mary,
      And, gathered all above,
   While mortals sleep, the angels keep
      Their watch of wondering love.

3 How silently, how silently
      The wondrous gift is given!
   So God imparts to human hearts
      The blessings of his heaven.
   No ear may hear his coming,
      But, in this world of sin,
   Where meek souls will receive him, still
      The dear Christ enters in.

4 Where children pure and happy
      Pray to the blessèd Child;
   Where misery cries out to thee,
      Son of the mother mild;
   Where Charity stands watching
      And Faith holds wide the door,
   The dark night wakes, the glory breaks,
      And Christmas comes once more.

5 O holy child of Bethlehem,
      Descend to us we pray;
   Cast out our sin, and enter in:
      Be born in us today!
   We hear the Christmas angels
      The great glad tidings tell;
   O come to us, abide with us,
      Our Lord Emmanuel!

Phillips Brooks (1835–93)

Phillips Brooks, when rector of Holy Trinity Church, Philadelphia (he later became a greatly respected Bishop of Massachusetts), was inspired to write this hymn after a visit to the Holy Land in 1865. On Christmas Eve, having ridden on horseback from Jerusalem, he stood in the field outside Bethlehem in which the annunciation to the shepherds is said to have occurred, and was later moved by the singing at the service in the Church of the Nativity. In 1868 he finally wrote down the hymn, which had been slowly gestating and seems to have been at least partly intended for the children of his Sunday School, and he asked his organist, Lewis Redner, to provide a setting. After much fruitless waiting on the muse, Redner awoke on Christmas Day 1868 with a tune (II) ringing in his ears, fully formed and harmonized. It was sung for the first time on 27 December that year, and his setting remains the standard one in the US.

Setting I, known as 'Forest Green', is Vaughan Williams's arrangement of the tune of the ballad 'The Ploughboy's Dream', and is now the best-known tune for this carol in England. It was collected by Vaughan Williams from a Mr Garman of Forest Green, near Ockley, Surrey, in December 1903. The curious lengthening of the first note of the final phrase (bar 12, ♩) which Vaughan Williams introduced into his arrangement is not untypical of the freedom with which folk singers will often lengthen particular notes, though it rarely fails to unsettle a congregation. There is no such lengthening in his transcription in the *Journal of the Folk-Song Society* (vol. 3, no. 8, pp. 203–4); we follow the many modern hymn-books that give the shorter upbeat.

Henry Walford Davies (setting III) was organist of the Temple Church, London, for twenty years, a prominent Master of the King's Music (1934–41), and a pioneer of music broadcasting. His original version of the carol gives two verses to a solo voice with piano, preceded by a recitative from St Luke; the choir sings only the final verse of the hymn. (It is published in *Carols for Choirs 3*, 1978, with the piano part arranged for organ by David Willcocks.) The composer also made the present adaptation, which is sung by many English congregations.

PERFORMANCE   I, II, III, voices and organ; III can also be effective with choir alone.

102

Drei Kön'ge wandern aus Morgenland
Three kings from Persian lands afar
(Die Könige)

(*Epiphany*)

Peter Cornelius (1824–74)
(Chorale by Philipp Nicolai, 1556–1608,
arr. editors)

Langsam, der begleitende Choral sehr breit
Lento, ben distinto il canto fermo

SOLO
Drei Kön' - ge   wan - dern aus Mor - gen - land;   ein Stern-lein führt sie zum
Three kings from   Per - sian lands a - far   To Jor - dan fol - low the

CHOIR
Wie   schön leuch - tet   der
How   bright - ly shines   the

PIANO

Cornelius was a poet as well as a composer, writing the librettos of his three operas (of which the best known is *Der Barbier von Bagdad*, 1858) as well as the words of many of his songs. He first set his poem 'Die Könige' in a simple, ballad-like style. The familiar setting was sketched in 1859 and published in a set of six *Weihnachtslieder* in 1871. The chorale by Nicolai that forms the piano accompaniment was suggested by Liszt when Cornelius showed him the sketch. (See 'Wie schön leuchtet der Morgenstern', 69, for Nicolai's chorale.)

This rather eccentric conjunction of Epiphany text and Christmas accompaniment may have arisen from an assumption that 'Wie schön leuchtet' is about the star that led the magi to Bethlehem; in fact, the 'Morgenstern' ('Morning Star') is Christ, and the subject is his birth.

Cornelius's song is for unspecified voice (treble clef) and piano. Choral arrangements are a recent phenomenon. We have made our own simple version for choirs that are not large enough to tackle the well-known arrangement by Ivor Atkins (published in *Carols for Choirs 1*, 1961). The translations are by William Mercer (1836–73) (chorale) and H. N. Bate (1871–1941) (solo text).

PERFORMANCE (*i*) Voice and piano; (*ii*) solo voice and choir, with piano or organ *ad lib*.

103

It came upon the midnight clear

I

(Christmas)

Richard Storrs Willis (1819–1900)
(arr. Uzziah Christopher Burnap, 1834–1900)

1. It came up-on the mid-night clear, That glo - rious song of old, From
an - gels, bend - ing near the earth To touch their harps of gold: 'Peace
on the earth, good - will to men From heaven's all - gra - cious King!' The
world in so - lemn still - ness lay To hear the an - gels sing.

II

(Christmas)

Traditional?
adapted by Arthur Sullivan (1842–1900)

1. It___ came up - on the___ mid - night clear, That glo - rious song___ of old, From an - gels, bend - ing near the earth To___ touch their harps of gold: 'Peace on the earth, good - will to men From heaven's all - gra - cious King!' The world in___ so - lemn still - ness lay To___ hear the___ an - gels sing.

2 Still through the cloven skies they come,
   With peaceful wings unfurled,
And still their heavenly music floats
   O'er all the weary world:
Above its sad and lowly plains
   They bend on hovering wing,
And ever o'er its Babel sounds
   The blessèd angels sing.

3 Yet with the woes of sin and strife
   The world has suffered long:
Beneath the angels' strain have rolled
   Two thousand years of wrong,
And man, at war with man, hears not
   The love-song which they bring:
O hush the noise, ye men of strife,
   And hear the angels sing!

4 And ye, beneath life's crushing load,
   Whose forms are bending low,
Who toil along the climbing way
   With painful steps and slow,
Look now! for glad and golden hours
   Come swiftly on the wing;
O rest beside the weary road,
   And hear the angels sing!

5 For lo! the days are hastening on,
   By prophet-bards foretold,
When, with the ever-circling years,
   Comes round the Age of Gold,
When peace shall over all the earth
   Its ancient splendours fling,
And the whole world give back the song
   Which now the angels sing.

Edmund H. Sears (1810–76)

This fine Christmas hymn is a meditation on man's wilful deafness to the message of the angels, and, not surprisingly, was written by a Unitarian minister: the Unitarian Church has a long and continuing history of social concern.

Sears was born in Massachusetts and spent his entire professional life there as pastor of various churches. His earlier Christmas hymn, 'Calm on the listening ear of night', is still sung in the United States. Unusually for one of his Church, he expressed unswerving belief in the divinity of Christ. 'It came upon the midnight clear' was written in 1849, during his second period as pastor of First Church (Unitarian) at Wayland, Massachusetts. It was first published in Boston in *The Christian Register* in 1850, but did not reach England until 1870, when it was included in Bicker-steth's *Hymnal Companion to the Book of Common Prayer*.

Both tunes had unusual origins. The American tune (I) comes from Willis's Organ Study No. 23, and was re-arranged as a hymn-tune by Uzziah Christopher Burnap. The one sung in Britain (II) is an adaptation by Sullivan of an eight-bar melody (bars 1–8) that was sent to him by a friend, which he slightly revised, completed, and harmonized. It was first published in *Church Hymns with Tunes* (1874) with the attribution 'Traditional Air rearranged'. There is, indeed, a strong resemblance to 'The Sussex Mummers' Carol' (see *The Oxford Book of Carols*, 1928, no. 45; also *Journal of the Folk-Song Society*, vol. 2, p. 130, and vol. 3, pp. 261–3).

PERFORMANCE   I and II, voices and organ.

104

Ding-dong ding!

(Christmas)

(*Piae Cantiones, 1582,*
arr. G. R. Woodward, 1848–1934)

Ding-dong ding!__ Ding-a-dong-a-ding! Ding-dong, ding-dong, ding-a-dong ding!

Up, good Christ-en Folk, and list-en__ How the mer-ry church__
Tell the sto-ry How from glo-ry__ God came down at Christ -

- bells ring, And, from stee-ple,__ Bid good peo-ple Come a-dore the
-mas-tide, Bring-ing glad-ness,__ Cha-sing sad-ness, Show'r-ing bless-ings

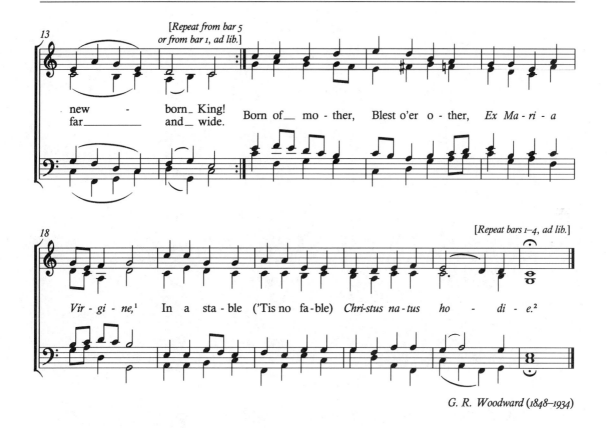

new - born_ King!
far_____ and_ wide. Born of__ mo - ther, Blest o'er o - ther, *Ex Ma - ri - a*

Vir - gi - ne,[1]   In a sta - ble ('Tis no fa - ble) *Chri-stus na-tus   ho   -   di - e.*[2]

G. R. Woodward (1848–1934)

[1] of the Virgin Mary   [2] Christ is born today

George Ratcliffe Woodward was one of the great forces for change in church music at the beginning of the twentieth century. An Anglican priest and a scholar, he was unique in combining musical and linguistic talents of a high order: his 'seventeenth-century' harmonizations of hymn-tunes, for example, are often indistinguishable from the real thing, and in his translations he refused to follow the easy road by replacing feminine endings with masculine, and adapting the tune to match. His researches into Continental hymnody, especially of the sixteenth and seventeenth centuries, resulted in *Songs of Syon* (1904), on which he collaborated with the Cambridge musician Charles Wood. This unique hymn-book was intended not only for use in churches but to serve as a model for other compilers. The reforms associated with *The English Hymnal* (1906), which jettisoned the prevailing Victoriana and aimed to include only music and verse of artistic worth, owed much to Woodward's researches.

Woodward also collaborated with Wood on *An Italian Carol Book* (1920; see notes, 107) and on the two series of *The Cowley Carol Book* (1901, 1919), written for the use of the Cowley Fathers' church of St John the Evangelist, Cowley, Oxford, which at that time was a stronghold of the English-medieval stream of Anglo-Catholicism, and had a choir-school attached. The Cowley book had a powerful influence on *The Oxford Book of Carols* (1928).

'Ding-dong ding!' comes from the first Cowley series, and is one of several 'English' carols ('Good King Wenceslas', 97, is another) that are contrafacta (retextings) of medieval Latin hymns preserved in the Scandinavian publication *Piae Cantiones* (1582). In 1910 Woodward produced an edition, with scholarly commentary, of a rare copy that had come to light, and he was foremost among those who translated and retexted the catchier tunes to create 'new' carols.

'Ding-dong ding!' is a contrafactum of the song 'O quam mundum, quam jocundum'. One of two monophonic songs that comprise the 'Concordia' section of the book, this is a joyful gloss on the opening of Psalm 133: 'Behold, how good and how pleasant it is for brethren to dwell together in unity!' The medieval melody begins with a melisma on the word 'O', to which Woodward wrote his 'Ding-dong ding!' refrain. He takes few liberties with the original, merely halving the lengths of two notes, but oddly he ignores the fact that bars 1–4 are repeated as a block at the end—it could be effective to repeat from the opening rather than from bar 5, and perhaps also to repeat bars 1–4 at the end, as is sometimes done.

PERFORMANCE   Choir.

105

Past three o'clock

(*Christmas*)

Traditional
(arr. Charles Wood, 1866–1926)

REFRAIN

Past three o'-clock, And a cold,__ frost-y morn - ing: Past three o'-

Fine VERSE

- clock: Good__ mor-row, mas - ters all!

1. Born is a Ba - by,
2. Se - raph quire sing - eth,

D.C.

Gen - tle as may be, Son__ of__ th' e - ter - nal Fa - ther su - per - nal.
An - gel bell ring-eth: Hark how they rime__ it, Time it and chime it!

3 Mid earth rejoices
  Hearing such voices
  Ne'ertofore so well
  Carolling 'Nowell'.

4 Hinds o'er the pearly,
  Dewy lawn early
  Seek the high stranger
  Laid in the manger.

378

5 Cheese from the dairy
   Bring they for Mary,
   And, not for money,
   Butter and honey.

6 Light out of star-land
   Leadeth from far land
   Princes to meet him,
   Worship and greet him.

7 Myrrh from full coffer,
   Incense they offer;
   Nor is the golden
   Nugget withholden.

8 Thus they: I pray you,
   Up, sirs, nor stay you
   Till ye confess him
   Likewise, and bless him.

Refrain traditional
Verses G. R. Woodward (1848–1934)

Woodward and Wood (see notes, 104) published this ripe but well-loved piece of 'Olde Englishry' in *The Cambridge Carol Book* (1924), on which they collaborated. Although it looks like a romantic concoction, it has a genuine connection with the music of the London waits, who in the Middle Ages were employed to patrol the town each night, keeping watch and sounding the hours.

By the late seventeenth century, town waits had become bands of civic musicians, of some standing in society, with few of the functions of the old watchmen. Yet most if not all the city groups maintained a link with their medieval predecessors in the form of a 'signature tune' which often derived from the old hourly calls. The call of the London waits was printed as a simple tune by John Playford in *The English Dancing Master* (third edn., 1665), and it was adapted by William Chappell in his *Popular Music of the Olden Time* (1853–9). Chappell added new harmonies and supplied the (authentic) words to the first section of the call (bars 1–8). The waits' Christmas repertory included carols, which they sang at civic occasions and on nocturnal street processions, evoking their watchmen ancestors. The crude 'folk' style in which these pieces were harmonized seems to have been one source of the later 'country' church style, though little more than hints and echoes survive of what it was actually like.

In *Popular Music* Chappell quotes a late seventeenth-century ballad, 'Song of the York Waits', which gives a vivid idea of the scene:

In a winter's night,
By moon or lanthorn light,
Through hail, rain, frost or snow,
Their rounds the music go;
And each in frieze [heavy cloth] or blanket
(For either Heaven be thanked),
Lin'd with wine a quart,
Or ale a double tankard
. . . Candles, four in the pound,

Lead up the jolly Round,
Whilst cornet shrill i' th' middle
Marches, and merry fiddle,
Curtal [dulcian] with deep hum, hum,
Cries, 'We come, we come, come!'
And theorbo loudly answers,
'Thrum, thrum, thrum, thrum, thrum.'
But, their fingers frost-nipt,
So many notes are o'er-slipt
. . . Then, Sirs, to hear their music
Would make both me and you sick.
And much more to hear a roopy [hoarse] fiddler call
(With voice, as Moll would cry,
'Come, shrimps or cockles buy!'),
'Past three, fair frosty morn,
Good morrow, my masters all.'

The tune of the ballad gives little hint of any York signature tune, but there may be a relic of the melody of an Irish waits' song in the air 'Past one o'clock' in Burk Thumoth's *Twelve Scotch and Twelve Irish Airs . . .* (London, 1745).

What Woodward and Wood did was to take the London call from Chappell, reharmonize it, and set words to the second section (bars 9–16): 'The refrain, *Past three o'clock*, is old, but the rest of the Carol [text] is newly composed by G. R. W . . .'. They were not the first to do this: in 1881 Chappell had issued a kind of parlour supplement to *Popular Music* called *Old English Ditties*, which consisted of excerpts from the parent volume, sometimes with new accompaniments and added texts. It includes a version of 'Past three o'clock', with non-Christmas words by J. Oxenford for the verses and an atmospheric piano accompaniment by G. A. Macfarren, the introduction of which gives out a sonorous 'three o'clock' in the bass. This setting must have been Woodward's inspiration.

PERFORMANCE Choir.

106

Blessed be that maid Marie

(Christmas)

Traditional
(arr. Charles Wood, 1866–1926)

¹ Rejoice! Jesus is born today of a virgin

2 In a manger of an ass
   Jesu lay and lullèd² was;
   Born to die upon the Tree
   *Pro peccante homine.*³

3 Sweet and blissful was the song
   Chanted of the angel throng:
   'Peace on earth, alleluya!
   In excelsis gloria.'⁴

4 Fare three kings from far-off land,
   Incense, gold and myrrh in hand;
   In Bethlem the Babe they see,
   *Stelle ducti lumine.*⁵

5 Make we merry on this fest,
   *In quo Christus natus est;*⁶
   On this Child I pray you call,
   To assoil⁷ and save us all.

*Fifteenth-century (Sloane MS,
rev. G. R. Woodward, 1848–1934)*

² soothed [with a lullaby]   ³ for sinful man   ⁴ glory in the highest   ⁵ led by the light of a star   ⁶ on which Christ was born   ⁷ absolve

This carol first appeared in Woodward and Wood's *Cowley Carol Book* (1901, 1919; see notes, 104). The patchwork text is basically a modernized and bowdlerized version of one of the carols in the fifteenth-century Sloane manuscript (British Library, MS 2593), a fragment of a larger volume without music. Verse 3 seems to be entirely by Woodward, and the first two lines of verse 5 are adapted from 'Make we joye nowe in this fest' (31).

The tune, 'Staines Morris', is one of a large and complex family of related morris tunes (see John M. Ward, 'The morris tune', *Journal of the American Musicological Society*, vol. 39, 1986, pp. 294–331). It is found set for solo lute in a late sixteenth-century manuscript (William Ballet's Lute Book) in the library of Trinity College, Dublin (see notes, 44). This was published by William Chappell in his *Popular Music of the Olden Time* (1853–9), which presumably was Wood's source.

PERFORMANCE   Choir.

107

Hail, blessed Virgin Mary!

(*Annunciation; Christmas*)

Italian traditional
(*arr. Charles Wood, 1866–1926*)

1. Hail, bless-ed Vir-gin Ma-ry! For so, when he did meet thee, Spake might-y Ga-bri-el, And thus we greet___ thee. Come weal, come woe, Our hymn shall ne-ver va-ry: 'Hail, bless-ed Vir-gin Ma-ry! Hail, bless-ed Vir-gin Ma-ry!'

2 *Ave, ave Maria!*

    To gladden priest and people

The Angelus shall ring

    From ev'ry steeple

To sound his virgin birth. Alleluia![1]

Ave, ave Maria!

3 Archangels chant 'Osanna!'

    And 'Holy! holy! holy!'

Before the Infant born

    Of thee, thou lowly

Aye-maiden[2] child of Joachim and Anna.

Archangels chant 'Osanna!'

G. R. Woodward (1848–1934)

---

[1] 'To be sung, as by the Eastern Church, as a word of five syllables.' (Woodward's note)   [2] perpetual virgin

One of the richest traditions on which Wood and Woodward (see notes, 104) drew for fresh carol material was that of Italian *laude*: the simple sacred songs, often with folk melodies, that were (and remain) the popular hymnody of Italy. The present carol is one of a large number that they adapted in their *Italian Carol Book* (1920), Wood providing stylistically apt harmonizations and Woodward new words, often unconnected with the original. In this case the original is a *lauda* in extravagant praise of the Virgin Mary (of no relevance to Christmas), 'Si, ch'io ti vuo' lodate, Maria Vergine bella' in the collection *Corona di sacre canzoni, o laude spirituali di più divoti autori* (Florence, 1689). Probably by design, the opening phrase is strongly reminiscent of the intonation to a well-known seventeenth-century plainchant *Credo* (*Liber Usualis, Credo* III), especially if the third melody note, possibly a misprint in the source, is corrected to a G (compare the beginning of the tune with bars 13 and 16, where, in the Italian as in the English, the opening of the text is repeated).

From the preface to *An Italian Carol Book*: 'It is much to be desired, though little to be expected, that the Compilers of future Hymnals will have respect to the words, or tunes, of these Italian Laude Spirituali, or that they will refrain from needlessly altering, "improving", mangling, and mismetring those carols which may happen to find favour in their sight.' For whatever reason, this carol seems to have escaped any such maltreatment (whereas John H. Hopkins's 'Three Kings of Orient', 99, has universally been altered, 'improved', mangled and, for all we know, mismetred, in spite of his prefatory threats of legal action).

PERFORMANCE   Choir.

108

Ding! dong! merrily on high

(Christmas)

Thoinot Arbeau (1520–95)
(arr. editors)

VERSE

1. Ding! dong! mer-ri-ly on high____ In____ heav'n the__ bells are ring - ing;
Ding! dong! ve-ri-ly the sky____ Is__ riv'n with an - gel sing - ing.

REFRAIN

Glo — — — —
Glo — — ria, glo — —
Glo — — ria,

- — — — ri - a! Ho - san - na__ in__ ex - cel - sis!
glo — — ri - a!

2 E'en so here below, below,

  Let steeple bells be swungen,

  And 'Io, io, io!'

  By priest and people sungen.

3 Pray you, dutifully prime

  Your matin chime, ye ringers!

  May you beautifully rime

  Your evetime song, ye singers!

G. R. Woodward (1848–1934)

Thoinot Arbeau (1520–95)
(arr. editors)

INSTRUMENTAL VERSION

Although this may seem to be the most traditional of carols, it is anything but. The tune is a dance in the *Orchésographie* (1589, 1596) of 'Thoinot Arbeau', an invaluable record of sixteenth-century music and choreography. It is just the kind of tune to which the French would add a *Noël* text, but for some reason it was left to an Englishman (Woodward) and an Ulsterman (Wood) to turn it into a carol (see notes, 104). Any good tune was grist to their mill as they combed the European past for material to set beside what seemed to them the limited supply of English folk carols, and despite Woodward's rather stilted text it has become one of the most popular of all carols.

The true author of the *Orchésographie* was Jehan Tabourot, a French ecclesiastic of wide learning who also published a work on astronomy and evidently enjoyed anagrams. He cast his dance tutor in traditional scholastic fashion as a vigorous dialogue between 'Capriol' and 'Arbeau'. *Capriol* means 'a caper [leap] in dancing' (Cotgrave's *Dictionarrie of the French and English Tongues*, London,

1611), and the character of that name represented the fifteen-year-old nobleman Guillaume Tabourot, the author's nephew, to whom the book is dedicated. There is probably a double pun in the name, since *capriole* is also a tendril of a vine, which twines round trees or wooden staves for support: 'Arbeau' has overtones of *arbre* (tree) and *arbreau* (shrub). Guillaume was not only being instructed by his uncle in the book, but was his legal heir in real life, so that their relationship was not unlike that of vine and support.

The tune is the 'Branle de l'official', a recently invented dance belonging to the huge family of branles. The name could just be a personal reference to Jehan, who had once held the ecclesiastical judicial post of *official*, though it is perhaps more likely to refer to *l'office*, the servants' hall. Servants in France were believed to experience life with an intensity denied their effete employers (witness Villiers de l'Isle-Adam's 'Live? Our servants can do that for us!'), and the description of this branle in the *Orchésographie* supports the interpretation: it is 'danced . . . with little springs like the *haut barrois*', which is 'danced by lackeys and serving wenches and sometimes by young men and maids of gentle birth masquerading as peasants and shepherds'. At one point the men take the women by the waist and help them to leap in the air, as in Queen Elizabeth's favourite lavolta. (Having had the dance explained to him, Capriol complains: '. . . it sounds to me very tiring. Besides which, its proper execution depends partly on the dexterity and agility of the maiden whom one must assist to jump, and some would attempt it who lacked the proficiency.' Arbeau replies: 'You will not find the gavotte branles [that follow] so tiring, in which there is no need to lift, but only to kiss, the young ladies.')

The vigorous tune is in the Ionian mode (the modern major mode), which at that time still had associations with hedonism and uninhibited enjoyment. For dancing, the tune would most often have been played on a single melody instrument, perhaps with drum. We know little about

alternative ways of performing it: our instrumental setting is modelled on published examples by Praetorius and others, which indicate how four-part instrumental groups might have played it. A crude two-part harmonization in Dubreuil's musical encyclopaedia *Essai sur la musique ancienne et moderne* (1780) throws further light on the tune (see ex. 1 below). It is the first of the 'airs de dance . . .' at the end of volume II, and no instruments are specified.

PERFORMANCE   Voices, with instruments *ad lib.*

The instrumental version can be played by a single melody instrument, perhaps with drum (a simple drum accompaniment might be ♩ ♩♩♩ ♩♩), or by a consort of string or wind instruments (e.g., three shawms and sackbut).

The two versions may be performed simultaneously (in G or A as appropriate).

EX. 1: *Dubreuil, 1780*

109

Lullay, my liking
I saw a maiden
Myn Lyking

I

(Christmas)

Gustav Holst (1874–1934)

al - le lord - es he is Lord, Of al - le king - es King.

(Repeat refrain)

VERSE 3
SOLO

3. There was mic - kle¹ me - lo - dy at that Child - es birth: Al - though

they were in hea - ven's bliss they ma - de mic - kle mirth.

(Repeat refrain)

VERSE 4
FULL

4. An - gels bright they sang that night, and said - en to that Child: 'Bless - ed be

thou, and so be she that is both meek and mild!'

(Repeat refrain)

VERSE 5
SOLO

5. Pray we now to that Child and to his mo - ther dear; God

grant them all his bless - ing that now ma - ken cheer!

(Repeat refrain)

Fifteenth-century
(Sloane MS, adapted)

¹ much

II

(Christmas)   Edgar Pettman (1865–1943)

2 This very Lord, he made all things,
   And this very God, the King of all kings.

3 There was sweet music at this child's birth,
   And heaven filled with angels, making
   much mirth.

4 Heaven's angels sang to welcome the child
   Now born of a maid, all undefiled.

5 Pray we and sing on this festal day
   That peace may dwell with us alway.

Fifteenth-century
(Sloane MS, adapted)

III

R. R. Terry (1865–1938)

(Christmas)

1. I saw a fair may-den syt-tin and sing: She
2. That same Lord is he that made al-le thing; Of
3. There was mic-kle[1] me-lo-dy at that Chyld-e's birth:
4. An-gels bright sang their song to that Chyld: 'Blyss-

lull - ed a lyt-tel childe, a swee-te lord - ing.
al - le lord - is he is Lord, of al - le kyng - es Kyng.
All that were in heav'n-ly bliss, they made mic - kle mirth.
-id be thou, and so be she, so meek and so mild!'

v. 1: cresc. e rit. / v. 2: rall.
v. 3: cresc. molto rall. / v. 4: cresc. molto rit.

[1] much

390

Fifteenth-century
(Sloane MS, adapted)

The same fifteenth-century carol from the Sloane Manuscript (British Library, MS 2593) is set by each composer, though the degree of updating and rewriting varies significantly. No fifteenth-century setting survives.

Holst's setting (I) has a spareness of approach that owes more to folk-song than to medieval models. It was written in 1916 for performance at one of the composer's successful Whitsun music festivals, in this case at the parish church in the Essex village of Thaxted. The incumbent at the time, Conrad Noel, was busily establishing the village as the mecca for the morris and the vast perpendicular church as a focus for Christian-socialist Sarum-ritists. The text we give is as amended in *The Oxford Book of Carols* (1928), where it is rather less modernized than in the original publication of 1919.

Edgar Pettman (II) was a well-known organist of St James's Church, Piccadilly, who maintained what can

seem like a production line in Christmas carols. He is best remembered for his version of the Basque carol 'Birjina gaztettobat zegoen' (196). The verse of the present carol is also set to a Basque tune, but the refrain is original.

Sir Richard Terry (III) was the first and most celebrated director of music at Westminster (Roman Catholic) Cathedral, where he established a musical regime of unrivalled enterprise and liturgical propriety. The hint of the parlour ballad in the refrain of this carol was perhaps calculated to appeal to the many Irish members of the cathedral congregation. (For the sake of economy we have condensed Terry's fully written-out carol, retaining his expressive variants but standardizing more minor differences.)

PERFORMANCE   I, choir; II (*i*) choir, (*ii*) choir and organ; III, choir and organ.

110

Love came down at Christmas

I

(*Christmas*)

R. O. Morris (*1886–1948*)

UNISON VOICES
1. Love came down at Christ - mas, Love all love - ly, Love di - vine;

ORGAN *or* PIANO

5 Love was born＿ at Christ - mas, Star and an - gels gave＿ the sign.

II

(*Christmas*)

Irish traditional
(*arr. editors*)

1. Love came down at Christ - mas, Love all love - ly,＿ Love di - vine;＿

Love was born at Christ - mas, Star and an - gels_ gave the sign.

2 Worship we the Godhead,
　　Love incarnate, Love divine;
　Worship we our Jesus:
　　But wherewith for sacred sign?

3 Love shall be our token,
　　Love be yours and love be mine,
　Love to God and all men,
　　Love for plea and gift and sign.

Christina Rossetti (1830–94)

Christina Rossetti, the younger sister of Dante Gabriel Rossetti, was a well-known poet and writer of mainly devotional literature. Reared in a bilingual Anglo-Italian family, her espousal of her mother's non-papalist Anglo-Catholicism resulted in the central crisis of her life, when incompatibility of religious views caused a breach with the man she loved deeply. From this time a pervasive melancholy sapped her artistic vitality, and, after completing the book of children's stories *Speaking Likeness* (1874), she turned from literature to works of piety which, ironically, brought her much more fame. Among these was *Time Flies: A reading diary*, published by the SPCK in 1885. This was a kind of late-Victorian *Christian Year*, providing short meditations and poems for the course of a single year, following the usage of *The Book of Common Prayer*. It was dedicated 'To my beloved example, friend, mother'. For 29 December, on which *BCP* has no feast, Rossetti gives the present poem, 'Christmastide', which is simpler and more heartfelt than the one she gives for Christmas Day itself. All the poems in the volume were later abstracted and combined with those in *Called to be Saints* (1881) and *The Face of the Deep* (1892) to form the section 'Songs for Strangers and Pilgrims' in the *Verses* (1893); there the final line of 'Love came down' is altered from the former 'Love

the universal sign.' The amendment also appeared in the 1904 *Poetical Works of Christina Rossetti* but not (presumably inadvertently) in the posthumous 1897 edition of *Time Flies*.

The poem was first used as a carol in *Songs of Praise* (1925). Market research by the editors had revealed 'a strongly felt need for short hymns', and this was one of many that were introduced. R. O. Morris's tune 'Hermitage' (I) was commissioned by the editors, and continues to be sung. At least as popular is the Irish melody (II) that was associated with the poem in the (Presbyterian) Church of Scotland's *Revised Church Hymnary* (1927). Known as 'Gartan' (after Lough Gartan, Co. Donegal), this 'chant, or hymn-tune' was supplied by the Revd James Mease of Freshford, Co. Kilkenny, to C. V. Stanford for his edition of the 'Petrie Collection' of Irish melodies (pt. II, 1907). Stanford described 'Gartan' as an 'old Irish church melody' in the fifth of his *Six Short Preludes and Postludes* (op. 101, 1907), which is based on it. The melody needed a little adaptation to fit Rossetti's words—bars 3, 4, and 7 each originally began with ♩ (rather than ♩ ♪).

PERFORMANCE　I, unison voices and organ or piano; II (*i*) choir; (*ii*) unison voices and organ.

111

In the bleak mid-winter

I

(Christmas)

Harold Darke (1888–1976)

In the bleak mid - win - ter A sta - ble-place suf - ficed The

Lord___ God al - might - y___ Je - - sus Christ.

D.C. for v. 3

mp [CHOIR *with* ORGAN *ad lib.*]
semplice

4. What can I give him, Poor as I am? If I were a

shep - herd___ I would bring a lamb;___ If I were a

Christina Rossetti (1830–94)

Christina Rossetti (see notes, 110) did not intend this fine poem as a hymn or carol. The free rhythm does not easily lend itself to a single-verse setting such as Holst's (II, overleaf), but the problem is effortlessly solved in Harold Darke's through-composed setting (I), an object-lesson in *multum in parve*. Darke was organist of the Church of St Michael, Cornhill (in the City of London), from 1916 to 1966, where he established a national reputation as a player and choral conductor. His setting dates from 1911. Holst's was composed for the first edition of *The English Hymnal* (1906), which (unlike most other hymn-books) did not censor the 'breastful of milk' in verse 3. Darke also sets that phrase but omits the original verse 4.

PERFORMANCE   I, soprano (verse 1) and tenor (verse 3) soli, choir, and organ. Darke does not specify forces for the other verses, but verse 2 provides an effective contrast if sung unaccompanied; his small notes in bars 37–40 imply optional organ accompaniment in verse 4.

II (*i*) choir with organ *ad lib.*, (*ii*) unison voices and organ.

II

(Christmas)

Gustav Holst (1874–1934)

VERSES 1, 4, 5

1. In the bleak mid - win - ter   Frost - y wind made   moan, ___
4. An - gels and arch - an - gels   May have ga - thered   there, ___
5. What ___ can I give him,   Poor ___ as I   am? ___

Earth stood hard as ir - on,   Wa - ter like a   stone:
Che - ru - bim and se - ra - phim   Thronged the ___ air: But
If I were a shep - herd   I would bring a   lamb;

Snow had fall - en, snow on snow,   Snow ___ on   snow,
on - ly his mo - ther   In her mai - den   bliss
If I were a wise ___ man   I would do my   part;   Yet

In the bleak mid - win - ter,   Long ___ a - go.
Wor - shipped the be - lo - ved   With ___ a ___ kiss.
what I can I give him—   Give ___ my ___ heart.

Christina Rossetti (1830–94)

See p. 397 for notes on this setting.

112

Bethlehem Down

(*Christmas*)

Peter Warlock (1894–30)

Very slow and quiet

1. 'When he is King we will give him the King's gifts,___
2. Beth - le - hem Down is___ full of the star - light—

Myrrh for its___ sweet - ness, and gold for___ a___ crown,___
Winds for the___ spi - ces, and stars for___ the___ gold,___

Beau - ti - ful___ robes,' said the___ young girl___ to___ Jo - seph,
Ma - ry for___ sleep, and for___ lul - la - by___ mu - sic

Fair___ with her___ first - born on Beth - le - hem Down.___
Songs of a___ shep - herd___ by Beth - le - hem fold.___

400

3. When he is King they will clothe him in grave - sheets,
4. Here he has peace and a short while for dream - ing, —

Myrrh for em - balm - ing, and wood for a crown, —
Close - hud - dled ox - en to keep him from cold, —

He that lies now in the white arms of Ma - ry,
Ma - ry for love, and for lul - la - by mu - sic

Sleep - ing so light - ly on Beth - le - hem Down. —
Songs of a shep - herd by Beth - le - hem fold. —

Bruce Blunt (1899–1967)

Peter Warlock (the pseudonym of Philip Heseltine) collaborated with Bruce Blunt, a friend and an amateur poet, on a number of vocal works. The genesis of 'Bethlehem Down' was somewhat undignified, as Blunt described in a letter to Gerald Cockshott (20 May 1943):

In December 1927 we were both extremely hard up, and in the hopes of being able to get suitably drunk at Christmas conceived the idea of collaborating on another carol which should be published in a daily paper. So, walking on a moonlit night between The Plough at Bishop's Sutton and The Anchor at Ropley, I thought of the words of 'Bethlehem Down'. I sent them off to Philip in London, the carol was completed in a few days and was published (words and music) in the *Daily Telegraph* on Christmas Eve. We had an immortal carouse on the proceeds and decided to call ourselves 'Carols Consolidated'.

(The carol is in fact inscribed 'Peter Warlock Eynsford. November 1927'.)

The *Telegraph* did them proud, reproducing Warlock's handwritten score, with its archaic diamond-headed notes. (It is also given in 'Peter Warlock's Choral Music', I. A. Copley, *Music and Letters*, vol. 45, no. 4, October 1964, p. 334.) A version for voice and piano was Warlock's last composition.

Other fruits of this collaboration include 'The First Mercy' ('Ox and ass at Bethlehem') for voice and piano (1927) and 'The Frostbound Wood', also for voice and piano and composed in 1930 for the Christmas pages of the *Radio Times*.

PERFORMANCE Choir.

113

Dormi, Jesu!
Sleep, sweet babe!
(The Virgin's Cradle Hymn)

I

(Christmas)

Edmund Rubbra (1901–86)

Dotted slurs and ties are for the English translation.

Traditional
(tr. Samuel Taylor Coleridge, 1772–1834)

II

(Christmas)

Anton Webern (1883–1945)

Two very different settings, composed within a short time of each other. The text is best known as the 'Schluss' (closing poem) of the final 'Kinderlieder' section of Brentano and von Arnim's great collection of German folk poems, *Des Knaben Wunderhorn* ('The Youth's Magic Horn', Heidelberg, 1805–8), which had so profound an

Quae tam dul - cem som - num vi - det, Dor - mi, Je - su,
Mo - ther sits be - side thee, smi-ling; Sleep, my dar-ling,

blan - du - le! Si non dor - mis, ma - ter plo - rat, In - ter fi - la
ten - der-ly! If thou sleep not, mo - ther mourn-eth, Sing-ing as her

can - tans o - rat, Blan - de, ve - ni, som - nu - le!
wheel she turn - eth: Come, soft slum - ber, balm - i - ly!

Traditional
(tr. Samuel Taylor Coleridge, 1772–1834)

influence on Gustav Mahler. It derives from a longer poem, one of many similar late-medieval hymns addressed to the infant Christ and couched in melting, almost erotic language. It begins: 'Dormi, Fili, dormi! Mater / Cantat Unigenito: / Dormi, Puer, dormi! Pater / Nato clamat Parvulo. / Millies tibi laudes canimus, / Mille, mille, millies.' This was sung as a chorale to a less than inspiring tune in German Catholic churches; there is a vernacular translation beginning 'Schlaf, mein Kindlein! Schlaf mein Söhnlein', and a good English translation in *Hymns and Lyrics* . . . (1867) by Gerard Moultrie.

Coleridge found the poem in about 1798, on 'a little print of the Virgin and Child in a small public house of a Catholic village' in Germany, and published his translation in the London *Courier* on 30 August 1811. It was first collected in *Sibylline Leaves* in 1817.

Rubbra's setting (I) dates from 1925, and he presumably encountered the text through Coleridge's translation (or perhaps through a setting published in 1892 by the Scottish composer Alexander Mackenzie, 1847–1935, for voice, violin/cello, and piano; see *Musica Brittanica*, LVI, 1989, no. 7).

Webern's setting (II) is a rare example of the twelve-tone Christmas carol. He presumably knew the verse from the *Wunderhorn*, and set it as no. 2 of his *Fünf Canons nach Lateinischen Texten* (op. 16, 1923–4) for soprano, clarinet, and bass clarinet. The odd-numbered movements are for all three; 'Dormi Jesu' is for voice and clarinet only. The carol is a simple and easily heard inverted canon (the soprano beginning a diminished twelfth above the opening of the clarinet's statement).

PERFORMANCE I, choir; II, soprano and clarinet.

114

Wither's Rocking Hymn

(Christmas)

Ralph Vaughan Williams (1872–1958)

1. Sweet ba - by, sleep! What ailes my dear?
2. Thou bless - ed soul, what canst thou fear?

What ailes my dar - ling thus to cry?
What thing to thee can mis - chief do?

Be still, my childe, and lend thine ear, To
Thy God is now thy Fa - ther dear, His

¹ i.e., the Church

*3 Though thy conception was in sin,
    A sacred bathing² thou hast had;
And, though thy birth unclean hath bin,³
    A blamelesse babe thou now art made.
Sweet babie, then, forbear to weep;
Be still, my dear; sweet babie, sleep!

4 Whilst thus thy lullabie I sing,
    For thee great blessings ripening be:
Thine Eldest Brother is a King,
    And hath a kingdome bought for thee.
Sweet babie, then, forbear to weep;
Be still, my babe; sweet babie, sleep!

5 Sweet babie, sleep, and nothing fear;
    For whosoever thee offends
By thy Protector threatned are,
    And God, and angels, are thy friends.
Sweet babie, then, forbear to weep;
Be still, my babe; sweet babie, sleep!

6 When God-with-us was dwelling here
    In little babes he took delight:
Such innocents as thou, my dear,
    Are ever precious in his sight.
Sweet babie, then, forbear to weep;
Be still, my babe; sweet babie, sleep!

7 A little infant once was hee,
    And strength in weaknesse then was
    laid
Upon his Virgin Mother's knee,
    That power to thee might be convaied.
Sweet babie, then, forbear to weep;
Be still, my babe; sweet babie, sleep!

*8 In this, thy frailty and thy need,
    He friends and helpers doth prepare,
Which thee shall cherish, clothe and feed,
    For of thy weal they tender are.
Sweet babie, then, forbear to weep;
Be still, my babe; sweet babie, sleep!

9 The King of Kings, when he was born,
    Had not so much for outward ease;
By him such dressings were not worn,
    Nor suchlike swadling-clothes as these.
Sweet babie, then, forbear to weep;
Be still, my babe; sweet babie, sleep!

*10 Within a manger lodged thy Lord,
    Where oxen lay and asses fed:
Warm rooms we do to thee afford,
    An easie cradle, or a bed.
Sweet babie, then, forbear to weep;
Be still, my babe; sweet babie, sleep!

² baptism   ³ [through original sin]

11 The wants that he did then sustain
    Have purchased wealth, my babe,
        for thee;
  And, by his torments and his pain,
    Thy rest and ease securèd be.
  My babie, then, forbear to weep;
  Be still, my babe; sweet babie, sleep!

*12 Thou hast (yet more!) to perfect this,
    A promise and an earnest[4] got
  Of gaining everlasting blisse,
    Though thou, my babe, perceiv'st it not.
  Sweet babie, then, forbear to weep;
  Be still, my babe; sweet babie, sleep!

George Wither (1588–1667)

---

[4] pledge

George Wither (or Withers) was one of the oddest and most prolific of seventeenth-century literary figures. His early work includes much fine lyric verse, and satirical prose which was sufficiently biting to get him imprisoned in the Marshalsea. A firm Royalist and Anglican, he later changed sides and, like Milton, devoted most of his output to the religious and political doctrines of Puritanism.

Wither is remarkable for having commanded (with conspicuous lack of success) troops of horse on both sides in the Civil War; captured by the Royalists during his Parliamentary phase, he was spared execution only through the intercession of the Royalist poet Sir John Denham, who pleaded that so long as Wither lived, he (Denham) would not be accounted the worst poet in England. ('Wither henceforth regarded Denham with very bitter feelings'—*Dictionary of National Biography*.)

In 1641 he published *Haleluiah or, Britains Second Remembrancer, bringing to remembrance (in praisefull and poenitentiall hymns, spirituall songs and moral-odes) meditations, advancing the glory of God, in the practice of piëtie and vertue; and applyed to easie tunes, to be sung in families, &c. Composed in a three-fold volume, by George Wither.* (*Britain's Remembrancer* was a pamphlet in which he had urged penitence in the wake of plague.) The general intention of the volume is set out in the address 'To the Reader': 'Some good men . . . have affirmed Poësie, to be the Language, and invention of the Devill . . . I have laboured according to my Talent, and am desirous . . . to become a means, by the pleasingness of Song, to season Childhood and young persons, with more Virtue and Pietie . . . in the hope that . . . I shall . . . prevent or dissolve the Devils Inchantments; by these lawful Charmes.'

Haleluiah is generally reckoned to be an isolated resurgence of Wither's earlier lyrical mastery, and this 'Rocking Hymn' (one of two) has always been prized as a poem. 'Applyed to easie tunes' in the title is ambiguous: unlike an earlier volume, *The Hymnes and Songes of the Church* (1623), for which Orlando Gibbons provided seventeen tunes (see notes, 45), here the poems are to be sung to any suitable tunes. Vaughan Williams's fine setting for *The Oxford Book of Carols* (1928) gives only verses 1, 4, 6, 7, 9, and 11. (Our complete text retains original spellings.) Like most of the poems in the first volume of *Haleluiah*, 'A Rocking Hymn' was intended for directly practical use, as Wither makes clear in a prefatory note: 'Nurses usually sing their Children asleep; and through want of pertinant matter, they oft make use of unprofitable (if not worse) Songs. This was therefore prepared, that it might help acquaint them, and their Nurse-Children, with the loving care and kindnesse of their heavenly Father.'

For another purely domestic carol see 'Watts's Cradle Hymn' (115).

PERFORMANCE (*i*) Solo voice and instrument (presumably keyboard; the instrument could substitute for the choir in the refrains); (*ii*) choir and organ or piano.

115

Watts's Cradle Hymn

(*Christmas*)

American traditional
(adapted and arr. editors)

1. Hush! my_ dear, lie still and_ slum - ber; Ho - ly_ an - gels
guard thy_ bed!_ Heav'n - ly_ bless - ings with - out_ num - ber
Gent - ly_ fall - ing on thy_ head. Sleep, my_ babe; thy_ food and_
rai - ment, House and_ home thy_ friends pro - vide:_ All with -

-out thy care or__ pay-ment, All__ thy__ wants are__ well__ sup - plied.

2 How much better thou'rt attended
　　Than the Son of God could be
When from heaven he descended
　　And became a child like thee!
Soft and easy is thy cradle,
　　Coarse and hard thy Saviour lay
When his birth-place was a stable
　　And his softest bed was hay.

*3 Was there nothing but a manger
　　Cursèd sinners could afford
To receive the heav'nly stranger?
　　Did they thus affront their Lord?
Soft! my child; I did not chide thee,
　　Though my song might sound too hard:
'Tis thy mother sits beside thee,
　　And her arms shall be thy guard.

*4 See the kindly shepherds round him,
　　Telling wonders from the sky!
Where they sought him, there they
　　found him,
　　With his Virgin Mother nigh.
See the lovely Babe addressing:
　　Lovely Infant, how he smiled!
When he wept, the mother's blessing
　　Soothed and hushed the Holy Child.

5 Lo! he slumbers in his manger,
　　Where the hornèd oxen fed;
Peace, my darling, here's no danger,
　　Here's no ox a-near thy bed.
May'st thou live to know and fear him,
　　Trust and love him all thy days;
Then go dwell for ever near him,
　　See his face and sing his praise!

Isaac Watts (1674–1748)

Watts's 'Cradle-Hymn' was first published in his *Moral Songs* (1706), at the end of what he called 'these Songs for Children'. In our verse 3 he gives 'nurse that' as an alternative to 'mother', with the note 'Here you may use the words, Brother, Sister, Neighbour, Friend etc.' We include ten of the fourteen four-line stanzas, omitting verse 8 as both anti-Semitic and absurd, and 12 (with its 'burning flame', 'bitter groans', and 'endless crying') as less than suitable for a tiny infant.

　　Although the hymn has appeared in several modern carol-books, the lack of a good tune denied it the popularity it deserves until Elizabeth Poston, in *The Second Penguin Book of Christmas Carols* (1970), married it to the tune that forms our bars 1–16. This was one of the most popular shape-note melodies (see Appendix 3), and may ultimately derive from a European folk tune. We have added a middle eight bars for variety, but those who wish may restore Watts's four-line stanzas and sing them to bars 1–16 only.

PERFORMANCE (*i*) Voice and instrument (guitar, harp, etc.); (*ii*) choir.

116

A Boy was born in Bethlehem

(Christmas)

Benjamin Britten (1913–76)

The text of this carol comprises three verses from Percy Dearmer's translation (in *The Oxford Book of Carols*, 1928) of the German chorale 'Ein Kind geborn zu Bethlehem' (54:II). Britten's setting is the theme of his choral variations *A Boy was born* (op. 3, 1933).

PERFORMANCE   Choir, with organ *ad lib.* (An optional organ part was added for the revised edition of 1958.)

117

A Hymn to the Virgin

(Christmas)

Benjamin Britten (1913–76)

¹ as the star of the sea ² mother and maiden

³ so holy ⁴ through Eve's sin ⁵ of you, his mother

⁶ of salvation   ⁷ of virtue

⁸ rose without a thorn ⁹ by divine grace ¹⁰ chosen

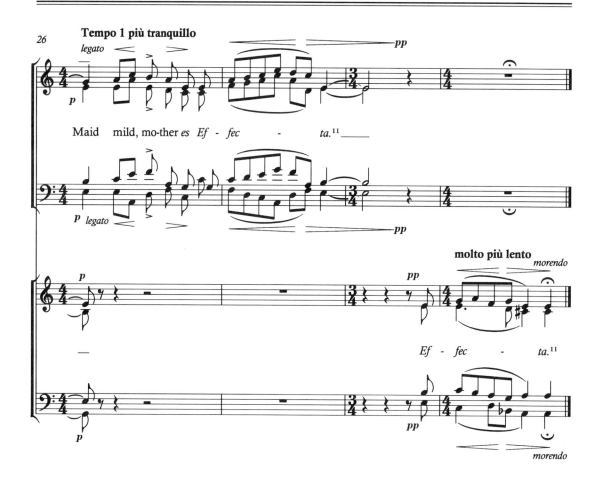

molto più lento

morendo

[11] you are made

This was one of Britten's earliest works, written during a period of confinement in his school sanatorium in 1930, when he was seventeen. He made small revisions in 1934, giving a harder and more characteristic edge to some of the harmonies, and published the carol the following year.

He found the text (in a modernized version) in *The Oxford Book of English Verse* (1900). It exists in two thirteenth-century manuscripts (Trinity College, Cambridge, MS 323, and British Library, Egerton MS 613) which are confused as to the order of the five verses. The Latin tags have not been traced, and are presumably by the poet. The verses Britten sets are probably the first, third, and second of the intended order in the Egerton manuscript, though the three modern scholarly editions we have consulted are at variance with each other. The 'es' in Britten's final verse is possibly a scribal misreading of 'ec' (also): the Trinity manuscript has 'moder milde ant [and] maidan ec'. The poem must have been particularly popular, since it continued in circulation until the fifteenth century, when it was recast as a carol with the refrain 'Enixa est puerpera', of which the music does not survive. (For the full poem and variants see R. L. Greene, *The Early English Carols*, 1977.)

PERFORMANCE   Choir with semichorus or solo quartet.

118

Torches

(Christmas; New Year)

John Joubert (b. 1927)

Alla marcia

mf UNISON VOICES

1. Tor-ches, tor-ches, run with tor-ches All the way to— Beth-le-hem! Christ is born and

ORGAN *mf*

simile

Ped.

1.

2.

now lies sleep-ing: Come and sing your song to him! Come and sing your song to him!

(unaccompanied ad lib.)

12 2. Ah, ro - ro, ro - ro,— my— ba - by, Ah,— ro - ro, my— love, ro - ro;

S. *p*

A.

Ro - ro,——————— ro - ro,———

T.

B. *p*

Joubert rescued this text from the pages of *The Oxford Book of Carols* (1928), where it was mutely enduring a joyless marriage to a debased and dimly harmonized version of its traditional melody (from Pedrell's *Cancionero musical popular* *español*, 1918–22). Torchlight processions in Galicia, as in Provence (see notes, 186, 187), played an important part in Christmas celebrations. Joubert's setting, published in 1952, has become perhaps the most popular of all modern carols.

Galician traditional
(tr. J. B. Trend, 1887–1958)

119

Make we joy now in this fest

(Christmas)

William Walton (1902–83)

¹ in which Christ is born   ² the Only-begotten of the Father

we__ of him__ and say__ 'Wel-come! *Ve - ni__ Re - demp - tor gen - ci - um.*'³

2 *Agnoscat omne seculum*⁴
   A bright star made three kings to come
   Him for to seek with their presents,
   *Verbum supernum prodiens.*⁵

3 *A solis ortus cardine*⁶
   So mighty a lord is none as he,
   And to our kind he hath him knit
   *Adam parens quod polluit.*⁷

4 *Maria ventre concepit,*⁸
   The Holy Ghost was aye her with.
   Of her in Bethlem born he is,
   *Consors Paterni luminis.*⁹

5 *O Lux beata Trinitas!*¹⁰
   He lay between an ox and ass,
   Beside his mother-maiden free:
   *Gloria tibi Domine!*¹¹

Fifteenth-century
(modernized)

³ come, Redeemer of the nations   ⁴ let every age perceive
(that)   ⁵ the high Word coming forth   ⁶ from the rising of
the sun   ⁷ which our father Adam defiled   ⁸ Mary
conceived in her womb   ⁹ sharing in the light of his Father
¹⁰ O Light of the Holy Trinity   ¹¹ Glory to thee, O Lord!

The text is a fifteenth-century carol found in two Bodleian
Library manuscripts and one in the British Library; the
English has been modernized. (For a fifteenth-century set-
ting and a note on this unusual text see 31.)

Walton produced a steady trickle of church music, including several Christmas carols, throughout his life. This
'old English carol for unaccompanied mixed voices' was
commissioned by *The Daily Dispatch* and was first published
in the issue of 24 December 1931.

PERFORMANCE Choir.

120

There is no rose of such virtue

(Christmas)

John Joubert (b. 1927)

Andantino semplice

1. There is no rose of such vir - tue As is the rose that bare Je - su: Al - - - le - lu - ia.

2. For in this rose con - tain - ed was Heaven and earth in
For in this rose con - tain - ed was Heaven and earth in
lit - tle space: Res mi - ran - da.
lit - tle space: Res mi - ran - da.

For a fifteenth-century setting and a note on the text see
'Ther is no rose of swych vertu' (28). Joubert's setting (his
op. 14) dates from 1954.

PERFORMANCE   Choir.

121

Adam lay ybounden

(*Christmas*)

Boris Ord (1897–1961)

¹ clergy   ² the Bible

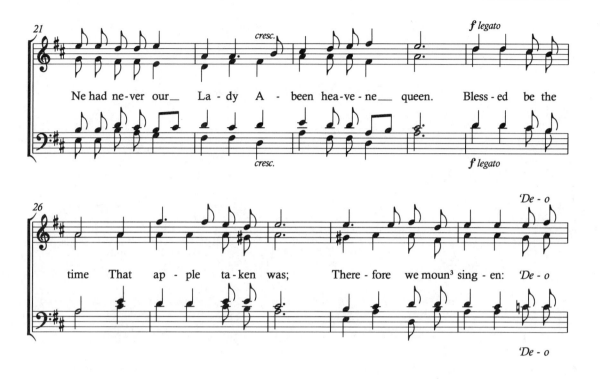

Fifteenth-century
(*Sloane MS, modernized*)

³ must

The text comes from the same fifteenth-century manuscript as 'Lullay, my liking' (109). No contemporary setting survives, but a number of twentieth-century composers have been attracted to the poem, including Peter Warlock and John Ireland. Boris Ord's beautiful carol was his only published composition. It has long retained its place in the Service of Nine Lessons and Carols at King's College, Cambridge, as a memorial to one of the chapel's most distinguished recent directors of music.

Ord's text follows that of Peter Warlock's setting in *The Oxford Book of Carols* (1928, no. 180).

PERFORMANCE Choir.

122

The Fader of heven

(Christmas)

Peter Maxwell Davies (b. 1934)

The Fa - der of he - ven, God om - ny - po - tent,___ That

sett alle on se - ven, His Son has he sent: My name couthe he ne - ven, And

lyght or he went. I con - ceyved hym full e - ven Thrugh myght as he ment,___ And

now is he borne. He kepe you fro wo: I

shalle pray him so; Telle furth as ye go, And myn on this morne.

TRANSLATION   The Father of heaven, God omnipotent, who created all things in seven days, has sent his Son. My name could he name, and [God] alighted [in me] before he departed. I conceived him [Christ] directly through his [God's] might, as he intended, and now is he [Christ] born. May he preserve you from sorrow—this I shall ask of him; proclaim [his birth] as you go, and remember this morning.

The seventh of the nine movements of Maxwell Davies's *O Magnum Mysterium*, which he wrote in 1960 for performance by the pupils of Cirencester Grammar School, Gloucestershire, where he was then director of music. The complete work comprises four carols (one a setting of the text of a Christmas matins responsory, which gives the work its title and is sung three times, in one, two, and four parts), two sonatas for instrumental ensembles based on Christmas plainchants, and a concluding organ fantasia on the *O Magnum Mysterium* setting. The composer notes that 'the carols may be performed separately, or as a small group together, in any combination'.

The words of 'The Fader of heven' are from the Second Shepherds' Play of the Towneley cycle of mystery plays, which is probably from Wakefield, Yorkshire, and is thought to have been written *c*.1450. Both the First and Second Shepherds' Plays are by the Wakefield Master, and seem to be alternatives. They have much material in common, but the second play is generally recognized as the greater, prefiguring Shakespeare in its easy mingling of poetry and rustic humour within a free-flowing dramatic structure. At the conclusion, the three shepherds, having been told of Christ's birth by an angel, come to the manger and present their gifts: cherries, a bird, and a ball, symbols of blood and death, divinity, and kingship which parallel the myrrh, frankincense, and gold of the magi. The Virgin then addresses them with the text that Maxwell Davies sets, and, with a few words of awe and concern, they depart, singing. The little speech is the dramatic climax of the play, a proclamation of the infant's divinity followed by an *envoi* to the shepherds and to the audience.

The meaning of Mary's speech is a matter of some contention; the word 'son' could be a scribal error for 'sond(e)' (messenger), since the scene in her mind is clearly that of the Annunciation. (Our translation differs from that given in the published score of *Four Carols from O Magnum Mysterium*, 1962.)

Maxwell Davies also composed a set of four *Christmas Carols* in 1961–2, one for four equal voices, three for four-part choir.

PERFORMANCE   High voices.

123

When Christ was born of Mary free

(Christmas)   *John Gardner (b. 1917)*

With bounce (♩ = 64)

VERSE

1. When Christ was born of Ma - ry free[1] In Beth - lem, in that
2. Herd - men be - held these an - gels bright— To them ap - pear - ed
3. This King is come to save his kind, In_____ the Scrip - ture
4. Then, dear Lord,_ for thy great grace, Grant us the bliss to

fair ci - ty, An - gels sung_ e'er with mirth and glee:_
with great light, And said: 'God's Son is born this night;
as we find; There-fore this_ song have we in mind: 'In ex - cel - sis
see thy face, Where we may_ sing to thy so - lace:_

REFRAIN

glo - ri - a.' 'Glo - ri - a, glo - ri - a, in ex-cel - sis glo - ri - a,'_____ Chri -

'Glo - ri - a, glo - ri - a, in ex-cel-sis glo - ri - a,'_____

- sto pa - re - mus can - ti - ca: 'In ex - cel - sis_ glo - ri - a.'[2]

_ Chri - sto pa - re - mus can - ti - ca:_____ 'In ex - cel - sis glo - ri - a.'[2]

[1] noble [2] to Christ let us give this song: 'On high [be] glory.'

A fifteenth-century text from a British Library manuscript (Harley 5396), modernized. No contemporary setting survives; Gardner's (op. 55) dates from 1963, and was commissioned for the anthology *Sing Nowell*.

PERFORMANCE Two-part voices, high or low, alternating or combined *ad lib.*; key to suit voices.

PART II

Traditional
Carols

124

The Boar's Head Carol

(Christmas)

English traditional
(Fyfe, 1860)

1. The boar's head in hand bear I, Be-decked with bays and rose - ma-ry; And I

pray you my mas - ters be mer - ry, Quot es - tis in con - vi - vi - o.[1]

Ca - put ap - ri de - fe - ro Red - dens lau - des Do - mi - no,

lau - des Do - mi - no, lau - des Do - mi - no, Do - mi - no.[2]

[1] as many as are at the feast [2] I bring in the boar's head, giving thanks to the Lord

ALTERNATIVE REFRAIN

(Queen's College, 1901)

Ca - put ap - ri   de - fe - ro   Red - dens lau - des Do - mi - no.

2 The boar's head, as I understand,
Is the bravest dish in all the land
When thus bedecked with a gay garland;
Let us *servire cantico*.[3]

3 Our steward hath provided this
In honour of the King of Bliss,
Which on this day to be servèd is
In Reginensi Atrio.[4]

English traditional
(Fyfe, 1860)

[3] serve it with a song   [4] in Queen's Hall

The carol sung every Christmas at the Queen's College, Oxford. An early version of the text is 'A caroll bringyng in the bores heed' in *Christmasse Carolles Newly Emprynted at London in the flete strete . . . by Wynkyn de Worde* (1521). No early musical setting survives, and the tune to which it has been sung from at least the eighteenth century probably derives from a Restoration bass pattern. The version we give was printed in William Wallace Fyfe's *Christmas, its Customs and Carols* (1860) and, unlike those in Rimbault's *Little Book of Christmas Carols* (1863) and Husk's *Songs of the Nativity* (1864), represents the carol as it was sung at that time. In 1901 the refrain was rewritten, and we give this as an alternative. (For a fifteenth-century boar's head carol see 'The Exeter Boar's Head Carol', 37.)

Boar's head feasts were particularly popular at Christmas—in Edward II's time the open season for boar-hunting ran from Christmas to Candlemas. Their origin was probably the Norse custom of sacrificing a boar to the goddess of fertility, Freyja, at her midwinter feast, a custom that persisted in the north of England and was adapted for various festivities. Queen's, a college with north-country connections and a strong attachment to tradition, almost certainly adopted rather than invented both feast and carol, and hung on to both even after the wild boar became extinct in seventeenth-century England. Ceremony, words, and music have all evolved over the years at Queen's, and the 1901 arrangement of the music is the one still sung. Nowadays the feast is held not on Christmas Night but on a Saturday shortly before, when old members are entertained at a 'gaudy'. The Provost and Fellows enter after a trumpet call and, the Provost having said grace, the boar's head is carried in by three chefs on its silver charger, surrounded by rosemary and gilded sprigs of bay, stuck with flags, and magnificently crowned. On either side are torch-bearers, and in front walks the solo singer and (proceeding backwards) the choir. The procession halts for each verse, moving forward during the refrains. When the charger is set down on the high table the Provost distributes the herbs among the choir and presents the solo singer with the orange from the boar's mouth.

PERFORMANCE   Choir.

125

Come all you faithful Christians

(Christmas)

English traditional
(Sharp, 1911, arr. editors)

1. Come all you faith - ful Christ - ians That_ dwell - eth__ here_ on__ earth: Come ce - le - brate the__ morn - ing of Our__ bless - ed Sa - viour's birth. This is the hap - py morn - ing, This is the bless - ed__ morn! To__ save our souls from ru - in The_ Son of__ God was_ born.

2 Behold, the angel Gabriel,
   In Scripture it is said,
Did with his holy message
   Come to the Virgin Maid.
'Hail, blest among all women!'
   He thus did greet her then;
'Lo! thou shalt be the mother
   Of the Saviour of all men.'

3 Her time being accomplished,
   She came to Bethlehem.
And then was safe delivered
   Of the Saviour of all men.
No princely pomp attended him,
   His honours were but small;
A manger was his cradle,
   His bed an ox's stall.

4 Now to that new-born Saviour
   Let all our praises be;
May we his footsteps follow,
   And he our pattern be.
So, when our lives are ended,
   We all may hear him call—
'Come, souls, receive the kingdom
   Preparèd for you all!'

English traditional
(*Oxford Book of Carols, 1928*)

Cecil Sharp collected verse 1 of this carol from Henry Thomas at Chipping Sodbury in Gloucestershire. Thomas could remember no more and believed the second quatrain to be a refrain, so when Sharp published the carol in his *English Folk-Carols* (1911) he added two suitable four-line verses from a carol called 'The Lamb' in a broadside by Pitt. The opening of the tune resembles 'The holly and the ivy' (126), which Sharp included in the same publication.

A more satisfactory text appeared under the title 'Hereford Carol' in *The Oxford Book of Carols* (1928), a conflation (with several verses omitted) of three sources: singers in Wales and in Worcestershire, and a ballad sheet published by R. Elliot of Hereford. There is no refrain, the tune (from the Welsh singer) is quite different, and the opening quatrain is clearly less corrupt than that which Thomas sang to Sharp.

We have married Thomas's more attractive tune to the Oxford text, substituting Thomas's 'dwelleth' for 'dwell' in verse 1, line 2 and his 'blessed' for 'dear' in line 4.

PERFORMANCE Choir.

126

The holly and the ivy

(*Christmas*)

English traditional
(Sharp, 1911, arr. editors)

436

2 The holly bears a blossom
   As white as the lily flower,
   And Mary bore sweet Jesus Christ
   To be our sweet Saviour.

3 The holly bears a berry
   As red as any blood,
   And Mary bore sweet Jesus Christ
   To do poor sinners good.

5 The holly bears a bark
   As bitter as any gall,
   And Mary bore sweet Jesus Christ
   For to redeem us all.

4 The holly bears a prickle
   As sharp as any thorn,
   And Mary bore sweet Jesus Christ
   On Christmas Day in the morn.

6 The holly and the ivy,
   When they are both full grown,
   Of all the trees that are in the wood,
   The holly bears the crown.

English traditional
(Sharp, 1911)

This text and tune are the now standard versions, taken down by Cecil Sharp from a Mrs Mary Clayton at Chipping Campden, Gloucestershire, and published in his *English Folk-Carols* (1911), the text supplemented and corrected from other sources.

The antiquity of this carol has been disputed: 'Although now so well known, the text of "The Holly and the Ivy", with the possible exception of the Cornish version ['Now the holly bears a berry', 127] . . . appears to derive from a single source, a Birmingham broadside published by Wadsworth, according to Husk [*Songs of the Nativity*, 1864] "about one-and-a-half centuries since", i.e. *c*.1710' (Margaret Dean-Smith, *A Guide to English Folk-Song Collections, 1822–1952*, 1954). We need not, however, assume that the carol was necessarily written for that broadside: it was presumably taken from a manuscript or previous printed source in the usual way. Although it may, certainly, have been worked up for publication and then been adopted by singers and by other publishers, a much earlier origin (for the verses at least) seems likely, particularly since so. many medieval 'holly and ivy' songs and carols are known.

The refrain is another matter. Incoherent and oddly irrelevant, it stands in the same aesthetic relationship to the verses as does Tower Bridge to the Tower of London, and is just the kind of 'Olde Englishe' trumpery that a canny broadside publisher of 1710 might have strung together from stock to eke out his product. The present first and last verse is surely the proper refrain, and we suspect (bearing in mind the early date) that Wadsworth's source would have given it in full at the beginning and end of the four-verse carol to indicate the old pattern of refrain–verse–refrain, etc. If Wadsworth interpreted this as a six-verse carol with no refrain, then his insertion of 'The rising of the sun . . .' was a bold completion of a supposedly defective source. Those who find the 'merry organ' and 'sweet singing' too quaint may easily restore what we believe was the original pattern by making verse 1 the refrain.

Holly and ivy were powerful male and female symbols in pagan times and they retained something of their ancient force in many English folk-songs and rituals, especially in some of those associated with the Christmas season when the old winter solstice custom of decorating houses with evergreens was kept up. Holly was also associated with good, and ivy (from its links with the druidic mistletoe) with evil. It is the 'goodness', not the 'maleness', of holly that permeates this carol and, most unusually, the plant is associated here with the Virgin. Perhaps it was simply the symbolic possibilities of holly that inspired the poet: the white blossom figuring Mary's virginity, the poisonous berry and the sharp thorn the pain of birth, the bitter-tasting bark the pain of Crucifixion—images so typically medieval as practically to rule out an eighteenth-century origin. (For an enjoyably fanciful interpretation see the article by E. Stredder in *Notes & Queries*, 8th series, ix, 1896, p. 4. For holly and ivy symbolism see R. L. Greene, *The Early English Carols*, second edn., 1977, pp. cxxii–cxxvii and notes to carols 136–139.1.)

PERFORMANCE Choir.

127

Now the holly bears a berry
(The St Day Carol)

English traditional
(*Oxford Book of Carols, 1928,*
arr. editors)

(*Christmas*)

1. Now the hol - ly bears a ber - ry as white as the milk, And_ Ma - ry bore_ Je - sus who was wrapped up in silk.
2. Now the hol - ly bears a ber - ry as green as the grass, And_ Ma - ry bore_ Je - sus who_ died on the cross.

And_ Ma - ry bore_ Je - sus Christ, our Sa - viour for to be, And the

first tree of the green-wood, it was the hol - ly; Hol - ly! hol -

- ly! And the first tree of the green-wood, it was the hol - ly.

3   Now the holly bears a berry as black as a coal,
     And Mary bore Jesus, who died for us all.

*4   Now the holly bears a berry as red as the blood,
     And Mary bore Jesus, who died on the rood.

vv. 1–3 English traditional
v. 4 W. D. Watson (Oxford Book of Carols, 1928)

The melody belongs to the vast family of 'A virgin unspotted' (143) variants and is remarkable for beginning each line with the same figure. The carol is also unusual in equating the holly with the Virgin: more usually holly is a masculine symbol, and it is ivy, its feminine counterpart, that is associated with Mary (see notes, 126).

The melody, together with the first three verses, was transcribed in the early twentieth century by the Revd G. H. Doble in St Day, near Redruth in Cornwall, from the singing of W. Daniel Watson, who had heard it sung by Thomas Beard when the latter was aged between fifty and sixty. Doble communicated his transcription to various editors, including those of *The Oxford Book of Carols* (1928).

Verse 4 is a modern addition, and was originally composed in Cornish by 'Tyrvab' (Watson) for his translation of Beard's carol, 'Ma gron war'n gelinen'.

Conventional notation rarely does justice to the subtleties of folk singing, and the recurring dotted figures (of which only the first two are from Doble—we have supplied the rest) should probably be sung as something closer to ♩♪.

St Day is thought to be the Breton St Dei, or Thei, a monk, and later abbot, of Landevennec. He was no doubt the titular saint of the village chapel prior to its dedication to the Holy Trinity in 1269.

PERFORMANCE   Choir.

128

The Cherry Tree Carol

I
The Cherry Tree [Part I]

(*Christmas*)

English traditional
(*Hutchens MS, arr. editors*)

1. Jo - seph was an old man, and an old__ man was__ he___ When he wed - ded__ Ma - ry in the land of Ga - li - lee,___ when he__ wed - ded Ma - ry in the land of__ Ga - li - lee.

2   When Joseph was married and Mary home had got,
    Mary proved with child, by whom Joseph knew not.

3   'Joseph and Mary walked through an orchard good,
    Where was cherries and berries, so red as any blood.

*4 'Joseph and Mary walked through an orchard green,
    Where was berries and cherries, as thick as might be seen.

5   O then bespoke Mary, so meek and so mild:
    'Pluck me a cherry, Joseph; they run so in my mind.'

6   O then bespoke Joseph, with words most reviled:
    'Let him pluck thee a cherry that brought thee with child.'

7   O then bespoke Jesus, all in his mother's womb:
    'Bow down, then, thou tallest tree, for my mother to have some!

*8 'Go to the tree, Mary, and it shall bow to thee,
    And the highest branch of all shall bow to Mary's knee.'

9   Then bowèd down the tallest tree, it bent to Mary's hand;
    Then she cried: 'See, Joseph, I have cherries at command.'

10 O then bespoke Joseph: 'I have done Mary wrong.
    But cheer up, my dearest, and do not be cast down!

*11 'O eat your cherries, Mary, O eat your cherries now!
    O eat your cherries, Mary, that grow upon the bough!'

12 Then Mary plucked a cherry, as red as any blood;
    And she did travel onward, all with her heavy load.

English traditional
(*Hone, 1822, adapted*)

II
Joseph and the Angel
[The Cherry Tree, Part II]

(*Christmas*)

English traditional
(*Terry, 1923, arr. editors*)

1. As Jo-seph was a-walk-ing, he heard an an-gel sing:___ 'This

night___ shall___ be born - ed our hea - ven-ly King._____

2 'He neither shall be bornèd in housen nor in hall,
   Nor in the place of Paradise, but in an ox's stall.

3 'He neither shall be clothèd in purple nor in pall,
   But in the fair white linen, as usen babies all.

4 'He neither shall be rockèd in silver nor in gold,
   But in a wooden cradle that rocks upon the mould.[1]

5 'He neither shall be christenèd in white wine nor red,
   But with the fair spring water with which we were christenèd.'

English traditional
(*Hone, 1822, adapted*)

[1] ground

III
Mary and Jesus
[The Cherry Tree, Part III]

(Christmas)

English traditional
(Sharp MS, arr. editors)

1. Then Ma - ry took her young son and set him on her knee, __ Say-ing:

'My dear son, __ tell __ me how __ this world shall __ be!', __ say-ing:

'My dear son, __ tell __ me how __ this __ world shall __ be!'

2 'O I shall be as dead, mother, as the stones in the wall,
And the stones in the streets, mother, shall mourn for me all.

3 'And upon a Wednesday my vow I will make,
And upon Good Friday my death I will take.

4 'And upon the third day my uprising shall be,
And the sun and moon together shall rise up with me.

443

5 'The people shall rejoice, and the birds they shall sing
To see the uprising of the heavenly King.'

English traditional
(*Hone, 1822, adapted*)

'We approached our last house high up on the hill, the place of Joseph the farmer. For him we had chosen a special carol, which was about the other Joseph, so that we always felt that singing it added a spicy cheek to the night. The last stretch of country to reach his farm was perhaps the most difficult of all. In those bare lanes, open to all winds, sheep were buried and wagons lost . . .

We grouped ourselves around the farmhouse porch, the sky cleared, and broad streams of stars ran down over the valley and away to Wales . . . Everything was quiet: everywhere there was the faint crackling silence of the winter night. We started singing, and we were all moved by the words and the sudden trueness of our voices. Pure, very clear, and breathless we sang:

> As Joseph was a walking
> He heard an angel sing:
> 'This night shall be the birth-time
> Of Christ the Heavenly King.
>
> He neither shall be bornèd
> In Housen nor in hall,
> Nor in a place of paradise
> But in an ox's stall . . .'

And two thousand Christmases became real to us then: the houses, the halls, the places of paradise had all been visited: the stars were bright to guide the Kings through the snow: and across the farmyard we could hear the beasts in their stalls. We were given roast apples and hot mince pies, in our nostrils were spices like myrrh, and in our wooden [collecting] box, as we headed back for the village, there were golden gifts for all.' (Laurie Lee, *Cider with Rosie*, 1959)

'The Cherry Tree Carol' is one of the most fascinating English ballads, with a profound meaning that can be half sensed beneath its mysterious narrative surface. Its roots are probably fifteenth-century, and, whether or not it was originally written by a single author, the surviving versions suggest that the unusual tripartite shape was planned and not fortuitous.

Centuries of use have woven a tangled web of variant texts, all of them marred by the vagaries and omissions of memory, by singers' mishearings and their replacement of idioms no longer understood, by their clipping or expansion of lines to fit different tunes, and by editorial inventions. A. H. Bullen, in *Carols and Poems from the fifteenth century to the present time* (London, 1886, p. 252) notes that no two copies of the text agree, and recommends an eclectic method to establish a satisfactory version. We have followed his recommendation, allowing ourselves unusual freedom in devising a text that is complete, narratively coherent, and with the relatively smooth fit of words to music that choral performance requires. The overt division into three sections is modern (most of the printed and oral versions consist of part I, parts I and II, parts II and III, or, less frequently, parts I and III). Only William Hone's text in his *Ancient Mysteries Described* (1822) (the longest, and the earliest in a printed book) preserves enough to suggest that the original form was of three balanced sections, and even here the so-called 'Eastertide verses' of part III can be only a portion of what once existed. (Laurie Lee's troop of Cotswold carollers were not alone in being moved by the carol: Hone writes that 'The admiration of my earliest days for some lines in the Cherry carol [part II, verses 3 and 4] still remains, nor can I help thinking that the reader will see somewhat of the cause for it.')

Hone's version is itself eclectic, having been assembled 'from various [broadside, etc.] copies of it printed at different times', and since it is the most satisfactory of the available versions we take it as our basic text. We take verse 12 from the unspecified version in A. L. Lloyd's *Folk Song in England* (1967) to avoid a bathetic and obviously wrong 'Then Mary went home', and we have also drawn on the Hutchens manuscript (see below) and on the versions given by F. J. Child in his *English and Scottish Popular Ballads* (1882–98), which also contains a useful commentary with details of the many Continental songs on the same subject.

Eight versions of both text and tune were collected by Cecil Sharp in England and North America (one from a 'wandering gypsy girl'), and there are numerous others in broadsides and various nineteenth-century publications, including Sandys's *Christmas Carols, Ancient and Modern* (1833) and *Christmastide* (*c.*1852); Rimbault's *Collection of Old Christmas Carols* (1861); Husk's *Songs of the Nativity* (1864) (a version taken from an eighteenth-century Worcester broadside which was probably one of Sandys's main sources); Bramley and Stainer's *Christmas Carols New and Old* (1871) (in which there seems to have been some editorial rewriting); and Bullen's *Carols and Poems*. We have taken note of what may be the earliest version of the tune, which is in three manuscript books of carols which Davies Gilbert bound up together (Houghton Library, Harvard, MS 25258.27.5*, part I, p. 22; the books seem to have come to the library together with the Child manuscripts early in the twentieth century).

The similarities between part I and the fifteenth play of the so-called *Ludus Coventriae* ('Coventry Play') mystery cycle have frequently been noted. The story derives from chapter 20 of the *Gospel of pseudo-Matthew*, but in both mystery play and ballad the original palm tree has been changed to a cherry and the event has been transposed from the post-natal flight into Egypt to the pre-natal journey to Bethlehem, with Christ effecting the miracle from within his mother's womb. The first change is typical of the ballads on this theme from all over western Christendom, but the second is found nowhere else, and suggests a possible direct connection between play and ballad. It allowed the writer to incorporate another apocryphal tale (from the *Protevangelium of James*), that of Joseph's doubts about the child's paternity. In mystery plays this was the basis of popular scenes in which Joseph is represented as a comic cuckold, his jealous anger giving way to penitence when an angel appears to enlighten him. In the ballad this jealousy is presented with a clever use of dramatic irony, since his waspish 'Let him pluck thee a cherry that brought thee with child' is followed by their immediate provision by the unborn Christ, who in theological terms is not to be differentiated from the Creator God who had indeed got Mary with child by the Holy Ghost.

The second change also allowed the writer to fit the cherry tree story into a coherent temporal scheme, for Joseph 'a-walking' in part II was calculated to evoke the mysterious episode in the *Protevangelium* account that ensues when he leaves Mary, now in labour, in a cave outside Bethlehem and goes to seek a midwife: 'Now I, Joseph, was walking, and yet I did not walk, and I looked up into the air, and saw the air in amazement . . .'. There follows an 'out-of-body', trance-like experience, similar to the ecstasies recorded by St Augustine. Part II is the still centre of the triptych, and its opening marks with allusive delicacy the unseen miracle that is taking place as Joseph walks. The angel's apparently prophetic account functions as a poetic substitute for a blunt birth narrative, concealing, as it were, the off-stage action rather as a drawn curtain might conceal it in a mystery or liturgical drama; this is one of several features of the ballad that suggest the hand of a playwright.

Part III has obvious links with the many fifteenth- and sixteenth-century carols in which the new-born Christ, seated in his mother's lap, foretells his life, death, and resurrection to her (see note, 132). By carrying the narrative forward to the final act of redemption, this balances a concealed background theme of the Fall of Man in part I which would have been apparent to those listeners who knew pseudo-Matthew's account or its retellings in popular legends and other books. The miraculous tree is an emblem of the Tree of Life in Genesis 2:9, which (commentators agree) bestowed notional immortality on Adam and Eve in Eden. By making it feed his mother, Christ symbolically confirms her immaculate conception as the New Eve; and (since the Tree of Life has its Jungian 'shadow' in the death-dealing Tree of the Knowledge of Good and Evil, from the wood of which the cross was believed to have been made) he simultaneously prefigures, as the moment of his birth approaches, the cancellation of the sin of the original Eve which his death will accomplish.

The subtlety of the scheme suggests the hand of a learned cleric, though the narrative surface and the carol's survival point to a popular origin. Perhaps the ballad was written to be sung on some convivial occasion in the Christmas season before an audience from a variety of educational backgrounds, such as a feast in a large clerical community or (just conceivably) of the trade guild that mounted the nativity play in the *Ludus Coventriae* cycle.

The ballad has been associated with several melodies. The received tradition, from the eighteenth century onward, is of a single tune for however much of the ballad is sung, though earlier practice may have been different. A single tune is perhaps best for solo performance, but we follow *The Oxford Book of Carols* (1928) in supplying separate ones for the three parts. Our three tunes correspond to those given (as tunes 1, 3, and 4) in the revised edition (1964) of that book.

Our tune I is one of the great English folk melodies, found in many variants on both sides of the Atlantic. It has a family resemblance to 'Love will find a way', which has been sung since at least the seventeenth century (see Claude M. Simpson, *The British Broadside Ballad and its Music*, 1966, fig. 295, and William Chappell, *Popular Music of the Olden Time*, 1853–9, vol. I, pp. 303–5), and to the ballad tunes 'Lamkin' and 'The Death of Queen Jane' (Bronson, 1959–72, nos. 93 and 170). Most of the many variants are in triple time, and some repeat the second half of each stanza. The 'traditional' version in Bramley and Stainer (very close to ours) had a powerful influence on Vaughan Williams, for whom it acted as an introduction to English folk-song when he encountered it as a boy in the 1880s: 'I remember clearly my reaction . . . which was more than simple admiration for a fine tune, though I did not then naturally realize the implications involved in that sense of intimacy' ('A Musical Autobiography', in *Some Thoughts on Beethoven's Choral Symphony*, 1953). Our version of the tune is given with carol 11 in the Hutchens manuscript of Cornish carols prepared for Davies Gilbert in or after 1816, though the carol was not included in Gilbert's *Some Ancient Christmas Carols* (1822; see Appendix 4). We have followed Husk in giving G♯ for E on the penultimate note (found in some versions collected later) and we have added passing notes in bar 3, which are found in many variants.

Tune II (unlike tunes I and III) is not known to have been sung to 'The Cherry Tree' before R. R. Terry set it to text II in his *Old Christmas Carols* (1923) and later publications, with the characteristically vague heading 'words and melody traditional'. (A quite different tune for text II is given in Fyfe's *Christmas, its Customs and Carols*, 1860, and is included in *The Oxford Book of Carols*. It sounds eighteenth-century, but we have found no record earlier than Fyfe.)

Tune III was transcribed in 1910 by Cecil Sharp from the singing of text II by a Robert Hughes, aged sixty-three, of 'Buckingham Union' (Sharp MS 489 in the Vaughan Williams Memorial Library, Cecil Sharp House, London). A virtually identical version was given as 'traditional' in Bramley and Stainer. We have added the repeat of the second half of each verse to give weight to this shorter third section and to link the setting to that of tune I.

PERFORMANCE   I, II, III (*i*) unaccompanied voice, perhaps using the same tune throughout; (*ii*) choir. The ballad can be sung complete or in one of the following forms: part I alone; parts I and II; part II alone; or parts II and III. Starred verses may be omitted without disturbing the narrative.

129

When righteous Joseph wedded was

(Annunciation; Immaculate Conception; Christmas)

English traditional
(Gilbert, 1822, arr. editors)

1. When right-eous Jo - seph wed - ded was To Is - rael's He-brew Maid
The an - gel Gab - riel came from heaven And to the_ Vir - gin said:

'Hail, bless - ed Ma - ry, full of grace, The Lord re - main on thee; Thou

shalt con-ceive and bear_ a Son, Our Sa - viour for to be.' *Then*

sing you all,— both great and small, Now well, now— well, now well! We

may re - joice to hear— the voice Of the an - gel— Ga - bri - el.

2 ''Tis wondrous strange', said Mary then,
    'I should conceive and breed,
Being never touched by mortal man,
    But pure in word and deed.'
The angel Gabriel thus replied:
    ''Tis not the work of man,
But as the Lord in heaven decreed
    Before the world began.'

3 This heavenly message she believed,
    And did to Jewry go,
There three months with her friends to stay,
    God's blessèd will to show;
And then returned to Joseph back,
    Her husband meek and mild,
Who thought it strange his wife should be
    Untouched and yet with child.

4 Then Joseph he, to shun the shame,
    Thought her for to forsake;
But then God's angel in a dream
    His mind did undertake:
'Fear not, just Joseph; this thy wife
    Is still a spotless maid;
And no consent of sin,' said he,
    'Against her can be laid.

5 'For she is pure, both maid and wife,
    And mother of God's own heir;
The Babe of Heaven and blessèd lamb
    Of Israel's flock so fair,
To save lost man from Satan's fold
    Which Adam lost by thrall,
When first in Eden paradise
    Did forfeit by the Fall.'

6 Thus Mary and her husband kind
    Together did remain,
  Until the time of Jesus' birth,
    As Scripture doth make plain.
  As mother, wife and virtuous maid,
    Our Saviour sweet conceived;
  And in due time to bring us him
    Of whom we were bereaved.

7 Sing praises all, both young and old,
    To him that wrought such things,
  And, all without the means of man,
    Sent us the King of kings;
  Who is of such a spirit blessed
    That with his might did quell
  The world, the flesh; and by his death
    Did conquer death and hell.

English traditional
(*Gilbert, 1822*)

One of many 'doubting Joseph' carols (see also 'The Cherry Tree Carol', 128, and 'O Joseph, being an old man', 130). It is from Davies Gilbert's *Some Ancient Christmas Carols* (1822; see Appendix 4). The melody may originally have been in a straightforward 4/4:

In Gilbert (or his source) the notes at the end of each phrase are lengthened (a common performing convention), while the strict 4/4 division is retained, which confusingly produces correct and incorrect stresses in alternate phrases:

Our rebarring is an attempt to resolve the problem. We have added upper parts to Gilbert's melody and bass.

The tune appears in Bramley and Stainer's *Christmas Carols New and Old* (1871) as the 'Devonshire' tune for 'The angel Gabriel from God was sent' (144). Both carols were sung to either melody. (See also 'The Lord at first did Adam make', 141: II, which has a related melody.)

PERFORMANCE Voices, with the tenor doubled at the higher octave, and instruments *ad lib.* (see Appendix 3).

130

O Joseph, being an old man truly
Joseph, being an aged man truly

I

(*Christmas*)

English traditional
(*Vaughan Williams, 1920*)

VERSES 1–4

1. O Jo - seph, being an old man tru - ly, He____ mar-ried a vir - gin fair and free; A pu - rer vir-gin could no man see Than he chose for his___ wife and his dear - est___ dear.

2. They li - ved both____ in joy and____ bliss; But now a strict com - mand-ment is: In Jew - ry - land___ no man should miss To___ go_____ a - long with his dear - est___ dear

3. Un - to_____ the place____ where he was___ born, Un - to the em - per-or to be sworn, To pay___ a tri - bute that's du - ly known, Both_ for_____ him - self and his dear - est___ dear.

4. And when____ they were____ to Beth - lehem come The____ inns were filled, both all and some; For Jo - seph en - treat - ed them ev - ery one, Both_ for_____ him - self and his dear - est___ dear.

VERSES 5–7

5. Then they were con - strain - ed pres - ent - ly With - in a sta - ble all night to lie, Where they___ did ox - en and ass - es tie, With_

*6. The Vir - gin pure___ thought it no___ scorn To___ lie in such___ a place for - lorn; But a - gainst the next morn - ing our Sa - viour was born, Even_

7. The King of all power was in Beth - lehem born, Who_ wore for our sakes a crown of thorn: Then God___ pre - serve us both even and morn, For____

449

his_____ true_ love and his dear - est_____ dear.
Je - sus___ Christ, our dear - est_____ dear.
Je - sus'___ sake, our dear - est____ dear!

II

English traditional
(arr. Ralph Vaughan Williams, 1872–1958)

Ah,_____ Ah,_____

†1. O Jo - seph, being an old man tru - ly, He__ mar-ried a vir - gin

Ah,_____ Ah,_____

Ah,_____

fair and free; A pu - rer vir - gin could no man see Than he

Ah,_____

Ah.

chose for his__ wife and his dear - est__ dear.

Ah.

† Follow music I for verses 2–7.

English traditional
(Sandys, 1833)

III

(*Annunciation; Christmas*)

English traditional
(*Lloyd, 1967, arr. editors*)

VERSES 1–3

1. Jo - seph, being an a - ged man tru - ly, He
2. The vir - gin pure there was no nay; The
3. The an - gel no soon - er this mes - sage said But

mar - ried a vir - gin fair and free; A pu - rer vir - gin could
an - gel Ga - briel to her did say: 'Thou shalt con - ceive a
all in heart she was a - fraid: 'How may this be, and

no man see Than he chose for his wife and his dear - est dear.
Child this day, The which shall be our dear - est dear.'
I a pure maid? Say then to me, my dear - est dear.'

VERSES 4–7

4. 'The Ho - ly Ghost,_ Ma - ry, shall come_ un - to thee; The
5. Jo - seph,_ being a_ per - fect mild_ man, Per -
6. Then an - swer - ed Ma - ry,_ meek_ and_ mild: 'I
7. But Jo - seph,_ think - ing her most_ un - just, Yield -

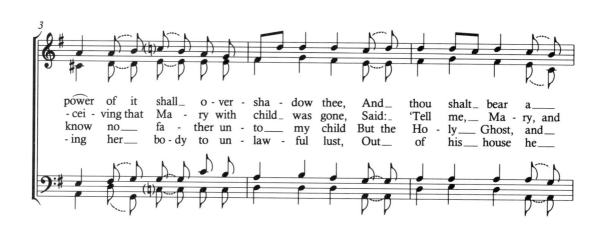

power of it shall_ o - ver - sha - dow thee, And_ thou shalt_ bear a_
-cei - ving that Ma - ry with child_ was gone, Said:_ 'Tell me,_ Ma - ry, and
know no_ fa - ther un - to_ my child But the Ho - ly_ Ghost, and_
-ing her_ bo - dy to un - law - ful lust, Out_ of his_ house he_

Son tru - ly, The_ which shall_ be_ our_ dear - est dear.'
do not_ frown, Who_ hath_ done_ this,_ my_ dear - est dear?'
I un - de - filed, That_ hath_ done_ this,_ my_ dear - est dear.'
thought for to thrust His_ own_ true_ love, his_ dear - est dear.

VERSES 8–11

8. But whilst in____ heart he____ thought the same The
9. Who said: 'Fear____ not to____ take____ to thee Thy
10. When Jo - seph a - rose from his sleep____ so sound His
11. The King of all power was in Beth - lehem born, Who

an - gel____ Ga - briel____ to____ him came As____ he lay sleep - ing____
true and____ faith - ful____ wife,____ Ma - ry: Most____ true and____ faith - ful is
love to____ Ma - ry did more____ a - bound; He____ would not____ for ten____
wore for____ our____ sakes a crown of thorn: Then God pre - serve us both

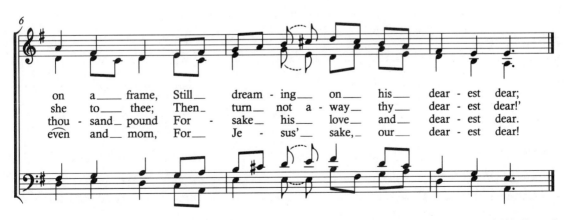

on a____ frame, Still____ dream - ing____ on____ his____ dear - est dear;
she to____ thee; Then____ turn____ not a - way____ thy____ dear - est dear!'
thou - sand____ pound For - sake____ his____ love____ and____ dear - est dear.
even and____ morn, For____ Je - sus'____ sake,____ our____ dear - est dear!

English traditional
(Sandys, 1833)

IV

(Christmas; Annunciation)

Cornish traditional
(Davey MS, arr. editors)

1. Jo - seph, being an___ a - ged man___ tru - ly, He___ mar - ried a___
2. The vir - gin___ pure___ there was___ no nay; The___ an - gel___
3. The an - gel no soon - er this mes - sage said But___ all___ in___

vir - gin fair___ and free; A pu - rer___ vir - gin could
Ga - briel to her___ did say: 'Thou shalt___ con - ceive___ a
heart___ she was___ a - fraid: 'How may___ this___ be,___ and

no___ man see___ Than he chose for his wife and his dear - est dear.
Child___ this day,___ The___ which shall be___ our dear - est dear.'
I a pure maid? Say___ then___ to me,___ my dear - est dear.'

4 'The Holy Ghost, Mary, shall come unto thee;
   The power of it shall overshadow thee,
   And thou shalt bear a Son truly,
      The which shall be our dearest dear.'

5 Joseph, being a perfect mild man,
   Perceiving that Mary with child was gone,
   Said: 'Tell me, Mary, and do not frown,
      Who hath done this, my dearest dear?'

6 Then answered Mary, meek and mild:
'I know no father unto my child
But the Holy Ghost, and I undefiled,
    That hath done this, my dearest dear.'

7 But Joseph, thinking her most unjust,
Yielding her body to unlawful lust,
Out of his house he thought for to thrust
    His own true love, his dearest dear.

8 But whilst in heart he thought the same
The angel Gabriel to him came
As he lay sleeping on a frame,
    Still dreaming on his dearest dear;

9 Who said: 'Fear not to take to thee
Thy true and faithful wife, Mary:
Most true and faithful is she to thee;
    Then turn not away thy dearest dear!'

10 When Joseph arose from his sleep so sound
His love to Mary did more abound;
He would not for ten thousand pound
    Forsake his love and dearest dear.

11 The King of all power was in Bethlehem born,
Who wore for our sakes a crown of thorn:
Then God preserve us both even and morn,
    For Jesus' sake, our dearest dear!

English traditional
(Sandys, 1833)

The text is from William Sandys's *Christmas Carols, Ancient and Modern* (1833; see Appendix 4). He gives no melody, and our tunes I/II and III were collected with different words. Tune I is Vaughan Williams's transcription of a 1908 gramophone recording of Mrs Esther Smith, a gypsy in Weobley, Herefordshire. She sang it to the popular Redemption hymn 'There is a fountain filled with blood', a favourite of nineteenth-century Christmas carollers (often sung to the tune of 'This is the truth', 150:I). Vaughan Williams, attracted by the tune but repelled by the 'rather unpleasant imagery' of the words, substituted a shortened version of the present text in his *Twelve Traditional Carols from Herefordshire* (1920) and subsequently in *The Oxford Book of Carols* (1928). 'Joseph and Mary', as the carol was named in the latter book, has now become quite popular in England.

Of the sixteen verses in Sandys, *The Oxford Book of Carols* gives 1, 11–14, and 16, and substitutes a new first line, supposedly to fit the folk tune. This version is now widely sung, so we give it without change except for the addition of verse 15 (as verse 6), along with Vaughan Williams's harmonization of the melody (II). However, it omits the substance of the carol, which is the story of Joseph's doubts about the paternity of Mary's child (told also in 'The Cherry Tree Carol', 128, and 'When righteous Joseph', 129, and

made much of in the medieval mystery plays). We therefore give verses 1–10 and 16, with a tune (III) collected by A. L. Lloyd in Woodbridge, Suffolk, to a ballad beginning 'A pretty young girl all in the month of May' (*Folk Song in England*, 1967, p. 185). The tune and bass of setting IV are from a manuscript of Cornish carols prepared for Gilbert in 1825 by John Davey, as sung in Zennor, near St Ives in Cornwall (see Appendix 4). The C in bar 11 may not always have been sharpened.

Cecil Sharp collected an equally fine variant of tune I to the words 'This is the truth sent from above' (150:II), and Gilbert's tune (in *Some Ancient Christmas Carols*, 1822) to 'Let all that are to mirth inclined' (140) is also related, and may be an eighteenth-century form from which the other more lyrical versions evolved. It seems that a single melody, varying according to location, was usually sung to both 'This is the truth' and 'There is a fountain', since the two are in the same metre and were frequently printed adjacently in Christmas broadsides.

PERFORMANCE I, solo voice, perhaps with a drone on A or A–E, or on a 'rocking' drone alternating between A–E and G–D, one chord per bar (two in bar 2).

II, choir.

III, IV (*i*) solo voice; (*ii*) choir.

131

The Seven Joys of Mary
The Seven Rejoices of Mary
The Blessings of Mary

I
The Seven Joys of Mary

(*Christmas*)

English traditional
(arr. R. R. Terry, 1865–1938)

VERSE

1. The first good joy that Ma-ry had, it was the joy of one:____ To

see her own__ Son, Je - sus, to suck at her__ breast - bone;____ To

suck at her breast - bone, good man,__ and bless - ed may he be:____ Sing

REFRAIN

456

Fa - ther, Son and Ho - ly Ghost, to all___ e - ter - ni - ty.___

2 The next good joy that Mary had, it was the joy of two:
To see her own Son, Jesus, to make the lame to go;

To make the lame to go, good man, and blessèd may he be,
Sing Father, Son and Holy Ghost, to all eternity.

3 The next good joy that Mary had, it was the joy of three:
To see her own Son, Jesus, to make the blind to see;

To make the blind to see, good man, (etc.)

4 The next good joy that Mary had, it was the joy of four:
To see her own Son, Jesus, to read the Bible o'er;

To read the Bible o'er, good man, (etc.)

5 The next good joy that Mary had, it was the joy of five:
To see her own Son, Jesus, to make the dead alive;

To make the dead alive, good man, (etc.)

6 The next good joy that Mary had, it was the joy of six:
To see her own Son, Jesus, to bear the Crucifix;

To bear the Crucifix, good man, (etc.)

7 The next good joy that Mary had, it was the joy of seven:
To see her own Son, Jesus, to wear the crown of heaven;

To wear the crown of heaven, good man, (etc.)

English traditional
(Brand, 1853–5; Sandys, 1833)

II
The Seven Rejoices of Mary

(Christmas)

Irish traditional
(Journal of the Irish Folk
Song Society, arr. editors)

VERSE

1. The first re - joice Our La - dy got, it was the re - joice of one:___ It

was the re - joice of her___ dear Son___ when he was born___ young,___ it

he was born___ young.___

REFRAIN

Glo - ry___ may___ he be, and
'Al - le - lu - i - a!' sweet

bless - ed now__ is she,_____ And those__ who sing the
'Al - le - lu - i - a!'_____ Sing 'Al - le - lu - ia! the

se - ven long ver - ses in hon - our of Our La - dy._____ Sing
hea - vens are true!'_ Sing 'Al - le - lu - i - - a!'_____

2 The second rejoice Our Lady got, it was the rejoice of two:
It was the rejoice of her dear Son when he was sent to school.

3 The third rejoice Our Lady got, it was the rejoice of three:
It was the rejoice of her dear Son when he led the blind to see.

4 The next rejoice Our Lady got, it was the rejoice of four:
It was the rejoice of her dear Son when he read the Bible o'er.

5 The next rejoice Our Lady got, it was the rejoice of five:
It was the rejoice of her dear Son when he raised the dead to life.

6 The next rejoice Our Lady got, it was the rejoice of six:
It was the rejoice of her dear Son when he carried the Crucifix.

7 The next rejoice Our Lady got, it was the rejoice of seven:
It was the rejoice of her dear Son when he opened the gates of heaven.

Irish traditional
(Journal of the Irish Folk Song Society)

III
The Blessings of Mary

(*Christmas*)

US traditional
(*Journal of American Folklore, 1935*)

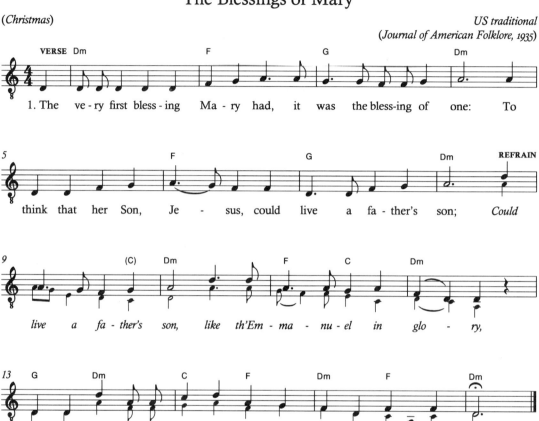

1. The ve - ry first bless - ing Ma - ry had, it was the bless-ing of one: To

think that her Son, Je - sus, could live a fa - ther's son; *Could*

live a fa - ther's son, like th'Em - ma - nu - el in glo - ry,

Fa - ther, Son and the Ho - ly Ghost, through all e - ter - ni - ty.

2   The very next blessing Mary had, it was the blessing of two:
    To think that her Son, Jesus, could read the Scriptures through;

    Could read the Scriptures through, like th'Emmanuel in glory, (etc.)

3   The very next blessing Mary had, it was the blessing of three:
    To think that her Son, Jesus, could set the sinner free;

    Could set the sinner free, (etc.)

4   The very next blessing Mary had, it was the blessing of four:
    To think that her Son, Jesus, could live for evermore;

    Could live for evermore, (etc.)

5   The very next blessing Mary had, it was the blessing of five:
    To think that her Son, Jesus, could bring the dead to live;

    Could bring the dead to live, (etc.)

6   The very next blessing Mary had, it was the blessing of six:
    To think that her Son, Jesus, could heal and cure the sick;

    Could heal and cure the sick, (etc.)

7   The very next blessing Mary had, it was the blessing of seven:
    To think that her Son, Jesus, could conquer hell and heaven;

    Could conquer hell and heaven, (etc.)

8   The very next blessing Mary had, it was the blessing of eight:
    To think that her Son, Jesus, could make the crooked straight;

    Could make the crooked straight, (etc.)

9   The very next blessing Mary had, it was the blessing of nine:
    To think that her Son, Jesus, could turn water into wine;

    Could turn water into wine, (etc.)

10 The very next blessing Mary had, it was the blessing of ten:
    To think that her Son, Jesus, could write without a pen;

    Could write without a pen, (etc.)

US traditional
(Journal of American Folklore, 1935)

The 'Joys of Mary' began as one of the innumerable and interconnected 'devotions' to the Virgin Mary which proliferated in the medieval church. It grew from the same roots as the Rosary, which consists of three groups of five 'Mysteries'. The 'Joyful Mysteries' centre on the divinity of Christ: the Annunciation to Mary by Gabriel (the moment of conception), the Visitation (John the Baptist recognizing the Messiah and leaping in the womb of Elizabeth), the Nativity, the Presentation of Christ in the temple (when Simeon hails him as the Messiah), and the Finding of the young Christ disputing among the doctors in the temple (when his earthly mission is first publicly revealed). The 'Sorrowful Mysteries' elicit pity and love at the Passion and death of Christ: the Agony in Gethsemane, the Scourging, the Crowning with Thorns, the Carrying of the Cross, and the Crucifixion. The 'Glorious Mysteries' elicit joy and longing for paradise: Christ's Resurrection, his bodily Ascension, the descent of the Holy Spirit at Pentecost, the Assumption (his joyful reunion with his mother as he raises her body to paradise after her death), and the Coronation of the Virgin (honouring her as chief among the saints). Beads, prayers, and sometimes biblical texts are used to concentrate the attention on the individual Mysteries.

Poems connected with the Joys show that they too were used for petitionary prayer (praying 'by the Five Joys', 'by the Five Wounds of Christ', etc.) and were connected with a strong personal love of the Virgin and her Son. The fourteenth-century poem 'As I me rod this ender day' begins like a secular *chanson d'aventure*, with four stanzas in which a young man tells how he rode by the forest, full of 'lovelonginge'; they conclude: 'Of alle things I love hire mest, / My dayes blis, my nyhtes rest; / Heo [she] counseileth & helpeth best / Bothe elde and yinge. / Nou I may yef I wole / The fif ioyes mynge [Now I may, if I wish, recite the Five Joys]'. He then recites five stanzas meditating on the Joys, with a final one pleading that he, after death, may also come to paradise.

Five remained the standard number of Joys in Britain until the fifteenth century, though the unofficial status of the devotion encouraged variation. The Epiphany was sometimes included, while the Crucifixion and the Coronation increasingly gained prominence. On the Continent, seven or fifteen Joys were usual, and the seven eventually acquired a companion set of 'Celestial Joys' which were said to have been communicated to St Thomas by the Virgin after her death. These were products of a general movement to give devotion to Mary a ritual status complementary (though inferior) to that of her Son. The original seven were renamed 'Terrestrial' and made to centre on Christ. In England the Five Joys underwent a similar transformation. One set of vernacular verses substitutes Doomsday for the Assumption, and a Five Joys carol of *c.*1600 in the commonplace-book of the London grocer Richard Hill (Balliol College Library, Oxford, MS 354) is almost entirely Christ-centred: Annunciation, Nativity, Resurrection, the Harrowing of Hell (oddly misplaced), and the Ascension. In time the five were gradually expanded to form a set of seven, often by the inclusion of representative miracles from Christ's life: this, and not a Protestant revision of the verses (as is usually supposed), is the source of the Joys of Mary in folk-song. (Medieval poems of the Five Joys can be found in *English Lyrics of the XIIIth Century*, ed. Carleton Brown,

1932 [nos. 18, 22, 41], and *Religious Lyrics of the XIVth Century*, ed. Carleton Brown, rev. G. V. Smithers, 1952 [nos. 11, 26, 31, 122]. In *Religious Lyrics of the XVth Century*, ed. Carleton Brown, 1939, nos. 30 and 31 are of Five Joys, no. 32 is of Seven Joys, and nos. 32–6 are of Seven Celestial Joys. Some of these are also in R. L. Greene, *The Early English Carols*, 1977 [nos. 230–33].)

The Joys as a devotion did not survive the Reformation, but, lacking the Marian emphasis which the repeated 'Ave Maria' prayers give to the Rosary, they were able to live on in the form of religious songs in Protestant folk culture. We do not know the process by which the many sets of Joys in British and North American folk-song evolved: partly from the simpler sets of 'literary' devotional verses, certainly, but there must also have been popular verses for the unlettered, sung to simple tunes. It is noticeable that all the folk-song versions are evocations rather than meditations, content with the mere naming of Joys, and this, too, may reflect a medieval folk tradition.

The numbers five, seven, and fifteen—resonant of the Five Wounds, the Seven Words from the Cross, the Seven Cardinal Virtues, the Seven Deadly Sins, the fifteen decades of the Rosary, and much else—reflect an obsessive medieval interest in number symbolism as well as a simple pleasure in enumeration rituals. These in particular lived on in folk culture, where songs of the Seven, Ten, or Twelve Joys take their place alongside others tracing the seven days of the week, the Ten Commandments, the twelve days of the Christmas season, the twelve Apostles, etc., and can be as straightforward as 'Ten green bottles' or as obscure as 'Green grow the rushes, O'. Seven is the most usual number in folk-song, though ten and twelve are also found, frequently with gaps. According to Husk (*Songs of the Nativity*, 1864), English carols of the Twelve Joys are confined to the north, 'being only found in broadsides printed at Newcastle late in the last or early in the present century'.

English folk carols of the Joys of Mary include those in Sandys's *Christmas Carols, Ancient and Modern* (1833, words only), W. H. Husk's *Songs of the Nativity* (1864, words only), Alice E. Gillington's *Old Christmas Carols of the Southern Counties* (1910), a Somerset version with an unusual tune in Sharp's *Folk Songs from Somerset* (1904–9) and *English Folk-Carols* (1911), and a number in the *Journal of the Folk-Song Society* (vol. 5, pp. 18–20, 319; vol. 18, pp. 18–21; vol. 33, pp. 115–16). The words alone appear on innumerable broadsides. (The five English versions collected by Sharp are given as no. 354 in *Cecil Sharp's Collection of English Folk Songs*, ed. Maud Karpeles, vol. 2, 1974.) A surprising metamorphosis of the usual traditional tune (pointed out by Erik Routley in *The English Carol*, 1958) is Ira Sankey's 'The Ninety and Nine' (*The English Hymnal*, 1906, no. 58).

The song was popular with those of the poor who sang carols for money, for whom the 'Chestnut' melody of 'God rest you merry, gentlemen' (151:1) was the catch-all tune for carols of this metre. Ralph Dunstan, in *A Second Book of Christmas Carols* (1925), gives an 'Advent images' carol which consists of a Joys text sung to 'Chestnut' but with the refrain 'It brings tidings of comfort and joy!' This carol survived well into the nineteenth century in northern counties of England, and was sung by groups of young girls or women calling at houses with a 'wassail', 'vessel', or even 'Wesley' box, originally 'going a-Thomasing' on St Thomas's Day, 21 December. The custom may have had a pagan origin: a typical box would contain two dolls lying on a bed of greenery, which were said to represent the Virgin and Child; this female 'Mystery' would be ceremonially unveiled and revealed to individuals in exchange for a small coin while the custodians sang the carol and drank from their 'vessel cup'. 'As unlucky as a man who hasn't seen the Advent images' was a saying in Yorkshire which reflected the importance of the rite.

Traditional Carols from Nova Scotia (Helen Creighton and Doreen C. Senior, 1950) has the 'Twelve Joys' sung to a variant of 'Chestnut', collected from a woman whose father, born in 1833, had learned it from village waits in England. (See Erik Routley, *The English Carol*, pp. 90–1.) The 'Twelve Joys' in Alice Gillington's collection, sung by New Forest gypsies, has a variant of 'Chestnut' with the refrain 'O the rising of the sun / And the lifting of the day', while the gypsies sang versions of the usual 'Joys of Mary' tune to several quite different carol texts.

Our version I takes its text for the verses from Brand's 'Advent images' carol (*Observations on the Popular Antiquities of Great Britain*, 1853–5), and the refrain from Sandys's *Christmas Carols, Ancient and Modern* (1833). Terry's admirably simple setting of a near-standard version of the tune is from his *Two Hundred Folk Carols* (1933). This form of the carol still has many living variants, but Bramley and Stainer's rather dull 1871 version (*Christmas Carols New and Old*) is usually sung in English churches. 'Bearing the Crucifix' (verse 6) was taken over from the Rosary, and is prominent in the Stations of the Cross (for example, 'Simon of Cyrene carries the Cross' and 'Jesus falls [beneath its weight] for the first/second time'). 'Wearing the crown of heaven' (verse 7) refers to the Resurrection.

Version II was collected by Alice (Mrs C.) Milligan Fox, who founded the Irish Folk Song Society and was an early advocate of collecting with the aid of a phonograph. She recorded it from a Mrs Lines, an elderly lady in Portlaw, Waterford, who had learned it from her mother, a native of Kille. Mrs Fox published it in her article, 'Folk song collecting in County Waterford' in the *Journal of the Irish Folk Song Society*, vol. 12, with the blunt opinion that 'it seems to be the product of some hedge schoolmaster'. 'Opening the gates of heaven' (verse 7) refers to the doctrine that no souls were able to enter heaven between the time of the Fall and the Resurrection. 'When he was sent to school' (verse 2) may be pious imagination or it may derive from one of the apocryphal gospels.

Mrs Fox does not underlay the music with text in her maddeningly ambiguous transcription, which has no slurs. There are five strains of music, with no indications of verse and refrain. The repeat of the second line of each verse to the music of strain 3, with its varied cadence, seems right to us on rhetorical grounds, and we assume that the double refrain is sung to strains 4–5 repeated. For a different interpretation see R. R. Terry, *Two Hundred Folk Carols* (1933, no. 26). Terry, almost as vague as Mrs Fox, states that 'The carol is included in the English section of this book as the Editor was informed (by an eminent authority of the Irish Folk Song Society) that although Mrs Millington Fox collected it in Ireland the *melody* is English in origin.' The 'eminent authority' cannot have been thinking of the present tune, and perhaps confused it with the 'New Forest Carol', a version of the 'Twelve Joys' with some rhythmic similarities to Mrs Fox's tune, which was collected by Alice Gillington from a half-gypsy woman and published in her *Old Christmas Carols of the Southern Counties* (1910).

Version III, a set of Ten Joys, was taken down by the American collector Richard Chase from the singing of a Mr Will Brady in Carthage, North Carolina, who remarked to Chase: 'That's a precious song: somebody ought to take care of it.' The transcription appeared in the *Journal of American Folklore* (vol. 48, 1935, no. 390; vol. 5, 1892, contains the words only of versions sung in Connecticut and Kentucky; *Folk Songs of the South*, ed. John Harrington Cox, 1925, has words from West Virginia; John Jacob Niles collected words and tune in the southern Appalachians, where others were collected by Cecil Sharp and Maud Karpeles. The song would seem to derive from a set of ten or twelve pre-Reformation Joys, but adapted and refracted through oral transmission among Protestant singers. 'Could live a father's son' (verse 1) probably means 'could take on human flesh'. 'Read the Scriptures through' (verse 2) derives from the Joy of the Finding of Christ in the temple, where he expounded the Scriptures rather than simply read them. 'Conquer hell and heaven' (verse 7) presumably derives from a verse including the two Joys of the Harrowing of Hell and the Ascension. 'Making the crooked straight' (verse 8, after Isaiah 40:4) is the healing of cripples. The 'writing without a pen' (verse 10), for all its overtones of Belshazzar's feast, is probably a corruption of something like 'sat on the throne/wore the crown (of heaven)'.

PERFORMANCE   I and II, choir; III, one or two voices, with guitar *ad lib.*

132

Tomorrow shall be my dancing day

I

English traditional
(*Sandys, 1833, arr. editors*)

(*Christmas*)

VERSE SOLO

1. To - mor - row shall be___ my dan - cing day; I
2. Then was___ I born of a vir - gin pure; Of
3. In a man - ger laid___ and wrapped I was, So

would___ my true___ love did___ so chance To___
her___ I took___ flesh - ly___ sub - stance. Thus___
ve - ry poor;___ this was___ my chance, Be -

see the le - gend of___ my play, To
was I knit___ to man's___ na - ture, To
- twixt an ox and a sil - ly poor ass, To

call my true___ love to___ the dance.
call my true___ love to___ the dance.
call my true___ love to my dance.

REFRAIN FULL

Sing O my___ love, O___ my love, my love, my

464

II

English traditional
(Sandys, 1833, arr. editors)

1. To - mor - row shall be___ my dan - cing day; I
2. Then was___ I born of a vir - gin pure; Of
3. In a man - ger laid___ and wrapped I was, So

would my true___ love did___ so chance To___ see the le - gend
her___ I took___ flesh - ly___ sub - stance. Thus was I knit___ to
ve - ry poor;___ this was___ my chance, Be - twixt an ox and a

of___ my play, To call my true___ love to___ the dance. *Sing*
man's_ na - ture, To call my true___ love to___ the dance. *Sing*
sil - ly poor ass, To call my true___ love to___ my dance.

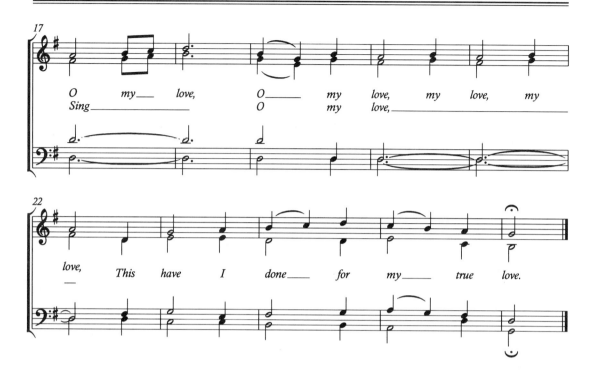

4 Then afterwards baptized I was;
    The Holy Ghost on me did glance,
My Father's voice heard from above
    To call my true love to my dance.

5 Into the desert I was led,
    Where I fasted without substance;
The devil bade me make stones my bread,
    To have me break my true love's dance.

6 The Jews on me they made great suit,
    And with me made great variance,
Because they loved darkness rather than light,
    To call my true love to my dance.

7 For thirty pence Judas me sold,
    His covetousness for to advance:
'Mark whom I kiss, the same do hold!'
    The same is he shall lead the dance.

8 Before Pilate the Jews me brought,
    Where Barabbas had deliverance;
They scourgèd me and set me at nought,
    Judged me to die to lead the dance.

9 Then on the cross hangèd I was,
    Where a spear my heart did glance;
There issued forth both water and blood,
    To call my true love to my dance.

10 Then down to hell I took my way
    For my true love's deliverance,
And rose again on the third day,
    Up to my true love and the dance.

11 Then up to heaven I did ascend,
    Where now I dwell in sure substance
On the right hand of God, that man
    May come unto the general dance.

English traditional
(Sandys, 1833)

From William Sandys's *Christmas Carols, Ancient and Modern* (1833; see Appendix 4), this is one of many carols traditionally sung at Christmas that trace the whole life of Christ. This particular one resists attempts to truncate it for carol services or concerts, and is perhaps best served by a flexible solo performance which will assimilate the many apparent misaccentuations. Our version I is designed to encourage such an approach. The melody, which Sandys gives with a rough-and-ready bass that may or may not be traditional, has close relatives in those of 136 (from Dorset) and 166 (from Wales).

The text has not been found in any other source, and the theme of the dance is unique among traditional carols, despite the origins of the strict carol form in the danced *carole* (see Introduction). Among several features that suggest a pre-Reformation origin are turns of phrase with a medieval ring ('fleshly substance', verse 2; 'this was my chance', verse 3; 'on me did glance', verse 4). The paucity of rhyme-words for 'dance' may perhaps be a sign of an inexperienced poet or adapter, and a typical sign of the post-Reformation oral transmission or adaptation of an earlier text is a non-rhyming line like the first of verse 9, where something like 'Then was I hangèd on the rood' would originally have rhymed with line 3.

The conceit whereby Christ addresses sinful man as his 'true love' is foreign to the verse of traditional and medieval carols but has several parallels in 'higher' forms of medieval poetry, typically in appeals from the cross. The biblical source of such imagery is the *Song of Songs*, of which the 'lover' and 'beloved' are interpreted by St Paul as Christ and the Church. The later middle ages, and Franciscan piety in particular, preferred to interpret the 'beloved' as the Christian soul, citing the 'We love him because he first loved us' of 1 John 4:19; the *locus classicus* for this quasi-nuptial relationship is the last, unfinished work of St Bernard (d. 1153), the series of thirty-eight sermons on the *Song of Songs*.

There are close medieval parallels to 'Tomorrow shall be' among the many fifteenth-century 'cradle prophecy' carols, in which the infant Christ foretells his future to his mother while seated in her lap, typically with lullaby refrains (see 23 and 39). Descended from these are two families of traditional carols. One preserves lullaby refrain and dialogue form (see Greene, *The Early English Carols*, 1977, no. 152 and notes; the mother–child dialogue is also preserved in part III of 'The Cherry Tree Carol', 128, which must have a medieval origin). The other, more widespread, transforms Christ's words into third-person narrative (see *The Oxford Book of Carols*, no. 17 and Greene's nos. 142B, *a* and *b* and his notes on no. 142).

The clue to the origin of the present carol is line 3 of the opening stanza: 'To see the legend ['story', especially 'life-story'] of my play', which implies a dramatic context. It has similarities to the 'banns' which advertised medieval mystery and morality plays: the *Comen Bans* of the Chester cycle were proclaimed at each station by the stewards, and those of the early fifteenth-century morality *The Castle of Perseverance* were proclaimed by members of a touring

company in each venue, a week or so ahead of performance. Far closer to the carol are the bann-like conclusions to the first and second parts of some of the three-day Cornish-language religious plays, a complete surviving example of which is the fourteenth- or fifteenth-century 'Macro' trilogy *Origo Mundi—Passio Domini—Resurrexio Domini* ('The Origin of the World—the Passion of our Lord—the Resurrection of our Lord'). William Jordan's *Creation of the World* (1611), probably the first day of an uncompleted cycle, ends with what E. K. Chambers calls 'a direction to minstrels to pipe for dancing, and an invitation to return on the morrow to see the Redemption' (*The Medieval Stage*, vol. II, p. 434). At the end of parts 1 and 3 of the Macro trilogy, too, 'minstrels are directed to pipe for a dance' (p. 434). In the late seventeenth century, when Cornish was a dying language, John Keigwyn, of Mousehole, made crude English translations of two of Jordan's dramas and (in 1682) of the lost Cornish original of the anonymous *Mount Calvary, or The History of the Passion, Death and Resurrection of our Lord and Saviour Jesus Christ*. This ends with a comparable verse injunction to what is unmistakably a 'general dance': 'This very day . . . you have seen every degree many matters done, / And the creation of the whole world. / . . . Come tomorrow betimes, / You shall see matters great, / And redemption granted, / . . . Minstrels, do you us pipe, / That we may together dance / As is the manner of the sport.' (From the edition by Davies Gilbert, London, 1826.) Such dramas were in many places enacted within a large circular round, known as a *platea* or 'place'; in Cornish a *Plan-an-Gwarry*. Examples survive at St Just-in-Penwyth (150 ft. in diameter and once encircled by seven tiers of stone) and at Perranzabuloe (130 ft. in diameter with earthen surround and central pit). The actors used the central area and stages ('scaffolds') around the perimeter; the audience was on the tiered seating and also moved freely within the *Plan*.

It seems possible that 'Tomorrow shall be' was devised to be sung and danced at the conclusion of the first day of a three-day drama, translated from the Cornish, which may itself have made use of the 'lover' and 'beloved' theme. The actor portraying Christ would have sung the verses and the whole company and audience the repeats of the refrains. The song would naturally have become familiar through repeated local use, and may even have been sung at Christmas: carols of the Passion were not unknown in the Christmas season. The increased popularity of 'Redemption' carols, following the eighteenth-century rise of the Methodist and Evangelical movements, would in any case have made it a natural choice for domestic carollers and village waits, by which time it would have lost the initial refrain and its origins within the drama would probably have been forgotten.

There are settings of the text by Holst and by Stravinsky (in his *Cantata*, 1952).

PERFORMANCE   I, verse, solo; refrain, three voices or choir.

II (*i*) choir, with instruments *ad lib.* (see Appendix 3); (*ii*) solo voice and a bass instrument.

133

The Twelve Days of Christmas

I

(Christmas; Twelfth Night)

English traditional
(arr. editors)

468

5. On the fifth day of Christ-mas my true love sent to me five_ gold_ rings,

four cal-ly-birds, three French hens, two tur-tle-doves, and a par-tridge in a pear tree.

6. On the sixth day of Christ-mas my true love sent to me six geese a - lay - ing,
7. On the seventh
8. On the eighth
9. On the ninth
10. On the tenth
11. On the eleventh
12. On the twelfth

seven swans a - swim-ming,
eight maids a - milk - ing,
nine la - dies dan - cing,
ten lords a - leap - ing,
eleven pi - pers pi - ping,
twelve drum-mers drum-ming,

English traditional
(Husk, 1864)

This song derives from a traditional forfeits game which was played on Twelfth Night (hence the twelve days). Each player would have to remember and recite the objects named by the previous players and then add one more. The game was probably universal, but the song seems to be of Gallic origin.

'Cally-' or 'colly-birds' are blackbirds; the 'gold rings' are perhaps a corruption of 'goldspinks' (Scottish dialect for goldfinches) or 'gulderer' ('gulder-cock' is a turkey); 'French' has the meaning 'exotic' in some English dialects. The origin of the mysterious pear tree may simply be *perdrix*, French for 'partridge'. However, the partridge and pear tree have been the subject of arcane speculation: the partridge as symbol of the devil, who reveals to Herod that the Virgin Mary is hiding behind a sheaf of corn; the folk belief that a girl who walks backwards towards a pear tree on Christmas Eve and walks round it thrice will see the image of her future husband; etc. (See *Journal of the Folk-Song Society*, vol. 5, pp. 277–81, which has five variant

tunes and notes by Cecil Sharp, Annie Gilchrist, and Lucy Broadwood; two more are in Sharp and Marson, *Folk Songs from Somerset*, 1904–9; and see *The Oxford Dictionary of Nursery Rhymes*, 1951, p. 122.)

The text appears in various forms in broadsides from the early eighteenth century onward. Version I is the now standard one, as printed by Husk 'for the first time in a collection of carols' (*Songs of the Nativity*, 1864). The tune is the usual modern one sung in England, with bars 18–19 dating only from Frederick Austen's 1909 arrangement. E is sometimes found for F as the seventh note, and the pause on 'rings' tends to lengthen from verse to verse.

Version II is the one still sung by the men of the Copper family from Sussex (Bob Copper, *Early to Rise*, 1976), who preserve an oral part-singing tradition (see also 'Shepherds, arise!', 147).

PERFORMANCE I, choir; II, voices.

469

II

English traditional
(Copper, 1976)

(*Christmas; Twelfth Night*)

1. On the first day of Christ-mas my true love sent to me   a   par - tridge in a pear tree.

2. On the   se-cond day of Christ-mas my   true love sent to me   two tur - tle-doves, and a

par-tridge in a pear   tree.   3. On the third day of Christ-mas my   true love sent to me

three French hens,   two tur - tle-doves, and a   par-tridge in a pear   tree.   4. On the

fourth day of Christ-mas my   true love sent to me   four ca - na - ry birds, three French hens,

two tur-tle-doves, and a par-tridge in a pear tree. 5. On the fifth day of Christ-mas my

true love sent to me five gold_ rings, four ca-na-ry birds, three French hens,

two tur-tle-doves, and a par-tridge in a pear tree.

6. On the sixth day of Christ-mas my
7. On the seventh
8. On the eighth
9. On the ninth
10. On the tenth
11. On the eleventh
12. On the twelfth

true love sent to me six geese a - lay - ing, five gold_ rings,
seven swans a - swim-ming,
eight deers a - run - ning,
nine lads a - leap - ing,
ten la - dies skip - ping,
eleven bears a - bait - ing,
twelve par-sons preach-ing,

four ca-na-ry birds, three French hens, two tur-tle-doves, and a par-tridge in a pear tree.

134

In those twelve days

(*Christmas*)

English traditional
(*Sandys, 1833, arr. editors*)

472

2   What are they which are but two?
    Two Testaments, as we are told:
    The one is New, the other Old.

3   What are they which are but three?
    Three persons in the Trinity,
    The Father, Son and Ghost Holy.

4   What are they which are but four?
    Four Gospels written true,
    John, Luke, Mark, and Matthew.

5   What are they which are but five?
    Five senses we have to tell,
    God grant us grace to use them well!

6   What are they which are but six?
    Six ages this world shall last;
    Five of them are gone and past.

7   What are they which are but seven?
    Seven days in the week have we,
    Six to work and the seventh holy.

8   What are they which are but eight?
    Eight beatitudes are given:
    Use them well and go to heaven.

9   What are they which are but nine?
    Nine degrees of angels high
    Which praise God continually.

10 What are they which are but ten?
    Ten commandments God hath given:
    Keep them right and go to heaven.

11 What are they which are but eleven?
    Eleven thousand virgins did partake
    And suffer death for Jesus' sake.

12 What are they which are but twelve?
    Twelve Apostles Christ did choose
    To preach the Gospel to the Jews.

English traditional
(Sandys, 1833)

From Sandys's *Christmas Carols, Ancient and Modern* (1833; see Appendix 4). He also gives an older version called 'A New Dyall' (the title referring to a clock-face or sundial) and a newer version called 'Man's Duty, or, Meditation for the Twelve Hours of the Day'. The 'eleven thousand virgins' (verse 11) were supposedly martyred at Cologne with St Ursula in the fifth century (their actual number seems to have been around ten).

The tune and bass are Sandys's, with small emendations. There is a very similar version of the melody in the Davey manuscript (c.1825; see Appendix 4).

PERFORMANCE Voices, with the tenor doubled at the higher octave, and instruments *ad lib.* (see Appendix 3).

135

The old yeare now away is fled

(New Year)

English traditional
(arr. editors)

1. The old yeare now a - way is fled, The new year it is en - ter - ed: Then
2. For Christ's cir - cum - ci - sion this day we keepe, Who for our sins did of - ten weepe; His

let us now our sins downe tread, And joy - ful - ly all ap - peare! Let's
hands and feet were wound - ed deepe, And his bless - ed side with a speare; His

mer - ry be this ho - ly day, And let us now both sport and play; Hang
head they crown - ed then with thorne, And at him they did laugh and scorne, Who

sor - row! Let's cast care a - way! God send you a hap - py new yeare!
for to save our soules was borne. God send us a mer - ry new yeare!

474

3 And now with new-yeare's gifts each
        friend
   Unto each other they doe send;
   God grant we may all our lives amend,
        And that the truth may appeare!
   Now, like the snake, cast off your skin
   Of evill thoughts, and wicked sin,
   And to amend this new yeare begin:
        God send us a merry new yeare!

4 And now let all the company
   In friendly manner all agree,
   For we are here welcome, all may see,
        Unto this jolly good cheere;
   I thanke my master and my dame,
   The which are founders of the same;
   To eate and drinke now is no shame:
        God send us a merry new yeare!

5 Come, lads and lasses, every one—
   Jack, Tom, Dick, Besse, Mary and Jone—
   Let's cut the meate up into the bone,
        For welcome you need not feare!
   And here for good liquor we shall not lack:
   It will whet my braines and strengthen my
        back;
   This jolly good cheere it must goe to wrack!
        God send us a merry new yeare!

6 Come, give's more liquor when I doe call:
   Ile drinke to each one in this hall!
   I hope that so loud I must not baule,
        But unto me lend an eare:
   Good fortune to my master send,
   And to my dame which is our friend;
   Lord blesse us all!—and so I end;
        And God send us a happy new yeare!

English traditional
(*New Christmas Carols*, *1642*)

The text is from *New Christmas Carols . . . Printed at London by E. P. for Francis Coles, dwelling in the Old Baily* (1642), which is in Anthony à Wood's collection of ballads in the Bodleian Library, Oxford (Wood 110 3*). The carol is headed 'A Carroll for New-yeares day. To the tune of, Greene Sleeves'.

'Greensleeves' is one of the many melodies that developed over the standard Italian dance basses which came to England around 1550—too late to support the popular belief that Henry VIII composed the tune. The earliest sources date from the 1580s, the first perhaps being the quotation of the melody and its bass in Byrd's Fantasia à 6, no. 2 (if Oliver Neighbour's dating is correct: see *The Consort and Keyboard Music of William Byrd*, 1978, p. 79). As with many other popular tunes of the period, by the end of the seventeenth century 'Greensleeves' had lost its bass and developed melodic variants that departed from the original harmony. (For a nineteenth-century choral setting see 'What child is this', 98.)

Early versions of the tune appear in both duple and compound time. Some set both halves to the *romanesca* bass (beginning on B♭), while others set the first half to the *passamezzo antico* (beginning on G in bars 1 and 5, but otherwise identical). We follow the latter, with the melody adapted from various early sources. (For an extensive list of versions see John M. Ward, 'And who but my Ladie Greensleeues?', in *The Well-Enchanting Skill*, 1990; details of the many texts sung to the tune are in Claude M. Simpson, *The British Broadside Ballad and its Music*, 1966, pp. 269–70.)

PERFORMANCE Voice, unaccompanied or with lute, guitar, keyboard, etc. Our plain version of the tune could be ornamented with more passing notes and dotted rhythms, or adapted to 6/8 rhythm.

136

Rejoice and be merry

(Christmas)

English traditional
(Oxford Book of Carols, 1928,
arr. editors)

1. Re - joice and be mer - ry in songs and in mirth; O praise our Re - deem - er, all mor - tals on earth! For this is the birth - day of Je - sus our King, Who brought us sal - va - tion: his prai - ses we'll sing.

2   A heavenly vision appeared in the sky;
    Vast numbers of angels the shepherds did spy,
    Proclaiming the birthday of Jesus our King,
    Who brought us salvation: his praises we'll sing.

3   Likewise a bright star in the sky did appear,
    Which led the wise men from the East to draw near;
    They found the Messiah, sweet Jesus our King,
    Who brought us salvation: his praises we'll sing.

4   And when they were come, they their treasures unfold,
    And unto him offered myrrh, incense and gold.
    So blessèd for ever be Jesus our King,
    Who brought us salvation: his praises we'll sing.

English traditional
(*Oxford Book of Carols, 1928*)

The words and tune are from an old church-gallery tune-book, Dorset, and were communicated to the editors of *The English Carol Book* (second series, 1919) by the Revd L. J. T. Darwall. The present whereabouts of the gallery book are not known.

The tune is closely related to those of 132 and 166.

PERFORMANCE   Choir.

137

The first 'Nowell!'
'Nowell and nowell!'

I

(*Epiphany; Christmas*)

English traditional (Sandys, 1833, arr. John Stainer, 1840–1901, adapted)

1. The first 'No - well!' the an - gel did say Was to cer - tain poor shep-herds in fields as they lay; In fields where they lay keep-ing their sheep On a cold win-ter's night that

was___ so deep. No - well!___ no - well! no - well!___ no -

- well!___ Born is the King___ of Is - ra - el!

2 They lookèd up and saw a star
  Shining in the east, beyond them far;
  And to the earth it gave great light,
  And so it continued both day and night.

3 And by the light of that same star
  Three wise men came from country far;
  To seek for a King was their intent,
  And to follow the star wheresoever it went.

4 This star drew nigh to the north-west:
  O'er Bethlehem it took its rest;
  And there it did both stop and stay,
  Right over the place where Jesus lay.

*5 Then did they know assuredly
  Within that house the King did lie;
  One entered in then for to see,
  And found the Babe in poverty.

6 Then entered in those wise men three,
  Full reverently, upon their knee,
  And offered there, in his presence,
  Both gold and myrrh, and frankincense.

*7 Between an ox-stall and an ass
  This Child there truly bornèd was;
  For want of clothing they did him lay
  All in the manger, among the hay.

8 Then let us all with one accord
  Sing praises to our heavenly Lord
  That hath made heaven and earth of
    nought,
  And with his blood mankind hath bought.

*9 If we in our lifetime shall do well
  We shall be free from death and hell,
  For God hath preparèd for us all
  A resting-place in general.

English traditional
(Sandys, 1833, adapted)

479

II

(*Christmas; Epiphany*)

English traditional
(recreation by the editors)

VERSE

1. 'No - well and no-well!'† the‿ an - gels did say, While shep - herds there in‿ the
2. And‿ then‿ there did ap - pear‿ a‿ star Whose glo - ry then‿ did

fields‿ did lay; Late in‿ the night‿ a - fold - ing‿ their sheep, A
shine‿ so far; Un - to‿ the earth‿ it gave a‿ great light, And

REFRAIN

win - ter's night‿ both cold‿ and bleak. *No - well‿ and‿ no - well! No -*
there it con - tin - ued a day and a night.

† Or 'O well and O well!' here and in the refrain—see notes.

-well_ and_ no - well!   Born is the__ King_____ of   Is - ra - el!

3 And by the light of that same star
  Three wise men came from country far;
  To seek a King was their intent:
  They followed the star wherever it went.

4 The star drew near unto the north-west:
  O'er Bethlehem city it took its rest
  And there it did both stand and stay,
  Right over the house where our Lord lay.

5 Then entered in those wise men three,
  With reverence, falling on their knee,
  And offered up, in his presence,
  Both gold and myrrh, and frankincense.

6 Between an ox-manger and an ass,
  Our blest Messiah's place it was;
  To save our souls from sin and thrall,
  He is the Redeemer of us all.

English traditional
(*Journal of the Folk-Song Society*, 5, adapted)

The text of 'The first "Nowell!"', which has its roots in the fifteenth century, is said to have appeared on (eighteenth-century?) broadsides printed at Helston, a town near the south coast of Cornwall, a few miles north of the Lizard, and home of the famous Furry Dance. The earliest known publication is of nine stanzas, without music, in the 1823 revised edition of *Some Ancient Christmas Carols* by Davies Gilbert, who came from Helston. Gilbert took it from the Hutchens manuscript, the collection of carols and their tunes prepared for him in or just after 1816 and now in the County Record Office, Truro (see Appendix 4).

The text and tune of the received modern form of the carol (I) derive from William Sandys's West Country collection *Christmas Carols, Ancient and Modern* (1833). We have made three small changes to the text. Verse 1: 'certain' for 'three' poor shepherds (as in Hutchens's and later texts); the gospel account does not specify the number, but three shepherds often feature in the mystery plays. Verse 7: 'bornèd was' for Sandys's (and Hutchens's) 'born he was'; granted the fifteenth-century origins of the text, 'y-bornèd' may have been rendered 'a-bornèd' at some stage, to mutate to 'born he' at a later date by oral transmission. Verse 9: 'lifetime' (from Hutchens) for 'life', to give a neater fit to the tune.

Setting I is Stainer's fine arrangement of the usual modern form of the carol (in Bramley and Stainer, *Christmas Carols New and Old*, 1871), which smooths away all the rough places of the tune as given by Sandys. The starred verses can seem a little down-at-heel in this urbane setting, and are normally omitted.

For a long time Sandys's tune was the only one known. Two features are so uncharacteristic of folk melody that they aroused suspicions of an unusual origin: the three virtually identical statements of the same phrase, suggesting a lapse of memory at some stage in the process of transmission, and the fact that all three strains cadence on the third degree of the scale, suggesting possible derivation from the upper part(s) of a 'gallery' harmonization.

From 1913 onwards, new versions of the carol began to emerge with Cecil Sharp's discovery of another and puzzlingly different version in Camborne, the refrain beginning 'Nowell and nowell!' (printed in the *Journal of the Folk-Song Society*, vol. 5, pp. 26–7, and in *Cecil Sharp's Collection of English Folk Songs*, ed. Maud Karpeles, 1974):

1. 'No-well and no-well!' the an-gels did say To

shep-herds there in the fields did lay, Lay-ing in one night and

fold-ing their sheep, A win-ter's night,— both

cold and bleak. No-well and no-well! No-well and no-well!

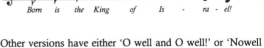

Born is the King of Is-ra-el!

Other versions have either 'O well and O well!' or 'Nowell and nowell' in both verse 1 and the refrain. We have taken text II from Sharp, as amended from the text taken 'from the old Helston broadsides' in Ralph Dunstan, *The Cornish Song Book* (1929).

The nature of Sandys's tune and its possible connection with the Camborne carol was exhaustively discussed by members of the Folk-Song Society in 1924 (see the *Journal*, vol. 8), by which time a second and very similar Camborne version had been collected (we have found a third, published by William Eade in Redruth in 1889) and a strong melodic link had been observed with a group of Cornish wassail-songs. No conclusion was reached, and there have subsequently been sporadic attempts to identify the tune to which 'The first "Nowell!"' was the 'descant'. But the missing tune was a chimera, and Sandys's tune is in fact the 'descant' to itself; or, in plainer terms, it evolved as an unconscious conflation of parts of the tune of the Camborne carol and the upper part(s) of some lost gallery setting(s). Setting II is our conjectural recreation of the kind of setting in which Sandys's tune could have evolved, with the Camborne tune forming the tenor in bars 1–4 and the refrain. The middle section ('Laying in one night' in the Camborne version) begins exactly like the first two strains of the best-known tune to 'On Christmas Night all Christians sing' (139), but seems to deviate to an upper part for 'a winter's night both cold and bleak'. We have replaced this with a continuation of the 'On Christmas Night' tune, which fits against the Camborne melody just as a tenor tune would fit beneath a treble.

Conflations of more than one voice-part were evidently commonplace in country choirs, and were certainly a recognized hazard when (as was customary) many of the singers learned their parts by ear. William Dewy, in Hardy's *Under the Greenwood Tree* (1872, chapter 4), was alert to the danger with the musically untutored altos of the Mellstock carollers: 'You two counter-boys [altos], keep your ears open to Michael's fingering [as he doubled their part on the violin], and don't ye go straying into the treble part along o'Dick and his [treble] set, as ye did last year . . .'. Unchecked, such inadvertent vagrancy would lead in time to the creation of a composite part. Ill-regulated galleries must have swarmed with such hybrid tunes, some of which would be passed on to new members, become generally sung within a particular voice-part, and then be repeated elsewhere—in unison street carol-singing, for example. Thereafter, the composite tune might be subject to the more normal processes of transmission, and what had begun as a mishearing in a gallery could end up as a tune notated in someone's manuscript carol-book or as a folk melody collected in the pages of the *Folk-Song Journal*. (See notes on 'A virgin most pure', 143, for evidence of the process in a publication of 1819.)

The most common confusions in gallery choirs were perhaps made by children singing treble, who would pick up their part by ear at rehearsal and could all too easily mistake the high and cadential sections of a tenor melody for their own line, since the tenor would normally be instrumentally and/or vocally doubled at the higher octave (see Appendix 3). Ian Russell, in *A Song for the Time* (1987), has investigated the phenomenon by comparing versions of the popular psalm tune usually called 'Foster' or 'Old Foster' (46:VII) as sung in the South Yorkshire singing pubs, which have preserved something of the tradition of gallery choirs after they were ousted from parish churches in the early nineteenth century. In one version he found that the soprano melody of the first strain is sung as the bass; in another the tenor line has become the melody; in a third a tune has evolved which is partly a mixture of Foster's original vocal lines, partly independent.

Most of the examples we have spotted are treble parts which have been significantly infiltrated by the tenor tune, and Sandys's tune for 'The First "Nowell!"' is a not dissimilar case, we believe. Of its three sections, the first and third (the refrain) are basically the treble part, but incorporate the strong opening of the tenor tune. The contrasting middle strain has been dropped, consciously or unconsciously, to be replaced by a virtual repeat of the first. A performance of setting II with the tenor melody at both octaves will show how easily the first and third sections of Sandys's tune could have evolved, particularly if a more florid version of the opening is used (see performance note).

Vaughan Williams's *The First Nowell* (1958), a Nativity play for soloists, choir and small orchestra, has a libretto adapted from medieval pageants and makes use of many traditional and folk carols, culminating in the present carol. 'The first "Nowell"' also opens and closes his masque *On*

Christmas Night (1926), and fragments of the tune are used in the *Fantasia on Christmas Carols* (1912) for baritone, choir, and orchestra.

PERFORMANCE   I, choir, with organ and congregation *ad lib.*

II (*i*) Solo voice, with unison voices on repeats of the refrain. Some singers might extemporize a little harmony in the refrain, perhaps culling a few figures from our treble, alto, and bass parts at cadences.

(*ii*) Voices, singing one or more parts: melody alone, or melody and bass, or melody, bass, and alto, or all four parts. Congregations could sing the tune in all four cases, either throughout or only in the repeats of the refrain. A more florid version of the tune for the opening of the verse and refrain could be used, as follows:

Whichever version is sung, the tenor should be doubled at the higher octave. Instruments *ad lib.* (see Appendix 3).

(*iii*) Voice and continuo. The following is a suggested bass and chordal pattern:

The repeat of the refrain is optional in all three schemes.

138

All hayle to the dayes

(*Christmas*)

English traditional
(Chappell, 1853–9, arr. editors)

1. All hayle to the dayes[1]___ That me - rite more praise___ Then all___ the rest of the yeare!___ And wel - come the nights__ That dou - ble de - lights As well for the poore as the peere![2] Good for - tune at-tend Each

2. The Court in all state___ Now o - pens her gate___ And bids a free wel - come to most:___ The Ci - ty, like - wise,__ Though some-what pre - cise,_ Doth wil - ling-ly part with her cost;___ And yet, by re-port, From

[1] those of the Christmas season [i.e., 25 December to 5 January]   [2] nobleman

mer - ry man's friend That doth bat³___ the best that he may, For -
Ci - ty and Court___ The coun - trey gets___ the day: More

- get - ting old wrongs With ca - rols and songs___ To drive the cold win - ter a - way.___
li - quor is spent, And bet - ter con - tent,___

3 The gentry there
   For cost do not spare
      (The yeomanry fast in Lent);
   The farmers and such
   Thinke nothing too much
      If they keep but to pay their rent.
   The poorest of all
   Do merrily call
      (Want beares but a little sway)
   For a song, or a tale,
   Ore a pot of good ale,
      To drive the cold winter away.

4 Thus none will allow
   Of solitude now,
      But merrily greete the time,
   To make it appeare
   Of all the whole yeare
      That this is accounted the prime:

December is seene
Apparel'd in greene,⁴
   And January, fresh as May,
Comes dancing along
With a cup and a song
   To drive the cold winter away.

5 This time of the yeare
   Is spent in good cheare;
      Kind neighbours together meet
   To sit by the fire
   With friendly desire
      Each other in love to greet;
   Old grudges, forgot,
   Are put in the pot,
      All sorrowes aside they lay;
   The old and the yong
   Doth caroll his song
      To drive the cold winter away.

³ serve, attend   ⁴ houses were decorated with greenery

6 To maske and to mum[5]
   Kind neighbours will come
      With wassels[6] of not-browne ale,
   To drinke and carouse
   To all in this house,
      As merry as bucks in the pale;[7]
   Where cake, bread and cheese
   Is brought for your fees
      To make you the longer stay,
   At the fire to warme
   Will do you no harme
      To drive the cold winter away.

7 When Christmastide
   Comes in like a bride,
      With holly and ivy clad,
   Twelve dayes in the yeare
   Much mirth and good cheare
      In every houshold is had;

The countrey guise[8]
Is then to devise
   Some gambole of Christmas play,
Whereas[9] the yong men
Do best that they can
   To drive the cold winter away.

8 When white-bearded Frost
   Hath threatned his worst
      And fallen from branch and brier,
   Then time away cals
   From husbandry hals[10]
      And from the good countryman's fire,
   Together to go
   To plow and to sow,
      To get us both food and array;[11]
   And thus with content
   The time we have spent
      To drive the cold winter away.

English traditional
(Pepys Collection broadside)

---

[5] to act and mime [in plays, games]   [6] wassail-cups
[7] enclosure   [8] custom   [9] whereat   [10] [farmers'] indoor
places of work   [11] clothing

'A pleasant Countrey new Ditty: Merrily shewing how To drive the cold Winter away', one of the ballads in the broadside collection of John Selden and Samuel Pepys (now in the Pepys Library, Magdalene College, Cambridge). The 'ditty' (poem) is also found in the Roxburghe broadside collection (in the British Library) and was included in *The Roxburghe Ballads* (W. Chappell and J. W. Ebsworth, eds., 1871–99). The broadside was printed for Henry Gosson (*fl.* *c.*1603–40), though the ballad itself may predate it. It is directed to be sung to the tune 'When Phoebus did rest', which is given by Claude M. Simpson in *The British Broadside Ballad and its Music* (1966) together with a second, distantly related tune called 'Drive the cold winter away', found in Playford's *The English Dancing Master* (1651) and

elsewhere. We follow *The Oxford Book of Carols* (1928) in giving an almost identical version of the second of the two tunes as it occurs in Chappell's *The Popular Music of the Olden Time* (1853–9). This was presumably the tune to which the words were usually sung. The ballad (and perhaps also the tune) may well date from the sixteenth century, as there is a Scots ballad (probably not a parody, as Chappell supposes) in the 1567 edition of *Ane Compendious Buik of Godly and Spirituall Sangis*, beginning 'The wind blowis cauld, furious and bauld', which has the same prosody and the occasional refrain '. . . keip the cauld wind away'.

The broadside text comprises twelve verses, of which we give eight. In verse 1, line 6 was originally 'As well the poore . . .'.

PERFORMANCE (*i*) Solo voice; (*ii*) voice with lute, guitar, keyboard, etc. (adapting our bass); (*iii*) choir.

139

On Christmas Night all Christians sing
(The Sussex Carol)

I

(*Christmas Night*)

English traditional (Journal of the Folk-Song Society, 2, arr. editors)

1. On Christ - mas Night all Christ - ians sing, To hear the news— the an - gels bring. an - gels bring:

News of great joy,— news of— great mirth,—

News of our— mer - ci - ful— King's birth.

II

English traditional
(arr. Ralph Vaughan Williams, 1872–1958,
adapted)

(Christmas Night)

2 Then why should men on earth be so sad,
  Since our Redeemer made us glad
  When from our sin he set us free,
  All for to gain our liberty?

3 When sin departs before his grace,
  Then life and health come in its place;
  Angels and men with joy may sing,
  All for to see the new-born King.

4 All out of darkness we have light,
  Which made the angels sing this night:
  'Glory to God and peace to men,
  Now and for evermore. Amen.'

English traditional
(after Bishop Luke Wadding, d. 1686)

The carol was collected by Vaughan Williams from Mrs Verrall, of Monk's Gate, near Horsham, Sussex, in 1904, and printed in the *Journal of the Folk-Song Society*, vol. 2, p. 127, alongside an unconnected tune and a 4/4 variant noted by Lucy Broadwood in 1892. Mrs Verrall was one of Vaughan Williams's most valued singers. The origin of the text is Luke Wadding's 'Another short caroll for Christmas Day' in his *Smale Garland of Pious and Godly Songs*, which he published in Ghent in 1684, shortly after his consecration there to the Roman Catholic diocese of Ferns, County Wexford, Ireland. The book became popular, and the post-humous London editions of 1728 and 1731 began a process of revision (in the present case, fairly drastic). Versions of the text close to Mrs Verrall's appeared in *A New Carol Book*, published by J. Guest (Birmingham, c.1830), and in the 1847 *Good Christmas Box*. See also Cecil Sharp, *English Folk-Carols* (1911), for a different tune. For an apparent connection with the tune of 'O well, O well' see notes, 137.

PERFORMANCE I, three men (one tenor could sing bars 1–4, the other the repeat); or men's choir, bars 1–4 perhaps solo, the remainder tutti (unison or harmony). II, unison voices and organ, or unaccompanied choir.

140

Let all that are to mirth inclined

(*Christmas*)

English traditional
(Gilbert, 1822, arr. editors)

VERSE

1. Let all that are to mirth in-clined Con - si - der well, and___
*2. Let all your songs and prai - ses be Un - to his heaven - ly___

bear in mind What our good God for___ us___ has done In
Ma - jes - ty; And e - ver - more a - mong your mirth Re -

send - ing his be - lo - ved Son.   *For to re - deem our___*
-mem - ber Christ our Sa - viour's birth.

REFRAIN

souls__ from thrall,   Christ   is   the   Sa - viour   of   us   all.

3 The twenty-fifth day of December
   We have good reason to remember:
   In Bethlehem, upon that morn,
   There was the blest Messiah born.

4 The night before that happy tide
   The spotless Virgin and her guide
   Were long time seeking up and down
   To find some lodging in the town.

5 But mark how all things came to pass!
   The inn and lodgings fillèd was,
   That they could find no room at all
   But in a silly¹ ox's stall.

6 That night the Virgin Mary mild
   Was safe delivered of a child
   According unto heaven's decree
   Man's sweet salvation for to be.

7 Near Bethlehem some shepherds keep
   Their flocks and herds of feeding sheep,
   To whom God's angel did appear,
   Which put the shepherds in great fear.

8 'Prepare and go', the angel said,
   'To Bethlehem—be not afraid:
   There shall you find, this blessèd morn,
   The princely Babe, sweet Jesus, born.'

9 With thankful heart and joyful mind
   The shepherds went, this Babe to find;
   And, as the heavenly angels told,
   They did our Saviour, Christ, behold.

10 Within a manger he was laid;
   The Virgin Mary by him stayed,
   Attending on the Lord of Life,
   Being both mother, maid and wife.

11 Three Eastern wise men from afar,
   Directed by a glorious star,
   Came boldly on, and made no stay
   Until they came where Jesus lay.

12 And, being come unto the place
   Whereas² the blessed Messiah was,
   They humbly laid before his feet
   Their gifts of gold and odours sweet.

¹ simple ² where

13 See how the Lord of heaven and earth
    Showed himself lowly in his birth;
    A sweet example for mankind
    To learn to bear an humble mind.

14 No costly robes nor rich attire
    Did Jesus Christ our Lord desire,
    No music nor sweet harmony,
    Till glorious angels from on high

15 Did in melodious manner sing
    Praises unto our heavenly King:
    'All honour, glory, might and power
    Be unto Christ, our Saviour!'

16 If choirs of angels did rejoice,
    Well may mankind with heart and voice
    Sing praises to the God of Heaven,
    That unto us his Son has given.

English traditional
(*Gilbert, 1822, adapted*)

This popular carol was found in several forms: see 'Good people all' (162), which has a different opening line and no refrain, but is otherwise remarkably similar. The text and setting (melody and bass) are from Gilbert's *Some Ancient Christmas Carols* (1822; see Appendix 4).

The text derives from a much longer ballad without refrain found in two black-letter broadsides in the British Library Roxburghe Collection. The older of the two (vol. II, p. 422^V) is headed 'The Sinners Redemption. Wherein is described the Nativity of our Lord Jesus Christ. Together with his Life on the Earth, and precious Death on the Cross for Mankind. Tune of, The bleeding heart. Or, In Creet, &c.', and it begins 'All you that are . . .'. The only ballad of 'The Sinner's Redemption' in the Register of the Stationers' Company is in 1656, and Claude Simpson has suggested that the broadside may actually predate this (see *The British Broadside Ballad*, 1966, pp. 362–5). The later Roxburghe broadside (vol. III, p. 552) is dated '*c.*1750' in the general catalogue of the British Library. It differs fairly extensively from the earlier version, and is cast in continuous verse like all the many Cornish texts of the carol we have seen (and unlike those from other regions). Gilbert's version follows the quatrains of the earlier broadside, consists of the Nativity portion only (rather less than half), adds a refrain, and incorporates some, but not all, of the emendations found in the later broadside. It seems likely that all the Cornish texts were taken from local chap-books or broadsides, which in turn derived from a single London broadside from sometime between about 1650–1750.

The tune is a church-gallery version of the folk melody usually sung to 'This is the truth sent from above' (150:1; see also notes, 130). (A simpler form of the tune, to the same text, is carol 26 in the Hutchens manuscript; see Appendix 4.) Verse 14, line 4 has been amended from the broadsides. Bar 2: broken type obscures the opening, which was probably intended thus:

This is not the same as either of the tunes mentioned in the earlier broadside. 'The bleeding heart' does not survive (or has not been identified), while 'In Creet', which Simpson gives in a version from William Ballett's lute-book, is not mentioned in the later broadside, and had presumably fallen from use.

PERFORMANCE Voices, with the tenor doubled at the higher octave, and instruments *ad lib.* (see Appendix 3).

141

The Lord at first did Adam make

I

(*Christmas Eve*)

English traditional
(Gilbert, 1822)

1. The__ Lord at first did__ A - dam make Out of the dust and clay,
2. And__ then with-in the__ gar - den he Com - mand - ed was to stay,

And__ in his nos - trils__ breath - ed life, E'en as the Scrip-tures say;
And__ un - to him in__ com - mand-ment These words the Lord did say:

And then in E - den's pa - ra - dise He pla - ced him to dwell,
'The fruit which in the__ gar - den grows To thee shall be for meat,

That he with-in it__ should re - main, To dress and keep it well.
Ex - cept the tree in the midst there - of, Of which thou shalt not eat.'

Now let good Christ - ians_ all be - gin An ho - ly life to live,

And to re - joice and_ mer - ry be, For this is Christ-mas Eve!

II

(Christmas Eve)

English traditional
(Sandys, 1833)

1. The Lord at_ first_ did A - dam make Out
2. And then with - in_ the gar - den he Com -

of the dust and_ clay, And in his_ nos - trils breath-ed life, E'en
-mand-ed was to_ stay, And un - to_ him_ in com-mand-ment These

494

3 'For in the day that thou shalt eat,
   Or to it then come nigh,
And if that thou dost eat thereof
   Then surely thou shalt die.'
But Adam, he did take no heed
   Unto that only thing,
But did transgress God's holy law,
   And so was wrapped in sin.

4 Now mark the goodness of the Lord,
   Which he to mankind bore:
His mercy soon he did extend,
   Lost man for to restore.
And then, for to redeem our souls
   From death and hellish thrall,
He said his own dear Son should be
   The Saviour of us all.

5 Which promise now is brought to pass
   (Christians, believe it well!),
†And by the coming of God's dear Son
   We are redeemed from hell.
Then, if we truly do believe
   And do the thing aright,
Then, by his merits, we at last
   Shall live in heaven bright.

6 Now for the blessings we enjoy
   Which are from heaven above,
Let us renounce all wickedness
   And live in perfect love.
Then shall we do Christ's own command,
   Even his own written word,
And when we die in heaven shall
   Enjoy our living Lord.

7 And now the tide is nigh at hand
   In the which our Saviour came;
Let us rejoice and merry be
   In keeping of the same.
Let's feed the poor and hungry souls,
   And such as do it crave;
Then, when we die, in heaven sure
   Our reward we shall have.

English traditional
(Gilbert, 1822, adapted)

† Setting II: coming of

Setting I is the first carol in Davies Gilbert's *Some Ancient Christmas Carols* (1822), where it is headed 'For Christmas Eve'. Setting II is from William Sandys's *Christmas Carols, Ancient and Modern* (1833; see Appendix 4) which has a very similar text. We have used Gilbert's text for both, with minor emendations from Sandys. The two settings together constitute a unique and extraordinary survival.

We give both as printed, except that II is transposed down a fourth and has been partly rebarred. Gilbert's (I) in particular, with its speech-rhythm melody and splendidly free-ranging instrumental bass, represents a style of per-formance which one might not have imagined but for this example. Yet there can be no doubt as to its authenticity. There is no evidence that Gilbert, or those that assisted him, ever tampered with their musical sources; if they had, it is scarcely conceivable that they would have produced anything so outrageous, and performance confirms what the printed page suggests—that there is a rough, peasant musicality about the setting as a whole to which a middle-class Georgian editor could hardly aspire. Sandys's bass line is less surprising, though still undoubtedly instrumental.

The fact that the refrain is specific to Christmas Eve

makes a domestic provenance almost certain, since Christmas Eve services were unknown in Protestant England. Gilbert's preface begins: 'The following Carols or Christmas Songs were chanted to the Tunes accompanying them, in the Churches on Christmas Day, and in private houses on Christmas Eve, throughout the West of England, up to the latter part of the late [eighteenth] century.' He describes the circumstances of domestic performance: 'The day of Christmas Eve was passed in an ordinary manner; but at seven or eight o'clock in the evening, cakes were drawn hot from the oven; cyder or beer exhilarated the spirits in every house; and the singing of Carols was continued late into the night.' Confirmation that instruments were used in this kind of domestic music-making (in some places, at least) can be found in 'a letter of reminiscence' quoted by K. H. MacDermott (*The Old Church Gallery Minstrels*, 1948, p. 8), which refers to a Northamptonshire village of the mid-nineteenth century where on every Sunday afternoon, when there was no church service, 'one would hear in every

cottage instrumental or vocal music blending in family harmony'.

Sandys's tune is related to that which Gilbert gives for 'When righteous Joseph' (129); Sandys calls it 'a specimen of the old minor key, with a flat seventh at the close . . . It appears harsh to modern ears, which expect G♯' (D♯ in our transposition).

Gilbert's second carol, 'When God at first created man' (142), for Christmas Day, is sung to a compound time version of I.

PERFORMANCE I, II, voices(s) and instrument (bassoon, cello, double bass, serpent, etc., taking the lower octave where possible; a violin might double the melody while other instruments busk harmonies). Solo verses and unison refrains might be ideal. Higher voices might prefer Sandys's setting (II) up a minor third.

For choral performance the words can be sung to the setting of 'When God at first created man' (142).

142

When God at first created man

(Christmas)

English traditional
(Gilbert, 1822, arr. editors)

1. When God at first cre - a - ted man, His i - mage for to be, And

how he made him by___ his power We may__ in Scrip - ture see: And

how he framed his help - mate Eve The Scrip - ture doth__ us tell; Being

free__ from sin, God placed them both in pa - ra - dise to dwell. Let

men__ there-fore then praise__ the Lord, Re - joice,__ and cease__ to mourn, Be -

- cause__ our Sa - viour, Je - sus Christ, This bless - ed day was born.

2 Man being entered in that place
  (We plainly understand),
The glory of it having seen,
  God gave them this command:
Be sure thou eat not of the tree
  Which in the midst doth stand;
In eating it thou sure shalt die,
  And perish from the land.

3 The serpent then hath Eve beguiled,
  That she thereof did eat,
And likewise gave unto the man,
  As Scripture doth repeat.
And so they both broke God's command,
  Committing of this thing;
Likewise the heavy wrath of God
  Upon them both did bring.

*4 Man, being now with grief oppressed,
    Not knowing where to go,
His soul, before being filled with joy,
    Is now oppressed with woe.
But see the mercy of the Lord!
    To save man's soul from hell,
His Son he promised to send down,
    That he with us might dwell.

5 An angel then from heaven was sent
    For to declare God's will,
And to the Virgin Mary came
    God's words for to fulfil.
A virgin sure, of life most pure,
    Of whom the Lord made choice,
To bear our Saviour in her womb,
    Man's heart for to rejoice.

6 Then Mary and her husband kind
    Together did remain,
And went to Bethlehem to be taxed,
    As Scripture doth make plain.
And so it was that, they being there,
    Her time being fully come,
Within a stable she brought forth
    Her first-begotten son.

*7 God grant us hearts for to believe,
    And likewise to consider
How that our Saviour suffered death
    Man's soul for to deliver:
The which, if rightly we believe,
    We shall with him be blessed,
And, when this mortal life is done,
    In heaven we hope to rest.

English traditional
(*Gilbert, 1822, adapted*)

This is Gilbert's Christmas Day companion to the Christmas Eve carol 'The Lord at first did Adam make' (141) in his *Some Ancient Christmas Carols* (1822; see Appendix 4). We give seven of his twelve verses, with small emendations from Sandys's *Christmas Carols, Ancient and Modern* (1833). We have transposed Gilbert's melody and bass down a minor third, and added upper parts. Bar 17 of Gilbert's melody was as follows (at our transposition):

The tune is a triple-time variant of the free-rhythm tune that Gilbert gives for 'The Lord at first'.

PERFORMANCE Voices, with the tenor doubled at the higher octave, and instruments *ad lib.* (see Appendix 3).

143

A virgin unspotted
A virgin most pure

I

(*Christmas*)

English traditional
(Chappell, 1853–9, arr. editors)

1. A___ vir - gin un - spot - ted, the___ pro - phet[1]_ fore - told,
Should bring_ forth a Sa - viour, which_ now we_ be - hold,

To___ be_ our Re - deem - er_ from_ death, hell_ and_

sin, Which A - dam's trans - gres - sion in - vol - ved_ us___ in.

[1] Isaiah

II

English traditional (*Journal of the Folk-Song Society, 5, arr. editors*)

(*Christmas*)

VERSE

1. A＿ vir - gin un - spot - ted, the＿ pro - phet[1] fore - told, Should

bring＿ forth a＿ Sa - viour, which now we be - hold,

To＿ be＿ our Re - deem - er＿ from death, hell＿ and sin, Which

REFRAIN *Then let＿ us be＿ mer - ry,＿ cast sor - row＿ a - way! Our＿*

A - dam's trans - gres - sion in - vol - ved＿ us in.
Sa - viour, Christ＿ Je - sus, was＿ born on＿ this day.

ALTERNATIVE REFRAIN

Then let＿ us be＿ mer - ry, cast sor - row＿ a - way! Our＿

Sa - viour, Christ＿ Je - sus, was＿ born on＿ this＿ day.

[1] Isaiah

2   Through Bethlehem city, in Jewry, it was
    That Joseph and Mary together did pass,
    And for to be taxèd when thither they came,
    Since Caesar Augustus commanded the same.
       [*Then let us be merry*, (etc.)]†

3   But Mary's full time being come, as we find,[2]
    She brought forth her first-born to save all mankind;
    The inn being full, for this heavenly guest
    No place there was found where to lay him to rest.

4   But Mary, blest Mary, so meek and so mild,
    Soon wrapped up in swaddlings this heavenly Child:
    Contented, she laid him where oxen do feed;
    The great God of nature approved of the deed.

5   To teach us humility all this was done;
    Then learn we from hence haughty pride for to shun.
    A manger his cradle who came from above,
    The great God of mercy, of peace and of love.

6   Then presently[3] after, the shepherds did spy
    Vast numbers of angels to stand in the sky;
    So merrily talking, so sweet they did sing:
    'All glory and praise to our heavenly King!'

English traditional
(Chappell, 1853–9)

† Refrain for setting II only.

[2] in the gospels   [3] immediately

III

(*Christmas*)

English traditional
(*Gilbert, 1822, arr. editors*)

1. A___ vir - gin___ most___ pure, as the pro - phets do___ tell,
Hath___ brought forth___ a___ ba - by, as it hath be - fell,

To be___ our Re - deem - er from___ death, hell___ and___ sin, Which

A - dam's trans - gres - sion hath___ wrap - ped___ us___ in. *Aye, and*

there - fore— be you mer - ry, Re - joice and be you mer - ry, Set sor - rows— a -

- side! Christ Je - sus,— our— Sa - viour, was— born on— this— tide.

2   In Bethlehem Jewry a city there was,
    Where Joseph and Mary together did pass,
    And there to be taxèd with many one more,
    For Caesar commanded the same should be so.

3   But when they had entered the city so fair,
    The number of people so mighty was there
    That Joseph and Mary, whose substance was small,
    Could find in the inn there no lodging at all.

4   Then were they constrained in a stable to lie,
    Where horses and asses they used for to tie;
    Their lodging so simple they took it no scorn,
    But against the next morning our Saviour was born.

5   The King of all kings to this world being brought,
    Small store of fine linen to wrap him was sought;
    When Mary had swaddled her young son so sweet,
    Within an ox-manger she laid him to sleep.

6   Then God sent an angel from heaven so high
    To certain poor shepherds in fields where they lie,
    And bade them no longer in sorrow to stay,
    Because that our Saviour was born on this day.

7   Then presently[1] after, the shepherds did spy
    A number of angels that stood in the sky;
    They joyfully talkèd and sweetly did sing:
    'To God be all glory, our heavenly King!'

English traditional
(Gilbert, 1822)

[1] immediately

One of the most venerable and widely distributed of all English Christmas carols, found in seemingly endless musical variants. (For an eighteenth-century American setting see 80.) The earliest known version of the text is in *New Carolls for this Merry Time of Christmas* (London, 1661), of which the only copy is in the Bodleian Library, Oxford. This version begins 'In Bethlehem city, in Jewry it was', and consists of thirteen stanzas, each of two eleven-syllable lines, with the refrain 'Rejoice and be merry' at the opening and 'And therefore be merry' after each stanza. There is no music, but it is directed to be sung to the tune 'Why weep ye', which has not been identified: it may be a Scottish ballad tune. The refrain–verse–refrain form would suggest a sixteenth-century origin at the latest, and the evidence of the text itself supports a sixteenth-century date. The familiar first verse, 'A virgin unspotted', had been added when the carol next surfaced in the eighteenth century, and is always found thereafter. The tune is found for the first time in *The Compleat Psalmodist* (1741) by John Arnold, of Great Warley, Essex, in a four-part setting.

Tune I is a variant of this from Chappell's *Popular Music of the Olden Time* (1853–9). Chappell sets the song 'Admiral Benbow' to the tune, but notes that 'in the month of January last, Mr Samuel Smith noted it down from the singing of some carollers at Marden, near Hereford, to the words commencing,—"A virgin unspotted the prophets foretold".'

Tune II was collected by Cecil Sharp on 19 December 1911 from the singing of the seventy-six-year-old Mr Samson Bates, of The Trench, Shropshire. It might appear to be independent of the usual tune, but its derivation is shown by a variant which is halfway between the two, collected by Sharp in October that year from two singers in Lilleshall, Shropshire. (See *Journal of the Folk-Song Society*, vol. 5, no. 18, pp. 24–5.)

Gilbert and Sandys (see Appendix 4) both published West Country versions, with texts beginning 'A virgin most pure'. The many differences from the usual text suggest a common derivation, perhaps from West Country broadsheets or chap-books. The versions they give are in fact variants of the same tune. Sandys's is deadly dull, and has unfortunately passed into common use through its inclusion in Husk's *Songs of the Nativity* (1864). (A very similar form of the tune given with 'This new Christmas Carol' in the Hutchens manuscript [see Appendix 4] suggests that this particular mutation was widely known.) The 3/4 tune is misbarred in 2/4; it is given as the soprano, with pianistic chords below; and there has clearly been a confusion between the tenor melody and the treble line. The problem arose because at that time tenor parts were sung at both octaves; there were thus two lines sounding at treble pitch. William Cole, of Colchester, is one of several writers to mention this process (*A View of Modern Psalmody*, 1819). Discussing the harmonization of psalm tunes in the context of the doubling of tenor parts (section IV), he points out that 'the greater part of those who sing in religious worship, being led entirely by the ear will of course follow the highest part, and form a melody compounded of the predominant notes.'

Sandys's tune (rebarred) begins:

The four-part source of this may have been something like this:

Similar confusions occur at the end of his second and last phrases.

Gilbert's splendid tune and bass (III)—all that he gives (in *Some Ancient Christmas Carols*, 1822)—must derive from gallery manuscripts (see Appendix 4). It is the most exotic of all the variants, though the recurring opening phrase is no more than an embellishment of Sandys's tune, such as

instrumentalists might automatically have provided:

The text is also taken from Gilbert. Verse 2, line 3: pronounce 'more' as 'mo'.

PERFORMANCE   I (*i*) solo or unison voices; (*ii*) choir.

II, one or two voices, with vocal or instrumental drone *ad lib.*:

Alternative refrain, choir.

III, voices, with the tenor doubled at the higher octave, and instruments *ad lib.* (see Appendix 3).

144

The angel Gabriel from God was sent

(Annunciation; Christmas)

English traditional
(Sandys, 1833, arr. editors)

1. The angel Gabriel from God Was sent to Galilee, And, when the angel thither came, He fell down on his knee, And, looking up in the

Unto a virgin fair and free, Whose name was called Mary; REFRAIN Then sing we all, both great and small, Nowell, nowell, nowell! We may rejoice to

vir - gin's_ face, He_ said:_ 'All_ hail,_ Ma - ry!'
hear the_ voice Of_ the an - gel_ Ga - bri - - el.

2 Mary anon looked him upon,
  And said: 'Sir, what are ye?
I marvel much at these tidings
  Which thou hast brought to me.
Married I am unto an old man,
  As the lot fell unto me;
Therefore, I pray, depart away,
  For I stand in doubt of thee.'

3 'Mary,' he said, 'be not afraid,
  But do believe in me:
The power of the Holy Ghost
  Shall overshadow thee;
Thou shalt conceive without any grief,
  As the Lord told unto me;
God's own dear Son from heaven shall
  come,
  And shall be born of thee.'

4 This came to pass as God's will was,
  Even as the angel told.
About midnight an angel bright
  Came to the shepherds' fold,
And told them then both where and when
  Born was the Child, our Lord;
And all along this was their song:
  All glory be given to God.

*5 Good people all, both great and small,
  The which do hear my voice,
With one accord let's praise the Lord,
  And in our hearts rejoice.
Like sister and brother let's love one
  another
  Whilst we our lives do spend.
Whilst we have space let's pray for grace:
  And so let my carol end.

English traditional
(Sandys, 1833)

From William Sandys's *Christmas Carols, Ancient and Modern* (1833; see Appendix 4). We take the melody and most of the bass (transposed down a tone) from Sandys's setting of 'When righteous Joseph wedded was'. He gives no music for 'The angel Gabriel' in his music section but prints it next to 'When righteous Joseph' in the body of his collection (a sign in broadsides, etc., that two texts share a melody): they have identical refrains and complementary themes, one the doubts of Mary, the other those of Joseph. There is no separate music for the refrain printed in Sandys's setting, though a double bar indicates the repeat point. (See also Gilbert's setting of 'When righteous Joseph', 129.)

PERFORMANCE Voices, with the tenor doubled at the higher octave, and instruments *ad lib.* (see Appendix 3).

145

God's dear Son, without beginning

(*Christmas*)

English traditional
(*Gilbert, 1822, arr. editors*)

1. God's dear Son, with-out be - gin - ning, Whom on earth vile men did scorn,
*2. In Beth - le - hem, King Da-vid's ci - ty, Ma - ry's Babe had sweet cre - a - tion:

The on-ly wise, with-out all sin - ning, On this bless - ed day_ was_ born To
God and Man, en - dued with pi - ty, And a Sa - viour of_ each na - tion. Yet

save us all from sin_ and thrall, Whilst we_ in Sa - tan's chains were bound; And
Jew - ry - land with cru - el_ hand Both first_ and last his power de - nied: Where

shed his blood to do us good, With many a bleeding purple wound.
he was born they did him scorn, And showed him malice when he died.

3 No place at all for our Saviour
    In Judea could be found;
  Mary sweet, with mild behaviour,
    Patiently upon the ground
  Her Babe did place in vile disgrace,
    Where oxen in their stall did feed;
  No midwife mild had this sweet Child,
    Nor woman's help at mother's need.

4 No kingly robes nor golden treasure
    Decked the birthday of God's Son;
  No pompous train at all took pleasure
    To this King of kings to run;
  No mantle brave could Jesus have,
    Upon his cradle for to lie;
  No music charms in nurse's arms,
    To sing the Babe a lullaby.

5 Yet, as Mary sat at solace
    By our Saviour's first beginning,
  Hosts of angels from God's palace,
    Sounding sweet, from heaven singing;

Yea, heaven and earth at Jesus' birth
    With sweet melodious tunes abound,
  And everything for Jewry's King
    Upon the earth gave cheerful sound.

6 Heaven perceiving small befriending
    Of this promised Prince of Might,
  From the crystal skies descending,
    Blazing glorious beams of light,
  A glorious star did shine so far
    That all the earth might see the same;
  And nations strange their faith did change,
    To yield him honour, laud and fame.

*7 Now to him that hath redeemed us
    By his precious death and Passion,
  And us sinners so esteemed us
    To buy dearly this salvation,
  Yield lasting fame, that still the name
    Of Jesus may be honoured here;
  And let us say that Christmas Day
    Is still the best day of the year.

English traditional
(Sandys, 1833, adapted)

The text is from the nine verses in William Sandys's *Christmas Carols, Ancient and Modern* (1833). Verse 1, line 2 was originally 'whom the wicked Jews. . .'. Other parts of the text are obviously corrupt in all sources. The tune and bass are from Davies Gilbert's *Some Ancient Christmas Carols* (1822; see Appendix 4). Bar 8, beat 4 had an opening repeat indication here (where the music of the refrain begins in comparable carols) followed by first- and second-time

bars at the end; neither Gilbert nor Sandys gives a refrain, and repetition of the half-verse would produce nonsense in some verses. In bar 16, the second bass note was originally C. The tune is a variant of the 'Chestnut' tune (151:1).

PERFORMANCE Voices, with the tenor doubled at the higher octave, and instruments *ad lib.* (see Appendix 3).

146

A Child this day is born

(Christmas)

English traditional
(Sandys, 1833, arr. editors)

VERSE

1. A___ Child this__ day is___ born, A Child of high re-nown, Most
2. These ti-dings shep-herds heard, In field watch-ing__ their fold, Were

wor-thy of__ a___ scep-tre, A scep-tre__ and a crown. No-
by__ an an-gel__ un-to them That night re-vealed and told.

REFRAIN

-vels,__ no-vels, no-vels! No-vels sing__ all__ we__ may, Be-

-cause the King of__ all_____ kings Was born_ this_ bless - ed day.

3 To whom the angel spoke,
      Saying: 'Be not afraid;
   Be glad, poor silly¹ shepherds,
      Why are you so dismayed?

4 'For lo! I bring you tidings
      Of gladness and of mirth,
   †Which cometh to all people by
      This holy Infant's birth.'

5 Then was there with the angel
      An host incontinent²
   Of heavenly bright soldiers,
      Which from the Highest was sent.

6 Lauding the Lord our God
      And his celestial King,
   'All glory be in paradise'
      This heavenly host did sing.

7 And as the angel told them,
      So to them did appear;
   They found the young child Jesus Christ,
      With Mary his mother dear.

*8 No pride at all was found
      In this most holy Child,
   But he being void of all sin,
      The Lamb of God most mild.

*9 His body unto bitter pains
      He gave to set us free:
   He is our Saviour Jesus Christ,
      And none but only he.

*10 To Father, Son and Holy Ghost
      All glory be therefore,
   To whom be all dominion
      Both now and evermore.

English traditional
(Sandys, 1833)

† Tenor (tune): people (vv. 6, 7, 9 similarly).

¹ simple   ² innumerable

The text and tune (the latter known as 'Sandys') are from Sandys's *Christmas Carols, Ancient and Modern* (1833; see Appendix 4), which gives twenty-one verses. 'Novels' (from

nouvelles) in the refrain probably reflects a French origin (see notes, 188).

PERFORMANCE Voices, with the tenor doubled at the higher octave, and instruments *ad lib.* (see Appendix 3).

147

Shepherds, arise!

(Christmas)

English traditional
(Copper, 1971)

VERSE

1. Shep - herds, a - rise! be not____ a - fraid; With_

ha - sty_ steps_ re - pair To_ Da-vid's ci - ty:_

With her blest In - fant

see_____ the maid With her blest In - fant there,_____

there,

_ with her blest In - fant there, with her_ blest_ In - fant there.

REFRAIN

Sing! sing all earth! sing! sing all earth! e - ter - -

2 Laid in a manger view the Child,
    Humility divine;
  Sweet innocence (how meek! how mild!),
    Grace in his features shine.

3 For us the Saviour came on earth,
    For us his life he gave
  To save us from eternal death
    And raise us from the grave.

4 To Jesus Christ, our glorious King,
    Be endless praises given;
  Let all on earth his mercies sing,
    Who made our peace in heaven!

English traditional
(Pickard-Cambridge, 1926)

This setting was transcribed from a recording made by the men of the Copper family from Rottingdean, Sussex, one of several rural families who preserve an oral part-singing tradition (see Bob Copper's *A Song for Every Season*, 1971; also 'The Twelve Days of Christmas', 133:11). It is given here in D, but their recorded performance is in F. The Copper version must derive from a fuging psalm tune: see the heavily 'corrected' version in W. A. Pickard-Cambridge's *Collection of Dorset Carols* (1926), which was based on the part-books in Winterborne Zelstone Parish Church.

Bob Copper's book has the first three verses of the text and the refrain, taken from the family song-book, copied in 1922 and 1936, which contains the words of all the songs. The verses are engagingly corrupt—verse 1 reads: 'Shepherds arise, be not afraid, / With hasty steps prepare / To David's city, sin on earth, / With our blest Infant there.' We have therefore followed Pickard-Cambridge's text, the only other source we could find, but have changed 'Bethlehem' to 'David's' in verse 1.

PERFORMANCE Voices, perhaps with soloists for the verses.

148

I saw three ships come sailing in

I

(*Christmas*)

English traditional
(Sandys, 1833)

1. I saw three ships come sail-ing in *On Christ-mas Day, on Christ-mas Day,* I

saw three ships come sail-ing in *On Christ-mas Day in the morn - ing.*

2 And what was in those ships all three?

3 Our Saviour Christ and his lady,

4 Pray, whither sailed those ships all three?

5 O they sailed into Bethlehem

6 And all the bells on earth shall ring

7 And all the angels in heaven shall sing

8 And all the souls on earth shall sing

9 Then let us all rejoice amain![1]

English traditional
(Sandys, 1833)

[1] greatly

II

(Christmas)

English traditional
(Bramley and Stainer, 1871, arr. editors)

1. I saw three ships come sail-ing in On Christ-mas Day, on Christ-mas Day, I

saw three ships come sail-ing in On Christ-mas Day in the morn - ing.

The text, from Sandys's *Christmas Carols, Ancient and Modern* (1833; see Appendix 4), is one of many variant versions, of which the earliest is in Forbes's *Cantus* (1666 edn.). They derive from the Mediterranean journeyings of the supposed relics of the magi, the 'Three Kings of Cologne', the splendour of whose final voyage has remained vivid in European folk memory. The Empress Helena, mother of Constantine the Great and discoverer of the True Cross, carried them to Constantinople in the fourth century, from where they were later taken by St Eustathius to Milan. In 1162 the skulls were gifted to Cologne Cathedral by Friedrich Barbarossa, and Bishop Renaldus brought them there, to rest in the jewelled caskets in which they remain to this day. A version of the carol collected from a boatman on the River Humber by Lewis Davis begins much as 'I saw three ships', but continues: 'I axed 'em what they'd got on board . . . They said they'd got three crawns [skulls] . . . I axed 'em where they was taken to . . . They said they was ganging to Coln upon Rhine . . .

I axed 'em where they came frae . . . They said they came frae Bethlehem . . .'. It is likely that in English versions of the song the voyage to Cologne has fused with the quite different tradition of symbolic ships, of which 'Es kommt ein Schiff, geladen' (179) is one of many German examples. (See Anne G. Gilchrist, 'The Three Kings of Cologne', *Journal of the Folk-Song Society*, vol. 5, pp. 31–40).

There are also many variants of the tune, which Sandys noted 'is very similar to one of the old Shakespearian tunes, "There lived a man in Babylon"', sung by Sir Toby Belch in *Twelfth Night*.

Setting II is of a slightly different tune in Bramley and Stainer's *Christmas Carols New and Old* (1871). For another variant see 'As I sat on a sunny bank' (149).

PERFORMANCE I (*i*) voice; (*ii*) voices in two parts; (*iii*) voice(s) and bass instrument.

II, choir.

149

As I sat on a sunny bank

(Christmas)

English traditional (Broadwood and Fuller Maitland, 1893, arr. editors)

1. As I___ sat on___ a sun-ny___ bank On___ Christ-mas Day, on Christ-mas Day, As I sat on___ a sun-ny___ bank On___ Christ-mas Day in the morn — ing.

2 I spied three ships come sailing by
   On Christmas Day, (etc.)

3 And who should be with those three ships
   On Christmas Day, on Christmas Day,
   And who should be with those three ships
   But Joseph and his fair lady!

4 O he did whistle and she did sing
   On Christmas Day, (etc.)

5 And all the bells on earth did ring
   On Christmas Day, (etc.)

6 For joy that our Saviour he was born
   On Christmas Day, (etc.)

*English traditional
(Husk, 1864)*

The text is the usual broadside form as given by W. H. Husk in *Songs of the Nativity* (1864). There are many variants of both texts and tune (see notes, 148). This form of the melody was collected by Lucy Broadwood from a Mrs Wilson, near Kings Langley, Hertfordshire. It was published in Broadwood and Fuller Maitland's *English County Songs* (1893).

PERFORMANCE (*i*) Choir; (*ii*) voice and lute, guitar, keyboard, etc. Suggested harmonies:

150

This is the truth sent from above

I

English traditional
(Sharp, 1911)

(Christmas)

1. This is the____ truth____ sent____ from a - bove, The truth of____ God, the
2. The first thing that____ I____ will re - late, That God at____ first did

God____ of____ love; There - fore don't____ turn me from____ the door,____ But
man____ cre - ate; The next thing____ which to you____ I tell— Wo -

Last verse

heark - en all,____ both____ rich and____ poor.
-man____ was made____ with____ him to____ dwell.

3 Then after that 'twas God's own choice
To place them both in paradise,
There to remain from evil free
Except they ate of such a tree.

4 But they did eat, which was a sin,
And thus their ruin did begin—
Ruined themselves, both you and me,
And all of our posterity.

5 Thus we were heirs to endless woes
Till God the Lord did interpose;
And so a promise soon did run:
That he'd redeem us by his Son.

6 And at this season of the year
Our blest Redeemer did appear,
And here did live, and here did preach,
And many thousands he did teach.

7 Thus he in love to us behaved,
To show us how we must be saved;
And if you want to know the way,
Be pleased to hear what he did say:

*8 'Go preach the Gospel,' now he said,
'To all the nations that are made!
And he that does believe on me,
From all his sins I'll set him free.'

*9 O seek! O seek of God above
That saving faith that works by love!
And, if he's pleased to grant thee this,
Thou'rt sure to have eternal bliss.

*10 God grant to all within this place
True saving faith, that special grace
Which to his people doth belong:
And thus I close my Christmas song.

English traditional
(A Good Christmas Box, 1847)

II

(*Christmas*)

English traditional
(arr. Ralph Vaughan Williams, 1872–1958)

1. This is the truth sent from a - bove, The truth of God, the God of love; There - fore don't turn me from the door, But hearken all, both rich and poor.

2 The first thing that I will relate,
   That God at first did man create;
   The next thing which to you I tell—
   Woman was made with him to dwell.

3 Then after that 'twas God's own choice
   To place them both in paradise,
   There to remain from evil free
   Except they ate of such a tree.

4 But they did eat, which was a sin,
   And thus their ruin did begin—
   Ruined themselves, both you and me,
   And all of our posterity.

5 Thus we were heirs to endless woes
   Till God the Lord did interpose;
   And so a promise soon did run:
   That he'd redeem us by his Son.

6 And at this season of the year
   Our blest Redeemer did appear,
   And here did live, and here did preach,
   And many thousands he did teach.

7 Thus he in love to us behaved,
   To show us how we must be saved;
   And if you want to know the way,
   Be pleased to hear what he did say:

*8 'Go preach the Gospel,' now he said,
   'To all the nations that are made!
   And he that does believe on me,
   From all his sins I'll set him free.'

*9 O seek! O seek of God above
   That saving faith that works by love!
   And, if he's pleased to grant thee this,
   Thou'rt sure to have eternal bliss.

*10 God grant to all within this place
   True saving faith, that special grace
   Which to his people doth belong:
   And thus I close my Christmas song.

English traditional
(A Good Christmas Box, 1847)

The text is from the sixteen verses given in *A Good Christmas Box* (1847). Tune I was collected by Cecil Sharp at Donnington Wood, Shropshire, and published in his *English Folk-Carols* (1911). Tune II was collected from Mr W. Jenkins of King's Pyon, Herefordshire (see *Journal of the Folk-Song Society*, vol. 4, no. 17). The setting was published in Vaughan Williams's *Eight Traditional English Carols* (1919). (See carols 130:1 and 140 for variants, and 160 for a choral setting.)

PERFORMANCE I, voice, perhaps with a one- or two-note drone; II, choir.

151

God rest you merry, gentlemen

I

(*Christmas*)

English traditional
(*arr. John Stainer, 1840–1901*)

VERSE

1. God rest¹ you mer - ry, gen - tle - men, Let no - thing you dis - may, For

Je - sus Christ, our Sa - viour, Was born up - on this

day To save us all from Sa - tan's power When we were gone a -

REFRAIN

- stray.___ O___ ti - dings of com - fort and joy, com - fort and

¹ keep

joy, ___ O___ ti - dings of com - fort and joy!

2 In Bethlehem in Jewry
    This blessèd Babe was born,
And laid within a manger
    Upon this blessèd morn;
The which his mother Mary
    Nothing did take in scorn.

3 From God our heavenly Father
    A blessèd angel came,
And unto certain shepherds
    Brought tidings of the same,
How that in Bethlehem was born
    The Son of God by name.

4 'Fear not,' then said the angel,
    'Let nothing you affright;
This day is born a Saviour
    Of virtue, power and might,
So frequently to vanquish all
    The friends of Satan quite.'

5 The shepherds at those tidings
    Rejoicèd much in mind,
And left their flocks a-feeding
    In tempest, storm and wind,
And went to Bethlehem straightway
    This blessèd Babe to find.

6 But when to Bethlehem they came,
    Whereat this Infant lay,
They found him in a manger
    Where oxen feed on hay;
His mother Mary, kneeling,
    Unto the Lord did pray.

7 Now to the Lord sing praises,
    All you within this place,
And with true love and brotherhood
    Each other now embrace.
The holy tide of Christmas
    All others doth efface.

West Country traditional
(Sandys, 1833)

II

(*Christmas*)

English traditional
(Dunstan, 1929, arr. editors)

VERSE

1. God rest¹ you mer - ry, gen - tle - men, Let no - thing you dis -
2. From God that is____ our Fa - ther The bless - ed an - gels

- may, Re - mem - ber Christ, our Sa - viour, Was born____ on Christ-mas
came Un - to some cer - tain shep - herds With ti - dings of the

Day To save____ poor souls____ from Sa - tan's power Which had
same: That there____ was born____ in Beth - le - hem The

REFRAIN

long time gone a - stray. *And____ it's ti - dings of com - fort____ and joy!*
Son of God by____ name.

¹ keep

3 'Go, fear not,' said God's angels,
　　'Let nothing you affright,
　For there is born in Bethlehem,
　　Of a pure virgin bright,
　One able to advance you
　　And throw down Satan quite.'

4 The shepherds at those tidings
　　Rejoicèd much in mind,
　And left their flocks a-feeding
　　In tempest storms of wind;
　And straight they came to Bethlehem
　　The Son of God to find.

5 Now when they came to Bethlehem,
　　Where our sweet Saviour lay,
　They found him in a manger,
　　Where oxen feed on hay;
　The blessèd Virgin, kneeling down,
　　Unto the Lord did pray.

6 With sudden joy and gladness
　　The shepherds were beguiled,
　To see the Babe of Israel
　　Before his mother mild;
　On them with joy and cheerfulness
　　Rejoice each mother's child.

7 Now to the Lord sing praises,
　　All you within this place,
　Like we true loving brethren
　　Each other to embrace,
　For the merry time of Christmas
　　Is drawing on apace.

8 God bless the ruler of this house,
　　And send him long to reign,
　And many a merry Christmas
　　May live to see again
　Among your friends and kindred
　　That live both far and near.

English traditional
(Oxford Book of Carols, 1928)

III

(Christmas)

West Country traditional
(Sandys, 1833, arr. editors)

VERSE

1. God rest[1] you mer-ry, gen-tle-men, Let no-thing you dis-may,
2. From God our heaven-ly Fa-ther A bless-ed an-gel came,

For Je-sus Christ, our Sa-viour, Was born up-on this day
And un-to cer-tain shep-herds Brought ti-dings of the same,

To save us all from Sa-tan's power When we were gone a-stray.
How that in Beth-le-hem was born The Son of God by name.

REFRAIN

O tidings, O tidings of com-fort and joy!

[1] keep

For___ Je - sus Christ, our_ Sa - viour, Was_ born on_ Christ - mas Day.

3 The shepherds at those tidings
   Rejoicèd much in mind,
   And left their flocks a-feeding
   In tempest, storm and wind,
   And went to Bethlehem straightway
   This blessèd Babe to find.

4 Now to the Lord sing praises,
   All you within this place,
   And with true love and brotherhood
   Each other now embrace.
   This holy tide of Christmas
   All others doth efface.

West Country traditional
(Sandys, 1833)

Text I is from William Sandys's *Christmas Carols, Ancient and Modern* (1833; see Appendix 4), where it is associated with tune III. This has now become the standard text. Text II is from an early nineteenth-century broadside (see *The Oxford Book of Carols*, 1928, no. 12). Text III is a shortened version of I. Both have minor emendations.

Tune I, the 'London' tune, is also known as 'Chestnut' from the title 'Chestnut (or Doves Figary)' in Playford's *The English Dancing Master* (1651). It is now ubiquitous in the form given in Bramley and Stainer's *Christmas Carols New and Old* (1871). It is also one of the endless variants of what A. L. Lloyd has called England's 'most persistent *quête* [luck-visit] tune'. Lloyd gives a version combining major and minor modes, to which modern Herefordshire carollers continued to sing Thomas Deloney's ballad on the London earthquake of 1580, 'Awake, awake sweet England' (A. L. Lloyd, *Folk Song in England*, 1967). He also gives related *quête* tunes from Hungary, Sweden, and Bulgaria, and from France, whence he believes the tune travelled to England. These European tunes correspond to the first eight bars of the present carol; the English derivatives vary widely in their later strains. These include 'God's dear Son without

beginning' (145), 'Come all you worthy gentlemen' (152), 'We've been a while a-wandering' (157), 'Here we come a-wassailing' (159:1), 'Wassail, O wassail all over the town' (158), and the 'Advent Images Carol' (see notes, 131). For a major-mode version see 'While shepherds watched' (46:III). An unusual version of both tune and text, beginning 'Sit you, merry gentlemen', is in the Cornish Hutchens manuscript (see Appendix 4).

Tune II is yet another variant, with a different refrain. This was printed in Ralph Dunstan's *Cornish Song Book* (1929), where it is described as 'formerly popular in Cornwall'. Dunstan claims to have taken both melody and harmony 'from a setting in MS (*c.*1845)', but as he generally shows little respect for lower parts in his sources (see notes, 91), we have replaced the ones he gives with our own.

Tune III is said to have been the usual West Country tune. Melody and bass are from Sandys.

PERFORMANCE I and II, (*i*) choir; (*ii*) voices and organ; III, voices, with the tenor doubled at the higher octave, and instruments *ad lib.* (see Appendix 3).

152

Come all you worthy gentlemen

(*Christmas; New Year*)

English traditional
(*Sharp, 1911, arr. editors*)

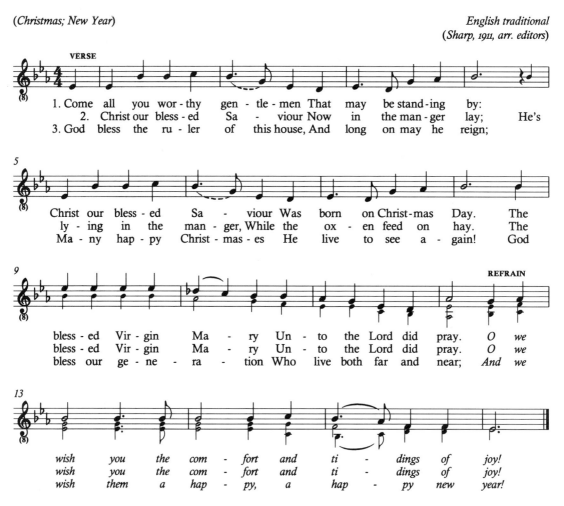

VERSE

1. Come all you wor-thy gen-tle-men That may be stand-ing by:
2. Christ our bless-ed Sa - viour Now in the man-ger lay; He's
3. God bless the ru-ler of this house, And long on may he reign;

Christ our bless-ed Sa - viour Was born on Christ-mas Day. The
ly - ing in the man-ger, While the ox - en feed on hay. The
Ma - ny hap-py Christ-mas-es He live to see a - gain! God

REFRAIN

bless-ed Vir-gin Ma - ry Un - to the Lord did pray. *O* we
bless-ed Vir-gin Ma - ry Un - to the Lord did pray. *O* we
bless our ge - ne - ra - tion Who live both far and near; *And* we

wish you the com - fort and ti - dings of joy!
wish you the com - fort and ti - dings of joy!
wish them a hap - py, a hap - py new year!

English traditional
(*Sharp, 1911*)

Cecil Sharp took this down from a Mr Rapsey, of Bridgwater, Somerset, who as a child used to sing it for money with bands of other children in the streets of Bridgwater at Christmas. 'Our generation' (family) in verse 3 was presumably originally 'his generation'; and Mr Rapsey sang 'say' for 'pray' in verses 1 and 2—Sharp corrected this in his *English Folk-Carols* (1911).

The tune and some of the text are reminiscent of 'God rest you merry, gentlemen' (151:1). The third phrase of the melody (bars 8–12) looks very like a harmony part, perhaps the tenor of a three-part setting, that has infiltrated the tune.

PERFORMANCE Voice(s), in unison or harmony.

153

We wish you a merry Christmas

English traditional
(arr. editors)

VERSE

1. We wish you a mer-ry Christ-mas, we wish you a mer-ry
2. Now bring us some fig-gy pud-ding, now bring us some fig-gy
3. O we won't go un-til we've got some, no, we won't go un-til we've
4. O we all like figgy pud-ding, yes, we all like fig-gy

Christ-mas, we wish you a mer-ry Christ-mas and a hap-py new year!
pud-ding, now bring us some fig-gy pud-ding, and bring it us here!
got some, we won't go un-til we've got some, So give it us here!
pud-ding, we all like fig-gy pud-ding, So bring it out here!

REFRAIN

Glad ti-dings we bring To you and your kin: We

wish you a mer-ry Christ-mas And a hap-py new year!

The remnant of an *envoie* much used by wassailers and other luck visitors, still in all too common use by modern doorstep carollers.

PERFORMANCE Voice(s), with refrain in unison or harmony.

154

Christemas hath made an end
Well-a-day!
(The Gooding Carol)

I

(*Candlemas Eve; Twelfth Night*)

English traditional
(*Chappell, 1853–9, arr. editors*)

1. Christ - e - mas___ hath made an end, *Well - a - day!___ well - a - day!*

[*Fine*]

Which___ was___ my dear - est friend, *More___ is___ the pi - ty!*

For with an hea - vy heart___ Must___ I___ from thee___ de - part,

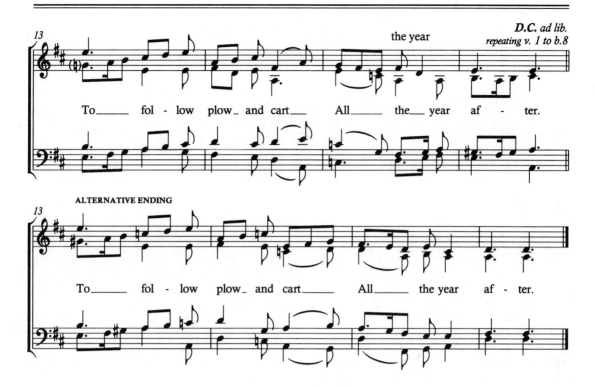

2 Lent is fast coming on,
    Well-a-day! well-a-day!
  That loves not anyone,
    More is the pity!
  For I doubt both my cheeks
  Will look thin from eating leeks;
  Wise is he then that seeks
  For a friend in a corner.

3 All our good cheer is gone,
    Well-a-day! well-a-day!
  And turnèd to a bone,
    More is the pity!
  In my good master's house
  I shall eat no more souse,[1]
  Then give me one carouse,
  Gentle kind butler!

4 It grieves me to the heart,
    Well-a-day! well-a-day!
  From my friend to depart,
    More is the pity!
  Christemas, I fear 'tis thee
  That thus forsaketh me:
  Yet for one hour, I see,
  Will I be merry.

(*New Carolls, 1661*)

[1] pickled meat or fish

II

(*Christmas*)

English traditional
(*Dunstan, 1925, arr. editors*)

Well - a - day!___ well - a - day!___ Christ - mas too__ soon goes a - way;
good - ing, pray; we can - not stay, We can - not stay__ but must a - way,

(2nd time)   *Fine*

Then your good - ing we__ do pray, For the good__ time will not stay.
For the Christ - mas will__ not stay; Well - a - day!_____ well - a - day!

We are not beg - gars That beg__ from door__ to door,
But neigh-bours' child - ren That you__ have seen__ be - - fore;___ So,

Text I is a carol for Candlemas Eve (1 February), from *New Carolls for this merry time of Christmas . . . to be sung to delight the Hearers. London. Printed by H. B. for Andrew Kemb, and to be sold at his shop near Saint Margarets hill in Southwark, 1661.* Candlemas (so called from the procession with candles before mass) is the feast of Mary's ritual purification in the temple at Jerusalem, forty days after the birth of her child, and it marked the official close of the Christmas season. For the seventeenth-century rustic, Christmas, when there was little work to be done in the fields, was the one extended period of leisure (summer holidays being unheard-of), though it rarely extended beyond Twelfth Night (5 January). The carol is the lament of such a man at the departure of Christmas, the return of unceasing labour, and the prospect of the privations of Lent. 'Christemas' is Sir Christemas, personification of the feast, who was one of the forebears of the modern Santa Claus. (See Samuel L. Macy, *Patriarchs of Time: Dualism in Saturn Chronos, Father Time, the Watchmaker God, and Father Christmas,* 1987. For a carol welcoming 'Syre Cristesmasse' see 'Nowell: Dieus wous garde, byewsser', 36.)

New Carolls cites the tune for the carol as 'Well-a-day'. This has caused some confusion, since there is a manuscript of English keyboard music (Paris, Bibliothèque Nationale, MS Rés. 1186, believed to have been copied *c.*1630–40) that contains two unrelated settings with this name; each has been taken to be that to which the carol was intended to be sung. The term 'well-a-day' was an expression of woe or desolation, and many ballads of lamentation were written with instructions that they were to be sung to a tune of this name (see Claude M. Simpson, *The British Broadside Ballad and its Music,* 1966). By far the most famous of these was 'A lamentable Dittie composed upon the death of Robert Devereaux late Earle of Essex', beginning 'Sweet England's pride is gone / welladay welladay', which was for sale on a broadside within two days of the execution of Queen Elizabeth's favourite in the Tower of London in 1601. It continued to be printed over the next few years, and was usually accompanied by a second ballad on the same theme, beginning 'All yow that crye O hone! O hone!' and directed to be sung to the tune 'Essex last goodnight'. A simple keyboard piece of this title is in a slightly later keyboard manuscript, *Elizabeth Rogers hir virginall booke* (British Library, MS Add. 10337), which is dated 'Ffebruary the 27 1656 [in modern terms, 1657]'. This is clearly related to the opening of the first of the 'Well-a-day' pieces in the Paris manuscript.

It might seem natural enough that two ballads on the same theme should be sung to a pair of related tunes, but William Chappell, who was aware of all three keyboard settings, seems to have concluded, very plausibly, that the tunes were variant forms of a single melody: in his *Popular Music of the Olden Time* (1859) 'Sweet England's pride is gone' is set to a remarkably free combination of the two tunes, and the section is headed 'Essex's Last Goodnight or Well-a-day'. H. E. Wooldridge, who issued a revised edition of Chappell's book in 1893 as *Old English Popular Music*, replaced the composite tune with the *second* 'Well-a-day' piece in the Paris manuscript as the more likely tune intended by the balladeers; Simpson made no mention of this and treated Chappell's two tunes as distinct entities; John Ward argued that Wooldridge had been right in his extended review 'Apropos The British Broadside Ballad and its Music' (*Journal of the American Musicological Society*, xx, 1967, pp. 28–86; see especially pp. 83–4); and there, for the moment, the matter rests.

We have nevertheless set Chappell's amalgamation (I), for it is an enchanting (if slightly unlikely) tune that carries the carol text well. Only Chappell's last strain seems to us to be weak, and we have replaced it with alternative adaptations: the first is freely amended, and leads to an entirely manufactured *da capo* refrain, while the second is closer to the Paris source than Chappell's version, and does not involve a refrain.

The 'Yorkshire Gooding Carol', (II) is another cobbling-together with a happy outcome. Ralph Dunstan published it in his *Second Book of Carols* (1925). 'In some parts of Yorkshire,' he explains, 'the following "Gooding" Carol was formerly sung from door to door on Christmas Morning by Children bearing a Christmas-Tree.' The custom seems to have been real enough, as shown by engravings in *The Illustrated London News* of Christmas Eve, 1864 (illustrating an article on carol-singing in Yorkshire), and in R. Chambers' *The Book of Days*, 1878). Dunstan took the text from Chambers, archaizing 'Christmas' into 'Christemas', and the 'Well-a-day' opening (if we assume it to be genuine) certainly appears to have been designed to go with the 'Well-a-day' tune—whichever that may be.

Dunstan undoubtedly lifted the tune from Chappell, covering his tracks by very slightly revising it, amputating the final strain, and replacing it with a repeat of the strain before it leading to a *da capo*. Whether anything like it ever existed in nature is likely to remain an open question: let us hope that it did.

To 'go a-gooding' was to pay a kind of luck-visit, though as early as the sixteenth century 'gooding' had also taken on the more general connotation of 'begging'. On St Thomas's Day (21 December), also known as 'Mumping [begging] Day', poor women would tour the better-off houses of their parishes, where they would be given money or food towards their Christmas celebrations. The custom still survived in the mid-nineteenth century in some areas, and was portrayed on the first Christmas card, designed for Henry Cole in 1843 and sold to the public in 1846. In many places it became institutionalized as a parish charity. Thomas Turner, churchwarden and overseer of the poor of the village of East Hoathly, Sussex, recorded the following in his diary on 21 December 1762: 'About 3.20 I arose and began to pay the people and finished about 10.20, having paid away £11, and I presume there had been 900 people.' Later, from his own pocket, he 'relieved' thirty more with 'one penny each and a draught of ale'. Luck-visits always involved an exchange of some kind, and singing carols in exchange for money was an established custom by at least the mid-eighteenth century. (Turner gave 3*d.* to 'some boys who came a-singing' one Boxing Day and to some men who did likewise one Epiphany). But the small fir-trees and bunches of greenery tied to sticks that the Yorkshire children are always portrayed as carrying may have derived from a specifically gooding custom, for John Brand (*Observations on the Popular Antiquities of Great Britain*, ed. Henry Ellis, 1853–5) notes that women going gooding 'appear to have presented their benefactors with sprigs of evergreens' and quotes an article in an issue of *The Gentleman's Magazine* following the mild winter of 1793–4, when 'The women who went a gooding . . . on St Thomas's Day, might in return for alms, have presented their benefactors with sprigs of palm and bunches of primroses.' Perhaps carol-singing children in Yorkshire took over both custom and name from female gooders.

PERFORMANCE   I (*i*) solo voice or four voices, with accompaniment *ad lib.*; (*ii*) choir.

II, children's voices.

155

Wassail! wassail all over the town!
(The Gloucestershire Wassail)

English traditional
(Oxford Book of Carols, 1928,
arr. editors)

(*Christmas*)

1. Was - sail!___ was - sail___ all o - ver the town!___ Our
2. So here is to Cher - ry and to his right cheek!___ Pray

toast it is white and our ale___ it___ is brown; Our___ bowl it___ is___ made of the
God send our mas - ter a good piece of beef, And a good piece of___ beef that___

white ma - ple tree: With the was - sail-ing bowl we'll drink___ to thee!
we all may see; With the was - sail-ing bowl we'll drink___ to thee!

3 And here is to Dobbin and to his right eye!
   Pray God send our master a good Christmas pie,
   And a good Christmas pie that we may all see;
   With our wassailing-bowl we'll drink to thee!

4 So here is to Broad May and to her broad horn!
May God send our master a good crop of corn,
And a good crop of corn that we may all see!
With the wassailing-bowl we'll drink to thee!

5 And here is to Fillpail and to her left ear!
Pray God send our master a happy new year,
And a happy new year as e'er he did see;
With our wassailing-bowl we'll drink to thee!

*6 And here is to Colly and to her long tail!
Pray God send our master he never may fail[1]
A bowl of strong beer; I pray you draw near,
And our jolly wassail it's then you shall hear.

*7 Come, butler, come fill us a bowl of the best,
Then we hope that your soul in heaven may rest;
But if you do draw us a bowl of the small,
Then down shall go butler, bowl and all!

*8 Then here's to the maid in the lily-white smock
Who tripped to the door and slipped back the lock;
Who tripped to the door and pulled back the pin,
For to let these jolly wassailers in.

English traditional
(*Oxford Book of Carols, 1928*)

---

[1] lack

Verses 1–5 and tune are as in *The Oxford Book of Carols* (1928), mainly taken by Vaughan Williams from 'an old person' in Gloucestershire. Verses 6–8 were collected by Cecil Sharp in the same county. At the close of the eighteenth century, the Revd John Brand recorded that Gloucestershire wassailers sang this carol carrying a large bowl decorated with ribbons and garlands (*Observations on the Popular Antiquities of Great Britain*, 1853–5).

White bread (verse 1) was a rich man's delicacy. Cherry and Dobbin are horses; Broad May, Fillpail, and Colly are cattle. Brand's copy left the names blank, to be supplied as required. 'Our master' in verses 2 and 3 is the leader of the wassailers. 'Christmas pie' in verse 3 was a huge game pie; Husk (*Songs of the Nativity*, 1864) gives an old recipe, which begins: 'Take pheasant, hare, and chicken, or capon, of each one; with two partridges, two pigeons, and two conies . . .'. Such pies were still common in Yorkshire in the mid-nineteenth century. Small beer (verse 7) was a watery second brew considered fit only for women, servants, and children.

PERFORMANCE   Voices (*i*) in unison; (*ii*) in three parts.

156

A wassail, a wassail throughout all this town!

(*Christmas; New Year*)

English traditional
(*Lloyd, 1967, arr. editors*)

VERSE

1. A was-sail, a was-sail through-out all this town! Our
2. Our was-sail is made of an__ el-der-berry bough, And

cup it is white__ and our ale it is brown; Our
so, my good neigh-bour, we'll drink un-to thou. Be -

was-sail is made of__ good ale and true, Some
-sides all on earth, you'll have ap-ples in store: Pray

REFRAIN

nut-meg and gin-ger, the best we could brew.__ *Fol the*
let us come in, for it's cold by the door.__ *Fol the*

dol, fol the dol-dy dol, fol the dol-dy dol, fol the dol-dy dee, Fol

dai-rol lol the dad-dy, sing too-ral aye do!

3 We hope that your apple trees prosper and bear,
   So we may have cider when we call next year;
   And where you've one barrel I hope you'll have ten,
   So we can have cider when we call again.

4 There's master and mistress sit down by the fire,
   While we poor wassailers do wait in the mire;
   So you, pretty maid, with your silver-headed pin,
   Please open the door and let us come in.

5 We know by the moon that we are not too soon;
   We know by the sky that we are not too high;
   We know by the stars that we are not too far;
   And we know by the ground that we are within sound.

6 Here's we jolly wassail boys growing weary and cold:
   Drop a bit of silver into our old bowl,
   And, if we're alive for another new year,
   Perhaps we may call and see who do live here.

English traditional
(Lloyd, 1967)

This little-known wassail is printed (a tone higher) in A. L. Lloyd's book *Folk Song in England* (1967). It was recorded from 'grand old Phil Tanner, before he died in a Gower [Wales] workhouse in 1947'. The strongly implied harmonies may reflect a dance or dance-song origin. The words of the refrain are a home-grown equivalent of 'Fa-la-la'.

PERFORMANCE Voices, with the verses solo or unison, perhaps with concertina accompaniment:

‖: Cm B♭ | Cm Gm | Cm | Gm :‖ E♭ B♭ | Cm Gm |

| B♭ Fm | Cm Gm Cm ‖

157

We've been a while a-wandering
(The Yorkshire Wassail Song)

(Christmas; New Year)

English traditional
(Vaughan Williams, 1919, arr. editors)

VERSE

1. We've been   a while   a - wan - der - ing   A - mongst   the leaves   so
2. We   are   not dai - ly   beg - gars   That   beg   from door   to

green,____ (v.4) But   now   we come   a - was - sail - ing,   So   plain - ly   to   be
door,____ But   we   are neigh-bours'   child - ren   Whom   you   have seen   be -

REFRAIN

seen: *For   it's   Christ-mas - time,   When   we   tra - vel   far   and   near,   May God*
- fore:

bless   you,   and   send   you   a   hap - py   new____   year!

3 We've got a little purse
   Made of stretching leather skin;
   We want a little money
   To line it well within:

4 Call up the butler of this house,
   Put on his golden ring;
   Let him bring us up a glass of beer,
   The better we shall sing:

5 So bring us out a table,
    And spread it with a cloth;
    And bring us out a mouldy cheese,[1]
    And then your Christmas loaf:

6 Good master and good mistress,
    While you're sitting by the fire,
    Pray think of us poor children
    That's wandered in the mire:

English traditional
(*Vaughan Williams, 1919*)

[1] blue cheese

From Vaughan Williams's *Eight Traditional English Carols* (1919), which had all been collected during the previous ten years. Vaughan Williams took this one down from a group of singers near Hooton Roberts, Yorkshire, and completed the text 'from another Yorkshire version sung to another tune'—presumably 'Here we come a-wassailing' (159). 'We've been a while a-wandering' may simply be a variant of that carol, which Husk (*Songs of the Nativity*, 1864) believed to be a mid-nineteenth-century conflation by northern wassailers, or one of its older sources: the fact that the wassailers remain outside but expect a table to be brought to them may suggest a source in an intermediate category between the older (in which the callers stay outside) and the newer (in which they expect to be asked in). The tune (like 159:1) is one of the endless variants of the old 'Chestnut' tune to 'God rest you merry, gentlemen' (151:1), most of which are associated with luck visits.

PERFORMANCE   Verse, solo voice or unison voices; refrain, voices in unison or harmony.

158

Wassail, O wassail all over the town!
(The Somerset Wassail)

(Christmas; New Year; Twelfth Night)

English traditional
(Somerset & Dorset Notes and Queries,
arr. editors)

VERSE 1

1. Was - sail,___ O was - sail___ all o - ver the town!
The cup___ it is white and the ale___ it is brown;

(4)

The cup___ it is made of the good___ ash - en tree, And___

9

so___ is the ale of the best___ bar - ley.

(12) **REFRAIN**

For it's your was - sail, and it's our___ was - sail, And I'm

17

jol - ly, come to our___ jol - ly was - sail!

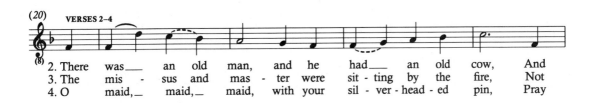

2. There was___ an old man, and he had___ an old cow, And
3. The mis - sus and mas - ter were sit - ting by the fire, Not
4. O maid,___ maid,___ maid, with your sil - ver - head - ed pin, Pray

how___ for to keep him he could___ not tell how. He
think - ing we poor tra - vellers were tra - velling in the mire; Come
o - pen the door and___ let___ us all in, And

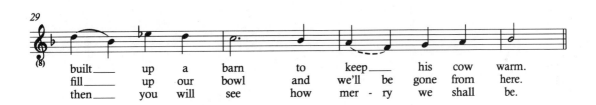

built___ up a barn to keep___ his cow warm.
fill___ up our bowl and we'll be gone from here.
then___ you will see how mer - ry we shall be.

(v.2) For no harm, boys, harm, no___ harm, boys,___
(vv.3, 4) For it's your was - sail, and it's our was -

harm, And a cup___ of good li - quor will do___ us no harm.
- sail, And I'm jol - ly, come to our___ jol - ly was - sail!

Wassailers in Drayton, Somerset, sing this song as they make their luck visits to the larger houses in the village on Twelfth Night (5 January) each year. BBC Television filmed them in 1977, and the ritual was described by G. R. Willey in an article in *Somerset & Dorset Notes and Queries*:

At the conclusion [of the song] the leader moves forward a pace or two and gives the toast 'God bless Missus and Master and all the family. Wishing you a merry Christmas and a bright and prosperous New Year; and many of 'em'—which is given a generous mutter of assent from the remainder. The host bids everyone welcome and a donation [nowadays to a village charity] and/or an invitation to step inside 'for a glass of something' is gratefully accepted. Inside, gossip, banter and perhaps a song or recitation are exchanged over refreshments. A lusty refrain of 'For they are jolly good people' (to the tune of 'For He's a Jolly Good Fellow') followed by additional seasonal greetings and then on to the next venue.

Willey gives the 1977 version of the text and melody, and compares them with the song as transcribed by Cecil Sharp

in September 1903 from the singing of a Miss Quick in the Drayton vicarage. We follow Sharp's transcription, from his notebooks in the library of Clare College, Cambridge. The later version has a smoothed-out melody and changes in the text; verses 3 and 4 are there reversed, and verse 5 has lost a line—not unusual, given an entirely oral tradition. What is surprising, however, is the thorough revision to which Sharp subjected the song before publishing it in Series V of his *Folk Songs from Somerset* (1909). He suppressed verse 5, substituting his own version of the famous 'girt dog' verse from the 'Langport Wassail Song', and he expanded the three-line verses to four lines, partly by analogy with the 'Curry Rivel Wassail Song', which he considered 'normal and trustworthy' in contrast to the 'corrupt' Drayton and Langport songs: altogether the kind of tidying-up process to which he was bitterly opposed.

The Drayton wassailers do not sing in harmony, and our lower parts are entirely optional.

PERFORMANCE   Voice(s), with refrain in unison or harmony.

159

Here we come a-wassailing
(Wassail Song)

(Christmas; New Year)

I

English traditional
(Oxford Book of Carols, 1928,
arr. editors)

VERSE

1. Here we come a-was-sail-ing A-mong the leaves so green;___ ⁊ Here we come a-wan-der-ing, So fair___ to be seen. *(v.4)*

2. Our was-sail cup is made___ Of the rose-ma-ry tree,___ And so___ is your beer___ Of the best___ bar-ley.

REFRAIN

Love and joy___ come_ to you, And to you your was-sail too, And God bless you, and send you a hap-py new year!___

543

II

(*Christmas; New Year*)

English traditional
(Bramley and Stainer, 1871, arr. editors)

VERSE

1. Here we come a - was - sail - ing A - mong the leaves so
2. Our was - sail cup is made___ Of the rose - ma - ry

green;___ Here we come a - wan - der - ing, So fair___ to be
tree,___ And so___ is your beer___ Of the best___ bar -

REFRAIN

seen. Love and joy come to you, And to you your was - sail
-ley.

too, And God bless you, and send___ you a hap - py new

year, And God send you a hap - py new year.

3   We are not daily beggars
    That beg from door to door,
  But we are neighbours' children
    Whom you have seen before.

4   Call up the butler of this house,
    Put on his golden ring;
  Let him bring us up a glass of beer,
    And better we shall sing.

5   We have got a little purse
    Of stretching leather skin;
  We want a little of your money
    To line it well within.

6   Bring us out a table,
    And spread it with a cloth;
  Bring us out some mouldy cheese,[1]
    And some of your Christmas loaf.

7   God bless the master of this house,
    Likewise the mistress too,
  And all the little children
    That round the table go.

8   Good master and good mistress,
    While you're sitting by the fire,
  Pray think of us poor children
    Who are wandering in the mire.

English traditional
(Husk, 1864)

---

[1] blue cheese

The text is from Husk (*Songs of the Nativity*, 1864), whose sources included a Manchester chap-book and a broadside printed in Bradford, Yorkshire, *c*.1850. He could find no older occurrence, and believed that the carol was a recent conflation by northern wassailers.

Tune II, from Bramley and Stainer (*Christmas Carols, New and Old*, 1871), was also from Yorkshire. Tune I (*The Oxford Book of Carols*, 1928) was taught to Martin Shaw by his father, who had often heard it sung in the streets of Leeds in the 1850s. It was still widely sung in the West Riding of Yorkshire more than sixty years later. (A very similar version, with identical verse and a longer, more adventurous refrain, was taken down by F. Kidson in Leeds and published in the *Journal of the Folk-Song Society*, vol. 5, p. 211. He estimated that it dated from 1860 or earlier.) The first eight bars are a variant of the 'London' tune to 'God rest you merry, gentlemen' (151:I), and the refrain is reminiscent of 'Brigg Fair', which is part of another great family of tunes (see A. L. Lloyd, *Folk Song in England*, 1967, pp. 79–83). 'We've been a while a-wandering' (157) may be a variant of the present wassail, or, if Husk is right, an older wassail that was one of its sources.

PERFORMANCE   I and II, voice(s), with refrain in unison or harmony.

160

The darkest midnight in December

I

(*Christmas Night*)

Irish traditional
(*Ó Muirithe, 1982*)

1. The darkest midnight in December, No snow nor hail nor winter's storm Shall hinder us for to remember The Babe that on this night was born. With shepherds we are come to see This lovely Infant's glorious charms; Born

2. No costly gifts can we present him, No gold nor myrrh nor o-dours sweet; But if with hearts we can content him, We humbly lay them at his feet. 'Twas but pure love that from above Brought him to save us from all harms; Then

of a____ maid,__ as pro - phets__ said, __ The__
let us____ sing__ and wel - come__ him, __ The__

God of_____ Love_____ in Ma - ry's arms.__
God of_____ Love_____ in Ma - ry's arms.__

3 Four thousand years from the Creation
   The world lay groaning under sin;
None could ever expect salvation:
   No one could ever enter heaven.
'Adam's fall had damned us all
   To hell, to endless pains forlorn;
'Twas so decreed we had ne'er been freed
   Had not this heavenly Babe been born.

*4 Have you not heard of the sacred story,
   How man was made those seats to fill
Which the fallen angels lost in glory
   By their presumption, pride and will?
They thought us mean for to obtain
   Such glorious seats and crowns in heaven:
So, through a cheat, got Eve to eat
   The fruit, to be revenged on man.

*5 If by a woman we were wounded,
   Another woman brings the cure;
If by a fruit we were confounded,
   A tree our safety would procure.
They laughed at man; but, if they can,
   Let Satan with his hellish swarms
Refuse to kneel and honour yield
   To the lovely Babe in Mary's arms.

6 Ye blessèd angels! join your voices,
   Let your guilded wings beat fluttering o'er,
Whilst every soul set free rejoices,
   And every devil must adore.
We'll sing and pray he always may
   Our Church and clergymen defend;
God grant us peace in all our days,
   A merry Christmas, and a happy end.

Irish traditional
(after Fr. William Devereux, fl. 1728)

II

English traditional
(Sharp, 1911, arr. editors)

(Christmas Night)

1. The dark - est___ mid - night___ in De - cem - ber, No snow nor___ hail nor win - ter's___ storm Shall hin - der___ us for to___ re - mem - ber The Babe___ that on___ this___ night was___ born.

(vv. 1,2,4)

2   Four thousand years from the Creation
    The world lay groaning under sin;
  No one could ever expect salvation:
    No one could ever enter heaven.

3   'Adam's fall had damned us all
    To hell, to endless pains forlorn;
  'Twas so decreed we'd ne'er been freed
    Had not this heavenly Babe been born.

4   'We like beasts lay in a stable,
    Senseless, blind, and dead by sin;
  To help ourselves we were not able,
    But he brings grace and life again.

5   'Twas but pure love that from above
    Brought him to save us from all harms:
  Then let us sing and welcome him,
    The God of Love in Mary's arms!

Irish traditional
(after Fr. William Devereux, fl. 1728)

The text, like 'Ye sons of men' (161), derives from Fr. William Devereux's 'A New Garland', a manuscript collection compiled in 1728 in imitation of Bishop Luke Wadding's *A Smale Garland* (1684; see notes, 139); the poem is probably by Fr. Devereux himself, and was perhaps meant to be sung before midnight mass. The original is lost, but the collection survives in the many manuscript copies of 'Fr. Devereux's Garland' made over the years by County Wexford singers. Eleven verses are printed in *The Wexford Carols*, ed. Diarmaid Ó Muirithe (1982), taken from 'Michael Murphy's MS', an 1803 copy of Devereux used by the carol-singers of Kilmore Parish Church, County Wexford, where an old local performance tradition survives. We give verse 1 as sung by Jack Devereux, leader of the Kilmore singers, who still perform this carol.

Tune I is as printed in *The Wexford Carols*, transcribed by Seóirse Bodley from a 1980 recording of the seventy-year-old Jack Devereux. The ornamentation is less daunting than it looks:

and ⬛ are grace-notes. ⬛ indicates an indefinite (sliding) approach to the melody note. The general tempo is very slow indeed (♪ = 72 is typical), and the ornaments and grace-notes are sung 'at a sufficiently slow pace to make them clear and unhurried in execution' (*The Wexford Carols*), rubato being used to accommodate the more complex figures.

The tune of setting II is adapted from the tune of 'This is the truth sent from above' collected by Cecil Sharp (150:II). The four-line stanzas have been selected and rearranged from Fr. Devereux's carol, with small adjustments.

PERFORMANCE   I (*i*) solo voice; (*ii*) two groups of three men, taking alternate verses (at any suitable pitch).
  II, choir

161

Ye sons of men, with me rejoice

I

(Christmas; Epiphany)

Irish traditional
(Ó Muirithe, 1982)

1. Ye_____ sons of men, with__ me re - joice, And____
2. Who_____ from his might - y__ throne a - bove Came__

praise__ the hea - vens with heart and voice! For joy - ful ti - dings_____
down__ to mag - ni - fy his love To all such as would_____

you we__ bring Of this heaven - ly Babe,__ the new - born King.
him em - brace And__ would be born__ a - gain__ in grace.

II

Irish traditional
(Ó Muirithe, 1982,
adapted and arr. editors)

1. Ye__ sons of men,_____ with__ me re - joice, And
2. Who__ from his might - y__ throne a - bove Came

praise_ the hea - vens with heart and voice! For joy - ful ti - dings
down_ to mag - ni - fy his love To all such as would

you we bring Of this heaven - ly Babe,_ the new - born King.
him em - brace And_ would_ be born_ a - gain_ in grace.

3 The mystery for to unfold:
   When the King of kings he did behold
   The poor unhappy state of man,
   He sent his dear belovèd Son.

4 The night of his nativity
   The people in the heavens did see
   Strange wonders which did them surprise,
   But none the reason could premise.

5 As earth with a new Son is blessed,
   So heaven with a new star is dressed.
   The shepherds warned by an angel were
   To Bethlehem straight to repair.

6 Within a manger there he lay;
   His dress was neither rich nor gay.
   In him you truly there might see
   A pattern of humility.

7   Three eastern kings came forth to see
    This heavenly Babe come from on high,
    Directed by a glorious star
    Which they espièd from afar.

8   Their gifts of gold and precious things
    They laid before the King of kings,
    Their homage paid with humble heart,
    And joyfully they did depart.

9   Let each good Christian, great and small,
    Repair unto the ox's stall.
    From these three kings example take:
    To this sweet Babe your offering make.

10 Give him your heart the first of all,
    Free from all malice, wrath and gall;
    And, now he's on his throne on high,
    He will crown you eternally.

Irish traditional
(*after Fr. William Devereux, fl. 1728*)

Like 'The darkest midnight in December' (160), the text may derive from Fr. William Devereux's 'A New Garland' (1728). The full twenty-seven verses are printed in *The Wexford Carols*, ed. Diarmaid Ó Muirithe (1982), all but the last from 'Michael Murphy's MS' (see notes, 160). The final verse is from another carol-book with the same derivation. This carol is far too rough to have been written by Devereux himself, and must be traditional.

Tune I is as printed in *The Wexford Carols*, transcribed by Seóirse Bodley from a 1980 recording of Jack Devereux, the seventy-year-old leader of the Kilmore singers. Notation:

see notes, 160. The melody has survived only through the devotion of the Devereux family, who have passed it on from singer to singer since the carol was last performed at Kilmore in 1850, when Jack Devereux's grandfather sang in the choir for the first time. The carol used to be sung before the priest came to the altar for the main mass of Christmas Day.

PERFORMANCE I (*i*) solo voice; (*ii*) two groups of three men, taking alternate verses (at any suitable pitch).
    II, choir.

162

Good people all, this Christmastime

(*Christmas*)

Irish traditional
(*Oxford Book of Carols, 1928,*
arr. editors)

1. Good peo - ple_ all,_____ this_ Christ-mas - time,___ Con - si - der well___ and

bear in mind What_ our good God___ for us has done___ In

send - ing his___ be - lo - ved Son. With Ma - ry ho - ly

we should pray To God, with love,＿ this Christ-mas Day: In

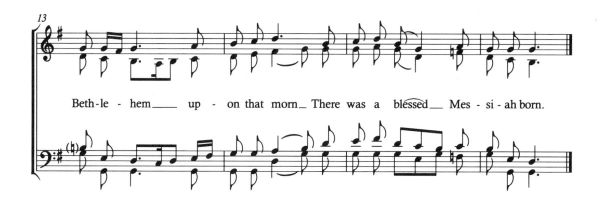

Beth-le - hem＿＿ up - on that morn＿ There was a blessed＿ Mes - si - ah born.

2   The night before the happy tide
     The noble Virgin and her guide
     Were a long time seeking up and down
     To find a lodging in the town.
     But hark how all things come to pass:
     From every door repelled, alas!
     As long foretold, their refuge all
     Was but an humble ox's stall.

3 Near Bethlehem did shepherds keep
   Their flocks of lambs and feeding sheep;
   To whom God's angels did appear,
   Which put the shepherds in great fear.
   'Prepare and go', the angels said,
   'To Bethlehem; be not afraid,
   For there you'll find, this happy morn,
   A princely Babe, sweet Jesus, born.'

*5 There were three wise men from afar,
    Directed by a glorious star,
    Came boldly on and made no stay
    Until they came where Jesus lay.
    And when they came unto that place,
    And looked with love on Jesus' face,
    In faith they humbly knelt to greet,
    With gifts of gold and incense sweet.

4 With thankful heart and joyful mind
   The shepherds went the Babe to find,
   And, as God's angels had foretold,
   They did our Saviour, Christ, behold.
   Within a manger he was laid,
   And by his side the Virgin Maid
   Attending on the Lord of Life,
   Who came on earth to end all strife.

6 Come, let us then our tribute pay
   To our good God, as well we may,
   For all his grace and mercy shown
   Through his Son to us, till then unknown;
   And when through life we wend our way
   'Mid trials and sufferings, day by day,
   In faith and hope, whate'er befall,
   We'll wait in peace his holy call.

Irish traditional
(Ó Muirithe, 1982)

The text is from *The Wexford Carols*, ed. Diarmaid Ó Muirithe (1982; see notes, 160). It is there called 'The Enniscorthy Christmas Carol', as it is taken from a modern broadside published by the County Wexford Museum in Enniscorthy, which gives the text as sung *c.*1912 by a Fr. Patrick Cummins; he had learned the words and tune from his mother, who in turn had been taught them by hers. Dr W. H. Grattan Flood (1859–1928) lived in Enniscorthy from 1895 until his death, and independently took down words and tune from a local singer; after revising the text, he sent the carol to the editors of *The Oxford Book of Carols*, who printed it as the 'Wexford Carol' (the only major differences are in verse 5; verse 6 appears in the broadside only).

The text is nevertheless English in origin: Vaughan Williams took the first verse from a Mr Hall, of Castleton, Derbyshire, and the first four-and-a-half verses are also in Shawcross's *Old Castleton Christmas Carols* (1904). Stanzas 1–5 in fact derive from the ballad beginning 'All you that are to mirth inclin'd' (see notes, 140). The final stanza is new,

and was perhaps written by an Irish poet: granted the Wexford provenance and the manner of the final stanza, it is not inconceivable that Fr. Devereux, author of 160 and 161, wrote it for his own adaptation of the English ballad, which has survived through oral transmission. (We suggest a similar provenance for 163.)

Grattan Flood's tune is in a traditional Irish style, though his transcription does not include ornaments. (Jack Devereux, the source of the melodies in *The Wexford Carols*, sang these words to the same tune as 'Ye sons of men', 161).

PERFORMANCE (*i*) (Melody only, at any suitable pitch) two groups of three men, taking alternate verses, with ornaments in the style of 'The darkest midnight in December' (160) and 'Ye sons of men' (161). (Although this carol is not now sung in Kilmore Parish Church, where this tradition of carol-singing survives, it may at one time have been sung there or in other Wexford churches observing the same custom.) (*ii*) Choir.

163

Christmas Day is come!

(Christmas)

Irish traditional
(Oxford Book of Carols, 1928,
arr. editors)

1. Christ-mas Day is come! let's all pre - pare for mirth, Which
Through both the joy - ous an - gels in strife[1] and hur - ry fly; With

fills the earth and hea - ven at this a - ma - zing birth.
Glo - ries and Ho - san - nas 'Ho - ly, ho - ly!' they cry.

The

In heaven the Church Tri - um - phant a - dores with all her choirs:

Mi - li - tant on earth with

The Mi - li - tant on earth with hum - ble faith ad - mires.

[1] 'The act of striving; strong effort' (*OED*)

556

2 But how can we rejoice? Should we not rather mourn
   To see the Hope of Nations thus in a stable born?
   Where is his crown and sceptre? Where is his throne sublime?
   Where is his train majestic that should the stars outshine?
   Is there no sumptuous palace, nor any inn at all
 † To lodge his heavenly mother, but in a filthy stall?

3 Why does he thus demean or thus himself disguise?
   Perhaps he would conceal him from cruel enemies.
   He trusts but two dumb beasts a-feeding on their hay;
   He steals to us at midnight, that none should him betray;
   And his supposèd father a carpenter must be,
   That none should yet discover the sacred mystery.

*4 Yet hath he no intention to shun his fate decreed;
   His death must be the ransom by which mankind is freed,
   With a long course of suffering for thirty years and three
   Which must be all completed upon Mount Calvary;
   For these he now preserves him, contented to begin
   In poverty and misery to pay for all our sin.

5 O cease, ye blessèd angels, such clamorous joys to make!
   The midnight favours silence: the shepherds are awake.
   And you, O glorious star, that with new splendour brings
   From earth's remotest corners the learnèd eastern kings,
   Turn some way else your lustre, your rays elsewhere display:
   Herod will[2] slay the Babe, and Christ must straight away.

6 Alas! to teeming Nature we offer rules in vain
   Which, big with such a prodigy, cannot itself contain,
   The rocks were split asunder to grieve our Saviour's death,
   And at his resurrection the dead sprung from the earth:
   Then can we now expect that at his joyful birth
   His creatures should conceal their triumph and their mirth?

---

² intends to
† Superscript notation for lower voice: ♩ ♪ ; verses 3, 4, and 8 likewise.

*7 Then let our joys abound now all his grief is o'er,
We celebrate his victory: his suffering we deplore.
Though 'twas in toil and slavery, his getting[3] was for us:
Be welcome, then, thrice welcome, divine Saviour Jesus!
Your Christmas is in glory: your torments all are passed:
Whate'er betide us now, grant us the same at last!

8 If we would then rejoice, let's cancel the old score,
And, purposing amendment, resolve to sin no more;
For mirth can ne'er content us without a conscience clear,
And thus we'll find true pleasure in all the usual cheer:
In dancing, sporting, revelling with masquerade and drum;
So be our Christmas merry, as Christians doth become.[4]

Fr. William Devereux? (fl. 1728)

[3] begetting   [4] as is becoming for Christians

The Irish musicologist Dr W. H. Grattan Flood sent the tune and verses 1, 5, 2, and 8 to Ralph Dunstan, who published them in his *Second Book of Christmas Carols* (1925). He also sent them to the editors of *The Oxford Book of Carols* (1928), and the carol has become fairly well known in Martin Shaw's campanological arrangement, despite the incoherence of the text. Flood presumably collected the carol from a folk singer in County Wexford (see notes, 162), and the Oxford editors attributed the text to the Franciscan scholar Bishop Luke Wadding (d. 1686), some of whose carols, published in *A Smale Garland* (1684), are still sung in that county (see notes, 139). But the present carol is clearly from the eighteenth century, and survives with others by Fr. William Devereux in the manuscript song-books of County Wexford that preserve his lost manuscript 'New Garland' (see notes, 160). Grattan Flood's four verses are consider-

ably less corrupt than the eight which are transcribed (without tune) from 'Michael Murphy's manuscript' in Diarmaid Ó Muirithe and Seoirse Bodley's *The Wexford Carols* (1982), but the latter show every sign of being the complete poem and in the correct order. We have therefore taken them as our basic text, but have amended verses 1, 2, 5, and 8 (mainly from Flood), and the remaining stanzas as necessary. The only major changes are: verse 4, line 1 (originally 'Yet does he not intend'); verse 4, line 5 ('For those he now reserves himself'); verse 6, line 2 ('When big of such a prodigy it can't itself contain'); and verse 7, lines 3 and 4 ('This was the toil and slavery that getting was for us, / Your welcome trice welcome divine Saviour Jesus').

PERFORMANCE (*i*) Solo voice; (*ii*) two solo voices; (*iii*) choir in two or (with octave doubling) four parts.

164

Oer yw'r gŵr sy'n methu caru
Soon the hoar old year will leave us
Deck the hall with boughs of holly
(Nos Galan)

I

(New Year's Eve)

Welsh traditional
(arr. Edward Jones, 1752–1824, adapted)

II

(New Year's Eve)

Welsh traditional
(Jones, 1784, arr. editors)

1. Oer yw'r gŵr sy'n me-thu ca-ru
1. Soon the hoar old year will leave us,
Fal, la, la, la, la, ———— la, la, la!

Hen fy-ny-ddoedd an-nwyl Cym-ru,
But the part-ing must not grieve us:
Fal, la, la, la, la, ———— la, la, la!

I-ddo ef a'u câr gyn-hes-af,
When the new year comes to-mor-row
Dad-le-a, dad-le-a, ———— la, la, la!

Gwyl-iau lla-wen flwy-ddyn nes-af,
Let him find no trace of sor-row,
Fal, la, la, la, la, ———— la, la, la!

2 I'r helbulus oer yw'r biliau,
  Sydd yn dyfod yn y gwyliau,
  Gwrando bregeth mewn un pennill,
  Byth na waria fwy na'th ennill.

3 Oer yw'r eira ar Eryri,
  Er fod gwrthban gwlanen arni,
  Oer yw'r bobol na ofalan',
  Gwrdd a'u gilydd, ar Nos Galan!

Welsh traditional

2 He our pleasures may redouble;
  He may bring us store of trouble;
  Hope the best and gaily meet him:
  With a jovial chorus greet him!

3 At his birth he brings us gladness:
  Ponder not on future sadness.
  Anxious care is now but folly:
  Fill the mead-cup, hang the holly!

tr. John Oxenford

III

(*New Year*)

1 Deck the hall with boughs of holly:
  'Tis the season to be jolly!
  Fill the mead cup, drain the barrel,
  Troll the ancient Christmas carol.

2 See the flowing bowl before us!
  Strike the harp and join the chorus!
  Follow me in merry measure,
  While I sing of beauty's treasure.

3 Fast away the old year passes,
  Hail the new, ye lads and lasses!
  Laughing, quaffing, all together,
  Heedless of the wind and weather.

Anon.

'Nos Galan' ('New Year's Eve'), as this dance-carol is known, originally had nothing to do with the festive season. It appears in the two editions of *Musical and Poetical Relicks of the Welsh Bards* . . . (London, 1784, 1794) by the harpist Edward Jones.

Jones played a leading part in London's professional musical life, and he also had a strong interest in the traditional music of his native Wales, which he did much to revive and encourage through the *eisteddfod* and other competitions, often supplying the prizes for harp-playing himself. Among his many publications are some specifically aimed at recording and popularizing Welsh folk music:

the *Relicks* (the second edition a considerable expansion of the first), *The Bardic Museum* (1802, published as the second volume of the *Relicks*), and *Hên Ganiadau Cymru: Cambro-British Melodies* . . . (1820, published as the third volume of the *Relicks*). He collected and preserved more than 200 melodies in these volumes, many of them from old people: 'It is very fortunate that I did so, because most of them are since dead' (*The Bardic Museum*). He regretted the decline in Welsh folk music in the later eighteenth century, attributing it to the influence of Methodism and other Nonconformist sects.

'Nos Galan' appeared in slightly different form in the two

editions of the *Relicks*, in each case as the theme of a set of harp variations, but with text supplied for vocal performance. Although Jones heads the song 'Nos Galan', he gives the text of a love-song, one of the many texts to which the melody was sung before it became specifically attached to New Year festivities. (The metre, trochaic tetrameters, is by far the most common in Welsh folk-song, and vast numbers of songs could have been sung to it.) 'Deck the hall' appeared, apparently from nowhere, in *The Franklin Square Song Collection*, selected by J. P. McCaskey, in 1881. It has little to do with the original song, but obstinately remains popular.

The tune belongs to the competitive *canu penillion* tradition, in which merrymakers would dance in a ring around the harpist. The verses (extemporized or remembered) would be thrown in by the dancers in turn, those who failed to produce something new falling out; and the 'answering' bars (3–4, etc.) were played by harp alone.

The steps of the dance to which 'Nos Galan' was performed are not known, but Jones's carefully indicated accents at the end of each phrase suggest a clapping/stamping element. The 'fal, la, la's' seem to have begun as substitutes when no harp was present. The last steps of the process can be seen in the two editions of the *Relicks*: 1784

has 'Fal, la, la . . .' for strains 1, 2, and 4 but 'Sym[phony]' for 3, whereas 1794 inserts 'Dadlea . . .' for strain 3. We have adapted the two settings to provide one for choir and one for voice and instrument: I is based on Jones's 1794 version, II on his 1784 one.

Nonsense syllables, misrepresented by one writer as incantations, eventually became a feature of Welsh folk-song, no longer being introduced as substitutes for the harpist but instead as a type of refrain. (See Phyllis Kinney, 'Vocal and instrumental interaction in earlier *Canu penillion'* in *Canu Gwerin: Journal of the Welsh Folk-Song Society*, no. 7, 1984.)

There is an arrangement by Haydn (or one of his pupils), to a newly written New Year text, for voice and piano with violin and cello *ad lib.* (Hob. xxxib:29).

PERFORMANCE   I, solo voice and harp (preferably not the modern concert instrument).

II, choir. The solo sections should be sung by a succession of voices, as in *canu penillion*.

There is a concise introduction to the pronunciation of Welsh in the appendix to Alan Luff, *Welsh Hymns and their tunes*, 1990.

165

O deued pob Cristion
Come all Christians, singing

(Christmas)

Welsh traditional
(arr. editors)

1. O__ deu - ed pob__ Crist - ion i Feth - lem yr__ awr - on, I__
1. Come all Christ - ians,_ sing - ing, our glad prai - ses_ bring - ing, In_

we - led_ mor_ dir - ion yw'n Duw; O__ ddyfn - der rhy - fedd - od! fe
thanks for_ the_ gift of God's love; With hearts full of_ yearn - ing, to

dref - nodd y__ Duw - dod Dra - gwydd - ol__ gy - fam - od i fyw! Daeth
Beth - le - hem_ turn - ing, We_ wor - ship_ with_ an - gels a - bove. The

Bren - in yr holl - fyd i oed - fa ein had - fyd Er sym - ud ein
Lord of Cre - a - tion sends down to each na - tion Sal - va - tion from

pen - yd a'n pwn; Heb le yn y llet - y, heb ae - lwyd, heb
sor - row and sin In Je - sus all ho - ly, now cra - dled so

we - ly, Na - do - lig fel hy - nny gadd hwn! Rhown glod i'r Mab
low - ly, For God found no room at the inn. Kneel down to the

by - chan, ar lin - iau Mair wiw - lan— Daeth Duw - dod mewn
Child there, and Ma - ry so mild there, For God - head by

Ba - ban i'r byd! Ei___ ras, O der - byn - iwn; ei haedd-iant cy -
this___ Babe is borne; So___ e - vil for - sa - king and grace hum - bly___

- hoedd - wn, A___ thros - to___ ef___ gweith - iwn i gyd.
ta - king Pro - claim we___ our___ Sa - viour this morn.

2　Tywysog tangnefedd wna'n daear o'r diwedd
　　　Yn aelwyd gyfannedd i fyw;
　Ni fegir cenfigen na chynnwrf na chynnen,
　　　Dan goron bydd diben ein Duw.
　Yn frodyr i'n gilydd, drigolion y gwledydd,
　　　Cawn rodio yn hafddydd y nef;
　Ein disgwyl yn Salem, i ganu yr anthem,
　　　Ddechreuwyd ym Methl'em, mae ef.
　Rhown glod i'r Mab bychan, ar liniau Mair wiwlan—
　　　Daeth Duwdod mewn Baban i'r byd!
　Ei ras, O derbyniwn! ei haeddiant cyhoeddwn,
　　　A throsto ef gweithiwn i gyd.

Welsh traditional
(*Llyfr Emynau a Thonau, 1927*)

2 All poor men and humble, all lame men who stumble,

    Come, haste ye, nor feel ye afraid,

For Jesus, our treasure, with love past all measure,

    In lowly poor manger was laid.

Though wise men who found him laid rich gifts around him,

    Yet oxen, they gave him their hay;

And Jesus in beauty accepted their duty:

    Contented in manger he lay.

Then haste we to show him the praises we owe him:

    Our service he ne'er can despise

Whose love still is able to show us that stable

    Where softly in manger he lies.

v. 1 tr. A. G. Prys-Jones, adapted
v. 2 K. E. Roberts (1877–1962)

The melody is one of an extended family of tunes generated by the English national anthem, first published in 1744 as 'God save our Lord the King'. The Welsh poets often took existing tunes and adapted them for their poetry, extending the melodic lines so as to give due weight to the internal assonance and rhyme that are an important feature of their art, and expanding the tunes overall to accommodate the generally larger stanza forms of Welsh poetry. Sometimes an imaginary ancient Celtic provenance was provided for foreign tunes taken over in this way, but in the present case the origin is proudly acknowledged, and already in the second half of the eighteenth century the generic title 'Duw Gadwo'r Brenin' ('God Save the King') is applied. The earliest known manuscript source of one of these tunes dates from *c.*1820, and gives the title 'Duw Gadwo'r Brenin Yr hen ffordd' ('God Save the King the old way'). Related versions in other manuscripts are called 'God Save the King the old Welsh way' or '. . . the old style'.

Some of the tunes are in the minor, some in the major, but all have been transcribed in triple time except 'O deued pob Cristion', and this can be attributed to the circumstances of its collection. Mrs Ruth (later Lady Herbert) Lewis, one of the pioneering figures in the early days of the Welsh Folk-Song Society, obtained it with the aid of a cylinder recorder in Caerwys, Flintshire (now Clwyd), in 1910, noting that 'several Caerwys people remember their fathers singing this carol'. Mrs Lewis was not musically trained, and employed young musicians to make the transcriptions, rejecting what she believed to be inac-

curacies. She herself explained the curious, limping rhythm of this carol as transcribed, and as it has become widely known (♩ |♩♩ ♫|♩♩ ♩|♩♩ ♩|♩♩ , etc.), by reference to the 'tendency among old singers to divide the lines into short phrases, prolonging the end note of each phrase [so as to emphasize the internal assonance] and giving the effect of syncopation'. She insisted on giving a 4/4 transcription, misrepresenting a subtle and varied lengthening of the assonant syllables as a duple-time straightjacket which consistently mis-stresses the text.

An English version harmonized by Canon Caradog Roberts, entitled 'Poverty', became well known from its inclusion in *The Oxford Book of Carols* (1928). Mrs Roberts's verse (our verse 2) is not a translation of the Welsh, but it has charm. The transcription of the Welsh text by Mrs Lewis, a non-Welsh speaker, is unreliable, so we give two of the traditional verses as printed in the standard Welsh Methodist hymnbook, *Llyfr Emynau a Thonau* (1927).

The carol would most often have been sung by three men in the *plygain* tradition (see notes, 166) or by a single voice, with or without harp accompaniment. Since no versions with bass survive, we provide a simple eighteenth-century-style harmonization in the spirit of the melody- and-bass format found in the several collections of Welsh carols published in England at that period.

PERFORMANCE Choir. Male-voice choirs should transfer the melody to the lower octave in the usual way.

166

Wel, dyma'r borau gorau i gyd

(*Christmas; Christmas Day*)

Welsh traditional
(*from the singing of Parti Fronheulog*)

1. Wel, dy-ma'r bo-rau go-rau i gyd_ Y rhoed_ i'r byd_ wy-bod-aeth, O e-ni'r gwa-raidd Ie-su gwynn I'n dwyn_ o'n syn_ gam-syn-iaeth. Fe ddaeth ein Bre-nin mawr a'n Brawd Dan wisg_ o gnawd ge-ned-ig; Rhy-fedd-ol gwe-led Mab_ Duw Nêr_ Ar fron-nau pêr_ For-wyn-ig.

2. Ag-or-wyd ffordd_ i'r ne-fol wlad_ Drwy'r me-ddyg rhad_ ca-re-dig; Hyn y-dyw'r gŵr_ sy'n ma-ddau bai_ Iach-aw-dwr rhai sych-ed-ig. Y sawl_ sy'n byw_ drwy Dduw a'i ddawn Wrth re-ol iawn_ ath-raw-iaeth, O fewn_ i hwn_ mae ys-bryd briw_ A delw_ Duw'n dyst-ti-ol-aeth.

v. 1 Dafydd Ddu Eryri (1759–1822)
v. 2 anon.

TRANSLATION 1 Behold! the best of mornings is here, on which the world was enlightened through the birth of gentle, loving Jesus, releasing us from our terrible error. Our great King and Brother came to us clothed in mortal flesh: it was glorious to see the Son of the Lord God at the breast of the blessed Virgin. This was an eternal wonder. O may the Comforter [the Holy Spirit] give wings to each talent that it may sing of joy and gladness! An ancient *aubade* is not pleasure enough for the believing soul, but [beholding] the blessed face of Jesus [is].

2 Freely given love, poured out upon mankind by redeeming grace, flowing from the very heart of God, ordained that through the blessed Trinity a blood-sacrifice should be offered and that a Great One should die to save the wretched of the earth from the dust; and when, through the enticement of a serpent, the Law was broken in the great and beautiful land of Eden, we wretches fell like a leaf into the clutches of death. Though for our sin we were brought down to desolation, yet is there come a Saviour who will raise us from our lowliness: a gentle Lamb, he saves mankind.

Plygain (literally 'matins') singing is a thriving Welsh tradition, particularly in the fertile Tanad Valley which runs from central Wales towards Shrewsbury. It is a technique of mainly three-man carol-singing that has its roots in the seventeenth century. It was largely improvisatory until the later nineteenth century, when clerical reaction against the old ballad tunes and verse forms led to the new type of composed and hymn-like settings which now, sadly, dominate the repertories of *plygain* groups. Parti Fronheulog, the trio of brothers from near Llangedwyn whose recorded performance is transcribed here, is one of a handful of groups who are conscious inheritors of an improvisatory tradition.

The texts have overriding importance: serious, scripture-based, and usually attributed, these are 'literary' productions that eschew the fantasy of the conventional folk carol. Before the nineteenth-century reforms, they were cast in a form that uniquely fused an intricate medieval alliterative technique with rhymed, free-metre verse, attuned to the cadences of the melodies for which they were written, so that what can seem excessively formal verse on paper springs to life when sung.

The first stanza is from a nine-stanza *canu plygain* of the old type, by the Caernarvonshire poet Dafydd Ddu Eryri (David Thomas), printed in his *Corph y Gaingc* (1810) and in many subsequent collections. The second verse is of unknown authorship.

The melody of the present carol, 'Ffarwel Ned Puw' ('Ned Puw's Farewell'), is one of the oldest of the surviving tunes. It takes its name from a legendary musician who is lost for ever within hillside caves and whose last tune—this one—can sometimes be heard emerging from potholes and crevices in the ground. The opening mirrors the tunes of two West Country carols, 'Tomorrow shall be my dancing day' (132) and 'Rejoice and be merry' (136), but this may simply have been a standard opening device. From the period 1550–1750 and onward, enormous numbers of ballads and carols have been written for this melody. (Performances were frequently monophonic, and it is thought that there was once a tradition analogous to that in County Wexford, in which two small unison groups sang alternate verses; see carols 160–2.)

The recording was made at one of the *plygain* services, which used to begin at anything between 3 and 6 a.m. on Christmas Morning. In some country places the night would be passed in making toffee and decorating the house, and sometimes dancing to the harp in people's homes would precede the service; elsewhere, mainly in towns, there would be festivity in the streets which would culminate in a torchlight procession leading the clergyman from his house to the church. There would be great quantities of candles, often of coloured wax, evidently symbolizing the coming of light to the world at Christ's nativity. The tradition seems to have arisen after the Reformation, as a substitute for the greatly revered midnight and dawn masses of Catholicism. There are strong links with the Manx midnight festival of *Oiel Verrey*, and with the old *Christnacht* services of German Lutheranism.

The service is an abbreviated form of the usual Anglican or Nonconformist morning service, interspersed with and followed by the singing of carols, some of them of enormous length. The service over, the *plygain* singing begins in earnest, with group after group stepping forward, without introduction or interruption, to sing a carol. It is a requirement not to sing a carol that has already been rendered by another group. Those unable to fulfil the requirements drop out, so that a winning group eventually emerges, whereupon a concerted carol and a special *plygain* breakfast follow. With the restoration of the midnight eucharist, modern *plygain* services are often held in the afternoon, but their general character is retained, and it is not uncommon for twenty groups to perform in a church, travelling round to others when they have sung.

The recording from which our transcription derives was made by the Welsh Folk Museum, St Fagans, Cardiff, and issued on disc as *Ar Gyfer Heddiw'r Bore*. See also the article 'The Christmas carol-singing tradition in the Tanad Valley', *Folk Life*, vol. 7, which contains the transcription we reproduce here.

PERFORMANCE Three men.

167

O Mary and the baby, sweet lamb!

(Christmas)

American traditional
(Poston, 1970, arr. editors)

The spiritual was transcribed by Elizabeth Poston (*The Second Penguin Book of Christmas Carols*, 1970) from a field recording of the singing of Ella Mitchell and Velma Wright (at Lubbock, Texas, 19 January 1937) by John A. Lomax, now in the Archive of Folk Song, Library of Congress, Washington, DC (AFS 913 B²). We have treated the song with some freedom, transposing it down a tone and restoring what we assume was the original verse–refrain form; on the recording there is (in our terms) no refrain after verses 1 and 2.

PERFORMANCE   The song may be sung (at whatever pitch) entirely by two solo voices (I and II), as on the recording (see above), or by a solo voice (I) alternating with three voices (II). In both of these cases the refrain is best omitted after the first verse, since it is identical; alternatively, it may

be taken by chorus (also divided into two groups), singing in unison (I) and in three parts (II). In this last case (with the chorus in three parts in both octaves) either or both of our refrain descants may be added. (Descant A is designed for a trio of 'soul sisters' using bold, slow portamenti.) A possible scheme might be:

Verse 1: solo alternating with three voices; refrain: chorus in one or three parts.

Verse 2: as verse 1 (different soloist); refrain as first time, but preceded by, then combined with, descant A.

Verse 3: as verse 1 (different soloist); refrain as first time, but preceded by, then combined with, descant B.

Verse 4: as verse 1 (different soloist); refrain as first time, but preceded by, then combined with, descants A and B together. (This last 'complete' refrain could be repeated at will.)

168

Mary had a baby

(Christmas)

American traditional
(Ballanta-Taylor, 1925, arr. editors)

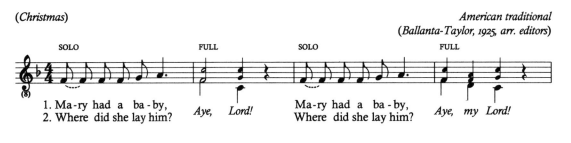

SOLO — FULL — SOLO — FULL

1. Ma-ry had a ba - by,
2. Where did she lay him?
Aye, Lord!
Ma-ry had a ba - by,
Where did she lay him?
Aye, my Lord!

5 SOLO — FULL

Ma-ry had a ba - by,
Where did she lay him?
Aye, Lord! The peo-ple keep a - co-ming and the train done gone.

3 Laid him in a manger, (*etc.*)

4 What did she name him? (*etc.*)

5 Name him King Jesus, (*etc.*)

6 Who heard the singing? (*etc.*)

7 Shepherds heard the singing, (*etc.*)

8 Star keep a-shining, (*etc.*)

9 Moving in the elements, (*etc.*)

10 Jesus went to Egypt, (*etc.*)

11 Travelled on a donkey, (*etc.*)

12 Angels went around him, (*etc.*)

American traditional

The tune and verse 1 are from *St Helena Island Spirituals*, ed. N. G. J. Ballanta-Taylor (1925). Verses 2–12 are as given by Elizabeth Poston in *The Second Penguin Book of Christmas Carols* (1970), 'as sung variously extempore' (see notes, 174). She suggests that the touchingly incongruous last line of each verse reflects 'the imaginative impact . . . of the advent of the railroad, 1830–40.'

PERFORMANCE Solo voice, alternating with unison chorus (high, low, or at both octaves) or three-part chorus (likewise).

169

Go tell it on the mountain

(*Christmas*)

American traditional
(*Fenner, 1909, arr. editors*)

1. In the time of Da - vid, Some call him a king, And if a child is true-born, Lord Je - sus will hear him sing:
2. When I was a seek - er I sought both night and day; I ask the Lord to help me, And he show me the way.
3. He made me a watch-man Up - on a ci - ty wall, And if I am a Christ-ian I am the least of all.

REFRAIN
Go tell it on the moun - tain, O - ver the hills and e - ve - ry-where;
Go tell it on the moun - tain That Je - sus Christ is born!

Text and tune: *Religious Songs of the Negro as Sung on the Plantations*, Thomas P. Fenner (1909).

PERFORMANCE Verse, solo voice; refrain, chorus in one, two, or three parts (high or low voices, or both).

170

Rise up, shepherd, and follow!

(*Christmas*)

American traditional
(Allen et al., 1867, arr. editors)

VERSE [SOLO]

1. There's a   star   in the East   on___   Christ - mas   morn—
2. If   you   take   good___ heed   to the   an - gel's   words—

[FULL] ... [SOLO]

Rise___ up,   shep-herd, and   fol-low!—   It - 'll   lead   to the place where the
You'll for - get   your_ flocks, you'll for -

[FULL]

Sa - viour's   born:___   *Rise   up,   shep - herd, and   fol - low!*
- get   your   herds:___

REFRAIN [FULL]

Leave your   sheep_ and   leave your_ lambs—   Rise_ up,   shep-herd, and   fol-low!

'A Christmas Plantation Song', first published in *Slave Songs of the United States*, ed. W. F. Allen, C. P. Ware, and L. McK. Garrison (1867). The songs were collected during the Civil War, mainly from slaves on the offshore islands of Georgia and South Carolina. The tune is related to various British folk-songs, including a Welsh carol (see

Canu Gwerin: Journal of the Welsh Folk-Song Society, vol. II, part 3, 1922, pp. 182 ff.).

PERFORMANCE Solo voice, alternating with unison chorus (high, low, or at both octaves) or three-part chorus (likewise).

171

Lullay, thou tiny little child

(Holy Innocents)

Appalachian traditional?
(Niles, 1935, arr. editors)

1. Lul - lay,— thou ti - ny lit - tle child; Bye - bye,— lul - le,— lul - lay;— Lul - lay,— thou ti - ny lit - tle child; Bye - bye, lul - le,— lul - lay.—

2 O sisters two, how may we do
     To persevere this day?
   To this poor childling, for whom we do sing:
     'Bye-bye, lulle, lullay.'

3 Herod the king, in his raging,
     Chargèd he hath this day
   His soldiers in their strength and might
     All children young to slay.

4 Then woe is me, poor child, for thee,
      And ever mourn and say,
      For at thy parting nor say nor sing:
      'Bye-bye, lulle, lullay.'

5 And when the stars ingather do,
      In their far venture stay,
      Then smile as dreaming, little one;
      Bye-bye, lulle, lullay.

(Niles, 1935)

Melody and words used by permission of G. Schirmer, Inc.

John Jacob Niles (1892–1980), the famed American folk-song collector, claimed to have taken this carol down 'from the singing of an old lady known to me only as "the old lady with the grey hat"' at an Old Timers' Day at Gatlinburg, Tennessee, on 16 June 1934 (*Ten Christmas Carols from the Southern Appalachian Mountains*, 1935). It would appear to be a descendant of 'Lully, lulla, thow littel tyne child' (40) from the Coventry Shearmen and Tailors' Pageant, though with an entirely different tune which, Niles suggested, could have been preserved in a shape-note song-book. No subsequent collector has ever found tune or words again, nor is the tune known from any shape-note book. Late in his life Niles confessed that his interference with the folk material he had published ranged from

alteration to entirely original composition, and it may be that the three excellent carols we have taken from his publications are among his original works rather than genuine survivals from a folk tradition. (See also 'I wonder as I wander', 172, and 'Sing we the Virgin Mary', 173.)

PERFORMANCE   (*i*) Choir, with octave doublings in the American primitive style (see Appendix 3); (*ii*) female voice(s), in unison or harmony; (*iii*) solo voice, perhaps with a simple instrumental or vocal accompaniment:

Lul - lay,   lul - lay,   lul - lay,   lul - lay._

172

I wonder as I wander

(*Christmas*)

Appalachian traditional?
(*Niles, 1934, arr. editors*)

1. I wonder as I wander, out under the sky, How Jesus the Saviour did come for to die For poor on-'ry peo-ple like you and like I; I won-der as I wan-der out un-der the sky.

2. When Mary birthed Jesus, 'twas in a cow's stall, With wise men and farm-ers and shep-herds and all; But high from the hea-vens a star's light did fall, And the pro-mise of a-ges it then did re-call.

3. If Je-sus had want-ed for a-ny wee thing, A star in the sky or a bird on the wing, Or all of God's an-gels in heaven for to sing, He sure-ly could have it 'cause he was the King.

John Jacob Niles (see notes, 171) claimed to have collected this in Murphy, Cherokee County, North Carolina, in 1933. He published it in his *Songs of the Hill-Folk* (1934), where verse 1 is repeated after verse 3. It has been suggested that the carol is 'neither so old nor so folk as we might suppose'.

PERFORMANCE Voice; the optional accompaniment may be adapted for any appropriate instrument.

173

Sing we the Virgin Mary

(*Christmas*)

Appalachian traditional?
(*Niles, 1945–7, arr. editors*)

1. Sing we the Vir - gin Ma - ry, Sing_ we that match - less_ one;_____ See_____ how the an - gels at - tend - ed her When she birth - ed God's own_ Son, when she_ birth - ed_ God's own Son.

2. So si - lent - ly came our Je - sus Un - to his sweet Ma - ry,_____ As_____ dew of Ap - ril_ fall - eth On_ flower so ten - der - ly, on_____ flower so_ ten - der - ly.

3 When Jesus was a-borning,
   To earth came heaven down,
   To lie upon a manger,
   Away in Bethlem's town.

4 Ah, blessèd Maiden Mother,
   Beknown to prophecy:
   Now Jesus is a-bornèd,
   And all men knoweth thee.

(*Niles, 1945–7*)

Niles claimed to have collected words and tune in Mayfield, Kentucky, in 1933, from members of the Mathers family, 'said to be tenants on a nearby farm' (*The Anglo-American Carol Study Book*, 1945–7; see notes, 171). If true, this would appear to be a near-miraculous survival of the fifteenth-century English carol text 'I sing of a maiden that is makeless' (British Library, Sloane MS 2593, where it appears without music). Other composers who have set that text include Benjamin Britten (in *A Ceremony of Carols*, 1943).

PERFORMANCE One or two voices, with optional accompaniment (guitar, etc.). (Niles used to accompany himself on a kind of cello with cross-shaped sound-holes.)

174

The Virgin Mary had a baby boy

(Christmas)

Trinidadian traditional
(*Connor, 1945, arr. editors*)

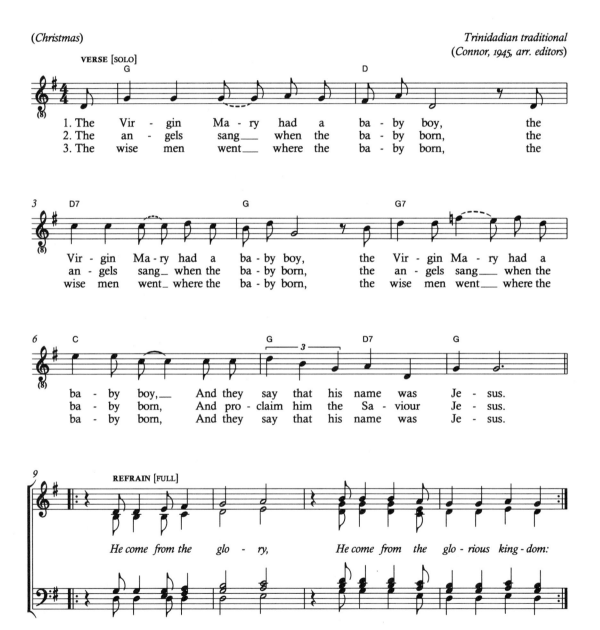

VERSE [SOLO]

1. The Vir - gin Ma - ry had a ba - by boy, the
2. The an - gels sang when the ba - by born, the
3. The wise men went where the ba - by born, the

Vir - gin Ma - ry had a ba - by boy, the Vir - gin Ma - ry had a
an - gels sang when the ba - by born, the an - gels sang when the
wise men went where the ba - by born, the wise men went where the

ba - by boy, And they say that his name was Je - sus.
ba - by born, And pro - claim him the Sa - viour Je - sus.
ba - by born, And they say that his name was Je - sus.

REFRAIN [FULL]

He come from the glo - ry, He come from the glo - rious king - dom:

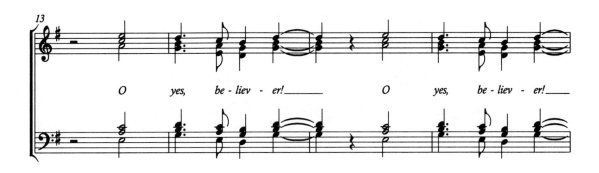

From *The Edric Connor Collection of West Indian Spirituals and Folk Tunes . . .* (1945). Connor explains: 'This, the only West Indian negro carol I found, was taught me by James Bryce, whose parents and grandparents were in Trinidad before the abolition of slavery in 1834. I met Bryce in 1942, when he was ninety-four years of age, but was still working, in rags, on a grapefruit plantation for 1s. 8d. a day. He died September 13 1943.' The music of the verse is in a calypso idiom, but the refrain, which may predate it, has powerful echoes of Africa and has been harmonized accordingly. (See *Sinful Tunes and Spirituals: Black folk music to the Civil War*, Dena J. Epstein, 1977, for many accounts of

the survival of African song and dance among the slaves of North America and the Caribbean.)

'They say that . . .' (verses 1 and 3) does not imply doubt—compare 'Some call him a king' in 'Go tell it on the mountain' (169).

PERFORMANCE   Verse, solo (perhaps with guitar); refrain, chorus in harmony.

The soloist could improvise further verses *ad lib.*, e.g., 'The shepherds came when the baby born', 'They left their gifts where the baby born', etc. (see 'Mary had a baby', 168, for a model).

175

Es sungen drei Engel
'Te Deum laudamus!' three angels sang

(Christmas)

German traditional
(Mainz Catholisch Cantual, 1605, arr. editors)

1. Es sun - gen drei En - gel ein'n süs - sen Ge -
1. 'Te De - um lau - da - mus!' three an - gels

- sang, der in dem ho - hen Him - mel klang.
sang, Through high - est heaven the sweet con - sort rang.

2 Sie sungen, sie sungen alles so wohl:
'Den lieben Gott wir loben soll'n.'

3 Wir heben an, wir loben Gott,
wir rufen ihn an, es tut uns not.

2 'Te Deum laudamus!' they chanted again,
God's praises their burden, their endless
refrain.

3 'Te Deum laudamus!' on earth must
resound;
We join with the angels, in duty bound.

4 All' unser Not und unser Pein,
das wandel' uns Mariae Kindelein.

German traditional
(*Mainz Catholisch Cantual, 1605*)

4 Our pain and woe he'll change for joy,
This Child of Mary, this heavenly boy.

Free tr., editors

The four verses of this haunting carol originally formed part of a much longer thirteenth-century hymn which had no Christmas connections. (One verse was a famous 'Marien-ruf'—literally, a cry to the Virgin Mary—which was used as a battle song by the German army.) Nine verses were extracted and printed in two Catholic chorale-books, the Mainz *Catholisch Cantual* (1605) and the Paderborn *Alte catholische geistliche Kirchengesänge* (1609). In popular usage these crystallized into two four-verse hymns of which verses 1 to 3 were very similar: the present carol, and the penitential 'Es sangen drei Engel', which is sung to a different tune and has a quite different fourth verse, 'Ach Gott, behüt uns vor der Höllischen Pein, / dass wir arme Sünder nicht kommen darein!' ('O God, save us from the pain of hell, that we poor sinners come not there!'). Interspersed with other penitential verses, the latter was much sung by begging children in the nineteenth century, sometimes at Christmas. A version was included under the title 'Armer Kinder Bettlerlied' in *Des Knaben Wunderhorn* (1805–8) and set by Mahler in the fifth movement of his Third Symphony (1896).

The usual modern form of the tune, which we give here, is very close to those in the Mainz book and in Corner's *Geistliche Nachtigall* (1649).

PERFORMANCE   Three voices, or three-part choir. The second half of each verse is sometimes repeated.

176

Maria durch ein' Dornwald ging
Blest Mary wanders through the thorn

(*Christmas*)

German traditional
(arr. editors)

2   Was trug Maria unter ihrem Herzen?

   Kyrieleison!

  Ein kleines Kindlein ohne Schmerzen,
  das trug Maria unterm Herzen!

   Jesus und Maria!

2   What clasps she to her breast so close?

   Kyrieleison!

  An innocent child doth there repose,
  Which to her breast she claspeth close.

   Jesu et Maria!

3 Da hab'n die Dornen Rosen getrag'n,
  Kyrieleison!
  Als das Kindlein durch den Wald getrag'n,
  da haben die Dornen Rosen getrag'n!
  Jesus und Maria!

3 Fair roses bloom on every tree,
  Kyrieleison!
  As through the thorn-wood passeth she
  Fair roses bloom on every tree.
  Jesu et Maria!

4 Wie soll dem Kind sein Name sein?
  Kyrieleison!
  Der Name, der soll Christus sein,
  das war von Anfang der Name sein!
  Jesus und Maria!

4 What shall this Infant callèd be?
  Kyrieleison!
  The Christ, he shall be called truly,
  Which Name he hath borne from eternity.
  Jesu et Maria!

5 Wer soll dem Kind sein Täufer sein?
  Kyrieleison!
  Das soll der Sankt Johannes sein,
  der soll dem Kind sein Täufer sein!
  Jesus und Maria!

5 This holy Name, who shall proclaim?
  Kyrieleison!
  Saint John Baptist shall do the same,
  This holy Name he shall proclaim.
  Jesu et Maria!

6 Was kriegt das Kind zum Patengeld?
  Kyrieleison!
  Den Himmel und die ganze Welt,
  das kriegt das Kind zum Patengeld!
  Jesus und Maria!

6 What christening-gifts to him are given?
  Kyrieleison!
  All things that be, the earth, the heaven,
  As christening-gifts to him are given.
  Jesu et Maria!

7 Wer hat erlöst die Welt allein?
  Kyrieleison!
  Das hat getan das Christkindlein,
  das hat erlöst die Welt allein!
  Jesus und Maria!

7 Who hath the world from sin set free?
  Kyrieleison!
  This Child alone, and only he,
  He hath the world from sin set free.
  Jesu et Maria!

German traditional

tr. editors

This has many of the characteristics of a fifteenth-century German folk carol, and the refrain 'Kyrieleison!' ('Lord, have mercy!') places it in the tradition of 'Leisen' or 'Leichen' (see notes, 59). The flowering rose is a favourite medieval image and the subject of a multitude of legends (see notes, 66). The barren thorn-wood is an image of the fallen world (Genesis 2:9; 3:18), and the birth of Christ, with its promise of Redemption, is symbolized by the return of the thorn trees to their prelapsarian condition. 'Seven long years', like the Hebrew 'forty days', denotes a long passage of time.

PERFORMANCE (*i*) Solo voice, with a unison group singing the refrains; (*ii*) four voices alternating with choir; (*iii*) choir.

177

Kommet, ihr Hirten
Come, all ye shepherds

(Christmas)

Bohemian traditional
(arr. editors)

[ENGEL:]
1. Kom - met,— ihr— Hir - ten,— ihr— Män - ner— und— Frau'n,
[ANGELS:]
1. Come, all— ye— shep - herds, O— come, fol - low— me!

kom - met,— das— lieb - li - che— Kind - lein— zu— schau'n.
Fa - thers— and— mo - thers— and— child - ren,— come— see!

Chri - stus, der Herr, ist heu - te ge - bo - ren, den Gott zum Hei - land
Born is the Christ, the Lord of Cre - a - tion, Cho - sen by God to

[HIRTEN:]

2 Lasset uns sehen in Bethlehems Stall,
   was uns verheissen der himmlische Schall.
   Was wir dort finden, lasset uns künden,
   lasset uns preisen in frommen Weisen:
   Halleluja!

[ALLE:]

3 Wahrlich, die Engel verkündige heut'
   Bethlehems Hirtenvolk gar grosse Freud',
   nun soll es werden Friede auf Erden,
   den Menschen allen ein Wohlgefallen:
   Ehre sei Gott!

(*rev.?*) *Carl Riedel* (*1827–88*)

[SHEPHERDS:]

2 Let us go see now, in Bethlehem's stall,
   What from the skies was revealed to us all;
   What there we find, abroad we'll be telling:
   Joyful our hearts, with God's praises swelling.
   Hallelujah!

[ALL:]

3 Truly the angels glad tidings revealed
   Unto the shepherds in Bethlehem's field:
   Tidings of joy to all men are given;
   Peace on the earth proclaimed from the
      heaven.
   Praise be to God!

tr. editors

Both Czech- and German-speaking Bohemians lay claim to this folk melody, though the truth of its origins will probably never be uncovered. The rise to its current popularity in German-speaking countries and the US began with the publication of the German version in a collection of *Altböhmische Gesänge* ('Ancient Bohemian Songs', 1870) arranged for mixed choir by the Leipzig chorus-master and composer Carl Riedel. Riedel's setting was for concert use, presumably made for his influential *Riedel-Whistling Verein* (the 'Riedel-Whistling Society'), but the dramatic nature of the words suggests that he adapted the text from one of the *Hirtenlieder* (shepherd songs) that abound in those parts and were sung as part of the shepherd dramas which were still popular in the more remote regions of Bohemia. These were the tail-end of a tradition extending from the semi-improvised Nativity folk dramas that had been played in the alleys and inns of medieval German towns. Gustav Jungbauer gives three in his *Bibliographie des deutschen Volks-*

liedes in Boehmen (1913): two begin 'Auf, auf, ihr Hirten!' and a third 'Kommet, kommet, ihr Hirten!', the last appearing in J. Kraus's publication of *Ein Weihnachtsspiel aus dem Erzegebirge* ('A Christmas Drama from the Erzegebirge', a mountainous region of northern Bohemia).

The Czechs sing the tune to a non-pastoral text beginning 'Nesem vám noviny'. They sing it, moreover, immensely slowly, and have been followed in this by the many American college choirs that have enthusiastically adopted the carol: but genre, German text, and tune surely suggest a quick, light style of singing.

PERFORMANCE (*i*) Two soloists (or two-part choir) with two-note drone *ad lib.*; (*ii*) choir. The scoring may be varied for performance within a Nativity play: verse 1 could be taken by two high voices, verse 2 by two men (both verses with instrumental drone), and all four soloists could join with the choir for verse 3.

178

Schlaf wohl, du Himmelsknabe du
O sleep, thou heaven-born Treasure, thou

(Christmas)

Nineteenth-century Bavarian
(Reimann, 1895, arr. editors)

1. Schlaf wohl, du Him - mels - kna - be du, _ schlaf wohl, _ du sü - sses
1. O sleep, thou heaven-born Trea - sure, thou, Sleep sound, thou dear - est

Kind! _____ Dich fä - cheln En - ge - lein in Ruh' _ mit
Child; _____ White an - gel-wings _ shall fan thy brow _ With

Kind! Dich fä - cheln En - ge - lein in Ruh' _
Child; White an - gel - wings _____ shall fan thy brow _

sanf - tem Him - mels - wind. _____ Wir ar - men Hir - ten
breez - es soft _ and mild. _____ We shep - herds poor are

Wir _ ar - men Hir - ten _
We _ shep-herds poor _ are _

588

sin - gen dir___ ein her - zig's Wie - gen - lied - chen für:_____
here to sing___ A sim - ple lul - lay to___ our King:_____

___ sin - gen dir___
___ here to sing___

'Schla - fe, schla - fe, Him - mels - söhn - chen, schla - fe!'
'Lul - la - by, lul - la - by, Sleep, sleep soft - ly, lul - la - by!'

'Schla - fe, schla - fe,
'Lul - lay, lul - lay,

2 Maria hat mit Mutterblick
   dich leise zugedeckt,
und Joseph hält den Hauch zurück,
   dass er dich nicht erweckt.
Die Schäflein, die im Stalle sind,
verstummen vor dir, Himmelskind.

2 See! Mary has, with mother's love,
   A bed for thee outspread,
While Joseph stoops him from above
   And watches at thy head.
The lambs within the stall so nigh,
That thou mayst sleep, have hushed their
   cry.

3 Bald wirst du gross, dann fliesst dein Blut
   von Golgatha herab,
ans Kreuz schlägt dich der Menschen Wut,
   da legt man dich ins Grab.
Hab immer deine Äuglein zu,
denn du bedarfst der süssen Ruh'.

3 When man thou art, thy blood will be
   Poured out, mankind to save,
And men will nail thee to the Tree,
   Men lay thee in the grave.
So sleep, my Baby, whilst thou may,
'Twill give thee rest against that day.

4 So schlummert in der Mutter Schoss
  noch manches Kindlein ein,
  doch wird das arme Kindlein gross,
  so hat es Angst und Pein.
  O Jesulein, durch deine Huld
  hilf's ihnen tragen mit Geduld.

German traditional
(Simrock, 1865)

4 On mother's knee doth man repose
  While he a child remains:
  But when the child to manhood grows,
  Then knows he woes and pains.
  O holy Child, give grace to all,
  That we endure whate'er befall.

vv. 1, 2, 3 (ll. 5–8)
tr. Charles Macpherson (1870–1927)
v. 3 (ll. 1–4), v. 4 tr. editors

This is the early nineteenth-century form of an ancient cradle-rocking carol (see notes, 55), and has been the subject of much confusion in English-speaking countries. It is generally known in Charles Macpherson's appealing 1904 arrangement for unaccompanied choir, which attributes the music to 'Carl Leuner, 1814'. 'Leuner' should in fact read 'Neuner', though this Bavarian musician could not have been Macpherson's real source. Neuner was musical editor of a serial publication of mainly religious music, the *Musikalischer Jugendfreund* ('Young Person's Musical Friend'), which was issued in monthly sections in 1814. It contains a version of 'Schlaf wohl', but only the first two strains correspond to Macpherson's tune: the rest is quite different.

Macpherson's actual source was Heinrich Reimann's *Das deutsche geistliche Lied von der ältesten bis auf unsere Zeit nach den Quellen* ('The German Sacred Song from the earliest times to our own time, after the sources', 1895), in which Romantic arrangements for voice and keyboard by Reimann are supplemented by brief notes on each piece. Reimann collected the tune from a folk singer in the Glatz region of Bohemia (Kłodzko in modern Poland), and called it 'Wiegenlied der Hirten an der Krippe zu Bethlehem' ('Cradle-song of the shepherds at the manger in Bethlehem'). He dates it from the beginning of the nineteenth century, and ascribes the text to C. F. D. Schubart (1739–91). The text did indeed appear in Schubart's *Sämtliche Gedichte* (1786), but it is not so much an original poem as a distillation of traditional verses. Karl Simrock gives thirty-five stanzas in his *Deutsche Weihnachtslieder* (1865), of which we give four. Macpherson made his own translations of the three in Reimann, bowdlerizing the third in a way that was then common, as though the details of Christ's Passion were an indecency to be hushed up.

The two tunes, different though they are, in fact have a common ancestor in the tune to which the carol had been sung for centuries in the German-speaking countries (and to which it mostly continues to be sung). Example 1 shows the traditional tune as sung in Basel (from Adèle Stoecklin, *Weihnachts- und Neujahrslieder aus der Schweiz*, 1921; there are many variants), Neuner's 1814 tune, and the tune transcribed by Reimann. The first is probably an eighteenth-century transformation (preserved by conservative folk singers) of a tune that dates back at least to 1566, when it was apparently printed in the *Kirchengesang* of the Bohemian Brothers. Neuner's tune looks like a half-way stage, bars 5–8 being close to the traditional one and bars 1–4 virtually identical to Reimann's later version. It already has an early Romantic feel, whilst Reimann's has developed into a heartfelt *Geistliches Lied* which could almost be from the hand of Schubert himself: very likely it is by some unknown composer of the Glatz region. ('Stille Nacht!', 86, written in 1818, very nearly came down to us as a 'folk' carol, too.)

There remains the puzzle of Macpherson's attribution to 'Carl Leuner'. We would guess that he wrote to libraries seeking the early nineteenth-century source that Reimann implies but does not name in his note, and received an incipit (opening phrase) of Neuner's version, which misled him into thinking that the entire melody must correspond to Reimann's.

Max Reger is one of several composers who made original settings for voice and piano of this favourite text.

PERFORMANCE Choir, with organ or piano *ad lib.*

EX. 1

179

Es kommt ein Schiff geladen
A ship there comes, a-laden
Uns kompt ein Schiff gefahren
There comes a ship a-sailing

I

(*Christmas*)

German traditional
(Catholische geistliche Gesänge, 1608,
arr. editors)

1. Es kommt ein Schiff ge - la - den bis an den höch - sten Bord, trägt
1. A ship there comes, a - la - den, And rich in - deed her hoard: The

Got - tes Sohn voll Gna - den, des Va - ters e - wig Wort.
Son of God the Fa - ther, And his e - ter - nal Word.

2 Das Schiff geht still im Triebe,
  trägt eine theure Last:
 das Segel ist die Liebe,
  der heilge Geist der Mast.

3 Der Anker schlägt zur Erden,
  so ist das Schiff am Land.
 Das Wort zu Fleisch soll werden,
  der Sohn ist uns gesandt.

2 The ship sails soft, her burden
  Of price all measure past.
 Her mainsail, it is charity,
  The Holy Ghost her mast.

3 The ship has dropped her anchor,
  Is safely come to land;
 The eternal Word in likeness
  Of man on earth doth stand.

592

4 Zu Bethlehem geboren
   im Stall ein Kindelein,
giebt sich für uns verloren;
   gepriesen müss es sein!

5 Und wer diess Kind mit Freuden
   umfangen, küssen will,
der muss erst mit ihm leiden
   der Pein und Marter viel.

6 Darnach auch mit ihm sterben
   und geistlich auferstehn,
das ewge Heil zu erben,
   wie an ihm ist geschehn.

German traditional
(Simrock, 1865)

4 In Bethlehem of Judah
   A Child to us is born:
Sing praises ever to him
   Who saves a world forlorn!

5 And whoso seeks that Infant
   In loving arms to hold,
Must share with him his anguish
   And sorrows manifold;

6 And then, with Jesus, dying,
   Again with Jesus, rise,
An heir of life eternal,
   Where Jesus gives the prize.

vv. 1–4 tr. Alan and Enid Luff, adapted
vv. 5, 6 tr. editors

II

(Christmas)

1 Uns kompt ein Schiff gefahren,
   es bringt ein' schöne Last,
darauf viel' Engelscharen,
   und hat ein' grossen Mast.

2 Das Schiff kompt uns geladen,
   Gott Vater hat's gesandt,
es bringt uns grossen Staden:
   Jesum, unsern Heiland.

3 Das Schiff kompt uns geflossen,
   das Schifflein geht am Land,
hat Himmel aufgeschlossen,
   den Sohn herausgesandt.

1 There comes a ship a-sailing
   With angels flying fast;
She bears a splendid cargo
   And has a mighty mast.

2 She seeks the harbour's shelter,
   The Father sent her here;
She brings a mighty helper:
   Jesus, our Saviour dear.

3 The ship comes on at leisure,
   The ship comes in to berth;
The heavens have loosed their treasure:
   The Son is come to earth.

4 Maria hat geboren
   aus ihrem Fleisch und Blut
das Kindlein, auserkoren,
   wahr' Mensch und wahren Gott.

5 Es liegt hier in der Wiegen,
   das liebe Kindelein,
sein G'sicht leucht' wie ein Spiegel,
   gelobet musst du sein!

6 Maria, Gottes Mutter,
   gelobet musst du sein!
Jesus ist unser Bruder,
   das liebste Jesulein.

7 Möcht' ich das Kindlein küssen
   an sein' lieblichen Mund,
und wär' ich krank, für g'wisse
   ich würd darvon gesund!

8 Maria, Gottes Mutter,
   dein Lob ist also b'reit:
Jesus ist unser Bruder,
   gibt dir gross' Würdigkeit.

German traditional
(Catholische geistliche Gesänge, 1608)

4 See Mary's Son appearing,
   Born of her flesh and blood,
Worthy of all revering,
   At once both man and God.

5 The holy Child, reclining
   Within the crib we see,
Like silvered mirror shining:
   Jesu, all praise to thee!

6 To Mary, God's dear mother,
   Be endless praises sung:
Jesus is born our brother,
   That dearest Child, thy Son.

7 O, could I but be near thee
   And kiss thy mouth so pure,
If I were sick, then, truly,
   That kiss would work my cure.

8 To thee, God's dearest mother,
   Our song again we raise;
Jesus is born our brother:
   To thee be endless praise.

v. 1 tr. Percy Dearmer (1867–1936)
vv. 2–8 tr. editors

A profoundly mystical folk carol, which dates from the fourteenth century and is one of many 'ship' carols (see notes, 148). Daniel Sudermann (1550–1631) printed a version in his *Etliche hohe geistliche Gesänge* (c.1626) which was taken from the writings of Johannes Tauler (1300–61); but, in the carefully chosen words of the editors of *The Oxford Book of Carols*, 'there is much doubt about Tauler's writings; and Sudermann seems to have rewritten the hymns in his collection.' The earliest reliable text, with five verses, is said to be in a manuscript of 1470–80, formerly in the Royal Library, Berlin (now divided between Berlin and Kraków).

Text I is taken from Karl Simrock's *Deutsche Weihnachtslieder* (1865) and is very close to Sudermann's version, the one normally sung in Germany today. The melody is from the *Catholische geistliche Gesänge* of 1608, where there is a different but related text of great beauty (II).

PERFORMANCE Voices, with organ *ad lib.*

180

O du fröhliche! O du selige!
O most wonderful! O most merciful!

I

(Christmas)

Italian traditional
(arr. anon, 1792)

1. O du fröh - li - che!__ O du se - li - ge! gna - den -
1. O most won - der - ful!__ O most mer - ci - ful! Christ, our

- brin - gen - de Weih - nachts - zeit! Welt__ ging ver - lo - ren,
Sa - viour, is born on earth! Sin - ners for - gi - ven,

Christ ward ge - bo - ren: Freu - e,__ freu - e dich, o Chri - sten - heit!
Sor - row for - got - ten: Greet, O__ greet we now his glo - rious birth!

II

(Christmas)

Italian traditional
(arr. Johannes Daniel Falk, 1768–1826)

1. O du fröh - li - che!___ O du se - li - ge!___
1. O most won - der - ful!___ O most mer - ci - ful!___

gna - den - brin - gen - de Weih - nachts - zeit!
Christ, our Sa - viour, is born on earth!

Welt___ ging ver - lo - ren, Christ___ ward ge - bo - ren:
Sin - ners for - gi - ven, Sor - row for - got - ten:

Freu - e,___ freu - e dich, o Chri - sten - heit!
Greet,___ O___ greet we now his glo - rious birth!

2   O du fröhliche!
   O du selige!
      gnadenbringende Weihnachtszeit!
   Christ ist erschienen,
   uns zu versühnen:
      Freue, freue dich, o Christenheit!

3   O du fröhliche!
   O du selige!
      gnadenbringende Weihnachtszeit!
   Himmlische Heere
   jauchzen dir Ehre:
      Freue, freue dich, o Christenheit!

2   O most wonderful!
   O most merciful!
      Christ, our Saviour, is born on earth!
   Christ comes among us,
   Christ will redeem us:
      Greet, O greet we now his glorious birth!

3   O most wonderful!
   O most merciful!
      Christ, our Saviour, is born on earth!
   Armies on high sing
   Praises unending:
      Greet, O greet we now his glorious birth!

v. 1 Johannes Daniel Falk (1768–1826)
vv. 2, 3 Heinrich Holzschuher (fl. 1819)

tr. Anne Ridler

Sung to the words 'O sanctissima! O piissima!' and known as 'The Sicilian Mariners' Hymn', this has established itself as a kind of honorary Christmas carol in English-speaking countries. The original text seems to have been a simple Latin prayer to the Virgin, unconnected with Christmas: 'O sanctissima! O piissima! / Dulcis Virgo Maria! / Mater amata, intemerata, / Ora, ora pro nobis!'

The earliest known version (setting I) was published in London in *The European Magazine and Review* for November 1792 (vol. xxii, pp. 185–6). The way the two upper parts move in thirds over a simple bass suggests the *zampogna* (see notes, 201), and this may have inspired the curious title: no link with any Sicilian mariner has ever been traced. The hymn rapidly became popular and was frequently reprinted. It was included in the Revd W. Tattersall's *Improved Psalmody* (1794), which contains settings of James Merrick's superior translations of the psalms (including several specially composed by Haydn), and it appeared in a number of broadsides coupled with 'Adeste, fideles' (70), presumably because of its Catholic provenance. Meanwhile, Johann Gottfried von Herder claimed to have collected the song on a trip to Italy in 1788, though he did not publish it until 1807 (in *Stimmen der Völker in Liedern*). At this stage 'O sanctissima!' had only one stanza, as in Beethoven's setting for three voices and piano with violin and cello *ad lib.* (written in 1814–15 for the Edinburgh publisher George

Thomson), in which the upper two voices are virtually identical with those in the 1792 publication.

The success of the melody is shown by its ranking as the seventh most common barrel-organ tune in the period 1790–1860 (Boston and Langwill, *Church and Chamber Barrel-Organs*, 1967). In Germany it was turned into a Christmas hymn by Johannes Falk and it remains very popular among German and American Lutherans. Falk was the warden of a Weimar orphanage, the Lutherhaus, and in 1819 he wrote a drama for his charges to perform called *Dr Martin Luther und die Reformation in Volksliedern* (published in 1830). This is a delightful piece of hagiography, with simple settings designed to appeal to children. (See 'Vom Himmel hoch', 60, which Luther wrote for his own children in a similar spirit.) 'O sanctissima!' appears there in versions for Christmas (with two additional verses by Heinrich Holzschuher, a Lutherhaus colleague), Easter, Whitsuntide, and for Luther's name-day, *Martinszeit*. (It also appears once with the Latin words put into the mouths of sailors of the Spanish Armada!) Only the Christmas version has established itself in churches.

PERFORMANCE   I, two voices and bass instrument and/or keyboard.

II, voices, with organ or piano *ad lib.*

181

O Tannenbaum
O Christmas tree
O Dannebom

I

(Christmas)

German traditional
(arr. editors)

1. O Tan - nen-baum, o Tan - nen-baum, wie grün sind dei - ne Blät - ter!
1. O Christ-mas tree, O Christ-mas tree, With faith-ful leaves un - chan - ging!

Du grünst nicht nur zur Som-mer-zeit, nein, auch im Win - ter, wenn es schneit. O
Not on - ly green in sum-mer's heat But in the win - ter's snow and sleet: O

Tan - nen-baum, o Tan - nen-baum, wie grün sind dei - ne Blät - ter!
Christ-mas tree, O Christ-mas tree, With faith-ful leaves un - chan - ging!

598

2 O Tannenbaum, o Tannenbaum,
    du kannst mir sehr gefallen.
   Wie oft hat doch zur Weihnachtszeit
   ein Baum von dir mich hoch erfreut.
   O Tannenbaum, o Tannenbaum,
    du kannst mir sehr gefallen.

3 O Tannenbaum, o Tannenbaum,
    dein Kleid soll mich was lehren:
   Die Hoffnung und Beständigkeit
   gibt Trost und Kraft zu jeder Zeit.
   O Tannenbaum, o Tannenbaum,
    dein Kleid soll mich was lehren!

Ernst Anschütz (fl. 1824)

2 O Christmas tree, O Christmas tree,
    Of all the trees most lovely!
   Each year you bring renewed delight,
   A-gleaming in the Christmas night:
   O Christmas tree, O Christmas tree,
    Of all the trees most lovely!

3 O Christmas tree, O Christmas tree,
    Your leaves will surely teach me
   That hope and love and faithfulness
   Are precious things I can possess:
   O Christmas tree, O Christmas tree,
    Your leaves will surely teach me.

tr. editors

II

(Christmas; general)

*German traditional
(arr. editors)*

1. O Dan - ne - bom, o Dan - ne - bom, du drägst 'ne grö - nen‿ Twig, den
2. 'Wo - rum schold ich nich grö - nen, da ich noch grö - nen‿ kann? Ick
3. 'Un de mi kann ver - sor - gen, dat is de le - ve‿ Gott, de

Win - ter, den‿ Som - mer, dat doert de le - ve Tid.
hebb nich Va - der un Mo - der, de mi ver - sor - gen kann.
leet mi was - sen und grö - nen, drum bin ich stark un grot.'

*German traditional
(Weber-Kellermann, 1982)*

TRANSLATION (II)   1 O fir tree, O fir tree, you bear a green leaf in winter and in summer, remaining the same all the time.

2 'Why should I not be green, since I am able to be green? I have no father and mother to care for me.

3 'And there is one who cares for me, the dear God, who lets me grow and be green so that I am big and strong.'

The symbol of the evergreen was too strongly rooted in the old European religions to be entirely eradicated with the coming of Christianity. The church tolerated these ancient symbols of the continuing life-force at the winter solstice and assimilated them as Christian symbols of the renewal of life at Christ's birth. As late as the nineteenth century, English churches were decorated with greenery at Christmas, though the old prejudice against mistletoe had lost none of its force, as a passage in Washington Irving's *Sketch Book* (1819–20) illustrates: 'On reaching the porch, we found the parson rebuking the gray-haired sexton for having used mistletoe among the greens with which the church was decorated. It was, he said, an unholy plant, profaned by having been used by the druids in their mystic ceremonies . . .' (Irving's imaginary parson, it has to be admitted, lived some 150 years in the past.)

Many Germans devoutly believe that Luther invented the Christmas tree, and there are several Romantic canvases portraying the Luther family enjoying his innovation. In reality the custom seems to have evolved in late medieval Rhineland, the Christmas tree being a symbolic descendant of the Tree of Life of the mystery plays. The first mention of it as an established custom is in an anonymous manuscript of 1605, by which time trees hung with glittering decorations were common in Strasbourg; candles were added later in the century. With the rise of German nationalism in the nineteenth century the ancient customs took on a romantic glow, and by 1850 the Christmas tree was universally pop-

ular in Germany, and was seen as a symbol of all that was best in the old Germanic Christmas tradition. Prince Albert introduced the tree to England in 1841, where it quickly caught on, and it made its first appearance in Paris in the same year.

Ernst Anschütz, a Leipzig schoolmaster, wrote 'O Tannenbaum' (I) in 1824 for his charges to sing, as Christmas trees were beginning to be common in the town. He took the melody of the song 'Es lebe doch' (published in 1799) and wrote an imitation of the first verse, inspired by the opening of the rather gnomic old folk-song 'O Dannebom' (II), which is not specifically a Christmas song but is much sung at that time. Anschütz added two more verses in the same vein, at the same time contriving to enlist the tree as an educational aid (see verse 3). The melody in fact predated 'Es lebe doch', having been sung by generations of students to the words 'Lauriger Horatius quam dixisti verum'. It is one of those formulaic tunes to which many different texts attach themselves: in this case 'Maryland, my Maryland', 'Delaware, my Delaware', 'Missouri, my Missouri', etc., and, more famously, 'The Red Flag'. James Smith, who wrote the words for this last, complained bitterly that they might as well have been sung to the 'Dead March' in *Saul*, and G. B. Shaw rather oddly remarked that the tune 'sounded like the funeral march of a dead eel.' (See 'Good tune, shame about the words' by Steve Race in the London *Independent*, 9 February 1989, and the ensuing correspondence.) Not that this has inhibited the popularity of the carol: though rarely sung in England, it is an essential part of the German and American Christmas.

The familiar translation derives from a later version of the German, with 'wie *treu* sind . . .' in verse 1 giving 'with *faithful* leaves'. 'Tannenbaum' actually means 'fir tree'.

PERFORMANCE   I, voices with or without piano.

II, one or two solo voices, with instrumental drone *ad lib*.

182

Žežulka z lesa vylítla
Out of the forest a cuckoo flew

(Christmas)

Czech traditional
(arr. editors)

1. Že - žul - ka z le - sa vy - lít - la, *ku - ku!* U sa - mých
1. Out of the fo - rest a cuc - koo flew, *cuc - koo!* Seek - ing the

je - sli - ček sed - la, *ku - ku!* Vzdá - vá čest
hea - ven - ly Babe to woo, *cuc - koo!* Near Je - sus'

a pro - zpě____ vu - je, Pá - na své - ho vy -
bed he gave____ in songs The praise that to our

-chva - lu - je, *Ku - ku, ku - ku, ku - ku!*
God____ be - longs, *Cuc - koo, cuc - koo, cuc - koo!*

2 Holoubek sedl na bani, *vrku!*

Dal se silně do houkani *vrku!*

Jest tomu take povd'ečen,

Že jest Ježíšek narozen,

    Vrku, vrku, vrku!

          Czech traditional

2 High in the rafters there sat a dove, *cooroo!*

Cooing to Jesus of his great love, *cooroo!*

His heart and voice so full of joy

That heaven sent this lovely Boy!

    Cooroo, cooroo, cooroo!

          (tr. George K. Evans, adapted)

This is the standard Czech version of the carol, also widely known in America. The variant printed in *The Oxford Book of Carols* (1928) was sent to the editors by a Czech schoolteacher from Polička, in the hills between Bohemia and Moravia.

PERFORMANCE Two solo voices, or two-part choir, at either or both octaves, with instrumental or vocal drone *ad lib.*

183

Hajej, nynej, Ježíšku
Jesu, Jesu, baby dear

(Christmas)

Czech traditional
(arr. editors)

1. Ha - jej, ny - nej, Je - žíš - ku, Je - žíš - ku, Pu - čí - me ti___ ko - žíš - ku.
1. Je - su, Je - su, ba - by_ dear, ba - by_ dear, We will rock your cra - dle_ here.

Bu - de - me tě ko - lí - ba - ti, A - bys_ moh' li - bé po - spa - ti,
We will rock you, rock you, rock you; Gent - ly_ slum - ber_ as we_ rock you;

Ha - jej, ny - nej, Je - žíš - ku, Pu - čí - me_ ti___ ko - žíš - ku.
Je - su, Je - su, do not_ fear: We_ who_ love_ you_ will_ be_ near.

2   Hajej, nynej, miláčku, miláčku,
    Marianský synáčku.
    Budeme tě kolíbati,
    Abys moh' libě pospati,
    Hajej, nynej, miláčku,
    Marianský synáčku.

                    Czech traditional

2   Jesu, Jesu, darling one, darling one,
    Gift of heaven, Mary's son.
    We will rock you, rock you, rock you;
    Gently slumber as we rock you;
    Jesu, Jesu, do not fear:
    We who love you will be near.

                    (*Free tr., Walter Ehret*)

A cradle-song known to all Czechs. A once-popular translation by the editors of *The Oxford Book of Carols* (1928), with lines such as 'Little Jesus . . . do not stir, / We will lend a coat of fur', is far removed from the original Czech.

'Hajej, nynej, Ježíšku' probably accompanied cradle-rocking, a medieval custom which began in Germany and spread through much of Europe (see notes, 55).

PERFORMANCE   (*i*) Children's voices with accompaniment; (*ii*) choir.

184

W żłobie leży
Infant holy, Infant lowly

(*Christmas*)

Polish traditional
(arr. editors)

1. W żło-bie le - ży, któż po-bie - ży ko-lę-do-wać Ma-łe-mu. Je-zu-so-wi,
1. In - fant ho - ly, In-fant low - ly, For his bed a cat-tle-stall; Ox-en low-ing,

Chrys-tu - so - wi, Dziś nam na - ro - dzo-ne-mu. Pa-stu-szko-wie
lit - tle know - ing Christ the Babe is Lord of all. Swift-ly wing-ing

przy-by - waj - cie, Je - mu pięk-nie przy-gry - waj-cie, Ja - ko Pa - nu na-sze-mu.
an-gels sing-ing, No-wells ring-ing, ti-dings bring-ing: Christ the Babe is Lord of all.

2 My zaś sami, z piosneczkami,
   Za wami pośpieszymy.
A tak tego Maleńkiego
   Niech wszyscy zobaczymy.
Jak ubogo narodzony,
Płacze w stajni położony
Więc go dziś ucieszymy.

Polish traditional

2 Flocks were sleeping, shepherds keeping
   Vigil till the morning new;
Saw the glory, heard the story,
   Tidings of a gospel true.
Thus rejoicing, free from sorrow,
Praises voicing, greet the morrow:
   Christ the Babe was born for you.

tr. Edith M. G. Reed (1885–1933), adapted

This carol is well known in the United States in the form in which it is sung in Poland, but it is still commonly sung in England in a version that misplaces the barlines and perpetuates an obvious misprint in the final cadence (C–B–G for B–A–G).

Edith Reed's telegraphese translation, first published in *Music and Youth* (vol. 1, no. 12, December 1921), a journal she founded and edited, is a clever solution to an almost impossible problem. It was written for the mis-stressed version, but fortunately it works (with a little help from the singers) when the barlines are correctly placed.

PERFORMANCE   Choir.

185

Guillô, pran ton tamborin!
Guillô, come, and Robin too

(Christmas)

Provençal traditional
(Barôzai, 1701, arr. editors)

1. Guil - lô,   pran ton tam - bor - in! Toi, pran tai fleû - te, _____ Ro -
1. Guil - lô,   come, and Ro - bin   too, Bring your pipe and   ta - bor,

Pa - ta - pan!   pa - ta - pa - ta - pan! _____
Rum - pum - pum!   rup - pa - pa - pa - pum! _____

-bin! Au son   de cés in - stru - man: *Tu - re - lu - re - lu!*   pa - ta - pa - ta -
do! Blow the   pipe and beat the   drum: *Tur - ra - lur - ra - lu!*   rup - pa - pa - pa -

— pa - ta - pan!   pa - ta - pa - ta - pan! _____
— rum - pum - pum!   rup - pa - pa - pa - pum! _____

-pan! Au son   de cés in - stru - man Je di - ron, No - ei _____ gai - man!
-pum! Blow the   pipe and beat the   drum, Sing 'No - well!': let _ none ____ be dumb!

— pa - ta - pan!   pa - ta - pa - ta - pan! _____
— rum - pum - pum!   rup - pa - pa - pa - pum! _____

2 C'étó lai môde autre foi
   De loüe le Roi dé Roi.
  Au son de cés instruman,
    Turelurelu! patapatapan!
  Au son de cés instruman
   Ai nos an fau faire autan.

3 Ce jor le Diale at ai cu,
   Randons an graice ai Jésu
  Au son de cés instruman,
    Turelurelu! patapatapan!
  Au son de cés instruman
   Fezon lai nique ai Satan.

4 L'homme et Dei son pu d'aicor
   Que lai fleûte et le tambor.
  Au son de cés instruman,
    Turelurelu! patapatapan!
  Au son de cés instruman
   Chanton, danson, sautons-an.

Provençal traditional
(Barôzai, 1701)

2 At our Saviour's birth we play:
   This hath ever been our way;
  Blow the pipe and beat the drum:
    Turralurralu! ruppapapapum!
  Blow the pipe and beat the drum,
   For the King of kings is come!

3 'Thanks be unto Christ!' we cry,
   For old Satan's end is nigh!
  Blow the pipe and beat the drum:
    Turralurralu! ruppapapapum!
  Blow the pipe and beat the drum,
   And your nose at Satan thumb!

4 Leap for joy and dance and sing,
   Drum and pipe re-echoing:
  Closer yet than pipe and drum,
    Turralurralu! ruppapapapum!
  Closer yet than pipe and drum
   God and man this day become!

Free tr., editors

A dance-like *noël* that remains popular throughout France as a sung carol. In Provence and Gascony it is also part of the pipe-and-tabor repertory of *noëls* and dances that are played at various points (including the elevation) in the Christmas midnight mass. In some rural churches the place of honour at this service is still given to local shepherds, who bear gifts to the *santon* (crib).

Both text and tune are in Gui Barôzai's *Noei borguignon* (1701), where the tune is called 'Ma mère, mariez-moi'. William Sandys printed an accurate version of the text as one of the 'French Provincial Carols' in his *Christmas Carols, Ancient and Modern* (1833; see Appendix 4).

The Provençal *tambourin* is a large tabor with a long cylindrical body and a snare on the upper head. It is hit with a single drumstick, usually in simple reiterated rhythmic patterns, and has a deep and resonant tone. The 'fleûte' is a fipple flute, the three-holed pipe (*flûte à trois trous*) or *flûtet*, which since the eighteenth century has more generally been known as the *galoubet*. Pipe and tabor were much used for dancing throughout the Middle Ages, and have continued to accompany folk dancing in Provence. The *tambourin* has a wide dynamic range, and the *galoubet* is relatively gentle in its lower register, and shrill in its high,

overblown octave. The present carol is perhaps most characteristically performed with loud drum and shrill pipe, and vocal performance might reflect this.

An oddity of the text is that two players are called on to play instruments that have always been played by one (the pipe has three holes so that it can be played with one hand only), even when the *tambourin* is used rather than the smaller tabor. Barôzai (or whoever wrote the text) may have been confusing pipe and tabor with fife and drum (also used for dancing in the Middle Ages and still popular in Provence), which are played by a pair of performers. On the other hand, Guillô and Robin are stock characters in Provençal carols: they bring food to the manger in 'Allons, bergers, partons tous', and, like Jeannette and Isabelle in 'Un flambeau' (187), are perhaps being used to suggest the idea of the entire village community.

PERFORMANCE (*i*) Voice, with one-note instrumental drone *ad lib.*; (*ii*) two voices with two-note drone; (*iii*) choir; (*iv*) pipe and tabor/*tambourin*, the latter playing a reiterated ♫♩ or ♩♫♩ rhythm.

'Turelurelu!' is in imitation of the pipe, 'patapatapan!' of the drum.

186

De matin ai rescountra lou trin
Ce matin j'ai rencontré le train
Far away, what splendour comes this way?
(Marcho di Rei)

(Epiphany)

Provençal traditional
(arr. Georges Bizet, 1838–75, adapted)

1. De ma - tin ai res - coun - tra lou trin De tres gran rei qu'a-na-voun
1. Ce ma - tin j'ai ren - con - tré le train De trois grands rois qui al-laient
1. Far a - way, what splen-dour comes this way? The wind is wa-ving ma - ny

en vou - ya - gi;___ De ma - tin ai res - coun - tra lou trin De
en voy - a - ge;___ Ce ma - tin j'ai ren - con - tré le train De
col - oured ban - ners;_ Far a - way, what splen-dour comes this way? I

tres gran rei des - su lou gran ca - min. Ai vis d'a - bor___ De
trois grands rois des - sus le grand che - min. Tout char - gés d'or Les sui -
see a ca - val-cade in fine ar - ray. O rich and fair Are the

gar - do cor, De gen ar - ma em' u - no trou-po de pa - gi; Ai
-vants d'a - bord, De grands guer - riers et les gar - des du tré - sor; Tout
robes they wear, And bright gold gleams on the har-ness of the ca - mels; O

vis d'a - bor__ De gar - do cor, Tou - tei doou - ra des - su sei just' oou cor.
char - gés d'or Les sui - vants d'a - bord, De grands guer-riers a - vec leurs bou - cli - ers.
rich and fair Are the robes they wear, And on their tur-bans glit - ter je - wels rare.

2 Dins un char dooura de touto par
Vesias lei rei moudeste coumo d'angi;
Dins un char dooura de touto par
Vesias briha de richeis estandar.
Oousias d'oouhouas,
De bellei vouas
Que de moun Dieou publiavoun lei louangi;
Oousias d'oouhouas
De bellei vouas
Que disien d'er d'un admirable chouas.

3 Tout ravi d'entendre aco d'aqui
Mi sieou rangea per veire l'equipagi;
Tout ravi d'entendre aco d'aqui
De luen en luen leis ai toujour suivi.
L'astre brihan
Qu'ero davan
Servie de guido e menavo les tres magi;
L'astre brihan
Qu'ero davan
S'aresté net quan fougué ver l' Enfan.

J. F. Domergue (fl. 1742)

2 Dans un char, doré de toutes parts,

On voit les rois, gracieux comme des anges;

Dans un char, doré de toutes parts,

On voit briller de riches étendards.

Entour les rois,

De belles voix

Qui du Seigneur proclamaient les louanges;

Entour les rois,

De belles voix

Qui tout en haut chantaient un air de choix.

3 Tout ravi de les entendre ainsi,

Me suis rangé pour voir leur équipage;

Tout ravi de les entendre ainsi,

De loin en loin les ai toujours suivis.

L'astre brillant,

Toujours devant,

Servait de guide et menait les trois mages;

L'astre brillant,

Toujours devant,

S'arrêta net, venu devant l'Enfant.

tr. Stephen Haynes

2 Kings, all three, such splendid men must be,

For each is brilliant as a golden sunrise;

Kings, all three, such splendid men must be,

Who on white stallions ride a King to see.

They all obey

Him who leads by day,

But every night by a star they have been
    guided,

They all obey

Him who leads by day;

His long white beard is seen from far away.

3 Now I hear the sound of music clear:

A page is singing with a voice of silver;

Now I hear the sound of music clear;

Such singing never heard I far or near.

O tell me why,

In a stable nigh,

They stoop so low to a baby in a manger?

O tell me why,

In a stable nigh,

They worship him who on a cross will die?

English version by Mary Barham Johnson

TRANSLATION (Provençal) 1 One morning I met a procession of three great kings who were travelling on a journey, . . . three great kings on the highway. First I saw their bodyguard of armed men with a group of pages, . . . their tunics all covered with gold.

2 In a carriage, gilded all over, you could see the kings, as comely as angels, . . . rich standards shining. You could hear beautiful voices singing the praises of our Lord, . . . a most choice melody.

3 Ravished by what I heard, I drew near to see the procession; . . . I continued to follow them mile after mile. The blazing star, which went before, guided and led the three magi, . . . stopped when it came before the child.

(tr. Stephen Haynes)

The tune as we know it began life in the seventeenth century as a military march entitled 'Marche de Turenne'. The celebrated military leader Henri de la Tour d'Auvergne (1611–75), Vicomte de Turenne, was created Marshal of France in 1643, and, after various vicissitudes, became a national hero in 1674–5, when he recovered the province of Alsace. The march was perhaps written at that time: it has been suggested, though not substantiated, that Lully was the composer, and the fine quality of the tune, together with Turenne's stature, make that by no means impossible.

The march is thought to have been written for the fifes and drums (*fifres* and *tambours*, not to be confused with the gentler pipe and tabor—*flûtet* and *tambourin*—which were used for dancing) to which the French army marched. It survived in Provence, where these instruments continued to be used by the many honorary companies of archers, musketeers, etc., whose brilliant uniforms and displays of marching were an essential part of the local *fêtes*.

The text was written in the following century to fit the tune—the usual way in which *noëls* were created. The author was presumably one of the family of Domergues, Avignois printers, since the firm published it as part of a series of *noël* collections: in the first edition (1763) it is attributed to 'J. F. D***', but the 1772 edition is less coy, crediting 'J. F. Domergue, doyen [leading citizen] d'Amaron'. Domergue's poem had previously appeared in print in a *Recueil de cantiques spirituels provençaux et françois* (Paris, 1759, generally known as 'the Abbé Dubreuil's collection'), and there is one source earlier still, a manuscript (no. 1256) in the Avignon Library, known as 'Castellant's collection' and dated 1742: there the poem is headed 'sur l'air de la Marche de Turenne'. (For full references to the textual and musical sources see J. Clamon, 'Bizet et le folklore provençal', *Revue de musicologie*, November 1938, pp. 150–3.)

It is quite likely that the carol was created specifically for performance at the processions of the three kings that made their way into the major Provençal towns on the eve of the Epiphany, of which it became an essential part. The march itself must already have been a feature of these processions, played by the military companies, and the text must surely have been inspired by the sight of the kings and their legions of attendants, camels, and banners, wending their way into the ancient towns. The Provençal poet Frédéric Mistral (1830–1914) recalls seeing such a procession in his boyhood, at Maillane:

A joyful shout rang from every throat as the magnificence of the royal pageant dazzled our sight. A flash of splendour and gorgeous colour shone in the rays of the setting sun, while the blazing torches showed the gleams of gold on crowns set with rubies and precious stones. The kings! The kings! See their mantles, their flags, and the procession of camels and horses which are coming . . .

We ran to the church. It was crowded, and, as we entered, the voices of all the people, accompanied by the organ, burst forth into the superbly majestic Christmas hymn: 'De matin ai rescountra lou trin'.

We children, fascinated, threaded our way between the women, till we reached the Chapel of the Nativity. There, suspended above the altar, was the beautiful star, and bowing the knee in adoration before the Holy Child we beheld at last the three kings: Gaspard, with his crimson mantle, offering a casket of gold; Melchior, arrayed in yellow, bearing in his hands a gift of incense; and Balthazar, with his cloak of blue, presenting a vase of the sadly prophetic myrrh. How we admired the finely dressed pages who upheld the kings' flowing mantles, and the great humped camels whose heads rose high above the sacred ass and ox; also the Holy Virgin and St Joseph besides all the wonderful background, a little mountain in painted paper with shepherds and shepherdesses bringing hearth-cakes, baskets of eggs, swaddling clothes, the miller with a sack of corn, the old woman spinning, the knife-grinder at his wheel, the astonished innkeeper at his window, in short, all the traditional crowd who figure in the Nativity, and, above and beyond all, the Moorish king.

Bizet used the carol in his incidental music to Daudet's drama of rustic passion, *L'Arlésienne* ('The Girl from Arles'), one of three tunes he took from a publication called *Tambourin* (1864) by the tabor player Vidal of Aix. The play has no connection with Christmas, but the *Marche* was too powerfully evocative of the region to be resisted. The overture begins with a set of variations on the tune, which returns chorally towards the tragic climax of the last act, first simply, then in canon, and finally in combination with another genuine Provençal tune from *Tambourin*, the 'Danso di Chivau Frus' ('Dance of the hobby-horses'), which has been heard earlier in the act as a *farandole*. We have stitched together a complete setting by Bizet from this last act, joining two halves that were originally in different keys and slightly adjusting the last two bars where Bizet writes in three parts.

PERFORMANCE (*i*) Solo voice or unison voices (with drone accompaniment); (*ii*) choir. One possible scheme (using Bizet's various treatments of the tune) is: v. 1, unison; v. 2, bars 1–8 unison sopranos and altos followed in canon by unison tenors and basses at a distance of two beats, bars 9–16 in harmony; v. 3, harmony.

187

Un flambeau, Jeannette, Isabelle!
Come with torches, Jeanette, Isabella!

(Christmas)

Provençal traditional
(arr. editors)

1. Un flam - beau,— Jean - nette, I - sa - bel - le! Un flam -
1. Come with tor - ches, Jean - ette, I - sa - bel - la! Run un -

- beau,— cou - rons au ber - ceau! C'est Jé - sus, bon - nes gens du ha -
- to— the cra - dle, run! Christ is born:— O come— be -

- meau,— Le Christ est né, Ma - rie ap - pel - le,
- fore— him! Ma - ry calls us to a - dore— him;

Ah! ah! ah! que la mère___ est bel - le,
Oh! oh! oh! such a love - ly mo - ther!

Ah! ah! ah! que l'En - fant___ est beau!
Oh! oh! oh! such a love - ly Son!

2 C'est un tort quand l'Enfant sommeille,
   C'est un tort de crier si fort.
   Taisez-vous, l'un et l'autre, d'abord!
   Au moindre bruit, Jésus s'éveille,
   Chut! chut! chut! Il dort à merveille,
   Chut! chut! chut! voyez comme il dort!

3 Doucement, dans l'étable close,
   Doucement, venez un moment!
   Approchez, que Jésus est charmant!
   Comme il est blanc! Comme il est rose!
   Do! do! do! que l'Enfant repose!
   Do! do! do! qu'il rit en dormant!

Provençal traditional
tr. Émile Blémont

2 Cease, good neighbours, your noisy prattle!
   Peace, good neighbours: let him sleep!
   Shame on him who the silence breaketh
   And the new-born Babe awaketh:
   Soft! soft! softly amid the cattle,
   Soft! soft! softly he slumbers deep.

3 Through the doorway softly filing,
   To his manger-bed we creep.
   Torches' glow the Babe discloses,
   Fair as snow, with cheeks like roses,
   Hush! hush! hushaby! sweetly smiling,
   Hush! hush! hushaby! fast asleep!

Free tr., editors

Torches have always played an important part in Provençal Christmas celebrations. Another tradition is the making of model villages, complete with crib and vividly characterized villagers. Both are reflected in this carol.

The French text by Émile Blémont first appeared in Julien Tiersot's *Noëls français* (1901) and is a version of the Provençal carol 'Vénès leou vieira la Pieoucelle', first published in Nicolas Saboly's *Recueil de noëls provençaux* (1836 edn.).

No melody for the Provençal carol is specified by Saboly.

Seguin's *Recueil de noëls composés en langue provençale* (1856) gives our tune; it derives from the drinking-song 'Qu'ils sont doux, bouteille jolie', which Charpentier wrote for later performances of Molière's *Le Médecin malgré lui* (1666). The Seguin melody was later adapted for Blémont's French text.

PERFORMANCE (*i*) Solo voice and continuo; (*ii*) choir. Ornaments: see notes, 189.

188

Noël nouvelet!

(Christmas; New Year)

French traditional
(arr. editors)

1. No - ël nou - ve - let! No - ël chan - tons i - cy;
1. *No - ël nou - ve - let! sing___ we this___ new No - ël!*

Dé - vo - tes gens, ren - dons à___ Dieu mer - ci;
Thank we now our God, and___ of his___ good - ness tell;

Chan - tons No - ël pour le Roi nou - ve - let:
Sing we No - ël to greet the new - born King:

No - ël nou - ve - let! No - ël chan - tons i - cy!
No - ël nou - ve - let! this___ new No - ël we sing!

2   Quand m'esveilly et j'eus assez dormy,
    Ouvris mes yeux, vis un arbre fleury,
    Dont il issait un bouton vermeillet.
    Noël nouvelet! Noël chantons icy!

3   Quand je le vis, mon coeur fut resjouy
    Car grande clarté resplendissait de luy,
    Comme le soleil qui luit au matinet.
    Noël nouvelet! Noël chantons icy!

4   D'un oysillon après le chant j'ouy,
    Qui aux pasteurs disait: 'Partez d'ici!
    En Bethléem trouverez l'Agnelet!'
    Noël nouvelet! Noël chantons icy!

5   En Bethléem, Marie et Joseph vy,
    L'asne et le bœuf, l'Enfant couché parmy;
    La crèche était au lieu d'un bercelet.
    Noël nouvelet! Noël chantons icy!

6   L'estoile vint qui le jour esclaircy,
    Et la vy bien d'où j'estois départy
    En Bethléem les trois roys conduisaient.
    Noël nouvelet! Noël chantons icy!

7   L'un portait l'or, et l'autre myrrhe aussi,
    Et l'autre encens, que faisait bon senty:
    Le paradis semblait le jardinet.
    Noël nouvelet! Noël chantons icy!

8   Quarante jours la nourrice attendy;
    Entre les bras de Siméon rendy
    Deux tourterelles dedans un panneret.
    Noël nouvelet! Noël chantons icy!

9   Quand Siméon le vit, fit un haut cry:
    'Voici mon Dieu, mon Sauveur,
        Jésus-Christ!
    Voicy celui qui joie au peuple met!
    Noël nouvelet! Noël chantons icy!

*10 Un prestre vint, dont je fus esbahy
    Que les paroles hautement entendy,
    Puis les mussa dans un petit livret.
    Noël nouvelet! Noël chantons icy!

*11 Et puis me dit: 'Frère, crois-tu cecy?
    Si tu y crois aux cieux sera ravy:
    Si tu n'y crois, va d'enfer au gibet!
    Noël nouvelet! Noël chantons icy!

12 Et l'autre jour je songeais en mon lict
    Que je voyais ung Enfant si petit
    Qui appelait Jésus de Nazareth.
    Noël nouvelet! Noël chantons icy!

*13 En douze jours fut Noël accomply;
    Par douze vers sera mon chant finy,
    Par chaque jour j'en ai fait un couplet.
    Noël nouvelet! Noël chantons icy!

French traditional
(*Grande Bible des noëls, 1721, adapted*)

2 Waking from sleep, this wonder did I see:
   In a garden fair there stood a beauteous tree,
   Whereon I spied a rose-bud opening.
   Noël nouvelet! this new Noël we sing!

3 How my heart rejoiced to see that sight divine,
   For with rays of glory did the rose-bud shine,
   As when the sun doth rise at break of day.
   This new Noël sing we: *Noël nouvelet!*

4 Then a tiny bird left off its song, to say
   Unto certain shepherds: 'Haste you now away!
   In Bethlehem the Lamb of God you'll see.'
   Noël nouvelet! this new Noël sing we!

5 Mary and Joseph in Bethlehem they found,
   Where the ox and ass the Infant did surround,
   Who in their manger slept upon the hay.
   This new Noël sing we: *Noël nouvelet!*

6 Then I saw a star which turned the night to day,
   Moving ever onward on its shining way,
   Leading to Bethlehem the kings all three.
   Noël nouvelet! this new Noël sing we!

7 Gold the first did carry; myrrh the next did bring;
   And the third bore incense, the garden perfuming,
   So that in paradise I seemed to dwell.
   Noël nouvelet! sing we this new Noël!

8 For forty days a nurse the Child sustained,
   Mary then a pair of turtle-doves obtained:
   In Simeon's hands she placed this offering.
   Noël nouvelet! this new Noël we sing!

9   Siméon saw the Child and lifted up his voice:
     'Lo! my God and Saviour, in whom I rejoice;
     Jesus, the Christ, the glory of Israël!'
     Noël nouvelet! sing we this new Noël!

*10   Greatly did I marvel Siméon's words to hear,
      Which a priest observed who shortly did appear,
      Within a book those words to store away.
      This new Noël sing we: *Noël nouvelet!*

*11   He of me demanded: 'Dost thou these words believe?
      If thou dost assent, the heavens shall thee receive;
      If thou dost deny, on hell's great gallows swing!'
      Noël nouvelet! this new Noël we sing!

12   I beheld these wonders as on my bed I lay,
      Dreaming of a Child all at the break of day:
      Jesus of Nazareth I saw in my dreaming;
      Noël nouvelet! this new Noël we sing!

*13   Twelve are the days that to Noël belong;
      Twelve are my verses, so doth end my song;
      A day for each verse: a verse for every day;
      This new Noël sing we: *Noël nouvelet!*

tr. editors

This is one of many early *noëls* that trace all or part of the Nativity narrative. A mysterious and enchanting *chanson d'aventure*, it has been reduced to banality in the versions of many carol-books. 'Noël nouvelet!' was sung at New Year, and was one of the most popular *noëls* in the sixteenth century. A copy in Villon's hand was found among his papers, while in Rabelais's *Pantagruel* (1532/3), Panurge describes his ideal spouse with a reference to verse 11: 'Ma femme sera cointe et jolie comme une petite chouette: Qui ne le croid, d'enfer au gibbet, Noel nouvelet!' ('My wife will be gentle and pretty, like a little owl: Whoever does not believe this, to the gallows of hell with him! *Noël nouvelet!*')

The earliest source is a late fifteenth-century manuscript (Paris, Bibliothèque Nationale, Arsénal MS 3653; copied 1491–8?), which does not include the usual *timbre* or reference to the opening lines of an existing song to which the poem should be sung. The Arsénal Manuscript, elegantly prepared for a noble or royal family, is a rare example of the careful presentation by a professional scribe of the quite different types of *noël* which were passed on within the oral tradition, and presumably there was no need to provide *timbres*, because these *noëls* were not parodies and their tunes were well known. (Such monodic or polyphonic *chansons rustiques* were an important part of popular culture, and also had a place on the theatrical stage. The internal refrain lines and repetitions characteristic of the genre were regarded with disdain by contemporary poets.)

No indication of the tune for this carol appears until the

seventeenth century. We give one of the two melodies to which 'Noël nouvelet!' is sung today; it has been associated with these words from the seventeenth century and may well be the original tune. The curious modal flavour derives from the quotation of the first five notes of the plainchant Marian hymn 'Ave, maris stella', which is used in a similar manner in several other early *noëls*.

No source gives a reliable text. Pierre Sargeant prints a version which has verses and refrains of three lines (presumably adapted for a different tune) in his *Les Grands Noelz nouvelles* . . . (Paris, *c.*1537), for which the Arsénal Manuscript was a source. Our text is from the *Grande Bible des noëls, tant vieux que nouveaux* (Troyes, 1721). Like all other sources, it gives 'trente jours' (thirty days) in the final verse, where only 'douze' makes sense. In verses 4 and 8 we have replaced 'Qu'aux' and 'deug' with Sargeant's 'Qui aux' and 'deux'. Verse 12 was cobbled together from lines of verses 9 and 13, and we have substituted the penultimate verse in Henri Lemeignen's scholarly edition of *Vieux Noëls* (Nantes, 1876, vol. I, pp. 33–4), which brings the narrative to a rounded close.

Nouvelet comes from the same root as *noël*, both originally denoting 'news' (*nouvelles* in modern French) or newness. New Year was the time when carols were most frequently sung, and general credence is given to Pierre Pansier's suggestion (in his article 'Les Noëls à Avignon du XVIe au XIXe siècle', *Annales d'Avignon et du Comtat Venaissan, 14e année*, 1928, pp. 124–276) that *nouvel an* became corrupted to *nouel* (compare the Cornish 'Novels, novels, novels!' refrain in 'A Child this day is born, 146) and eventually to *noël*. By the sixteenth century, *noël* had taken on its modern meanings of 'Christmas' and 'Christmas song', and refrains of the 'chantons noël' type are at least as common as 'sing nowell' refrains had been in fifteenth-century English carols. The addition of *nouvelet* suggested both the New Year and that this was a 'new-made' *noël* for the 'new-born King' (verse 1). The priest (verses 10, 11) is perhaps a personification of St Luke, the only Evangelist to describe the Purification, and his words reflect those of Simeon when he blessed Joseph and Mary: 'Behold, this child is set for the fall and rising again of many in Israel; and for a sign . . . that the secrets of many hearts shall be revealed' (Luke 2:34–5).

PERFORMANCE   (*i*) Solo voice; (*ii*) choir. Verses 10 and 11 are not entirely suitable for singing in church. Verse 13 will make sense only when the whole *noël* is sung. Possible shortened versions are: verses 1–5, 12; 1–7, 12; 1–5, 8–9, 12; 1–9, 12.

189

Dans cette étable
Cradled all lowly

(Christmas)

French traditional
(arr. editors)

1. Dans cette é - ta - ble Que Jé - sus est char - mant, Qu'il est ai -
1. Cra - dled all low - ly, Be - hold the Sa - viour Child, A be - ing

- ma - ble___ Dans son a - bais - se - ment!___ Que d'at - traits à la
ho - ly___ In dwell - ing rude___ and wild!___ Ne'er yet was re - gal

fois!___ Tous les pa - lais des rois___ N'ont rien de com - pa -
state___ Of mon - arch proud and great,___ Who grasped a na - tion's

619

2 Que sa puissance

    Paraît bien en ce jour,

Malgré l'enfance

    Où l'a réduit l'amour!

Notre ennemi dompté,

L'enfer déconcerté,

    Font voir qu'en sa naissance

Rien n'est si redouté

    Que sa puissance.

2 No longer sorrow,

    As without hope, O earth;

A brighter morrow

    Dawned with that Infant's birth!

Our sins were great and sore,

But these the Saviour bore,

And God was wroth no more:

His own Son was the Child that lay

    in Bethlehem.

3 Sans le connaître,
   Dans sa divinité
Je vois paraître
   Toute sa majesté:
Dans cet Enfant qui naît,
À son aspect qui plaît,
   Je découvre mon maître
Et je sens ce qu'il est
   Sans le connaître.

*4 Plus de misère!
   Un Dieu souffre pour nous
Et de son Père
   Apaise le courroux;
C'est en notre faveur
Qu'il naît dans la douleur;
   Pouvait-il pour nous plaire
Unir à sa grandeur
   Plus de misère?

French traditional
(*after Bishop Esprit Fléchier, 1632–1710*)

3 Babe, weak and wailing,
   In lowly village stall,
Thy glory veiling,
   Thou cam'st to die for all.
The sacrifice is done,
The world's atonement won
Till time its course hath run.
O Jesu, Saviour! Morning Star
   of Bethlehem!

English version by Henry Farnie

The text was originally published in the 1728 edition of *Cantiques spirituels* by Fléchier, Bishop of Nîmes. We give the usual modern text, the result of gradually accumulating changes in later editions.

At the beginning of the eighteenth century the melody was sung to words beginning 'Dans le bel âge / Tout est fait pour aimer'. It is found in both simple and compound time; the latter version has become well known in English-speaking countries through the setting by Gounod.

Ornaments: + most commonly indicates a trill, but other (unspecified) ornaments are sometimes implied; ⌣ indicates a lower appoggiatura, ⌢ an upper.

PERFORMANCE (*i*) Solo voice, or four voices, and continuo; (*ii*) choir and organ.

Possible instrumentations of the ritornello: recorders/flutes/oboes/violins with bass viol/bassoon and/or chordal continuo; alternatively, keyboard solo.

190

Entre le bœuf et l'âne gris
Oxen and asses stand around

(Christmas)

French traditional
(arr. editors)

1. En - tre le bœuf et____ l'â - ne gris, Dors, dors,
1. Ox - en and ass - es____ stand a - round Je - sus,

dors le pe - tit Fils: *Mille an - ges di - vins,* *Mil - le sé - ra - phins,*
Je - sus sleep - ing sound; *From the skies a - bove* *An - gels ho - ver near,*

Vo - lent à l'en - tour____ De ce Dieu d'a - mour.
Round the God of Love____ In the man - ger here.

2   Entre les deux bras de Marie,
    Dors, dors le Fruit de la Vie;

3   Entre les roses et les lys,
    Dors, dors, dors le petit Fils;

4   Entre les pastoureaux jolis,
    Dors, dors, dors le petit Fils;

5   En ce beau jour solennel,
    Dors, dors, dors l'Emmanuel;

French traditional

2   Mary's arms are clasped around
    Jesus, Jesus sleeping sound;

3   Rose and lily twine around
    Jesus, Jesus sleeping sound;

4   Shepherds are piping all around
    Jesus, Jesus sleeping sound;

5   Round his cradle now we sing:
    Jesus, born to be our King!

tr. editors

The text was first published in Henri Lemeignen's *Vieux Noëls* (1876) and is thought to have originated in Brittany. The tune is one of many variant versions.

PERFORMANCE   (*i*) Solo voice and continuo; (*ii*) choir. Ornaments: see notes, 189.

191

Quelle est cette odeur agréable
Shepherds, what fragrance, all-perfuming

(Christmas)

French traditional
(arr. editors)

[1er BERGER:]
1. Quelle est cette odeur agréable,
[1st SHEPHERD:]
1. Shepherds, what fragrance, all-perfuming,

Bergers, qui ravit tous nos sens?
Sweetly our senses now doth seize?

S'exhale le t'il rien de semblable
Did ever flowers, at spring-tide blooming,

S'exhale le t'il rien de semblable
Did ever flowers, at spring-tide blooming,

S'exhale le t'il rien de semblable
Did ever flowers, at spring-tide blooming,

624

D.C. al Fine

Au mil - ieu des fleurs du_____ prin - temps?
Breathe forth such balm - y scents_____ as these?

[DEUXIÈME BERGER:]

2 Mais quelle éclatante lumière
   Dans la nuit vient frapper les yeux?
L'astre du jour, dans sa carrière,
   Fût-il jamais si radieux?
Mais quelle éclatante lumière
   Dans la nuit vient frapper les yeux?

[TROISIÈME BERGER:]

3 Voici beaucoup d'autres merveilles!
   Grand Dieu! qu'entends-je dans les airs?
Quelles voix! Jamais nos oreilles
   N'ont entendu pareil concerts.
Voici beaucoup d'autres merveilles!
   Grand Dieu! qu'entends-je dans les airs?

[CHŒUR D'ANGES:]

4 Ne craignez rien, peuple fidèle,
   Écoutez l'Ange du Seigneur;
Il vous annonce une merveille
   Qui va vous combler de bonheur.
Ne craignez rien, peuple fidèle,
   Écoutez l'Ange du Seigneur.

[SECOND SHEPHERD:]

2 Whence comes this dazzling radiance, rending
   The gloomy shadows of the night?
Did e'er the Morning Star, ascending,
   Shed from his car a ray so bright?
Whence comes this dazzling radiance, rending
   The gloomy shadows of the night?

[THIRD SHEPHERD:]

3 Hark! on the trembling air, such singing
   As hath our souls to wonder stirred!
Choirs, in sweet concord, earthwards winging:
   Strains that no mortal ear hath heard!
Hark! on the trembling air, such singing
   As hath our souls to wonder stirred!

[ANGEL CHOIR:]

4 O trusty shepherds, nothing fear ye:
   Hark to the Angel of the Lord!
Tidings from highest heaven hear ye:
   Joys without end shall they afford!
O trusty shepherds, nothing fear ye:
   Hark to the Angel of the Lord!

[GABRIEL:]

5 A Bethléem, dans une crèche,
     Il vient de vous naître un Sauveur;
   Allons, que rien ne vous empêche
     D'adorer votre Rédempteur!
   A Bethléem, dans une crèche,
     Il vient de vous naître un Sauveur.

[CHŒUR D'ANGES *ou* TOUS:]

6 Dieu tout-puissant, gloire éternelle
     Vous soit renduë jusqu'aux cieux!
   Que la paix soit universelle,
     Que la grâce abonde en tous lieux!
   Dieu tout-puissant, gloire éternelle
     Vous soit renduë jusqu'aux cieux!

French traditional

[GABRIEL:]

5 In Bethlehem, God's will obeying,
     Born is the Saviour of mankind;
   Come and adore! make no delaying:
     In yonder stall ye shall him find.
   In Bethlehem, God's will obeying,
     Born is the Saviour of mankind.

[ANGEL CHOIR *or* TUTTI:]

6 Glory to God in highest heaven:
     Let all below his praises sound!
   O may such grace to earth be given
     That peace may everywhere abound!
   Glory to God in highest heaven:
     Let all below his praises sound!

Free tr., editors

The tune, in one form or another, occurs in English sources as early as *c.*1710 (British Library, G. 307 [210]) and in French sources from at least 1717 (*La Clef des Chansonniers*, Paris, 1717). To the words 'Fill ev'ry glass', John Gay used it in *The Beggar's Opera* (1728) as a drinking song, as did Thomas D'Urfey before him (*Wit and Mirth: Or Pills to Purge Melancholy*, 1719–20). It was also a favourite on the French stage, and featured in *La Chercheuse d'esprit* (1741), an *opéra comique* by C. S. Favart, to the words 'Ne les laissons point seuls ensemble'.

The poem dates from the seventeenth century, and is said to be from Lorraine. It is a little *scena* based on the annunciation to the shepherds in Luke 1. Although there are no indications of the different characters in the sources we have seen, the division between shepherds (often three in number in traditional dramas) and angels is clear from the text. It may be that Gabriel sings both verses 4 and 5, the angel choir singing only verse 6, but the sense of the French suggests our division. The verses may be distributed between four solo voices and consort or choir, but non-dramatic performance is more likely to represent eighteenth-century practice.

PERFORMANCE   (*i*) Voice and continuo; (*ii*) vocal consort/choir and continuo; (*iii*) four tenor/baritone soloists and consort/choir, with continuo *ad lib*. Verse 6 should perhaps be sung tutti only when a choir participates.

192

Quittez, pasteurs
O leave your sheep

(Christmas)

French traditional
(arr. editors)

1. Quit - tez, pas - teurs, Vos bre - bis, vos houl - et - tes, Vo -
1. O leave your sheep, Your lambs that fol - low af - ter! O

- tre ha - meau Et le soin du trou - peau! Chan - gez___ vos___
leave the brook, The pas - ture and the crook! No lon - ger___

pleurs___ En u - ne joie par - fai - te! Al - lez tous a - do - rer
weep:___ Turn weep - ing in - to laugh - ter! O shep - herds, seek your goal:

Un
The

[SOLI]

[SOLI] Un
The

2 Vous le verrez
   Couché dans une étable
Comme un enfant
Nu, pauvre, languissant;
Reconnaissez
   Son amour ineffable
Pour nous venir chercher:
Il est le fidèle Berger!

3 Rois d'Orient!
   L'étoile vous éclaire;
A ce grand Roi
Rendez hommage et foi!
L'astre brillant
   Vous mène à la lumière
De ce Soleil naissant;
Offrez l'or, la myrrhe et l'encens.

2 You'll find him laid
   Within a simple stable,
A Babe new-born,
In poverty forlorn;
In love arrayed,
   A love so deep 'tis able
To search the night for you;
'Tis he! 'tis he, the Shepherd true!

3 O kings so great,
   A light is streaming o'er you,
More radiant far
Than diadem or star.
Forgo your state;
   A Baby lies before you
Whose wonder shall be told:
Bring myrrh, bring frankincense and gold!

*4 Esprit Divin,
    A qui tout est possible,
Percez nos cœurs
De vos douces ardeurs!
Notre destin
    Par vous devient paisible;
Dieu prétend nous donner
Le ciel en venant s'incarner.

French traditional
(Garnier, 1723)

*4 Come, Holy Ghost,
    Of blessings source eternal!
Our hearts inspire
With thy celestial fire!
The heavenly host
    Praise Christ, the Lord supernal,
And sing the peace on earth
God gives us by his holy birth!

vv. 1–3 tr. Alice Raleigh
v. 4 tr. John Rutter

The text of this carol is from P. Garnier's *La Grande Bible renouvelée de noëls* (1723). The tune is a Besançon melody, also associated with the song 'Nanon dormait'.

PERFORMANCE (*i*) Choir; (*ii*) voice and harpsichord. Ornaments: see notes, 189.

193

Il est né, le divin Enfant!
Christ is born a Child on earth!

(Christmas)

French traditional
(arr. editors)

REFRAIN [FULL]

Il est né, le di - vin En - fant! Jou - ez, haut-bois, ré - son - nez, mu - set - tes!_
Christ is born a_ Child on earth! Shawm and_ bag - pipe,_ sound his prai - ses!_

Il est né, le di - vin En - fant! Chan - tons tous son a - vè - ne - ment!
Christ is born a_ Child on earth! Sing we all his_ ho - ly_ birth!

VERSE [S. A. SOLI]

1. De - puis plus de qua - tre_ mille ans Nous le pro - met - taient les pro - phè - tes;
1. Twice two thou - sand years_ and_ more Pro - phets have fore - told his co - ming;

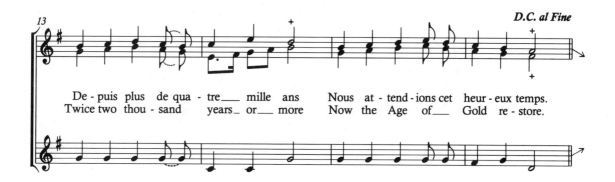

D.C. al Fine

De - puis plus de qua - tre___ mille ans   Nous at - tend - ions cet heur - eux temps.
Twice two thou - sand   years_ or__ more   Now the Age of__ Gold re - store.

2 Ah! qu'il est beau, qu'il est charmant!
   Ah! que ses grâces sont parfaites!
   Ah! qu'il est beau, qu'il est charmant!
   Qu'il est doux, ce divin Enfant!

3 O Jésus, O Roi tout-puissant,
   Tout petit Enfant que vous êtes,
   O Jésus, O Roi tout-puissant,
   Régnez sur nous entièrement!

French traditional

2 See his grace and beauty mild;
   See his charms in all perfection!
   See his grace and beauty mild;
   Soft he lies, this holy Child!

3 Jesu, man and God in one,
   Helpless babe and King all-powerful;
   Jesu, man and God in one,
   Hail thy rule on earth begun!

tr. editors

The text was first published in Dom G. Legeay's *Noëls anciens* (1875–6). The earliest publication of the tune seems to be R. Grosjean's *Airs des noëls lorrain* (1862), where it is called 'Ancien air de chasse'; the old Normandy hunting tune 'Tête bizarde' is very similar, though in 6/8 time. Perhaps the most likely origin is an eighteenth-century piece in rustic style, and we have harmonized it accordingly.

PERFORMANCE   (*i*) Solo voice (or four solo voices) and continuo; (*ii*) soprano and alto duet with bass viol playing the second stave throughout; (*iii*) choir. Ornaments: see notes, 189.

194

Berger, secoue ton sommeil profond!

Shepherd, shake off your drowsy sleep!

(Christmas)

French traditional
(arr. editors)

1. Ber - ger, se - coue ton som - meil pro - fond! Lève - toi et lai - sse tes
1. Shep-herd, shake off your drow - sy sleep! Rise and leave__ your

mou - tons jou - er! An - ges du ciel, chan - tant très fort,____
sil - ly sheep! An - gels from heaven a - round are sing - ing,

Ap - por - tez nous la gran - de___ nou - vel - le. *Ber - ger, en chœur chan -*
Ti - dings of___ great joy___ are bring - ing. *Shep-herd, the cho - rus*

- tez   No - ël!   O____ chan - tez,____ chan - tez____ No - ël!
come   and   swell!   Sing____ No - el!____ O   sing____ No - el!

2 Vois comme les fleurs s'ouvrent de nouveau,
   Vois que la neige est rosée d'été,
  Vois les étoiles brillent de nouveau,
   Jetant leurs rayons les plus lumineux.

2 See how the flowers all burst anew,
   Thinking snow is summer dew;
  See how the stars afresh are glowing,
   All their brightest beams bestowing.

3 Berger, levez-vous, hâtez-vous!
   Allez chercher l'Enfant avant le jour.
  Il est l'espoir de chaque nation,
   Tous en lui trouveront la rédemption.

3 Shepherd, then up and quick away!
   Seek the Babe ere break of day.
  He is the hope of every nation,
   All in him shall find salvation.

French traditional

Traditional translation

The text is possibly eighteenth-century; the tune was included in *La Clef des chansonniers* (1717) among the tunes 'more than a century old', and associated with the words 'L'Échelle du temple'.

PERFORMANCE (*i*) Solo voice (or four solo voices) and continuo; (*ii*) choir, with organ *ad lib*. Ornaments: see notes, 189.

195

Les anges dans nos campagnes
Angels we have heard on high
Angels, we have heard your voices

I

(Christmas)

French traditional
(arr. editors)

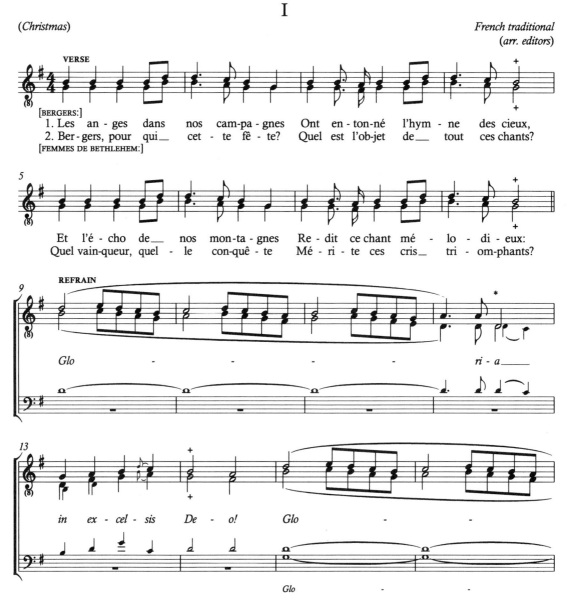

VERSE

[BERGERS:]
1. Les an - ges dans nos cam-pa-gnes Ont en-ton-né l'hym - ne des cieux,
2. Ber - gers, pour qui__ cet - te fê - te? Quel est l'ob-jet de__ tout ces chants?

[FEMMES DE BETHLEHEM:]

Et l'é - cho de__ nos mon-ta-gnes Re - dit ce chant mé - lo - di - eux:
Quel vain-queur, quel - le con-quê - te Mé - ri - te ces cris__ tri - om-phants?

REFRAIN

Glo - - - - ri - a____

in ex - cel - sis De - o! Glo - -

Glo - -

*See performance note.

634

- - - ri - a_____ in ex - cel - sis De - o!

- rīa, glo - ri - a_____

[BERGERS:]

3 Ils annoncent la naissance
    Du Libérateur d'Israël;
  Et, pleins de reconnaissance,
    Chantent en ce jour solennel:

[FEMMES:]

4 Cherchons tous l'heureux village
    Qui l'a vu naître sous ses toits;
  Offrons-lui le tendre hommage
    Et de nos cœurs et de nos voix:

[TOUS:]

5 Dans l'humilité profonde
    Où vous paraissez à nos yeux,
  Pour vous louer, Dieu du monde,
    Nous redirons ce chant joyeux:

[BERGERS:]

*6 Déjà, par la bouche de l'ange,
    Par les hymnes des chérubins,
  Les hommes savent les louanges
    Qui se chantent aux parvis divins:

[FEMMES:]

*7 Bergers, quittez vos retraites,
    Unissez-vous à leurs concerts,
  Et que vos tendres musettes
    Fassent retentir les airs.

[TOUS:]

*8 Dociles à leur exemple,
    Seigneur, nous viendrons désormais
  Au milieu de votre temple,
    Chanter avec eux vos bienfaits:

French traditional
(Smidt, 1932)

TRANSLATION 1 [SHEPHERDS:] The angels have sung the celestial hymn on our plains, and the echo of our mountains repeats this melodious song: Glory to God in the highest!

2 [WOMEN OF BETHLEHEM:] Shepherds, what do you celebrate? Why all these songs? What victor, what conquest, inspires these triumphant cries? Glory to God in the highest!

3 [SHEPHERDS:] They [the angels] announce the birth of the Saviour of Israel; and, full of gratitude, they sing on this solemn day: Glory to God in the highest!

4 [WOMEN:] Let us all seek the fortunate village which has seen him born beneath its roofs! Let us offer to him the loving homage of both our hearts and our voices: Glory to God in the highest!

5 [ALL:] In the deep humility in which you appear to our eyes, to praise you, God of all the world, we repeat this joyful song: Glory to God in the highest!

6 [SHEPHERDS:] Already, from the mouth of the angel, from the hymns of the cherubim, men know the praises which are sung in the courts of heaven: Glory to God in the highest!

7 [WOMEN:] Shepherds, forsake your haunts: join with their concerts, and let your sweet bagpipes make melodies resound! Glory to God in the highest!

8 [ALL:] Obedient to their [the angels'] example, O Lord, we shall come henceforth into the midst of your temple, to sing with them your blessings: Glory to God in the highest!

II

(*Christmas*)

French traditional
(*arr. Edward Shippen Barnes, 1887–1958*)

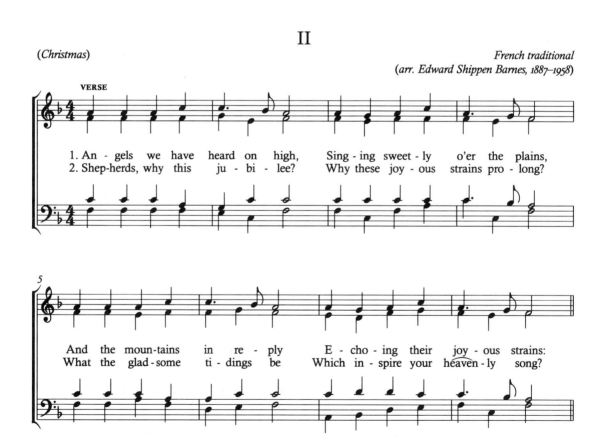

1. An - gels we have heard on high, Sing - ing sweet - ly o'er the plains,
2. Shep-herds, why this ju - bi - lee? Why these joy - ous strains pro - long?

And the moun-tains in re - ply E - cho - ing their joy - ous strains:
What the glad - some ti - dings be Which in - spire your heaven - ly song?

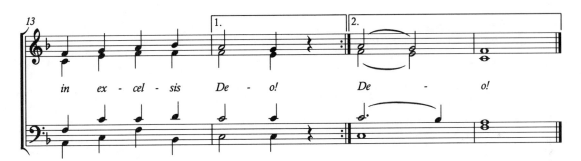

3 Come to Bethlehem and see
   Him whose birth the angels sing;
   Come, adore on bended knee
   Christ the Lord, the new-born King!

4 See him in a manger laid,
   Whom the choirs of angels praise;
   Mary, Joseph, lend your aid,
   While our hearts in love we raise.

H. F. Hémy (1818–88),
after James Chadwick (1813–82)

III

(*Christmas*)

1 Angels, we have heard your voices,
   Sweetly singing o'er the plains;
   Mount, and crag and hill replying,
   Echo still your joyous strains:

2 Shepherds, why this jubilation?
   Why this ecstasy of song?
   Tell us what may be the tidings
   That inspired the heavenly throng?

3 Come and see in Bethlem's city
   Him whose birth the angels sing;
   And, on bended knee, adore him,
   Christ the Lord, the new-born King!

4 See, within a manger lying,
   Jesus, Lord of heaven and earth;
   Aid us, Mary, aid us, Joseph,
   To acclaim our Saviour's birth.

Free tr., R. R. Terry (1865–1938)

'Les anges dans nos compagnes' (I) is described by J. P. Migne (*Troisième et Dernière Encyclopédie théologique, tome 63, Dictionnaire de noëls et cantiques,* 1867) as an 'old *noël* from Lorraine', but no printed source has been found earlier than the Abbé Lambillotte's *Choix de cantiques sur des airs nouveaux* (1842). (Exhaustive inquiries among elderly French-Canadian singers by Ernest Myrand, for his *Noëls anciens de la Nouvelle-France,* Quebec, 1907, confirmed that these carols had been unknown in their childhood but suddenly appeared and achieved wide popularity in the 1840s. Since Lambillotte's book was on sale in Canada from 1842, this would appear to be the source.) J. R. H. de Smidt (*Les Noëls et la tradition populaire,* 1932) dates the carol *c.*1800, but both text and music would seem to support the more general belief that it is an eighteenth-century *noël,* probably from Lorraine or Provence; and since it was usual for such texts to be written for existing tunes (no newly composed *noël* tune is known from the whole of the eighteenth century), the melody may well be older.

We have taken the text from Smidt, who follows Henri Lemeignen's *Vieux Noëls composés en honneur de la naissance de Notre-Seigneur Jésus-Christ* (Nantes, 1876, vol. III). Verses 1–4 and 7 indicate that it originated as a dialogue, though we have not found it printed as such in any source. The 'women of Bethlehem', etc., are thus our invention.

The clipped form of the tune in setting II is the one that was always sung in England until it was displaced by Martin Shaw's harmonization of another variant in *The Oxford Book of Carols* (1928). It is still sung by American congregations. (For Shaw's harmonization see 'Angels, from the realms of glory', 96:1. Montgomery's text, to which it is set, has no connection with the *noël* text. The Oxford editors brought the two together because of the coincidental similarity of Montgomery's first line to that of the *noël*.) The tune is found in virtually identical form in W. A. Pickard-Cambridge's *Collection of Dorset Carols* (1926, harmonized by the editor) and in the 1940 and later editions of the standard American Episcopalian *Hymnal* (with the harmonization by Edward Shippen Barnes which we give here).

The English text seems to have originated as 'The angels we have heard on high', a free imitation of the French by James Chadwick (1813–82), Roman Catholic Bishop of Hexham and Newcastle. It first appeared, with the 'English' tune, in *The Holy Family Hymns* (London, 1860). The adaptation of Chadwick's text that we give (II) was included in the Newcastle composer Henri Friedrich

Hémy's *The Crown of Jesus Music* (1864), and many different versions followed. The carol somehow passed into common use in the West Country: R. R. Chope gives it in his *Carols for Use in Church* (1877) as 'Bright angel hosts are heard on high', describing it as 'Cornish, alt[ered] by R. R. C.', while in Pickard-Cambridge's *Collection of Dorset Carols* (where it is marked 'West Country generally') it begins as Hémy but diverges in verse 4 (as does Chope) to avoid calling on Mary and Joseph:

> See, within a manger laid,
> Jesus, Lord of heaven and earth,
> Lend your voices, lend your aid,
> To proclaim the Saviour's birth!

R. R. Terry's adaptation (III), described as 'a cento from Bishop Chadwick', appeared with his own setting in his *Two Hundred Folk Carols* (1933), the clipped endings of lines 2 and 4 having been restored.

A revised version of Hémy's adaptation, by Earl Marlatt, appeared in H. Augustine Smith's 1937 Episcopalian *New Church Hymnal* (of which both Barnes and Marlatt were associate editors), and it was taken up in the same form in the 1940 *Hymnal,* from which it passed into common use in many denominations.

G. R. Woodward's 'Shepherds in the fields abiding' (*Songs of Syon,* 1910), sometimes sung to the tune in England, is a free translation 'after an ancient Antiphon'.

PERFORMANCE I, four voices or four-part choir. The shepherds' verses may be taken by tenors and basses, singing the upper parts in the refrain to bar 14 (the basses taking the small notes in bars 12–13), the full choir singing the repeat of 'Gloria' (bars 15–21). The women of Bethlehem's verses may be taken by sopranos and altos in a similar fashion. In the full verses, bars 1–8 may be sung at both octaves.

Alternatively, our dialogue instructions might be ignored, and high and low voices could split each verse between them (bars 1–4, 5–8) or alternate from verse to verse.

Ornaments: see notes, 189.

II, voices and organ. An element of dialogue might be introduced (as in I, above) in a scheme such as the following: verse 1, men's voices (choir); verse 2, upper voices (choir); verse 3, full choir; verse 4, choir and congregation. Refrains: bars 9–14, full choir; bars 15–21, choir and congregation.

196

Birjina gaztettobat zegoen
The angel Gabriel from heaven came

I

(Annunciation; Christmas)

Basque traditional
(Bordes, 1895, arr. editors)

1. Bir - ji - na gaz - te - tto - bat ze - go - en_____ Kre -
2. Ain - gu - ri - a sar - tzen, di - o - la - rik:_____ 'A -

-a - za - le Jao - na - ren o - thoi - tzen,_____ Nou -
-gour, gra - zi - az zi - ra be - ther - ik,_____ Jao -

-iz et' ain - gu - ru - bat le - hi - a - tu - ki Bei -
-na da zou - re - kin, be - ne - di - ka - tu_____ Zi -

-tzen ze - lu - tik jai - tchi Min - tza - tze - ra_____ ha - ren._____
-ra e - ta_____ hai - ta - tu E - ma - tzen ga - ñe - tik.'_____

3 Maria ordian duluratu,
Eta bere beithan gogaratu
Zeren zian ouste gabe entzuten
Houra agour erraiten,
Hanbat zen lotsatu.

4 'Etzitela, ez, lotza, Maria:
Jinkoatan bathu' zu grazia:
Zuk duzu sabelian ernaturen,
Eta haorbat sorthuren
Jesus datiana.'

639

5 Harek, duluraturik, harzara:
  'Bena noula izan daite hola,
  Etzu danaz gizounik ezagutzen,
  Ez eta ezaguturen
  Batere sekula?'

6 'Ezpiritu saintiak hountia
  Izanen duzu hori, Maria.'
  Zu zirateke, ber ordian, ama
  Bai et'ere birjina,
  Mundian bakhoitza.

7 Mariak arrapostu ordian:
  'Hao naizu Jinkoren zerbutchian,
  Zuk errana nitan biz konplitu.'
  Jaona aragitu
  Heren sabelian.

8 O Jinkoaren ama saintia,
  Bekhatugilen urgaitzarria,
  Zuk gitzatzu lagunt, bai Jinkoaren,
  Baita berthutiaren
  Bihotzez mait hatzen.

Eighteenth-century (?) Basque
(Bordes, 1895)

TRANSLATION 1 A young maiden was worshipping the Lord of Creation when an angel descended precipitously from the heavens to speak with her.

2 The angel entered, saying: 'Hail! thou who art full of grace; the Lord is with thee; thou art blessed and elect above all women.'

3 Mary was troubled, and wondered why she was hearing the angel greet her in this fashion; she was sore afraid.

4 'Be not afraid, Mary! Thou hast found grace with God; thou shalt conceive in thy womb and shalt bring forth a Son who shall be Jesus.'

5 She, troubled once more, [replied]: 'But how may this come to pass, since I know not a man, nor shall know one—no, not one?'

6 'The Holy Spirit will take care of all that, Mary. Thou shalt be at the same time a mother and also a maiden: thou alone of all the world.'

7 Mary replied thus: 'Behold the handmaid of God! May what you speak of come to pass in me!' And the Word was made flesh within her womb.

8 O Mary, blessed saint of God, refuge of sinners, teach us to love with all our heart both the Saviour and virtue.

II

(*Annunciation; Christmas*)

Basque traditional (Bordes, 1895,
arr. Edgar Pettman, 1865–1943)

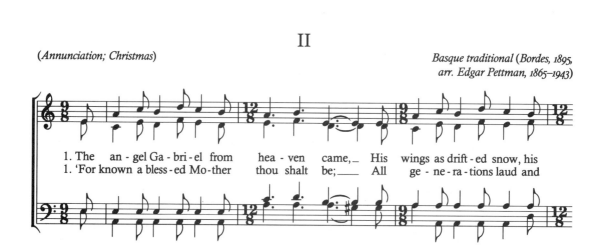

1. The   an - gel Ga - bri - el from   hea - ven   came,   His   wings as drift - ed snow, his
1. 'For known a bless - ed Mo - ther   thou shalt   be;   All   ge - ne - ra - tions laud and

† See notes.

3 Then gentle Mary meekly bowed her head;
'To me be as it pleaseth God!' she said.
'My soul shall laud and magnify his holy
Name.'
Most highly favoured lady! Gloria!

4 Of her Emmanuel, the Christ, was born,
In Bethlehem, all on a Christmas morn;
And Christian folk throughout the world
will ever say:
Most highly favoured lady! Gloria!

English version by
Sabine Baring-Gould (1834–1924)

One of the best-known Basque carols in England. It was collected by Charles Bordes and appeared at the beginning of his volume *Douze Noëls populaires* in the series *Archives de la tradition basque* (1895), to which he also contributed the volume *Dix Cantiques populaires basques*.

Bordes was an active musician, a composer and an assiduous scholar with an interest in early music, and he had already been active in collecting French folk music. In 1889–90 the Bureau des Archives de la Tradition Basque, which had been set up by the Ministère de l'Instruction Publique, commissioned him to travel in the French Basque country, 'and there he received from the mouth of the people over 200 songs of various kinds, almost all of them unpublished'. His publication stands head and shoulders above similar collections, and remains a primary source. The melodies are unharmonized, and the texts are edited by J.-F. Larrien, who also provided French prose translations. Bordes's work on Basque music stimulated him to compose a *Suite basque* for flute and string quartet (1888) and a *Rhapsodie basque* for piano and orchestra (1890).

Whatever the provenance of 'Birjina gaztettobat zegoen' and 'Oi Betleem!' (197), the texts are sophisticated literary productions, presumably by a Basque cleric. Perhaps they are from a publication (of the eighteenth century?) which caught the public imagination, and came to be sung to folk tunes; or, as in the usual French tradition, perhaps the texts were written to fit existing folk-song melodies.

Dix Cantiques populaires basques has a notice which throws light on the motives of the Bureau: 'It is felt that the memory of the people preserves a lost Basque culture which is to be restored to scholars and artists in the hope of a new flowering in imitation of the old.' The patrimony of the people was to be returned into their hands, to which end a cheap 'Edition vulgaire [in the Basque tongue] à l'usage des populations rurales' was printed in addition to the French edition. Whether the rural Basques bought back their patrimony we do not know, but the French edition was avidly seized upon by several British musicians, always eager for fresh carol material. R. R. Terry set a number of items (including the present one and 'Oi Betleem!'), and George Oldroyd set the entire volume, both composers using English translations. But it was Pettman's settings of 'Birjina' and 'Oi Betleem!' that caught the public's fancy, and they have remained extremely popular.

Pettman was organist of St James's Church, Piccadilly, and a prolific composer of Christmas carols. He had a flair for simple, characterful arrangements, and few scruples about altering his material to suit his whim (see 'I saw a maiden', 109:II, for a Basque melody to which he fitted an old English text and added new music for the refrain). In the present case he changed the cadences in bars 4 and 8 of his setting (II) to conform with the 'Olde Englishe' taste of the time, and so deeply imprinted on the English choir-master's psyche have his flattened leading notes become that we have even seen 'corrected' copies of Oldroyd's setting of Bordes's original melody. The small notes in the penultimate bar are alternatives: Pettman published both readings.

The other great merit of Pettman's settings of this carol and 'Oi Betleem!' is their texts, which do not attempt to mirror the Basque, a spacious language which has English translators searching for words to fill up the long lines. In this case, Baring-Gould (see notes, 197) conveys the gist of the original eight stanzas in four of great refinement.

PERFORMANCE   I, one or two voices, at any suitable pitch, with instrumental or vocal drone; II, choir.

In the Basque text all pairs of vowels except 'ia', 'oa', and 'oe' are to be treated as a single syllable.

197

Oi Betleem!
Sing lullaby!

I

(Christmas)

Basque traditional
(Bordes, 1895, arr. editors)

1. Oi Bet - le - em! A - la e - gun zou - re glo - ri - ak, Oi Bet - le - em! Ha - nitch bei - tu dis - ti - at - zen! Zou - re ga - nik hel - tu ar - gi - ak, Be - that - zen tu baz - ter gu - zi - ak, Oi Bet - le - em!

2 Zer ouhoure!
　Ala beizira goratia,
Zer ouhoure!
Zer grazia, zer fabore!
　Zeliak zira haitatia
　Jesus haorraren sorlekhia,
Zer ouhoure!

3 Askenekoz
　Hor heltzen da Jesus maitia,
Askenekoz.
Ougun laida bihotz oroz;
　Hersi nahi du ifernia,
　Et' ireki gouri zelia
Askenekoz.

4 Gouregatik
　Jinkobat photerez bethia,
Gouregatik
Jaichten da zelu goratik:
　Bai sortzen da Jinko Semia,
　Bitima thonarik gabia,
Gouregatik.

5 Manjateran
　Dago haorrik aberatsena,
Manjateran.
Nourk othe zukian erran
　Zeru lurren jabia dena
　Ikhousiren zela etzana
Manjateran?

6 Artzañekin

   Jiten niz lehiaz zugana

Artzañekin.

   Haien antzo nahiz egin;

     Adoratzen zutut, Mesia,

     Zouri' maiten bihotz guzia

Artzañekin.

7 Eztut deusik

   O Jesus! zouri eskeutzeko,

Eztut deusik,

Bihotz ogendunbat baizik:

     Eskerren zouri buhurtzeko

     Hanbat dohanen phakatzeko,

Eztut deusik.

Basque traditional
(Bordes, 1895)

TRANSLATION 1 O Bethlehem! Ah! how your glory today shines out brightly! The light that comes from you fills every corner.

2 What honour! for you are raised up on high. What grace! What favour! You are chosen of God as the birthplace of the child Jesus.

3 At last we see there the beloved Jesus. Let us praise him with all our heart; he has closed up hell and has opened up heaven for us.

4 For us an all-powerful God comes down from the heights of heaven; yes, he is born the Son of God, the spotless victim.

5 In the manger is the richest of children. Who would ever have predicted that the Lord of heaven and earth would be found lying in a manger?

6 With the shepherds I am impelled to come to you, wishing to do as they do; I worship you, the Messiah, give you all my heart, with the shepherds.

7 I have nothing, O Jesu, to offer you but a guilty heart, to show you my gratitude for all my benefits.

II

(*Christmas*)

Basque traditional (Bordes, 1895, arr. Edgar Pettman, 1865–1943)

1. Sing lul-la-by! Lul-la-by ba-by, now re-cli-ning, Sing lul-la-by! Hush! do not wake the in-fant
2. Sing lul-la-by! Lul-la-by ba-by, now a-sleep-ing, Sing lul-la-by! Hush! do not wake the in-fant

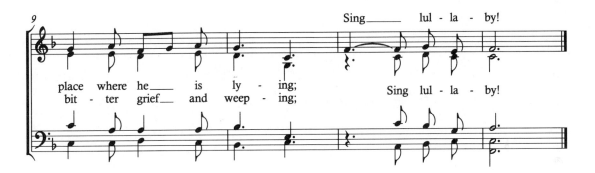

3 Sing lullaby!

Lullaby baby, now a-dozing,

Sing lullaby!

Hush! do not wake the infant King!

Soon comes the Cross, the nails, the piercing,

Then in the grave at last reposing;

Sing lullaby!

4 Sing lullaby!

Lullaby, is the Babe a-waking?

Sing lullaby!

Hush! do not wake the infant King!

Dreaming of Easter, gladsome morning,

Conquering death, its bondage breaking;

Sing lullaby!

Sabine Baring-Gould (1834–1924)

From the same source as 'Birjina gaztettobat zegoen' (196). Pettman's changes to the melody are here confined to the stretching-out of the final cadence.

The text is by Sabine Baring-Gould, clergyman, hagiographer, novelist, religious philosopher, hymn-writer (author of 'Onward! Christian soldiers' and 'Through the night of doubt and sorrow', among others), and an important collector of folk-songs. Unfortunately, the first and last of these roles were often in conflict, and he was frequently horrified at the *doubles entendres* in the songs he transcribed. (It is his bowdlerized version of 'Strawberry Fair' that has preserved the innocence of generations of schoolchildren.)

Baring-Gould had a remarkable gift for providing English texts of real poetic merit for foreign carols. They are not necessarily translations, but contrive to capture the atmosphere of the originals with great accuracy. For 'Oi Betleem!' he produced an entirely new text which is no less effective for imitating such German folk carols as 'Schlaf wohl, du Himmelsknabe du' (178) in its mingling of a lullaby for the infant Christ with anticipation of his Passion and Resurrection.

PERFORMANCE I, two voices, at any suitable pitch, with instrumental or vocal drone *ad lib.*; II, choir.

In the Basque text all pairs of vowels except 'ia', 'oa', and 'oe' are to be treated as a single syllable.

198

El desembre congelat
Cold December's winds were stilled

(*Christmas*)

Catalan traditional
(arr. editors)

1. El de-sem-bre con-ge-lat, Con-fús es re-ti-ra.
1. Cold De-cem-ber's winds were stilled In the month of snow-ing.

Ab-ril de flors co-ro-nat, Tot el món ad-mi-ra,
Though the world with dark was filled, Spring-time's hope was grow-ing.

Quan en un jar-di d'a-mor Neix u-na di-vi-na flor. D'u-na
Then a rose-tree blos-somed new: One sweet flower up-on it grew; On the

ro-, ro-, ro-, D'u-na -sa, -sa, -sa, D'u-na ro-, d'u-na -sa, D'u-na
tree once bare Grew a rose so fair, Ah! the rose, ah! the rose, Ah! the

ro - sa bel - la,   Fe - cun - da y _ pon - cel - la.
rose tree bloom - ing,   Sweet the air_ per - fu - ming.

2 El primer Pare causá   2 When the darkness fell that night,
      La nit tenevrosa   Bringing sweet reposing,
   Que a tot el mon ofusca   All the world was hid from sight,
      La vista penosa   Sleep men's eyes was closing.
   Mes en una mitja nit   All at once there came a gleam
   Brilla el sol que n'és eixit   From the sky: a wondrous beam
   D'una bel-, bel-, bel-,   Of a heavenly star
   D'una -la, -la, -la,   Giving light afar.
   D'una bel-, d'una -la,   Ah! the star, ah! the star,
   D'una bella aurora   Ah! the star-beam glowing,
   Que el cel enamora.   Brightness ever-growing.

3 El més de maig ha florit,   3 Now the month of May was there,
      Sense ser encara,   Filled with God's own radiance;
   Un lliri blanc y polit   Bloomed a lily, white and fair,
      De fragráncia rara,   Flower of sweetest fragrance;
   Que per to el món se sent,   To the people, far and near,
   De Llevant fins a Ponent,   Came a breath of heavenly cheer.
   Tota sa, sa, sa,   O the incense rare
   Tota dul-, dul-, dul-,   Of the lily there!
   Tota sa, tota dul-,   Ah! the scent, ah! the scent
   Tota sa dulcura   Of the lily blooming,
   I olor, amb ventura.   All the air perfuming!

Catalan traditional   *vv. 1, 2 anon., v. 3 tr. George K. Evans,*
                                              both adapted

We have been unable to trace a Spanish source for this folk carol, which is popular in both the United States and Britain.

The flowering rose tree features in innumerable medieval legends (see notes, 66, 176): here the rose flower is Christ. The star in verse 2 is the Star of Bethlehem; the lily in verse 3 is the traditional emblem of Mary, to whom the month of May is dedicated.

The melody derives from an old drinking-song, 'C'est notre grand pèr Noé', also sung as a *noël* to a variety of texts, including 'Bon Joseph, écoute moi' and 'Quand Dieu naquit à Noël'. There are keyboard settings of the tune by Daquin and others.

PERFORMANCE Choir.

199

Veinticinco de diciembre
Twenty-fifth day of December

(Christmas)

Spanish traditional
(arr. editors)

1. Vein - ti - cin - co de di - ciem-bre, *¡Fum, fum, fum!* *fum!* Na - ci -
1. Twen - ty-fifth day of De - cem-ber, *¡Fum, fum, fum!* *fum!* For the

- do ha por nues-tro a - mor, El Ni - ño Dios, el Ni - ño Dios; Hoy de
love of man is given The ho - ly In - fant, Son of Heaven; Of the

la Vír-gen Ma - rí - a En es - ta no - che tan frí - a, *¡Fum, fum, fum!*
ho - ly Vir - gin spring-ing, Peace on earth and good will bring-ing, *¡Fum, fum, fum!*

2 Pajaritos de los bosques,
  ¡Fum, fum, fum!
Vuestros hijos de coral
Abandonad, abandonad,
Y formad un muelle nido
A Jesús recién nacido,
  ¡Fum, fum, fum!

3 Estrellitas de los cielos,
  ¡Fum, fum, fum!
Que a Jesús miráis llorar
Y no lloráis, y no lloráis,
Alumbrad la noche oscura
Con vuestra luz clara y pura,
  ¡Fum, fum, fum!

                    Spanish traditional

2 Birds that live within the forest,
  Fum, fum, fum!
All your fledglings leave behind,
And seek the infant Saviour kind.
Build, as well as you are able,
Downy nest to be his cradle,
  Fum, fum, fum!

3 Little stars up in the heavens,
  Fum, fum, fum!
If you see the baby cry,
O do not answer with a sigh!
From the skies your radiance beaming,
Pierce the darkness with your gleaming,
  Fum, fum, fum!

                    tr. George K. Evans

In the English-speaking countries this is perhaps the most popular of all Spanish folk carols. It sounds like a dance-song, and the recurring 'Fum, fum, fum!' may imitate the sound of a drum (or perhaps the strumming of a guitar).

PERFORMANCE   (*i*) Voice and guitar; (*ii*) choir.

200

El Noi de la Mare
The Son of the Virgin

(Christmas)

Catalan traditional
(arr. editors)

1. Qué li da - rem a n'el Noi de la Ma - re? Qué li da - rem que li
1. What shall we give to the Son of the Vir - gin? What can we give him that

Ah! _____ Ah! _____

sá - pi - ga bon?___ Li da - rem pan - ses en u - nes ba - lan - ces,
he will en - joy?___ First, we shall give him a tray full of rai - sins,

Li da - rem fi - gues en un pa - ne - ró.___ un pa - ne - ró.
Then we shall of - fer sweet figs to the boy.___ figs to the boy.

650

2 Qué li darem el fillet de Maria,
Qué li darem a l'hermós Infantó?
Panses i figues i nuez i olives,
Panses i figues i mel i mató.

2 What shall we give the belovèd of Mary?
What can we give to her beautiful Child?
Raisins and olives and figs and sweet honey,
Candy and figs and a cheese that is mild.

3 Tam patantam, que les figues son verdes,
Tam patantam, que ja madurarán.
Si no maduren el dia de Pasqua,
Madurarán en el dia del Ram.

3 What shall we do if the figs are not ripened?
What shall we do if the figs are still green?
If by Palm Sunday they still have not ripened,
Yet shall that ripeness at Easter be seen.

Catalan traditional

tr. George K. Evans, adapted

A song of the shepherds. In the third verse the green fig is the innocent Child, its ripening his work of redemption.

PERFORMANCE (*i*) Solo voice or unison voices, with instrumental or vocal drone (on E♭, or E♭ and B♭, throughout); (*ii*) two voices or two-part choir with drone (in this case the first two alto E♭s in the last bar should be sung as Ds); (*iii*) choir.

201

Quando nascette Ninno
When Christ, the Son of Mary

(Christmas)

Neapolitan traditional
(arr. editors)

1. Quan - do nas-cet - te Nin - no a Bet - te - lem - me,__ E - ra not-te a pa-
1. When Christ, the Son of Ma - ry, in Beth - le - hem was born,__ 'Twas night, and yet the

- re - a mmie-zo juor - no! Ma - je le stel - le Lus - te - re
light____ was bright as sum - mer's morn! Stars__ were gleam - ing, Bright - ly

bel - le, Se - ve - det - te - ro ac - cu - si!____ La chiù lu - cen -
beam - ing O'er__ the town__ of Beth - le - hem;____ A bright - er star__ there

- te____ Jet - te à chiam - mà li Ma - gi, in O - ri - en - te.____
shone__ For ma - gi far, a gui - ding star that led them on.____

2 No n'cerano nemice ppe la terra,
La pecora pascia co lo lione,
  Co le crapette
  Se vedette
Lo liopardo pazzià:
  L'urzo e o vitiello,
  E co lu lupo 'npace u pecoriello.

3 Guardavano le pecore lu pasture;
E l'angelo, sbrennente chiù de lu sule,
  Comparette,
  E le dicette:
  'Nò ve spaventate, nò!
  Contento e riso;
  La terra è arrenventata paradiso!'

Neapolitan traditional

2 When Christ, the Son of Mary,
  within her arms was laid,
The lion with the lamb,
  the bear with fatling strayed.
Close to the shepherd
Wandered the leopard,
Every creature was at peace;
  The great and small were one;
For calf or lamb that night no fright,
  but joy, did come.

3 When Christ, the Son of Mary,
  within the crib did lie,
There came to shepherds drowsy
  a voice which sang on high:
'Peace on the earth
Is come with this birth;
Go, seek the Babe in yonder stall,
  Your King, though weak and small;
The world's true light is come this night
  to save you all.'

tr. Gordon Hitchcock, adapted

For many centuries, during the period before Christmas mountain shepherds have descended on Rome, Naples, and other cities in southern Italy and Sicily, clad in sheepskin cloaks and wide-brimmed hats and playing pastoral music on their pipes. William Hone gives an account in his *Ancient Mysteries Described* (1822): 'During the last days of Advent, Calabrian minstrels enter Rome, and are to be seen in every street saluting the shrines of the Virgin mother with their wild music, under the traditional notion of charming her labour-pains on the approaching Christmas. Lady Morgan observed them frequently stopping at the shop of a carpenter . . . the workmen who stood at the door said that it was done out of respect for St Joseph.'

The shepherds traditionally perform 'Quando nascette Ninno' in small groups. If there are two shepherds, one sings while the other plays the *ciaramella* (a small shawm), and then the latter sings while the former plays the *zampogna*, a large, sweet-toned bagpipe with two drones and two chanters, which is played mostly in thirds and sixths with some embellishment. If there are three shepherds, one will usually play the *zampogna* while the other two alternate between vocal duet and voice and *ciaramella*. When there are four, two will sing while the other two play the two instruments. The carol can also be played by *zampogna* alone, or by the two instruments together.

Many eighteenth-century composers used the pastoral *siciliana* rhythm of the Italian shepherds to suggest Christmas: the aria 'And he shall feed his flock' in Handel's *Messiah* is remarkably similar to the melody of 'Quando nascette Ninno', and it is possible that Handel heard it during his time in Rome as a young man, in 1707–9. (The *Pifa* or 'Pastoral Symphony' in the same work uses similar melodic material.) Rimbault, in the preface to his *Collection of Old Christmas Carols* (1861), reproduces an almost identical melody which he claims came from an early seventeenth-century manuscript of Italian *inni* (hymns), but perhaps this is one of his fabrications.

Italian *piffari* and other itinerant musicians were a common sight on the streets of London in the nineteenth century. One of them was interviewed by Henry Mayhew, author of *London Labour and the London Poor* (1851):

I worked on the ground at Naples, in the country, and I guarded sheep . . . In my country they call my instrument de 'zampogna'. All the boys in my country play on it . . . There are four clarinets to it. There is one for the high and the other the low. They drone to make harmony . . . The 'Pastorelle Neapolitan' is very pretty, and so is the 'Pastorelle Romaine' . . . When I go out to guard my sheep I play my zampogna, and I walk along and the sheep follow me . . . sometimes I go into the mountains . . . I can hear the guardians of the sheep playing all around me in the mountains . . . sixteen, twelve, or fifteen, on every side . . . Every night in my village there are four or six who play together instruments like mine, and all the people dance . . . (*Mayhew's London*, 1969).

PERFORMANCE   (*i*) Two voices, or two-part choir, with vocal or instrumental drone; (*ii*) choir; (*iii*) two voices with *zampogna* and *ciaramella* (see above).

APPENDIX 1

Pronunciation of Fifteenth-Century English

No brief discussion of such an intricate subject can hope to be in any way definitive or comprehensive, especially as spellings are such inconsistent indicators of pronunciation. However, much more is known about the sounds of the English language in earlier periods than is commonly supposed, and to ignore the often stronger colours of earlier pronunciation in vocal music can be to lose a vital ingredient. The following suggestions, based on the work of Professor E. J. Dobson, imagine the singer to be an educated mid-fifteenth-century Londoner, and use examples from the texts of carols 24–38. In the pronunciations below, 'modern English' ('mod. Eng.') refers to what is familiar to many as 'BBC English'.

Similar guides to thirteenth- and fourteenth-century English pronunciation may be found in E. J. Dobson and F. Ll. Harrison, *Medieval English Songs* (1979), Appendix 1.

VOWELS

In general, vowels should be brighter, more clearly characterized, and produced further forward in the mouth than in modern English. More words had short vowels, as in current northern English (e.g., *after*, *pass*, *past*, *path*), and the different characters of short and long vowels should not be lost in singing when, for example, a short vowel has to be sung to a long note.

SPELLING	EXAMPLES	PRONUNCIATION	IPA SYMBOL
a (*short*)	sange, whan, what;	as French *patte* (or mod. northern Eng. *man*, *pass*);	a
	all, als, celestiall	before *ll*, or *l* + consonant = au (see below)	
a (*long*)	grace, make, Mary, save, wake	as *a* in mod. Eng. *father*, but to front of mouth	a:
ai/ay	maide; day, hayl, lullay	diphthong, as mod. Eng. *time*	ai
au/aw	aungel, commaund, graunt, servaunt; baw	diphthong, as mod. Eng. *house*	au
e (*short*)	*stressed*: mery, vertu;	as mod. Eng. *men*;	ɛ
	unstressed: Lordes	as *er* in mod. Eng. *father*, sounding of final *e* (as in 'loude') had disappeared from speech and was optional in verse	ə
e (*long*)	credil (*also* pees, conceyve)	as *è* in French *frère*	ɛ:
ee	see (*also* meke, slepe, we)	as *ie* in German *Liebe* (purer than mod. Eng. *see*)	i:
ei/ey	heile, seid; peyne	diphthong, as mod. Eng. *time* (=ai/ay; see above)	ai
eu/ew	bewy, byewsser, natewre, new, trew	diphthong, ee + oo (a clearer version of mod. Eng. *few*)	iu
i/y (*short*)	birde, blis, hir; nyght	as mod. Eng. *bit*	ɪ
i/y (*long*)	milde; aryse, wyf	dipthong, as Australian *tea* (unstressed short e + ee)	əi
o (*short*)	God, Lorde;	as German *Gott* (almost mod. Eng. *god*);	ɔ
	wold;	before *ll*, or *l* + consonant = ou (see below);	

SPELLING	EXAMPLES	PRONUNCIATION	IPA SYMBOL
o (*short*)	com, som	= short u (see below)	
o (*long*)	alone, borys, holi, rose, told, wo	as Italian open *o* (almost as mod. Eng. *laud*, but with lips well rounded)	ɔː
oo	Yoolis (*also* blode, dothe, moder)	as German *gut* (almost as mod. Eng. *boot*, but with a pure vowel)	uː
oi/oy	coynt, joye	diphthong, as mod. Eng. *joy*, with lips initially rounded	ɔɪ
ou/ow	loude, thou, your; down, lullow, now, owt;	diphthong, u (as mod. Eng. *cut*) + oo (as French *fou*), or similar to mod. Eng. *know*;	ʌu
	thought	o (as mod. Eng. *short*) + oo (as French *fou*)	ɔu
u (*short*)	burd, cumpany, murning (*also* com, som)	as mod. Eng. *pull*	ʊ
u (*long*)	humilite, pure (*in most French-derived words*)	diphthong, as eu/ew (see above)	iu
y		see i/y above	
yw	nywe	= eu/ew (see above)	

CONSONANTS

Rarely silent; as in mod. Eng., with the following exceptions or qualifications:

SPELLING	EXAMPLES	PRONUNCIATION
ch	charity, chere, lordchip, worchyp	as mod. Eng. *cheese* (rarely as mod. Eng. *chivalry*)
g (*soft*)	herytag, messag	as mod. Eng. *heritage*, *message*
gh	bright; doghter	as German *Licht* (after *ei* or *i/y*); as German *ach* (after *au* or *o(u)*)
gn		at the front of a word ('gnash') with a hard *g* before the *n*; in the middle of a word ('signal') either as mod. Eng. or as *ngn* in 'dyngnyte' (see below); in 'sign' etc. as mod. Eng. *sign*
h	herytag, humilite; Jhesu	silent (as the first letter of French-derived words); silent
kn	knave, kne, knele	with both consonants sounded
ld	shuld, wold	with both consonants sounded
ng	dyngnyte, kynge, syng	as mod. Eng. *finger* (both consonants fully sounded)
r	birde, hir, mirthe, werk	always lightly trilled
sch	flesch, sche	as mod. Eng. *flesh*, *she*
th	that, thre	voiced or unvoiced, as in mod. Eng. equivalents (but probably voiced in 'merthis')
wh	whan, what	generally with both consonants sounded, the *h* before the *w* (but 'who' often as in mod. Eng.)
wr	wrong	with both consonants sounded

ANDREW PARROTT

The Post-Reformation Hymn:
Liturgical Context and Performance

I. THE GERMAN TRADITION
II. PERFORMANCE SCHEMES IN THE GERMAN TRADITION
III. ENGLISH ORGAN ACCOMPANIMENTS, INTERLUDES, AND GIVINGS-OUT

This Appendix is concerned with the Christmas hymnody of Germany and England between the sixteenth and the mid-nineteenth centuries, and in particular with the role of the organ.

A reverential approach is rarely appropriate to repertories of this kind. A four-voice chorale setting by Michael Praetorius is not a finished art work; it is *Gebrauchsmusik*: a well-crafted piece of performing material, frequently with the most diverse potential and to be used as taste and circumstances dictate. When approaching a particular item, it can be helpful to begin by asking the most basic questions concerning genre, period, location, function, and treatment, whether or not some specific historical context is envisaged in performance: What kind of hymn is this? When and where might it have been sung? What was its status within which service(s)? Who would have sung it, and what forces and what kind of presentation would have been appropriate? The answer to the last question will obviously depend on those previously given: 'Resonet in laudibus' (55), for example, would have been performed very differently at Christmas vespers in a fifteenth-century Rhineland community, at Christmas matins in fifteenth-century Leipzig, at a catechism service in sixteenth-century Hamburg, in the little court chapel at Weimar when Bach was organist, and at evensong in Magdalen College, Oxford, under Sir John Stainer.

The answers to such questions and the various options they raise can help to infuse a much-needed variety into the hymn-singing at Christmas services and concerts. Restoration of some of the lost splendours of historical hymn performance could also help raise what is too often mere mechanical repetition onto a higher artistic level, so lessening the divide between choirs and congregations or carol-concert audiences, and drawing all concerned into a richer and more thoughtful relationship with the sung texts.

I. THE GERMAN TRADITION

A limited number of vernacular hymns were firmly established before the Reformation, and the old tradi-tions of performance were retained and amplified by both Catholics and Lutherans. Luther gave the hymn a central place in Protestant worship, however, and the repertory was greatly expanded by the early reformers, reaching a peak of richness and diversity in the larger town churches, court chapels, etc. between the 1580s and the onset of the Thirty Years War in 1618. Most of the settings of German Christmas hymns that we give in this book are either products of this golden age of Lutheran church music or our own settings in the style of the period.

Germany probably has a wider repertory of traditional Christmas songs—loosely, carols—than any other country, but these found a limited place in the Lutheran song-books. The Catholic Church (which, broadly speaking, retained the southern parts of the German-speaking areas) gave equal status to all permitted non-liturgical song, so that the carol repertory was much more strongly represented in Catholic books. But it was not until the turn of the century that Catholic song-books began to be produced in any numbers, and many of the carol tunes we give—even those with medieval roots—tend as a consequence to have a pronounced early seventeenth-century flavour. Because the Catholic books rarely provide more than text and melody, the harmonizations here are mostly our own, though these, again, often adopt a seventeenth-century idiom.

Congregational song

By tradition, congregations sang *choraliter*: that is unaccompanied, in unison, and at a markedly steady pace. (A *Choral*—chorale—was a plainchant, or any other unison hymn-like melody, though the term eventually came to mean both the tune and the text of a hymn.) The singing was led by a cantor (normally the master of the municipal Latin school) who usually stood in the centre of the nave, in the midst of the congregation. He was often assisted by a professional *chorus choralis* (the unison choir which had sung the concerted plainchant in pre-Reformation times), by the Latin school boys (who would in many places sing the weekday services), or by an amateur *Cantorei*, a kind of middle-class

Friendly Society which rehearsed congregational song privately and led it in the service. In some conservative cities and regions, unaccompanied hymn-singing in unison was still a feature of services well into the eighteenth century and even into the nineteenth in more remote areas; but as the *chorus choralis* gradually fell out of use, the *chorus musicus*, a professional choir singing in harmony, increasingly led the congregational hymns, as it did in St Mary's, Lübeck, and the Leipzig churches from about the mid-eighteenth century. Congregations sang almost entirely in the vernacular, except in such special cases as the services of Latin schools and universities.

In the early days of Lutheranism, the hymns and their unharmonized tunes were issued in unpretentious little books, from which the cantors and clergy taught the new repertory to their congregations. The rhythmic forms of many of the new tunes were difficult for congregations to memorize, and they were by no means universally sung as notated. Some, indeed, had been composed as unmeasured melody, and had only subsequently been rhythmicized, in the manner of the subtle solo art of the *Meistersinger*; others had been lifted direct by the printers from the elaborated forms used as the tenors of polyphonic settings, which were quite inappropriate to unison performance. As cantors and congregations assimilated the new tunes, they automatically simplified and adapted the notated rhythms, sometimes according to local conventions or folk-song traditions. Where pre-Reformation songs and hymns were still used (their texts purged of unacceptable doctrines), the local forms of the tunes were usually retained, whatever the 'official' notated version might be. In this way a multitude of local variants developed at an early stage (in many cases even within a single town).

The tunes mutated further as fashions changed over the years and the rhythmic subtleties of the early Lutheran tunes came to seem wilfully irregular. The process was partly conscious, in the published songbooks, and partly automatic, as the rhythmic features of the old chorales were ground away under the weight of massed singing at ever slower speeds. In the course of the seventeenth century the two oldest strata of specifically Lutheran tunes, those from the founding fathers and from the later sixteenth century, were generally transformed into a single, monorhythmic, 'solemn' type: a succession of equal note values varied only by the double-length concluding note of each line.

A contrary tendency towards elaboration was apparent from the later seventeenth century onward. The old tunes, having been rhythmically (and often melodically) simplified, were now progressively adorned with passing notes and other figures. The old hymn and carol tunes were similarly elaborated in the Catholic tradition, so that the tune of 'Joseph, lieber' (55:IV), for example, was sung in Mozart's Salzburg with its bold triadic opening softened into a flowing, conjunct-motion line—which is how he set it in an early symphony (see notes, 55).

In the later seventeenth century the natural tendency of unaccompanied singing to slow down was exacerbated by the concern of the increasingly dominant Pietist faction for 'seemliness' and a 'devotional character' in congregational singing. (The Methodists, in contrast, their eighteenth-century near-equivalents in Britain, preferred lively tunes and played an important part in reversing the same process there.) After the sustained final note of each line, the singers would take a *Luftpause*: a break during which they would draw breath while reading or recalling the following line. The *Luftpausen* became gradually longer as the singing slowed down, and organists began to fill these gaps with the passagework or other figuration of interline interludes, which are discussed below.

The slowing-down process continued into the nineteenth century in many places. Where there were no organs, as in much of rural Sweden before the twentieth century, speeds became so phenomenally slow as to precipitate a process analogous to the 'old way of singing' in seventeenth-century England, elaborate congregational embellishment effectively subdividing the unsingably slow pulse of the chorale melody into smaller units. Elsewhere, such extremes cannot have been reached, and the overall picture has been confused by the widespread credence given to what must be a misinterpretation by Arno Werner in his *Vier Jahrhunderte im Dienste der Kirchenmusik* ('Four centuries in the service of church music', 1932) of a nineteenth-century report of the singing at Baden. 'Each syllable' of a chorale is said to have been held for four slow beats, with the last note of each line dragged out to ten or twelve. There is a confusion of terminology here, and what was being described was almost certainly the prolongation of the final syllable (= note) of each line for four beats, while the last of each verse was extended to ten or twelve, enabling the organist to improvise (*präludieren*) a *Choralschluss* or 'chorale ending' against it. Volume III of Justin Heinrich Knecht's *Vollständige Orgelschule* (1795–8) gives examples of such perorations, to be substituted in his model chorale accompaniments for the last cadence of the final verse only: these typically last for ten beats, with a final pause. Perhaps the Baden practice was identical, or perhaps a *Choralschluss* was applied to every verse there.

We can get an idea of just how slow was 'slow' in Bach's Weimar from the notation of his accompaniments to congregational Christmas hymns (discussed below). As with English examples of interline preludes, an optimum speed for the passagework is usually fairly easy to establish—not so fast as to be unplayable, nor so slow as to lose its brilliant effect—and from this the speed of the melody which he had in mind can generally be worked out: it is by no means as slow as those suggested by comparable English examples.

We follow the modern Lutheran consensus in favouring the melodic forms (and in our case the settings) of the first half of the seventeenth century, when the earliest tunes had lost what to modern ears seems their primitive strangeness yet still retained their freshness. Such forms of the tunes, moreover, are as yet unwarped by the slowing-down process, and they lend themselves equally readily to unison and to harmonized or accompanied performance. This is one reason for our concentration on the settings of Praetorius, which were published in the first decade of the century.

The chorus musicus: complex performance schemes

Quite separate from the *chorus choralis* was the *chorus musicus* (also called the *chorus figuralis*). This was a professional choir which in many places drew its trebles and altos from the boys of the local Latin school. It sang chorales in harmony, and its contributions might be accompanied by the main organ and (in larger churches) by instruments, supplemented by those of the town waits on major festivals. The usual home of the *chorus musicus* was the western organ loft. By 1600 many larger churches had additional smaller organs and regals, permanently installed or portable, which would be deployed in galleries and other locations around the building. Soloists and small groups of voices and instruments (some with these organs, others in more remote spots with non-organ continuo) would combine in the grandest hymns on high feast-days. The smaller groups might even be hidden from view, to increase the surprise and delight of the congregation as the invisible musicians contrasted or combined with the main body of performers.

A favourite inherited tradition was the singing of hymns in verse-by-verse alternation with the congregation, one of the many forms of *Wechselgesang* (antiphonal song). Sometimes the choir would sing each verse in Latin and the congregation repeat it in German translation, the contrast in speeds and between harmonized/unison singing being an integral part of the effect. Or the *chorus musicus* might take alternate verses (usually the odd-numbered ones; when there was an odd number overall, the congregation would sing the final pair). Some ancient Christmas hymns took the *Wechselgesang* principle yet further, intermingling the stanzas of different hymns and sharing them among different groups in the church (see carols 55, 57, and 59). The various groups (including the congregation) would divide each verse between them, combining for the last section. Smaller groups might interpose individual phrases within a long stanza: in 'Resonet in laudibus/Joseph, lieber Joseph mein' (55), for example, three sections of the long refrain could be spread around the building; the little phrase 'Eia! eia!' could

come from one (or two) hidden groups, or the second 'Eia!' could be tutti. The variations are endless, the one basic rule being that the same pattern should be adhered to in each verse. We provide a full complement of English singing translations of most of the relevant hymns, in the hope that choirs will begin to recover some of the glories of this fascinating performing tradition.

Friedrich Blume (*Protestant Church Music*, 1974) emphasizes the 'multiplicity of performance possibilities' for hymns, and the freedom with which music directors would deploy them: 'The [ecclesiastical] performance practice of the time . . . probably made practical use of all types of musical presentation.' Published and documented schemes by no means exhaust these possibilities; the same striving for freshness and variety that characterized the treatment of individual hymns must equally have been a feature of festal services in their entirety, though always governed by liturgical needs and propriety. The main gradual hymn of the day or feast, for example, might be performed with the maximum of contrast and splendour; another might be sung quite straightforwardly. Among the options was the performance of a hymn entirely by congregation, choir, or organ. Communion hymns could be very extended affairs, with different techniques of organ interluding or replacement. Some of the extended sets of chorale partitas and variations from the later baroque period may have been interspersed with sung verses, for example, or may have replaced them entirely during the lengthy distribution of communion, their expressive interpretation of the unheard text being followed devoutly by the worshippers.

The earliest publication of chorales with music (Johann Walter's *Geistliches Gesangbüchlein*, 1524, produced under Luther's supervision) gives tunes not in the simple congregational form that we might expect, but as *cantus firmi* within ornate polyphonic settings. Typically the tune is in the tenor, freely embellished, and like the plainchant of a contemporary Catholic setting it also permeates the other parts. Walther also pioneered a much simpler style of four-part choral setting based on the style of the *Tenor-Lied*, with the melody in the tenor and the part-writing tending towards homophony and more modern, non-modal harmony. From the beginning, then, there was a two-directional thrust in Lutheran hymn settings: towards the complexity of traditional Catholic polyphony, and towards a new simplicity which would soon give rise to the homophonic, treble-tune harmonizations of the Cantional tradition (see below). Thus the seeds of this second (and eventually triumphant) strand of congregational singing, with choral and/or instrumental harmonic support, were present from the earliest days.

Both types of setting could be performed in two ways: with voices on each line or with the *cantus firmus* melody sung by a soloist and the other parts taken by instruments or organ. They were normally printed with the text of only the first verse underlaid, but this had no special significance. The elaborate first type might most naturally precede and/or replace the congregational first verse, or follow or replace the last; it could also replace any particularly important verse(s) within the hymn. The simpler second type could very effectively replace or alternate with the congregational verses.

In Lucas Osiander's 1586 collection of hymns and metrical psalms, the *Fünffzig geistliche Lieder und Psalmen*, we find for the first time choral hymn settings that are professedly designed for congregational participation—the choir sings in simple, root-position, note-against-note harmony, with the tune clearly audible in the soprano. This inaugurated a whole new line of similar but less restricted Cantional settings and books, amongst which volumes V, VI, and VII of Praetorius's *Musae Sioniae* (1605–10) are by far the most encyclopaedic, covering the bulk of the local variants and providing the widest possible variety of settings. The Osiander note-against-note style is followed in Praetorius's volume VII, which is devoted specifically to congregational settings.

Although we draw freely on Praetorius in this book, we have preferred the rather more varied choral harmonizations of volume V, in deference to the usual modern practice of verse-by-verse repetition of a single setting. It could on occasion be effective to confine the setting that we give to choir and organ (and/or instruments), alternating it with congregation and organ verses sung to a volume VII setting. Those in volumes VI and VII are well suited to incorporation within abbreviated versions of the more extended multi-verse schemes of volume V, which are intended to be mined as well as used complete. Care should be taken to choose either the same version of the melody or a similar one, adapting the music if necessary so that the two match: there is nothing sacrosanct about such *Kapellmeister* music. See the performance schemes below for ways in which carols in this book can be combined with other Praetorius settings to put together many different schemes.

Organ accompaniment

In the early sixteenth century, Catholic and Lutheran organists tended to be 'coarse and obstinate fellows' (in Blume's phrase), endlessly in dispute with the church authorities, constantly exhorted to play sacred music rather than love-songs and dances, and silently tolerated rather than specified or banned in the early Lutheran church orders. But there seems to have been a gradual improvement in standards and attitudes, culminating among Lutherans in a carefully worded statement by the Wittenberg Theological Faculty in 1597 which characterized organ music as 'unobjectionable'.

Coming from the nearest thing to a centralized authority in the Lutheran Church, this virtually constituted official acceptance.

Organ accompaniment for congregational hymns was almost unknown in the sixteenth century. The earliest references are to sporadic use (in the Hamburg *Melodeyen Gesangbuch*, 1604, and a Danzig regulation of 1609 requiring organ accompaniment during communion hymns), but it spread only slowly and was by no means universal even in the nineteenth century.

The different ways in which the organ could be involved in congregational hymns from *c*.1600 to the early nineteenth century may be summarized as follows (see Peter Williams, *The Organ Music of J. S. Bach*, vol. 3, 1984, pp. 10–12):

(*i*) The organ provides a prelude and inter-verse interludes, but is silent during the actual singing.

(*ii*) The organ provides a prelude, accompanies the verses (in vocal-style four-part harmony, from a figured bass, or in an idiomatic keyboard style), and provides short interline interludes.

(*iii*) As (*ii*) but without the interludes.

(*iv*) As (*ii*) but with a pitch-setting intonation or *praeambulum* rather than a full-scale prelude.

See the performance schemes below for typical procedures *c*.1600 and a full range of more specialized schemes from Praetorius.

Giving out the tune: chorale preludes

The organ made individual contributions in the Lutheran service more impressively, on a larger scale, and in a less 'reformed' manner than in any other Protestant Church. In most ways Catholic practice paralleled that of the Lutherans.

When a hymn involving the organ was to be sung, the organist's job was to 'give out' the whole, or only half, of the tune in what is nowadays generally called a 'chorale prelude' (*Choralvorspiel*). (When there was some liturgical activity to be covered after the singing of a chorale, the organist might also provide a postlude in a comparable style, though this was much less usual.) The tendency in such 'preluding' was always away from the functional and towards the decorative, and embellishments, contrapuntal elaborations, and bravura flourishes would routinely throw up a smoke screen around the tune, giving rise to periodic demands for reform. (It was to deal with this problem that hymn-boards were introduced, as early as 1701 in Buxtehude's church of St Mary's, Lübeck, and in 1714 in Bach's court chapel at Weimar; in St Mary's, from the mid-eighteenth century the organ prelude seems to have been replaced by choral givings-out, from a complete collection of simple four-part settings which had been assembled by the cantor.) It is possible that the preludes of Bach's *Orgelbüchlein* were intended as models, combining as they do decorative figuration, which 'expresses' or 'interprets' the text, with a clearly audible presentation of the melody.

Short pitch-setting intonations in the Italian tradition were common, and were particularly appropriate for a single stanza sung after the communion, for instance (the published *intonazioni* of the two Gabrielis are late sixteenth-century examples). In some places at least, these seem to have developed into more impressive contrapuntal *praeambula*, some of which made use of the chorale melody. Alternatively, the organist might introduce a hymn with a short dance or an excerpt from some other secular or sacred work in the rag-bag collections of bits and pieces that he would keep by him to cover pauses during the service—the practice was by no means confined to the early period. (Ammerbach's *Tabulaturbuch*, 1571/83, intended for students of any keyboard instrument, includes some suitable dances and transcriptions, and is available in a modern edition. It also yields clues as to a plausible style for later sixteenth-century givings-out. No. 3, for example, is an elaboration of a chorale melody, and has every appearance of being a prelude to no. 2, four simple settings of the tune which are perhaps *alternatim* organ verses.) Lighter introductions of the above kinds are perhaps suitable for the predominantly Catholic repertory of traditional Christmas songs: it would be absurd to 'give out' 'Es ist ein Roess entsprungen' (66:1), let alone 'Maria durch ein' Dornwald ging' (176), with the ritual solemnity of a Lutheran choral prelude.

Organ verses

The extended schemes of Praetorius's *Musae Sioniae* volume III, with settings for each verse, are supplemented in the case of certain Latin hymns with organ verses. In every case the melody is in long notes in the bass, which is texted to indicate the intended verse: the setting of 'Veni, Redemptor gencium' (2) can substitute for the choral setting of verse 4; the two organ settings of 'A solis ortus cardine' (4) are for the first and last verses, the latter working up to an extended and virtuosic conclusion. Such verses had grown out of the medieval tradition of strict alternation between organ and voices, which both Catholics and Lutherans had retained for Magnificats and other liturgical movements. But Lutherans allowed themselves considerable freedom where hymns were concerned, and organ verses seem frequently to have been additional to the sung ones. They might conceivably have preceded each verse where there was no *chorus musicus* (or merely for the sake of variety within a particular service); more usually they would be components of more complex schemes. The practice continued into the nineteenth century in some places.

Interline interludes

Interline interludes, improvised to fill the *Luftpause* at the end of each line when a chorale was sung by the congregation at a slow speed, were an integral part of the art of congregational accompaniment. They came into use with the marked slowing down of congregational singing in the seventeenth century (see above), and were still common in Lutheran Germany two centuries later. Peter Williams plausibly suggests that interludes (*Zwischenspielen*) may have developed out of the *Choralschluss* or 'chorale ending', a peroration played during the final note of the last verse.

There were two types of interline interludes in Germany. Examples of the more musically satisfying kind are found in the earliest published source, Georg Friedrich Kauffmann's *Harmonische Seelenlust* (Leipzig, 1733). Here the chorales are in the form of melody and figured bass, and the singers' breaks after each line are filled with simple organ passagework, which a competent player would probably vary from verse to verse. Simple scalic passages separate the lines in a pair of idiomatic chorale accompaniments included in H. F. Quehl's *Der zur Beförderung göttlicher Ehre* of the following year, and may represent the most primitive form of *Zwischenspiel*. The interlude principle is raised to a high art form in many of the organ chorales and vocal chorale fantasia movements of Bach and, to a lesser extent, his near contemporaries. His organ chorales with interline interludes are generally recognized as being, in some sense, notations of congregational accompaniments. They probably predated the publications of Kauffmann and Quehl, and give some idea of what the improvised tradition at its finest must have been like. Bach's interludes tend to be flourishes in free tempo, and would presumably have been varied from verse to verse, or perhaps even omitted in certain verses for the sake of variety. In the most exhilarating examples it is as if the organ leaves the singers momentarily earthbound to catch their breath between lines, swooping down to snatch them up once more.

Three of Bach's settings of Christmas chorales, 'Gelobet seist du, Jesu Christ', 'In dulci jubilo', and 'Vom Himmel hoch', survive in parallel forms that could be useful to organists interested in developing an improvised interline technique on this model. In the simpler forms, BWV 722a, 729a, and 738a, the melodies of the chorales are simply set, with no more than a figured bass, and the interline flourishes are schematic rather than fully worked out. Their better-known counterparts, BWV 722, 729, and 738, stand in the same relation to them as a finished oil painting does to a preliminary sketch. Whatever the connection between the pairs may be (a matter of speculation), they can be seen as, respectively, rough reminders and worked-out examples of the kind of accompaniments that Bach would improvise for joyful Christmas hymns in his younger days. The 'oil paintings' could conceivably serve for final verses, the 'sketches' supplying the basis for rather more sober accompaniments to earlier ones.

Many local song-books from the century or so after 1780 give examples of interline interludes, clearly in response to demand. Adlung (1783) suggests that interludes should be omitted in penitential chorales, or at least that brilliant passagework should be avoided. Knecht (1795–8) feels that shorter interludes are appropriate to lively chorales and longer to slower ones. His examples (*Vollständige Orgelschule*, pp. 153–71) are in the Bach tradition, though debased, and are intermediate between the 'higher' type above and a more mechanical type that appears to have been cultivated by less skilled organists, in which there is a halt on the final chord of a verse, followed by a lead-in to the opening line once more. Such 'mechanical' interludes correspond to those known from English prints of the late seventeenth to mid-eighteenth century, in which every line, including the last, leads into the line following, and there is no suggestion of the kind of variation from verse to verse that the 'higher' variety allows. Charles Burney, himself an organist and composer of hymn-tunes, encountered the *Choralzwischenspiel* at its horrific worst in the Lutheran cathedral in Bremen in 1772:

I found the congregation singing a dismal melody, without the organ. When this was ended, the organist gave out a hymn tune, in the true dragging style of Sternhold and Hopkins . . . the playing was more old-fashioned, I believe, than anything that could have been heard in our country towns, during the last century. The interludes between each line of the hymn were always the same . . . After hearing this tune, and these interludes, repeated ten or twelve times, I went to see the town, and returning to the cathedral, two hours after, I still found the people singing all in unison, and as loud as they could, the same tune, to the same accompaniment. I went to the post office, to make dispositions for my departure; and, rather from curiosity than the love of such music, I returned once more to this church, and, to my great astonishment, still found them, vocally and organically, performing the same ditty, whose duration seems to have exceeded that of a Scots Psalm, in the time of Charles I.

Inter-verse interludes

The whole subject of inter-verse interludes in Germany is riddled with doubts and ambiguities. There are several apparent references to inter-verse 'preluding' in organists' contracts, orders of service, etc., but none is unambiguous, and they usually make equally good sense as referring to one of the types of verse substitution mentioned above. Peter Williams points out that even a denunciation of lengthy preluding before the *Schlussvers* (literally 'final verse') is much less likely to refer to a free interlude before the last stanza of a chorale than to the improvised voluntary which in many places preceded the single-stanza *Schlussvers* of dismissal at the end of the service. Moreover, there are

no extant examples, and the likelihood is that the inter-verse interlude was at best an occasional extravagance on the part of an organist, and in no way part of the central German tradition.

II. PERFORMANCE SCHEMES IN THE GERMAN TRADITION

In the following schemes, *choraliter* signifies singing of the chorale melody by the congregation and *chorus choralis* (led by the cantor), unaccompanied and in unison; *figuraliter* signifies singing by the *chorus musicus*, which probably sang exclusively in harmony and is understood to have been accompanied by organ and/or instruments. When the congregation and *chorus musicus* alternate, the solemn *choraliter* verses, sung at a dignified pace, contrast strongly with the rather faster *figuraliter* ones.

Typical schemes for hymn-singing, c.1600

(*i*) German hymn sung by congregation. Order: organ prelude; v. 1 *choraliter,* preceded by cantor's intonation of the first line or verse; the remaining verses without intonation. (See above for the possible use of inter-verse organ interludes.)

(*ii*) German hymn sung by congregation alternating with choir or organ. Order: as (*i*), but with the even-numbered verses taken either by *chorus musicus, figuraliter,* or by organ alone; the last verse is always sung by congregation.

(*iii*) Latin and German hymns sung together *in Wechsel.* Latin sung by *chorus musicus, figuraliter,* German (either a translation or an independent hymn) by congregation, *choraliter.* Order: organ prelude (at *choraliter* speed?); v. 1 Latin; v. 1 German, preceded by cantor's intonation of the first line or verse; v. 2 Latin, etc.

Schemes from Praetorius's Urania

Praetorius's enthusiasm for the involvement of congregations in choral settings followed his visits to the Electoral chapel at Kassel in 1605 and 1609. The schemes set out in the introduction to *Urania* (1613) provide a unique overview of the gamut of possibilities, from some of the most straightforward ways in which choirs and congregations combined to sing hymns around 1600 to the more enterprising procedures in some of the more advanced churches and chapels of this first golden age of Lutheran music. His schemes (*Arten*, literally 'manners', or 'ways') may be performed just as he gives them, or they may be used as a source of authentic procedures for more general application. (We have adjusted Praetorius's numbering and have not indicated all his many ambiguities.)

See the list of additional settings by Praetorius (below) for alternative settings from his collections which may be used to supplement those given in the present book in certain schemes.

Scheme 7, describing polychoral performance, refers specifically to his chorale settings for 2, 3, and 4 choirs in *Urania*, designed for congregational participation (a Kassel innovation). It is nevertheless directly applicable to simple SATB harmonizations such as the ones we provide in this book. Instead of giving different settings to the different choirs, a very similar effect may be obtained by sharing out sections of an SATB setting among different groups, a common north-Italian technique of the time.

Praetorius only mentions spreading groups around the church in connection with four-choir settings, but he only details doubling and continuo instruments in that context too. He probably intends all these to be equally applicable to two-, three-, and four-choir schemes as well, and spatial contrast is always effective when the scheme permits it. Likewise, he only occasionally mentions organ introductions, but the organ would always set the pitch with a giving-out or *praeambulum* (see above). After this, the cantor would probably only intone the first line or verse if the congregation was to sing v. 1.

Scheme 1. Organ prelude; v. 1 congregation, *choraliter*; v. 2 *chorus musicus*, *figuraliter* but with congregation joining in with the melody; v. 3 as v. 1; v. 4 as v. 2, etc.; last verse always as v. 2.

Scheme 2. The entire hymn *figuraliter* by choir and organ, with or without congregation.

Scheme 3. v. 1 *choraliter* (as scheme 1, v. 1); v. 2, etc. as scheme 2.

Scheme 4. v. 1, line 1 *choraliter*, the remainder *figuraliter*; subsequent verses (*i*) as v. 1; (*ii*) *figuraliter* throughout; or (*iii*) alternately *figuraliter* and *choraliter*.

Scheme 5. For hymns of seven- and eight-line stanzas; 'suitable only for small churches or princely chapels'. (The organ is not mentioned, but a free *praeambulum* might be appropriate.) The following applies to each verse: lines 1, 3, 5, and 7, either a good tenor soloist (unaccompanied), or SATB soli with 'lovely, pure voices singing gently'; lines 2, 4, 6, [and 8,] all the voices and instruments of the *chorus musicus*, loudly.

Scheme 6. For hymns of five or seven stanzas. (The organ is not mentioned, but a free *praeambulum* might be appropriate.) v. 1 either two/three trebles singing a setting à 2 or à 3 from *Musae Sioniae* IX, or four, five, or more mixed voices singing some other chorale-motet setting; vv. 2 and 4 *choraliter*, 'sung immediately' (i.e., without any organ preluding?); vv. 3 and 5 a simple *figuraliter* setting. (The last verse is not mentioned, but presumably it would be *choraliter* however the previous verse had been sung, following the normal rule.)

Scheme 7. This covers polychoral performance, and is only suited to multi-verse hymns. (It is divided into two *Arten*, but the second concerns through-composed works and is irrelevant here.)

(*i*) With two choirs
Choir 1: four soli (or more if available). Choir 2: one or two trebles, singing the melody, and organ 'with an attractive stop'.

vv. 1, 3 choir 1 and congregation; vv. 2*, 4* choir 2 and congregation; v. 5 tutti. The same pattern repeats, with the last verse as v. 5 and with *organo pleno*.

The same SATB setting may be used throughout, or one or more others (ideally with contrasting harmony and more movement of parts) may be sung in the starred verses.

(*ii*) With three choirs
The three choirs may be formed in two ways.

(*a*) *Without congregation*
  Choir 1: *chorus musicus*.
  Choir 2: solo S or T (singing the chorale melody) and organ.
  Choir 3: either four bright-toned solo voices ('Vocales & viva voce canentes') or cornetts and trombones or strings with at least a S or T (see four-choir scoring, (*iii*) below).

(*b*) *With congregation*
  Choir 1: congregation.
  Choir 2: four bright-toned voices.
  Choir 3: either as (*a*) choir 2 or as (*a*) choir 3 alternatives.

The basic scheme is that vv. 1, 2, 3, and tutti are taken by choirs 1, 2, 3, and tutti; at least one later stanza is sung by choirs 1 and 2 combined; the final stanza is always tutti. Alternatively, v. 1 may be tutti, the procedure from v. 2 being as from the beginning of the basic scheme.

Three distinct SATB settings should be used if possible, the first very simple. The verses for two and three choirs should ideally divide an SSATB setting among the voices, the two S parts being sung at both treble and tenor pitch. Alternatively, the choir 1 setting may be used. In either case, the basses of one choir should 'sing high' and the others 'sing low' (i.e., use contrary motion where the bass moves in fourths and fifths).

(*iii*) With four choirs
Choir 1: *chorus musicus* or four solo voices ('Cantores oder vocales Musicos').
Choir 2: wind instruments, e.g., cornett and trombones.
Choir 3: recorders and flutes, with curtal on the bass, or 'crumhorns and other such instruments, when the *Stadtpfeifer* are available,' or four solo voices.
Choir 4: strings ('to which it would be pleasant to add a lute, harpsichord, harp, or theorbo; or, if none is

available, then an organ, *positif*, or regal should be used'.

In choirs 3 and 4, at least one vocal soloist with a 'good, clear voice' ('ein feine reine Stimme') must sing the chorale melody at treble, alto, or tenor pitch.

At the end of *Urania* Praetorius gives a similar but more detailed specimen four-choir scoring in tabular form:

Choir 1: SATB, four singers alone or with organ 'etc.'.

Choir 2: SAB strings and TB voices; or four viols, with one or more lutes and pandora, or regal.

Choir 3 s cornett, A singer and flute or recorder, T trombone, B *Pommer* or curtal.

Choir 4: T voice and four trombones, with theorbo or harpsichord or other stringed keyboard instrument.

Praetorius refers the reader to part III of his *Syntagma Musicum* for further suggestions.

There is no set pattern for the verses in four-choir schemes, which may be ordered on the principles of those for two and three choirs. Different SATB settings (see (*i*) above) may be used for choirs 2–4 when they sing alone or combine without choir 1. No congregation is mentioned, but there could be no objection to it singing the melody in tutti verses; or it could sing with the *chorus musicus* if this forms choir 1. A possible scheme for an eight-stanza hymn might be: v. 1 choir 1; v. 2 choir 2; v. 3 choirs 1 and 2; v. 4 choir 3; v. 5 choir 4; v. 6 choirs 3 and 4; v. 7 choirs 2, 3, and 4; v. 8 tutti.

Additional settings by Praetorius

The settings listed here may be combined in a variety of ways with those given in this book (including the editorial arrangements in early seventeenth-century style): see above and performance notes on the individual carols.

The verse-by-verse settings in *Musae Sioniae* V (1607) are all underlaid with stanza 1 only, but are intended either for the successive verses of a complete performance (however ordered) or to be extracted and used at will. Elsewhere, the different underlaid stanzas represent Praetorius's intentions, but may similarly be extracted and used for any stanza.

Other simple SATB harmonizations will be found in *Musae Sioniae* VIII (1610). *Musae Sioniae* VI and VII (both 1609) have individual settings of different local forms of tunes, with their associated forms of texts. The small-scale settings in *Musae Sioniae* IX (1610) are specifically to be inserted at will within existing schemes. *Musae Sioniae* II (1607) has double-choir settings underlaid with first verses.

Puer natus in Bethlehem (54). *Musae Sioniae* V: no 84 *à* 4; no. 85 *à* 5; no. 86 is an 'expanding' verse-by-verse scheme *à* 2, *à* 3, *à* 4, *à* 5, *à* 6 which is sung twice through for the ten stanzas. (Our setting I, which is *Musae Sioniae* VI, no. 34, or our setting III could be

sung congregationally after each choral verse; see performance notes for the textual alternatives.)

Musae Sioniae IX: settings *à* 2 (ss); *à* 3.

Resonet in laudibus/Joseph, lieber Joseph mein (55).

(*Resonet*) *Musae Sioniae* V: no. 92 *à* 5 (SSATB), a simple setting that could alternate with our setting III. It could also alternate with:

(*Joseph*) no. 87 *à* 5 (Walther, 1544). This could alternate with no. 92 ('Resonet', above) or could be sung either by full choir or by ss and organ to precede our given setting (IV).

Nun komm, der Heiden Heiland (58). *Musae Sioniae* V: successive settings, no. 51 *à* 3; no. 52 *à* 4 (*voces aequales*); no. 53 *à* 4 (SATB); no. 54 *à* 5 (Walther, 1524); no. 55 *à* 6 (of the type which Praetorius says may be performed by two trebles and organ).

Musae Sioniae II: double-choir setting of v.1.

Musae Sioniae IX: settings *à* 2, *à* 3.

In dulci jubilo (59). *Musae Sioniae* V: no. 80 *à* 2; no. 81 *à* 3; no. 82 *à* 4 (SSST, *voces aequales*); no. 83 *à* 4 (our setting I).

Musae Sioniae II: double-choir setting.

Musae Sioniae IX: *à* 2 (ss)

Vom Himmel hoch, da komm' ich her (60). *Musae Sioniae* V: no. 71 *à* 3 (high clefs—down a fourth for SAT); no. 72 *à* 4 (SSSA *ad aequales*); no. 73 *à* 4 (SATB; could alternate with our setting I, which is from *Musae Sioniae* VI); no. 74 *à* 5 (of the type Praetorius says may be performed by two trebles and organ). Nos. 68–70 set the same tune to a different text.

Musae Sioniae IX: two settings *à* 2 (v. 1); one setting *à* 3 (first and last verses).

Christum wir sollen loben schon (61). *Musae Sioniae* V: no. 57 *à* 4 (composer unidentified; could alternate with our given setting by Osiander).

Hymnodia Sionia (1611): eleven vocal settings underlaid with various stanzas; two organ verses (first and last).

Wachet auf (68). *Musae Sioniae* V: no. 97 *à* 2 (ss); no. 98 *à* 7 (SSA/SATB); no. 99 *à* 4 (high clefs—down a fourth for SATB; melody differs slightly from ours).

III. ENGLISH ORGAN ACCOMPANIMENT, INTERLUDES, AND GIVINGS-OUT

The pre-Victorian English tradition of organ accompaniment had much in common with its German counterpart, though it began virtually from scratch in the later seventeenth century and attained real artistic maturity for only a brief period from around 1800 when the German church music tradition was mostly in a state of decadence. In England, as in Germany, the very slow speed of the singing of psalms in the seventeenth century necessitated interludes between the lines if a steady tempo was to be maintained and the congregation were to draw breath. But as the eighteenth century progressed, the combined influences of the Handelian aria, the Evangelical movement in general, and the growth of Methodism led to a gradual quickening of tempos, and interline interludes were no longer necessary to urge the juggernaut forward. Anglican organists in particular turned to inter-verse interludes, a type that offered more scope for the fancy. Those of Samuel Sebastian Wesley (1810–76) are the summit of the art.

Most published interludes were designed for psalm rather than hymn-tunes, since the metrical psalm continued to dominate parish church music (except in the Evangelical tradition) far into the Victorian period. There is no doubt, however, that the same techniques were applied to hymn-singing as it continued to gain ground in the remainder of the Established Church during the early nineteenth century. The English tradition of giving-out, accompaniment, and interluding is less well known than the German, and a list is therefore given below of selected sources in which examples can be found. The techniques are particularly applicable to some of the English eighteenth- and early nineteenth-century settings (e.g., 70–3, 92, and 96:II), and can be used more generally for any hymns from those periods except the English 'gallery' and American 'primitive' settings. The performing tradition for these, which in the case of the gallery carols involved the use of instruments other than the organ, is described in Appendix 3.

The few organs in English parish churches which survived the Reformation were almost all destroyed by the Puritans during the Commonwealth. Most households large enough to have private chapels would also have employed musicians, and here four-part settings performed by groups of instruments and voice(s) were probably to be heard, as in Lutheran and Calvinist households on the Continent (see 'While shepherds watched', 46:I, for an early example of such a setting, by Richard Alison). A few domestic chapels could boast an organ, and virginals and other keyboard instruments were readily available. Organs began to reappear in Wren's rebuilt City churches from *c.*1670, generally with one manual and a split keyboard allowing different registrations in the right and left hands. On Sundays the singing would be led from galleries by the children of the parish 'charity schools', who were in a few instances joined by the young men of the parish religious society to form four-part choirs. The organist would give out the tune of a psalm, and then accompany in a two- or simple three-part texture. The typical choir of charity children, if we are to believe reports, sang in unison with shrill unmusicality, and the generally mechanical, expressionless style of singing was matched by a lack of variation in organ registration

from verse to verse. From the beginning of the eighteenth century, organs were installed in parish churches in increasing numbers, at first mainly in major cities and in the more musical north of England, where full SATB gallery choirs were already occasionally to be found.

From at least the beginning of the eighteenth century, when the first notated examples appear, the giving-out of the tune to set the pitch and speed, and an improvised accompaniment of the verses, were already part of the stock-in-trade of the professional parish-church organist, a relatively new breed which had emerged in the late seventeenth century in response to the proliferation of new organs and the rise of amateur music-making around the country. A strict giving-out of the entire tune was the usual rule, but, as in Germany, sometimes only the first half was played, and lavish embellishments often obscured it. Arthur Bedford, a musical high churchman with a passionate concern for seemliness in worship, pleads for the givings-out to be 'as plain as possible, that the meanest Capacity may know what the Tune is. The Notes . . . are often plaid with such variety and Divisions that none in a Common Congregation can tell what is meant' (*The Great Abuse of Musick*, 1711).

A considerable advance in accompanying techniques since the 1670s is evident in four sources dating from between 1700 and *c.*1731. The first two, Daniel Purcell's *The Psalmes Set Full for the Organ or Harpsichord* (1718) and *The Psalms by Dr Blow Set Full for the Organ or Harpsichord* (1703), represent a much earlier style in Nicholas Temperley's view (see 'Organ music in parish churches, 1660–1730', *Journal of the British Institute of Organ Studies*, 5, 1981, pp. 33–45). The other two are manuscript collections by John Reading (1685/6–1764), a pupil of Blow (1649–1708). Now in the library of Dulwich College in south London, they were made during Reading's time as organist of two leading London parish churches, St John's, Hackney, and St Mary, Woolnoth.

There are no givings-out in Blow's volume, but those of Daniel Purcell (d. 1717) blend contemporary ornament with an antique style of division (stylized pattern-making around the notes of a melody) and they often leave the melody obscured. Reading's givings-out are on a rather higher level, but none can bear comparison with the late seventeenth-century masterpiece of the genre, the *Voluntary on the Old Hundredth*, which exists in versions for one- and two-manual organ with ascriptions to both Henry Purcell and Blow. The tune is stated twice, in the bass and on a cornet stop, with none of the mechanical ornamentation of later settings.

On accompaniment, Bedford exhorts that 'the Notes, which are play'd when the Congregation sings, are to be one with the singing . . . without any Graces or Flourishes, except what nature teaches them all to use'—the latter including many that any modern congregation would regard as far from natural. The sample verse accompaniments in the Purcell and Blow collections are plain settings of the tune with idiomatic keyboard writing, while the passagework in the interludes confirms that speeds for the verses were very slow. Comparison of these early sources reveals a style of verse accompaniment close to that of near-homophonic figured bass realization.

Bedford has sound advice about interline interludes:

In the Interludes between the Lines, Care should be taken that the congregation should be sensible when to begin and when to leave off. For this reason, it is necessary, that an Interlude not only begins with swifter Notes after the End of the Line, but that there is a Preparation [cadential trill] made for the first Note of the next Line . . . the extempore Organist being not always equal in the Length of his Interlude, there must be uncertainty when to begin.

Reading makes his accompaniment to the sung lines of the psalms in his collection as sonorous as possible, so that the contrast of the mainly two-part interludes encourages the singers to come off their last note, and he scrupulously leads them back in with single, double, or even triple trills; furthermore, against all the odds he manages to invest many of these linking 'maggots' (as Bedford calls them) with character, often developing a contrapuntal idea or musical motif in successive interludes. Precisely the opposite approach, but one reflecting eighteenth-century practice, is recommended a century later by William Cole of Colchester in his *A View of Modern Psalmody* (London, 1819). Cole echoes Bedford when he complains that the organ is 'frequently too powerful', and suggests that organists should play mainly in two parts, with some full chords: 'This occasional introduction of chords would produce a much better effect than a constant monotony of full harmony' (section III, 'Remarks on the use of an organ in religious worship').

It was standard practice in the earlier eighteenth century either for all the verses of a psalm to be sung equally loudly, or for loud and soft verses to alternate regularly, regardless of the content of the text. The ridiculing of this convention towards the end of the century reflects a growing sensitivity to the words, which was associated with the increasing prominence of the hymn and the emergence of a more expressive manner of congregational singing. Tastes were changing: more lively tunes were being introduced, in contrast to the old, slow-moving psalm tunes, and the interline interlude was increasingly abandoned. The first known example of the inter-verse interlude which replaced it is in the later of Reading's Dulwich College collections (up to 1731), and it may even be that he introduced the practice. The earliest published inter-verse interludes, beginning with the *c.*1767 edition of the *Organist's Pocket Companion*, are mostly light and curiously incon-

sequential, but there must have been a more substantial tradition: one cannot imagine the composer of 'Christians, awake!' (71), for example, being content with such *galant* trifles.

In London, a bewildering range of charitable hospitals, proprietary chapels, temples, and tabernacles sprang up to cater for the manifold tendencies of free-enterprise Protestantism, but only the Methodists had produced music of any great worth before the closing years of the eighteenth century. It was the Methodists, too, who took the lead in the fight against female degradation: the Magdalen Hospital (for penitent prostitutes) and the Lock (for venereal patients) were two liberal institutions in which the emergent sect's social and musical concerns were brought into fruitful partnership. Pre-eminent in both fields was Martin Madan, presiding genius at the Lock Hospital until reaction against his more radical proposals brought him down (see notes, 72). Here, and in a few other large female institutions, the more musically gifted women formed highly-trained and much-admired choirs, which were in stark contrast to the ranks of untrained charity children in the metropolitan parish churches. They sang (from concealed positions) psalms, anthems, and—especially—hymns for two voices and organ in the airy trio-sonata-like style that was then fashionable. The music's naïve charm, allied to the poetic genius of Charles Wesley and his fellow hymn-writers, had an appeal which was rarely to be found in the psalm-bound services of the Established Church. Madan's 'Lock Collection' (*A Collection of Psalm and Hymn Tunes*, 1769) towers over most comparable hymn-books of the time, and was reprinted in expanded and revised editions well into the nineteenth century.

The Methodist hospitals particularly favoured a recurring ritornello (usually called 'symphony' and often reminiscent of secular styles) which was played between the verses of their hymns. The symphony, and other unobtrusive methods of punctuating the singing, were favoured also by some Anglican organists. William Cole (1819) recommends 'short symphonies, strict and adapted to the melody of the tune [setting]', or else a repetition by the organ of the last line (or the last two lines) of each stanza, with the minimum of embellishment. John Gay, in the lengthy introduction to his *Sacred Music* (published in London in 1827, but composed much earlier) notes that he has provided 'no symphonies' for all except one of his psalm tunes, but has 'left it to the performer's extemporaneous abilities and discretion; recommending something in character with the piece, such as the last strain, with a little variation.' On the other hand, Cole puts it beyond doubt that eighteenth-century printed interlude models tell only half the story: 'We . . . too often find that an organist, after tickling the ears of his audience with a succession of unmeasured flourishes, and exhibiting the dexterity of his fingers at the expense of his judgement, returns abruptly to the subject without any previous preparation. Hence the people, being taken by a kind of surprise, are unable to join in the beginning of the next stanza.'

Towards the end of the eighteenth century, a group of London musicians led by Samuel Wesley (1766–1837) was responsible for fulfilling the promise of Reading's better work and raising the giving-out and the inter-verse interlude to an artistic level that had been no more than hinted at in earlier printed examples. The great influence was that of J. S. Bach, in particular the *Well-tempered Clavier*. Benjamin Jacob (1778–1829), organist of the Surrey Chapel, Blackfriars Road, was reckoned one of the best organists in England, setting new standards of programme planning in his recitals at the chapel, in which the music of Bach predominated. His *National Psalmody: A collection of tunes with appropriate symphonies* (1819) shows a new attitude to the performance of psalmody. For each psalm he provides 'a Tune adapted as nearly as possible to the spirit of it . . . A little observation will suggest the true manner of performing, so as to make sound and sense agree. And to this end the Symphonies are written or attempted in the style of their respective tunes.' Jacob's symphonies are quite free of the *galant* influence which pervades Methodist examples. Many are in a Bachian contrapuntal idiom, and a few tunes are given introductory as well as inter-verse symphonies.

Samuel Sebastian Wesley (1810–76), son of Samuel Wesley, was the greatest English improviser of his age. The two editions of his *Selection of Psalm Tunes* (1834 and 1842) provide model examples of subtly varied accompaniment, though always within the limits of a sober, ecclesiastical style. Contrast of length, mood, and dynamics within a set of interludes is now a striking feature (see carol 92). It may have been the influence of Bach's chorale preludes that led Wesley and other Victorian composers to take a further step away from the English tradition by occasionally basing an interlude on the melody of the hymn or psalm.

Varied accompaniments for verses can also be found in *A Choral Book* (*c*.1855) by Henry Smart, whose playing at St Pancras New Church resulted in congregational singing famed for its volume and unanimity (see notes, 96). Smart provides models of different manners of giving out the psalm tune, as well as representative verses with choir in harmony and idiomatic organ accompaniment. (See Nicholas Temperley, *The Music of the English Parish Church*, vol. 2, ex. 82 for two givings-out and a verse of 'London New' by Smart.)

The tradition of organ interludes is appropriate for modern use in all kinds of ways. On a practical level, organ interludes have the advantage of being adaptable in length according to need. More importantly, per-haps, carefully judged interludes can help revivify the singing of well-known hymns and carols. Although the hymn takes longer, the participants have time to meditate on texts which normally fly past only half-understood. But in the twentieth century, interluding is a pale shadow of its former self and the art of giving out has all but disappeared. Perhaps the last serious practitioner of both was George Thalben-Ball (1896–1987), organist of the Temple Church, London. No examples of his interludes have been published, but his *113 Variations on Hymn Tunes for Organ* (1969) are, despite the title, givings-out in the classical tradition. His variation on the tune 'Irby' ('Once in royal David's city') is one of many fine models for imitation that the collection provides.

Following historical practice in the performance of earlier interludes is not always straightforward. Interluding in an eighteenth-century style would involve not using the pedals, for example, and this is perhaps only worthwhile where a suitable organ gives the opportunity for appropriate period registration. As so often with miniature forms, timbre plays a vital part in the musical effect, and genuine eighteenth-century pipework, tuned and voiced in the old manner, can often give apparently banal interludes an unexpected appeal. When a selection is made from sets of psalm interludes for use with hymns, choice can be severely limited by the convention that if the tune begins with an anacrusis, then so, normally, should the interludes (Samuel Wesley is the one composer who frequently breaks this rule).

Provided that the giving-out, accompaniment, and interludes match in style (or are creatively mis-matched), there is nothing to prevent organists from rifling any suitable collection for examples—short extracts from other composed works can sometimes be effective—and deploying them at will. Variety between the interludes became increasingly prominent in the later tradition: all surviving inter-verse sets exploit differences of texture, and the later ones also vary length and even key. The playing of only a few interludes, or of just one before the final verse, was also an option in the eighteenth century. However flexible the schemes created with pre-existing examples, though, improvisation (a sadly declined art in Britain) will always be the ideal.

Selected sources of givings-out, accompaniment, and interludes in the English tradition

Daniel Purcell, *The Psalms Set Full for the Organ or Harpsichord* (London, 1718); also included in *The Harpsichord Master Improved*, Daniel Wright (London, 1718).

John Blow, *The Psalms by Dr Blow Set Full for the Organ or Harpsichord as they are play'd in churches or chapels* (London, advertised 1703, earliest known copy 1731).

John Reading, two large manuscript collections of organ music in the library of Dulwich College, London, MS 92B (before 1727) and MS 92A (up to *c*.1731). Both were clearly intended for publication, with a number of psalm tunes in common but presented differently. There is a third collection of his organ music in the Henry Watson Music Library, Manchester (MS BRm. 7105. Rf. 31).

The Organist's Pocket Companion (London, *c*.1751; later editions *c*.1767 and 1782).

Eighteen Preludes or Short Fugues for the organ or harpsichord proper for interludes to the psalms (London?, *c*.1770).

William Gawler, *Harmonia Sacra, or a Collection of Psalm Tunes, with Interludes, & a Thorough Bass* (London, 1781).

Musica Sacra, or, a collection of easy tunes (London, *c*.1783).

John Valentine, *Thirty Psalm Tunes in four parts with Symphonies, Interludes and an Instrumental Bass* (Leicester, *c*.1785). Valentine includes instrumental interludes, and some of the three- and four-part organ interludes have the appearance of being for instruments too.

John Keeble and Jacob Kir(c)kman, *Forty Interludes to be played between the verses of the psalms: twenty-five by Mr. J. Keeble, & fifteen by Mr. J. Kirkman* . . . (London, *c*.1787). Kirckman (d. 1812) was probably a nephew of Jacob Kirckman (1710–92, founder of the London firm of harpsichord and piano makers). He succeeded Keeble as organist of St George's, Hanover Square, on his death in 1786, the year before this collection was probably published. It was one of the most widely used collections of interludes.

John Hill, *Hill's Church Music, containing psalm tunes and anthems, with hymns for Christmas and Easter, interspersed with proper symphonies*, 2 vols. (London, 1788–91).

Francis Linley, *A Practical Introduction to the Organ* (London, 1800).

Cornelius Bryan, *Effusions for the Organ, containing eight Voluntaries, One Hundred Interludes and Three Psalms* [London, 1815 or earlier].

Benjamin Jacob, *National Psalmody: A collection of tunes with appropriate symphonies, set to a course of psalms selected from the New Version* (London, 1819).

Ralph Bradshaw, *Twenty-four Psalms and Hymns, with Interludes, and Pedals to the 3rd verses* (London, *c*.1820).

—— *A Second Set of Twenty-four Psalms and Hymns* . . . (London, 1825?).

Samuel Wesley, *Parochial Psalm Tunes* and *A Book of Interludes for Young Organists*. Both titles are mentioned in *Letters of Samuel Wesley to Mr Jacob*, ed.

Eliza Wesley (London, 1875; reprinted with an introduction by Peter Williams as *The Wesley–Bach Letters*, London, 1988). We have not yet found a published copy of either, but the music, prepared for publication, has been identified by Blaise Compton in British Library Add Ms. 34999 (bequeathed by Eliza Wesley in 1895).

S. S. Wesley, *A Selection of Psalm Tunes* (London, 1834; second, revised ed. London, 1842).

Vincent Novello, *The Psalmist*, 4 parts (London, 1835–42; new ed. 1863). Part I contains six interludes by Novello (1781–1861) in a simple style 'for Psalms of Long Measure'; Part III contains three interludes by James Turle (1802–82) and one each by Mendelssohn, Samuel Wesley, and John Gauntlett (to the tune 'Oxford'). The 1863 edition contains two sets of three interludes by Thomas Adams.

Thomas Adams, *Ninety Interludes in the most familiar major and minor keys for the organ or pianoforte suited to psalm tunes in common or triple time* (London, 1837).

Joseph Warren (1804–81), *One Hundred Interludes* (mid-century).

Novello's Interludes, 3 series, extracted from *National Psalmody* [by Benjamin Jacob; see above], 'newly arranged, and with proper stops marked for each, intended as a guide to young organists, by John Hiles' (London, 1851).

Edward Travis and J. R. Dyer, *The Amateur Interludist, a Collection of 144 Short Preludes to play between the verses of the Psalms* (London?, post-1852).

Henry Smart, *A Choral Book . . . containing a selection of tunes employed in the English Church* (London?, *c*.1855). Contains four givings-out of 'London New' and three varied accompaniments. Four other tunes have two or three accompaniments.

Henry Smart, *Fifty Preludes and Interludes* (London, 1862).

Edward Thirtle, *Ninety Short Interludes for Organ or Harmonium, Composed and Arranged for Psalm and Hymn Tunes* (advertised in the *Musical Times*, August 1862; they are 'interspersed for Solo Stops' and have a separate pedal part.)

Edward Travis, *Ninety Interludes in the most familiar Major and Minor Keys for the Organ or Pianoforte, suited to Psalm Tunes in common and triple time* (advertised in the *Musical Times* in the mid-1860s).

Cleveland Wigan, *A Modulating Dictionary, consisting of 552 Modulations, by three intermediate chords from and into the twenty-four major and minor keys; with the return Modulations* (London, 1859).

George Thalben-Ball, *113 Variations on Hymn Tunes for Organ* (London, 1969).

HUGH KEYTE

APPENDIX 3

The English 'Gallery' and American 'Primitive' Traditions

I. THE ENGLISH GALLERY CHOIRS AND BANDS
II. THE AMERICAN TRADITION

This book differs from previous comparable collections in its inclusion of a substantial number of composed carols that do not conform to conventional notions of 'correct' harmony. Many musicians who are at home with concepts of rough, improvised harmony in folk music nevertheless find it difficult to take seriously notated pieces which are riddled with 'forbidden' consecutives, 'irrational' harmonic clashes, and 'bare' (that is, open) fifths: signs, surely, of straightforward incompetence. But there is real pleasure to be had from such music, as long as we approach it not as an amusing sport of musical nature but as the product of a long and coherent tradition with its own characteristic conventions of performance. Nicholas Temperley, who has almost single-handedly brought the English gallery tradition to the attention of performers and scholars, maintains that 'eighteenth-century psalmodists had as much right to change the conventions of musical style as twentieth-century dodecaphonists', and suggests one possible approach: 'Some of the music . . . makes little sense by the standards of the élite music of the time. But it is possible nowadays . . . to think of it as a form of folk music, as it would surely have been considered had it survived to the present time' (*The Music of the English Parish Church*, 1979, vol. 1, pp. 192, 162).

The American tradition began as a transplantation of the English, but soon branched out in unexpected directions and grew rich and strange in the new land. Wilfrid Mellers' comments on two of the most individual of the New England composers, William Billings of Boston (1746–1800) and Supply Belcher (1752–1836) could stand for all American primitive music: '[Billings] is the true American *naïf* in that his "art" is an overflow of wonder, of energy, of released delight . . . It is as though he—and we—were experiencing music for the first time.' 'This [Belcher's music] is how Handel might sound, with a wilderness behind him instead of Augustan England' (*Music in a New Found Land*, 1964, pp. 15, 12).

If conventional eighteenth-century Christmas hymnody has had a raw deal in the modern carol anthology, hymns and carols in the primitive tradition have been virtually wished out of existence, especially in England. Even those that have appeared have not become popular. One reason, we believe, has been a failure to seek out the best of the primitive repertory; another is that many editors of gallery music have 'corrected' or 'improved' the music beyond repair, and anthology editors in search of one or two token gallery settings have mostly lifted them uncritically from such flawed collections. Then there is the question of performance style: this music wilts and dies when sung either in the mannered English cathedral tradition or with the mollifying vibrato of many American choirs. The editors' experience is that most amateur and professional choirs are able to adapt their performing style quite radically once inhibitions about ecclesiastical propriety have been overcome, and that the music leaps to life as a result.

I. THE ENGLISH GALLERY CHOIRS AND BANDS

From the Reformation until the last decade of the seventeenth century few, if any, hymns would have been sung in English parish churches. Miles Coverdale had produced a number of translations of chorales in his *Goostly psalms and spirituall songes* (c.1535) that might have formed the basis of a hymn-singing tradition, but England lacked Germany's experience of vernacular congregational song, and it was the Calvinist rule—that only biblical texts should be sung in services—which triumphed. The unison metrical psalm, not the hymn, became the staple congregational music. Hymns were only very slowly accepted by Anglicans. The combined influence of the great Independent poet Isaac Watts (1674–1748) and of the Wesley brothers was a major force for change, but it was not until late in the eighteenth century that hymn-singing began to gain whole-hearted acceptance, beginning in the urban Evangelical churches.

With rare exceptions, sung metrical psalms did not replace those appointed in the prayer-book office, which were recited (in some places chanted) in Coverdale's prose translations. In country churches a sung psalm, in the 'Old Version' paraphrases of Sternhold and Hopkins, would precede the morning service, and another would follow it; in the evening only one would normally be sung. In both Britain and the US, the parish clerk or his Dissenting counterpart would recite or 'line out' each line of the psalm before it was sung, since congregations had no books. The Puritan parliament ordained in 1644 that 'the minister, or some fit person appointed by him' should 'read the psalm line by line before the singing thereof'. But what had been intended as a temporary expedient became an essential part of the performing style; regular dismembering of the verses into individual lines did little for the poetry and opened the way to extraordinary musical abuses. At first the clerks spoke the lines, and later gave them in a chant-like nasal sing-song, but in each case the final syllable of the line would be raised in a glissando to the congregation's first sung note, since it was also the clerk's duty to lead their singing. In many churches and dissenting chapels there was a gradual progression from lining out individual lines to lining out couplets and eventually entire verses.

The speed of the massed unison singing of the old Geneva-type psalm tunes became ever slower in the course of the seventeenth century (cf. the Lutheran chorale in Appendix 2), and the extraordinary 'old way' of singing developed in country churches. In theory, this was merely the unison singing of highly embellished versions of psalm tunes; in practice, a combination of widely varying speeds, held notes, and individual embellishment was wilfully exploited to produce an awe-inspiring heterophony. This may still be heard in the Gaelic psalmody of the Strict Presbyterian churches of the Isle of Lewis, in the outer Hebrides (see *The New Grove Dictionary of Music and Musicians*, 1980, vol. 15, p. 375, for an example), and in the exotic-sounding 'surge songs' of the southern-American blacks (see George Pullen Jackson, *White and Negro Spirituals*, 1943).

With the appearance of the *New Version of the Psalms* by Nahum Tate and Nicholas Brady in 1696, the days of the 'old way' of singing were numbered. Choirs began to be formed to sing Tate and Brady's superior translations to harmonized settings, though it was more than a century before the 'Old Version' was effectively displaced. (The emergence of choirs was not inevitably associated with the *New Version*; some churches sang the *New Version* without choirs, and some churches with choirs were still singing the 'Old Version' after 1800.) It became the custom in parish churches for Christmas hymns and carols to replace the metrical psalms on Christmas Day, and during the Christmas season in at least some places. To begin with, they were sung to familiar psalm tunes, and some of these have come down to us, transformed and embellished, in association with particular carols. The young men's religious societies, which spread rapidly through the parishes in the reign of Queen Anne (1702–14), quickly adopted psalm-singing as a godly recreation, and, by helping to establish the new texts and the tunes that went with them in the service, often acted as the advance guard of what was a very radical change for unlettered country congregations. From leading the congregational singing, with their members placing themselves strategically in the church, they developed into parish choirs in many cases, joined by boys', girls', and young women's voices. Many parish churches had their own singers' pew, but in the course of time these tended to be replaced by west-end galleries, particularly when the new choirs began to be supported by instruments. This was partly to remove from the congregation's view the distracting sight of string players tuning and wind players emptying their instruments, and partly for acoustical reasons. Churches had been building nave galleries to accommodate rising populations since the mid-sixteenth century, and one of these would normally be taken over for the choir. Others were newly built, occasionally incorporating the fronts of the old rood-lofts which had been removed from above their screens following an Elizabethan ordinance.

The Methodists, as they gradually drew away and built their own chapels, used gallery choirs as extensively as the Anglicans, often sharing the services of the same village choir in rural areas, where attendance at church in the morning and chapel in the afternoon was a common practice. The Independents (Congregationalists) and Baptists introduced similar choirs, though music always played a comparatively minor part in their services.

Single bass instruments began to appear in the gallery choirs from at least the 1740s, usually a bassoon or a 'bass viol' (cello or double bass). By the 1770s these had in many places been augmented by treble instruments, so that the soprano and alto parts, which had often been inaudible or even omitted in the past, could be heard much more clearly. The very common custom of singing in only two parts (the tenor melody, sung also at the higher octave, and the bass — a much richer sound than we might imagine) gradually gave way in all but the most primitive churches to a more evenly balanced four-part texture, which in turn led composers to abandon the old tenor-melody format and to adapt and compose settings with the melody in the soprano.

A typical small English parish-church choir of *c.*1800 would consist of some ten to fifteen voices, with three instruments supporting the bass and the two highest parts. Some choirs boasted large bodies of competent players: the choir at Puddletown, Dorset, with which Thomas Hardy's family was involved from 1841, had fourteen instrumentalists (see notes, 87). The lists of instruments in Sussex churches given by Canon K. H. MacDermott in *Sussex Church Music in the Past* (1922) show an amazing diversity, the most common being flute, oboe, clarinet, bassoon, serpent, trombone, violin, and cello/double bass.

The independence of such choirs was absolute, and the choice of music was in most cases entirely in their hands. Where the parish clerk directed them, he would choose the music; elsewhere he might select the words and leave the choice of tune to the choir; or, very commonly, the choir itself would communicate to the clerk its choice of psalms or Christmas hymns before the service; or the choir leader might simply announce them. George Gay, in the preface to his *Sacred Music* (1827), remembers 'a clerk who made it a rule of holding up a certain number of fingers, as a private guide to the choir at the opposite end of the chapel' to indicate the metre of the text, so that they could choose a tune as he announced it and lined out the first verse.

When the parish clerk had announced a psalm or carol and lined out the first stanza, the band would set the pitch for the singers. In some places this was done by playing through a verse instrumentally, no doubt with vigorous embellishment from the treble and bass in some instances. Other bands had their own little introductory phrase, which they would adapt to whatever key was required. MacDermott quotes the rules of Petworth Church, Sussex, which are recommended for general use in the introduction to a collection of Petworth psalms and hymns published before 1816: the clerk reads the first verse; the band plays the tune over; the clerk sings the first line of verse 1 on the opening note; the performance begins.

Fuging tunes

In the mid-eighteenth century there developed a new type of setting in which the main formal element was a contrast between the fugal treatment of at least one line of the text and the homophonic setting of the remainder. A typical example for a four-line verse would set lines 1/2 and 3/4 as distinct halves, each half with one line fuging and one homophonic; the second half was normally repeated. When congregations participated they might sing only the homophonic sections, leaving the rest to the choir, or they might 'busk' their way through the fugal sections. Some nineteenth-century urban Methodist congregations were trained to sing entirely in harmony.

John Wesey and other Methodist leaders strongly opposed fuging tunes because the words were obscured by the imitative entries, and they only began to appear in Methodist collections after Wesley's death in 1791. There is evidence, however, that they were sung in at least some Methodist chapels in Wesley's lifetime. Eventually officially admitted at a time when it had fallen from Anglican favour, the genre enjoyed an Indian summer between 1791 and *c.*1830 at the hands of such composers as Thomas Clark, a Canterbury cobbler, in whose later examples delicate counterpoint and tuneful homophony are skilfully balanced. We include examples of the fuging tune in its early days and in its Methodist heyday, both sung to 'While shepherds watched' (see 46: IV, V, and notes).

The later gallery settings

A rich variety of forms and styles gradually displaced the fuging tune and other rigid formulae towards the end of the eighteenth century in England, and these lasted until the gallery choir began to die out from *c.*1830. The fuging tune persisted in Dissenting (and New England) churches, and Dissenters developed the 'repeating tune', a non-fugal setting in which phrases and complete lines would be repeated, with a powerful rhetorical (though sometimes unintentionally comic) effect. The Methodist predilection for repeating tunes led to their becoming popularly known as 'Methodist tunes'. ('Adeste fideles', 70, is an example, despite its Roman Catholic provenance and its original 'plainchant' character).

The constant demand for carols by village choirs (in the church gallery and in their other role as village waits) meant that new settings were produced in astonishing numbers, both in printed publications and in manuscript, and eagerly transcribed into the singers' part-books. (A great mass of compositions still awaits cataloguing, let alone transcription and publication.) Some cathedral musicians published easy settings especially for country choirs, often imitating the mannerisms of rural composers, and the latter assimilated elements of the cathedral style, along with other influences. By the beginning of the nineteenth century the best gallery music used conventional harmonic procedures, and had lost much of the old 'primitive' style. Even rural settings, though, such as those in the carol-book of Thomas Hardy II (father of the novelist), need no special pleading: irregular their harmony and part-writing may sometimes be, but the language is by now firmly established, and handled with assurance (see carols 87, 88, and 90).

From the 1830s onward, the overwhelmingly Oxbridge-educated clergy began to wage a century-long war of attrition against the gallery choirs, replacing them with barrel-organs and harmoniums, which were both more seemly and less rebellious. Surpliced chancel choirs were introduced in imitation of the cathedral service, often under the romantic illusion that this had been pre-Reformation custom in parish churches (in reality, clerks had sung the chant, and sometimes polyphony, from the rood-loft). The rebuilt Leeds Parish Church of 1841 gave an impressive lead in what was initially a high-church reform, and clergy of all degrees of churchmanship were not slow in following suit.

Vocal scoring

In early four-part harmonizations of psalm tunes, such as those by Tallis, the melody is found not in the treble, but in the tenor. This manner of setting both sacred and secular tunes was common to all sixteenth-century Europe (and it was still the norm in certain of the more conservative English and American churches well into the nineteenth century).

When part-singing was reintroduced in English parish churches, for the first time since the Reformation, it was to this tenor-tune tradition (kept alive in domestic music-making and by the town and country waits) that the country composers turned. Choirs were often set up by peripatetic singing teachers —parish clerks and others—who also composed and published the settings of psalms, hymns, carols, anthems, and simple service music which were to be their staple fare. These men were generally the self-taught practitioners of an 'additive' method of composing reminiscent of medieval practice. To the tenor melody they would first add a bass, often with considerable toleration of—even fondness for—the sound of 'forbidden' parallel unisons, octaves, and fifths. (More important to the abler composers, to judge from their music, was the melodic freedom of part writing permitted by such an approach.) Soprano and alto parts would be added in turn, often with progressively greater dissonance: as long as each new part was consonant with the tune, a high degree of discord was acceptable. The massed voices on the melody and the weight of the bass (which was routinely reinforced as instruments began to be used) meant that dissonant upper voices must have sounded less alarming than their appearance on paper might suggest. As well as the prevalence of such 'irrational' dissonance, the virtual absence of 'rational' dissonance in the form of suspensions (one of the main methods of articulating conventional bass-led harmony) is one of the distinguishing features of 'primitive' music in both Britain and America.

When a mixed congregation joined choir and/or instruments in performing tenor-tune settings, the melody would be heard at both octaves. It was customary in country choirs for some sopranos—boys or women—to sing the tune with the tenors, an octave higher, even in set pieces, anthems, etc. when the congregation was silent. The tenor and bass were the backbone of four-part settings, and although it was more usual to give all the parts, the upper ones were often omitted from publications. The melody-and-bass format can be traced from the 1623 Wither/Gibbons *Hymns and Songs of the Church* (see carol 45), through the psalm and hymn tunes in the 1708 sixth edition of the Supplement to Tate and Brady's *New Version of the Psalms*, to the rural mid-eighteenth-century settings in Davies Gilbert's 1882 *Some Ancient Christmas Carols* (see Appendix 4). Four-part settings were frequently sung in only two parts (TB), or in three, either ATB (omitting the treble part) or TTB (with the alto part omitted and the treble part sung by tenors at the lower octave). In all three cases the tenor melody was again doubled at the higher octave by some trebles.

The new gallery choirs sang from vocal scores, or from individual part-books copied from them, with both the alto and tenor notated in the newly adopted 'transposing treble' clef still used by modern tenors. Sometimes only those on treble, alto, and bass lines would be paid by the parish, and the tenor tune would be taken by a larger group of less skilled and mostly musically illiterate singers, together with some bolder members of the congregation. Alto parts could be something of a problem, and were taken variously by boys or women, by high tenors, or sometimes by a combination of all three; falsettists were rare in rural parish choirs, and where they were found they usually sang the treble part.

An admirable summary of the central eighteenth-century tradition of voice types and singing style is given in *The Psalm-Singer's Assistant* (written in 1774 or 1776, published London, 1778) by John Crompton, of Southwold, Suffolk:

As to the treble, women, girls, and some boys [*sic*] voices are naturally adapted to that part, and [it] should never be attempted by men . . . Suitable voices for the middle, or counter part [alto] are rather difficult to find; but let no-one, for that reason, attempt it with a feigned [falsetto] voice, however there is but few wanted in comparison with the number who engage in other parts, and better quite omitted than not performed with a natural voice; therefore let a voice be chosen with great care, it should be soft, clear, and very manageable, for this part may be compared to a thread run through the whole, and anything harsh, rough or grating, rends the music all to pieces. For leading the tenor [melody] a person should be chosen who has a pleasant, strong, and manageable voice; for much depends upon him; no less than the whole air of the tune; he should be master of a distinct and proper diction and his voice should be easily distinguished from the rest . . . even in the bass, the upper notes are much better touched soft and pleasant; the middle and lower ones will admit that you be full and strong upon them, and at a cadence or close, never break off abruptly; but let all the voices die away gradually, the bass being heard rather after the other parts.

Between about 1750 and 1830 there was a gradual change-over to modern practice, with the tune migrating from the tenor to the treble part. From *c.*1770 many tenor-tune settings were updated in new editions of psalm books, causing terrible confusion. Between *c.*1790 (William Dixon, *Six Anthems for Country Choirs*) and 1830 (Vincent Novello, *The Psalmist*), exasperated prefaces continue to spell out the modern system, inveighing against the misunderstandings that had established themselves in many country churches. Alto parts in the 'transposing treble' clef (written an octave higher than they sounded) were being gamely tackled at the wrong octave by confused sopranos ('women or boys squealing out counter, as in some places I have lately heard'—George Gay, in the preface to his *Sacred Music*, 1827). In some places boys and women had clung to their old practice of doubling the tenor part, even though it no longer carried the tune, while elsewhere men had begun to double the treble tune from sheer necessity. Gay admits that 'for want of good trebles . . . octaves at all times cannot be well avoided', but he did not like the result:

From my childhood . . . before I knew anything of music, I could not bear to hear a tenor voice interfering with the women's part, which I found the most captivating . . . nor could I ever endure to see a man placed in front of a gallery with half a dozen women, bawling out the chief melody and murdering the main part (the treble, I mean) he pretended to support . . . Such octaves, in my opinion, are unpleasant and grating in one or two parts: and though they may be partly drowned in the full chorus, yet I still think them unpleasant: and moreover they rob other parts of their beauty, making a confused mixture of the whole.

The men of many congregations added a sub-bass doubling of the tune, which became increasingly objectionable with the more evenly balanced choirs of the treble-tune era. Many writers rage against them, and Gay differentiates between 'more refined congregations, where only one octave below the tune is sung' and others containing some who 'sing two octaves below the treble'.

Gay's description of the ideal voices required for each part agrees closely with Crompton's of fifty years earlier, except that he is prepared (with reservations) to allow falsettists on to the treble line (now singing the tune):

The treble demands delicacy without tameness, the counter a peculiar sweetness, the tenor a medium between feminine softness and masculine robustness, and the bass pomp and solidity. Low notes should be sung firm and steady; high notes not too strong, but firm and sweet, without any tremulous motion of the voice . . . The treble being the principal part, had better be too strong than too weak . . . some men will feign [in falsetto] a pretty good treble; but if care be not taken, they will get into a disagreeable tone, which will entirely spoil the music.

The following summary of the principal scoring possibilities is drawn mainly from prefaces to gallery collections and from Nicholas Temperley's *The Music of the English Parish Church*.

(*i*) In unison. This was the usual way of singing when there was no choir to provide harmony. (It can be heard again today with powerful effect in, for example, some London Methodist churches with West Indian congregations.)

(*ii*) In two parts, the melody sung at both tenor and treble octaves, basses either with a single doubling instrument which takes the lower octave where possible, or (where there are several instruments) with at least one at the lower octave throughout.

(*iii*) In three parts, ATB, the lower parts as (*ii*), the alto (which, like the tenor, is sung an octave lower than

notated) instrumentally doubled at pitch, or at the higher octave, or at both octaves.

(*iv*) In four parts (SATB), ATB as (*iii*), with the trebles at notated pitch and any doubling treble instruments moving between the higher octave and notated pitch.

(*v*) In four parts, with the treble and tenor (melody) parts reversed and all parts sung in the modern SATB manner (a participating congregation, though, will obviously sing the tune at both octaves). Instruments double the bass at the lower octave where possible, with those on the upper parts playing an octave above the voices at times.

Instruments

A typical choir might have begun in the 1750s with voices only and acquired a single bass instrument in the 1770s. Especially when sounding an octave below the bass voices, this would help to assert the melody–bass polarity of the early settings, and would help the singers with their tuning. Two or even three treble instruments might have been added by the turn of the century, and their doubling of the upper voices would have been part of a move towards a more even balance of parts. (Tenor-range instruments were scarcely ever found in gallery bands.) During the great period of gallery music—from around 1780 through the first few decades of the nineteenth century—more instruments might have been added on an *ad hoc* basis, availability, ease of playing, and ability to withstand the cold and damp of the church in winter months being important factors in their choice.

Nicholas Temperley has found 'nothing to show that any parish choirs were supported by instruments before the 1740s' (p. 148, and see his tables, p. 149), and they scarcely appear at all in records before then. But evidence is slowly accumulating which suggests that in a few places, at least, instruments may have been used from the earliest days of gallery choirs. There must have been privately owned instruments in many villages, used to accompany dancing, dramatic entertainment, domestic music-making, and perhaps even for carolling, and such instruments would not necessarily show up in churchwardens' accounts when they first began to be used in church galleries during services. (Temperley's earliest record, from 1742, is indeed for the rehairing of a bow, not the purchase of an instrument.) Publications for country choirs begin to assume the possibility of instruments as early as the mid-century, implying an established tradition and yet preceding documentary evidence of more than the odd single instrument in galleries. In *The Psalm Singer's Compleat Tutor and Divine Companion* (2nd ed., 2 vols., 1750) by Thomas Moore of Glasgow, the three upper voices are all in G clefs (as in a modern vocal score) rather than the old C clefs, these being 'more commodious for persons who play on the violin, flute, hautboy [oboe], and many other instruments'. A setting in the third and earliest known edition of *Church Harmony Sacred to Devotion* (1760) by Joseph Stephenson of Poole, Dorset, has obbligato parts and a sinfonia for flute, two violins, and a bass instrument.

The most comprehensive list of gallery instruments that we have found is in Noel Boston and Lyndsay G. Langwill's *Church and Chamber Barrel-Organs* (1967, pp. 111–16), though even the 157 English and Welsh churches for which they give details represent little more than a scratching of the surface. The list covers the whole period of the church bands' existence, and some of the instruments they cite may have been in use consecutively rather than simultaneously; but the size and distribution of this sampling is such that a clear and convincing picture of the relative numbers of the different types of instrument emerges. Wind instruments are vastly more common than stringed (partly, no doubt, because they stood up to the harsh conditions better), and bassoons are by far the most frequently encountered instruments of all. If we exclude the more unusual examples (and there are plenty of them), treble instruments mentioned are clarinets (54), flutes (including one piccolo and a few flageolets) (41), violins (20), and oboes (11). The most common bass instruments are bassoons (89), cellos and double basses (28—the frequency of the generic term 'bass viol' prevents distinction between them), and serpents (12).

Specific scorings, such as the one quoted from Stephenson's book above, would in many cases have had to be adapted to suit whatever instruments were available, and this was often a very haphazard collection indeed. Some churches had only bass instruments: five bassoons at Alfriston, Sussex (MacDermott, *Sussex Church Music in the Past*, 1922); seven at Feock, Cornwall (Boston and Langwill); nine at Brightling, Sussex (MacDermott—the sound of all nine closing on bottom F was said to 'sound like heaven'); and two bassoons, a 'bass horn', and a bass serpent at Heathfield, Sussex. Contrary to what Hardy puts into the mouths of his band in *Under the Greenwood Tree* (part I, chapter 4), string bands were great rarities, and we know only of those at Stinsford (which the novelist's grandfather founded), Kirkwhelpington, Northumberland, and the famous Yorkshire Big Set, which still plays for carolling. A few bands appear to have been set up with a specific timbre in mind, but these are the exceptions and the majority seem to have been assembled with no such concern.

Each player in a small gallery band specialized in a single part, and each part had its peculiar technique of doubling. A single bass instrument—bassoon, cello, serpent, double bass—might double the bass, the first three always 'playing low' where possible. If there were three treble instruments, they would double the

soprano, alto, and tenor voices, the 'tenor' instrument always playing at the higher octave (no transposition was involved, since the part would normally be notated in the 'transposing treble' clef). The players doubling the alto and treble parts might play either at pitch or (much more commonly) an octave higher, but an 'alto' instrument playing at pitch would normally 'play high' when the part went low (though clarinets would have no difficulty with the range). Similarly, a 'treble' instrument playing at the upper octave would 'play low' when the part went high—above extended first position for violin, for example; this 'half-and-half' technique was the standard one for doubling the treble line. If there were only two treble instruments, one would generally double the tenor, the other either the alto or treble. A composer writing two obbligato parts, however, would usually place them on the treble and alto lines, as in carol 88. Here the second instrument is expected to play the 'alto' line throughout, and the original notation makes it clear that both instruments play at the higher octave when doubling the voices but at normal pitch in the symphonies and even in the little interpolation in bar 46. Such a scheme must also apply to settings with independent music for four instruments (such as carols 77 and 90): the 'treble', 'alto', and 'tenor' instruments all play an octave higher when doubling the voices, but at pitch when playing alone.

The scoring in larger bands could be more problematical. The band at Knowle, Warwickshire, in 1824 consisted of '1st clarionette, 2nd clarionette, German flute, basson, cello, tramboon, trumpet, horn' (Boston and Langwill), and it may have been for forces like these, where the instruments outnumber the parts to be doubled, that the indications of upper and lower octaves sometimes found in manuscript scores have been made. We would suggest the following as the most likely way of interpreting these octave indications for general use. In the case of two bass instruments, one would play at written pitch, the other would 'play low', with embellishment. The tenor (whether or not this was the melody part) would normally be doubled at the upper octave by one, two, or more instruments. Where two instruments double the alto, one could operate at pitch exactly as described above, while the other would double at the higher octave throughout. In the case of the treble, one would play with the 'half-and-half' technique, with embellishment, while the other doubled plainly, and entirely at pitch.

The more conventional musicians were troubled by the effects of instrumental doubling at the octave—successions of fourths would sound as fifths, for example. To avoid this, William Dixon (in the preface to *Six Anthems*, c.1790) urged that tenor and, especially, alto parts written in the 'transposing treble' clefs should be played only at the lower octave, in unison with the voices; on the other hand, George Gay (*Sacred Music*,

1827) was prepared to countenance instruments playing alto and tenor lines at the higher octave so long as the treble line was also played an octave higher and the bass an octave lower.

A typical later nineteenth-century scoring of a treble-tune setting for a choir of moderate size is illustrated by the part-books from Widecombe in the Moor, Devon, investigated by Rollo Woods (see notes, 77). The voices are doubled as follows: treble, violin 1 playing at written pitch; alto, flute playing at the upper octave; tenor, violin 2 playing at the upper octave; bass, cello playing mostly at pitch, sometimes at the lower octave. Here the flute often sounds highest, with the two violins approximately equal in register at about a fourth or so below it.

At Winterbourne St. Martin, Dorset, there was a choir of about twenty in 1820, including two adult male 'counters', and a band of four clarinets, an oboe, and a 'bass viol'. Two clarinets doubled the treble line and two the alto (one presumably playing high, the other low in each case), the oboe doubled the tenor at the higher octave, and the 'viol' played the bass. Abbotsbury, most unusually, had an intermediate-pitch instrument, a viola, which played the alto line at pitch. Given that the known instrumental combinations for gallery bands are almost infinitely flexible, all the examples we provide can be no more than a guide.

George Eliot (1819–90) gives a vivid description of a country parish choir with instruments in her novella *The Sad Fortunes of the Reverend Amos Barton* (from her first publication, *Scenes of Clerical Life*, 1858, set 'five-and-twenty years ago'). Her portrait of the fictional Shepperton gallery musicians draws on vivid memories of the parish church of Chilvers Coton, Warwickshire, which she attended as a child, evoking both the drab mid-Victorian gentility of the 'restored' church fabric and the accumulation of architectural styles that had been replaced: the choir was as much a part of the pervasive Georgian ethos as the little gallery it sat in, and both were swept away by the clergy with scarcely a regret. The music Eliot describes may simply be a typical 'country' anthem of the later eighteenth century, with instrumental passages in a trio-sonata texture (keyed-bugles could easily cope with virtuosic violin writing), but she could possibly be referring to extemporized ornamentation.

Shepperton Church was a very different-looking building five-and-twenty years ago . . . Now there is a wide span of slated roof . . . ; the windows are tall and symmetrical; the outer doors are resplendent with oak-graining; . . . Pass through the baize doors and you will see the nave filled with well-shaped benches . . . Ample galleries are supported on iron pillars, and in one of them stands the crowning glory, the very clasp or aigrette of Shepperton church-adornment—namely, an organ, not very much out of repair, on which a collector of small rents . . . will accompany the alacrity of your departure after the blessing, by a sacred minuet or an easy 'Gloria'.

. . . I recall with a fond sadness Shepperton Church as it was in the old days, with its outer coat of rough stucco, its red-tiled roof, its heterogeneous windows . . . No low partitions allowing you . . . to see everything at all moments; but tall dark panels, under whose shadow I sank with a sense of retirement through the Litany, only to feel with more intensity my burst into the conspicuousness of public life when I was made to stand up on the seat during the [spoken prose] psalms or the singing.

And the singing was no mechanical affair of official routine; it had drama. As the moment of psalmody approached, by some process to me as mysterious and untraceable as the opening of flowers or the breaking-out of the stars, a slate appeared in front of the gallery, advertising in bold characters the psalm about to be sung, lest the sonorous announcement of the clerk should leave the bucolic mind in doubt on that head. Then followed the migration of the clerk to the gallery, where, in company with a bassoon, two key-bugles, a carpenter understood to have an amazing power of singing 'counter', and two lesser musical stars, he formed the complement of a choir regarded in Shepperton as one of distinguished attraction, occasionally known to draw hearers from the next parish. The innovation of hymn-books was as yet undreamed of; even the New Version was regarded with a sort of melancholy tolerance . . . But the greatest triumphs of the Shepperton choir were reserved for the Sundays when the slate announced an ANTHEM, with a dignified abstinence from particularisation, both words and music lying far beyond the reach of the most ambitious amateur in the congregation:—an anthem in which the key-bugles always ran away at a great pace, while the bassoon every now and then boomed a flying shot after them.

Ornamentation

From *c.*1800 onward the evidence is that both treble and bass instruments would have been expected to add ornaments (we have come across no evidence that the instruments doubling the alto and tenor lines would do so). Two of our west country settings, carols 89 and 96:III, have an idiosyncratic type of instrumental ornamentation, supplied from unspecified manuscript sources by Ralph Dunstan. The decorated lines have much in common with the renaissance tradition of division, whereby both singers and instrumentalists would 'divide' long notes, substituting conventional patterns of short notes for sections of the melodic line (though Dunstan's examples use mainly classical, not renaissance, patterns). An earlier style of division had characterized the 'old way' of singing psalm tunes in the seventeenth century, and must have lived on in rural music-making; it was perhaps the largely extemporized tradition of country dance music that had kept the technique alive among instrumentalists. There are other examples of ornamented instrumental parts in Dunstan's *Christmas Carols* (1923) and *The Cornish Song-Book* (1929) (possibly tidied up and/or centonized from different manuscripts). A number of eighteenth-century publications for country choirs give ornamented bass parts, generally for bassoon and usually more regular and 'composed' than the Dunstan examples. The tenor-tune settings in John Valentine's

Thirty Psalm Tunes (op. 7, *c*.1785) are a rich source of eighteenth-century models for imitation.

Ornamentation was as appropriate for the simpler tunes of psalms, hymns, and carols (in which the congregation joined) as for the more complex, anthem-like offerings of the choir alone. Simpler settings certainly were ornamented, in some places at least, though just how enterprisingly it is difficult to guess: settings of a more primitive type did not imply a single manner of performance. Those in Gilbert's *Some Ancient Christmas Carols* (1822) and Sandys's *Christmas Carols, Ancient and Modern* (1833) could be ornamented in a variety of ways with perfect propriety, and the same applies to our editorial completions of carols from those collections and to any others which are in a fairly primitive style and have the tune in the tenor. When there were many instruments (normally with larger choirs), it is not known how many would ornament. Practice probably varied, and it may have been quite acceptable for players to do so in different ways simultaneously.

Thomas Hardy's innumerable references to 'bowing' in gallery music almost certainly refer to ornamentation. A well-known example is the poem 'To My Father's Violin', from *Moments of Vision & Miscellaneous Verses* (1917). His dead father is gone 'Where no fiddling can be heard . . . / No bowing wakes a congregation's wonder.' Many other examples in Hardy make it clear that extempore embellishment is what is meant.

Performance style

As must now be apparent, there was no single 'gallery style', either of composition or of performance. At one extreme is sophisticated music such as carols 71 and 76:ɪɪ, which would follow normal eighteenth-century performance practice; at the other, music too crude for inclusion here. Performance can be tailored to the type of setting being used, but three vital aspects of the country style remain constant: precise tuning (which makes the simple, open harmonies wonderfully sweet and resonant), an absence of imposed 'expression', and a vocal production which seems to have been at best incisive and natural, at worst shrill. In *Sussex Church Music in the Past* (1922), K. H. MacDermott quotes the observation of a Dr Burton in 1750 that 'The more shrill-toned [Sussex singers] are, the more they are valued . . . [In church] they bellow to excess and bleat out some goatish noise with all their might'. MacDermott's findings are widely cited, as the only detailed study of a gallery tradition, made at a time when a few choirs and bands still survived and reliable reminiscences of many others could easily be obtained. However, his observations on vocal timbre should not be taken as automatically applicable to areas such as Lancashire, Yorkshire, and the south-west of England, where gallery music was part of a musical culture that was generally much more advanced and varied. Sussex was a poor and

backward county in the nineteenth century, largely untouched by the industrial revolution, and with few towns of any size to give a lead in changing fashions.

There can be no doubt that in some of the more rural areas the tone quality and vocal mannerisms that we would now associate with folk singing were cultivated: witness the descriptions (denunciations, rather) in so many of the psalm-book prefaces of the nasal timbre of country singers, their habits of sliding up to high notes and dropping a fourth on coming off a final note, and so on. But the more sophisticated part of the tradition, especially the urban Methodist churches, almost parodied normal eighteenth-century style in some ways, with abundant ornamentation (both vocal and instrumental) and the use of *piano* and *forte* to imply 'soli' and 'full'; at the cruder end of the spectrum, soloists seem to have been sparingly used. The more sophisticated the setting (in terms of conventional harmony and part-writing), the more applicable is the emphasis placed by such skilled choirmasters as Crompton and Gay on balance between the parts, and on sweetness of timbre allied to firmness of tone.

II. THE AMERICAN TRADITION

The American equivalent of gallery music grew from English practice, but soon developed distinct styles of performance and composition. The Pilgrim Fathers had brought with them Henry Ainsworth's *Book of Psalmes* (1612), which included an appendix of thirty-nine melodies. As in Britain, harmonized tunes were initially heard only in domestic worship and recreation; in church they were always sung in unison. Speeds were fast at first, but the same gradual slowing-down occurred and the 'old way' of singing was soon adopted, drawing on English publications as a guide. The 'Old Version' of Sternhold and Hopkins was sung, and the hymns of Isaac Watts were as popular with American Dissenters as with their British counterparts. In 1640 the *Bay Psalm Book* was issued—new metrical translations by members of the colony of Massachusetts Bay—but this did not include tunes until its ninth edition in 1698. Its influence was such that echoes of the English seventeenth century continue to be audible even in many of the shape-note hymns composed in the nineteenth-century south. The *Bay Psalm Book* was followed by others, so that a whole repertory of English psalmody became the common property of the Anglican and Dissenting sects (see Richard A. Crawford, *The Core Repertory*, 1984).

Native composers began to write their own settings in the eighteenth century, beginning by imitating the English published collections of country and 'conventional' music which were widely circulated among the American urban churches. Like the English country composers, the Americans treated word-stress with great freedom, producing a creative tension between accentuation and the underlying pulse. This is also a characteristic of Anglo-American folk-song, and the simple productions of the early composers may, as Temperley suggests for their English counterparts, be regarded as a species of composed folk music.

There was far greater antagonism to the introduction of harmony in church than there had been in England, since Puritans of all shades (including those within the Episcopalian Church) had a Calvinist distrust of its sensual appeal. The link between harmony and the introduction of the *New Version of the Psalms* was much more direct than in England, and in the 1720s there was a bitter war throughout New England between those for and those against both the *New Version* and the settings that went with it. The eventual victory of harmony, in all but the most conservative rural churches, owed much to a well-timed 'discovery' by Thomas Walter, a young Harvard graduate at the head of the campaign for reform. In 1721 he demonstrated to general satisfaction that King David had personally directed the singing of his psalms in the temple at Jerusalem by antiphonal three-part choirs of male voices. A decade of struggle still lay ahead, but with this trumpet of Joshua in the hands of the reformers, citadel after citadel fell easily to the armies of harmony.

The essential difference between the New England 'primitive' tradition and the music of the English galleries is that the Americans made scarcely any use of instruments. William Billings of Boston (1746–1800) used octave writing for the bass voices quite deliberately to give the added sonority that was provided in England by bass instruments playing at the lower octave, and the frequent division of the upper vocal parts by many composers was perhaps to compensate for the lack of treble-doubling instruments. The resulting sonority is distinctive, and quite different from that of English gallery choirs (see Harriet Beecher Stowe's description, below).

Billings, a Congregationalist, was by far the greatest of the eighteenth-century 'primitive' composers in either country. He anticipated many later New England composers in the individual and ruggedly intellectual approach to composition that he evolved. 'Every composer should be his own Carver,' he once wrote, and he and followers such as Supply Belcher (1752–1836) carved out a distinctively northern American style from the material to hand. Billings was a passionate *aficionado* of the fuging tune and of the fugal principle in general: 'The words are seemingly engaged in a musical warfare . . . each part . . . striving for Mastery, and sweetly contending for Victory . . . now here, now there, now here again. O enchanting! O ecstatic! Push on, push on, ye Sons of Harmony!' (*The Continental Harmony*, 1794). His rough-hewn but endlessly inventive counterpoint pushes on with a

vengeance, making the most extrovert fuging tune by an English master of the form such as Thomas Clark seem almost effete by comparison. Billings's outstanding characteristic, shared by few of his counterparts in either country, is his melodic gift: all three of his Christmas settings (carols 78, 79, and 80) have memorable tunes, and all three have modal inflexions derived from folk music, which give his very diatonic style much of its sweetness.

Harriet Beecher Stowe (1811–96) gives a vivid description in her story 'Poganuc People' of the singing of Billings's first setting of 'The Lord descended from above' ('Majesty') in the meeting-house of her childhood in Litchfield, Connecticut (quoted in Crawford, *The Core Repertory*, p. xliii):

There was a grand, wild freedom, an energy of motion in the old 'fuging tunes' of that day, that well expressed the heart of the people courageous in combat & unshaken in endurance. . . Whatever the trained musician might say of such a tune as old Majesty, no person of imagination or sensibility could hear it well rendered by a large choir without deep emotion. And when back and forth from every side of the church came the different parts shouting—

> On cherubim and seraphim
> Full royally He rode,
> And on the wings of mighty winds
> Came flying all abroad,

there went a stir and thrill through many a stern and hard nature, until the tempest cleared off in the words—

> He sat serene upon the floods
> Their fury to restrain,
> And He as Sovereign Lord and King
> For evermore shall reign.

Shape-note music

Although the 'primitive' tradition did not die out immediately upon Billings's death, a great blandness descended on the music of the urban churches, typified by the work of the German-trained Presbyterian Lowell Mason (1782–1872). The Great Defuger of fuging tunes, Mason filleted away most of the character from the tune 'Comfort' while worrying that it might still be too raw for church performance (see notes, 76). But in Billings's lifetime the northern 'primitive' tradition had already put out roots in rural America, and these produced a new and vigorous growth with no counterpart in other countries—the music of the shape-note composers.

The lost history of the shape-note tradition has been methodically and lovingly unravelled in a series of books by George Pullen Jackson. Shape notes were the American counterpart of Hullah's tonic sol-fa in Britain, a system of teaching sight-singing to the masses. Each differently shaped note-head denoted a different degree of the scale (there were different patent systems) so that it was not necessary to understand clefs or key signatures to sight-read with ease. The system was ideal for a rhythmically straightforward diatonic idiom. Whereas the success of Hullah and his followers led to the creation of innumerable oratorio choirs, the sight-singing movement in the US unlocked a flood of musical creation and performance in a new and democratic style that was closely linked with the church choir tradition. The movement began in New England, but spread to the south just in time, for the northern triumph of European respectability was at the door. The new music belonged as surely to the rural poor whites as did the blues to later generations of urban blacks.

The arrival of the shape-note movement in the south coincided with the mass religious revivals which had begun with the successful Methodist missions from England in the 1770s and 80s. At the mass hymn-singings of the Great Revival, and of the Great Awakening which followed, the Wesleys' ideals of hymn-singing were realized in spontaneous, folk-derived music in which the simplest and (in theory) the most sophisticated could join. At the camp grounds, various national, and especially British, traditions of extemporized harmony emerged, and have been preserved in shape-note pieces such as 'Ye nations all, on you I call' (82), with its modal harmonies and free doublings of lines. These traditions also interacted with the partly African-derived black American tradition to produce the riches of the black spiritual repertory.

The most original shape-note music built on such extempore folk music to create a body of hymnody which is the special possession of the Southern Baptists and similar sects. The harmonies and melodic contours of some settings in this vast repertory—the woeful ones in particular—recall the music of Orlando Gibbons and other English composers who appear in the *Bay Psalm Book* and its successors. Yet others present versions of English country settings, reworked operatic arias (often with startling harmonies), or any other music that came to hand; the music which has lived on, though, is that closest to the musical traditions of the people who sang

it. This has meant that styles and procedures long relegated to musical history in England, their country of origin, have survived (if fitfully) in an apparently unbroken line of performance in remote corners of the New World.

There are three special features of the shape-note performing style. One is that accidentals are sometimes to be supplied which are not implied by the shapes: Jackson testifies to having heard this done consistently in certain settings. Another is what is always described as its easy, 'jogging' rhythm, which nothing is allowed to interrupt and which is allied to an impassive vocal delivery not unlike that of the traditional folk singer. Crawford (p. xvi) quotes a correspondent to the *Boston Columbian Centinel* in 1811, whose defence of fuging passages has a much wider application: 'Here is none of your disgusting expression, none of your crescendo and diminuendo, but all is most elevating and delightful.'

The third and most essential feature of shape-note music in performance involves the doubling of the tenor at the higher octave *and* the treble at the lower. This has been widely misapplied to American 'primitive' music in general; the likelihood is, though, that the doubling of treble parts by tenors was a specifically shape-note expansion of the existing English gallery and New England 'primitive' practice of doubling the tenor only. (It may have arisen from the folk-music background of the singers and from the ease of sight-singing from shape-note notation, which meant that a singer was not confined to a single voice-part that had to be learnt but could select any part in a suitable vocal range.) Both three- and four-part settings are greatly enriched by the characteristic sonority which the two doublings produce. We would therefore suggest that early American music in conventional notation is best served by doubling of the tenor part only, whilst the shape-note composers probably constructed their settings with the expectation of treble doubling as well.

HUGH KEYTE

Davies Gilbert, William Sandys, and the Revival
of the English Folk Carol

The classifications 'from Gilbert' or 'from Sandys' are the commonest feature of every modern carol-book. But the original publications of these two collectors seem (I cannot discover why) to be as much of a mystery as were the sources of the Nile. Not only do modern reprints labelled 'Gilbert' or 'Sandys' differ widely from the originals, but they also differ considerably from each other . . . There is a popular belief . . . 'in quires and places where they sing', that 'Gilbert and Sandys' constitute a rich mine of folk-carols from which—as yet—only a few gems have been hewn. But Gilbert (1822) published only eight carols with tunes. Sandys (1833) published only eighteen tunes. (R. R. Terry, in the preface to his *Gilbert and Sandys' Christmas Carols with six collateral tunes*, 1931.)

Sir Richard Terry was right that the number of carols published by Gilbert and Sandys is small, but it would be quite wrong to underestimate the overall significance of their work. Though the number of carols they preserved is not great, many are of exceptional quality: 'The First Nowell!'; the 'West Country' tune of 'God rest ye merry'; 'Tomorrow shall be my dancing day'; 'A virgin unspotted'; 'A child this day is born'; and several others. Without the interest in the English folk carol that their books aroused, the whole nineteenth-century carol revival might have taken place much later, by which time many carols that they and their successors recovered would probably have been irretrievably lost. Moreover, there is reason to believe that Sandys's influence extends beyond his published collections of 1833 and c.1853 to include at least two others, *A Garland of Christmas Carols* (1861) and *Songs of the Nativity* (1864); the latter brought the folk carol to popular (as distinct from antiquarian) attention. And we now know (as Terry had no way of knowing) that Gilbert preserved many more carols than the few that he published in his 1822 book and its 1823 second edition: a great mass of Cornish texts and tunes is only now coming to light (too late, for the most part, to be included in the present book), including several of the first order which are not otherwise known.

Terry was also right about the modern reprints of the tunes, versions which date from the revisions of Victorian editors such as William Husk (*Songs of the Nativity*, 1864) and Sir John Stainer (Bramley and Stainer, *Christmas Carols New and Old*, 1871). But despite his restoration of the original tunes in his 1931 edition, Terry rejected the bass parts which are their essential adjuncts. The musical milieu in which he lived was such that it probably never occurred to him that the 'settings' which Gilbert and Sandys provided might not be their own, but represent (with varying degrees of success in the latter case) the way the carols were performed by rural gallery musicians, domestic carollers, and village waits of the mid-eighteenth century. The basses have until now been either ignored or derided by editors: 'Such "harmony" as either Gilbert or Sandys attempted is too bad for reproduction . . . Neither shows the smallest knowledge of the rudiments of music,' as Terry put it.

Quite apart from the nature of the basses, Terry was disconcerted by the fact that no other parts are given. He would have been unaware that the two parts in many cases had constituted a kind of adapt-it-yourself kit: it was fairly common for eighteenth-century 'country' collections to provide only the tenor melody and the bass from existing three- or four-part settings, the buyer being expected either to perform the arrangements in two parts (not at all unusual in the smaller churches, and often surprisingly effective) or else to add his own upper voices. Our completions of the carols from Gilbert's volume (and a number of others, some from Sandys's) are therefore no more than what the buyers of such a collection would have been expected to provide for themselves. We take Gilbert's basses seriously, and have added upper parts in the 'additive' (as distinct from the 'simultaneous') manner of country composers (see Appendix 3), but we have in general fought shy of quite the degree of dissonance that many arrangers would have produced, since a modern choir will probably have a more even balance of parts than that of a typical eighteenth-century Cornish country church, making much more apparent clashes which might scarcely have been noticed when the melody and bass parts predominated. All our four-part tenor-tune completions of these tune-and-bass settings can be performed in two ways. The first option is to sing them straightforwardly as printed, with some sopranos doubling the tenor melody an octave higher (see Appendix 3). Alternatively, the treble and tenor parts may be exchanged, which is what many performers would automatically have done in line with the late eighteenth-century updating of tenor-tune settings, as described in Appendix 3.

Davies Gilbert (1767–1839)

Resourceful, energetic, and multi-talented, Davies Gilbert played important roles in many aspects of late-Georgian public life. He was born in 1767 at his family's seat of Tredrea, just outside St Erth, in the south-west of Cornwall. His clergyman father was from an old Cornish family, and Davies was successively Member of Parliament for Helston (from 1804) and Bodmin (1806–32). As treasurer (1820) and then president (1827–30) of the Royal Society, the oldest and most prestigious scientific society in Britain, he witnessed and promoted the great technological advances of the age: he energetically pleaded the cause of science in Parliament, was closely involved with Richard Trevithick and his pioneering smooth-rail locomotive of 1804, encouraged the young Humphrey Davy, was responsible for selecting Isambard Kingdom Brunel's design for the Clifton Suspension Bridge over the Avon Gorge at Bristol, and published on many scientific matters. (See Arthur Dodd's biography, *Beyond the Blazes*, 1967, which ignores Gilbert's musical activities). He was an active member of the Royal Cornish Institution and the Society of Antiquaries, wrote a *Parochial History of Cornwall* (1838), and issued editions of two Cornish mystery plays and other records of Cornish memorabilia.

Eighteenth-century Cornwall was one of the most remote and conservative regions of England: 'the land of West Barbary', as some contemporary writers called it, with 'the worst roads in England' (letter to the *Gentleman's Magazine*, 1754). In this staunchly Royalist duchy (Cornwall was—and remains—the property of the heir to the throne) some aspects of the medieval age lived on until the later eighteenth century, when Methodism, the decline of the Cornish language, and improved transport began to reduce the county's isolation. A richer soil for the growth and retention of folksongs and customs could hardly be imagined, and Cornwall has been beyond doubt the prime British source of folk carols. From the early part of the century there was a vigorous tradition of 'gallery' music in local churches (see Appendix 3), and each village took pride in its own repertory of traditional carol tunes, which were sung not only in church but also in the cottages on Christmas Eve and by the village waits (who usually also comprised the church-gallery choir and band) on Christmas Night visits to each house in the parish. The identities of the composers who adapted and set the carols were rarely recorded, and are now mostly lost.

The Christmas Eve carolling in the cottages of the farm labourers had its echo in the houses of the gentry, and the tradition may indeed have lasted longer there in some places. It was Gilbert's experience of domestic carolling, as much as of the village waits and of the gallery choir of his father's church, that gave him his lifelong love of the carol. Within his own family he very actively 'kept up the carol', and was saddened to see the traditional texts and their old gallery settings being superseded, partly under the influence of the Methodist and Evangelical movements, which had little time for their pre-Reformation concentration on such topics as the Fall of Man and Mary as Virgin Mother. Gilbert was likewise pained at the decline of domestic and street carolling, which he represented as things of the past (whereas Sandys, eleven years later, describes them as still current). In the accepted antiquarian manner, Gilbert affected merely to be 'desirous of preserving [the carols] . . . as specimens of times now passed away, and of religious feelings superseded by others of a different cast'. But, more personally, he was also anxious to preserve them 'on account of the delight they afforded him in his childhood', when the village waits would sound beneath his window in the silence and dark of Christmas Night at Tredrea.

Some Ancient Christmas Carols, with the tunes to which they were formerly sung in the West of England (1822, followed by a second edition with additional carol texts in 1823) is a model publication, elegantly printed by a firm in Parliament Street with which Gilbert presumably had come into contact as an MP. Both music and texts are impeccably edited, though whether Gilbert's involvement went beyond selection of the items and the provision of an introduction is doubtful, since we know that he employed competent acquaintances to copy and transcribe music and texts. The settings are manifestly taken from the manuscript books of unidentified church-gallery musicians. Though short, the 1822 book preserves unique gallery versions of some of the most important carols in the old Cornish repertory. Many of the most characteristic melodies are interlinked and may have had a common ancestor, and this, together with the striking unity of the settings, suggests that they may all derive from a single location, perhaps near Gilbert's birthplace. Music and texts have an eighteenth-century accent, though quite a number of items must have seventeenth-century origins. One type of carol that scarcely exists elsewhere is overwhelmingly represented: folk tunes adapted for gallery use by a regularization of rhythm and the provision of a bass part.

An attraction of the eighteenth-century Cornish repertory is that the anonymous musicians adapting the tunes in this way were working within the folk tradition, not outside it, developing a style in which the melodies are set in a wholly sympathetic manner. A. L. Lloyd, the leading folk-song scholar of the generation after Sharp and Vaughan Williams, reports an exchange with a perceptive Yorkshireman who had been singing carols both with a traditional carol group and with a male-voice choir. Lloyd asked him what he thought of the choral arrangers, and after a moment's thought the singer pinpointed the problem: 'They don't know how to bass 'em.' The Cornish musicians most definitely *did* know how to 'bass 'em', and they also perfected a manner of clipping the melodies to fit into a regular metrical shape which still allowed them their power of flight. It is a general rule with rural settings that the more primitive the composer, the more mal-adroit the bass line; the energetic, free-ranging basses in Gilbert's collection, with their Ivesian scorn for the trammels of academic harmony, are a glorious excep-tion—the work, perhaps, of a composer or arranger of real talent, who had forged his own style remote from the influence of published 'country' settings, which were often either composed by conventional musicians or 'improved' by the publisher.

No manuscript source for the carols in Gilbert's book has yet been identified, but the 'Hutchens' manuscript, prepared for Gilbert in or around 1817, appears to have supplied him with ten out of the eleven additional car-ols printed (without music) in the expanded 1823 edi-tion of the book. (The eleventh was 'Christians, awake!', 71.) The Hutchens collection contains the texts of thirty-nine carols with twenty-four tunes; some texts and tunes are otherwise unknown, and there are two non-Christmas carols, one 'On the coming of the Prince of Orange' (William III, in 1689) and another headed 'A Song for Easter Day'. It is now in the Davies Gilbert archive in the Cornwall County Record Office, Truro, which also contains other carol material, includ-ing eighteenth-century manuscript word-books.

Other manuscripts confirm that Gilbert's work on the Cornish folk carol was far more extensive than has been realized. A manuscript headed 'Some ancient Carol-Tunes' was made for Gilbert in 1825 by John Davey (1770–1845), the mathematician-poet of St.-Just-in-Penwith, who assisted Gilbert with his paper *The Mathematical Theory of Suspension Bridges* (1826). It contains the underlaid melodies of eight carols (one with bass) 'pricked off all by memory in manner as they were formerly sung in the parish of Zennor', and a ninth, with a four-part refrain, copied from a late eigh-teenth-century publication. The manuscript was discov-ered in the 1960s by Inglis Gundry, together with another from 1822 (with the words of a single carol) and a manuscript book of carol texts that Davey pre-pared for his own use at Zennor Church in 1795. (The location of the first two manuscripts is now unknown, though Mr Gundry has retained photocopies which he has generously made available to us; the third is now in the British Library, MS Add. 52421.) Three eighteenth-century word-books also survive in the Houghton Library of Harvard University, bound together by Gilbert and interleaved with carol tunes, possibly as the basis of a much larger publication that never material-ized (see below).

William Sandys (1792–1874)

William Sandys, like Gilbert, was a practical and pro-fessional man of some social standing, a prominent London lawyer and antiquary and a member of a well-known family of Cornish gentlefolk. He was born in Fleet Street, the eldest of the six surviving children of Hannibal Sandys, of Helstone, Cornwall. He was edu-cated at Westminster School, and was taught the cello and given a thorough musical grounding by the com-poser Thomas Linley senior. His famous carol collec-tion of 1833 is entitled *Christmas Carols, Ancient and Modern, including the most popular in the west of England, with the tunes to which they are sung. Also specimens of French Provincial carols.*. In *c*.1852 he published *Christmastide, its history, festivities and carols*, a somewhat sentimental popular history of the customs of the sea-son, expanded from the introduction to his 1833 vol-ume and recycling some of its carols and tunes (the settings marginally improved) with the addition of Wainwright's 'Christians, awake!' in a setting almost identical to that in Gilbert's 1823 book. He was also co-author of what was for a long time a standard work, *The History of the Violin and other instruments played on with the bow* (1864, with Andrew Forster). Like Gilbert, Sandys was much interested in Cornish antiquities, and was a member of the Society of Antiquaries. He con-tributed three articles to the *Journal of the Royal Institution of Cornwall*; in the first, on 'The Cornish Drama' (vol. 1, no. III, pp. 1–18), he is sharply critical of Gilbert's translations. He was a leading freemason, and author of *A Short View of the History of Freemasons* (1829).

Christmas Carols, Ancient and Modern is literary in emphasis, and folk carols are only one of its concerns. After the introduction there are three main sections, each impeccably edited: part I gives the texts of thirty-four 'Ancient Carols and Christmas Songs from the early part of the fifteenth to the end of the seventeenth century'; part II comprises the texts of forty folk carols, a selection from carols 'still used in the West of England' (in contrast to Gilbert's 'formerly sung in the West of England'); and part III has the texts of six Provençal *noëls*, including 'Guillô, pran ton tamborin!' (185). Then follow a composite 'Christmas Play of St George as represented in Cornwall', nine pages of notes, explanations of Provençal words ('French Provincialisms'), four pages of publishers' advertise-ments, and, last and emphatically least, twelve pages of tunes for eighteen of the forty folk carols that comprise part II.

In stark contrast to the rest of the book, the eighteen tunes are amateurishly lithographed, with major omis-sions and mistakes, and the musical transcriptions themselves are mostly on a low level: some are mis-barred; several seem to be fumbling transcriptions from performance, with a peculiar style of chordal 'vamping' in the bass stave which indicates the harmonies without giving the parts. Such basses as are given are shapeless and repetitive, and cannot bear comparison with the coherent and independent basses in Gilbert's book; moreover, someone seems to have tried to bring them into conformity with the rules of classical harmony. Mismatches between underlaid and printed texts are not infrequent ('certain/three poor shepherds' in 'While shepherds watched', for example) and suggest that two hands were at work. The inescapable impression is that Sandys delegated the entire musical side to someone else of limited competence, perhaps a Cornish contact.

Despite the shortcomings of the musical transcriptions, Sandys's carols are as invaluable in their way as those of Gilbert, provided that the music is interpreted in the light of the earlier collection. Sandys has a wider cross-section of West Country practice, and one or two carols, such as 'God rest you merry, gentlemen' (151:III), have what are probably genuine gallery basses. Whereas Gilbert's attitude to such 'primitive' music had been coloured by happy childhood memories of the Tredrea waits and domestic carolling, that of the London-born Sandys was much more equivocal. Waits had very different connotations for him: 'In the metropolis, a solitary itinerant may be occasionally heard in the streets, croaking out "God rest you merry, gentlemen", or some other carol, to an ancient and simple tune' (from the 1833 preface). Far more than Gilbert, Sandys was in the line of those antiquaries in the related field of balladry who had consigned a wealth of tunes to oblivion by their resolute concentration on texts (his brief introduction to the tunes in the 1833 book concludes: 'As it would have encumbered the work to have printed a greater number, I may, from the difference of taste in these matters, have omitted some, more prized by the singers, but I have endeavoured to bring forward the best'). For all his apparent lack of sympathy with the music, however, Sandys was a more active figure in the revival of the folk carol than has been appreciated, and he may have been an *éminence grise* behind several carol publications after 1833: at least one carol collection, *A Garland of Christmas Carols* by 'Joshua Sylvester' (1861), is generally believed to have been the work of Sandys in partnership with William Husk.

There are striking parallels between *Christmas Carols, Ancient and Modern* and *Some Ancient Christmas Carols*. Both rescue many West Country carols that would otherwise have been lost; both give an overview of the customs associated with carolling in their prefaces; both give a full range of carol types, including domestic carols and waits' music. Each gives a 'debased' local version of Joseph Stephenson's 'Hark! hark what news the angels bring' (75) in three parts, and each has what we believe is a domestic setting of the Christmas Eve carol 'The Lord at first did Adam make' (141) for voice(s) and a bass instrument. The parallels between the two

books are matched by the shared interests of their compilers: both were of Cornish extraction and active members of the Royal Cornish Institution; both understood Cornish and translated vernacular drama; both were members of the Society of Antiquaries. There was even a distant family connection, for Davies Gilbert was one of the co-heirs of the Barony of Sandys. The fact that Gilbert may have planned a much larger sequel to his 1822 collection prompts the speculation that he may have asked Sandys to take over the task of publishing more Cornish carols, perhaps finding that his public life left him too little time to bring the project to fruition.

W. H. Husk (1814–87)

If Gilbert and Sandys were the pioneers, William Henry Husk was the popularizer. Husk was a leading musical scholar of his day, librarian of the Sacred Harmonic Society (whose published catalogue he compiled), author of *An Account of the Musical Celebrations on St Cecilia's Day in the 16th., 17th., and 18th. Centuries* (1857), and a contributor of many articles to Sir George Grove's *Dictionary of Music and Musicians* (1878–90). His influential *Songs of the Nativity* was published in 1864 by the printer of the *Garland of Christmas Carols*, and the standard modern forms of many well-known carols derive from it. Husk makes frequent reference to a 'garland . . . published pseudonymously' as a source, and his notes draw heavily on Sandys's *Christmastide*. The likelihood is, as Margaret Dean-Smith has argued in her *Guide to English Folk-Song Collections 1882–1952*, (1954, pp. 20, 27), that the two men worked closely together and that Husk had access to Sandys's collection of carols in broadsides and chapbooks which the latter mentions in *Christmastide* (1853) as having been amassed during the previous thirty years. (The present whereabouts of this collection are unknown.)

Husk's versions of tunes from Gilbert's and Sandys's collections (and others from elsewhere) have been stripped of their rhythmic crudities and melodic idiosyncrasies so as to render them notionally 'correct' and more suited to conventional harmonization. It was his book, with its decorative borders and 'Olde-Englishe' ambiance, that captured the imagination of the general public, and his versions of the tunes, further refined through the high-Victorian arrangements of Bramley and Stainer, that became the basis of the repertory on which most of us have been raised. No such amiable tunes and bland texts ever existed in nature, of course. But if Husk's work on the carol was disturbingly reminiscent of mid-Victorian 'restorations' of Gothic stonework—all too often restorations of what people thought should have been there, rather than what had in fact existed—we should remember that it was he, as much as Gilbert and Sandys, who saved the English folk carol for posterity. Without such processing, few of the raw melodies and rough texts of eighteenth-century Cornwall would ever have crossed the cultural divide that separated the gallery bands and choirs of the rural west from the upright piano in the heavily-draped Victorian drawing-room or the surpliced choir in the echoing chancel.

Ultimately, though, the post-Victorian age is in Gilbert's debt for resisting the temptation to bowdlerize. Despite the declaration in the preface to *Some Ancient Christmas Carols* that he was 'desirous of preserving [these carols] in their actual forms, however dis-torted by false grammar or obscurities', he must have been aware that it is precisely through the 'false grammar' and 'obscurities' that the vigorous life of the genre finds its most obvious expression. Gilbert's personal taste for the wild honey of the genuine folk carol is also that of the modern age, and his work of preservation allows us to follow the track back past the docile Victorian domestications to the more primitive stock beyond.

HUGH KEYTE

BIBLIOGRAPHY

This bibliography contains all books and musical publications mentioned in the notes and appendices, with the exception of a few peripheral items. A few other books that we have found particularly useful are also included, but we have not attempted a bibliography of the carol nor listed general works on the history of music, the liturgy, performance practice, etc.

We have examined a wide range of hymn- and carol-books, but only include here those whose contents we have drawn upon or which have introductions that contain original information. Collections of carols and hymns have generally been referred to by title in the notes and are accordingly entered thus here, though library catalogues are more likely to include them under compilers or editors. Standard thematic catalogues of composers' works appear under the name of the composer, where relevant.

Items listed in the 'Selected sources of givings-out, accompaniment, and interludes in the English tradition' (Appendix 2) are not repeated here. Manuscripts are normally cited fully enough in the text to require no further identification, though we have given guidance here towards further information on Conradus, Davey, Hutchens, and Laufenberg. Fuller details of medieval and renaissance manuscripts may be found in the *Census-Catalogue of Manuscript Sources of Polyphonic Music 1400–1550* and *Répertoire international des sources musicales*. Periodicals are omitted, unless the citation in the body of the book needs amplification; we have, for instance, given a summary of the complex numbering of the *Journal of the Folk-Song Society*.

Subtitles are abbreviated, capitalization standardized, and various forms of words in any language for 'edited by' and 'compiled by' are usually simplified into 'ed.'. Dates of publication are in square brackets if surmised (they do not necessarily appear on the title-page), though the bibliographic practice of using square brackets for dates taken from anywhere other than the title-page has been ignored. Details of modern reprints, editions, and facsimiles are quoted where possible.

Generally, only the place of publication is given for pre-1900 material (though some familiar publishers' names are also given for earlier editions), but the publisher is also included for items after 1900. Places of publication are not repeated when stated or implied by the name of the publisher; no further indications are given for university presses (abbreviated UP), even though some English universities have published in London and some American universities have state rather than town names. No distinction is made between the Clarendon Press and OUP. When a book is nominally published in various places, the place where the book was primarily produced is preferred.

Achtliederbuch: see *Etlich christlich Lider*

Adeste fideles: see Thomas GREATOREX

ADLUNG, Jakob, *Anleitung zu der musikalischen Gelahrtheit* (Berlin, 1758; new edn., Berlin, 1783).

AINSWORTH, Henry, *The Book of Psalmes Englished both in prose and metre* (Amsterdam, 1612).

ALCOCK, John, *The Pious Soul's Heavenly Exercise* (Lichfield, 1756).

ALEXANDER, Mrs Cecil Frances, *Hymns for Little Children* (London, 1848). First edition gives only the initials C. F. H[umphreys]., her maiden name. First edition with music, *Hymns for Little Children, by the author of 'The Baron's Little Daugther', etc. Set to music, with pianoforte accompaniment, by H. J. Gauntlett* (London, 1858).

ALISON, Richard, *The Psalmes of David in Meter* (London, 1599); facs. edn., ed. I. Harwood (Scolar Press, Menston [W. Yorkshire], 1968).

ALLEN, William Francis, Charles Pickard Ware, and Lucy McKim Garrison, *Slave Songs of the United States* (New York, 1867; new edn., Oak Publications, New York, 1965).

ALLON, Henry: see *The Congregational Psalmist*

Alte catholische geistliche Kirchengesänge [known as the *Speyer Gebetbuch*] (Cologne, 1599).

Alte catholische geistliche Kirchengesänge [known as the *Paderborn Gesangbuch*] (Paderborn, 1609).

AMELN, Konrad and Wilhelm Thomas, *Der Quempas geht um: Vergangenheit und Zukunft eines deutschen Christnachtbrauches* (Bärenreiter, Kassel, 1965).

AMMERBACH, Elias Nicolaus, *Orgel oder Instrument Tabulaturbuch (1571/83)*, ed. Charles Jacobs (OUP, 1984).

Analecta Hymnica Medii Aevi, ed. G. M. Dreves et al., 55 vols. (Leipzig, 1886–1922).

Andernacher Gesangbuch (1608): see *Catholische geistliche Gesänge*

ANDERSON, Gordon A., *Notre Dame and Related Conductus* (Institute of Mediaeval Music, Henryville [Pennsylvania], 1979–). Vols. 3, 5, 6, and 8 of the projected 10 vols. published before Anderson's death.

Antiphonale Sarisburiense (facs.), ed. W. H. Frere (Plainsong and Mediaeval Music Society, London, 1901–24; repr., 6 vols., Gregg Press, 1966).

ARBEAU, Thoinot [anagram of Jehan Tabourot], *Orchésographie* (Lengres, 1589; repr. 1596, 1597); facs. edn. (Minkoff,

Geneva, 1972); tr. Mary Stewart Evans (Dover Books, New York, 1967).

ARLT, Wulf, *Ein Festoffizium des Mittelalters aus Beauvais in seiner liturgischen und musikalischen Bedeutung*, 2 vols. (Arno Volk Verlag, Cologne, 1970).

ARNIM, Achim von: see *Des Knaben Wunderhorn*

ARNOLD, John, *The Compleat Psalmodist* (London, 1741, and subsequent edns.).

Around the World with Christmas: A Christmas exercise. Words arranged by W. E. Hewitt. Music by John Sweeney and Wm. J. Kirkpatrick (Cincinnati, 1895).

ASHWORTH, Caleb, *A Collection of Tunes* (London, 1760).

ATTEY, John, *The First Book of Ayres of Four Parts* (London, 1622); facs. edn., ed. D. Greer (Scolar Press, Menston [W. Yorkshire], 1967); ed. E. H. Fellowes, *English Lute Songs*, I, 9 (Stainer & Bell, London, 1926).

Auserlesene catholische geistliche Kirchengesänge (Cologne, 1623).

AUSTIN, Frederic (arr.), *The Twelve Days of Christmas* (Novello, London, 1909).

BABST, Valentin, *Geystliche Lieder* (Leipzig, 1545); facs. edn. as *Das Babstche Gesangbuch* (1966).

BACH, Johann Sebastian: Wolfgang Schmieder, *Thematisch-systematisches Verzeichnis der musikalischen Werke von Johann Sebastian Bach* (Breitkopf & Härtel, Leipzig, 1950; rev. edn., 1990).

——*Johann Sebastian Bach vierstimmige Choralgesänge*, ed. C. P. E. Bach, 2 vols. (1765–9).

BALLANTA-TAYLOR, N. G. J., *St Helena Island Spirituals* (Schirmer, New York, 1925).

BALLET, William: Eire, Dublin, Trinity College, MS D.1.21/II; see *Lute Society Journal*, x (1968), p. 15.

BARNICOAT, Ben, *Old Cornish Carols* (Polperro Press, Polperro [Cornwall], 1927).

BARÔZAI, Gui, *Noei borguignon* (1701).

BAYLEY, Daniel, *The New Harmony of Zion* (Newburyport [Massachusetts], 1788).

Bay Psalm Book: see *The Whole Booke of Psalmes*

BEDFORD, Arthur, *The Excellency of Divine Musicke*, with appendix 'A Specimen of Hymns for Divine Musick' (London, 1733).

——*The Great Abuse of Musick* (London, 1711). See also *Divine Recreations*.

BELCHER, Supply, *The Harmony of Maine* (Boston [Massachusetts], 1794).

BENTLEY, William, *The Diary of William Bentley, D.D., pastor of the East Church, Salem, Massachusetts*, 4 vols. (Salem [Massachusetts], 1905–14).

BERLIOZ, Hector: for bibliographic information see D. Kern Holoman, *Catalogue of the Works of Hector Berlioz* (*New Berlioz Edition*, 25) (Bärenreiter, Kassel, 1987).

BICKERSTETH, Edward Henry, *A Hymnal Companion to the Book of Common Prayer* (London, 1870).

BILLINGS, William: *The Complete Works*, 4 vols., ed. Karl Kroeger (1, 3, 4), Hans Nathan (2), and Richard Crawford (American Musicological Society and Colonial Society of Massachusetts, Virginia UP, 1977–90).

——*The Continental Harmony* (Boston [Massachusetts], 1794); facs. edn., ed. Hans Nathan (Harvard UP, 1961).

——*Music in Miniature* (Boston, 1779).

——*The New-England Psalm-Singer* (Boston, 1770).

——*The Psalm-Singer's Amusement* (Boston, 1781).

——*The Singing Master's Assistant* (Boston, 1778).

——*The Suffolk Harmony* (Boston, 1786).
  See also David P. McKAY and Richard Crawford, *William Billings of Boston*.

BINDI, Cesare, *Corona di sacre canzoni* (Florence, 1689).

BIZET, Georges, *L'Arlésienne* [vocal score and full score with editorial orchestration] (Choudens, Paris, [c.1875)]; of original version (King's Music, Huntingdon [Cambridgeshire], 1990).

BLOCK, Adrienne, *The Early French Parody Noël* (*Studies in Musicology*, 36), 2 vols. (UMI Research Press, Ann Arbor [Michigan], 1983).

BLUME, Friedrich, *Geschichte der evangelischen Kirchenmusik* (Bärenreiter, Kassel, 1964); English edn., rev. L. Finscher, *Protestant Church Music: A History* (Norton, New York, 1974). The English edition has additions, including a chapter by Robert Stevenson, 'Protestant Music in America'.

BODENSCHATZ, Erhard, *Florilegium Portense* (Leipzig, 1618).

Bohemian Brethren: see *Kirchengesang* (1566)

The Booke of the Common Prayer (London, 1549); repr. in *The First and Second Prayer-Books of King Edward the Sixth* (Dent, London [1910]). A revised version of the 1559 edition was in use until 1645 and a new version was published in 1662, which remained in use in the Church of England until the 20th century.

BOOTH, Edwin, *The Wesleyan Psalmodist* (London, 1843).

BOSTON, N. and L. G. Langwill, *Church and Chamber Barrel-Organs* (1967; 2nd edn. [by Langwill and Boston], Langwill, Edinburgh, 1979).

BORDES, Charles, *Douze Noëls populaires en dialecte souletin* (Bureau des Archives de la Tradition Basques, Paris [1895]).

BRAMLEY, Henry Ramsden: see *Christmas Carols New and Old*

BRAND, John, *Observations on the Popular Antiquities of Great Britain*, arranged, revised and greatly enlarged by Henry Ellis, 3 vols. (Bohn, London, 1853–5). Completed by Brand in 1795; first (posthumous) edn., 1813.

BRENTANO, Clemens: see *Des Knaben Wunderhorn*

BRETT, Philip: see *Musica Britannica*, XXII

Breviarium ad Usum Insignis Ecclesiae Sarum [ed. F. Procter and C. Wordsworth], 3 vols. (Cambridge, 1876–86).

BRITTEN, Benjamin, *A Ceremony of Carols* (Winthrop Rogers [Boosey & Hawkes], London, 1943).

BRITTON, Allen Perdue and Irving Lowens, *American Sacred Music Imprints 1698–1810: A bibliography*, completed by Richard Crawford, introduction by Richard Crawford (American Antiquarian Society, Worcester [Massachusetts], 1990).

BROADWOOD, Lucy: see *English County Songs*

BRODERIP, John, *A Second Book of New Anthems and Psalm Tunes* (London, 1750; repr. 1764).

BRONSON, Bertrand Harris, *The Singing Tradition of Child's Popular Ballads* (Princeton UP, 1976). A one-volume abbreviation of the following title.

——*The Traditional Tunes of the Child Ballads*, 4 vols. (Princeton UP, 1959–72).

BROOKE, William Thomas, *The Altar Hymnal* (London, 1884).

BROOME, Michael, *Collection of Church Musick*, I (c.1725).

BROWN, Carleton, *English Lyrics of the XIIIth Century* (OUP, 1932).

——*Religious Lyrics of the XIVth Century*, 2nd edn., rev. G. V. Smithers (OUP, 1952).

——*Religious Lyrics of the XVth Century* (OUP, 1939).

BROWNING, Robert, *The Compleat Psalmist*, 4th edn. (London, 1756).

BULLEN, A. H., *Carols and Poems from the fifteenth century to the present time* (London, 1886).

BURNEY, Charles, *The Present State of Music in Germany, the Netherlands, and United Provinces*, 2 vols. (London, 1773).

BYROM, John, *Miscellaneous Poems* (1773).

CALDWELL, John, *The Oxford History of English Music*, vol. 1 (OUP, 1991).

CALDWELL, William, *Union Harmony or Family Musician* (Maryville [Tennessee], 1837).

CALVISIUS, Seth, *Geistliche Chormusik*, ed. Albrecht Tunger (Hänssler, Stuttgart, 1965). Incorporates *Vier Weihnachtsmotetten* by the same editor and publisher, 1960.

——*Hymni Sacri Latini et Germanici* (Erfurt, 1594).

——*Joseph, lieber Joseph mein*, ed. Percy M. Young (Broude Brothers, New York, 1975).

The Cambridge Carol Book: see Charles WOOD and George Ratcliffe Woodward

Cancionero de Uppsala: see *Villancicos de diversos autores*

Carols for Choirs, vol. 1 ed. Reginald Jacques and David Willcocks, vols. 2–4 ed. David Willcocks and John Rutter (OUP, 1961–80).

Carols for Christmas-tide: see George Ratcliffe WOODWARD

Carols for Christmas-tide, set to ancient melodies, ed. Thomas Helmore and J. M. Neale (Novello, London, 1853–4).

The Castle of Perseverance: see Peter HAPPÉ, *Four Morality Plays*

CASWALL, Edward, *Hymns and Poems* (London, 1873).

——*The Masque of Mary, and other poems* (London, 1858).

Catholisch Cantual oder Psalmbücherlein [known as the Mainz *Cantual*] (Mainz, 1605).

Catholische geistliche Gesänge [known as the *Andernacher Gesangbuch*] (Cologne, 1608); facs. edn., *Denkmäler Rheinischer Musik*, 13 (Düsseldorf, 1970).

CAWLEY, A. C. and Martin Stevens, *The Towneley Cycle: A facsimile of Huntington MS 1* (*Leeds Texts and Monographs, Medieval Drama Facsimiles*, 2) (Leeds UP, 1976).

CENNICK, John, *A Collection of Sacred Hymns* (5th edn., London, 1752).

Census-Catalogue of Manuscript Sources of Polyphonic Music 1400–1550, compiled by the University of Illinois Musicological Archives for Renaissance Manuscript Studies (*Renaissance Manuscript Studies*, 1), 5 vols. (American Institute of Musicology/Hänssler, Stuttgart, 1979–88).

CHAMBERS, E. K., *The Medieval Stage*, 2 vols. (OUP, 1903).

CHAPPELL, William, *Old English Ditties* (London, 1881).

——*Popular Music of the Olden Time*, 2 vols. (London, 1853–9; repr. Dover, New York, 1965).

——and J. W. Ebsworth, *The Roxburghe Ballads* (London, 1871–99).

CHARPENTIER, Marc-Antoine: *Les Œuvres de Marc-Antoine Charpentier, catalogue raisonné*, H. Wiley Hitchcock (Picard, Paris, 1982). Carol 187 is listed as 460*c*.

Cheetham's Harmonist: see John HOULDSWORTH

CHETHAM, John, *A Book of Psalmody* (London, 1718).

CHILD, Francis James, *The English and Scottish Popular Ballads*, 5 vols. (Houghton, Mifflin & Co., Cambridge [Massachusetts], 1882–98; repr. Dover, New York, 1965); shortened edn., ed. H. C. Sargent and G. L. Kittredge (1904). For musical companion see Bertrand Harris BRONSON.

CHOPE, Richard R., *Carols for Use in Church* (London, 1877). See also *Congregational Hymn and Tune Book*.

The Christian Register (Boston, 1850).

Christmas Carols [ed. Bishop Brant] (SPCK, London, 1833).

Christmas Carols New and Old, ed. Henry Ramsden Bramley and John Stainer (London, 1871).

Christmasse Carolles Newly Emprynted (Wynkyn de Worde, London, 1521).

The Church Hymnary (with Supplement), ed. David Evans (OUP, 1927).

Church Hymns (SPCK, London, 1871).

Church Hymns with Tunes, ed. Arthur Sullivan (SPCK, London, 1874).

CLARK, Thomas, *The Congregational Harmonist, or Clark's Companion* (London, 1828).

——*The Sacred Gleaner* (London, 1830; new edn. as supplement to the above, London, 1843).

——*A Set of Psalm and Hymn Tunes* (London, 1805).

——*The Union Tune Book* (Sunday School Union, London, 1837, and subsequent edns.).

La Clef des chansonniers (1717).

COLERIDGE, Samuel Taylor, *Sibylline Leaves* (London, 1817).

Cologne *Gesangbuch* (1599): see *Alte catholische geistliche Kirchengesänge* (Cologne, 1599)

Cologne *Gesangbuch* (1623): see *Auserlesene catholische geistliche Kirchengesänge*

Companion Tunes to Gadsby's Hymn Book (C. J. Farncombe, London, 1927).

Ane Compendious Buik of Godly and Spirituall Sangiss: see John, James, and Robert WEDDERBURN

Congregational Hymn and Tune Book, ed. Richard R. Chope (Bristol, 1857).

The Congregational Psalmist, ed. Henry Allon and H. J. Gauntlett (London, 1858–79).

CONNOR, Edric, *The Edric Connor Collection of West Indian Spirituals and Folk Tunes* (Boosey & Hawkes, London, 1945).

CONRADUS, Frater: Trier MS 2363/2304; more information available in *Kirchenmusikalisches Jahrbuch*, 41, 1957, pp. 64–7.

COPEMAN, Harold, *The Pocket Singing in Latin* (the author, Oxford, 1990).

——*Singing in Latin; or, Pronunciation Explor'd* (the author, Oxford, 1990).

COPPER, Bob, *Early to Rise* (Heinemann, London, 1976).

——*A Song for Every Season: A hundred years of a Sussex farming family* (Heinemann, London, 1971). Recordings by the Copper family are on Leader LEAB 404.

CORNELIUS, Peter, *Weihnachtslieder*, op. 8 (Leipzig, 1871); also in *Musikalische Werke*, 1 (Breitkopf & Härtel, Lepzig, 1905).

CORNER, David Gregor, *Geistliche Nachtigall* (Vienna, 1649).

Corph y Gaingc: see David THOMAS

CORSI, Cesare and Pierluigi Petrobelli, *Le polifonie primitive in Friuli è in Europa* (Edizioni Torre d'Orfeo, Rome, 1989).

COTTERILL, Thomas, *A Selection of Psalms and Hymns for Public Worship* (London, 1810; 8th edn., London, 1819).

Coventry Cycle: see Peter HAPPÉ, *English Mystery Plays*

The Cowley Carol Book: see Charles WOOD and George Ratcliffe Woodward

COX, John Harrington, *Folk Songs of the South* (Harvard UP, 1925).

CRAIG, Hardin, *Two Coventry Corpus Christi Plays* (Early English Text Society [*Extra Series*, 87], London, 1902; 2nd edn., 1957).

CRAWFORD, Richard, *The Core Repertory of Early American Psalmody* (*Recent Researches in American Music*, 11–12) (A–R Editions, Madison [Wisconsin], 1984).

CREIGHTON, Helen and Doreen C. sen., *Traditional Carols from Nova Scotia* (Ryerson Press, Toronto, 1950).

CRISP, William, *Divine Harmony* (London, 1755).

CROMPTON, John, *The Psalm-Singer's Assistant* (London, 1778).

The Crown of Jesus Music: see Henri Friedrich HÉMY

CUTTS, John P., *Bishop Smith's Part-Song Books in Carlisle Cathedral Library: Roger Smith, his booke* (American Institute of Musicology, Rome, 1972).

Dafydd Ddu Eryri: see David THOMAS

DANKÓ, Joseph, *Vetus Hymnarium Ecclesiasticum Hungaricae* (Budapest, 1893).

DAVENPORT, Uriah, *The Psalm-Singer's Pocket Companion* (London, 1755).

DAVEY, John, *Joannis Davey ejus Liber Carminum* (1795); British Library, Add. MS 52421. (See Appendix 4.)

DAVIES, Peter Maxwell, *Four Carols from 'O Magnum Mysterium'* (Schott, London, 1962).

DAVISSON, Ananias, *The Kentucky Harmony* (Lexington [Kentucky], 1816; 2nd edn., Harrisonburg [Virginia], 1817).

DAY, John, *The Whole Book of Psalmes* [known as *Day's Psalter*] (London, 1562).

DEAN-SMITH, Margaret, *A Guide to English Folk-Song Collections 1882–1952* (Liverpool UP, 1954).

DEARMER, Percy: see *The English Carol Book*; *The English Hymnal*; *The Oxford Book of Carols*; *Songs of Praise*

Das deutsche Kirchenlied: Kritische Gesamtausgabe der Melodien, ed. Konrad Ameln et al., vol. I, (Bärenreiter, Kassel, 1975). This catalogue of sources is also part of the series *Répertoire international des sources musicales*, vol. B^{viii} 1.

DEVEREUX, William, 'A New Garland Containing Songs for Christmas'. A manuscript compiled in 1728 whose contents survive in various later copies, including one dated 1803 by Michael Murphy, repr. in Diarmaid Ó MUIRITHE, *The Wexford Carols*.

Divine Recreations (London, 1736–7). A quarterly publication ascribed to Arthur Bedford.

DIXON, William, *Six Anthems in Score, designed for the use of Country Choirs* (London, *c.*1790).

DOBSON, E. J. and F. Ll. Harrison, *Medieval English Songs* (Faber & Faber, London, 1979). See also Frank Ll. HARRISON, *Now Make We Merthe*.

DOMERGUE, J. F., *Noëls* (Avignon, 1763, 1772). See also Nicolas SABOLY.

DONOVAN, Richard Frank, *Old French and Czecho-Slovakian Carols* (*Carol Society Publications*, 8) (Stainer & Bell, London, 1931).

DUBREUIL, Abbé, *Essai sur la musique ancienne et moderne* (1780). See also *Recueil de cantiques spirituels*.

DUNSTAN, Ralph, *Christmas Carols* (Reid, London, 1923).

——*Cornish Dialect and Folk Songs* (Jordan's Bookshop, Truro [Cornwall], 1932; repr. Lodenek Press, Padstow [Cornwall], 1972).

——*The Cornish Song Book* (London, Reid, 1929; selections repr. by Lodenek Press, Padstow, 1973).

——*A Second Book of Christmas Carols* (London, Reid, 1925).

EADE, William, *Cornish Carols* [ed. with preface by R. H. Heath], pt. I (Redruth, 1889).

EAST, Thomas, *The Whole Booke of Psalmes, with their wonted tunes* (London, 1592).

EAST, William, *The Second Book of the Voice of Melody* (Waltham [Leicestershire] and Grantham [Lincolnshire], 1750).

Easy Hymn Tunes (London, 1851).

ECCARD, Johannes, *Geistlicher Lieder* (Königsberg, 1597; new edn., Wolfenbüttel, 1928).

EHRET, Walter: see *International Book of Christmas Carols*

Elizabeth Rogers Hir Virginall Booke, ed. Charles J. F. Cofone (Dover, New York, 1975).

Enchiridion oder eyn Handbuchlein (Erfurt, 1524).

ENGLAND, George and A. W. Pollard, *The Towneley Plays* (Early English Text Society [*Extra Series*, 71], London, 1897).

The English Carol Book, ed. Martin Shaw and Percy Dearmer, 2 vols. (Mowbrays, London, 1913, 1919).

English County Songs, Lucy Broadwood and J. A. Fuller Maitland (London, 1893).

The English Hymnal [ed. Percy Dearmer and R. Vaughan Williams] (OUP, London, 1906; new edn., 1933).

EPSTEIN, Dena J., *Sinful Tunes and Spirituals: Black folk music to the Civil War* (Illinois UP, 1977).

ERK, Ludwig, and Franz M. Böhme, *Deutscher Liederhort: Auswahl der vorzüglicheren deutschen Volkslieder*, 3 vols. (Leipzig, 1893–4).

An Essay on the Church Plain Chant [thought to have been compiled by J. F. Wade and Samuel Webbe] (J. P. Coghlan, London, 1782; repr. 1789).

Etlich cristlich Lider Lobgesang und Psalm [known as the *Achtliederbuch*] (Wittenburg [in fact, Nuremberg], 1524); facs. edn. (Bärenreiter, Kassel, 1957).

The European Magazine and London Review (London, 1782–1826).

EVANS, David: see *The Church Hymnary*

EVANS, George K.: see *International Book of Christmas Carols*

The Evening-Office of the Church [thought to have been compiled by J. F. Wade] (J. P. Coghlan, London, 1760; 2nd edn., 1773).

EVERIST, Mark, *Polyphonic Music in Thirteenth-Century France: Aspects of sources and distribution* (Garland, New York, 1989).

EVISON, James, *A Compleat Book of Psalmody* (2nd edn., London, 1751; 5th edn., London, 1769).

FALK, Johannes Daniel, *Dr Martin Luther und die Reformation in Volksliedern* (Weimar, 1830).

FAVART, Charles Simon, *Acajou: opera-comique en trois actes en vaudevilles* (Paris, 1744).

——*La chercheuse d'esprit: Opéra-comique* (Paris, 1741).

FENNER, Thomas Putnam, *Cabin and Plantation Songs as sung by the Hampton students* (Hampton [Virginia], 1854); new edn. as *Religious Folk Songs of the Negro as sung on the plantations* (Hampton, 1909).

The Fitzwilliam Virginal Book, ed. J. A. Fuller Maitland and William Barclay Squire, 2 vols. (Breitkopf & Härtel, Leipzig, 1899; repr. Dover, New York, 1963).

FLÉCHIER, Valentin Ésprit, *Cantiques spirituels* (1728).

Folk Music Journal: see *Journal of the Folk-Song Society*

FORBES, John, *Cantus, Songs and Fancies* (Aberdeen, 1662; 2nd edn., 1666; 3rd edn., 1682).

FOSTER, John, *A 2d Collection of Sacred Music Consisting of Anthems, Psalms & Hymns* (York, *c.*1820).

——*While shepherds watched*, orchestral score and parts, ed. Clifford Bartlett (King's Music, Huntingdon, 1991).

FRIESE, A. R., *Vier ächte Tyroler Lieder* (Dresden, [1833]).

FROST, Maurice, *English and Scottish Psalm and Hymn Tunes c.1543–1677* (SPCK, London, 1953). See also *Hymns Ancient and Modern, Historical Companion*.

FULLER MAITLAND, J. A.: see *English County Songs*

FYFE, William Wallace, *Christmas, its Customs and Carols* (London, 1860).

GABRIEL, Charles Hutchinson, *Gabriel's Vineyard Songs* (Louisville [Kentucky], 1892).

GABRIELI, Andrea and Giovanni, *Intonazioni d'organo* (Venice, 1593).

GABRIELI, Andrea, *Intonationen*, ed. Pierre Pidoux (Bärenreiter, Kassel, 1959).

GABRIELI, Giovanni, *Composizioni per organo*, ed. Sandro dalla Libera (Ricordi, Milan, 1957–8). *Intonazioni* are in vol. 1.

GARNIER, P., *La Grande Bible renouvelée de noëls* (1723).

GATTY, Alfred, *A Life at One Living* (London, 1884).

GAUNTLETT, Henry John, *Christmas Carols*, nos. 1–4 (London, 1849). See also Mrs Cecil Frances ALEXANDER; *The Congregational Psalmist*.

GAWLER, William, *Harmonia Sacra* (London, 1781).

GAY, George, *Sacred Music* (London, [1827]).

Gesangbuch (Dresden, 1723).

Gesangbuch (Trier, 1871).

GESIUS, Bartholomaeus, *Geistliche deutsche Lieder* (Frankfurt an der Oder, 1601).

GIBBONS, Orlando, *Full Anthems, Hymns and Fragmentary Verse Anthems* (*Early English Church Music*, 21), transcribed and ed. David Wulstan (Stainer & Bell, London, 1978). Includes the music from George Wither, *The Hymnes and Songes of the Church*.

GIFFORD, William, *Twelve New Psalm Tunes* (London, 1805).

GILBERT, Davies, *Some Ancient Christmas Carols* (London, 1822; 2nd edn., London, 1823).

GILLINGTON, Alice E., *Old Christmas Carols of the Southern Counties* (J. Curwen, London, 1910).

A Good Christmas Box (Dudley, 1847); facs. edn., ed. M. and J. Raven (Wolverhampton Folk Song Club, 1967).

Grande Bible des noëls, tant vieux que nouveaux (Troyes, 1721).

GREATOREX, Thomas (arr.), *Adeste, fideles, 'Portugese Hymn' . . . (1797)*, orchestral score and parts, ed. Clifford Bartlett (King's Music, Huntingdon, 1991).

GREEN, John and James, *A Collection of Choice Psalm Tunes* [various editions with slightly different titles; 4th edn. onwards by James Green only] (Nottingham and London, 1713–51).

GREENE, Richard Leighton, *The Early English Carols* (OUP, 1935; 2nd edn., 1977).

GRESHAM, William, *Psalmody Improved* (London, c.1797).

GROSJEAN, R., *Airs de noëls lorrain* (1862).

GROVE, George, *A Dictionary of Music and Musicians*, 4 vols. (London, 1878–90, and subsequent edns.). See also *The New Grove Dictionary of Music and Musicians*.

GRUBER, Franz Xaver, *Weihnachtslied 'Stille Nacht! Heilige Nacht'* (*Denkmäler der Musik in Salzburg, Einzelausgaben*, 4) (Comes-Verlag, Bad Reichenhall, 1987).

GUNDRY, Inglis, *Now Carol We: Twelve carols from an old Cornish manuscript* (OUP, 1966).

HAEUSSLER, Armin, *The Story of Our Hymns: The handbook to the Hymnal of the Evangelical and Reformed Church* (Eden Publishing House, Saint Louis, 1952).

HALL, William John, *Psalms and Hymns adapted to the services of the Church of England* [known as *The Mitre Hymn Book*] (London, 1836).

HANDEL, George Frideric: for bibliographic information see the thematic catalogue in *Händel-Handbuch*, vols. 1–3 (Deutscher Verlag für Musik, Leipzig, and Bärenreiter, Kassel, 1978–86).

HAPPÉ, Peter, *English Mystery Plays: A selection* (Penguin Books, Harmondsworth, 1975).

——*Four Morality Plays* (Penguin Books, Harmondsworth, 1979).

HARRISON, Frank Ll., 'Benedicamus, conductus, carol: a newly discovered source', *Acta Musicologica*, xxxvii (1965), pp. 35–48.

——*Now Make We Merthe* [with texts edited by E. J. Dobson], 3 vols. (OUP, 1968).

See also E. J. DOBSON and F. Ll. Harrison, *English Medieval Songs*.

HARRISON, Ralph, *Sacred Harmony* (London, 1784 6).

HARVEY, Wallace, *Thomas Clark of Canterbury (1775–1859)* (Emprint, Whitstable, 1981).

HAWKES, Thomas, *A Collection of Tunes* (Watchet [Somerset], 1833).

HAYDN, Joseph, *A Select Collection of Original Welsh Airs*, vol. 2 (London, 1803); facs. edn. (King's Music, Huntingdon [Cambridgeshire], 1991).

HAYM VON THEMAR, Johann, *Schöne christenlichen catholisch weihnächt- oder kindtlesswiegen Gesäng* (Augsburg, 1590).

HELMORE, Thomas: see *Carols for Christmas-tide, set to ancient melodies*; *The Hymnal Noted*

HÉMY, Henri Friedrich, *The Crown of Jesus Music* (London, 1864).

HERDER, Johann Gottfried von, *Stimmen der Völker in Liedern* (Tübingen, 1807).

The Hereford Breviary, 1505, ed. W. H. Frere and L. E. G. Browne, 3 vols. (Henry Bradshaw Society, London, 1903–13).

HILL, Geoffrey, *Wiltshire Folk Songs and Carols* (W. Mate, Bournemouth, [1904]).

HOFFMANN VON FALLERSLEBEN, August Heinrich, *Geschichte der deutschen Kirchenlieder*, 3rd edn. (Hamburg, 1861).

HOLFORD, William, *Voce di melodia* (London [c.1834]).

HOLST, Gustav: Imogen Holst, *A Thematic Catalogue of Gustav Holst's Music* (Faber Music, London, 1974).

The Holy Family Hymns, and *Music for the Holy Family Hymns* (Archfraternity of the Holy Family, London, 1860).

HONE, William, *Ancient Mysteries Described* (London, 1823).

HOPKINS, John Henry, *Carols, Hymns, and Songs* (New York, 1865).

HOULDSWORTH, John, *New and Enlarged Edition of Cheetham's Psalmody* (Halifax, 1832).

HUNTINGTON, Jonathan, *The Apollo Harmony* (Northampton [Massachusetts], 1807).

HUSK, William Henry, *Songs of the Nativity* (London, 1864).

HUTCHENS, John, *A Book of Carols Collected for Davies Gilbert*. A manuscript in the Cornwall Record Office, Truro, Davies Gilbert Record, DG 92. A photocopy was kindly supplied to the editors by Inglis Gundry.

HUTCHINS, Charles Lewis, *Sunday School Hymnal and Service Book* (Medford [Massachusetts], 1876).

The Hymnal Noted, ed. Thomas Helmore and J. M. Neale (Novello, London, 1851); accompanying harmonies [with introduction and bilingual texts] (Novello, London, 1852); Part 2 (London, 1854).

Hymnarium Sarisburiense, cum rubricis et notis musicis (London, 1851); see also *Early Tudor Organ Music*, I (*Early English Church Music*, 6), transcribed and ed. John Caldwell (Stainer & Bell, London, 1966), which includes critical editions of Sarum hymns.

The Hymner, containing translations of the hymns from the Sarum

Breviary and other English service-books (Cambridge, 1891; 2nd edn., Convent of St Mary the Virgin, Wantage, and the Plainsong and Mediæval Music Society, London, 1904).

Hymns Ancient and Modern (William Clowes, London, 1861, and various later revised edns.); *Historical Edition* [ed. W. H. Frere] (London, 1909); *Historical Companion*, ed. Maurice Frost (London, 1962).

Hymns and Psalms: A Methodist and ecumenical hymn book (Methodist Publishing House, London, 1983).

Hymns for the Use of Churches (London, 1864).

INGALLS, Jeremiah, *The Christian Harmony, or Songster's Companion* (Exeter [New Hampshire], 1805); facs. edn., ed. David Klocko (New York, 1981).

The International Book of Christmas Carols, musical arrangements by Walter Ehret, translations and notes by George K. Evans (Prentice Hall, Englewood Cliffs [NJ], 1963).

IRVING, Washington, *The Sketch Book of Geoffrey Crayon, Gent.* (New York, 1819–20).

An Italian Carol Book: see Charles WOOD and George Ratcliffe Woodward

JACKSON, George Pullen, *Spiritual Folk-Songs of Early America* (New York, 1937; repr. Dover, New York, 1964).

——*White and Negro Spirituals* (J. J. Augustin, New York, 1943).

——*White Spirituals of the Southern Uplands* (N. Carolina UP, 1933).

JAMES, Montague Rhodes, *The Apocryphal New Testament* (OUP, 1924). Contains the *Book of James* (*Protevangelium*) (pp. 38–49).

JOHNSON, Mary Barham, *20 European Carols* (Schirmer, New York, 1960).

JONES, Edward, *Musical and Poetical Relicks of the Welsh Bards* (London, 1784; augmented and improved, London, 1794).

——*The Bardic Museum* [vol. 2 of the above] (London, 1802).

——*Hên Ganiadau Cymru: Cambro-British Melodies* [vol. 3 of the above] (London, 1820).

Journal of the Folk-Song Society (London, 1899–1931). The numbering is confusing, with a cumulative series of issue numbers as well as volume numbers; pagination is consecutive through each volume, which contains issues from several years. Vol. 1 (nos. 1–5), 1899–1904; vol. 2 (nos. 6–9), 1905–6; vol. 3 (nos. 10–13), 1908–9; vol. 4 (nos. 14–17), 1910–13; vol. 5 (nos. 18–20), 1914–17; vol. 6 (nos. 21–5), 1918–21; vol. 7 (nos. 26–30), 1922–6; vol. 8 (nos. 31–5), 1927–31. Publication continued as the *Journal of the English Folk Dance and Song Society* from 1932 to 1964, and it became the *Folk Music Journal* in 1965.

The Joy of Christmas: Words and music of traditional and local carols, compiled and presented by Worral Male Voice Choir (1982).

JULIAN, John, *A Dictionary of Hymnology* (London, 1892); rev. edn. with new supplement (London, 1907; repr. Dover, New York, 2 vols., 1957).

JUNGBAUER, Gustav, *Bibliographie des deutschen Volksliedes in Boehmen* (Prague, 1913).

KARPELES, Maud, *An Introduction to English Folk Song* (OUP, 1973); repr. with a new foreword by Peter Kennedy (OUP, 1987). See also Cecil SHARP, *Cecil Sharp's Collection of English Folk Songs*.

KAUFFMANN, Georg Friedrich, *Harmonische Seelenlust* (Leipzig, 1733); ed. Pierre Pidoux (Bärenreiter, Kassel, 1951).

KELE, Richard, *Christmas Carolles newly Inprynted* (London [*c*.1550]).

Kirchengesang . . . , II, *Geistliche Lieder*, [Eibenschitz (Ivančice)] (1566) [songbook of the Bohemian Brethren].

KIRKPATRICK, William J.: see *Around the World with Christmas*

Das Klugsche Gesangbuch: see Martin LUTHER, *Geistliche Lieder*

Des Knaben Wunderhorn, ed. Achim von Arnim and Clemens Brentano, 3 vols. (Heidelberg, 1805–8).

KNECHT, Justin Heinrich, *Vollständige Orgelschule für Anfänger und Geübtere*, 3 vols. (Leipzig, 1795–98); facs. edn., ed. Michael Ladenburger (Breitkopf & Härtel, Wiesbaden, 1989).

LAMBILLOTTE, Louis, *Choix de cantiques sur des airs nouveaux* (Paris, 1842).

LAUFENBERG, Heinrich: texts from MS dated 1445 (formerly Strasbourg, Archives et Bibliothèque Municipale, B.120.4°), which does not survive, are printed in Wackernagel, *Das deutsche Kirchenlied*, II, nos. 701–98.

LAWN, Andrew, *A Collection of Hymn Tunes* (Cheshire [Connecticut], 1783).

LAWLEY, S. C.: see *The York Breviary*.

LEAVER, Robin A., *'Goostly Psalmes and Spirituall Songes': English and Dutch metrical psalms from Coverdale to Utenhove 1535–66* (OUP, 1991).

LEGEAY, Georges, *Noëls anciens*, 2 series (Paris, 1875–6).

LEGG, J. Wickham, *The Processional of the Nuns of Chester* (*Henry Bradshaw Society*, 18) (London, 1899).

——*The Sarum Missal* (OUP, 1916).

LEIGHTON, William, *The Teares or Lamentacions of a Sorrowfull Soule* (London, 1614); ed. Cecil Hill in *Early English Church Music*, vol. 11 (Stainer & Bell, London, 1970).

LEMEIGNEN, Henri, *Vieux Noëls composés en honneur de la naissance de Notre-Seigneur Jésus-Christ* (Nantes, 1876).

The Liber Usualis, with introduction and rubrics in English (Desclée, Tournai, 1963).

Little Children's Book for Schools and Families, by authority of the General Council of the Evangelical Lutheran Church in North America (Philadelphia, 1885).

LLOYD, Albert L., *Folk Song in England* (Lawrence & Wishart, London, 1967).

Llyfr Emynau a Thonau (Calvinistic Methodist Church, Caernarvon, 1927).

LOSSIUS, Lucas, *Psalmodia, hoc est cantica sacra veteris ecclesia selecta* (Nuremberg, 1553, and later edns.).

Ludus Coventriae: see Peter HAPPÉ, *English Mystery Plays*

LUFF, Alan, *Llyfyr Carolau Deiniol: The St Deiniol Carol Book* (Cyhoeddedig gan Bwyllgor Cerdd Esgobaeth, Bangor, 1974).

——*Welsh Hymns and their tunes* (Stainer & Bell, London, 1990).

LUTHER, Martin, *Geistliche Lieder auffs new gebessert* [known as *Das klugsche Gesangbuch*, after its printer] (Wittenberg, 1533, rev. edn. 1535); facs. of 1533 edn. (Bärenreiter, Kassel, 1954). First edition (1529) not extant, but see Robin Leaver, *'Goostly Psalmes and Spirituall Songes'*, pp. 281–5.

——*Luthers geistliche Lieder und Kirchengesänge: Vollständige Neuedition in Ergänzung zu Band 35 der Weimarer Ausgabe* (*Archiv zur Weimarer Ausgabe der Werke Martin Luther, Texte und Untersuchungen*, 4), ed. Markus Jenny (Böhlau, Cologne, 1985).

——*Works, 53: Liturgy and Hymns*, ed. Ulrich S. Leupold (Fortress Press, Philadelphia, 1965).

LYON, James, *Urania* (Philadelphia, 1761); facs., ed. Richard Crawford (Da Capo, New York, 1974).

MacDermott, Kenneth Holland, *The Old Church Gallery Minstrels* (SPCK, London, 1948).

——*Sussex Church Music in the Past* (Moore & Wingham, Chichester, 1922; 2nd edn., 1923).

Macy, Samuel L., *Patriarchs of Time: Dualism in Saturn Chronos, Father Time, the Watchmaker God, and Father Christmas* (Georgia UP, 1987).

Madan, Martin, *A Collection of Psalm and Hymn Tunes* [the 'Lock Collection'] (London, 1769).

——*Thelyphthora, or a treatise on female ruin* [published anonymously] (London, 1780).

Mainz *Cantual* (1605); see *Catholisch Cantual oder Psalmbüchlein*

Mason, Lowell, *Carmina Sacra* (Boston, 1841).

——*The Modern Psalmist* (Boston, 1839).

——*The National Psalmist* (Boston, 1848).

——*Occasional Psalm and Hymn Tunes, selected and original* (Boston, 1836).

Mauburn, Johann, *Rosetum Exercitiorum Spiritualium* (Zwolle, 1494).

Mayhew, Henry, *London Labour and the London Poor* (London, 1851).

——*Mayhew's London*, ed. Peter Quennell (Spring Books, London, 1969).

McCaskey, J. P., *The Franklin Square Song Collection* (New York, 1881).

McKay, David P. and Richard Crawford, *William Billings of Boston* (Princeton UP, 1975).

Mellers, Wilfrid, *Music in a New Found Land* (Barrie & Rockliff, London, 1964).

Mendelssohn-Bartholdy, Felix, *Festgesang* (Breitkopf & Härtel, Leipzig, 1840); also in *Werke*, 15 (Breitkopf & Härtel, Leipzig, 1874–7); English vocal score (Ewer, London, 1844).

The Methodist Hymn Book (Methodist Conference Office, London, 1933).

Migne, J. P., *Troisième et Dernière Encyclopédie théologique, tome 63, Dictionnaire de noëls et cantiques . . . par Fr. Pérennès* (Paris, 1867).

The Mitre Hymn Book: see William John Hall

Monson, Craig, *Voices and Viols in England, 1600–1650: The sources and the music* (*Studies in Musicology*, 55) (UMI Research Press, Ann Arbor [Michigan], 1982).

Montgomery, James, *The Christian Psalmist* (Glasgow, 1825).

Moore, Thomas, *The Psalm Singer's Compleat Tutor and Divine Companion* (2nd edn., Manchester, 1750).

Moultrie, Gerard, *Hymns and Lyrics* (London, 1867).

Muirithe, Diarmaid Ó [sometimes catalogued under O'Muirithe], *The Wexford Carols*, ed. Seóirse Bodley (Dolmen Press, Mountrath [Portlaoise, Eire], 1982). Contains William Devereux's 'A New Garland'.

Murray, Francis Henry, *A Hymnal for Use in the English Church* (London, 1852).

Murray, James R., *Dainty Songs for Little Lads and Lasses* (Cincinnati, 1887).

——*Royal Praise for the Sunday School* (Cincinnati, 1888).

Musica Britannica, IV, *Mediæval Carols*, ed. John Stevens; 2nd, rev. edn. (Stainer & Bell, London, 1958).

——XVIII, *Music at the Court of Henry VIII*, ed. John Stevens (Stainer & Bell, London, 1962).

——XXII, *Consort Songs*, ed. Philip Brett (Stainer & Bell, London, 1967).

Musicalische Jugendfreud [ed. Carl Neuner] (Munich, 1814–15).

Die Musik in Geschichte und Gegenwart: allgemeine Enzyklopädie der Musik [known as *MGG*], 17 vols. (Bärenreiter, Kassel, 1949–86).

Myrand, Ernest, *Noëls anciens de la Nouvelle-France*, 2nd edn. (Laflamme & Proulx, Quebec, 1907).

Neale, J. M., *Hymns of the Eastern Church* (London, 1861). See also *Carols for Christmas-tide, set to ancient melodies*; *The Hymnal Noted*.

Neighbour, Oliver, *The Consort and Keyboard Music of William Byrd* (Faber & Faber, 1978).

Neuner, Carl: see *Musikalische Jugendfreud*.

New Carolls for this merry time of Christmas (London, 1661). Copy in Oxford, Bodleian Library.

New Christmas Carols (London, 1642). Copy in Oxford, Bodleian Library.

The New Church Hymnal, ed. H. Augustin Smith (D. Appleton-Century, New York, 1937).

The New Grove Dictionary of Music and Musicians, ed. Stanley Sadie, 20 vols. (Macmillan, London, 1980).

The New Office Hymn Book (W. Knott, London, 1908).

Nicolai, Philipp, *Frewden Spiegel dess ewigen Lebens* (Frankfurt, 1599).

Niles, John Jacob, *The Anglo-American Carol Study Book* (*Schirmer's American Folk-Song Series*, 24 and 26) (G. Schirmer, New York, 1945–8).

——*Songs of the Hill-Folk* (*Schirmer's American Folk-Song Series*, 14) (G. Schirmer, New York, 1934).

——*Ten Christmas Carols from the Southern Appalachian Mountains* (*Schirmer's American Folk-Song Series*, 16) (G. Schirmer, New York, 1935).

Novello, Vincent, *The Psalmist* (London, 1830).

——*Congregational and Chorister's Psalm and Hymn Book* (London, 1843).

Nunn, William, *A Selection of Psalms and Hymns* (Manchester, 1827).

Office de St. Omer (St. Omer, 1822).

Orchard, Bernard, *A Catholic Commentary on Holy Scripture* (Nelson, London, 1953).

Osiander, Lucas, *Fünfftzig Geistliche Lieder und Psalmen* (Nuremberg, 1586); ed. F. Zelle (Berlin, 1903).

The Oxford Book of Carols, by Percy Dearmer, R. Vaughan Williams, and Martin Shaw (OUP, 1928; rev. edn., 1964).

Paderborn *Gesangbuch* (1609): see *Alte catholische geistliche Kirchengesänge* (Paderborn, 1609)

Page, Christopher, *Voices and Instruments of the Middle Ages: Instrumental practice and songs in France 1100–1300* (J. M. Dent, London, 1987).

Pearce, Samuel, *Sacred Music* (London, [c.1776)].

Pedrell, Felipe, *Cancionero musical popular español* (E. Castells, Valls, 1918–22; 2nd edn., 1936).

The Pepys Ballads, ed. H. E. Rollins, 7 vols. (Harvard, 1930).

Petrie Collection: see Charles Villiers Stanford

Piae Cantiones ecclesiasticae et scholasticae veterum episcoporum, ed. Theodoricus Petri of Nyland (Greifswald, 1582); facs. edn. (*Documenta Musicae Fennicae*, 10) (Helsinki, 1967); revised and re-edited, with preface and explanatory notes, by G. R. Woodward (Plainsong and Mediaeval Music Society, London, 1910); ed. H. Andersén and Timo Mäkinen [including additions from the 1625 edition] (Edition Fazer, Helsinki, 1967).

Pickard-Cambridge, William Adair, *A Collection of Dorset Carols* (A. W. Ridley, London, 1926; repr. Dorchester, 1980).

PLAYFORD, John, *The English Dancing Master* (London, 1651, and later edns.); complete contents from all edns. in *The Complete Country Dance Tunes from Playford's Dancing Master*, ed. Jeremy Barlow (Faber Music, London, 1985).

POSTON, Elizabeth, *The Penguin Book of Christmas Carols* (Penguin Books, Harmondsworth, 1965).

——*The Second Penguin Book of Christmas Carols* (Penguin Books, Harmondsworth, 1970).

POULAILLE, Henry, *La Grande et Belle Bible des noëls anciens de XIIᵉ au XVIᵉ siècle* (Albin Michel, Paris, 1942).

——*La Grande et Belle Bible des noëls anciens. XVIIᵉ au XVIIIᵉ siècles* (Albin Michel, Paris, 1950).

——*La Grande et Belle Bible des noëls anciens, noëls régionaux et noëls contemporains* (Albin Michel, Paris, 1951).

——*La Grande et Belle Bible des noëls anciens* [an abridged edn. of the preceding three items] (Albin Michel & Club des Éditeurs, Paris, 1958).

PRAETORIUS, Hieronymus, *Magnificat on the Fifth Tone . . . with two carols, 'Joseph lieber' and 'In dulci jubilo'*, ed. Gordon Dodd (Mapa Mundi, London, 1980); also published in *Denkmäler deutscher Tonkunst*, vol. 23, rev. edn. (Breitkopf & Härtel, Leipzig, 1958).

PRAETORIUS, Michael, *Gesamtausgabe der musikalischen Werke*, 22 vols. (Kallmeyer, Wolfenbüttel, 1928–40, 1960).

—— *Eulogia Sionia* (Wolfenbüttel, 1611) [*Gesamtausgabe*, 13].

—— *Hymnodia Sionia* (Wolfenbüttel, 1611) [*Gesamtausgabe*, 22].

—— *Megalynodia Sionia* (Wolfenbüttel, 1611) [*Gesamtausgabe*, 14].

—— *Musae Sioniae*, 9 vols. (Regensburg, etc., 1605–10) [*Gesamtausgabe*, 1–9].

—— *Polyhymnia Caduceatrix et Panegyrica* (Wolfenbüttel, 1619) [*Gesamtausgabe*, 17].

—— *Puericinium* (Frankfurt, 1621) [*Gesamtausgabe*, 19].

—— *Sämtliche Orgelwerke* (Breitkopf & Härtel, Wiesbaden, 1990).

—— *Syntagma Musicum* (Wolfenbüttel, 1614–19).

—— *Terpsichore* (Wolfenbüttel, 1612) [*Gesamtausgabe*, 15].

—— *Urania* (Wolfenbüttel, 1613) [*Gesamtausgabe*, 16].

The Primitive Methodist Hymnbook (1889).

PROCTER, Francis, *A New History of the Book of Common Prayer*, rev. Walter Howard Frere (Macmillan, London, 1901).

—— and Christopher Wordsworth, *Brevarium ad Usum Insignis Ecclesiae Sarum* (Cambridge UP, 1882).

Protevangelium of James: see Montague Rhodes JAMES

PRUDENTIUS [Aurelius Prudentius Clemens, *Poems*], with an English translation by H. J. Thomson (*The Loeb Classical Library*), 2 vols. (Harvard UP, 1949–53).

Psalms and Hymns for Divine Worship, ed. Henry Smart (London, 1867).

Psalms and Hymns for the Worship of God (Richmond [Virginia], 1867).

QUEHL, H. F., *Der zur Beförderung göttlicher Ehre* (Nuremberg, [1733 or 1734]).

RAINBOW, Bernarr, *English Psalmody Prefaces: Popular methods of teaching 1562–1835* (Boethius Press, Clarabricken [Co. Kilkenny], 1982).

RAVENSCROFT, Thomas, *Melismata* (London, 1611); facs. edn., *Pammelia, Deuteromelia, Melismata* (*Publications of the American Folklore Society, Bibliographical and Special Series*, 12) (Philadelphia, 1961).

Recueil de cantiques spirituels provençaux et françois [known as the Abbé Dubreuil's Collection] (Paris, 1759).

REIMANN, Heinrich, *Das deutsche geistliche Lied von der ältesten bis auf unsere Zeit*, 6 vols. (Simrock, Berlin, 1895).

Répertoire international des sources musicales, Series Bⁱᵛ. 1, *Manuscripts of Polyphonic Music, 11th–early 14th century*, ed. Gilbert Reaney; 2, *Manuscripts of Polyphonic Music (c.1320–1400)*, ed. Gilbert Reaney; 3, 4 *Handschriften mit mehrstimmiger Musik des 14., 15. und 16. Jahrhunderts*, ed. Kurt von Fischer and Max Lütolf; (Henle, Munich, 1966–72).

RHAU, Georg, *Newe deudsche geistliche Gesenge* (Wittenberg, 1544); facs. edn. (Bärenreiter, Kassel, 1969); ed. H. J. Moser (Breitkopf & Härtel, Wiesbaden, 1958).

RHEZELIUS, Haquinus, *Några Psalmer* (Stockholm, 1619).

RIDER, Charles, *Psalmodia Britannica* [Manchester, c.1830].

RIEDEL, Carl, *Altbömische Gesänge* (Leipzig, 1870).

RIMBAULT, Edward Francis, *A Collection of Old Christmas Carols* (London, 1861).

—— *A Little Book of Christmas Carols* (London, 1863).

ROLLINS, Hyder Edward, 'Ballads from Additional MS. 38,599' [the Shanne Commonplace Book], *Publications of the Modern Language Association of America*, 38 (1923), pp. 133–53. See also *The Pepys Ballads*.

ROQUES, Léon, *40 Noëls anciens* (Durand, Paris, 1930).

ROSSETTI, Christina, *Poetical Works* (Macmillan, London, 1904).

—— *Time Flies: A reading diary* (SPCK, London, 1885).

ROUTLEY, Erik, *The English Carol* (Herbert Jenkins, London, 1958). See also *The University Carol Book*.

RUSSELL, Ian, *A Song for the Time: Village carols from the Black Bull* (Village Carols, Unstone [nr. Sheffield], 1987).

SABOLY, Nicolas, *Recueil des noëls provençaux* (Avignon, 1699); 3rd edn. (J. F. D[omergue], Avignon, 1737); new edn., ed. F. Seguin, *Receuil des noëls composés en langue provençale* (Avignon, 1856).

The Salvation Army Tune Book for Congregational Singing (London, [c.1950]).

SANDON, Nick, *The Use of Sarum* (Antico Edition, Newton Abbot, 1984–).

SANDYS, William, *Christmas Carols, Ancient and Modern* (London, 1833).

—— *Christmastide, its history, festivities and carols* [1852].

Sarum Antiphonal: see *Antiphonale Sarisburiense*; for hymns, see *Hymnarium Sarisburiense*

Sarum Gradual, see Nick SANDON, *The Use of Sarum*

SCHEIDT, Samuel, *Tabulatur-Buch hundert geistlicher Lieder und Psalmen . . . für die Herren Organisten* (Görlitz, 1650); modern edn. (Peters, Leipzig, 1941).

—— *Werke* (Ugrino Verlag, Hamburg, 1923–).

SCHEIN, Johann Hermann, *Cantional, oder Gesangbuch Augspurgischer Confession* (Leipzig, 1627; enlarged 1645); modern edn., *Neue Ausgabe sämtlicher Werke*, 2 (Bärenreiter, Kassel, 1965).

SCHEMELLI, George Christian, *Musikalisches Gesangbuch* (Leipzig, 1736); facs. edn. (G. Olms, Hildesheim, 1975).

SCHMAUS, Alois and Lenz Kriss-Rettenbeck, *Silent Night, Holy Night: History and circulation of a carol* (University Press Wagner Co., Innsbruck, 1968).

SCHUBART, Christian Friedrich Daniel, *Sämtliche Gedichte*, 2 vols. (Stuttgart, 1786).

SCHUMANN, Valentin, *Geistliche Lieder* (Leipzig, 1539).

SEGUIN, François-Marie-César, see Nicholas SABOLY

SENFL, Ludwig, *Varia Carmina Genera* (Nuremberg, 1534); modern edn. in *Sämtliche Werke*, 6 (Möseler, Wolfenbüttel, 1961).

SERGEANT, Pierre, *Les Grands Noelz nouvelles* (Paris, [*c*.1537]).

SHARP, Cecil, *Cecil Sharp's Collection of English Folk Songs*, ed. Maud Karpeles, 2 vols. (OUP, 1974).

—— *English Folk-Carols* (Novello, London, 1911).

—— *English Folk Song: Some conclusions* (Simpkin, London, 1907); 4th (rev.) edn. prepared by Maud Karpeles (Mercury Books, London, 1965).

—— and C. L. Marson, *Folk Songs from Somerset*, 5 vols. (Simpkin, Marshall, Hamilton Kent & Co., London, 1904–9).

SHARP, Thomas, *The Pageant of the Shearmen and Taylors, in Coventry* (Coventry, 1817).

—— *Dissertations on the Pageants or Dramatic Mysteries, anciently performed at Coventry* (Coventry, 1825).

SHAW, Martin: see *The English Carol Book*; *The Oxford Book of Carols*; *Songs of Praise*

SHAWCROSS, W. H., *Old Castleton Christmas Carols* (London, 1904).

SIMPSON, Claude M., *The British Broadside Ballad and its Music* (Rutgers UP, 1966). See also John M. WARD, 'Apropos the British broadside ballad and its music'.

SIMROCK, Karl Joseph, *Deutsche Weihnachtslieder . . . Neue Ausgabe* (Leipzig, 1865).

SMART, Henry Thomas: see *Psalms and Hymns for Divine Worship*

SMIDT, J. R. H. de, *Les Noëls et la tradition populaire* (Amsterdam, 1932).

SMITH, Benjamin, *The Harmonious Companion* (London, 1732).

SNYDER, Kerala J., *Dietrich Buxtehude: Organist in Lübeck* (Schirmer, New York, 1987).

The Social Harp, ed. John G. McCurry (Philadelphia, 1855); facs. edn., ed. Daniel W. Patterson and John F. Garst (Georgia UP, 1973).

Songs of All Time (Co-operative Recreation Service, n.d.).

Songs of Praise, ed. Percy Dearmer, Ralph Vaughan Williams, and Martin Shaw (OUP, London, 1926; revised and enlarged edn., 1931).

Songs of Syon: see George Ratcliffe WOODWARD

The Southern Harmony: see William WALKER

SPANGENBERG, Cyriacus, *Christliches Gesangbüchlein* (Eisleben, 1568).

SPANGENBERG, Johann, *Grammaticae Latinae Partes* (Nuremberg, 1546).

Speyer Gebetbuch: see *Alte catholische geistliche Kirchengesänge* (Cologne, 1599)

STAINER, John: see *Christmas Carols New and Old*

STANFORD, Charles Villiers, *The Complete Collection of Irish Music as notated by George Petrie* (Boosey, London, 1902–5).

STÉPHAN, Jean, 'The Adeste Fideles: a study on its origin and development' (Buckfast Abbey Publications, Buckfastleigh [Devon], 1947).

STEPHENSON, Joseph, *Church Harmony Sacred to Devotion* (3rd edn., London, 1760; 4th edn., London, [*c*.1775]).

—— *The Musical Companion* (London, [*c*.1775]).

STERNHOLD, Thomas and John Hopkins, *The Whole Booke of Psalmes* [known as the 'Old Version'] (London, 1562). There were innumerable subsequent editions, usually printed in a format suitable for binding with *The Book of Common Prayer*.

STEVENS, John, '*Angelus ad virginem*: the history of a medieval song', in *Medieval Studies for J. A. W. Bennett*, ed. P. L. Heyworth (OUP, 1981), pp. 297–328.

—— 'Carol', in *The New Grove Dictionary of Music and Musicians* (Macmillan, London, 1980).

—— *Music and Poetry in the Early Tudor Court* (Methuen, London, 1961).

—— *Words and Music in the Middle Ages* (Cambridge UP, 1986). See also *Musica Britannica*, IV, XVIII.

STEVENSON, Robert M., *Christmas Music from Baroque Mexico* (California UP, 1974).

STOECKLIN, Adèle, *Weihnachts- und neujahrslieder aus dem Schweiz* (Schweizerischen Gesellschaft für Volkskunde, Basel, 1921).

SUDERMANN, Daniel, *Etliche hohe geistliche Gesänge* (Strasbourg, [*c*.1626]).

SULLIVAN, Arthur: see *Church Hymns with Tunes*

SUSO [SEUSE], Henrich, *Das Büchlein der ewigen Weisheit, 1328*, in *The Life of Blessed H. Suso, by Himself*, tr. T. F. Knox (London, 1865).

SYLVESTER, Joshua, *A Garland of Christmas Carols* (London, 1861). Sylvester is thought to be a pseudonym for William Sandys and W. H. Husk.

TANSUR, William, *The Royal Melody Compleat* (London, 1754–5; 3rd edn., 1764–6).

TATE, Nahum and Nicholas Brady, *A New Version of the Psalms of David, fitted to the tunes in use in churches* (London, 1696; supplement, London, 1700). Innumerable subsequent editions, usually printed in a format suitable for binding with *The Book of Common Prayer*.

TATTERSALL, William D., *Improved Psalmody* (London, 1794 [score], 1795 [parts]).

TEMPERLEY, Nicholas, *The Music of the English Parish Church*, 2 vols. (Cambridge UP, 1979).

—— 'Organ music in parish churches, 1660–1730', *BIOS* [*British Institute of Organ Studies*] *Journal*, 5 (1981), pp. 33–45.

—— 'Organs in English parish churches, 1660–1830', *Organ Yearbook*, 10 (1979), pp. 83–100.

—— 'The origins of the fuging tune', *RMA* [*Royal Musical Association*] *Research Chronicle*, 17 (1981).

—— and Charles G. Manns, *Fuging Tunes in the Eighteenth Century* (Information Coordinators, Detroit, 1983).

TERRY, Richard R., *Gilbert and Sandys' Christmas Carols with six collateral tunes* (Burns Oates, London, 1931).

—— *A Medieval Carol Book* (Burns Oates, London, 1931).

—— *Old Christmas Carols*, part 1 (Burns Oates, London, 1923).

—— *Two Hundred Folk Carols* (Burns Oates, London, 1933).

THEMAR, Johann Haym von: see HAYM VON THEMAR

THEODORICUS PETRI: see *Piae Cantiones*

THOMAS, David [Dafydd Ddu Eryri], *Corph y Gaingc* (Dolgellau [Gwynedd], 1810).

THUMOTH, Burk, *Twelve Scotch and Twelve Irish Airs with Variations* (London, 1745).

TIERSOT, Julien, *Noëls français* (Heugel, Paris, 1901).

TIMBRELL, Francis, *The Divine Musick Scholar's Guide* (London, [*c*.1720–35]).

TOMKINS, Thomas, *Musica Deo Sacra* (London, 1668).

The Towneley Plays: for edn. see George ENGLAND and A. W. Pollard; for facs. see A. C. CAWLEY and Martin Stevens

TOWNSEND, A. D., *The Mellstock Carols* (Serpent Press, Witney [Oxon.], 1989).

Trente et Six Chansons musicales (Attaingnant, Paris, 1530).

TRILLER, Valentin, *Ein schlesich Singbüchlein aus göttlicher Schrifft* (Breslau, 1555); rev. edn., *En christlich Singebuch für Layen und Gelerten, Kinder und Alten und in Kirchen zu singen* (Breslau, 1559).

TURNER, Thomas, *The Diary of Thomas Turner, 1754–1765*, ed. David Vaisey (OUP, 1984).

TYE, Christopher, *The Actes of the Apostles, translated in English Metre* (London, 1553); ed. John Morehen in *Christopher Tye: I, English Sacred Music* (*Early English Church Music*, vol. 19) (Stainer & Bell, London, 1977).

ULLATHORNE, William Bernard, *The Autobiography of Archbishop Ullathorne* (London, 1891–2).

The University Carol Book, ed. Erik Routley (Freeman, Brighton, 1961). This incorporates many of the carols issued in 50 pamphlets under the same title between 1952 and 1965.

VAUGHAN WILLIAMS, Ralph, *Eight Traditional English Carols* (Stainer & Bell, London, 1919).

—— *Some Thoughts on Beethoven's Choral Symphony, with writings on other musical subjects* (OUP, 1953); repr. in *National Music and Other Essays* (OUP, 1963).

—— *Twelve Traditional Carols from Herefordshire* (Stainer & Bell, London, 1920).

See also *The English Hymnal*; *The Oxford Book of Carols*; *Songs of Praise*.

The Village Harmony, or Youth's Assistant to Sacred Musick (Exeter [New Hampshire], 1795).

Villancicos de diversos autores [known as *Cancionero de Uppsala* or *Cancionero del Duque de Calabria*] (Venice, 1556). Modern edns. ed. Jesús Bal y Gay (Mexico City, 1944) and Rafael Mitjana and Leopoldo Querol Rosso (Madrid, 1980); facs. (Emiliano Escolar, Madrid, 1983).

VOPELIUS, Gottfried, *Gesangbuch* (Leipzig, 1682).

WACKERNAGEL, P., *Das deutsche Kirchenlied von den ältesten Zeit bis zum Anfang des XVII. Jahrhunderts* (Leipzig, 1864–77).

WADDING, Luke, *A Smale Garland of Pious and Godly Songs* (Ghent, 1684); repr. in Diarmaid Ó MUIRITHE, *The Wexford Carols*.

WADE, John Francis: see *An Essay on the Church Plain Chant*; *The Evening-Office of the Church*

WAINRIGHT, John, *A Collection of Psalm-Tunes* (London, 1766).

WALKER, William, *The Christian Harmony* (Philadelphia, 1867).

—— *The Southern Harmony* (Spartanburg [S. Carolina], 1835); facs. edn., ed. Glenn C. Wilcox (Pro Musicamerica, Los Angeles, 1966).

WALTER (WALTHER), Johann, *Geystliches gesangk Buchleyn* (Wittenberg, 1524); modern edn. in *Werke*, vols. 1–3.

—— *Sämtliche Werke*, 6 vols. (Bärenreiter, Kassel, 1953–73).

WARD, John M., 'And who but my Ladie Greensleeues?', in *The Well Enchanting Skill: Music, poetry, and drama in the culture of the Renaissance. Essays in honour of F. W. Sternfeld*, ed. John Caldwell, Edward Olleson, and Susan Wollenberg (OUP, 1990), pp. 181–211.

—— 'Apropos the British broadside ballad and its music', in *Journal of the American Musicological Society* [*JAMS*], xx (1967), pp. 28–86.

WARLOCK, Peter, *The English Ayre* (OUP, 1926).

WATTS, Isaac, *Horae Lyricae* (London, 1687).

—— *Hymns and Spiritual Songs*, 3 vols. (London, 1707); modern edn. by Selma L. Bishop, with collation of 1707–48 edns. (Faith Press, London, 1962).

—— *Moral Songs* (London, 1706).

—— *The Psalms of David imitated in the language of the New Testament* (London, 1719).

WATTS, Joseph, *A Choice Collection of Church Musick* (Fennycompton and Banbury, 1749).

WEBBE, Samuel, *A Collection of Motetts or Antiphons* (London, 1792). See also *An Essay on the Church Plain Chant*.

WEBER-KELLERMANN, Ingeborg, *Weihnachtslieder* (Schott, Mainz, 1982).

WEDDERBURN, John, James, and Robert, *Ane Compendious Buik of Godly and Spirituall Sangis* [often called *The Gude and Godlie Ballatis*] (Edinburgh, 1567, and subsequent edns.); ed. A. F. Mitchell (*The Scottish Text Society*, 39) (Blackwood, Edinburgh, 1897).

WESLEY, Charles, *Hymns and Sacred Poems* (London, 1739).

—— *Hymns of Intercession for all Mankind* (London, 1758).

—— *Select Hymns with Tunes Annex'd* (London, 1765).

WESLEY, John, *A Collection of Hymns for the use of the people called Methodists* (London, 1779, and many subsequent edns.).

WHITEFIELD, George, *Hymns for Social Worship* (London, 1753). Later editions entitled *A Collection of Hymns*.

The Whole Booke of Psalmes [the *Bay Psalm Book*] (Cambridge [Massachusetts], 1640). Music first included in the 9th edn. (1698).

WILKINS, Matthew, *A Book of Psalmody, containing a choice collection of psalm tunes* (Great Milton [Oxon.], [c.1760]); 2nd edn., ed. Elizabeth Wilkins (Great Milton, [c.1775]).

—— *A Book of Psalmody, containing some easy instructions* (Great Milton [Oxon.], [c.1730]).

WILLCOCKS, David: see *Carols for Choirs*

WILLIAMS, Peter, *The Organ Music of J. S. Bach*, 3 vols. (Cambridge UP, 1980–4).

WITHER, George, *Haleluiah, or, Britains Second Remembrancer* (London, 1641).

—— *The Hymnes and Songes of the Church* (London, 1623). The music by Gibbons is transcribed in *Orlando Gibbons II: Full Anthems, Hymns and Fragmentary Verse Anthems* (*Early English Church Music*, 21), ed. David Wulstan (Stainer & Bell, London, 1978).

—— *The Psalms of David Translated into Lyrick-Verse* (London, 1632).

—— *The Songs of the Old Testament* (London, 1621).

WITZEL, Georg, *Psaltes Ecclesiasticus* (Cologne, 1550).

WOOD, Charles and George Ratcliffe Woodward, *The Cambridge Carol Book* (SPCK, London, 1924).

—— *The Cowley Carol Book*, 2nd series (Mowbray, Oxford, 1919). For 1st series see George Ratcliffe WOODWARD.

—— *An Italian Carol Book* (Faith Press, London, 1920).

WOODWARD, George Ratcliffe, *Carols for Christmas-tide*, series 1 (Pickering & Chatto, London, 1892).

—— *The Cowley Carol Book* [1st series] (1901); revised and enlarged edn. (Mowbray, Oxford, 1902; repr. 1908). For 2nd series see Charles WOOD.

—— *Songs of Syon: A collection of psalms, hymns and spiritual songs* (Schott, London, 1904; 4th edn., 1923). See also *Piae Cantiones*.

WORDE, Wynkyn de: see *Christmasse Carolles Newly Emprynted*

WULSTAN, David, *An Anthology of Carols* (J. & W. Chester, London, 1968).

WYETH, John, *Repository of Sacred Music*, part second (Harrisburg [Pennsylvania], 1813); facs. of 2nd edn., 1820 (Da Capo, New York, 1964).

The York Breviary, ed. S. W. Lawley (*Surtees Society*, 71, 75), 2 vols. (Durham, 1880–83).

ZAHN, Johannes, *Die Melodien der deutschen evangelischen Kirchenlieder* (Gütersloh, 1889–93; repr. George Olms, Hildesheim, 1963).

ZASLAW, Neal, *Mozart's Symphonies: Context, performance, reception* (OUP, 1989).

INDEX OF FEASTS AND SEASONS

This list comprises specific feasts and seasons other than Christmas. Since carols appropriate for use at Christmas constitute the bulk of the contents, they are not listed here. Each carol is followed by its item number.

INDEX OF SOURCES FOR MUSIC AND TEXT

This index incorporates all the information from the music and text ascriptions to the carols: authors, translators, composers, arrangers, printed and manuscript sources (entered under both title and author, where the latter is known), etc. Editorial arrangements, adaptations, and translations (and authors of prose translations) are not given. References are to carol number throughout; occasional reference is also made to the Appendices where an entry is discussed in some detail there.

Adam de la Halle 7
Alexander, Mrs Cecil Frances 93
Alison, Richard 46:I
Allen et al., *Slave Songs of the United States* (1867) 170
Alte catholische geistliche Kirchengesänge (1599) 66:II
Ambrose, St 2, 58
Ancient Mysteries Described (Hone, 1822) 128
An Essay on the Church Plain Chant (1782) 70
Anglo-American Carol Study Book, The (Niles, 1945–7) 173
Anschütz, Ernst 181:I
Aosta MS 9–E–17 10:I
    MS 9–E–19 9:II, 11, 12, 55:I
Arbeau, Thoinot 108
Around the World with Christmas (Kirkpatrick, 1895) 100:I
Arundel MS 248 8:I
Asti MS 17 14:II
Auserlesene catholische geistliche Kirchengesänge (1623) 62:I, 64

Bach, J. S. 54:II, 58:II, 59:II, 60:II, 67:II, 68:I, 69:I
Baker, Theodore 62:II, 66:I
Ballanta-Taylor, *St Helena Island Spirituals* (1925) 168
Baring-Gould, Sabine 196:II, 197:II
Barnes, Edward Shippen 195:II
Barnicoat, *Old Cornish Carols* (1927) 91
Barôzai, *Noei borguignon* (1701) 185
Bate, H. N. 102
Bedford, *The Excellency of Divine Music* (1733) 47:I
    (see also Appendix 2, III)
Belcher, Supply 81
Berlioz, Hector 94
Biblioteca del Seminario Vescovile, MS 17 14:II
Biblioteca Medicea-Laurenziana, MS Plut. 29.1 9:I
Bibliothèque Nationale, fonds latin MS 10581 16
Billings, William 78, 79, 80
    The Singing Master's Assistant (1778) 80
    (see also Appendix 3, II)
Birkitt, Francis Crawford 68
Bizet, Georges 186
Blémont, Émile 187
Blunt, Bruce 112
Bodleian Library MS Eng. poet. e. 1 26
    MS Selden b. 26 29, 30, 31, 32, 33, 34, 35
Book of Psalmody, A (Wilkins, c.1760) 74
Bordes, *Douze Noëls populaires* (1895) 196, 197
Borderies, E. F. J. (de) 70
Bramley, H. R. 60
Bramley and Stainer, *Christmas Carols New and Old* (1871) 148:II, 159:II
Brand, *Observations on the Popular Antiquities of Great Britain*

(1853–5) 131:I
British Library MSS
    Add. MS 5665 24, 38
    Add. MS 38599 42, 43
    Arundel MS 248 8:I
    Cotton Fragments 8:III
    Egerton MS 274 6
    Egerton MS 2971 44:II
    Harley MS 5396 123
    MS Royal App. 58 39
    MS Sloane 2593 106, 109
Britten, Benjamin 116, 117
Broadwood and Fuller Maitland, *English Country Songs* (1893) 149
Brooke, W. T. 70
Brooks, Phillips 101
Burnap, Uzziah Christopher 103:I
B[urney], C[harles] 92:II
Byrom, John 71

Caldwell, William 84:I
Calvisius, Seth 58:I
Cambridge University Library MSS
    Add. MS 710 8:II
    Add. MS 5943 23
    MS Ff. I 17 15:II
Caswall, Edward 95
Catholische geistliche Gesänge (1608) 179
'C. B.' 92:II
Cennick, John 72:I
Chadwick, James 195:II
Chappell, *The Popular Music of the Olden Time* (1853–4) 138, 143:I, 154:I
Choice Collection of Church Musick, A (Watts, 1749) 46:IV
Chorley, H. F. 94
Christmas Carols, Ancient and Modern (Sandys, 1833) 45, 130, 131:I, 132, 134, 137:I, 141:II, 144, 145, 146, 148:I, 151:I, 151:III
    (see also Appendix 4)
Christmas Carols New and Old (Bramley and Stainer, 1871) 148:II, 159:II
Christmas, its Carols and Customs (Fyfe, 1860) 124
Church Harmony Sacred to Devotion (Stephenson, c.1775) 75:II
Clark, Thomas 46:V, 76:II
Coleridge, Samuel Taylor 113
Collection of Dorset Carols, A (Pickard-Cambridge, 1926) 90, 147
Collection of Psalm and Hymn Tunes, A (Madan, 1769) 73, 92:II
    (see also Appendix 2, III)
Compleat Book of Psalmody, A (Evison, 1769) 75:I

INDEX OF FIRST LINES AND TITLES

Where titles differ from first lines, they are shown in *italic*. Each carol is followed by its item number.